Managerial Accounting

About the Authors

Dale C. Morse

Dale Morse is the Charles E. Johnson Professor of Accounting and Chairman of the Accounting Department at the University of Oregon. He received his M.B.A. in accounting from the University of Oregon and his Ph.D. in accounting from Stanford University. He was a faculty member at Cornell University in Ithaca, NY, from 1978–1991 and has held Visiting Professorships at the University of Auckland; the Dalian Institute of Technology, China; the University of Helsinki; the Universitas Merdeka Malang, Indonesia; and Koc University, Turkey. He also held a Fulbright Scholar position at the University of Nairobi, Kenya.

Dr. Morse's research has appeared in the *Journal of Accounting Research, Journal of Accounting and Economics, The Accounting Review,* and *Accounting Horizons.* His monograph, "Efficient Capital Markets and Accounting: A Critical Analysis," (with Tom Dyckman) is part of the Prentice-Hall "Contemporary Topics in Accounting" series. Dale Morse is a member of the American Accounting Association, American Finance Association, Institute of Management Accountants, and the Western Finance Association.

Jerold L. Zimmerman

Jerry Zimmerman is Alumni Distinguished Professor at the William E. Simon Graduate School of Business Administration, University of Rochester. He holds an undergraduate degree from the University of Colorado, Boulder, and a doctorate from the University of California, Berkeley. While at Rochester, Dr. Zimmerman has taught a variety of courses spanning accounting, finance, and economics. A deeper appreciation of the challenges of managing a complex organization was acquired by spending four years as Deputy Dean of the Simon School.

Dr. Zimmerman publishes widely in accounting on topics as diverse as cost allocations, municipal accounting, budgeting, taxes, auditing, financial accounting theory, mergers and acquisitions, trade unions, capital markets, and executive turnover. His paper, "The Costs and Benefits of Cost Allocations," won the 1978 American Accounting Association's competitive Manuscript Contest. He is recognized for developing Positive Accounting Theory. This work, co-authored with Ross Watts, also at the University of Rochester, received the 1978 and 1979 American Institute of Certified Public Accountants' Notable Contribution to the Accounting Literature Awards for "Towards a Positive Theory of the Determination of Accounting Standards" and "The Demand for and Supply of Accounting Theories: The Market for Excuses." Both papers appeared in the *Accounting Review.* They are also co-authors of the highly cited textbook, *Positive Accounting Theory* (Prentice Hall, 1986). Jerry Zimmerman was a founding editor of the *Journal of Accounting and Economics,* published by North-Holland, a scientific journal that is one of the most highly referenced accounting publications.

MANAGERIAL ACCOUNTING

Dale C. Morse
University of Oregon

Jerold L. Zimmerman
University of Rochester

Irwin
McGraw-Hill

Boston, Massachusetts   Burr Ridge, Illinois   Dubuque, Iowa
Madison, Wisconsin   New York, New York   San Francisco, California   St. Louis, Missouri

To Leslie, Jared, Tyler, Danielle, and Amy

Irwin/McGraw-Hill
*A Division of The **McGraw·Hill** Companies*

Managerial Accounting

Material from the Certified Management Accountant Examination, copyright © 1982–1990 by the Institute of Certified Management Accountants, is adapted with permission.

Copyright © 1997 by The McGraw-Hill Companies, Inc. All rights reserved. Printed in the United States of America. Except as permitted under the United States Copyright Act of 1976, no part of this publication may be reproduced or distributed in any form or by any means, or stored in a data base or retrieval system, without the prior written permission of the publisher.

This book is printed on acid-free paper.

3 4 5 6 7 8 9 0 VNH/VNH 9 0 9 8 7

ISBN 0-256-18955-2

Publisher: *Michael W. Junior*
Executive editor: *Jeff Shelstad*
Development editors: *Kelly Lee/Burrston House, Ltd.*
Marketing manager: *Heather L. Woods*
Project editor: *Karen M. Smith*
Production supervisor: *Dina L. Genovese*
Prepress buyer: *Charlene R. Perez*
Designer: *Larry J. Cope*
Photo research: *Burrston House, Ltd.*
Photo research coordinator: *Keri Johnson*
Compositor: *Weimer Graphics, Inc., Division of Shepard Poorman Communications Corp.*
Typeface: *10/12 Palatino*
Printer: *Von Hoffmann Press, Inc.*

Library of Congress Cataloging-in-Publication Data

Morse, Dale (date)
    Managerial accounting / Dale C. Morse, Jerold L. Zimmerman.
  —1st ed.
      p. cm.
    Includes index.
    ISBN 0-256-18955-2
    1. Managerial accounting.   I. Zimmerman, Jerold L., 1947- .
II. Title.
HF5657.4.M67   1997
658.15′1—dc21
                                        96-46238

http://www.mhcollege.com

PREFACE

During their professional careers, managers in all organizations, large and small, profit and not-for-profit, interact with the organization's accounting systems. Managers often use their accounting system to acquire information for making planning decisions such as what products or services to offer and at what prices. At other times, the accounting system can be used to measure the performance and influence the behavior of employees. In this way, an accounting system within an organization is both a source of information for making planning decisions as well as part of the organization's control mechanism.

Managerial Accounting provides students with an understanding and appreciation of the strengths and limitations of an organization's accounting system. Users of this textbook will become more intelligent users of the information generated by the accounting system. Students will begin to think critically about this system and will be able to analyze proposed changes to the system. *Managerial Accounting* very clearly demonstrates that the practice of managerial accounting is an integral part of the firm's organizational infrastructure, not an isolated set of computational topics.

> **"This book will make "traditional" managerial accounting texts obsolete."**
> [Eric Johnson, University of Toledo]

INTENDED AUDIENCE

> **"Logical and internally consistent, comprehensive, easy to read, and contemporary without being trendy."**
> [Eric Johnson, University of Toledo]

Managerial Accounting is written with the premise that the future user is the primary audience. While preparation of accounting information is an important skill, this text focuses on the analysis of the information generated by the accounting system for both planning and control decisions. For this reason, business majors and current and future managers will benefit greatly from the material presented. Future accounting majors will also gain a better understanding of how accounting information is used for effective planning and control within all types of organizations.

DISTINGUISHING CONTENT FEATURES

EMPHASIS ON GAINING AN UNDERSTANDING OF ORGANIZATIONS

Managerial Accounting will expose students to many different organizational settings. They will gain an understanding of the different roles of managers within organizations and will see the importance of cross-functional skills to achieving a successful managerial career. Students will understand the

> **"Morse and Zimmerman have done an excellent job of demonstrating that managerial accounting is an integral part of an organization's infrastructure."**
> [Wilfred Devine, Villanova University]

underlying importance of accounting information within an organization, as it is consistently related to the dichotomy of planning and control decisions.

ORGANIZATIONAL EXAMPLES IN EACH CHAPTER

Every chapter's text material is complemented by examples from organizations whose product and/or service is very familiar to students. For example, chapters are built around organizations such as a

> **"Morse and Zimmerman have a knack for examples that cut to the essence of accounting techniques."**
> [Hugh Warren, California State University-LA]

compact disc store, a skateboard manufacturer, and the department of motor vehicles. Organizational examples are typically of smaller businesses, and many of them deal with the increasingly vibrant service sector. These organizational examples are consistently referenced throughout the chapter, making them vital to a chapter's understanding and contributing to the ease of comprehension and student interest in the material.

> **"The running example in each chapter is outstanding at showing the student how the theory fits into real world situations."**
> [Gwen Pate, University of Southern Mississippi]

RELEVANCE OF MATERIAL

Business majors, accounting majors, and all potential future managers will find *Managerial Accounting*

> **"A clear, no-nonsense presentation of the critical concepts for management accountants."**
> [Melvin Jolly, University of Idaho]

stimulating, challenging, and rewarding. The organizational examples in each chapter provide consistent proof that the material under review is important to a successful career. The focus on analysis and decision making will challenge students to become broader thinkers and more critical analyzers of business and accounting information.

> **"One of the greatest strengths of the text."**
> [Eric Johnson, University of Toledo]

END-OF-CHAPTER MATERIAL

The extensive end-of-chapter material has many options for instructor use and student reinforcement. The numerical examples presented throughout the chapters are complemented by many additional numerical problems in the problem material. Additionally, many thought-provoking discussion problems

> **"The numerical and discussion problems are significantly stronger than those in competing textbooks. They are much more diverse, challenging, and realistic."**
> [Frank Luh, Lehigh University]

serve to reinforce the important concepts in each chapter. Cases are used to tie several concepts together and present a more comprehensive learning

> **"Very good match of questions and problems to chapter material. It is not just that the questions fit the topics, but that the questions fit the tone of the material."**
> [Leslie Oakes, University of New Mexico]

experience for the student. Several spreadsheet problems are identified and templates provided for

> **"I have been very impressed with the end-of-chapter material throughout the text. There is a good mix of complexity and the chapter material has generally been covered well."**
> [Paul Juras, Wake Forest University]

each chapter. Finally, cooperative learning examples and writing exercises are included in most chapters.

CONCEPTUAL FRAMEWORK

Managerial Accounting offers, for the first time, a conceptual framework for the study of this important subject. The concepts of opportunity cost and organization theory serve as the underlying framework

> "The text lays out a framework that accountants and others can use to solve problems that involve accounting information. This framework can be applied to a much larger number of institutions and decisions than the cost systems that continue to be the focus of many textbooks."
> [Leslie Oakes, University of New Mexico]

to organize the analysis. In the early chapters when planning decisions are being explored, opportunity cost serves as the foundation for this discussion. When the focus of the text moves to the control function, recent discussions of organization theory provide the foundation.

> "The authors effectively tie in various parts of managerial accounting into a seamless fabric."
> [David Lesmond, SUNY-Buffalo]

TRADE-OFFS

Accounting systems cannot always fulfill the two demands of making planning decisions and controlling managerial actions. It is common for accounting systems used primarily as a control mechanism to be less effective as a planning tool. Existing texts do not emphasize the trade-off between designing an accounting system for planning decisions and designing it for control. For example, activity-based costing presumably improves the accounting sys-

UNIQUE PEDAGOGY

Besides the consistent use of organizational examples throughout each chapter, which are unique to *Managerial Accounting*, several other pedagogical de-

tem's ability for making planning decisions like product design and product pricing. Existing texts fail to address how implementing activity-based costing affects control. *Managerial Accounting* pays attention to these trade-offs.

> "The trade-offs are described clearly with good, simple examples."
> [Roby Sawyers, North Carolina State University]

LOGICAL SEQUENCE

Due to the earlier mentioned conceptual framework, the chapters in *Managerial Accounting* clearly build on each other. The first chapter focuses on the business environment, recent advances in management accounting, and the dual role of the accounting sys-

> "A major strength is the early focus on management decision making rather than product costing."
> [Joyce Strawser, Seton Hall University]

tem. Chapters 2–5 focus on planning decisions within organizations. Chapters 6 and 7 return to the foundation of organization theory and identify organizational problems of control. Chapters 9–12 develop the basic theme of the trade-off that exists when using an accounting system for both planning and control decisions. Chapter 12 continues the discussion of new manufacturing methods, and many of these are used to critically analyze the basic themes of the book. The final three chapters (13, Capital Budgeting; 14, Standard Costing; and 15, Managerial Accounting in International Organizations) can be taught at the end of the course or after Chapter 6 at each individual instructor's own discretion.

> "Overall I find the organization and development to be excellent."
> [Ram Ramanan, University of Notre Dame]

vices are used to enhance student understanding and to develop the reader's critical thinking skills.

Learning Objectives and Concept Reviews

Presented at the beginning of each chapter, learning objectives are used to provide a road map for the students. Making sure one understands the learning objectives as one progresses through the chapters is vital to gaining a complete understanding of the material being presented. To better facilitate this learning, *Managerial Accounting* provides Concept Reviews at periodic points throughout the chapters. These Concept Reviews ensure that students have fully comprehended the presentation before continuing their study of the chapter. Answers appear at the end of this book.

> **CONCEPT REVIEW**
> 1. How do decision rights cascade from top-level managers to the rest of the employees of the organization?
> 2. How does linking decision rights and knowledge benefit an organization?
> 3. How does the transfer of knowledge allow for linking knowledge and decision rights and still allow for control?

What's Happening Sidebars

> **WHAT'S HAPPENING**
> A labor strike recently idled General Motors' plants around the United States, forcing the company to lay off thousands of workers. Analysts estimated that General Motors was losing $300 million a week in lost sales. At the same time it was noted that the company had 82 days of finished cars in inventory. What is the opportunity cost to General Motors of this strike?

These sidebars, sometimes as many as 3–4 per chapter, present a scenario that students have observed and/or experienced in their own lives. By presenting a unique twist to this experience, students will be challenged to rethink their experience and perhaps gain a new and different understanding. Students can find explanations for this feature at the end of this book.

Team Decisions Regarding . . .

Once in every chapter, students will be shown how the book team for *Managerial Accounting* made various decisions regarding the execution of this product. As future users of accounting information, students will no doubt benefit from a better understanding of why certain accounting information was useful in executing this unique new textbook. Business students might also gain a better understanding of a discipline that will ultimately be their career of choice. Most importantly, students will consistently see that accounting is not an isolated set of computational activities, but rather a crucial function that plays a role in the success of all products and services and, ultimately, all organizations.

> **THE STORY OF MANAGERIAL ACCOUNTING**
> **Team Decisions Regarding Strategy**
> The *Managerial Accounting* book team was faced with an initial strategic decision. Irwin Publishing already had the best-selling management accounting book in the United States. One possible solution was to modify that management accounting book to accommodate the changing educational environment. Such a change, however, might cause the company to lose many satisfied customers. The other alternative was to develop a new management accounting book that would compete with the existing management accounting book. How should Peggy, the team accountant, use the notion of opportunity cost to help the team make this strategic decision?

Numerical Examples and Solutions

At relevant points throughout the chapters, *Managerial Accounting* provides numerical examples that reinforce the key quantitative skills that students need in order to successfully complete this course. Numerical examples are then revisited in the end of chapter material, where as many as three numerical problems are provided for each numerical example in the chapter. To help the student fully understand how to solve numerical problems, the authors refer the student to a specific numerical example in the text.

NUMERICAL EXAMPLE 2.7

Jackson Company makes computers. They estimate that the annual fixed costs are $100,000 and variable costs are $100 per unit. What are total expected costs if the company makes 500 computers per year? What are total expected costs if the company makes 700 computers per year?

■ **SOLUTION** Total expected costs if Jackson Company makes 500 computers per year is the sum of fixed costs ($100,000) and variable costs ($100 × 500 = $50,000), or $150,000. Total expected costs if Jackson Company makes 700 computers per year is the sum of fixed costs ($100,000) and variable costs ($100 × 700 = $70,000), or $170,000.

NP 2–17: Variable and Fixed Costs (LO 6; NE 2.7) The school newspaper editor estimates that the fixed cost of an edition is $10,000. The variable cost is $.03 per copy.

a. What is the expected cost of an edition if 3,000 copies are produced?
b. What is the expected cost of an edition if 5,000 copies are produced?

SUMMARY, KEY TERMS, SELF-STUDY PROBLEMS, NUMERICAL PROBLEMS, DISCUSSION PROBLEMS, AND CASES

These additional elements make up the end-of-chapter material in each chapter.

INSTRUCTOR SUPPLEMENTS

SOLUTIONS MANUAL

Prepared by the authors, this manual contains detailed solutions for all end of chapter material in *Managerial Accounting*. The Solutions Manual has been accuracy checked by independent parties. It is also available in Microsoft Word® format for those who want to manipulate the material for alternative classroom use.

INSTRUCTOR'S RESOURCE MANUAL

Prepared by the authors, this manual includes detailed teaching ideas for *Managerial Accounting*. The authors discuss ways to divide the text into class size sections for 3- or 4-credit quarters or semester courses, problem material is classified according to difficulty, and alternative teaching strategies are given for end of chapter material (including ways to use end of chapter material to promote cooperative learning). Conversion notes to make the transition from leading competitors to *Managerial Accounting* are also provided and will highlight some of the material available to adopters of *Managerial Accounting*. The Instructor's Resource Manual also provides additional "real-life" scenarios. These scenarios include references to simple organizations that students understand and current events of better-known, larger organizations. This manual also includes a disk in Microsoft Word® format for easiest use and maximum flexibility.

SOLUTION TRANSPARENCIES

All numerical problems presented in *Managerial Accounting* will have their solutions available in acetate format for classroom projection.

PRAXIS READY SHOWS

Prepared by Jon A. Booker, Charles W. Caldwell, Susan C. Galbreath, and Richard S. Rand, all of Tennessee Technological University, Ready Shows is a comprehensive package of multimedia lecture enhancement aids that use PowerPoint® software to illustrate chapter concepts.

PRAXIS READY SLIDES TRANSPARENCY MASTERS

Selected PowerPoint® slides from the Ready Shows product are available to adopters in a master format for easy classroom use. In addition, adopters of *Managerial Accounting* may utilize the Ready Shows disks to facilitate use of the entire slide package.

TEST BANK

Prepared by Jay Holmen of the University of Wisconsin–Eau Claire and Eric Johnson of the University of Toledo, this comprehensive test bank contains over 1,200 items. For each chapter of *Managerial Accounting*, adopters will have their choice of objective questions, numerical problems, discussion problems, and "What's Happening" questions.

COMPUTERIZED TESTING SOFTWARE

A computerized version of the manual test bank for more efficient classroom use is also available in either Macintosh, Windows, or DOS versions.

TELETEST

By calling a toll-free number, adopters of *Managerial Accounting* can specify the content of exams and have a laser-printed copy of the exams mailed to them.

RICHARD D. IRWIN MANAGERIAL/COST VIDEO LIBRARY

These short, action-oriented videos provide the impetus for lively classroom discussion. This six-volume library includes videos of international and service companies as well as many manufacturing examples, as outlined below:

Volume I: "Behind the Bill"
            "The Vancouver Door Company"
            "How Many Bucks in a Bag"

Volume II: "Moving the Merchandise"
            "Ogre Mills, after the Curtain Fell"

Volume III: "Lean Production"
            "Quality"
            "The Manufacturing Process"

Volume IV: "Computer-Integrated Manufacturing"
            "Inventory Management"
            "Service"

Volume V: "Manufacturing"
            "Supplier Development Outreach Program"
            "Accounting Careers"

Volume VI: "Atlas Foundry and Machine Company"
            "Management Accounting and Concepts"
            "International Accounting"

STUDENT SUPPLEMENTS

STUDY GUIDE

Students will find this essential in preparing for exams. The Study Guide allows the students to practice what they have learned by providing a variety of multiple choice, true/false, matching, and short answer questions, as well as numerical problems with solutions. Students can also use the Study Guide for a review of learning objectives, chapter summaries, and outline of topical coverage.

WINDOWS TUTORIAL

Irwin Windows Tutorial summarizes the essential points in each chapter and tests students' knowledge using objective questions and exercises. Students will find it an effective way to prepare for exams.

WEB TUTORIAL

Now students will be able to go on-line to review concepts presented in *Managerial Accounting*. Offering true-false and multiple-choice review, this tutorial will give enterprising students another learning option.

PRAXIS READY NOTES

Selected screens are printed from the PRAXIS Ready Shows product to enable students to be efficient note takers during classroom presentations. Ready Notes are available to students at a nominal cost and again will be an effective exam preparation tool.

SPATS *(Spreadsheet Applications Template Software)*

Selected numerical problems in the end of chapter material are available in Excel® for Windows® template format for student problem solving. These templates are available for duplication from a master or are shrinkwrapped with *Managerial Accounting* for a nominal charge.

RAMBLEWOOD MANUFACTURING, INC.

This computerized practice set was recently updated by Leland Mansuetti and Keith Weidkamp, both of Sierra College. This software simulates the operations of a company that manufactures customized fencing. It can be used to illustrate job-order costing systems with JIT inventory in a realistic setting. The entire simulation requires 10–14 hours to complete. A new feature prevents files from being transferred from one disk to another without detection. It is available in DOS and Windows formats and soon will be available in a multimedia format.

ROOM ZOOM: THE CPA SOURCE DISC

This multimedia, interactive CD-ROM provides an exciting guide to a CPA career. Students will be able to experience a day in the life of the CPA, review salary statistics, learn about scholarships and internships, understand the technology inherent in the profession, learn about the CPA exam, and much more. Available to students for a nominal charge when purchased from Irwin with *Managerial Accounting,* this innovative technology component would also be perfect for the first day of class.

ACKNOWLEDGMENTS

From the outset, we wanted to create a unique, yet accessible undergraduate textbook—one that would set the standard for future texts. To the extent we have succeeded in achieving our goals, this success is attributable to the efforts of numerous individuals. Much of the intellectual capital in the book is drawn from our colleagues at Cornell University, University of Oregon, and the University of Rochester, especially Tom Dyckman, Ron Hilton, John Elliott, Ray Ball, James Brickley, Clifford Smith, and Ross Watts. Some of the ideas in *Managerial Accounting* owe their existence to the extensive review and development process underlying *Accounting for Decision Making and Control* by Jerold Zimmerman (Burr Ridge, IL: Richard D. Irwin, 1995). Steve Ault and Kechia Anderson helped on earlier drafts by reading and providing comments. Barbara Schnathorst and Kate Walsh did a superb job of copyediting. Kathy Jones provided enormous assistance with the manuscript and solutions manual.

Managerial Accounting would not have been possible without the dedicated professionalism of our colleagues at Richard D. Irwin: Jeff Shelstad, Executive Editor, Michael Junior, Publisher, Kelly Lee, Developmental Editor, and Heather Woods, Marketing Manager. Cathy Crow and Glenn Turner at Burrston House provided enormous help in the development process. Their collective vision, commitment to excellence, and numerous suggestions have made *Managerial Accounting* a much better book.

Besides providing editorial and production assistance, the publisher manages the outside review process. The very useful comments and suggestions from the following reviewers are greatly appreciated:

Janice Ammons, New Mexico State University
Progyan Basu, Boston College
James Borden, Villanova University
Marvelyn Burnette, Wichita State University
Marybeth Caldwell, University of Arkansas
Peter Cheng, Purdue University
Won Choi, Rutgers University–Camden
Maureen Crane, California State University–Fresno
Stephen Dempsey, University of Vermont
Wilfred Devine, Villanova University
Timothy Farmer, University of Missouri–St. Louis
Marci Flanery, University of Kansas
Michael Haselkorn, Bentley College
Jay Holmen, University of Wisconsin–Eau Claire
Eric Johnson, University of Toledo
Melvin Jolly, University of Idaho
Paul Juras, Wake Forest University
Donald Keller, Cal State University–Long Beach
Joseph Kerstein, Baruch College–CUNY
Robert Koehler, Pennsylvania State University
Paul Koogler, Southwest Texas State University
Robert Lin, California State University–Hayward
Frank Luh, Lehigh University
David Lesmond, SUNY–Buffalo
Gary Marchant, University of Connecticut
David Marcinko, SUNY–Albany
Lawrence Metzger, Loyola University
Leslie Oakes, University of New Mexico
Richard Palmer, University of Tennessee–Martin
Gwen Pate, University of Southern Mississippi
Kenneth Pelfrey, Ohio State University
Mary Louise Poloskey, University of Texas
Madhav Rajan, University of Pennsylvania
Khalid Razaki, Illinois State University
Ram Ramanan, University of Notre Dame
Anne Rich, Quinnipiac College
J. Timothy Sale, University of Cincinnati
Kathryn Savage, Northern Arizona University
Roby Sawyers, North Carolina State
FW Schaeberle, Western Michigan University
Shirish Seth, California State University–Fullerton
William Shenkir, University of Virginia
Jae Shim, California State University–Long Beach
Jenice P. Stewart, University of Missouri–Columbia
Donald Stone, University of Massachusetts
Joyce Strawser, Seton Hall University
Bente Villadsen, Washington University
Hugh Warren, California State University–Los Angeles
Mary Pat Waterhouse, University of Hawaii
Jim Weglin, North Seattle Community College
Michael Welker, Drexel University
Gwendolen White, Ball State University

We wish to express special appreciation to Jay Holmen of University of Wisconsin–Eau Claire and Eric Johnson of University of Toledo for their preparation of the Test Bank.

To all the above individuals, our most heartfelt appreciation. The patience of our families is also recognized as a critical success factor in writing this book. In order to continually improve the book, we invite your comments.

Dale C. Morse
Jerold L. Zimmerman

Contents in Brief

Chapter 1
Organizations and Accounting — 2

Chapter 2
The Nature of Costs — 30

Chapter 3
Cost Estimation — 60

Chapter 4
Estimating Product Costs and Activity-Based Costing — 100

Chapter 5
Product Planning Decisions — 134

Chapter 6
Controlling Organizations — 170

Chapter 7
Role of Accounting within Decentralized Organizations — 196

Chapter 8
Budgets and Budgeting — 238

Chapter 9
Cost Allocations — 286

Chapter 10
Traditional Absorption Cost Systems — 338

Chapter 11
Problems with Absorption Cost Systems and Possible Solutions — 384

Chapter 12
Management Accounting in a Changing Environment — 434

Chapter 13
Investment Decisions — 470

Chapter 14
Standard Costs and Variance Analysis — 516

Chapter 15
Managerial Accounting in Multinational Organizations — 564

Endnotes   593

Thoughts on "What's Happening" Questions   597

Answers to Concept Reviews   601

Photo Credits   609

Index   611

Contents

Chapter 1
Organizations and Accounting   2

- **1.1** Management Accounting in a Changing Environment   4
  - Changing Technology   4
  - Global Competition   6
- **1.2** The Nature of Organizations   8
- **1.3** The Role of Managers   10
  - Making Planning Decisions   10
  - Control: Managing, Motivating, and Monitoring People   11
- **1.4** The Role of the Accounting System   12
  - Use of Accounting for Making Planning Decisions   13
  - Use of Accounting for Control   14
  - Use of Accounting by External Parties   14
- **1.5** Trade-Offs in Using the Accounting System for Multiple Purposes   16
  - Trade-Off between Making Planning Decisions and Control   16
  - Trade-Off between Making Planning Decisions and External Reporting   16
  - Trade-Offs between Control and External Reporting   17
- **1.6** Multiple Accounting Systems   18
- **1.7** The Evolution of Management Accounting: A Framework for Change   19
- **1.8** Types of Management Accountants   21
- **1.9** Ethics and Management Accounting   22
- **1.10** Summary   24

Chapter 2
The Nature of Costs   30

- **2.1** Making Planning Decisions   32
  - Using Cost/Benefit Analysis   32
  - Opportunity Costs   35
  - Sunk Costs   38
- **2.2** Opportunity Costs and the Rate of Output   40
  - Opportunity Costs of Initiating Operations   40
  - Opportunity Costs of Normal Operations   40
  - Opportunity Costs of Exceeding Capacity   41
  - Graphical Analysis   41
  - Marginal and Average Costs   41
- **2.3** Approximations of Opportunity Costs   43
  - Fixed and Variable Costs   43
  - Historical Costs   45
- **2.4** The Benefit and Cost of Information   46
- **2.5** Summary   48

Chapter 3
Cost Estimation   60

- **3.1** Estimating Costs for Planning Decisions   62
  - Planning Decisions Related to the Cost of Products and Services   62
  - Planning Decisions Related to the Cost of Activities or Processes   67
  - Planning Decisions Related to the Cost of Organizational Subunits   70
  - Planning Decisions Related to the Cost of Customers   71
  - Planning Decisions Related to Suppliers   72
  - Planning Decisions Related to Costs Associated with Periods   74
- **3.2** Estimating Costs through Tracing: Direct and Indirect Costs   75
- **3.3** Estimating Costs through the Identification of Variable and Fixed Costs   78
  - Estimating Variable and Fixed Costs through Account Classification   79

Visually Fitting Historic Cost Data   82

3.4 A Framework of Costs for Planning Purposes   85

3.5 Summary   86

Appendix: Using Regression to Estimate Fixed and Variable Costs   87

CHAPTER 4

Estimating Product Costs and Activity-Based Costing   100

4.1 Product Life Cycle and Product Costs   102

4.2 Estimating Direct Product Costs   106

4.3 The Nature of Indirect Product Costs   108

Unit-, Batch-, Product-, and Facility-Level Costs   109

4.4 Using Cost Drivers to Trace Indirect Costs to Products   111

Tracing Indirect Product Costs Using a Single Cost Driver   111

Problems with Using a Single Cost Driver to Trace Indirect Costs   115

4.5 Activity-Based Costing (ABC)   117

4.6 Summary   122

CHAPTER 5

Product Planning Decisions   134

5.1 Pricing Decisions   136

Pricing to Maximize Value   136

Cost-Based Pricing   138

Cost as a Lower Boundary for Price   140

5.2 Cost-Volume-Profit Analysis   142

Break-Even Analysis   144

Achieving a Specified Profit   146

Graph of CVP Analysis   147

Problems with CVP Analysis   148

5.3 Product Mix Decisions   149

Decision to Add a Product or Service   150

Decision to Drop a Product or Service   151

Decision to Make or Buy a Product or Service   152

Decision to Process a Service or Product Further   153

Decision to Promote a Product or Service   154

5.4 Product Mix Decisions with Constraints   155

Product Mix Decisions with a Single Constraint   155

Theory of Constraints   156

5.5 Summary   159

Appendix: Achieving a Specified After-Tax Profit   160

CHAPTER 6

Controlling Organizations   170

6.1 Control within an Organization   172

6.2 Knowledge and Decision Making within an Organization   173

6.3 Motivating Individuals toward the Goals of an Organization   176

Self-Interested Behavior   177

Monitoring Costs   177

Performance Measurement   178

Rewarding Performance through Contracts   181

6.4 Organizational Structure and the Framework for Change Revisited   182

6.5 Separating Planning Decision Process from Decision Control   184

Steps of a Decision Process   185

Examples of Internal Control Systems   186

6.6 Summary   188

CHAPTER 7

Role of Accounting within Decentralized Organizations   196

7.1 Controllability Principle   198

7.2 Responsibility Centers and Performance Measures   200

Cost Centers   200

Profit Centers   202

Investment Centers   204

Identifying Responsibility Centers   212

7.3 Transfer Pricing   212

Existence of a Competitive Market for the Intermediate Product or Service   216

No Competitive Market Exists for the Intermediate Product or Service   218

Choosing Transfer Prices: Control and Making Planning Decisions   220

7.4 Summary   223

CHAPTER 8

Budgets and Budgeting   238

8.1 The Purpose of Budgets   240

Budgeting for Planning Decisions   240

Budgeting for Control   241
8.2 Conflict between Planning and Control   243
8.3 How Budgeting Helps Resolve Organizational Problems   245
Short-Run versus Long-Run Budgets   245
Line-Item Budgets   246
Budget Lapsing   247
Static versus Flexible Budgets   249
Incremental versus Zero-Base Budgets   251
8.4 Comprehensive Master Budget Illustration   252
Description of the Firm: NaturApples   253
Overview of the Budgeting Process   253
Sales Budget   255
Production Budget   256
Selling and Administration Budget   257
Capital Investment Budget   258
Financial Budget   258
Budgeted Financial Statements   259
8.5 Summary   265
Appendix: Monthly Cash Flow Estimates and Spreadsheets   266

Chapter 9

Cost Allocations   286

9.1 Allocating Indirect Costs   288
9.2 Reasons for Allocating Indirect Costs   289
Satisfying External Requirements   290
Cost Allocation for Planning Purposes   294
Cost Allocation for Control Reasons   296
9.3 Basic Steps of Cost Allocation   299
Defining the Cost Objects   299
Accumulating the Indirect Costs in Cost Pools   300
Choosing an Allocation Base   301
Estimating an Application Rate   303
Distributing Indirect Costs Based on Usage of the Allocation Base   307
9.4 Segment Reporting   308
9.5 Summary   310
Appendix: Allocating Costs of Service Department with Interactions   312

Chapter 10

Traditional Absorption Cost Systems   338

10.1 Absorption Costing in Organizations   340
10.2 Job-Order Costing   341
10.3 Cost Flows through the Accounts   345
10.4 Allocating Overhead to Jobs   348
Over- and Underabsorbed Overhead   349
Why Worry about Over- and Underabsorbed Overhead?   351
Accounting for Over- and Underabsorbed Overhead   352
Multiple Allocation Bases   354
Allocation of Overhead by Departments   357
10.5 Process Costing   359
10.6 Summary   362
Appendix: Cost of Goods Manufactured and the Cost of Goods Sold and Alternative Cost Flow Methods for Inventory   364

Chapter 11

Problems with Absorption Cost Systems and Possible Solutions   384

11.1 Criticisms of Absorption Cost Systems   386
Incentive to Overproduce   386
Underuse of Allocation Base Used to Allocate Fixed Costs   389
Misleading Product Costs   390
Alternatives to Traditional Absorption Costing Systems   391
11.2 Allocating Overhead Based on Practical Capacity   392
11.3 Variable Costing   395
11.4 Activity-Based Costing/Activity-Based Management   398
Planning Decisions through Activity-Based Management   399
Control Decisions through Activity-Based Management   401
Acceptance of ABC   403
11.5 Joint Costs   406
11.6 Summary   410
Appendix: Allocating Joint Costs   411

Chapter 12

Management Accounting in a Changing Environment   434

12.1 An Integrative Framework for Change and Management Accounting   436
Environmental and Competitive Forces Affecting Organizations   436

Investment Opportunities 437

Organizational Structure 440

Making Planning Decisions and the Value of the Organization 440

The Role of Management Accounting and Change 441

12.2 Innovations and Management Accounting Systems 442

Productivity and Productivity Measures 443

Total Quality Management and Quality Measures 446

Just-in-Time (JIT) Processes 453

12.3 When Should Management Accounting Be Changed? 458

12.4 Summary 459

Chapter 13

Investment Decisions 470

13.1 Long-Term Investment Decisions 472

The Capital Budgeting Process 472

Opportunity Cost of Capital 473

13.2 Investment Criteria Ignoring the Opportunity Cost of Capital 476

Payback 476

Accounting Rate of Return 477

13.3 The Net Present Value of Cash Flows 479

Estimating Cash Flows for Calculating Present Values 481

Adjusting the Discount Rate for Risk 484

13.4 Internal Rate of Return (IRR) 486

13.5 Capital Budgeting Methods Used in Practice 490

13.6 Summary 491

Appendix: Interest Rate Mathematics 493

Chapter 14

Standard Costs and Variance Analysis 516

14.1 Standard Costs 518

Reasons for Standard Costing 518

Setting and Revising Standards 519

14.2 Direct Labor and Direct Materials Variances 522

Direct Labor Variances 522

Direct Materials Variances 527

14.3 Incentive Effects of Direct Labor and Materials Variances 532

Incentive to Build Inventories 532

Externalities 533

Discouraging Cooperative Effort 533

Mutual Monitoring Incentives 534

Satisficing Behavior 534

14.4 Overhead Standard Costs and Variances 535

Expected, Standard, and Actual Usage of the Allocation Base 536

Budgeted, Applied, and Actual Overhead 537

Incentive Effects of Overhead Standards and Variances 538

14.5 Variance Investigation 540

14.6 Costs and Benefits of Using Standard Costing Systems 541

14.7 Summary 543

Appendix: Overhead Variances 545

Chapter 15

Managerial Accounting in Multinational Organizations 564

15.1 International Trade and Multinational Organizations 566

15.2 Different Currencies 568

Exchange Rates 568

Managerial Importance of Exchange Rates 570

15.3 Multiple Taxing Authorities 571

15.4 Accounting Standards for External Reporting 573

15.5 Cultural Differences 575

15.6 International Transfer Pricing Issues 576

Tax Minimization 577

Political Considerations 579

Trade-Offs with Planning Decisions and Control 580

15.7 Performance Evaluation 581

Appendix: Other Government Taxes and Regulations 585

Endnotes 593

Thoughts on "What's Happening" Questions 597

Answers to Concept Reviews 601

Photo Credits 609

Index 611

Managerial Accounting

CHAPTER 1

Organizations and Accounting

LEARNING OBJECTIVES

1. Explain how technological innovation and global competition can affect an organization and its management accounting system.

2. Identify the basic processes of an organization's structure.

3. Describe the role of managers in organizations.

4. Explain the critical role played by management accounting in making planning decisions and controlling managers to work toward organizational goals.

5. Identify the trade-offs that exist in using information for making planning decisions, control, and external reporting.

6. Describe the advantages and disadvantages of having multiple accounting systems.

7. Identify the roles of different types of management accountants.

8. Recognize the role of judgment and ethics in making management accounting choices.

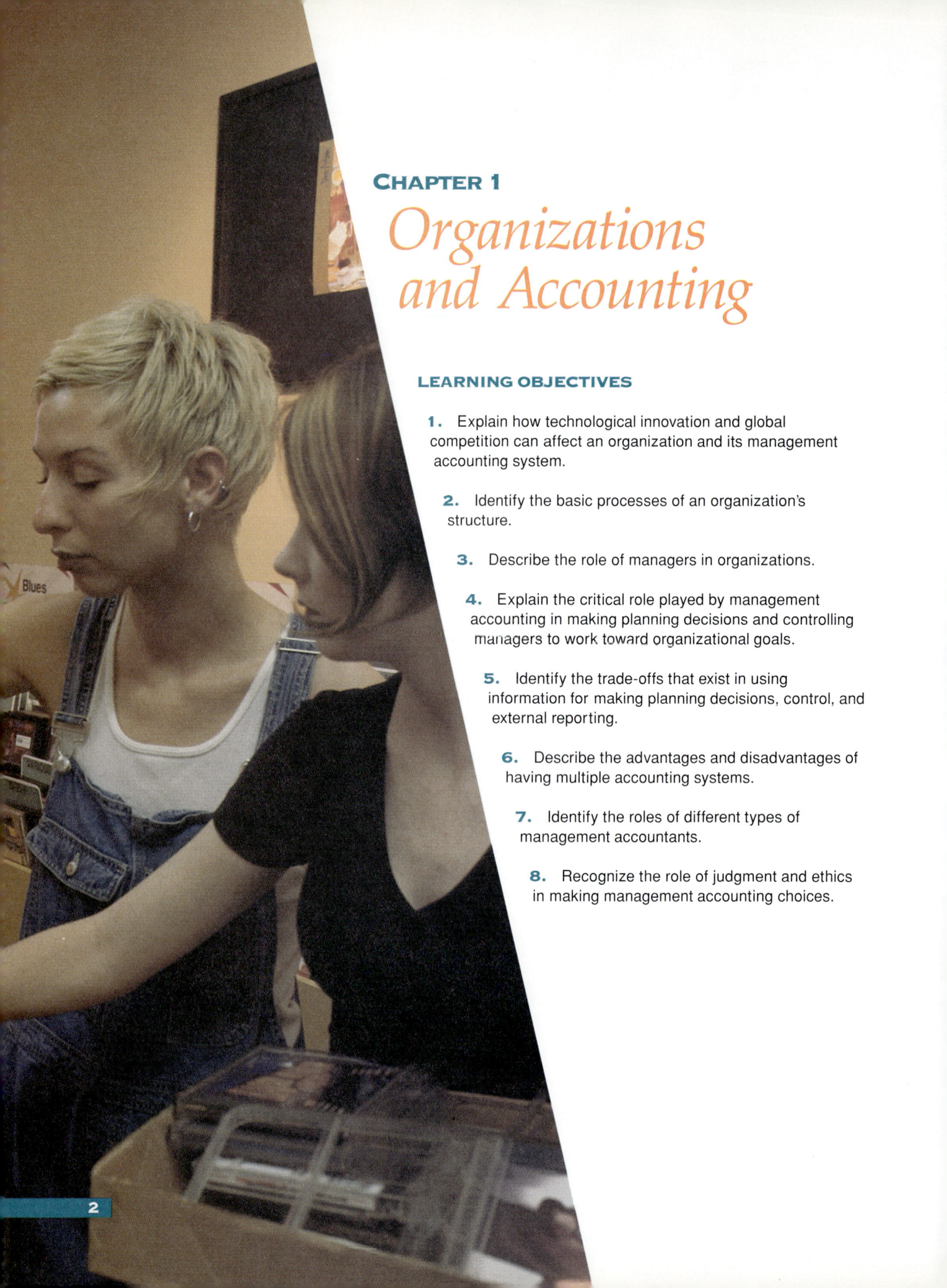

COMPACT DISC STORES

When Diane Johnson approached her friend, Janice Nishimura, about investing in a compact disc store, Janice was not very excited. But Diane persisted. She explained that music stores don't have to pay for compact discs (CDs) until they are sold and any unsold CDs are returned to the producer of the CD. Therefore, there are no initial investment requirements for inventory and no risk of unsold inventory.

Diane's business strategy was to have low markups on CDs and attempt to sell large volumes. Diane also wanted to support local recording artists by reserving some shelf space for their CDs.

Diane eventually convinced Janice to invest $50,000 along with her own $50,000 to form a partnership. Diane would receive an annual salary of $30,000 for managing the store and the remaining profits would be shared equally. Janice would not be involved in management. They borrowed $200,000 from a bank and leased space in the center of town for the initial Compact Disc Store. After sales exceeded expectations, two more Compact Disc Stores were opened in the suburbs. Managers were hired to operate the two stores in the suburbs.

With the growth of the business, problems began to arise. Sales were not as high as expected at one store in the suburbs, and the other store appeared to suffer from considerable shoplifting. Competition in the retail CD business has increased with a national chain opening a store near one of the stores in the suburb. In addition, further expansion would require another loan from the bank.

Diane and Janice must make some decisions about how to react to the threat of increased competition. They realize that the stores must be much more sensitive to their customers and operate more efficiently, but they aren't sure exactly what to do.

1.1 Management Accounting in a Changing Environment

Management accounting includes the design and use of accounting within organizations. Management accounting is not composed of a fixed set of rules. Management accounting methods are chosen to help an organization achieve its goals through better decision making and management of the members of the organization. Because organizations have different goals and are composed of different members, there are no universal rules of management accounting. Management accounting must adapt to each organization.

If organizations were static entities, management accounting methods could be designed for each organization to match the specific needs of that organization. But organizations change as individuals join and leave the organization. Even organizations with the same individuals change because of changes in lifestyle preferences. Organizations must also adapt to a changing environment. The two major forces affecting organizations today are changes in technology and global competition. Organizations that fail to adapt to these forces will not be able to survive in the long run.

Organizations are dependent on their management accounting systems to provide information in a dynamic environment. If the evolution of the management accounting system lags behind the evolution of the organization, the system will act as an anchor preventing the organization from successfully dealing with a changing environment. Organizations must adapt to changing environments and management accounting must adapt to a changing organization. Therefore, the study of management accounting is a study of a process, not a study of a set of procedures. The process of management accounting is linked to the characteristics of the organization, which are constantly changing. To understand management accounting, you must understand organizations and the forces that affect them.

The following sections describe two major forces, technological change and global competition, that have affected organizations. Organizations have chosen to adapt to these forces in different ways. Some of these adaptations, such as total quality management (TQM) and just-in-time (JIT), have become well publicized. These adaptations and others are described in the following sections. In identifying and understanding these changes in organizations, we can appreciate the role and process of management accounting.

Changing Technology

Technology has changed the way we live. Computers, telecommunications, transportation systems, and medical and scientific discoveries have affected the way we work, eat, and recreate. Organizations have been similarly influenced by changing technology and will be continually influenced by breakthroughs in the future.

Information Acquisition and Dissemination

Probably the biggest impact of technology on organizations recently is the proliferation of products and services related to information. The telecommunications and computer industries have revolutionized the way organizations operate. Organizations can communicate with their members, suppliers, and customers almost instantly through devices such as cellular phones, fax machines, and the Internet. Information on changing demand for products and demographics is easily accessible. And computers can manipulate information and simulate different scenarios to allow organizations to make better predictions of the future.

To be successful, organizations must recognize the advantages of greater access to information.

A recent survey of financial executives indicated that many accounting systems are not adapting rapidly enough to new technology. Of the financial executives surveyed, 80% indicated that their company's accounting system produced useful data too slowly and inefficiently. Smithkline-Beecham recently installed software to reduce the time to make certain budgeting comparisons from two to three weeks to two to three days.[1] Other companies are experimenting with real-time management with information available almost immediately.

Computers

Computers have changed the way organizations operate. Computers allow organizations to process and communicate information much more quickly. Computers also allow organizations to make better quality products more efficiently through automation and precise operations.

Computer-integrated manufacturing (CIM) is the term used to describe an organization that has all its systems linked by computer. These links begin with **computer-assisted design (CAD),** which allows engineers and designers to create new product ideas using three-dimensional plans. Daimler-Benz, the manufacturer of Mercedes-Benz cars, recently spent $10 million to buy software for all 3,000 engineers to enable them to use CAD.[2]

The computer design is then linked to the manufacturing process. **Computer-assisted manufacturing (CAM),** for example, allows organizations to make products through programmed machines. Programmable machines are commonly used in the manufacture of cars to perform welding and in the electronics industry to insert components in a circuit board. In addition to saving on some labor costs, these machines have the advantage of being more precise and faster than humans.

The CIM organization also has the advantage of real-time information. Coors' new production facility in Virginia is designed to be a CIM facility. The reporting system is tied to the manufacturing system and provides minute-by-minute displays. These systems feed process and operational data into a database that can be accessed by many users. All the employees at the Coors plant are trained to use the computer system.[3]

Through computer-assisted design (CAD), engineers can create car designs without paper. When CAD is tied to the manufacturing and management accounting systems, managers have a powerful tool for planning. What are some of the ways in which this technology has changed industry?

Global Competition

Global competition has been a major force affecting business organizations in the last 30 years. In 1960 almost all cars and televisions purchased in the United States were made in the United States. The manufacturers of those products did not have to concern themselves with competition from other countries. Today, however, most of the televisions and many of the cars purchased in the United States come from abroad. In many cases, parts for a product are made in many different countries. With the reduction of tariffs due to treaties such as the North American Free Trade Agreement (NAFTA), business organizations must consider the whole world as a source of competition and an opportunity for new customers.

To be successful in a global economy, business organizations must be more concerned about customer demands and operate more efficiently. Organizations generally compete by providing better customer service and selling products and services at a lower cost. Better customer service requires the organization to have a customer orientation. Lower costs require the organization to operate more efficiently.

Although the global economy has been blamed for the failure of some organizations and the loss of jobs in some countries, the global economy has benefited many organizations that can compete for customers around the world. Each organization must look for its comparative advantage in the global economy. Also, customers have benefited from the global economy. With increased competition, product and service prices are lower and the quality is higher.

Customer Orientation and Total Quality Management (TQM)

In a global economy, customers have more choices. No longer are they limited to purchasing from a dominant national supplier. With customers free to choose, organizations must recognize and satisfy customer demands. Increased customer orientation of organizations is obvious in advertising slogans such as Ford's "Quality is Job #1" and United Airlines's "Fly the Friendly Skies of United."

The move to customer orientation has been formalized through **total quality management (TQM).** TQM is a philosophy of continually lowering costs and improving the provision of services and products to customers. Quality is defined by the customer and designed into the product. TQM involves everyone within the organization. A shift to TQM means the organization will seek to continually improve its operations and customer services.

The Value Chain and Efficient Operations

One of a customer's greatest concerns is the price of the product or service. Because customers are price conscious, organizations must be concerned with efficiency in supplying the product or service. In a global economy, the low-cost producer has a competitive advantage.

To operate efficiently, an organization must identify the processes that are critical to satisfying the customer. These processes make up the **value chain.** The value chains of products or services may differ, but a typical value chain for a manufacturer may look like the following:

Research and development → Design and Engineering → Production → Distribution → Customer service

Any processes that are not on the value chain are considered **non–value-added activities.** Non–value-added activities do not provide value for customers. Examples of non-value-added activities include the moving and storing of products and many administrative tasks. Elimination of non–value-added activities

Automatic teller machines (ATMs) have revolutionized the way people use banks. Customers who now get cash at many convenient locations and "just in time" for their activities can hardly imagine the days when cash was only available from tellers during regular bank operating hours. A combination of technology and competition has turned banks into customer-oriented organizations.

allows the organization to save resources and sell its products and services at a lower price without reducing the value to customers.

Just-in-Time (JIT) Procedures

Just-in-time (JIT) is a process of providing products and services on demand. Manufacturing organizations using JIT make a product when an order is received rather than make it in advance and hold it until it is sold or discarded. Service organizations using JIT must adjust operations such that customers are served upon demand. With JIT, customers should no longer have long waits for delivery of the product or service. To make JIT work, the organization must design systems that operate efficiently and without delay. JIT is designed to eliminate non–value-added activities. One result of JIT is the elimination of costly inventory. By making the product only when ordered, there is no wasted product due to obsolescence or lack of demand.

JIT only works if the product or service can be supplied quickly when demanded. If customers have to wait, they will go elsewhere for the product or service. Organizations are able to shift to JIT, in part, because of technological changes. For example, the advent of bar-coding and the instant reporting of sales to suppliers of grocery stores allow stores to hold less inventory of a particular item and suppliers to replenish inventory when needed. CAM allows manufacturers to change production quickly to accommodate unexpected changes in demand. Toyota's automated plants are designed to reduce the time of changing over from making one type of car to another. And computers allow service organizations to satisfy customer demands more quickly. Automatic teller machines (ATMs) allow bank customers to obtain cash when needed rather than wait for normal operating hours.

WHAT'S HAPPENING

McDonald's restaurants maintain an inventory of many cooked hamburgers, but Burger King restaurants cook their hamburgers after they are ordered. What are the advantages and disadvantages of each method?

CONCEPT REVIEW

1. Why is management accounting an evolving process?

McDonald's and Burger King have been active competitors for over 30 years. This competition has driven each organization to provide better service. "You deserve a break today!" and "Have it your way!" reveal the customer orientation of each organization. Burger King's slogan emphasizes its individual preparation of orders.

2. How can technological innovations affect an organization?
3. Why should organizations be worried about global competition?
4. What is the philosophy of TQM?
5. What is the advantage of identifying the value chain of a product?

COMPACT DISC STORES (CONTINUED)

By opening stores that sell CDs, Diane was fortunate to reap the benefits of being at the forefront of a technological revolution in the music business. But Diane knows she must be aware of technological innovations that may make CDs obsolete. She also has identified some innovations that will help in operating her business. Bar-coding of the CDs allows for the tracking of inventory by Diane and the suppliers of the CDs. Also, antitheft magnetic tapes help reduce shoplifting.

Diane is also concerned about competition. Although her stores sell CDs for low prices, she has ignored other aspects of customer satisfaction. Are customers finding the CDs they want? Do customers receive friendly service? Should more listening rooms be constructed? Diane realizes that her sales goal and her goal to help local artists are dependent on having satisfied customers. This means surveying customers to discover what they want and restructuring the organization to recognize the importance of customers. She plans to attend a seminar on TQM in the near future to learn more about making the organization more sensitive to customers.

1.2 The Nature of Organizations

Organizations are groups of individuals that have joined together to perform particular tasks to achieve particular goals. Organizations include schools, businesses, clubs, religious groups, hospitals, and governmental bodies. Organizations are formed because groups of individuals can perform particular tasks more easily than individuals operating alone. For example, schools are formed because the process of educating can be performed more easily with a structured curriculum and classes. An alternative to a school is to have each individual arrange for his or her own education. This would be a difficult process. Even individuals involved in home schooling usually join together to provide some joint educational experiences.

An organization performs tasks to achieve goals. The goals of an organization reflect the interests of the stakeholders of the organization. The **stakeholders** of the organization are any parties that are affected by the organization. Stakeholders include owners, creditors, employees, customers, and society. Typical goals might include providing cash or nonmonetary benefits to the owners, maximizing profits, satisfying customers, improving the welfare of members of the organization, and providing services to society.

Although organizations are formed to perform a particular task, not all individuals within the organization will agree on how the task should be performed. In addition, disagreements may exist as to how responsibilities are divided among the different individuals within the organization, how the individuals are evaluated, and how any rewards are shared. Organizations develop structures to help solve these problems. An organization's structure is composed of three related processes: (1) the assignment of responsibilities, (2) the measurement of performance, and (3) the rewarding of individuals within the organization.

The first component of the organizational structure is to determine the responsibilities of the different members of the organization. **Decision rights** define the duties that a member of an organization is expected to perform. The decision rights of a particular individual within an organization are specified by that person's job description. Checkout clerks in grocery stores have the decision rights to collect cash from customers but don't have the decision rights to accept certain types of checks. A manager must be called for that decision. A division manager may have the right to set prices on products, but not the right to borrow money through issuing debt. The right to issue debt is usually retained by the president or the board of directors.

Organizations must also motivate individuals to perform their duties consistent with the goals of the organization. Individuals have their own goals, which are not necessarily congruent with the goals of the organization. To motivate individuals within the organization, organizations must have a system for measuring performance and rewarding individuals. **Performance measures** are direct or indirect measures of output of individuals or groups of individuals within the organization. Performance measures for a salesperson could include total sales and customer satisfaction based on a survey of customers. Performance measures for a manufacturing unit could include number of units produced and percentage of defective units.

Performance measures are extremely important because rewards are generally based on performance measures. Rewards for individuals within organizations include wages and bonuses, prestige and greater decision rights, promotions, and job security. Because rewards are based on performance measures, individuals and groups are motivated to act to influence the performance measures. Therefore, the performance measures influence the direction of individual and group efforts within the organization. A poor choice of performance measures can lead to conflicts within the organization and derail efforts to achieve organizational goals. For example, measuring the performance of a college president based on the number of students attending the college will encourage the president to allow ill-prepared students to enter the college and reduce the quality of the educational experience for other students.

Designing and implementing an organizational structure is difficult. Goals must be identified, and processes to achieve those goals must be planned. These processes, which include assigning decision rights, measuring performance, and rewarding the members of the organization, must consider the environmental conditions that affect the organization. The processes become more complicated as organizations grow. Some organizations have decided to downsize (get smaller) because their organizational structure has become too cumbersome. For example, in 1995 General Motors decided to separate its automobile manufacturing business from its electronic data processing business because the existing organizational structure did not accommodate the diverse goals and processes of the two business units.

CONCEPT REVIEW

1. Why do organizations form?
2. What are the three basic processes of an organization's structure?

COMPACT DISC STORES (CONTINUED)

> Diane realizes that she has not had time to carefully consider the organizational structure of Compact Disc Stores. Now she begins to do so by examining the decision rights that she has delegated. Presently, managers control the daily operations of their respective stores in the suburbs. The managers also make their own inventory decisions because Diane feels that the managers have a better understanding of the preferences of their own customers. Diane currently uses total sales as a performance measure and frequently visits the stores in the suburbs to verify that appropriate shelf space is reserved for local recording artists. The reward system for the managers, however, is not based on any performance measure. Managers are paid $20,000 whether sales are high or low. Diane decides that a bonus based on sales will provide additional incentives for the managers, but she is not sure whether sales is the appropriate performance measure and whether she has given her managers too few or too many decision rights.

1.3 The Role of Managers

Managers are individuals within the organization who make planning decisions. Historically only individuals at the top of the organizational chart had decision rights. The remaining employees had no decision rights and simply did what they were told. Modern organizations, however, have recognized that most individuals within the organization have knowledge that can be useful for decision making. Laborers in manufacturing organizations often have better knowledge of the manufacturing process than their superiors. Salespeople usually know their customers better than the sales manager does. To take advantage of this specialized knowledge, modern organizations have given these employees more decision rights. This delegation of decision rights is known as **worker empowerment.** With worker empowerment, every member of the organization has some decision rights and, therefore, is a manager.

In addition to making decisions, managers are also responsible for managing, motivating, and monitoring other people within the organization. In a typical corporation, the board of directors supervises the president, the president supervises the vice presidents, the vice presidents supervise the division managers, and so on. In traditional corporations, an organizational chart similar to Figure 1.1 provides the lines of authority in determining who is responsible for supervising others.

Making Planning Decisions

To accomplish the goals of the organization, managers must make decisions on what tasks should be performed and how to complete those tasks. The planning

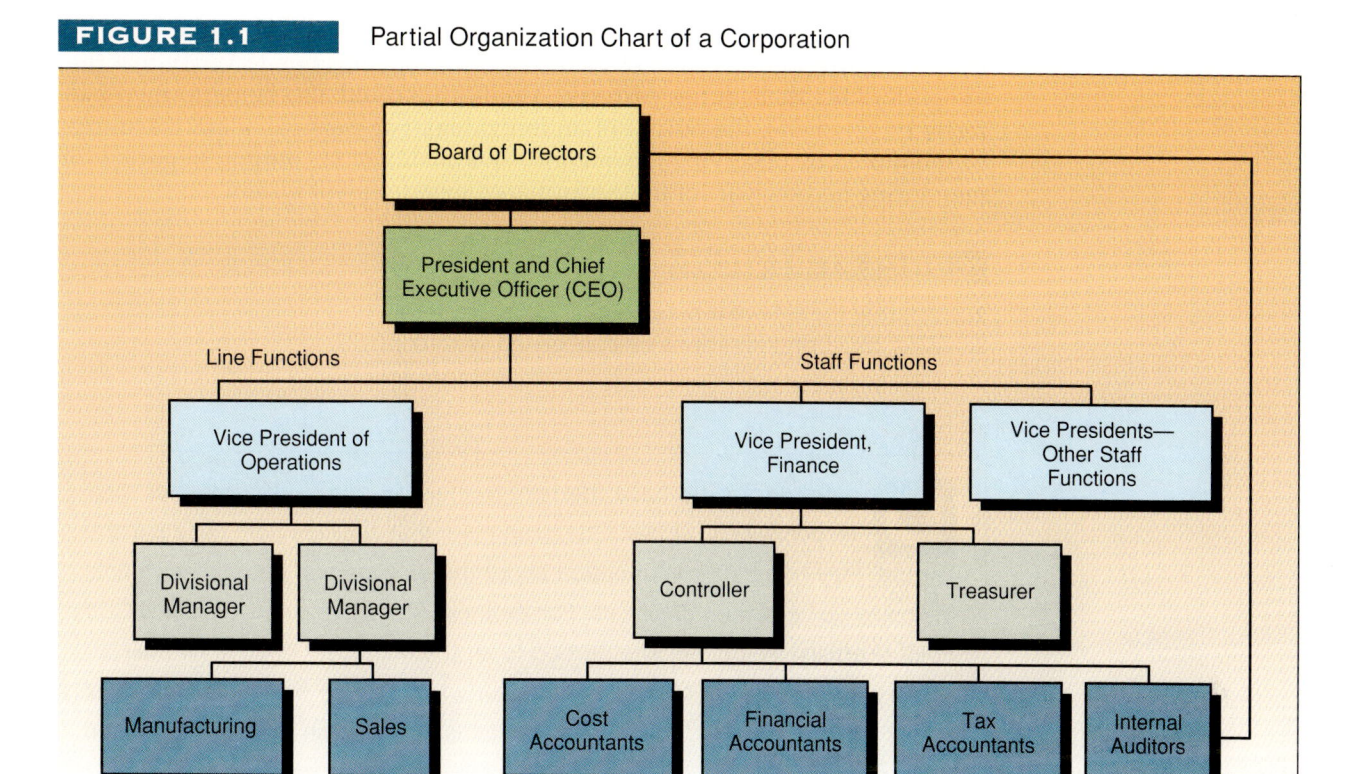

FIGURE 1.1 Partial Organization Chart of a Corporation

```
                    Board of Directors
                            |
                  President and Chief
                  Executive Officer (CEO)
                            |
        ┌───────────────────┴────────────────────┐
   Line Functions                          Staff Functions
        |                              ┌──────────┴──────────┐
  Vice President of              Vice President,      Vice Presidents—
     Operations                      Finance          Other Staff Functions
        |                                |
   ┌────┴────┐                    ┌──────┴──────┐
Divisional  Divisional         Controller      Treasurer
 Manager     Manager                |
   ┌────┴────┐          ┌───────┬───┴────┬──────────┐
Manufacturing  Sales   Cost   Financial  Tax      Internal
                    Accountants Accountants Accountants Auditors
```

decisions occur at all levels of the organization. Long-term planning decisions tend to be made by the top-level managers while shorter term planning decisions tend to be made by managers with fewer decision rights. For example, the president of the organization is likely to make decisions on what product lines to offer and long-term financing. The division managers make decisions on specific products or services to offer. The manufacturing managers make decisions on how to make the product. And the shop floor managers make decisions on how to route products among the different machines.

This book primarily focuses on planning decisions to choose the products or services to be provided and the pricing of those products and services. But managers make other types of planning decisions. For example, long-term investment decisions are discussed in Chapter 13. Also, managers may make planning decisions about operational processes, marketing, and customers.

Control: Managing, Motivating, and Monitoring People

The managing, motivating, and monitoring of other people within the organization is called **control.** The purpose of control is to encourage members of the organization to work for the goals of the organization. Because of diverse individual preferences, organizational goals and individual member's goals may not always coincide. For example, the goal of the organization may be to maximize profits. Maximization of profits, however, may mean more hours of overtime for employees, which may not be in the best interest of the employees.

The organizational design and assignment of decision rights help control manager decisions. For example, a purchasing manager is constrained to follow specific rules in making a purchase and can only make purchases above a specified amount with approval from a superior.

Control also encompasses the choice of performance measures and a reward system. Performance measures and rewards based on those performance measures are used to motivate members of the organization.

Organizations also control members through **monitoring.** Monitoring includes the direct observation of members of the organization to verify that they are performing their duties correctly. Monitoring could also be performed indirectly by observing the output of an individual. For example, a craftsman may be monitored by observing the quantity and quality of his output. Reports from monitoring become part of the performance measurement system.

CONCEPT REVIEW

1. What is the role of a manager?
2. Why must organizations be concerned with control?

COMPACT DISC STORES (CONTINUED)

> Diane's managers have the right to make inventory decisions for their respective CD stores. She gave them that decision right because she felt that they had better information about their customers, but she still wants to control some of their decisions. For example, she wants them to display CDs of local artists. Therefore, she agreed to let the managers choose all their inventory except for 5% of the shelf space, which will be designated for local artists chosen by Diane. Diane also maintains the decision rights for any large investments.

1.4 The Role of the Accounting System

The accounting system traditionally identifies events affecting the organization and measures and communicates those effects in monetary terms. For example, the purchase of a building by the organization is measured by the cash outlay for the building. A sale on credit is identified as a receivable for the organization and measured in terms of the money owed to the organization. Because the events are all measured in a common monetary unit, the accounting systems can aggregate the effect of different events and make comparisons. Accumulated accounting data is communicated in accounting reports for managers of the organization and users outside the organization.

In modern organizations the role of accounting need not be limited to recording dollar amounts of past events. To fulfill the information demands of managers and external users, the accounting system should also encompass nonfinancial information such as production data, consumer demand forecasts, customer satisfaction statistics, service calls, and industry benchmarks. By integrating financial and nonfinancial information, the accounting system can better serve its users.

Accounting information related to the organization is used by different parties. Figure 1.2 describes the different roles of the accounting system of the organization. **Management accounting** involves the use of accounting information by managers to help achieve the organization's goals. Managers receive this information in the form of reports such as sales reports, inventory reports, budgets, and monthly operating reports. Management accounting provides information for two general functions: making planning decisions and control. Accounting allows for better planning decisions through more knowledge of the problem. Managers use accounting for control through influencing members of the organization to make decisions that are consistent with the organizational goals. Preferred characteristics of management accounting include accurate measures of

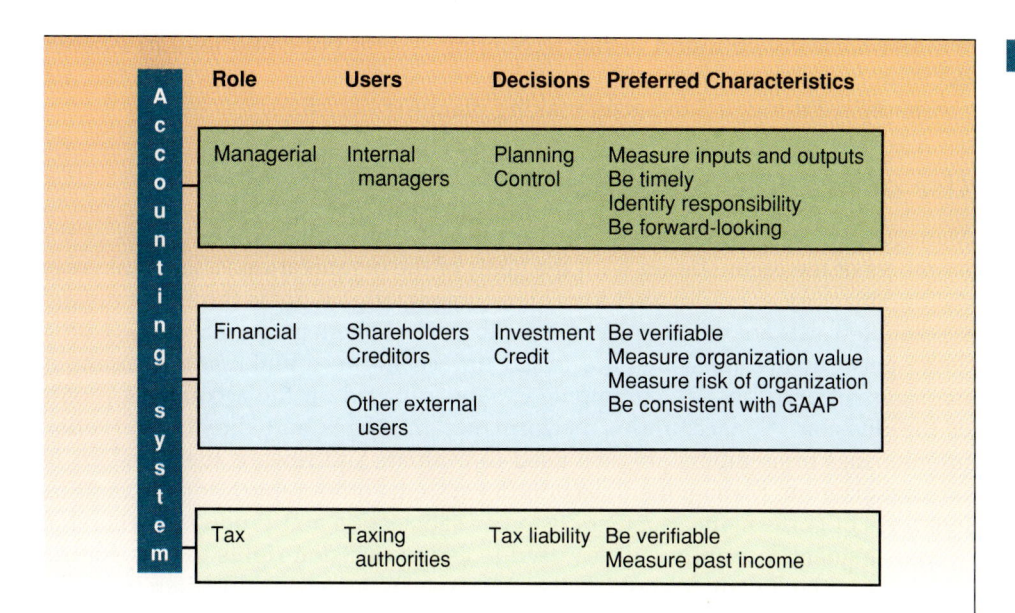

FIGURE 1.2

The Accounting System Serves Different Purposes

Role	Users	Decisions	Preferred Characteristics
Managerial	Internal managers	Planning Control	Measure inputs and outputs Be timely Identify responsibility Be forward-looking
Financial	Shareholders Creditors Other external users	Investment Credit	Be verifiable Measure organization value Measure risk of organization Be consistent with GAAP
Tax	Taxing authorities	Tax liability	Be verifiable Measure past income

multiple inputs and outputs of the organization, timeliness, identification of responsibility, and the capacity to be forward-looking.

The accounting system must also meet the requirements of constituents outside the organization. **Financial accounting** is used to report to investors, creditors, and other interested parties outside the organization. These parties are primarily interested in information for making investment and credit decisions. Preferred characteristics of financial accounting include verifiability, measures of organizational value, measures of risk of the organization, and consistency with financial reporting regulations, known as *generally accepted accounting procedures (GAAP)*.

Tax accounting is used to calculate income taxes and report to government taxing authorities, such as the Internal Revenue Service (IRS) in the United States. Taxing authorities prefer accounting to be verifiable and to measure past income consistent with tax regulations.

Use of Accounting for Making Planning Decisions

Planning decisions are made to help an organization achieve its goals. Increased knowledge about the impact of a decision on the organization allows managers to make more informed choices. For example, the forecast of sales is used to determine the amount of product to be manufactured. If a customer survey is performed, a more accurate sales forecast will lead to better production decisions.

Management accounting is not the only source of information to improve decision making. Information about the political, legal, and competitive environment also leads to better decisions within an organization. The advantage of management accounting information is the conversion of events into a common unit of measure, the monetary unit. Conversion of events into dollars allows managers to compare the impact of various decisions on the organization. The decision to automate or continue to produce handmade products can be analyzed by converting both events into dollar outlays and comparing the dollar outlays of each alternative. But other nonfinancial information may also be useful, especially if the organization has goals other than minimizing dollar outlays. The organization may also be concerned about the welfare of its employees. Automation may improve or harm the employees' welfare. This type of information will not normally be found in the accounting system but could lead to a better decision.

Chapters 2 through 5 focus on making planning decisions.

Use of Accounting for Control

Management accounting assists in control by helping align the interests of the members of the organization with the goals of the organization. The members of the organization are motivated to achieve organizational goals through a reward system. Rewards are based on achieving sufficiently high performance measures. Some performance measures are based on accounting numbers. For example, managers of divisions are commonly evaluated based on the accounting profits of the division. Nonaccounting performance measures and direct observation (monitoring) of members are also used to evaluate and reward the members of the organization. Management accounting systems often report non-accounting measures of performance such as customer satisfaction and product defect rates.

Management accounting is also used to assign decision rights to help control members of the organizations. Limits on actions by managers are often based on accounting numbers. For example, a salesperson may have the right to grant credit to a customer only up to $1,000. The communication of these decision rights often occurs through management accounting documents such as the budget.

Designing a system to align the interests of the members of the organization with the goals of the organization is not an easy task. Chapters 6 and 7 focus on control issues, and Chapters 8 through 15 look at the combined use of management accounting for making planning decisions and for control.

Use of Accounting by External Parties

Financial reporting is the accounting process of communicating with parties outside the organization such as shareholders and creditors. These outsiders use financial reports to evaluate the financial progress and current state of the organization and the success of the top-level managers in achieving the organization's financial goals. Top-level managers are often rewarded based on numbers in the financial reports, such as the firm's reported profits. For example, presidents often receive bonuses if profits are greater than a predetermined target. The financial reports of corporations commonly include a balance sheet, income statement, changes in stockholders' equity, a cash flow statement, and footnotes explaining those statements. Other types of organizations have similar statements in their financial reports.

WHAT'S HAPPENING

Boeing Corporation, a large manufacturer of commercial airplanes, has many people performing accounting duties, but only about 4% of those accountants are working on financial and tax accounting issues. Accountants in smaller organizations, however, spend a higher proportion of time on financial and tax accounting. Why do financial and tax issues take more precedence in a small organization?

The procedures used in financial accounting for corporations are dictated by generally accepted accounting principles (GAAP), which are consistent with the pronouncements of the Financial Accounting Standards Board (FASB) and the Securities and Exchange Commission (SEC). Although financial accounting reports must follow certain basic rules, managers can influence financial accounting reports because GAAP allow some discretion to managers for changing accounting estimates or accounting methods.

Many organizations must also file accounting reports with a taxing authority. In the United States, these accounting reports are sent to the Internal Revenue Service (IRS). The rules governing these accounting reports are determined by the U.S. Congress and court cases and may differ from the rules for financial reports sent to shareholders and

The complexity of assembling a Boeing 777 requires planning and control. Boeing hires a large number of accountants to help coordinate functions such as the purchase and delivery of parts, controlling the cost of parts, and the management of Boeing's thousands of employees.

creditors. The goal of most organizations is to minimize taxes within the rules of the taxing authority.

Financial reporting and income tax reports are not the primary focus of this book. But reporting to external parties cannot be ignored in management accounting, especially when numbers from the accounting system are used for both external reporting and for planning decisions and control. The next section identifies the trade-offs that exist when using a common accounting system for multiple purposes.

CONCEPT REVIEW

1. How is management accounting used for making planning decisions?
2. What is the role of management accounting for control?
3. Who are external users of the accounting system?

COMPACT DISC STORES (CONTINUED)

Diane has not paid much attention to the accounting system of Compact Disc Stores. When she started the first store, she purchased software for her personal computer to record expenditures and cash receipts. At the end of the year, she hired a CPA to generate financial statements and fill out income tax forms. The financial statements are sent to Janice Nishimura, her partner, and the bank that made the loan. As long as sales were strong, Diane did not worry about using the accounting system for managing the stores. But sales have declined and Diane is thinking about how she can make better decisions. In particular, she must decide whether to open another store. An examination of the profit of her existing stores should help in this decision.

In measuring profit by stores, Diane is also able to establish new performance measures for the managers of the stores. Managers evaluated based on profit will consider the effect of their decisions on both revenues and expenses.

1.5 Trade-Offs in Using the Accounting System for Multiple Purposes

Figure 1.2 describes a single accounting system that generates accounting numbers for multiple purposes. But one accounting system is unlikely to be appropriate for all the different decisions being made by internal and external users of accounting. For example, a manager might like to know the cost of alternative methods of manufacturing a product, but a creditor would want to know the impact of the method chosen on cash flows available to pay interest.

Because a single accounting system will not provide appropriate information for all decisions, trade-offs must be made among the different roles for accounting. This theme of trade-offs among different uses of accounting information is referred to throughout this book. The following sections provide examples of these trade-offs.

Trade-Off between Making Planning Decisions and Control

Managers generally have specialized information that is useful for making planning decisions. To make the best planning decision, the person with the best information about a choice should make the decision. But there is the problem of motivating the individual to make decisions consistent with the goals of the organization. For example, a computer specialist may be the best informed individual on the relative qualities of different computers. If the computer specialist is given the decision rights to purchase a computer for the organization, he may choose the most powerful and expensive computer available. Having the most expensive computer may not be in the best interest of the organization if the organization has a greater need of cash for other purposes.

Instead of delegating decision rights to the manager with specialized knowledge, the organization could request the manager to communicate the specialized knowledge to higher level managers, who would make decisions related to the information. But the communicated information could also be used to evaluate the manager with the specialized knowledge. Knowing that any information a manager communicates can be used for evaluation may cause the manager to alter the information and make the information less useful for making planning decisions. For example, a manufacturing manager may know how to modify a machine to reduce processing time. This information would be useful for general management in making investment decisions for new machinery. But the manufacturing manager is evaluated based on number of units produced daily. The manufacturing manager can modify the machine to achieve production goals more easily, but knowledge of this modification by general management would eventually lead to higher expectations about the performance of the manufacturing manager. The use of information to reward the manufacturing manager inhibits the communication of information useful for planning decisions.

Trade-Off between Making Planning Decisions and External Reporting

External reporting is for users outside the organization. Current regulations set forth by the FASB, the SEC, and the IRS specify the use of **historical costs** to measure the value of most assets of the organization. The historical cost of an object is its acquisition price or the value of resources used to acquire the object. For example, land purchased 10 years ago for $70,000 may now have a market value of $200,000, but the land is still recorded at $70,000 in the financial reports, and no gain due to the increase in market value is recognized in financial or tax reports until the land is sold.

An advantage of using historical costs is their objective nature. Historical costs depend less on the subjective judgment of managers because they reflect actual transactions. Outside investors, creditors, and taxing authorities generally prefer accounting numbers that are not susceptible to manipulation by managers. But historical costs are not necessarily the costs that managers should use for decision making within the organization.

Managers of organizations often make planning decisions. Estimates of future costs would be useful for these planning decisions. Historical costs are only good estimates of future costs if the economic, competitive, and operational environments have remained the same. For example, the historical cost of a gold watch is not a very good estimate for making another gold watch if the cost of gold has changed. Therefore, financially reported (historical cost) numbers should be used with care for planning as they can lead to inappropriate decisions.

Trade-Offs between Control and External Reporting

If a financial report based on historical costs is the only available method of evaluating managers, managers will work to affect the financial report. But maximizing profit based on historical costs may not be consistent with the shareholder goal of maximizing shareholder value. For example, the maintenance of machines, which increases the value of the organization, is an immediate expense and reduces present profit figures. By cutting maintenance, managers increase current profit at the expense of future profits.

To achieve the goals of the organization through control, performance measures should be closely associated with those goals. Financial reports based on historical costs may not be closely linked to the goals of the organization and could lead to dysfunctional behavior by members of the organization.

COMPACT DISC STORES (CONTINUED)

Diane Johnson wants to estimate future cash flows to determine if she can expand Compact Disc Stores without going to the bank. These plans require accurate estimates of future sales, but Diane is worried that the managers will provide her with low estimates of future sales if she rewards them based on sales or profits. The managers will want to establish a low benchmark, so that bonuses for high sales and earnings can be achieved easily.

In deciding whether to expand to another CD store, Diane must estimate the cost of purchasing and remodeling a building. She has recently opened two new stores . The cost of opening those two new stores is reflected in the balance sheet of her financial reports. She could use those historical cost figures as an estimate of the cost of opening a new store, but she knows that real estate prices have increased since she opened her last store. Therefore, the financial accounting reports are not relevant. Diane must acquire more data about present real estate prices to make the decision.

Diane has decided to compensate her managers based on the accounting profit generated from their respective stores. But her music store managers are young and looking for other work opportunities. She is worried they aren't

> concerned about the long-term interests of Compact Disc Stores. She recently visited one of the stores in the suburbs and found customers grumbling about not enough staff available to provide customer service. When she approached the manager about this problem, the manager responded that he cut the number of sales positions to reduce costs and improve profits. Diane is worried that customers will not return to any of the Compact Disc Stores if they are disappointed with service at this suburban store. Therefore, she decides to perform customer surveys as an additional performance measure to be used jointly with accounting profit to reward the managers.

CONCEPT REVIEW

1. Why does the use of accounting numbers for both planning decisions and control lead to trade-offs?
2. Why may historical costs from financial reports be inappropriate for making planning decisions?
3. Why may the profit number in financial reports be inappropriate for evaluating managers?

1.6 Multiple Accounting Systems

The trade-offs that exist among the various uses of an accounting system could be solved by using multiple accounting systems. Separate accounting systems could be established for making planning decisions, control, and financial and tax reporting. The problem with this solution is the cost of establishing multiple accounting systems. Many small organizations have the resources for only a single accounting system. Because financial reports are often required by regulations and banks, the financial accounting system may be the only accounting system that is available within the organization. Larger organizations, however, are likely to have two or more accounting systems for different purposes.

Multiple accounting systems are at times confusing. With multiple accounting systems, items may be reported at different costs. One accounting system might report that a particular division made profits of $6.2 million and the other accounting system reports its profits at $5.8 million. Managers will be forced to spend time reconciling the differences. Remember the old proverb: "A man with one watch knows what time it is. A man with two watches is never sure."

An accounting system with only monetary measures is not the only source of information to assist in making planning decisions and control. Planning decisions are likely to be at least partially based on nonmonetary factors. For example, planning decisions to achieve goals such as employee satisfaction would use employee surveys as an information source. Control could also be implemented using nonmonetary performance measures. For example, a manufacturing manager could be evaluated based on the percentage of defective units produced.

This book recognizes that most organizations do not have separate accounting systems for different purposes, and trade-offs will exist in using accounting numbers for different types of decisions. The trade-off between making

WHAT'S HAPPENING

Before a recent modification of the accounting system for management accounting purposes, engineers at Tektronix had developed their own accounting system separate from the organization's accounting system. Why did these engineers become accountants?

planning decisions and control will be the primary focus of this book, but financial and tax reporting issues will also be recognized.

COMPACT DISK STORES (CONTINUED)

The CPA hired by Diane Johnson has determined that the financially reported profit of Compact Disc Stores is $32,000 before income taxes. But the auditor has also suggested that a more conservative accounting method could be used for tax reporting to obtain a profit before income taxes of $28,000. Both Diane and her investment partner, Janice Nishimura, are thrilled to pay less taxes, but they are confused about which profit number to use to divide profits among the partners.

CONCEPT REVIEW

1. What are the advantages of having multiple accounting systems?
2. Why do some organizations only have one accounting system?

1.7 The Evolution of Management Accounting: A Framework for Change

Management accounting has evolved with the nature of organizations. Prior to the most recent 200 years, most business organizations were small and operated by family members. Management accounting was less important for these small organizations. It was not as critical for planning decisions and control reasons because the owner could observe directly the whole environment of the organization. The owner or a family member made almost all of the decisions, so there was little delegation of decision rights and no need to worry about motivation. Only as organizations grew larger would management accounting become more important.

Most of today's modern management accounting techniques were developed in the period from 1825 to 1925, with the growth of large organizations.[4] Textile mills in the early 19th century grew by combining the multiple processes (spinning the thread, dying, weaving, etc.) of making cloth. These large firms developed systems to measure the cost per yard or per pound for the separate manufacturing processes. The cost data allowed managers to compare the cost of conducting a process inside the firm versus purchasing the process from external vendors. Similarly, the railroads of the 1850s–1870s developed cost systems that reported cost per ton-mile and operating expenses per dollar of revenue. These measures allowed managers to increase their operating efficiencies. In the early 1900s, Andrew Carnegie (at what was to become U.S. Steel) devised a cost system that reported detailed unit cost figures for material and labor on a daily and weekly basis. This system allowed senior managers to maintain very tight controls on operations and also gave them accurate and timely information on marginal costs for pricing decisions. Merchandisers such as Marshall Field's and Sears, Roebuck developed gross margin (revenues less cost of goods sold) and stock-turn ratios (sales divided by inventory) to measure and evaluate performance. Manufacturing companies such as Du Pont Powder Company and General Motors were also active in developing performance measures to control their growing organizations.

Large organizations such as General Motors have benefited from modern management accounting techniques. GM recognized early the importance of developing performance measures to control the growing organization. The organizational structure in conjunction with management accounting enables a large organization to motivate employees to achieve organizational goals.

In the period 1925–1975, management accounting was heavily influenced by external considerations. Income taxes and financial accounting requirements (e.g., the Financial Accounting Standards Board) were the major factors affecting management accounting.

Since 1975, two major environmental forces have changed organizations and caused managers to question whether traditional management accounting procedures (pre-1975) are still appropriate. These environmental forces are: (1) factory automation and computer/information technology and (2) global competition. To adapt to these environmental forces, organizations must reconsider their organizational structure and their management accounting procedures.

The history of management accounting from 1825 to the present illustrates how management accounting has evolved in parallel with the organizations' structure. Management accounting is used to provide information for planning decisions and control. It is useful for assigning decision rights, measuring performance, and determining rewards for individuals within the organization. Because management accounting is part of the organizational structure, it is not surprising that management accounting evolves in a parallel and consistent fashion with other parts of the organizational structure.

Figure 1.3 is a framework for change within an organization. Environmental forces such as technological innovation and global competition change the investment opportunities of the organization. To meet these new investment opportunities, organizations must adapt their organizational structure, which includes management accounting. The new organizational structure provides incentives for members of the organization to make planning decisions, which leads to a change in the value of the organization. The roles of accounting in this framework are assisting in the control of the organization through the organization's structure and providing information for planning decisions. This framework for change will be referred to throughout the book.

CONCEPT REVIEW

1. What historical circumstances made management accounting important for organizations?
2. Why must organizations and management accounting evolve together?

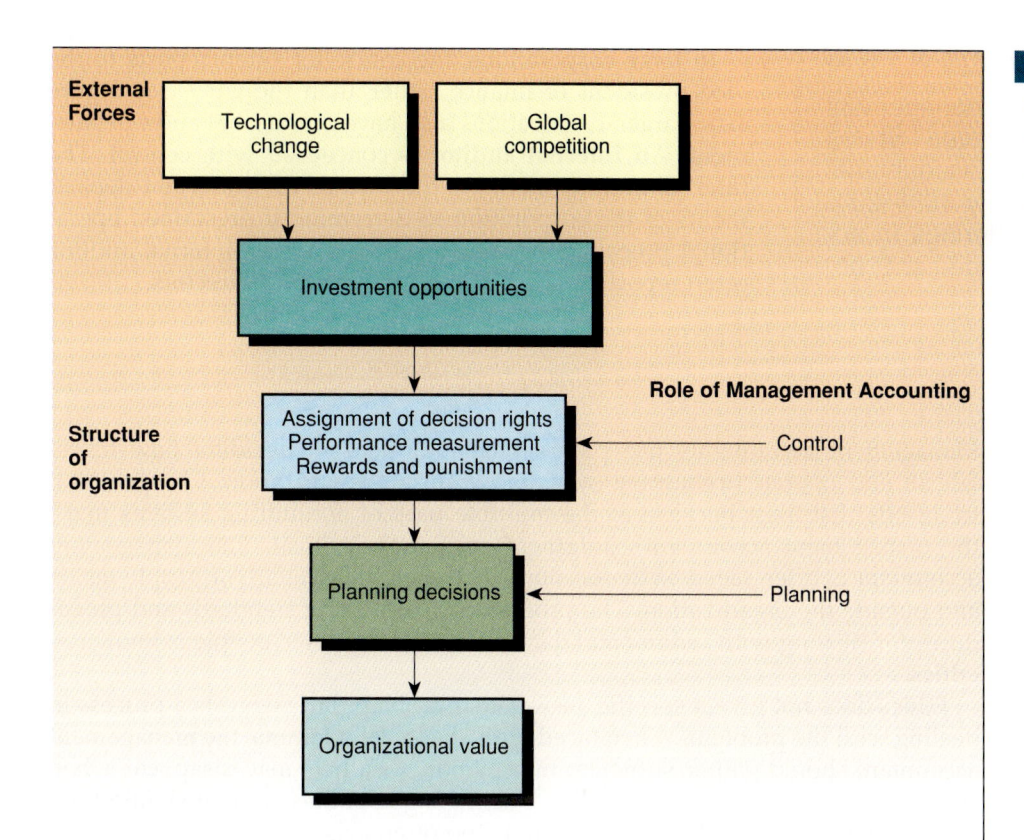

FIGURE 1.3

Framework for Organizational Change and Management Accounting

External Forces: Technological change, Global competition → Investment opportunities

Structure of organization: Assignment of decision rights, Performance measurement, Rewards and punishment → Planning decisions → Organizational value

Role of Management Accounting: Control, Planning

COMPACT DISC STORES (CONCLUDED)

By adjusting the decision rights of the managers and changing the performance measurement and reward systems of Compact Disc Stores, Diane feels that her business can be a success. But these changes are only the first of many. As Compact Disc Stores grows and the technology and competition change, the organizational structure and management accounting system will have to evolve.

1.8 Types of Management Accountants

Management accountants are responsible for the accounting system within the organization. The accounting system should be designed to assist in making planning decisions, in control, and in financial and tax reporting. The management accounting function in very small organizations is normally performed by a bookkeeper who records transactions. An outside accountant often assists in the creation of financial statements and tax returns. The emphasis on financial reporting means that managers may not have relevant information easily available for planning purposes. Control is unlikely to be important because the manager making the decisions is likely to be the owner.

In larger organizations, someone is normally assigned the responsibilities of a management accountant. That person is usually called the **controller.** The controller assists managers in making decisions and reports to the president or chief executive officer (CEO). The controller may also have assistant controllers. Controllers are more than just compilers of information; they also are members of planning teams and act as interpreters and advisors. Controllers are expected to add value to the management process.[5]

Organizations and Accounting

WHAT'S HAPPENING

There are more management accountants in the United States than all other types of accountants combined. Why are only 10%–20% of university course offerings in accounting in the management accounting field?

In large corporations, the controller often reports to the vice president of finance rather than the CEO (see Figure 1.1). Larger corporations also have an internal audit department. An **internal auditor** is concerned with control. The internal auditor monitors the various divisions and departments of the corporation to determine if prescribed operational procedures are being followed. The internal auditor often reports to the CEO and the board of directors.

1.9 Ethics and Management Accounting

Management accountants use professional judgment in deciding how to establish and operate accounting systems within an organization. The potential trade-offs that exist because of the multiple uses of accounting systems make the management accountant's judgment even more critical. The management accountant is often faced with decisions that affect the welfare of people inside and outside the organization. The process of determining standards and procedures for dealing with judgmental decisions affecting other people is known as **ethics**.

Ethics does not give a specific answer to a problem but suggests a process in dealing with the problem. When faced with an ethical dilemma, the management accountant should gather sufficient information. Conflicts may disappear when sufficient information comes to light. The management accountant should then determine how stakeholders are affected. Too often crises arise when the effect on some individual or group is forgotten or ignored.

For example, a controller may find inventory items that are outdated by newer models. The old inventory items can only be sold below their historic cost. Their sale or write-down will cause a reported loss on the accounting statements and will harm the chances of the divisional employees' obtaining a bonus. The controller could simply ignore the old inventory; however, there is a cost of continuing to store the inventory. Although the current employees may be harmed by recognizing the loss associated with the old inventory, there are other parties that would be harmed by continuing to ignore the old inventory. The owners would have to continue to pay storage costs, and bonuses of future employees may be harmed if the loss is postponed. Once the effect on all the parties is examined, the controller will have more information to make a judgment.

The management accountant may be assisted in making judgment decisions by a code of ethics. Organizations frequently have a code of ethics that deals with standard problems facing the management accountant.

Employees of an organization must make judgmental decisions that affect customers, suppliers, owners, the community, and other members of the organization. BellSouth recognizes the importance of providing guidance through training and ethical codes to enable employees to make appropriate choices.

THE STORY OF MANAGERIAL ACCOUNTING

Team Decisions Regarding Change

The modern approach to management is a team-based decision process. Teams composed of members from different functional areas are formed to solve organizational problems. In order to publish *Managerial Accounting*, a book team was formed in 1994.

Including team members from different functional areas creates a team with diverse backgrounds and skills to allow for more creative, comprehensive, and efficient solutions. Often, organizational teams are short-lived and disbanded upon providing a solution to the current day's problem. With *Managerial Accounting*, our book team worked together on this First Edition and may be reconvened for future revisions.

Teams help an organization manage change. The *Managerial Accounting* book team was formed because management accounting education is changing. The book's publisher, Richard D. Irwin, recognized the importance of remaining competitive in a changing world. Note that an accountant is included on the team. Why should cross-functional teams have accountants? The *Managerial Accounting* book team is composed of the following members:

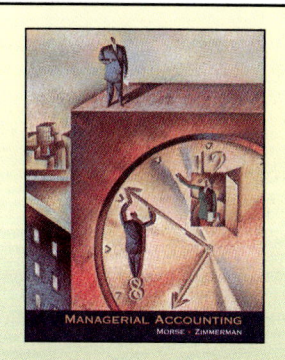

Person	Title	Duties
Jeff	Executive Editor	Team leader
Heather	Marketing Manager	Studies effective product positioning, then plans and coordinates marketing strategy
Kelly	Developmental Editor	Manages product through manuscript development
Charlene	Prepress Buyer	Solicits and reviews bids and selects typesetter; sets up schedule
Karen	Project Supervisor	Guides manuscript, art, and proof through editing and production cycles
Larry	Designer	Plans and oversees book interior design, cover design, and page layout
Dina	Production Supervisor	Oversees manufacturing (typesetting, printing, and binding)
Peggy	Accountant	Makes financial analyses and reports costs

BellSouth recognizes that workers face increasingly ambiguous situations in their work environment and consequently has developed an infrastructure to assist employees in using high ethical standards. In particular, the company has created training exercises, communication, and systems to promote ethics.[6] The establishment of ethical standards in an organization is important for helping members make appropriate choices.

The professional body of management accountants also has a code of ethics. The Institute of Management Accountants (IMA) has prescribed the following set of ethical standards:

1. **Competence.** Management accountants should be professionally competent to perform their duties of providing relevant and reliable information in accordance with relevant laws, regulations, and technical standards.
2. **Confidentiality.** Management accountants should refrain from disclosing confidential information or using confidential information to their own advantage.
3. **Integrity.** Management accountants should avoid (a) conflicts of interest by refusing compromising gifts and favors, (b) subversion of organizational objectives, (c) communication of biased information, and (d) activities that could discredit the profession.

4. *Objectivity.* Management accountants should communicate information fairly and objectively and disclose all relevant information.

This code of ethics is not sufficient to solve all ethical problems, but it provides some direction for the management accountant. In the case of the controller who found the old inventory, the integrity section of the code of ethics suggests that the decision to recognize the loss immediately is consistent with the communication of unbiased information. On the other hand, the current employees should not be held responsible for the loss because old inventory reflects a decision in prior years to produce extra inventory.

The IMA also administers a program that qualifies certified management accountants (CMAs). Applicants must pass an examination in management accounting and in the related fields of economics, finance, financial accounting, organizational behavior, and decision analysis.

CONCEPT REVIEW

1. Describe the roles of controllers and internal auditors in organizations.
2. Why should management accountants have a code of ethics?

1.10 Summary

1. Explain how technological innovation and global competition can affect an organization and its management accounting system. Technological innovation offers opportunities for new products and services and more efficient methods of operations. Global competition forces organizations to be more concerned about their customers and operating efficiently. The management accounting system must adapt to the changes in the organization.

2. Identify the basic processes of an organization's structure. An organization's structure includes the assignment of decision rights, performance measures, and a reward system.

3. Describe the role of managers in organizations. Managers make planning decisions and manage, motivate, and monitor others within the organization (control).

4. Explain the critical role played by management accounting in making planning decisions and controlling managers to work toward organizational goals. Management accounting improves planning decisions by providing decision makers with more information to make better decisions. Management accounting also supports control by assisting in the assignment of decision rights and establishing performance measures to motivate individuals.

5. Identify the trade-offs that exist in using information for making planning decisions, for control, and for external reporting. Using the same accounting system for making planning decisions, for control, and for external reporting leads to trade-offs. Employees will bias information used for planning purposes if the information is also used as a benchmark for measuring performance. External reports will similarly be affected if also used to evaluate performance.

6. Describe the advantages and disadvantages of having multiple accounting systems. Having multiple accounting systems allows managers to generate different accounting numbers for different purposes. Multiple accounting systems, however, are expensive and sometimes confusing.

7. Identify the roles of different types of management accountants. Controllers are responsible for the accounting systems within the organization. Internal auditors monitor members of the organization to determine if prescribed procedures are being followed.

8. **Recognize the role of judgment and ethics in making management accounting choices.** The management accountant must use judgment in resolving trade-offs arising from different uses of accounting information. This judgment should recognize the effect of decisions on all involved parties. A code of ethics assists the management accountant in making decisions.

Remainder of Book. Chapters 2 through 5 are devoted to making planning decisions. Various management decisions are examined and the appropriate information and decision rules are identified. These decisions include pricing decisions, product mix decisions, and capital budgeting decisions. Chapters 6 and 7 focus on the nature of organizations. Decision rights and control issues are examined. Chapters 8 through 15 consider the problem of adapting accounting systems to satisfy both planning and control demands for information.

Key Terms

Computer-assisted design (CAD) Use of computers for designing new products.

Computer-assisted manufacturing (CAM) Use of programmable robots to assist in the manufacturing of products.

Computer-integrated manufacturing (CIM) A manufacturing plant with all its systems linked by computer.

Control Use of information systems to influence members of the organization to make decisions that are consistent with organizational goals.

Controller The person within an organization responsible for the accounting system.

Decision rights The duties that a particular individual in an organization is expected to perform.

Ethics The process of determining standards and procedures for dealing with judgmental decisions affecting other people.

Financial accounting The accounting system used to report to investors, creditors, and other interested parties outside the organization.

Historical cost The acquisition cost of an object.

Internal auditor A person within the organization who monitors various divisions and departments of the organization to determine if prescribed operational procedures are being followed.

Just-in-time (JIT) Process of providing products and services at the time they are needed.

Management accounting The accounting system used within the organization to help the organization achieve its goals.

Monitoring The process of indirectly or directly observing members of the organization to determine if they are performing their duties appropriately.

Non–value-added activities Activities in an organization that do not benefit the customers of the organization.

Performance measure Direct or indirect measures of actions of individuals or groups of individuals within the organization.

Rewards Include wages and bonuses, prestige and greater decision rights, promotions, and job security.

Stakeholders Parties that are affected by an organization.

Tax accounting The accounting system used to calculate taxable income and to report to government taxing authorities.

Total quality management (TQM) A philosophy of continually lowering costs and improving the provision of services and products to customers.

Value chain The sequence of critical organizational processes to satisfy customers of the organization

Worker empowerment The delegation of greater decision rights to members of the organization.

DISCUSSION PROBLEMS

DP 1–1: Using Accounting for Making Planning Decisions (LO 4)
The owner of a small software company felt his accounting system was useless. He stated, "Accounting systems only generate historical costs. Historical costs are useless in my business because everything changes so rapidly."

a. Are historical costs useless in rapidly changing environments?
b. Should accounting systems be limited to historical costs?

DP 1–2: Goals of a Corporation (LO 2)
A finance professor and a marketing professor were recently comparing notes on their perceptions of corporations. The finance professor claimed that the goal of a corporation should be to maximize the value to the shareholders. The marketing professor claimed that the goal of a corporation should be to satisfy customers.

What are the similarities and differences in these two goals?

DP 1–3: Accounting and Control (LO 4,7)
The controller of a small private college is complaining about the amount of work she is required to do at the beginning of each month. The president of the university requires the controller to submit a monthly report by the fifth day of the following month. The monthly report contains pages of financial data from operations. The controller was heard saying, "Why does the president need all this information? He probably doesn't read half of the report. He's an old English professor and probably doesn't know the difference between a cost and a revenue."

a. What is the probable role of the monthly report?
b. What is the controller's responsibility with respect to a president who doesn't know much accounting?

DP 1–4: Control and Internal Auditors (LO 7)
A recent accounting graduate was hired by a large diversified company as an internal auditor. He was thrilled by this opportunity. The company trained him to provide assistance to the managers of the various divisions in achieving the goals of the organization. He would be able to learn about many different aspects of the business in the role of an internal auditor as he rotated among the various divisions. The internal auditor position seemed to be an ideal position that would lead to early advancement in the company. His first outing to a division, however, was not particularly successful. The managers of the division barely tolerated his criticism of their operating processes. Instead of being perceived as a person helping the organization achieve its goals, he was shunned by the divisional managers.

a. Why were the divisional managers not appreciative of the internal auditor?
b. How could the organization improve the role of the internal auditor?

DP 1–5: Financial Reporting and Ethics (LO 8)
The president of the company has come to the controller at the end of the fiscal year. He says, "We've had a pretty bad year. Sales have been off, but I think we'll do better next year. Can you do something about the annual financial report to make us look a little better and get us through until next year? Otherwise, I might get fired."

a. What can the controller do to make the annual financial report look better?
b. What other factors should the controller consider in responding to the president?

DP 1–6: One Cost System Isn't Enough (LO 6)
Robert S. Kaplan in "One Cost System Isn't Enough" (*Harvard Business Review*, Jan.–Feb. 1988, pp. 61–66) states:

> No single system can adequately answer the demands made by diverse functions of cost systems. While companies can use one method to capture all their detailed transactions data, the processing of this information for diverse purposes and audiences demands separate, customized development. Companies that try to satisfy

all the needs for cost information with a single system have discovered they can't perform important managerial functions adequately. Moreover, systems that work well for one company may fail in a different environment. Each company has to design methods that make sense for its particular products and processes.

Of course, an argument for expanding the number of cost systems conflicts with a strongly ingrained financial culture to have only one measurement system for everyone.

Critically evaluate the preceding quote.

DP 1–7: Tax Reporting and Accounting Systems (LO 5)

Tax laws in Japan tie taxable income directly to the financial statements' reported income. A Japanese firm's tax liability is the net income as reported to shareholders multiplied by the tax rate. In contrast, with a few exceptions, U.S. firms can use different accounting procedures for calculating net income for shareholders (financial reporting) and income for calculating taxes.

Given these differences in the tax laws between the United States and Japan, what effect would you expect these institutional differences in tax laws to have on internal accounting and reporting?

DP 1–8: Making Planning Decisions and Financial Reporting (LO 5)

The controller is complaining to her friend about the crazy requests that come from the top managers. "The CEO has requested that I calculate product costs to include research and development and selling costs. Doesn't he know that according to GAAP research and development and selling expenditures are expensed during the period incurred and are not product costs."

Evaluate the controller's comments.

DP 1–9: Role of the Divisional Controller (LO 7)

The Arjohn Corporation is a multidivisional firm. Each division has a manager who is responsible for division operations. The controller for each division is assigned to the division by the corporate controller's office. The division controller manages the division's accounting system and provides analysis of financial information for the division management. The division manager evaluates the performance of the division controller and makes recommendations for salary increases and promotions. However, the final responsibility for promotion evaluation and salary increases rests with the corporate controller.

Each division of Arjohn is responsible for product design, sales, pricing, operating costs and expenses, and profits. However, corporate management exercises tight control over the financial operations of the divisions. For example, all capital expenditures for buildings and equipment above a very modest amount must be approved by corporate management. The method of financial reporting from the division to corporate headquarters provides further evidence of the degree of financial control. The division manager and the division controller submit to corporate headquarters separate and independent commentary on the financial results of the division. The corporate management maintains that the division controller is there to provide an independent view of the division's operations and not as a spy.

Arjohn Corporation's dual reporting systems for decisions may create problems for the division controller.

a. Identify and discuss the factors that make the division controller's role difficult in this type of situation.
b. Discuss the effect of the dual reporting relationship on the motivation of the division controller.

(CMA adapted)

DP 1–10: Decision Rights, Information, and Performance Measures (LO 2)

Steve Johnson sells baskets for a wholesaler to retail shops. Retail shops like to have 30 days to pay after receipt of the goods. Unfortunately, retail shops often have financial difficulties and fail to make timely payments and in some cases, no payments at all. Steve's manager, who has never visited the retail shops, makes the decision whether to require collection on delivery (COD) or allow the store to pay in 30 days. Forcing the store to make payment on delivery often deters the shop from making a purchase. Steve, who visits each store, argues that he should have the right to make the decision on allowing for payment within 30 days.

a. How would the organization wholesaling baskets benefit from Steve's making the decision to allow for payment within 30 days?
b. What types of performance measures should be used for Steve if he is not given the decision right to allow for payment within 30 days?
c. What types of performance measures should be used for Steve if he is given the decision right to allow for payment within 30 days?

DP 1–11: Global Competition (LO 1)   Jim Jensen has opened a small business making hand-crafted guitars. His guitars sell for around $4,000 apiece and he only sells about 40 each year. When warned about potential competition from a producer in another country, Jim said, "I'm not worried about competition from abroad. Although my guitars are very expensive, I work hard to satisfy my customers. I will never be a low-cost producer."

Should Jim worry about global competition and change his business?

DP 1–12: The Role of Managers (LO 3)   The activities of managers can be categorized as either planning or control. Label each of the following manager activities as either a planning decision or a control activity.

a. Choosing a price for a product.
b. Explaining to an employee how to operate a machine.
c. Deciding which supplier of a part to use.
d. Congratulating the engineering department for a wonderful design.
e. Planning a building site for a new factory.
f. Asking an employee to provide service to a customer.
g. Creating a new process for manufacturing.
h. Deciding how to finance a new project.
i. Keeping track of the hours worked by the employees.

DP 1–13: Total Quality Management (TQM) (LO 1)   The owner of a jewelry store has just heard about TQM as a way of managing. The owner sees no reason to invest any further in TQM. As he told a friend, "TQM may be relevant for some of the cheap jewelry shops in town, but I only sell the highest quality diamonds and jewelry. I am already the top-quality retail shop of jewelry in town. TQM has nothing further to offer me."

Evaluate the jewelry store owner's comments.

DP 1–14: Computer-Aided Manufacturing (CAM) (LO 1)   CAM welding machines can be programmed to make different types of welds. Software is inserted into the machine to change the welding pattern. The Kipling Box Company makes steel boxes that require only one type of weld. The president of the company is trying to decide if the company should invest in a CAM welding machine.

What are the advantages and disadvantages of investing in the CAM welding machine?

DP 1–15: Just-In-Time (JIT) (LO 1)   A hospital administrator has just read a book about JIT. She feels that JIT is a good idea for manufacturing companies but doesn't think that JIT would be of much use to a service organization.

Describe how JIT could be used in a hospital.

DP 1–16: Computer-Integrated Manufacturing (CIM) (LO 1)   A recent *Wall Street Journal* article indicated that top-level managers do not understand CIM.[7] Only about 20% of the conversions to CIM began with top-level managers. The push for CIM usually begins with shop-floor engineers.

What are the advantages of implementing a change from the top versus the bottom of the organization?

CASE

C 1–1: Ethical Behavior (LO 8)   FulRange Inc. produces complex printed circuits for stereo amplifiers. The circuits are sold primarily to major component manufacturers, and any production overruns are sold to small manufacturers at a substantial discount. The small-manufacturer market segment appears very profitable because the basic operating budget assigns all fixed production expenses to the major manufacturers, the only predictable market.

A common product defect that occurs in production is a "drift" that is caused by failure to maintain precise heat levels during the production process. Rejects from the 100% testing program can be reworked to acceptable levels if the defect is drift. However, in a recent analysis of customer complaints, Scott Richardson, the cost accountant, and the quality control engineer have ascertained that normal rework does not bring the circuits up to standard. Sampling shows that about one-half of the reworked circuits will fail after extended, high-volume amplifier operation. The incidence of failure in the reworked circuits is projected to be about 10% over one- to five-years' operation.

Unfortunately, there is no way to determine which reworked circuits will fail because testing does not detect this problem. The rework process could be changed to correct the problem, but the cost/benefit analysis for the suggested change in the rework process indicates that it is not feasible. FulRange's marketing analyst has indicated that if the problem is not corrected, it will significantly affect the company's reputation and customer satisfaction. Consequently, the board of directors would interpret this problem as having serious negative implications on the company's profitability.

Richardson has included the circuit failure and rework problem in his report that has been prepared for the upcoming quarterly meeting of the board of directors. Due to the potential adverse economic impact, Richardson has followed a long-standing practice of highlighting this information.

After reviewing the reports to be presented, the plant manager and his staff are upset and indicate to the controller that he should control his people better. "We can't upset the board with this kind of material. Tell Richardson to tone that down. Maybe we can get it by this meeting and have some time to work on it. People who buy those cheap systems and play them that loud shouldn't expect them to last forever."

The controller calls Richardson into his office and says, "Scott, you'll have to bury this one. The probable failure of reworks can be referred to briefly in the oral presentation, but it should not be mentioned or highlighted in the advance material mailed to the board."

Richardson feels strongly that the board will be misinformed on a potentially serious loss of income if he follows the controller's orders. Richardson discusses the problem with the quality control engineer, who simply remarks, "That's your problem, Scott."

(CMA adapted)

Case Questions

a. Discuss the ethical considerations that Scott Richardson should recognize in deciding how to proceed in this matter.
b. Explain what ethical responsibilities should be accepted in this situation by each of the following: controller, quality control engineer, and plant manager and staff.
c. What should Richardson do in this situation? Why?

Chapter 2
The Nature of Costs

LEARNING OBJECTIVES

1. Use differential costs and benefits to assist in cost/benefit analysis.

2. Identify and measure opportunity costs for making planning decisions.

3. Ignore sunk costs for making planning decisions.

4. Determine how opportunity costs vary with the rate of output.

5. Calculate marginal and average costs.

6. Approximate opportunity costs using variable and fixed costs.

7. Recognize advantages and disadvantages of using historical costs as an approximation for opportunity costs.

8. Use cost/benefit analysis to make information choices.

Jones and McLean, Certified Public Accountants

The firm of Jones and McLean, Certified Public Accountants (CPAs), provides auditing, tax, and consulting services for its clients. The clients' annual financial reports are audited by Jones and McLean to determine that the financial statements are not misleading and follow generally accepted accounting principles. In performing the audit, the firm of Jones and McLean checks the accuracy of the financial statements by examining items such as receivables, inventory, and fixed assets and their corresponding documentation. Much of this work is performed just after the completion of the fiscal year of the client, which is often December 31. Therefore, January and February are very busy audit months.

The firm of Jones and McLean also completes tax returns for its clients. Tax returns should be sent to the Internal Revenue Service two and one-half months after the end of the fiscal year for corporate clients and three and one-half months for individual clients. Extensions can be requested, but the firm prefers to submit all tax returns on a timely basis. Therefore, January, February, March, and the first part of April are busy months for taxes at Jones and McLean.

The consulting services provided by Jones and McLean include advice on management information systems, product development, and executive compensation. There is a demand for consulting services throughout the year.

The firm of Jones and McLean is composed of 10 CPAs: two partners (Ed Jones and Mary McLean), two managers, and six professional staff. All the CPAs can perform audits, prepare tax returns, and provide consulting services, but at least one partner must check the work for each client. The support staff includes five secretaries.

The two managers and six professional staff members receive annual salaries with no overtime pay. The CPAs generally incur considerable overtime during the first four months of the year and take longer vacations during other times of the year to compensate for the overtime. The support staff is paid on an hourly basis with a 40% increase for overtime. The support staff generally work one hour for every two hours of work by CPAs. Other costs of operating the office include rent, utilities, computing equipment, copiers, and office supplies. The partners share the profit.

The firm of Jones and McLean has the opportunity to audit the local municipality, Grove City. Like most cities, Grove City has a fiscal year-end on June 30, so much of the audit work must be done in July and August. The initial audit of the municipality will require more CPA time than subsequent audits because the firm of Jones and McLean would have to learn about the accounting systems of Grove City. Grove City will pay $10,000 for the audit. Jones and McLean must decide if the $10,000 is sufficient to accept the audit.

2.1 Making Planning Decisions

Chapter 1 describes the dual roles of management accounting in providing information for making planning decisions and for control. This chapter focuses on making planning decisions. Typical planning decisions made within an organization include:

What customers should the organization target and satisfy?
How should the organization finance its operations?
What products or services should the organization provide?
What processes should be used to provide the products or services?
How should products or services be priced?

The criteria for making these decisions depend on the goals of the organization. Some aspects of a decision will help the organization achieve its goals. These aspects are called **benefits.** For example, the goal of the La Leche League is to promote breast-feeding. A direct mailing of information on breast-feeding to pregnant women would be consistent with the goal of the organization and be considered a benefit. Benefits, however, are seldom achieved without a cost. The **cost** of a decision is the use of organizational resources to achieve a benefit. The cost of the promotional campaign by the La Leche League is the cost of writing, printing, and mailing the information on breast-feeding.

Decisions should be made after a careful analysis of benefits and costs. The benefits and costs to the organization, however, may be different than the benefits and costs to the manager within the organization who is making the decision. Managers may have goals different from the organization's and will tend to make the decision that leads to the greatest net benefit to themselves. The problem of control is to motivate the managers to align their individual goals with the organizational goals. Control problems are taken up again in Chapter 6. In Chapters 2 through 5, the goals of the managers and the organization are assumed to be the same.

Using Cost/Benefit Analysis

Cost/benefit analysis is the process of analyzing alternative decisions to determine which decision has the greatest expected benefit relative to its cost. We all informally use cost/benefit analysis in making day-to-day decisions. For example, a common decision may be whether to ride your bicycle or drive your car to school. The benefit of riding a bicycle is more exercise, but the cost is a longer commute time and possibly the need to take a shower after arriving at school.

Microsoft Windows® and Windows 95® are two of the most successful products for computers. They are made by the same company yet compete with each other. Therefore, any cost/benefit analysis should consider the products jointly.

The benefit of driving a car is a faster commute time, but the cost is the payment of parking fees or fines. There are also some uncertainties. For example, the probability of rain, an accident, or a traffic jam should affect the expected benefits and costs of traveling to work. To make a decision, you identify, measure, and compare the expected benefits and costs of each alternative and choose the alternative with the greatest net benefits (total benefits less total costs). Managers should use cost/benefit analysis to make organizational decisions, but the benefits and costs are not always easily identified and measured.

One method of avoiding the measurement of all the benefits and costs of each alternative is to compare only those costs and benefits that are different among the alternative decisions. The difference in benefits is known as the **differential benefit** and the difference in costs is known as the **differential cost.** A comparison of the differential benefits and costs will lead to the same decision as a comparison of all the benefits and costs because the remaining costs and benefits are not affected by the decision. For example, Microsoft recently had to decide on its television marketing for Windows 95, an operating system for computers. The differential benefit of marketing Windows 95 on television is the increase in sales due to the televised marketing campaign. The differential cost of marketing Windows 95 on television is the cost of producing the advertisements, the cost of having the advertisements aired on television, and the cost of making the additional units of Windows 95 that are sold because of the television advertisements. Microsoft should market Windows 95 on television as long as the differential benefits exceed the differential costs. The remaining benefits and costs generated by Microsoft are irrelevant to the television marketing decision because they are the same whether Microsoft decides to market Windows 95 on television or not.

NUMERICAL EXAMPLE 2.1

The manager of Kemp Sports must decide whether to rent only mechanical or only manual stringing machines for tennis rackets it manufactures. A mechanical stringer can string 60 rackets per hour and requires one operator. A manual stringing machine can string 10 rackets per hour and each machine requires one operator. The rental cost for a mechanical stringing machine is $100 per hour and the rental cost of a manual stringing machine is $10 per hour. The cost of electricity for a mechanical stringer is $5 per hour.

Labor cost is $10 per hour. Kemp must produce 120 tennis rackets per hour to meet customer demand. To produce 120 rackets, either 2 mechanical or 12 manual machines are required. The other manufacturing processes are not affected by the choice of stringing machines.

Managers perform cost/benefit analysis to identify less costly methods of processing products. To manufacture tennis rackets, numerous processes must be completed. The costs and benefits of each process should be analyzed to determine the most efficient process.

■ **SOLUTION** Because the rest of Kemp Sports is not affected by the choice of stringing machines and the revenues will be the same with a sufficient number of stringing machines (2 mechanical or 12 manual), the decision hinges on the differential costs of the two types of machines. The differential costs for each type of machine are:

Type of Cost	Manual Method	Mechanical Method	Difference
Rent	(12)($10) = $120	(2)($100) = $200	$ −80
Labor	(12)($10) = $120	(2)($10) = $ 20	+100
Electricity		(2)($5) = $ 10	−10
Totals	$240	$230	$ 10

The use of mechanical stringing machines causes lower costs and is the preferred choice.

The expected profit of an activity is a form of a cost/benefit analysis. Revenues represent the benefits and expenses represent the costs. The profit in reports to external users of accounting, however, use historical costs and accrual accounting methods to measure revenues and expenses. These measures may not be appropriate for making planning decisions.

Problems in Identifying and Measuring Benefits

The benefits of making a particular decision depend on the goals of the organization. The achievement of some goals is not easily identified and measured. For example, most car dealerships have the goal of customer satisfaction. When you purchase a new car, you receive a survey from the dealership asking you if you are satisfied with your new car and the services provided. Because many buyers never return these surveys, the measurement of customer satisfaction is not necessarily accurate.

Benefits to organizations are often measured in terms of cash inflows. But the cash inflow from a decision is not always known and must often be estimated. For example, the benefit of introducing a new product would be measured based

The synergies (benefits of combining) involved in Disney acquiring ABC are quite obvious. One produces entertainment and the other broadcasts entertainment. In another takeover CBS, the broadcasting company, was acquired by Westinghouse. The synergies of this combination were not directly obvious because Westinghouse is known for its electronic systems and power generation. But Westinghouse also owns television stations, satellite communications, and program production that will be used by CBS.

on marketing estimates of future sales. Because these cash inflows occur in the future, there will be some uncertainty in measurement. Also, cash flows from different time periods should be adjusted for the time value of money before they are accumulated. The time value of money is discussed in Chapter 13.

Not all the benefits of a decision have immediate monetary implications. Benefits such as learning and training, improved working environment, and greater worker satisfaction are difficult to identify and measure in terms of dollars. These benefits have monetary consequences in later years.

Disney recently purchased ABC/Capital Cities. In making that decision, the executives of Disney attempted to measure the benefits of owning ABC. Some of the benefits are obvious. ABC is a successful television network that generates a profit. Other benefits, however, are less direct. By owning ABC, Disney had an additional vehicle for its programming. Disney also felt that owning ABC would give the company a competitive advantage over rivals. These benefits are more difficult to measure.

Problems in Identifying and Measuring Costs

Costs are the use of organizational resources. Costs are easy to identify and measure when cash is the resource being used. For example, the purchase price of a new drilling machine is easily identified and measured in monetary terms. Some costs, however, do not have immediate or obvious monetary implications. For example, requiring employees to work overtime may adversely affect employee morale and have long-term cost implications.

Measuring the cost of using noncash resources is also a problem. For example, what is the cost of using raw materials in inventory? Possible answers include the purchase price (historical cost), the current market price, or the future replacement cost. What is the cost of using the existing labor pool or the existing facilities? Once again there are numerous possible answers. The next section introduces the concept of opportunity cost to answer these questions.

Opportunity Costs

Using the resources of an organization, whether the resource is cash, inventory, buildings, or employee time, leads to forgone opportunities. If a resource is used for one purpose, it can't be used for another purpose. If cash is used to buy a machine, it can't be used to hire a new employee. If a building is used to house the assembly division, it can't be used by the marketing department or sold to another party. If an employee is designing a project, that employee can't be cleaning the plant at the same time. Cost is defined as the use of resources. The measurement of costs is based on the forgone opportunities of using those resources for other purposes. The size of the forgone opportunity of using a resource is the **opportunity cost.**

You use opportunity costs to make decisions every day. For example, the opportunity cost of accepting a job is the forgone opportunity to do something else with your time. If your best alternative to working is to relax, the opportunity cost of working is the forgone opportunity to relax. If the opportunity to relax has a value greater than the benefits of working, you will choose to relax. Another example is the opportunity cost of going to an early morning class. The forgone opportunity is being able to sleep later. Also, the opportunity cost of going to a movie is the forgone opportunity of using the time and money for another activity. In each case, a decision to use a resource prevents the resource from being used for another purpose.

The concept of opportunity cost is consistent with cost/benefit analysis. Opportunity costs provide a means of measuring the cost of a particular decision. The costs of each alternative decision should be identified and measured in terms of the forgone opportunity of using the resources for other purposes.

Measuring Opportunity Costs

The forgone opportunity of using a resource is the opportunity cost to an organization. If a decision involves the use of many different resources, the opportunity cost of using each resource should be measured in monetary terms. The opportunity costs of using each resource are then added and compared with the benefits derived from the decision.

To measure opportunity costs, the next best use of the resource should be identified. Forgone opportunities of using a resource include selling the resource or using the resource for another project. Generally, however, a similar resource can be purchased, so the use of the resource does not necessarily prevent the other projects from occurring. For example, raw materials can be replaced with further purchases, additional machines and buildings can be bought, and more employees can be hired.

If the next best use of the resource is to sell the resource, the sales price of the resource is the opportunity cost of using the resource. For example, suppose you are considering keeping this book as a reference after completing the class. The opportunity cost of keeping the book is the used book sales price of $12 at the bookstore.

If the use of the resource means that further resources must be purchased for other projects, the cost of replacing the resources is the opportunity cost. The forgone opportunity of a new-car dealership selling a car is the inability to sell the same car to another customer. But the new-car dealership can buy another car from the manufacturer. Therefore, the opportunity cost of selling a new car is the cost of replacing the car.

If the next best use of the resource is for another project and replacement is not feasible, then the loss in value to the organization of not being able to do the other project is the opportunity cost. For example, the time of an employee who has specialized knowledge of the organization's computer network is limited and cannot be easily replaced by hiring another employee. If the employee has no free time, use of the employee on one project prevents the employee from doing some other project. The opportunity cost to the organization of using the employee's time is the loss in value caused by not being able to do the other project.

The following numerical examples illustrate the identification and measurement of opportunity costs.

NUMERICAL EXAMPLE 2.2

Doris Wheaton has 10 bags of cement in her garage. The bags cost $4 per bag last year when they were purchased. The store now sells the cement for $5 per bag but doesn't take returns. A neighbor, however, told Doris he would buy the cement from her for $3 per bag if she didn't want them. Doris is considering using the cement to make a patio.

a. If Doris uses the 10 bags of cement to make her patio and has no other use for the cement, what is the opportunity cost of using the cement?
b. If Doris must also rebuild her front steps (which requires 20 bags of cement), what is the opportunity cost of using the cement for the patio?

■ SOLUTION

a. If Doris has no other use of the cement, the next best alternative to using the cement for the patio is to sell the cement. She can sell the cement to her neighbor for $3 per bag for 10 bags, or $30. Therefore, the opportunity cost of using the cement is $30.
b. Using the cement for the patio means that the cement must be replaced to make the front steps. The replacement cost of $5 per bag for 10 bags, or $50, is the opportunity cost of using the 10 bags of cement for the patio.

NUMERICAL EXAMPLE 2.3

A copy center has hired a permanent employee to operate a copy machine for large jobs. The permanent employee is paid $7 per hour whether or not copy jobs must be performed. Temporary help can be hired for $8 per hour.

Each service provided by a copy center such as Kinko's has an opportunity cost. Opportunities are forgone when using equipment, labor, and space. For example, a walk-up copier prevents that floor space from being used for computers. Thus, the opportunity cost of the walk-up copier includes the forgone profits from not using that space for computers.

a. What is the opportunity cost per hour of using the permanent employee to copy a job if there is no other work for the employee to perform?
b. What is the opportunity cost per hour of using the permanent employee if the employee could be working on another copy job that would generate a value of $6 per hour of work?
c. What is the opportunity cost per hour of using the permanent employee if the employee could be working on another copy job that would generate a value of $10 per hour of work?

■ **SOLUTION**

a. If there is no alternative use of the employee's time, the opportunity cost of using the employee is $0 per hour.

b. Because the cost of hiring a temporary employee ($8/hour) is greater than the increased value of performing the other work ($6/hour), the organization will not hire the temporary employee. Therefore, using the permanent employee prevents the employee from performing the other work and generating a value of $6 per hour. Under these circumstances, the opportunity cost of using the employee is $6 per hour.

c. Because the cost of hiring a temporary employee ($8/hour) is less than the increased value of performing the other work ($10/hour), the organization will hire the temporary employee if the permanent employee doesn't have time. Therefore, using the permanent employee on another project causes the copy center to hire a temporary employee. The opportunity cost of using the permanent employee is the cost of hiring a temporary employee, or $8 per hour.

NUMERICAL EXAMPLE 2.4

An importer rents a building for storage. The rental cost is $1,000 per month. Presently, the importer is using only half of the building space. She could sublet the remaining space for $300 per month. She is considering a new line of products to import that would use the remaining space. What is the opportunity cost of using the building to add the new line of products?

■ **SOLUTION** The opportunity cost is the forgone opportunity to sublet the remaining space, or $300 per month.

WHAT'S HAPPENING

A labor strike recently idled General Motors' plants around the United States, forcing the company to lay off thousands of workers. Analysts estimated that General Motors was losing $300 million a week in lost sales. At the same time it was noted that the company had 82 days of finished cars in inventory. What is the opportunity cost to General Motors of this strike?

WHAT'S HAPPENING

Financial statements to external parties are based on historical costs. Historical costs, however, are sunk costs. Why don't financial statements use opportunity costs?

The identification and measurement of opportunity costs may appear cumbersome and difficult, but *opportunity costs are the appropriate costs for making planning decisions.* Later in this chapter we will look at different methods of approximating opportunity costs.

Sunk Costs

Sunk costs are costs that have already been incurred and cannot be changed no matter what action is taken. Because they have already been incurred and are, therefore, the same for all possible alternative decisions in the present and the future, sunk costs are irrelevant for cost/benefit analysis. Ironically, we often find ourselves using sunk costs for making decisions. For example, many people use the past purchase price of their house to decide on the price to sell their house. Other people stay to the last inning of a baseball game to "get their money's worth" even though the weather has turned miserable and the home team is down by 10 runs.

NUMERICAL EXAMPLE 2.5

Paul Hardy is struggling to assemble a wooden chair. He has spent five hours on the process and estimates at this rate he will complete the assembly in two more hours. Joan Jiminez walks into the room and notifies Paul that he is doing it the hard way. She describes a simpler method that will only take one hour to disassemble the work Paul has performed over the last five hours and assemble the chair completely. What should Paul do?

■ **SOLUTION** Paul should follow Joan's advice because the remaining time to completion is less. The five hours of work he has performed is a sunk cost.

JONES AND MCLEAN, CERTIFIED PUBLIC ACCOUNTANTS (CONTINUED)

The firm of Jones and McLean has two alternatives: (1) accept the offer to audit Grove City or (2) reject the offer to audit Grove City. Ed Jones and Mary McLean will presumably make the decision that most benefits the firm, but there may not be complete agreement on the goals of the firm. Ed Jones prefers to fish in the summer, while Mary McLean needs extra money to pay for her daughter's college expenses. This type of conflict is a control problem and may be partially resolved by adjusting the partners' method of sharing profit and work. In this chapter, we assume that Ed Jones and Mary McLean both want to increase the long-term profitability of the firm.

To Jones and McLean the immediate cash benefit of auditing Grove City is the $10,000 fee. But there could be other benefits that are less obvious. For example, by auditing Grove City, Jones and McLean could be in the position to acquire other municipal audits. The learning that will occur in auditing Grove City could be applied to these other municipalities. Accepting the audit also provides the firm with the option of continuing to audit Grove City in the future. If another CPA firm audits Grove City this year, Jones and McLean are not likely to have the opportunity to audit Grove City in the near future.

In deciding whether to accept or reject the Grove City audit, Jones and McLean should determine the opportunity costs of using materials, labor, and facilities and ignore sunk costs. The materials such as forms and paper will all be replaced, so the replacement cost should be used for the opportunity cost. The seasonal nature of the auditing business means that the firm of Jones and McLean has excess labor and capacity during the summer months. The opportunity cost of using the CPAs, who are paid an annual salary, would be reduced employee morale from lost free time. Their annual salary, however, is a sunk cost. The support staff is paid on an hourly basis, so any increased support staff hours from the audit of Grove City creates an opportunity cost equal to the additional hours times the wage rate, or 1.4 times the wage rate if overtime is incurred. Overtime may be avoided by hiring temporary help. The costs of the facilities appear to be sunk costs. The rent has already been paid and the equipment has already been purchased. There will be some costs of learning how to do the municipal audit. There also may be a slight increase in utilities if the Grove City audit is accepted.

CONCEPT REVIEW

1. How does the use of differential costs and benefits help in performing cost/benefit analysis?
2. Why are some costs and benefits difficult to measure?
3. What should be considered in determining the opportunity cost of using a resource?
4. Why should sunk costs be ignored for planning purposes?

2.2 Opportunity Costs and the Rate of Output

Many planning decisions are related to the rate of output. An organization must decide how many units to produce or how many hours of service to provide during a certain time period. Ford Motor Company must decide how many cars of each model to produce each week. United Airlines must decide whether to fly a 200-passenger jet or a 130-passenger jet between Denver and Dallas next month. The opportunity cost of increasing or decreasing the rate of output is an important part of that decision. Each product or service and the corresponding method of manufacturing products or providing services is likely to have different opportunity costs as the rate of output during a period of time changes. The general pattern of opportunity costs with changing rates of output for most products and services, however, has some common characteristics.

Opportunity Costs of Initiating Operations

Certain costs must be incurred before operations begin. Machines and facilities must be purchased or rented. Employees must be hired. Suppliers must be found. Marketing channels must be opened. Therefore, the cost of starting operations and producing the first few units or providing the first few hours of service may be extremely high. The opportunity cost per unit of output is likely to be very high if only a few units are made.

Opportunity Costs of Normal Operations

During normal operations, an organization's output can be achieved without being constrained by the size of the facility, suppliers, machines, or employees. Producing one type of output does not impose costs on the production of other types of output. The operating process is in place and working smoothly. At normal rates, the opportunity cost of making additional units is relatively small.

What are the opportunity costs to United Airlines of providing this flight? What are the additional costs of having one more passenger?

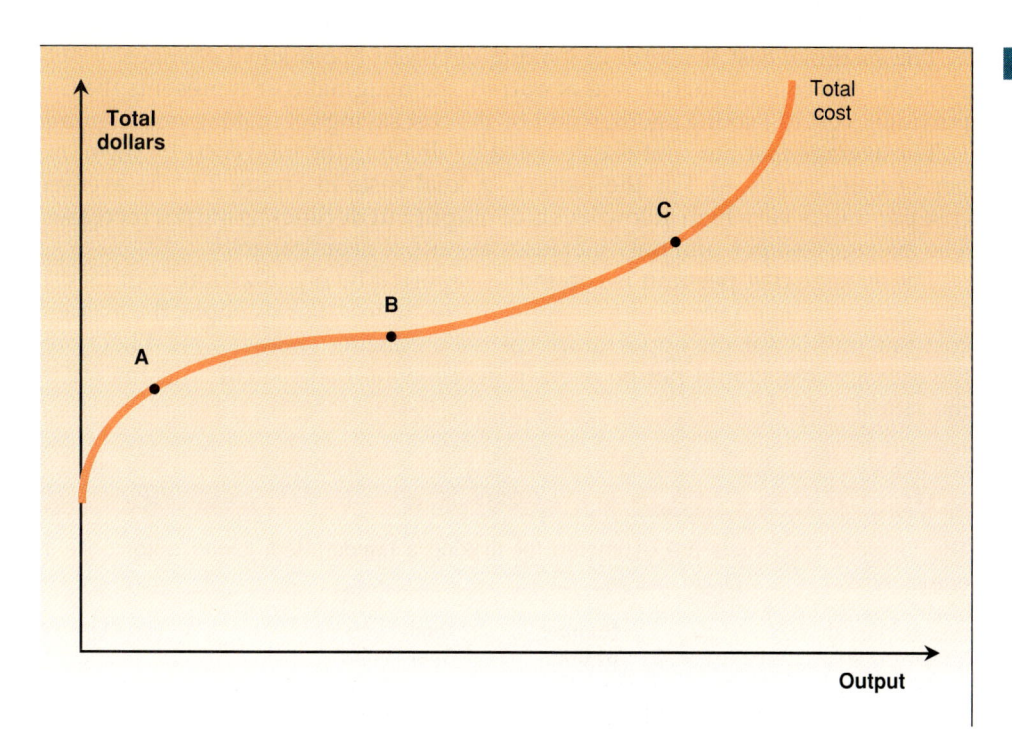

FIGURE 2.1
A Nonlinear Cost Curve

These opportunity costs would include the cost of additional labor and material to make more units.

Opportunity Costs of Exceeding Capacity

Capacity is a measure of the constraints on operations. Capacity constraints include the physical size of the plant, the number of machine hours available, and employee time. When the rate of output of a product nears capacity, costs are imposed on other products because of constraints on the use of space, machines, and employees. Machines are more likely to fail when operating at capacity. Labor costs increase because employees are paid for overtime. An organization can increase capacity, but the cost of buying a new factory or hiring and training a new set of employees may be very high, especially if the organization must do it quickly. Therefore, the opportunity cost of making additional units when operating near capacity is higher than under normal operations.

Graphical Analysis

The common characteristics of how opportunity costs change with increased output during a period of time are graphed in Figure 2.1. The curve represents total cost at different rates of output. The total costs might rise sharply at low rates of output (point A) because of start-up costs. Opportunity costs then increase moderately when normal operating rates are achieved (point B). When output rates near capacity (point C), total costs begin to rise sharply again because of congestion and alternative uses of facilities.

Marginal and Average Costs

The **marginal cost** is the cost of producing one more unit of output given the existing rate of output. The marginal cost is the slope of the total cost curve in Figure 2.1 at each rate of output. The steeper the slope, the higher the marginal cost. The marginal cost is highest at very low output rates (point A) and output rates near capacity (point C). The marginal cost is lowest at normal operations (point B) between these extreme rates of output.

The marginal cost is useful in making decisions about small changes in output rates. Given a particular rate of output, the marginal cost represents the opportunity cost of making another unit or the cost savings of making one less unit.

The **average cost** per unit is calculated by dividing the total costs by the number of units produced. For the pattern of total costs in Figure 2.1, the average cost per unit is very high at low levels of output but declines as output increases. The average cost per unit only increases as output nears capacity.

The average cost per unit is commonly reported by organizations, but its use for certain decisions can lead to inappropriate choices. For example, the average cost per unit is not the opportunity cost of producing another unit. Therefore, the average cost should not be used in decisions to make small adjustments to the rate of output.

NUMERICAL EXAMPLE 2.6

The following total costs are estimated for making a handcrafted, luxury automobile in one month:

Number of Units	Total Cost
1	$100,000
2	150,000
3	190,000
4	220,000
5	250,000
6	280,000
7	320,000
8	370,000
9	470,000
10	600,000

a. What are the marginal and average costs for each level of output?
b. The company is currently making and selling eight cars per month. The company has an offer from a customer to buy a ninth car for $90,000. Should the company accept the offer?

■ **SOLUTION**

a.

Number of Units	Total Cost	Marginal Cost	Average Cost
1	$100,000	$100,000	$100,000
2	150,000	50,000	75,000
3	190,000	40,000	63,333
4	220,000	30,000	55,000
5	250,000	30,000	50,000
6	280,000	30,000	46,667
7	320,000	40,000	45,714
8	370,000	50,000	46,250
9	470,000	100,000	52,222
10	600,000	130,000	60,000

b. The company should not accept the offer because the marginal cost of making the ninth car is $100,000. The average cost of $52,222 should not be used in this decision.

CONCEPT REVIEW

1. Why are opportunity costs of making the first few units of a product or service likely to be relatively high?

2. Why should capacity be a factor in determining opportunity costs?
3. What type of decisions should use marginal costs?
4. Why is the average cost inappropriate for some decisions?

JONES AND MCLEAN, CERTIFIED PUBLIC ACCOUNTANTS (CONTINUED)

Before auditing Grove City, the firm of Jones and McLean would have to learn about government audit requirements and acquaint themselves with Grove City's accounting system. These start-up costs would make the audit of Grove City more costly than if Jones and McLean were already performing municipal audits. If Jones and McLean tried to audit too many municipalities, however, they could find themselves nearing capacity in terms of office space and support personnel. Increased congestion and delays would impose costs on the other services provided by Jones and McLean. These congestion costs would be opportunity costs of accepting too many municipal audits.

2.3 Approximations of Opportunity Costs

Opportunity costs are not always easy to estimate. The opportunity forgone to use a resource depends on the alternative uses of the resource. The opportunity cost curve in Figure 2.1 requires knowledge of alternative uses of facilities and labor as the rate of production increases. Such estimates are difficult to measure, so managers often use approximations of opportunity costs. One method of approximation is to describe opportunity costs in terms of fixed and variable costs. Another approximation method is to use historical costs.

Fixed and Variable Costs

An approximation of Figure 2.1 using straight lines is provided in Figure 2.2. The approximation assumes that there is a cost of setting up and starting operations called a **fixed cost** (intersection of the cost axis in Figure 2.2). Fixed costs do not change with the rate of output. Fixed costs include the opportunity cost of using the facilities, purchasing machines, paying senior managers, and using other resources that do not change with the rate of output.

Once the fixed costs are incurred, there are additional operational costs to produce output. The costs that increase with the rate of output are called **variable costs.** In Figure 2.2 the linear representation of opportunity costs assumes that the variable cost of producing each additional unit is constant over all rates of output. The **variable cost per unit** is represented by the slope of the line in Figure 2.2. Variable costs include the opportunity cost of using additional labor, materials, and other resources to make more units.

In Figure 2.2 the straight line is the fixed and variable cost approximation of opportunity costs. The line is closest to the opportunity costs in the range of normal operations. This range is called the **relevant range.** The relevant range encompasses the rates of output where the combined fixed and variable costs are close approximations of the opportunity costs. Because the slopes of the opportunity cost curve and the fixed and variable cost curve are about the same, the variable cost per unit is a close approximation of the marginal cost. In the relevant range, the variable cost can be used to estimate the cost of making additional units of output.

For output quantities below the relevant range of output, the total fixed and variable costs tend to overestimate opportunity costs. The fixed and variable

FIGURE 2.2

Fixed and Variable Cost Approximation of Opportunity Costs

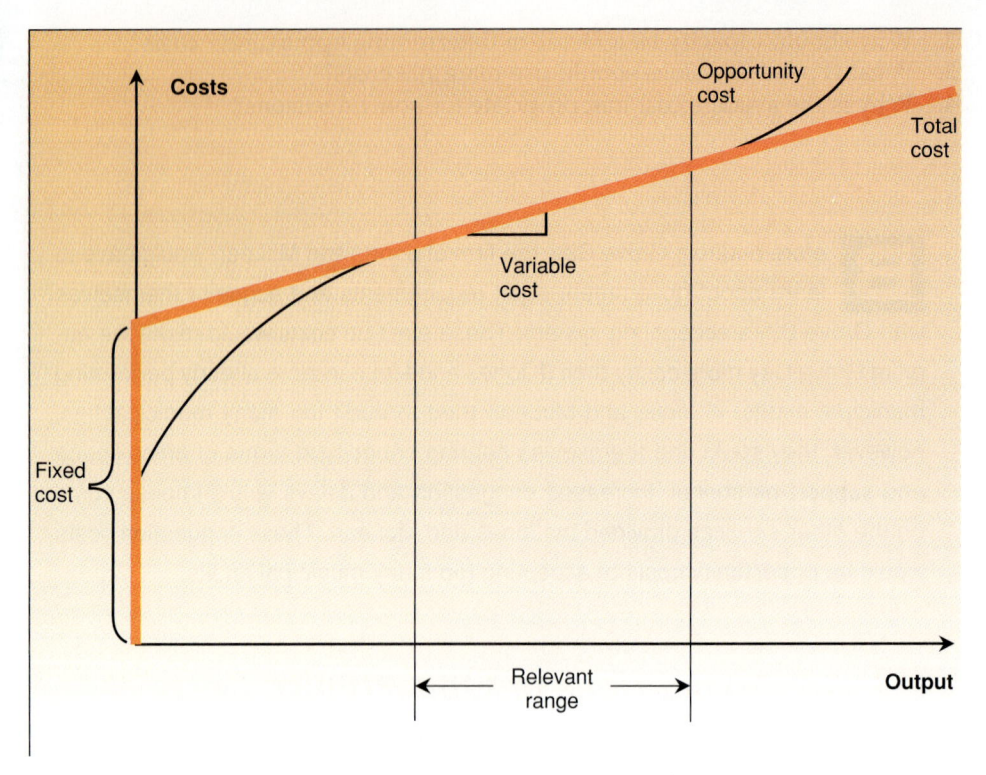

cost curve is flatter than the opportunity cost curve, implying the variable cost per unit underestimates the marginal cost below the relevant range. Therefore, the marginal cost of making the first few units tends to be higher than the variable cost. Above the relevant range, the total fixed and variable costs tend to underestimate the opportunity costs. Once again, the fixed and variable cost curve is flatter than the opportunity cost curve, implying the variable cost per unit underestimates the marginal cost above the relevant range. The marginal cost is greater than the variable cost as the rate of output approaches capacity.

The total costs in terms of variable and fixed costs can be described by the following equation:

$$\text{Total costs} = \text{Fixed costs} + \text{Variable costs}$$

or

$$\text{Total costs} = \text{Fixed costs} + (\text{Variable cost per unit})(\text{Number of units})$$

NUMERICAL EXAMPLE 2.7

Jackson Company makes computers. They estimate that the annual fixed costs are $100,000 and variable costs are $100 per unit. What are total expected costs if the company makes 500 computers per year? What are total expected costs if the company makes 700 computers per year?

■ **SOLUTION** Total expected costs if Jackson Company makes 500 computers per year is the sum of fixed costs ($100,000) and variable costs ($100 × 500 = $50,000), or $150,000. Total expected costs if Jackson Company makes 700 computers per year is the sum of fixed costs ($100,000) and variable costs ($100 × 700 = $70,000), or $170,000.

In this chapter, fixed and variable costs are defined as costs that are fixed or vary with the rate of product output. But fixed and variable costs can be defined in terms of output of other activities within the organization. For example, the cost of the output of the accounting department could be described as a fixed cost plus a variable cost that varies with the number of transactions recorded. Chapter 4 describes these alternative approaches to fixed and variable costs in more detail.

> **WHAT'S HAPPENING**
>
> There are only a few companies in the world that make large airplanes. Why is it so difficult to enter this industry?

Historical Costs

The historical cost of a resource reflects the cost at the time of acquiring the resource. At the time of acquisition of a resource, the historical cost is usually a close approximation of the opportunity cost. Except for somewhat arbitrary write-downs (depreciation and amortization), however, the historical cost of the resource remains the same as long as the resource is held by the organization. The opportunity cost, on the other hand, depends on the opportunity forgone in using the resource. The opportunity forgone to use a resource is likely to vary over time. For example, one forgone opportunity to use a resource is the opportunity to sell that resource. The sales price of the resource is likely to change over time.

Financial reporting to outside investors is based on historical costs. Most internal accounting reports also use historical costs. The popularity of historical cost accounting reports is somewhat surprising. Although the historical cost approximates the opportunity cost of a resource at the time of purchase, the historical cost is a sunk cost subsequent to the purchase and should not be used for planning purposes. As prices and alternative uses of resources change over time, the opportunity cost of using a resource is likely to deviate from its historical cost.

Given potential deviations between historical costs and opportunity costs, there is reason to question why historical cost accounting has survived. In the last century, regulations may have been partly responsible for its survival. Financial reporting requirements around the world are based on historical costs. But the demand for opportunity costs by external parties for making planning decisions (e.g., investment decisions) should ultimately have some affect on regulations.

Another reason for the continued popularity of historical costs is their use for control decisions. Verifying the actions of managers is an important part of control. The historical costs may be more useful than opportunity costs for control because they reveal the past actions of managers. Historical costs are easily verifiable and less subject to the discretion of the managers whose performance is being measured by the historical costs. This historical cost data can be used to motivate and reward managers.

Historical costs are still sometimes used for making planning decisions. Historical costs or simple adjustments to historical costs may be reasonable approximations of opportunity costs. If the environment does not change very much from the time of the resource acquisition, the historical cost may remain a close approximation of the opportunity cost. Using rules of thumb such as increasing historical costs by expected price inflation to approximate opportunity costs may also be effective.

The problem for managers is to determine when to use historical cost numbers as approximations and when to incur further efforts to determine the opportunity costs. This cost/benefit decision related to acquiring more information is discussed next in this chapter.

> **CONCEPT REVIEW**
>
> 1. How does a fixed cost change with the rate of output?
> 2. What do variable costs approximate?
> 3. Why is the use of historical costs still popular?

JONES AND MCLEAN, CERTIFIED PUBLIC ACCOUNTANTS (CONTINUED)

For Jones and McLean, the fixed cost of performing a municipal audit is learning the governmental regulations on auditing municipalities and the accounting systems of municipalities. Jones and McLean estimate these fixed costs to equal $5,000. Jones and McLean estimate variable costs in terms of CPA time. These variable costs include the opportunity cost of using supplies, secretarial help, and the cost of motivating the CPAs to work during the summer. Jones and McLean estimate that the variable cost per hour of CPA time for all these costs is $60. They also estimate that the Grove City audit will require 100 hours of CPA time. Therefore, the total estimated cost of auditing Grove City is $5,000 + (100 hours)($60/hour) or $11,000. If Jones and McLean only performed one municipal audit (Grove City) this year, the $10,000 revenue would not cover the $11,000 opportunity cost of performing the audit. If Jones and McLean performed more municipal audits this year, however, most of the fixed costs related to doing municipal audits would already have been incurred. Therefore, Jones and McLean must decide whether to audit more municipalities than just Grove City.

Jones and McLean must also consider the option to audit Grove City next year. If some of the fixed costs of auditing Grove City this year will not be incurred next year, the trade-off between losing money this year and making money in subsequent years should be compared. Chapter 13 on discounting future cash flows describes this type of comparison.

The firm of Jones and McLean has past accounting reports based on historical costs. If the firm had audited Grove City in previous years, the historical cost of performing those audits could yield a reasonable approximation of the opportunity cost if conditions and the nature of the audit have not changed. If Grove City was not audited in previous years, the historical cost of an equivalent audit might be useful in estimating opportunity costs. But Jones and McLean have never performed a municipal audit. Hence, the historical costs are not of much use in making the decision to accept the Grove City audit.

2.4 The Benefit and Cost of Information

Cost/benefit analysis described in this chapter applies to all types of planning decisions. One planning decision is whether to choose to gather further information before making another planning decision. The manager may ask for another accounting report or a marketing survey. How should the manager make the decision to gather further information? Once again, a cost/benefit analysis is appropriate. If the benefit of further information is greater than the cost, the

The Benefit and Cost of Information

THE STORY OF MANAGERIAL ACCOUNTING

Team Decisions Regarding Strategy

The *Managerial Accounting* book team was faced with an initial strategic decision. Irwin Publishing already had the best-selling management accounting book in the United States. One possible solution was to modify that management accounting book to accommodate the changing educational environment. Such a change, however, might cause the company to lose many satisfied customers. The other alternative was to develop a new management accounting book that would compete with the existing management accounting book. How should Peggy, the team accountant, use the notion of opportunity cost to help the team make this strategic decision?

additional information should be produced or purchased. The problem is measuring the cost and benefit of the information.

The opportunity cost of more information includes the cost of acquiring, modifying, communicating, and analyzing the information. Resources including cash and employee time are used in the process. Each of these resources has an opportunity cost.

The benefit of information comes from improved decisions. If reading *The Wall Street Journal* leads to better investment decisions, then the *WSJ* has a benefit. If reading the *WSJ* does not change any decisions, then the *WSJ* has no benefit as an information system. The differential benefit of new information is the difference between the expected benefit of making a decision with the new information and the expected benefit of making the decision with existing information. For example, you can choose an MBA program without further information. But information on the quality and nature of alternative MBA programs would be beneficial in deciding which MBA program matches your preferences.

The benefit of new information depends on the decision being made. A weather report is unlikely to have much value in choosing an investment but is

Although The Wall Street Journal *has many entertaining articles, most people read* The Wall Street Journal *for assistance in making better investment decisions. Investors view the cost of acquiring and reading* The Wall Street Journal *as small relative to potential investment gains.*

likely to improve the choice of whether to have a picnic or when to plant a field of corn. In doing a cost/benefit analysis for information choice, the decision context must be known. Information that improves more than one decision is likely to be more valuable. Firms that choose to purchase only one accounting system should choose the accounting system that provides the greatest benefit for a large number of decisions. The ability of an accounting system to satisfy the demands of many users increases its benefit.

JONES AND McLEAN, CERTIFIED PUBLIC ACCOUNTANTS (CONCLUDED)

> The firm of Jones and McLean has the option of gathering more information before deciding to audit Grove City. Further study may provide more accurate estimates of hourly requirements for the audit and a better measure of the cost of the audit. The study will be costly, however, and should not be performed if the results of the study will not affect the decision. The study should only be performed if the expected benefits of an improved decision are greater than the cost of the study.

CONCEPT REVIEW

1. What is the cost of information?
2. What is the benefit of information?

2.5 Summary

1. Use differential costs and benefits to assist in cost/benefit analysis. Differential analysis identifies the costs and benefits that vary across alternative decisions. Only differential costs and benefits are relevant for decisions because all other factors are the same for each possible decision.

2. Identify and measure opportunity costs for making planning decisions. Opportunity cost is defined in terms of alternative uses of a resource. The size of the forgone opportunity to use the resource is the measure of the opportunity cost.

3. Ignore sunk costs for making planning decisions. Sunk costs are costs that have already been incurred. Sunk costs are not relevant for planning decisions.

4. Determine how opportunity costs vary with the rate of output. The opportunity costs of the first several units of production tend to be relatively high. At normal production levels, the opportunity cost of making another unit tends to be lower. When production nears capacity, the opportunity cost of making another unit tends to rise.

5. Calculate marginal and average costs. The marginal cost is the opportunity cost of making one more unit, which is the slope of the total cost curve. The average cost is the total cost of a product or service divided by the number of units produced.

6. Approximate opportunity costs using variable and fixed costs. Approximating opportunity costs by fixed and variable costs assumes there is a cost of initiating production, which is the fixed cost. Subsequent units are assumed to cost the same amount per unit, which is the variable cost per unit.

7. Recognize advantages and disadvantages of using historical costs as an approximation for opportunity costs. Historical costs may approximate opportunity costs if the economic environment and operational procedures have not changed significantly. Historical costs are usually easier to identify and measure than opportunity costs.

8. Use cost/benefit analysis to make information choices. More information should be gathered if the benefit of improved decision making is greater than the cost of the information.

KEY TERMS

Average cost The total costs of production divided by the number of units produced.

Benefit Aspects of a decision that help the organization achieve its goals.

Capacity Measure of the constraints on the operations of an organization.

Cost Use of organizational resources to achieve a benefit.

Cost/benefit analysis The process of making decisions by comparing the costs and benefits of alternative choices.

Differential benefits The difference in benefits among alternative decisions.

Differential cost The difference in costs among alternative decisions.

Fixed cost The cost of initiating production, which does not vary with the number of units produced.

Marginal cost The additional cost of producing one more unit given a certain level of output.

Opportunity cost The forgone opportunity of using a resource for another purpose.

Relevant range The range of output levels over which variable costs are reasonable approximations of opportunity costs.

Sunk cost A cost that has already been incurred and cannot be changed.

Variable cost Any cost that increases with output. Also, the variable cost per unit times the number of units produced.

Variable cost per unit The slope of the total cost line. The variable cost per unit is an approximation of the marginal cost using fixed and variable costs.

SELF-STUDY PROBLEM I

Identifying Opportunity Costs Western State University is contemplating dropping all athletic scholarships because the administration thinks that the university can't afford them. The athletic department is arguing that the cost of dropping athletic scholarships will be high. The athletic teams will no longer be competitive and the school may be dropped from the Big 17 Conference. Ticket revenues will drop. Alumni will not provide as many donations. Because many of the athletes are on partial scholarships, the university may lose the remaining tuition. The school will get less publicity, especially in the sports pages of newspapers and on television.

What are the benefits and opportunity costs of providing athletic scholarships?

Solution

The arguments of the athletic department reveal benefits of having athletic scholarships. The benefits, however, are difficult to measure. For example, donations and ticket revenues are likely to be higher with more competitive teams. Publicity will also probably be higher, but the value of that publicity is also difficult to measure. The value of being in an athletic conference depends on the quality of the other institutions in the league.

Being in the Ivy League, for example, gives those institutions a certain amount of prestige, which is difficult to value. Athletes on partial scholarships also pay some tuition.

These benefits should be offset against the opportunity costs of having athletic scholarships. What are the forgone opportunities of providing scholarships? The opportunity cost of any cash payments to athletes for books, housing, and food can be measured directly. But most of the scholarship is the waiving of tuition and providing free education to the athletes. The opportunity cost depends on whether providing free education to athletes prevents a tuition-paying student from attending the university. If the university is at capacity and the athlete takes the place of a tuition-paying student, the forgone opportunity to the university is the lost tuition. If the university is not at capacity, the forgone opportunity is the marginal cost (approximated by the variable cost) of educating an additional student. The variable cost of educating a student may not be very high because most costs at a university are fixed.

SELF-STUDY PROBLEM II

Approximating Opportunity Costs with Variable and Fixed Costs

Frank Choi, the president of Trace Products, understands product costs, but he feels that estimating opportunity costs for his gold ore processing plant is difficult. Instead, he tells his controller to worry only about fixed and variable costs. The controller estimates that the variable cost of processing gold ore is $1,000 per ton of gold ore. The fixed costs are $50,000.

a. What is the estimated cost of processing 60 tons of gold ore?
b. What is the danger of approximating opportunity costs with variable and fixed costs?

Solution

a. The estimated cost of processing 60 tons of gold ore is

$$(60 \text{ tons})(\$1,000/\text{ton}) + \$50,000 = \$110,000$$

b. The danger of estimating opportunity costs with variable and fixed costs is being outside the relevant range. In the relevant range, the estimates from variable and fixed costs should be fairly close to the opportunity cost. If output levels are extremely low or near capacity, however, the fixed and variable cost estimate tends to differ from the opportunity cost.

NUMERICAL PROBLEMS

NP 2–1: Differential Costs and Revenues (LO 1; NE 1)   A grocery store is deciding how to use a particular space in the store. One option is to lease a freezer to put in the space and sell ice cream bars. The ice cream bars should generate annual revenues of $10,000 but will reduce revenues from other ice cream sales by $2,000 annually. The freezer leases for $1,000 per year, the electricity for the freezer should cost $500 per year, and the cost of the ice cream bars will be $5,000 per year. The other option is to rent shelving for $500 per year and sell bakery items. The revenues from the bakery items should be $7,000 per year and cost of the bakery items should be $3,000. The bakery items should not cause any other loss of revenue. Other costs are the same for the two options.

What should the grocery store do with the space?

NP 2–2: Differential, Variable, and Fixed Costs (LO 1, 6; NE 1, 7)

Darien Industries operates a cafeteria for its employees. The operation of the cafeteria requires fixed costs of $4,700 per month and variable costs of 40% of sales. Cafeteria sales are currently averaging $12,000 per month.

Darien has an opportunity to replace the cafeteria with vending machines. Gross customer spending at the vending machines is estimated to be 40% greater than current sales because the machines are available at all hours. By replacing the cafeteria with vending machines, Darien would receive 16% of the gross customer spending and avoid all cafeteria costs.

A decision by Darien Industries to replace the cafeteria with vending machines will result in a monthly increase (decrease) in operating income of how much?

(CMA adapted.)

NP 2–3: Differential Costs and Revenues (LO 1; NE 1)

A hardware store is considering opening on Sunday. The differential costs of paying for salespeople and utilities is $1,000 per Sunday. Sales each Sunday are expected to be $10,000. The sales price of an item is determined by taking the purchase price of the item and adding 20%.

a. If sales on Sunday do not affect sales the rest of the week, should the hardware store open on Sundays if the goal is to increase profit?
b. Should the hardware store open on Sundays if 60% of the sales on Sundays would have occurred on other days of the week at the hardware store?

NP 2–4: Opportunity Cost of Space (LO 2; NE 4)

JP Max is a department store carrying a large and varied stock of merchandise. Management is considering leasing part of its floor space for $72 per square foot per year to an outside jewelry company that would sell merchandise. Two areas are being considered: home appliances is 1,000 square feet and televisions is 1,200 feet. These departments had annual profits of $64,000 for appliances and $82,000 for televisions. Fixed costs have been allocated at the rate of $7 per square foot.

Considering all the relevant factors, which department should be leased and why?

NP 2–5: Opportunity Cost of Using Materials (LO 2, 3; NE 2, 5)

Emrich Processing is a small custom stainless-steel parts processor. Customers send new and used stainless-steel parts to Emrich for cleaning in various acid baths to remove small imperfections or films on the surface. These parts are used in a variety of applications, ranging from nuclear reactors to chemical and medical applications. Depending on the foreign substance to be removed, Emrich chooses the acid bath mixture and process.

Such chemical cleaning operations require highly skilled technicians to handle the dangerous acids. Environmental Protection Agency (EPA) and Occupational Safety and Health Administration (OSHA) regulations are closely followed. Once the part is treated in the proper chemical bath using other chemicals, a benign waste solution results that can be disposed of via the city sewer system.

On May 12, Emrich ordered a 50-gallon drum of a specialty acid known as GX-100 for use in a May 15 job. It used 25 of the 50 gallons in the drum. The 50 gallons cost $1,000. GX-100 has a shelf life of 30 days after the drum is opened before it becomes unstable and must be discarded. Because of the hazardous nature of GX-100 and the other chemicals Emrich uses, Emrich works closely with Environ Disposal, a company specializing in the disposal of hazardous wastes. At the time of ordering the GX-100, Emrich anticipated no other orders in the May–June time period that could use the remaining 25 gallons of GX-100. Knowing it would have 25 gallons remaining, it built $1,000 into the cost of the job to cover the cost of the GX-100 plus an additional $400 to cover the cost of having Environ dispose of the remaining 25 gallons.

On June 1, a customer called and asked for a price bid for a rush job to be completed on June 5. This job will use 25 gallons of GX-100. Emrich is preparing to bid on this order.

What cost amount for the GX-100 must be considered in preparing the bid? Justify your answer.

NP 2–6: Opportunity Cost of Using Display Space (LO 2; NE 4)

Home Auto Parts is a large retail auto parts store selling the full range of auto parts and supplies for do-it-yourself auto repair enthusiasts. Annual store sales are $5 million. The store is arranged such that there are three prime display areas: front door, checkout counters, and end-of-aisles. These display areas receive the most customer traffic and contain special stands that display the merchandise with attractive eye-catching posters. Each display area is set up at the beginning of the week and runs for one week. Three items are scheduled next week for special display areas: Texcan Oil, windshield wiper blades, and floor mats. The table below provides information for the three promotional areas scheduled to run next week:

	Planned Displays for Next Week		
	End-of-Aisles	Front Door	Cash Register
Item	Texcan Oil	Wiper blades	Floor mats
Sales price	69¢/can	$9.99	$22.99
Projected weekly volume	5,000	200	70
Unit cost	62¢	$7.99	$17.49

Based on past experience, management finds that virtually all display area sales are made by impulse buyers. The display items purchased do not reduce the sales of similar items in the store because people attracted to the displays did not enter the store to buy these items. The display items are extra purchases by consumers attracted by the exhibits.

After the above table is prepared but before the store manager sets up the display areas, the distributor for Armadillo car wax visits the store. She says her firm wants its car wax in one of the three display areas and is prepared to offer the product at a unit cost of $2.50. At a retail price of $2.90, management expects to sell 800 units during the week if the wax is on special display.

a. Home Auto has not yet purchased any of the promotion items for next week. Should management substitute the Armadillo car wax for one of the three planned promotion displays? If so, which one?

b. A common practice in retailing is for the manufacturer to give free units to a retail store to secure desirable promotion space or shelf space. The Armadillo distributor decides to sweeten the offer by giving Home Auto 50 free units of car wax if it places the Armadillo wax on display. Does your answer to (a) change?

NP 2–7: Opportunity Cost of Time (LO 2; NE 3)

The Indo Corporation is considering leasing a private jet to fly between the corporate offices in Rochester, New York, and the firm's main plant in Tucson, Arizona. The commercial carrier has one flight leaving Rochester each morning and one returning flight departing Tucson in the afternoon. Ten executives take this seven-hour (one-way) trip every day and 10 make the return flight each day. A recent study showed that business travelers are unable to work while traveling on either a commercial flight or a private jet. The average salary (including fringe benefits) of an executive is $200,000. On average, they work 2,500 hours per year. Round-trip airfare on the commercial carrier averages $500.

Two alternative private jets are available for leasing. The following table summarizes various operating statistics for the two jets:

Model	Number of Seats	One-Way Flight Time	Total Daily Operating Cost
Lx-0100	10	6 hrs	$5,100
Lx-0200	7	4 hrs	$5,200

The leased plane will duplicate the existing commercial carrier's scheduled departure times. The Lx-0200 cannot make more than one round trip a day.

Which alternative air transportation should the firm undertake? (Show calculations.)

NP 2–8: Marginal and Average Costs (LO 5; NE 6) Allan Brothers Company has designed a machine for sorting apples. The machine is able to detect bruises on an apple. Those apples that are bruised are used for making apple sauce. The apples without defects are shipped to grocery stores. Managers at Allan Brothers are uncertain of the demand for these sorting machines but have estimated the following opportunity costs of making different numbers of the machines:

Number	Total Costs
1	$100,000
2	150,000
3	190,000
4	220,000
5	250,000
6	280,000
7	340,000
8	400,000
9	500,000

a. Prepare a table showing how the marginal cost of sorting machines varies with the number of machines manufactured.
b. Why does the marginal cost increase after six machines?
c. What is the average cost of making five sorting machines?
d. If the sorting machines can be sold for $70,000, how many machines should be produced?

NP 2–9: Fixed and Variable Costs (LO 6; NE 7) A manufacturer of skis has determined that the fixed cost of making skis is $1,000,000 and the variable cost is $100 per pair of skis. During normal operations the firm plans to make 20,000 pairs of skis.

a. What is the expected cost of making 20,000 pairs of skis?
b. What is the expected cost of making 30,000 pairs of skis using the fixed and variable costs?
c. Why might the variable and fixed costs be poor predictors of costs when 30,000 pairs of skis are made?

NP 2–10: Fixed, Variable, and Average Costs (LO 5, 6; NE 6, 7) Midstate University is trying to decide whether to allow 100 more students into the university. Tuition is $5,000 per year. The controller has determined the following schedule of costs to educate students:

Number of Students	Total Costs
4,000	$30,000,000
4,100	30,300,000
4,200	30,600,000
4,300	30,900,000

The current enrollment is 4,200 students. The president of the university has calculated the cost per student in the following manner: $30,600,000/4,200$ students = $7,286 per student. The president was wondering why the university should accept more students if the tuition is only $5,000.

a. What is wrong with the president's calculation?
b. What are the fixed and variable costs of operating the university?

NP 2–11: Cost Behavior Patterns (LO 4; NE 7)

For each question below, draw a graph that depicts how costs vary with volume. Completely label each graph and axis.

a. The Medford plant operates 40 hours per week. Management can vary the number of workers. Currently, there are 200 workers being paid $10 per hour. The plant is near capacity. To increase output, a second 40-hour per week shift is being considered. To attract workers to the second shift, a 20% wage premium will be offered. Plot total labor costs as a function of labor hours per week.

b. The Dallas plant has a contract with the Texas Gas Company to purchase up to 150 million cubic feet of natural gas per month for a flat fee of $1.5 million. Additional gas can be purchased for $0.0175 per cubic foot. The Dallas plant manufactures aluminum cans. One thousand cans require 10 cubic feet of gas. Plot total gas costs as a function of can production.

NP 2–12: Variable and Fixed Costs (LO 6; NE 7)

The MedView brochure refers to a new radiology imaging system that MedView rents for $18,000 per month. A "scan" refers to one imaging session that is billed at $475 per scan. Each scan requires that the patient receive a chemical injection and that the X ray negative be exposed and developed. MedView claims that 45 scans per month are sufficient to cover the cost of renting the machine plus any additional variable costs.

What variable cost per scan is MedView assuming in calculating the 45 scans per month amount?

NP 2–13: Fixed and Variable Costs (LO 6; NE 7)

Chen Industries is planning to build a computer chip factory to make 10,000 chips per month. The company has two different options in manufacturing the chips. A CAM approach will cause fixed costs to be equal to $1,000,000 per month and variable costs to be $20 per chip. A more manual approach will cause fixed costs of $500,000 per month and variable costs of $50 per chip.

Which method should the company use to minimize costs?

NP 2–14: Opportunity Costs (LO 2, 3; NE 2, 3, 5)

Shanti Debi must decide whether to build a fence around her garden or pay someone $300 to build the fence for her. If Shanti makes the fence, she could use some leftover fencing materials from a previous job. Those materials cost $60, but she can't sell them and has no other use for them. In addition she would have to buy materials that would cost $100. Shanti estimates she would spend 15 hours purchasing the materials and putting up the fence. If she didn't make the fence, she could spend the time playing tennis. She values her tennis-playing time at $10 per hour.

Should Shanti build the fence or pay someone else to make the fence?

NP 2–15: Opportunity Costs (LO 2, 3; NE 4, 5)

The First Church has been asked to operate a homeless shelter in part of the church. To operate a homeless shelter, the church would have to hire a full-time employee for $1,200/month to manage the shelter. In addition, the church would have to purchase $400 of supplies per month for the people using the shelter. The space that would be used by the shelter is rented for wedding parties. The church averages about five wedding parties a month that pay rent of $200 per party. Utilities are normally $1,000 per month. With the homeless shelter, the utilities will increase to $1,300 per month.

What is the opportunity cost to the church of operating a homeless shelter in the church?

NP 2–16: Opportunity Costs (LO 2; NE 3)   Ken Morrow is returning from his accounting class. As he passes the student union building, he thinks about visiting the video game room. For $5 he could play the video games for one hour. The best alternative to playing video games is to study for the accounting exam. One more hour of studying should raise his grade from a B+ to an A−. The higher grade would give Ken an opportunity to get a higher paying job. Ken estimates that the higher grade is worth about $200 in job opportunities.

What is the opportunity cost of playing the video games for an hour?

NP 2–17: Variable and Fixed Costs (LO 6; NE 7)   The school newspaper editor estimates that the fixed cost of an edition is $10,000. The variable cost is $.03 per copy.

a. What is the expected cost of an edition if 3,000 copies are produced?
b. What is the expected cost of an edition if 5,000 copies are produced?

NP 2–18: Average, Variable, and Fixed Costs (LO 5, 6; NE 6)   A university has 5,000 students but a capacity of 6,000 students. The fixed cost of operating the school is $1,000,000 per month. The variable cost is $100 per student per month.

a. What is the average cost per student of operating the university given 5,000 students?
b. What is the cost of adding 50 more students?

NP 2–19: Average, Variable, and Fixed Costs (LO 5, 6; NE 6)   A soccer ball manufacturer plans to make 100,000 balls per year. The following annual costs are estimated:

	Utilities	$ 10,000
	Machines	50,000
	Administration	100,000
	Marketing	120,000
	Labor	200,000
	Materials	150,000
	Total	$630,000

Labor and materials are variable costs and the remaining costs are fixed.

a. What are the annual fixed costs of making soccer balls?
b. What is the variable cost per soccer ball?
c. What is the average cost per ball?
d. If the manufacturer is operating normally and not near capacity, what is the expected cost of making 1,000 more balls?

NP 2–20: Fixed and Variable Costs (LO 6; NE 7)   The university athletic department has been asked to host a professional basketball game at the campus sports center. The athletic director must estimate the opportunity cost of holding the event at the sports center. The only other event scheduled for the sports center that evening is a fencing match that would not have generated any additional costs or revenues. The fencing match can be held at the local high school, but the rental cost of the high school gym would be $200. The athletic director estimates that the professional basketball game will require 20 hours of labor to prepare the building. Cleanup depends on the number of spectators. The athletic director estimates the time of cleanup to be equal to two minutes per spectator. The labor would be hired especially for the basketball game and would cost $8 per hour. Utilities will be $500 greater if the basketball game is held at the sports center. All other costs would be covered by the professional basketball team.

a. What is the variable cost of having one more spectator?
b. What is the opportunity cost of allowing the professional basketball team to use the sports center if 10,000 spectators are expected?
c. What is the opportunity cost of allowing the professional basketball team to use the sports center if 12,000 spectators are expected?

DISCUSSION PROBLEMS

DP 2–1: Variable and Fixed Costs (LO 6)

Fast Photo operates four film developing labs in upstate New York. The four labs are identical. They employ the same production technology, process the same mix of films, and buy raw materials from the same companies at the same prices. Wage rates are also the same at the four plants. In reviewing operating results for November, the newly hired assistant controller, Matt Paige, became quite confused over the numbers:

	Plant A	Plant B	Plant C	Plant D
Number of rolls processed	50,000	55,000	60,000	65,000
Revenue ($000s)	$500	$550	$600	$650
Less:				
Variable costs	(195)	(242)	(298)	(352)
Fixed costs	(300)	(300)	(300)	(300)
Profit (Loss)	$ 5	$ 8	$ 2	($ 2)

Upon further study, Matt learned that each plant had fixed overhead of $300,000. Matt remembered from his cost accounting class that as volume increases, average fixed cost per unit falls. Because plant D had much lower average fixed costs per roll than plants A and B, Matt expected plant D to be more profitable than plants A and B. But the numbers show just the opposite.

Write a concise but clear memo to Matt that will resolve his confusion.

DP 2–2: Opportunity Costs and Executive Stock Options (LO 2)

A large public accounting firm, reporting findings of a survey on corporate directors' compensation, remarked, "Since there are usually greater growth rates in smaller companies, stock options offer directors a good chance at investment appreciation at no cost to the company."

Suppose one three-year stock option is granted to a director at today's stock price of $10. Then, at any time over the next three years, the director can buy one share of stock from the company at $10. If next year the stock rises to $14, the director can exercise the option by paying $10 to the company and receiving one share of stock, which can then be sold in the market for $14, thereby realizing a $4 gain.

Critically evaluate the *quoted* sentence.

DP 2–3: Opportunity Cost of Using Inventory (LO 2)

After the Iraqi invasion of Kuwait in August 1990, the world price of crude oil doubled to over $30 per barrel in anticipation of reduced supply. Immediately, the oil companies raised the retail price on refined oil products even though these products were produced from oil purchased at the earlier, lower prices. The media charged the oil companies with profiteering and price gouging, and politicians promised immediate investigations.

Critically evaluate the charge that the oil companies profited from the Iraqi invasion. What advice would you offer the oil companies?

DP 2–4: Differential Costs of a New Product (LO 1)   Indurin Company is the maker of Syndex, a popular drug for headaches. Indurin has felt the increased competitive pressure from other manufacturers of headache medicine as they have developed new products. The president of Indurin is considering the introduction of a new product, which will be called Syndex Plus. This product will be for people who want added strength in their drugs. The president wants a prediction of the additional profit from this new drug. In his management accounting course, he had learned that he should compare differential revenues with differential costs. He has figured that total expected sales of Syndex Plus is equal to differential revenues because there was no previous sales of Syndex Plus. Differential costs would be those additional costs necessary to make Syndex Plus. Because there is extra space and labor available, these costs are expected to be very low.

The controller, when asked to compute the expected costs, asked, "What about the effect of introducing Syndex Plus on the sales of Syndex?" The president replied, "The decision to introduce a new product should only be based on a comparison of differential costs and revenues."

Evaluate the decision rule of the president.

DP 2–5: Opportunity Cost of Attracting Industry (LO 2)   The Itagi Computer Company from Japan is looking to build a factory for making CD-ROMs in the United States. The company is concerned about the safety and well-being of its employees and wants to locate in a community with good schools. The company also wants the factory to be profitable and is looking for subsidies from potential communities. Encouraging new business to create jobs for citizens is important for communities, especially communities with high unemployment.

Wellville has not been very well since the shoe factory left town. The city officials have been working on a deal with Itagi to get the company to locate in Wellville. Itagi officials have identified a 20-acre undeveloped site. The city has tentatively agreed to buy the site for $50,000 for Itagi and not require any payment of property taxes on the factory by Itagi for the first five years of operation. The property tax deal will save Itagi $3,000,000 in taxes over the five years. This deal was leaked to the local newspaper. The headlines the next day were: "Wellville Gives Away $3,000,000+ to Japanese Company."

a. Do the headlines accurately describe the deal with Itagi?
b. What are the opportunity costs and benefits to the citizens of Wellville of making this deal?

DP 2–6: Opportunity Cost of Using Military Forces (LO 2, 3)   Recent excursions by the U.S. military in other countries have been costed by the Government Accounting Office (GAO). The calculation is based on the cost of paying and supplying personnel, movement of material and personnel to the problem area, depreciation on equipment, and armaments used. Newspaper accounts indicate that some of these actions provided training for personnel and experimentation for new weapons. Also some older armament was used without any intention of replacement.

How would you calculate the opportunity cost of using military forces?

DP 2–7: Historical Costs Approximating Opportunity Costs (LO 7)
Maverick Productions organizes rock concerts. Last year the company rented the local high school football stadium for a rock concert that included the Rolling Rocks. The concert was a big success and Maverick Productions made $10,000 on the concert. This year Maverick Productions is planning to bring the Rolling Rocks back to town for another concert. The company plans to rent the university football stadium, which is larger, but

still plans to use the same ticket agency and vendors. Maverick Productions has detailed accounting records of the revenues and costs of the previous Rolling Rocks concert and would like to use these accounting records to make plans for the concert this year.

a. What are some of the advantages and disadvantages of using the past concert accounting records to make estimates of the costs and benefits of the concert this year?
b. Are there ways of adjusting the past accounting records to make them better predictors of costs and benefits?

DP 2–8: Cost/Benefit Analysis of Information (LO 8)

A paper manufacturer feels that he needs better information on the quality of paper the plant is producing. He is considering purchasing a scanning machine that would identify defects in the paper as it is being produced. The scanner would have to be operated full-time by an employee.

What factors should the manufacturer consider in determining the costs and benefits of the scanning machine?

CASE

C 2–1: Opportunity Costs (LO 2)

Steve Martinez was saddened when he heard of the death of his uncle but was shocked when he heard that he had inherited a 1,000 acre ranch in Wyoming, called Windy Acres. The ranch currently had a house, bunkroom for help, and a barn. The inheritance also included 500 head of cattle. When Steve arrived in Wyoming to check on his inheritance, he found the buildings and fences in need of repair. The manager of the ranch greeted Steve with a handshake and the financial statements from the end of the most recent fiscal year, which was about three months ago. The accounting report included only a balance sheet and an income statement:

WINDY ACRES
Balance Sheet
12/31/96

Assets		Liabilities	
Cash	$2,000	Mortgage	$200,000
Equipment	100,000		
Buildings	184,000	**Owner's Equity**	
Accumulated depreciation	(52,000)	Owner's share	34,000
Total assets	$234,000	Total liabilities and equities	$234,000

WINDY ACRES
Income Statement
Year of 1996

Sale of cattle	$ 50,000
Cost of supplies	(10,000)
Manager's salary	(15,000)
Depreciation	(10,000)
Interest on mortgage	(20,000)
Net loss	($ 5,000)

Steve looked a little worried after seeing the financial statements. He was relieved, however, when he noticed that the cattle were not on the balance sheet. "Well, at least there is some additional value on this ranch that is not recorded in the financial statements," he said.

The manager replied, "We decided not to report the cattle as an asset because the number varies throughout the year and we're never sure exactly how many cattle are out there. I'd like to keep working for you, but my feeling is that you should sell this place. A neighbor is willing to buy the place for $300,000. I think it is a good offer and you should accept it."

Steve Martinez is reluctant to accept the offer without further investigation of the operations of Windy Acres.

Case Questions

a. How does the offer to buy Windy Acres provide a benchmark for Steve?
b. How should Steve use the balance sheet and income statement to value Windy Acres?
c. If Steve decides to continue operating Windy Acres as a cattle ranch, how should he decide on the appropriate number of cattle to raise?

Chapter 3
Cost Estimation

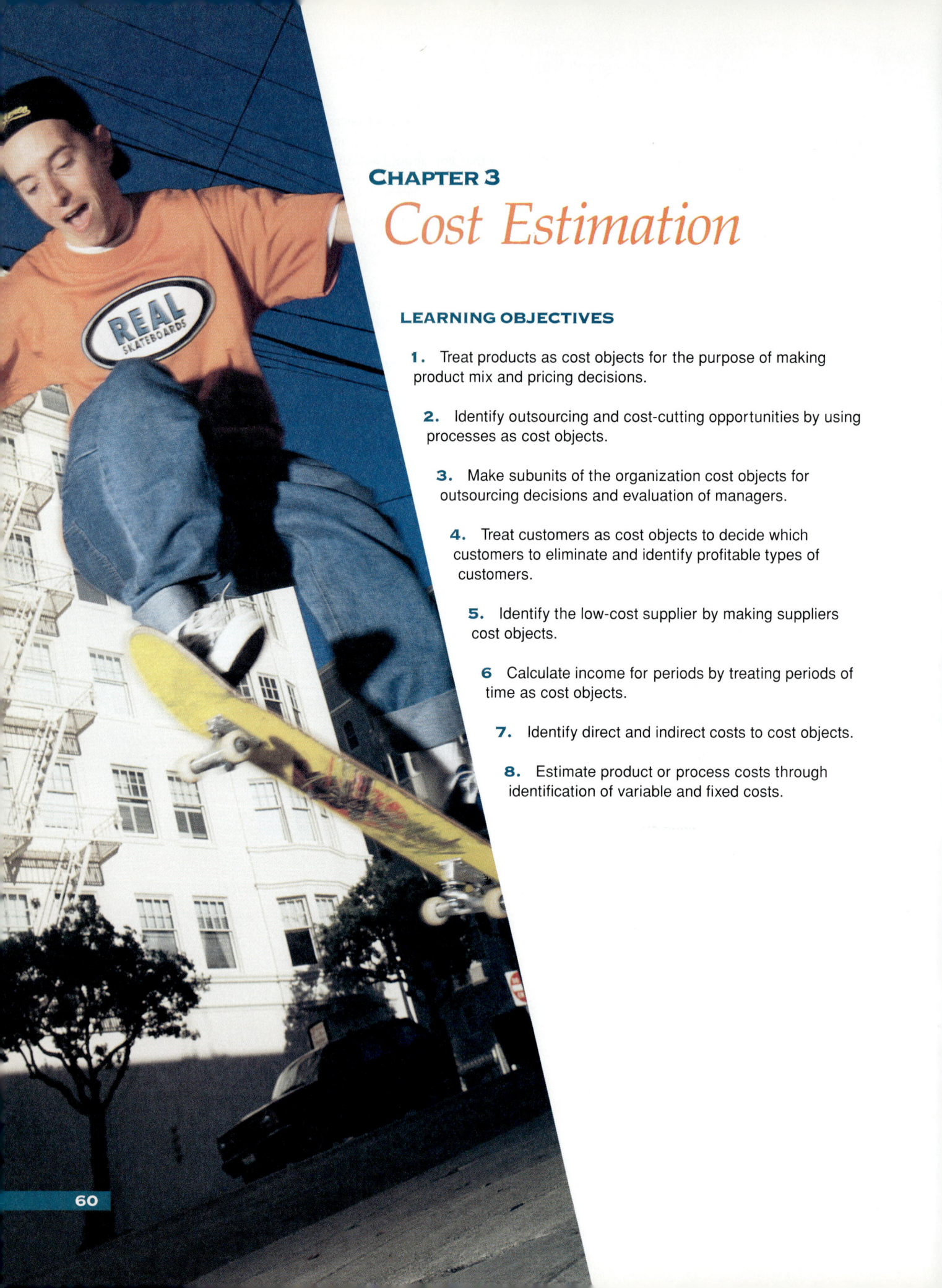

LEARNING OBJECTIVES

1. Treat products as cost objects for the purpose of making product mix and pricing decisions.

2. Identify outsourcing and cost-cutting opportunities by using processes as cost objects.

3. Make subunits of the organization cost objects for outsourcing decisions and evaluation of managers.

4. Treat customers as cost objects to decide which customers to eliminate and identify profitable types of customers.

5. Identify the low-cost supplier by making suppliers cost objects.

6. Calculate income for periods by treating periods of time as cost objects.

7. Identify direct and indirect costs to cost objects.

8. Estimate product or process costs through identification of variable and fixed costs.

Snake Skateboards—I

Snake Skateboards has been operating for five years. The company has two products: a flat skateboard sold to large discount chains and a molded skateboard sold to specialty shops. Snake Skateboards has been successful in recent years with the popularity of skateboarding, but the management must make some decisions about changing the products manufactured, the prices of products, the processes of manufacturing, and its choice of suppliers and customers.

A skateboard is constructed much like plywood. Thin layers of wood veneer are glued together with the grain of the wood of adjacent layers going in opposite directions. This alternating pattern gives the skateboard strength and some flexibility. The layers of wood veneer of the flat skateboard are glued and squeezed together using a flat press. Ten flat skateboards can be pressed at once so the flat skateboards are normally produced in batches of ten. The molded skateboards are pressed in individual molds. Because there are five molds, the molded skateboards are made in batches of five. The molded skateboards also have a layer of plastic glued to the bottom of the skateboard to allow the skateboard to slide when the rounded bottom comes in contact with rough surfaces. Both types of skateboards use the same polyurethane wheels and axle assemblies, which are purchased from another company and attached at Snake Skateboards. The flat skateboards are painted with a single color, while the molded skateboards are multicolored with a variety of designs.

Snake Skateboards is owned by Jeff Williams, who also manages the company and designs new products. Jeff has hired four managers for the following departments: administration, purchasing, production, and marketing. The cost accounting system has separate accounts for the cost of operating each of the departments and the cost of materials and labor used to make the skateboards. Jeff has projected the following costs for next year given the assumption that 50,000 flat skateboards and 5,000 molded skateboards will be produced and sold:

Materials	$ 60,000
Labor	300,000
Administrative	90,000
Purchasing	50,000
Production (excluding labor and materials)	210,000
Marketing	100,000
Total expected costs	$810,000

Snake Skateboards has competitors that make similar skateboards. The competitors sell flat skateboards to large discount stores for $15 and molded skateboards to specialty shops for $25. Projected revenues for Snake Skateboards at those prices are:

Flat skateboards: (50,000 units at $15/unit)	$750,000
Molded skateboards: (5,000 units at $25/unit)	125,000
Total expected revenues	$875,000

3.1 Estimating Costs for Planning Decisions

In making planning decisions, the opportunity costs and benefits of different decisions must be estimated. For example, the decision to purchase a computing system for an organization is based on the estimated costs and benefits associated with each possible computing system. The comparison of estimated costs with estimated benefits helps managers identify the best choice for the organization. Management accounting assists in this process through estimating the benefits and costs associated with each decision. This chapter focuses on the cost estimation process.

The first step in the cost estimation process is to decide what item of the organization to cost. The item to be costed, called the **cost object,** depends on the decision being made. The primary cost objects described in Chapters 4 and 5 are the products or services provided by the organization. But cost objects may also include activities or processes, subunits of the organization, customers, suppliers, and time periods. Each of these cost objects is related to different planning decisions. Some of those planning decisions are described in this section.

Planning Decisions Related to the Cost of Products and Services

Estimating the opportunity cost of a product or service is very useful in making decisions about what products or services to provide and determining a price for those products and services. The cost of using resources to provide a product or service is called the **product** or **service cost.** For simplification purposes, the term *product cost* is used in this book for both product and service costs. The procedures for estimating service costs are the same as the procedures for estimating product costs.

The opportunity cost of using resources yields the appropriate product cost for making planning decisions. The actual procedures for estimating product costs, however, are delayed until Chapter 4. This chapter focuses primarily on decisions related to products and other cost objects. The product mix decision and the pricing decision discussed in this section are examples of planning decisions based on product costs.

Product Mix Decision

The role of managers in an organization is to help the organization achieve its goals. Most organizational goals, from satisfying customers to generating a profit for owners of the organization, are related to the products and services that or-

Estimating Costs for Planning Decisions

Mrs. Fields may have started with the chocolate chip cookie, but now the company sells many kinds of cookies and brownies and has even expanded into supermarkets with the introduction of Mrs. Fields' frozen cookie dough. How was cost information used in the introduction of each new product?

ganizations provide. Managers of organizations must decide which products and services to offer. The choice of what products and services to offer is known as the **product mix decision.** For example, McDonald's must decide what types of food to offer in their restaurants. Not all McDonald's have the same product mix. For example, McDonald's restaurants in Southeast Asia have durian milkshakes on the menu as durians are a popular fruit in that part of the world.

An organization is usually established to provide a certain product or service. But as the organization evolves, other products and services are frequently offered. A bakery may start by making bread but will have to decide whether to branch into pastries. Ford Motor started by making black Model T's but now has a wide variety of types of cars, trucks, and vans in multiple colors. The product mix of an organization will continually evolve as new opportunities arise and competitive pressures affect existing products and services.

The product cost provides information to managers that is useful in making the product mix decision. The organization with a higher product cost for a particular product will be at a competitive disadvantage. A computer chip manufacturer that makes a chip that costs $500 is at a competitive disadvantage if the chip is currently being made by a competitor for $400. AT&T recently dropped its personal computer line because the company was not competitive in the personal computer market. AT&T continues to be a major supplier of long-distance services but is also looking for opportunities to expand into other areas of communication where the company may have a comparative advantage.

An organization must continually analyze its existing and new products or services to determine whether the organization has a comparative advantage in offering those products and services. For example, an organization may identify a service it can provide at a low cost due to having special skills. Microsoft has personnel who have an intimate knowledge of the Windows® operating system that allow them to produce other software at a low cost. A low-cost provider of services has a comparative advantage over its competitors and is likely to include that service in its service mix. On the other hand, a high-cost producer is unlikely to continue to include that product or service in its mix unless there are some other benefits to offering the product.

The ultimate decision on choosing a product mix is based on a comparison of the benefits of the product with the opportunity costs of providing the product. If the benefits exceed the costs, a product is included in the product mix. The benefits of the product are usually measured in terms of revenues generated from sales. But an organization must consider other benefits of having a product. For example, having a particular product in a product mix may be important to the sales of other products. Car dealerships want a wide variety of products to give customers a comprehensive selection. If car dealerships limited their inventory to only the most profitable models, customers might be less likely to shop at the dealership. The benefits of having a product may also be related to the employees of the organization. Dropping a product from the product mix can mean layoffs of employees. Managers must continually deal with ethical issues related to the welfare of employees versus the welfare of the owners of the organization. Most of the problems and examples in this book focus on revenues as the primary benefit of having a product or service, but other benefits should be considered.

Estimating the opportunity costs of providing a product is also difficult. This chapter provides some conceptual direction on estimating product costs, but actual procedures are delayed until Chapter 4. In the examples and problems in this chapter, the product costs are provided without much explanation of their estimation.

NUMERICAL EXAMPLE 3.1

A grocery store is considering adding a locally made salsa to its product mix. The salsa costs $1 a jar to purchase from the supplier. The supplier does all the shelving, but the grocery store could generate an additional $100 in profit monthly if the shelf space is used to sell ketchup. The grocery store expects to sell 200 jars of the salsa a month at $1.40 per jar. Should the grocery store include the salsa in its product mix if there are no other significant costs or benefits?

■ **SOLUTION** The monthly revenues are (200 jars)($1.40/jar), or $280. The cost of buying the jars is (200 jars)($1/jar), or $200, and the opportunity cost of using the shelf space is $100. Therefore, the profit from including the salsa in the product mix is $280 − $200 − $100, or −$20. Because the revenue is less than the opportunity costs, the salsa should not be included in the product mix.

Pricing Decision

Part of the product mix decision is based on the demand for the product or service. If the price of the product or service is too high, consumers will not buy it. If the price is too low, making and selling the product will reduce the value of the organization. Determining the price of a product or service, the **pricing decision,** is another important planning decision managers must make.

Starbucks made considerable profits in the early 1990s by selling high-priced, specialty coffee. Starbucks' success, however, did not go unnoticed, and other companies entered the competition with their own coffee outlets like this Brothers Gourmet Coffee Bar.

Product costs are also used to help make pricing decisions. The product cost serves as a lower boundary in making a pricing decision. If products and services are sold below their opportunity cost, there are alternative uses of the resources used to make the product or service that would be preferable. For example, if an umbrella manufacturer estimates the cost of making an umbrella is $3, then the forgone opportunity of using the resources to make the umbrella is equal to $3. If the umbrella is sold for less than $3, the organization is forgoing a preferable use of those resources.

Although cost information is useful in pricing decisions, information about the demand for products and services and competitor prices should also be considered. In the Pacific Northwest, the sale of specialty coffees has become extremely competitive. Drive-through coffee outlets are located at almost every major intersection. Most business is from repeat customers getting their daily fix, so customers quickly learn about the quality and prices of the various outlets. The coffee outlets must compete on both quality and price dimensions. If a competitor down the street is selling the same quality coffee for $1.50 per cup, a coffee outlet will soon lose its competitors if it tries to sell the identical coffee for $1.75 per cup.

The pricing decision is complicated and requires knowledge of your own product costs, knowledge of your customers, and knowledge of your present and potential competitors. The pricing decision is covered more completely in Chapter 5. In this chapter, we assume that prices should be somewhere between the opportunity cost of providing the product and the price of primary competitors.

As a reminder, the historical cost of the product is irrelevant in the pricing decision except to the extent that it approximates the opportunity cost. Once a product is purchased or produced, the purchase price or production cost no longer necessarily represents the opportunity cost. The sales price should be chosen with the alternative use of the resources to make the product in mind.

NUMERICAL EXAMPLE 3.2

A textile manufacturer can make the following products: slacks, jeans, shirts, dresses, and socks. The product costs of each item and competitor prices are listed below:

Product	Product Cost	Competitor Price
Slacks	$10	$15
Jeans	9	8
Shirts	6	9
Dresses	13	20
Socks	2	1

a. What products should be in the product mix of the textile manufacturer?
b. What is the possible range of prices that the textile manufacturer could offer for the products in the product mix?

■ **SOLUTION**

a. The textile manufacturer should not make products with a product cost higher than the competitor's price unless the product provides other benefits. Therefore, the company should only make slacks, shirts, and dresses.
b. The range of possible prices should be between the product cost and the competitor's price. Therefore, the prices should be in the following ranges:

Product	Price Range
Slacks	$10–$15
Shirts	$6–$9
Dresses	$13–$20

Some organizations price their products based on some markup on product cost. For example, if a product had a cost of $10 and the organization chose to mark up products 30%, then the sales price for the product would be (1 + .30)($10), or $13. This procedure ignores competition and demand for the product and can lead to pricing decisions that lower the value of the organization. Pricing and product mix decisions are discussed further in Chapter 5.

Target Costing

Recently, some organizations have first chosen the price based on demand and competition and then attempted to design and make the product at a low enough cost to make a profit. This procedure is known as **target costing.** With target costing, a product opportunity is identified first. The product opportunity is a description of all of the functional characteristics of the product. At the same time, a price is identified that would make that product competitive. The product opportunity and the necessary functional characteristics are then turned over to the design and engineering department to determine if the product can be made at a sufficiently low cost to provide a profit for the organization.

Target costing is performed during the product design stage. This often allows managers to remove costs through the design as opposed to reducing costs through efficiencies in the production stage. For example, by using fewer different parts in the product, purchasing costs, inventory holding costs, and production labor are lowered, thereby reducing the product cost.

Toyota was one of the first companies to use target costing in 1965. Members of the sales division, who are closest to the customers and understand their preferences, identify cars with characteristics that are particularly attractive to customers. For example, dual-side air bags are a characteristic that most customers expect in the cars they buy. The sales staff then establishes a price for such a car and estimates the amount of sales for that model. A target cost is then chosen to give Toyota a sufficient profit. Then the company seeks a design that will allow Toyota to reduce costs without losing the functional characteristics. Target costing has allowed Toyota to reduce costs but still manufacture a high-quality car.

Snake Skateboards—I (continued)

Jeff Williams of Snake Skateboards is considering a change in product mix and prices. Currently, about 91% of the skateboards Snake produces are flat and 9% are molded. The current prices for these skateboards reflect prices of competitors, but Jeff Williams feels that by lowering the price, he could sell more skateboards. Before making those decisions, however, Jeff must determine the cost of each type of skateboard. If the cost of one of the skateboards is greater than the competitors' prices, then Jeff should drop that skateboard from the product mix. If the cost of one of the skateboards is less than the competitors' prices, then Jeff has some flexibility in reducing the price of that skateboard to increase sales. The present accounting system, however, gives no indication of the cost of either type of skateboard. Also, Jeff is not sure that the company is currently operating very efficiently. Even if he could determine the costs of his products, he may be able to reduce the product costs further by cutting costs. Before he can identify cost-cutting opportunities, however, he must gain a better understanding of the processes operating in his company.

Planning Decisions Related to the Cost of Activities or Processes

In deciding which products and services to offer, managers must decide on the series of activities or processes necessary to provide products and services. (The terms *process* and *activity* will be used interchangeably in this book.) For example, manufacturing organizations must make decisions on design, engineering, acquisition of raw materials, use of personnel, manufacturing processes, inventory warehousing, transportation, marketing, and customer service. All of these activities have a cost.

Managers must initially identify the activities in the organization. American Express recently analyzed the process of transferring funds. Figure 3.1 provides an indication of the detail that might occur in identifying the subactivities of a process. For example, to process an American Express card transaction requires three specific activities: capture the transaction, process the transaction, and—if necessary—resolve exceptions.

The benefit of an activity is the added value to the organization from performing the activity. Activities add value to the organization by supporting the generation of products and services for consumption by customers. The activities that add value to the organization are called the **value chain.** The links in the value chain identify only those activities that add to the product to enhance its

FIGURE 3.1 Activity Hierarchy of Transferring Funds

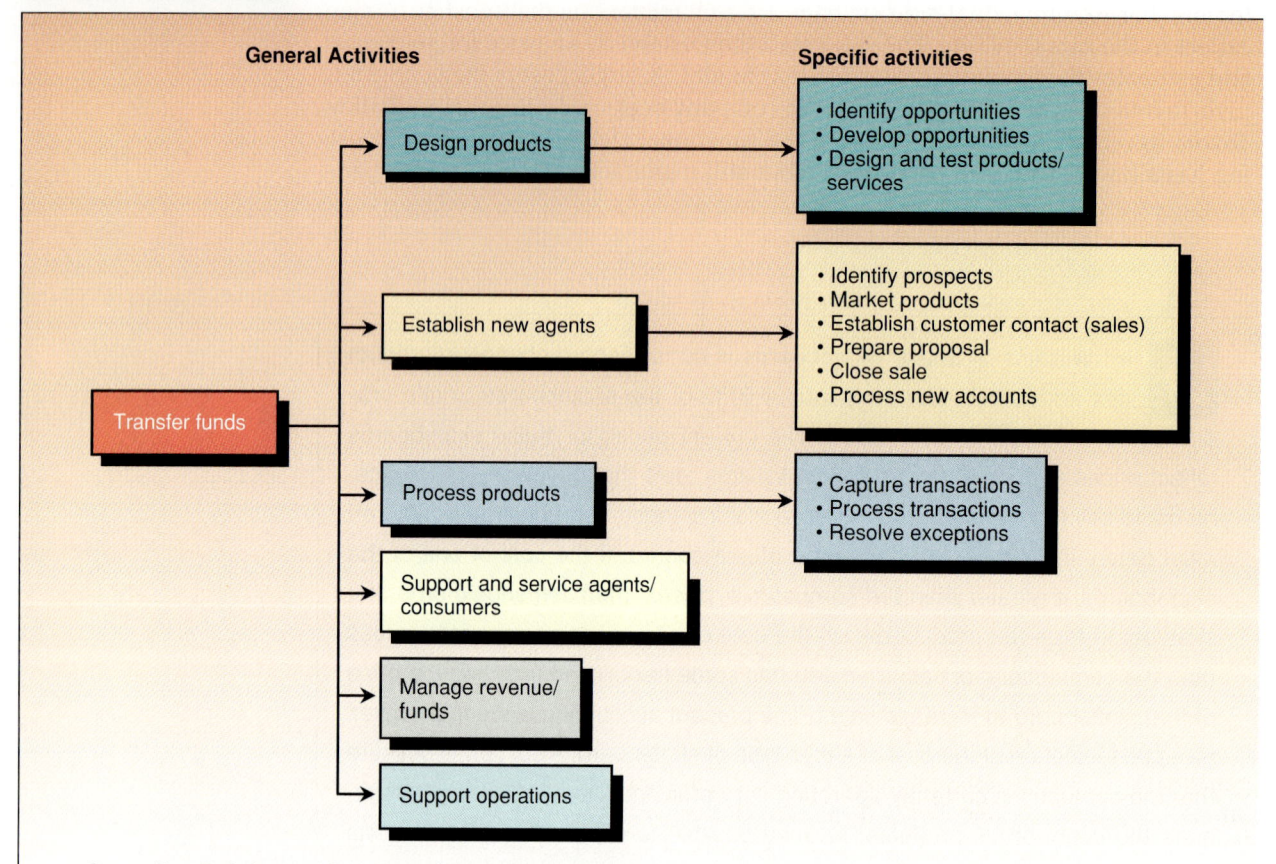

General Activities

Transfer funds →
- Design products
- Establish new agents
- Process products
- Support and service agents/consumers
- Manage revenue/funds
- Support operations

Specific activities

Design products →
- Identify opportunities
- Develop opportunities
- Design and test products/services

Establish new agents →
- Identify prospects
- Market products
- Establish customer contact (sales)
- Prepare proposal
- Close sale
- Process new accounts

Process products →
- Capture transactions
- Process transactions
- Resolve exceptions

Source: From D. Carlson and S. M. Young, "Activity-Based Total Quality Management at American Express," *Journal of Cost Management*, Spring 1993, pp. 48–58.

---

use by a customer. An oak chair manufacturer, for example, would have the following value chain:

$$\text{Design} \to \genfrac{}{}{0pt}{}{\text{Acquisition}}{\text{of materials}} \to \text{Cutting} \to \text{Sanding}$$

$$\to \text{Assembly} \to \text{Finishing} \to \text{Distribution} \to \genfrac{}{}{0pt}{}{\text{Customer}}{\text{service}}$$

Each of these activities is critical to making the oak chair and satisfying the customer. But each activity is costly to perform and the cost of the product or service reflects the cost of the activities of the value chain.

Service organizations would likely have different types of value chains. For example, a university might have a value chain that looks like the following:

$$\genfrac{}{}{0pt}{}{\text{Research and}}{\text{development}} \to \text{Teaching} \to \genfrac{}{}{0pt}{}{\text{Student}}{\text{services}} \to \text{Placement} \to \genfrac{}{}{0pt}{}{\text{Alumni}}{\text{relations}}$$

Research and development includes activities such as developing curriculum, making teaching plans, and acquiring knowledge for use in the classroom. Teaching is the activity of communication and discovery in the classroom. Student services include other learning activities and advising. Job placement involves helping the student find employment. And alumni relations maintains communication with alumni. These activities add value for the student but are part of the cost of educating students.

Organizations also perform activities that are not on the value chain. These activities are called non-value-added activities. Non-value-added activities do not have any effect on customer satisfaction. For example, customers are not affected if products are moved from the manufacturing floor to inventory, by products remaining in inventory for any length of time, or by setting up machines for a production run. Also, many administrative activities have no direct effect on customer satisfaction. Each of these activities has a cost without any direct benefit to the customer. Therefore, the identification and measurement of non-value-added activities give some indication of cost-saving opportunities for an organization.

The cost of a value-added activity can also be used for planning purposes. Many organizations decide to outsource certain activities. **Outsourcing** is a decision to pay some other organization to perform certain activities. The decision to outsource an activity is based on the opportunity cost of performing the activity in-house versus the cost of paying some other organization to perform the activity. Richard D. Irwin, the publisher of this book, outsources many of its activities. For example, the editing and printing activities are performed by other organizations. Irwin has determined that the opportunity cost of editing and printing in-house is greater than the cost of purchasing these services from other organizations.

The outsourcing decision should also consider quality and timely delivery. If outsourcing a process means reduced quality control or late deliveries, the organization should reconsider its decision. Many U.S. companies outsource certain processes to organizations in other countries because of lower costs. But if lower costs are accompanied by reduced quality and slow delivery, the U.S. company may be better off performing the process in-house.

There is also an ethical dimension associated with outsourcing. A recent strike at General Motors indicated the problem. Workers at a brake factory of General Motors went on strike because the workers were worried that General Motors was outsourcing the manufacture of brakes on new models. If this

WHAT'S HAPPENING

Some organizations have identified the existing management accounting process as non-value-added. These organizations have encouraged management accountants to change their roles so that they will be involved in value-added activities. How can the management accountant become part of the value chain?

Nike is the world's largest seller of athletic shoes, but the company doesn't actually make shoes. Shoes are designed at their Beaverton, Oregon, headquarters, but all the shoes are manufactured by other companies, primarily in Asia. Why does Nike outsource manufacturing?

practice continued, the workers would eventually lose their jobs. On the other hand, General Motors is trying to operate efficiently to remain competitive and to reward shareholders. The strike was resolved by General Motors agreeing to update the brake factory in the United States to make it more competitive, but General Motors maintained the right to outsource in the future if it is cost effective.

Determining the cost of activities is also the initial step in determining the cost of products. Because activities use resources to make a product or service, activities are part of the product cost. For example, word processing is an activity in a law office that is part of the cost of providing legal services. Determining the product cost from the different activities used to create the product is described further in Chapter 4.

NUMERICAL EXAMPLE 3.3

A brewery makes canned beer, which is shipped in boxes. A machine is available that can box 10,000 cans of beer a day. The daily cost of operating the machine, which includes electricity, an operator, maintenance, and the decline in value of the machine, is $500. Instead of using a machine, the company could use manual labor to box the cans of beer. One person can box 2,000 cans of beer a day. The daily cost of a person boxing cans of beer, which includes wages, health and retirement benefits, employee taxes, and other personnel costs, is $80. Which activity should the food processor use to box cans of beer?

■ **SOLUTION** Five employees can perform the same work as the boxing machine. Because the daily cost of one employee is $80, the cost of 5 employees boxing cans of beer is (5)($80), or $400. Using employees instead of the machine to box the beer is less costly and therefore preferable. The decision, however, is a short-run decision. As employees become more expensive and machinery less expensive, the brewery may decide to change to boxing by machine.

SNAKE SKATEBOARDS—I (CONTINUED)

The accounting system of Snake Skateboards presently identifies costs by departments (administration, purchasing, production, and marketing). Although these departments represent general processes in the organization, Jeff Williams needs more information about subprocesses. For example, the production process is composed of the following subprocesses: warehousing and handling raw materials, cutting, gluing, setting up molds, painting, and assembling. Of these subprocesses, the warehousing and handling of raw materials and the setting up of molds are identified as non-value-added. Therefore, Jeff should focus his cost-cutting efforts on those processes, but he is still not sure of the costs of each of these processes.

Planning Decisions Related to the Cost of Organizational Subunits

Most organizations are divided into subunits, which are also treated as cost objects. These subunits could be divisions, departments, or even individuals. Cost/benefit analysis with respect to subunits determines whether the subunit is adding value to the organization. For example, a subunit could be a division of a company for making and selling a family of products. A measure of the costs and benefits of that division could be the profit generated by that division. If the benefits generated by the subunit are greater than its costs (positive profits), the subunit is adding value to the organization. If the subunit's costs are greater than the benefits (negative profits), the organization should consider eliminating the division.

For some subunits, the benefits to the organization are difficult to isolate. For example, the engineering department provides a valuable service for a manufacturing company, but the value of that service is difficult to measure. A cost measure of the engineering department may still be viable and could be used to decide whether to outsource engineering.

Treating subunits as cost objects is also part of the process of evaluating the performance of managers responsible for the subunits. Determining performance measures for different subunits within the organization is discussed further in Chapter 7.

Planning Decisions Related to the Cost of Customers

Until recently, most organizations thought any customer was a good customer. But organizations have begun to evaluate customers and found that some customers are not as good as other customers. Why do customers differ? Some customers buy more than others. Some customers are farther away and require higher delivery costs. Some customers are chronic complainers or need additional customer service. To evaluate customers, the different customers are treated as cost objects. Costs related to customers are compared with the benefits of having the customer. In some cases the cost of having a customer is higher than the benefit. For example, insurance companies often find that drivers with a history of accidents tend to create greater costs than the premiums they pay. If so, the insurance company might refuse to provide insurance for those high-risk drivers or increase their premiums.

Some organizations may also choose to educate customers to make them more profitable. For example, golf courses try to educate golfers on appropriate behavior on the golf course. Slow play and damage to greens can be costly for the golf

The victims of Hurricane Andrew in Miami are expensive customers for property insurance companies. Insurance companies measure the cost of providing homeowner's insurance in Florida and other states and price their policies accordingly. Why is homeowner's insurance more expensive in Florida than in Maine?

course, so most golf courses have rangers on the golf course to encourage customers to play faster and respect the golf course.

A cost/benefit analysis of customers is not only beneficial in identifying unprofitable customers, but should also reveal the type of customer that is most profitable to the organization. When the preferred type of customer is identified, marketing efforts can be focused on those customers. For example, life insurance companies have identified nonsmokers as good customers and many insurance companies seek nonsmokers as customers.

NUMERICAL EXAMPLE 3.4

James Wilson, a contractor, purchases 1,000 windows annually from Clear Windows, a window manufacturer, for $120,000. The product cost of $80/window includes the cost of designing and manufacturing the windows but doesn't include transportation or customer service. The cost to Clear Windows of delivering the 1,000 windows to James Wilson is $10,000. Employees at Clear Windows spend 80 hours a year taking orders, answering questions, and offering other assistance for James Wilson. The cost of using employee time is $20 per hour. What is the annual net benefit to Clear Windows of having James Wilson as a customer?

■ **SOLUTION** The benefit of having James Wilson as a customer is the revenue generated from sales, or $120,000. The costs include:

Cost of goods sold (1,000 windows)($80/window)	$80,000
Cost of transportation	10,000
Cost of service ($20/hour)(80 hours)	1,600
Total costs of James Wilson as customer	$91,600

The net benefit is the benefit ($120,000) less the cost ($91,600), or $28,400.

SNAKE SKATEBOARDS—I (CONTINUED)

> **J**eff Williams of Snake Skateboards is considering dropping some of his discount store customers. Jeff knows the amount of revenue he generates from each store, but he doesn't know the cost of having each store as a customer. First he must determine the cost of the product sold to the customer. Then he must determine if the store causes Snake Skateboards any additional costs. He feels that one discount store in particular is a very costly customer because the store is always returning skateboards with questionable defects. The cost of handling those returns is part of the marketing cost figure, but Jeff is not sure how big that extra handling cost is.

Planning Decisions Related to Suppliers

An organization generally wants to use the lowest cost supplier. If the organization needs raw materials, parts, or services, the organization should find the supplier that will provide those inputs at the lowest cost. The traditional method of searching for the lowest cost producer has been to ask for bids from suppliers. The supplier with the lowest credible bid would win the opportunity to supply the organization.

An example of an effective supplier/company relationship is that between Sonoco Products Company and Ludlow Corp. Ludlow has an exclusive contract to supply the liners and bands for the Sonoco fiber drums being manufactured here. The companies have worked together to achieve higher standards of quality.

With the advent of just-in-time (JIT) and total quality management (TQM), however, organizations are taking a closer look at their relations with suppliers. Just because an organization submits the lowest bid for a part or service does not mean it is the lowest cost supplier. Suppliers affect an organization's costs in many different ways. The timeliness of the delivery of the parts or services affect costs. A late delivery can shut down an organization and be extremely expensive. The packaging of parts or products from suppliers can also affect costs. Some packaging is difficult to dismantle and discard. Ideally, an organization would like the supplier to package their parts or products so they are ready for immediate use and do not have to be initially unpacked and warehoused.

The quality of the supplier's products or services also has an effect on the costs of an organization. Even if an organization can return defective parts, the cost of inspecting and handling those defects can be large. A high-quality part is much easier to assemble and can reduce customer service costs because of reduced customer complaints.

Suppliers also cause purchasing costs. Purchasing costs are incurred by an organization because purchase agents must contact and communicate with suppliers and write purchase orders. Also, accountants must record transactions and the treasurer must write checks. Some suppliers require more purchasing costs than other suppliers.

Treating the supplier as a cost object can help identify whether a supplier is truly low cost. To determine the cost of a supplier, the costs related to delivery, inspection, warehousing, quality, and purchasing must be added to the purchase price of the part or service.

SNAKE SKATEBOARDS—I (CONTINUED)

Snake Skateboards currently has separate suppliers for the wood, glue, plastic, and wheel assemblies. Jeff Williams has been unhappy with the supplier of the wheel assemblies because of late deliveries. The supplier of the plastic sheets, who has always made timely deliveries, can also provide the

> wheel assemblies, but they would cost $1,000 more. But Jeff figures that he can save $2,000 on purchasing costs by reducing the number of suppliers for Snake Skateboards, and the wheel assemblies would more likely arrive on time. Therefore, Jeff decides to change suppliers for the wheel assemblies.

Planning Decisions Related to Costs Associated with Periods

Financial reporting to external parties such as shareholders or taxing authorities is based on treating a period of time as the cost object. The revenue recognition principle attempts to determine in which period of time a revenue occurs. The matching principle then matches costs to revenues. Some costs, such as research and development and selling and administrative, are treated as **period costs.** Period costs are assigned to the period of time in which they were incurred. Depreciation is an example of a process of assigning the cost of certain fixed assets to different periods. The revenues and costs of a certain time period are then compared to determine the profit for that period.

In calculating profit, only the product costs of the products sold during the period are treated as costs of that period. The product costs of products sold are called **cost of goods sold.** The product costs of products not sold are treated as an asset and called *inventory.* Inventory costs only become cost of goods sold when the inventory is sold.

NUMERICAL EXAMPLE 3.5

The Pebble Book Store opens on January 1, 1997. During the year the book store purchases $500,000 of books. The freight charges to have the books delivered are $50,000 and are treated as product costs. During the year, the book store has the following other costs, which are treated as period costs:

Rent	$12,000
Advertising	$30,000
Salaries	$80,000

Pebble Book Store has revenues of $800,000 during 1997 and has 20% of its books unsold at the end of the year. Make an income statement for the bookstore for 1997.

■ **SOLUTION** Because the freight charges are treated as product costs the total product costs during the year are $550,000. Because 80% of the books are sold during the year, the cost of goods sold is (80%)($550,000), or $440,000. The remaining product costs—(20%)($550,000), or $110,000—remain as an asset called inventory. The period costs are completely expensed during 1997.

PEBBLE BOOK STORE
Income Statement
Year of 1997

Revenues	$800,000
Cost of goods sold	(440,000)
Rent	(12,000)
Advertising	(30,000)
Salaries	(80,000)
Net income	$238,000

It is important to recognize that the product cost used to calculate the cost of goods sold for external reporting purposes is usually different than the estimate of product costs used for planning purposes. The cost of goods sold for external reporting is based on historical costs. Also, the cost of goods sold in the external reports does not include many of the costs associated with products, such as research and development. In general, the cost of goods sold only includes the purchase and manufacturing costs of products. But the opportunity cost of providing a product includes many costs before and after the manufacturing stage, such as designing, engineering, distribution, marketing, and customer service.

Making the period of time the cost object is not consistent with any specific internal planning decisions. Tracing costs and revenues to a particular period of time allows for the estimation of the increased value or income of the organization during the period. This measure provides information to external users about the value of debt and ownership shares of the organization and also provides information for owners to evaluate senior managers. For internal purposes, however, a measure of period income only gives an indication of how well the existing organizational strategy is working. A loss during a period would indicate that the organization needs to reexamine its strategy.

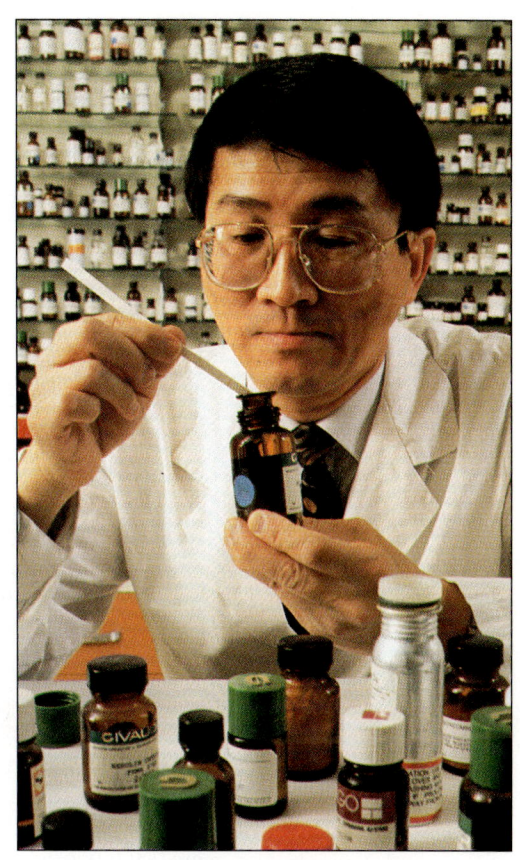

This technician is testing flavors in a food research laboratory. Laboratory work is an indirect cost of making many products. What would be a good cost driver to trace laboratory costs to products?

CONCEPT REVIEW

1. How are cost objects chosen?
2. What decisions are based on product and service costs?
3. Why measure the cost of activities?
4. What is the advantage of identifying the value chain of a product?
5. How does treating an organizational subunit as a cost center relate to control decisions?
6. What are the advantages of treating customers as cost objects?
7. What costs should be considered when evaluating suppliers?
8. How are financial reports used by shareholders?

3.2 Estimating Costs through Tracing: Direct and Indirect Costs

Estimating the cost of a cost object requires the identification and measurement of all the costs associated with the cost object. Linking costs with cost objects is called *tracing*. Some costs are easily traced to a cost object, but other costs may only be peripherally related to the cost object. Those costs that are easily identified as belonging to a particular cost object are called **direct costs.** For example, the direct cost of making a desk includes the wood, nails, screws, and labor to assemble the desk. Each of these costs is easily traced to making that desk.

Other costs that can't be easily traced to a particular cost object are called **indirect costs.** Indirect costs are difficult to trace because they are associated with multiple cost objects. The indirect cost of making the desk includes the cost of machines that are used for other products, the plant manager's salary, and the cost of the personnel office. These indirect costs are organizational costs that support the making of a desk but also support other products.

Direct and indirect costs depend on the cost object. A direct cost of a subunit of an organization may be an indirect cost of a product. For example, the salary of a manager who works with many different products would be an indirect cost of a particular product. If the manager only works within one subunit of the organization, however, the manager's salary is a direct cost of that subunit.

Although the tracing of indirect costs to a cost object appears to be problematic, a careful analysis of the cause of the indirect costs can provide some direction. Indirect costs occur because an organization performs an activity or process that is related to multiple cost objects. These activities are triggered by some event called a **cost driver.** A cost driver is the cause of the cost of an activity. For example, maintenance is an activity used by many departments. Maintenance costs occur because maintenance workers are requested and used by the other departments. Therefore, cost drivers for maintenance costs could include maintenance requests or hours of maintenance time. The more maintenance requests or maintenance time a department uses, the more maintenance costs it causes. The maintenance costs can, therefore, be traced to the different departments based on how much of the cost driver each department uses.

NUMERICAL EXAMPLE 3.6

A company has three customers: the U. S. government, General Motors, and Du Pont. A customer service department has been established to deal with complaints from the customers about the product. The estimated costs of the customer service department are $400,000 and the number of complaints is identified as the cost driver for tracing customer service costs to the different customers. The company estimates that the U.S. government will make 50 complaints, General Motors will make 200 complaints, and Du Pont will make 150 complaints. In estimating the cost of the different customers, how much of the customer service department costs are traced to each of the customers?

■ **SOLUTION** There are a total of 400 estimated complaints. The percentage of the expected cost driver usage by each of the customers and the corresponding tracing of customer service costs are:

Customer	% of Cost Driver Usage	Customer Service Costs
U.S. Government	50/400 = 12.5%	($400,000)(.125) = $50,000
General Motors	200/400 = 50%	($400,000)(.50) = $200,000
Du Pont	150/400 = 37.5%	(400,000)(.375) = $150,000

More customer service costs are traced to General Motors because General Motors used more of the cost driver.

Cost drivers are ideal tracers of indirect costs when the usage of the cost driver is proportional to the indirect costs. When proportionality exists between cost driver usage and the indirect costs of an activity, each cost driver used causes the same activity cost. The proportional relationship is described in Figure 3.2.

If a proportional relation does not exist between cost driver usage and indirect activity costs, usage of a cost driver will cause activity costs that depend on total cost driver usage. If there are start-up costs for the activity, the initial usage of the cost driver will cause more activity costs than subsequent usage. This will make the tracing of costs by the cost driver more difficult.

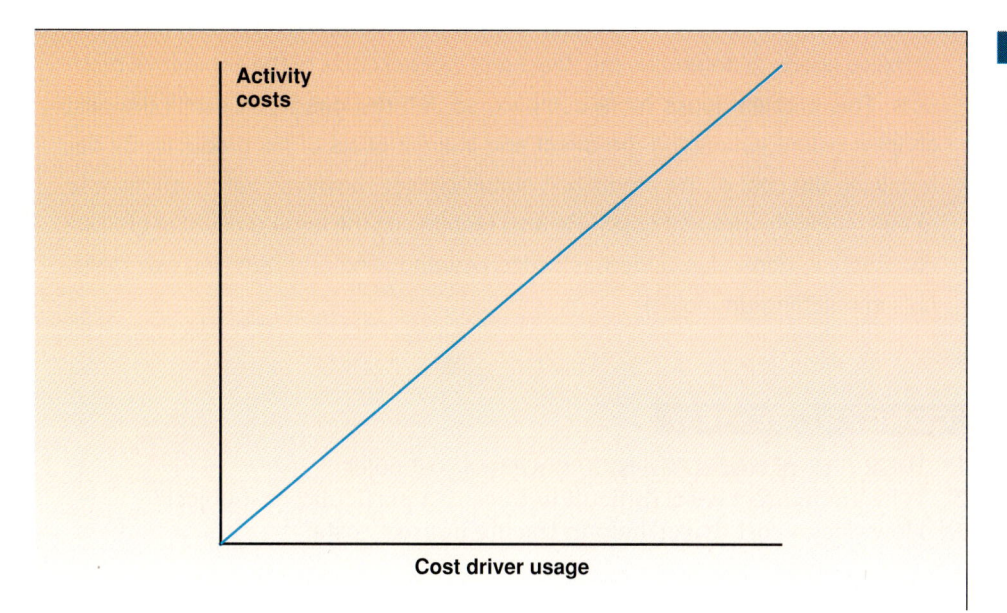

FIGURE 3.2

Proportionality of Cost Driver Usage and Activity Costs

(Graph: Activity costs vs. Cost driver usage showing a straight line through the origin)

SNAKE SKATEBOARDS—I (CONTINUED)

On closer examination, Jeff is able to trace the different production costs to the subprocesses. Most of the production costs were direct costs. Only the $25,000 production manager's salary was associated with all the subprocesses. The number of hours working with each subprocess is used to trace the production manager's salary to each of the subprocesses.

Production Subprocess	Percentage of Manager's Time	× Manager's Salary	= Indirect Costs
Warehousing and handling raw materials	10%	$25,000	$2,500
Cutting	30%	25,000	7,500
Gluing	5%	25,000	1,250
Setting up molds	20%	25,000	5,000
Painting	20%	25,000	5,000
Assembly	15%	25,000	3,750
Total	100%		$25,000

The total costs traced to each of the subprocesses given Jeff's estimates of direct costs are:

Production Subprocesses	Indirect Costs	Direct Costs	Total Costs
Warehousing and handling raw materials	$ 2,500	$ 15,500	$18,000
Cutting	7,500	42,500	50,000
Gluing	1,250	8,750	10,000
Setting up molds	5,000	50,000	55,000
Painting	5,000	30,000	35,000
Assembly	3,750	38,250	42,000
Total	$25,000	$185,000	$210,000

Jeff also needs to determine the direct and indirect costs of the company's products. This problem looks more complex, so Jeff decides to wait until the next chapter before estimating the direct and indirect costs of his products. By determining the cost of the production subprocesses, however, Jeff is on his way to estimating the product costs. He also recognizes the large amount of production costs in non-value-added activities (warehousing and handling raw materials and setting-up molds).

CONCEPT REVIEW

1. What type of cost is easiest to trace to a cost object?
2. Why are indirect costs difficult to trace to a particular cost object?
3. How does a cost driver help in tracing indirect costs?

3.3 Estimating Costs through the Identification of Variable and Fixed Costs

Estimating the cost of processes, including the making of products, can be performed by identifying the fixed and variable costs of those processes. This approach assumes that all the costs associated with a process can be traced to the process, but these costs vary with the output of the process. Fixed and variable costs are defined by their relation with the output of the process. For example, the output of the process of hiring employees is the number of employees hired. The process of hiring has costs that vary with the number of employees that are hired. Process costs that vary with the output of the process are called *variable costs*. Process costs that don't vary with the output are called *fixed costs* of the process. Once the variable costs per unit of output and the fixed costs are estimated, the total costs of the process can be estimated using the following equation:

$$\text{Total process costs} = \left(\begin{array}{c}\text{Variable cost per}\\ \text{unit of output}\end{array}\right)\left(\begin{array}{c}\text{Number of units}\\ \text{of output}\end{array}\right) + \text{Fixed costs}$$

The equation assumes that the process is operating within its relevant range. In other words, the process is not operating at an unusually low level or near capacity.

NUMERICAL EXAMPLE 3.7

The variable cost of processing loan applications is $50 per application. The fixed costs are $60,000. What is the expected cost of processing loan applications if 500 loan applications are processed? (Assume 500 loan applications are in the relevant range.)

■ **SOLUTION** The expected cost of processing loan applications is $60,000 + (500 applications)($50/application), or $85,000.

The problem with estimating process costs through fixed and variable costs per unit is making the estimates of the fixed and variable costs. This section describes two methods of estimation: the account classification method and the visual-fitting of historical data. The appendix of this chapter describes a method using regression analysis.

Estimating Variable and Fixed Costs through Account Classification

Accounting systems aggregate costs within different categories called *accounts*. For example, all maintenance costs may be aggregated within a single account. Or all electricity costs may be aggregated within a single account. The costs in these accounts are treated as if they are all the same and have predictable relations with the output of different processes. For example, the costs in the electricity account are assumed to be similar and have predictable relations with different processes such as accounting and machining. In the case of accounting, the major use of electricity is for lighting. The cost of electricity for lighting is not likely to change much with the output of the accounting department, which could be described in terms of number of transactions recorded or hours of work performed by accountants. Under these circumstances, the cost of electricity would be considered fixed with respect to accounting. In the case of machining, the major use of electricity is the operation of the machines. The more the machines operate, the more electricity is used. The cost of electricity for machining is likely to change with the change in output of machining, which could be described in terms of machine hours or number of units machined. Under these circumstances the cost of electricity would be considered variable with respect to machining.

The account classification method assumes that each cost account associated with the process of interest can be identified as either fixed or variable with the output of the process. If the costs of an account do not change with the output of the process, the account is classified as fixed. If the costs of an account increase proportionally with the units of output of a process, the account is classified as variable. Figure 3.3 demonstrates the fixed and variable relation.

In reality, very few cost accounts can be described as either exactly variable or exactly fixed with respect to a process. Cost accounts generally have some of both characteristics and tend to curve instead of being linear as they are in Figure 3.3. The account classification method, however, requires the identification of cost accounts as either fixed or variable.

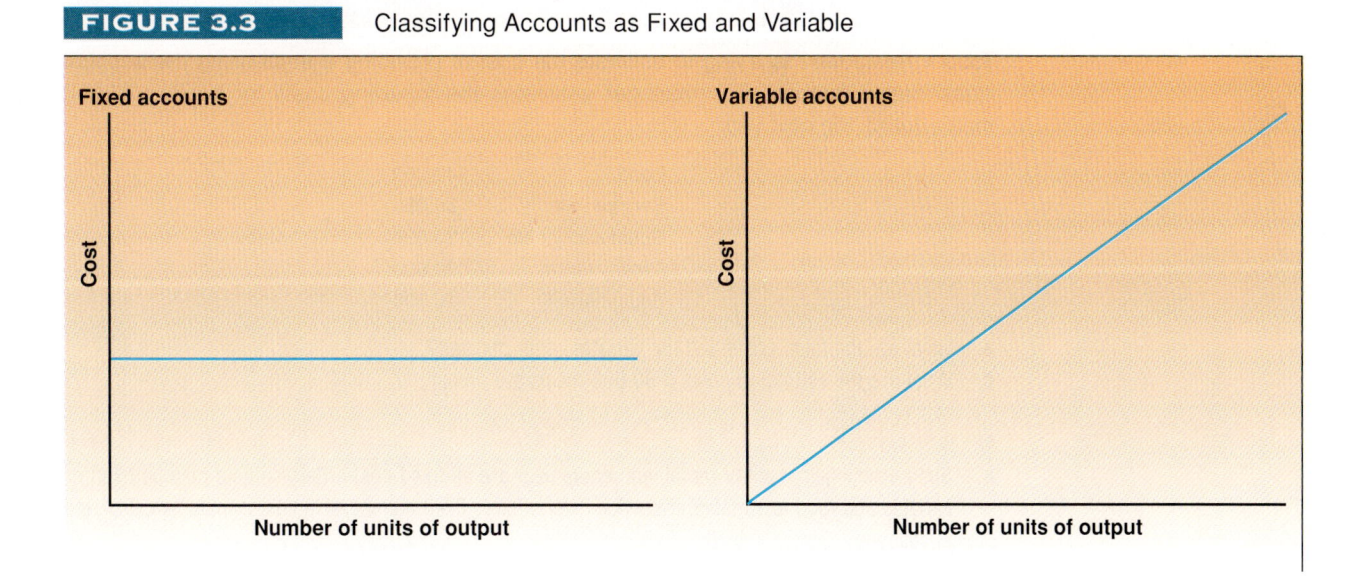

FIGURE 3.3 Classifying Accounts as Fixed and Variable

There are several ways of preparing and selling meals. Caterers typically work out of kitchens in homes or warehouses and deliver meals to the customers. Restaurateurs prepare and serve meals at the restaurant. What differences would you expect in the fixed costs of the two types of operations?

Once the cost accounts are classified as fixed or variable, all of the costs in each category are aggregated. The total costs of the fixed cost accounts are the fixed costs of the process. The total costs of the variable cost accounts are divided by the expected units of output of the process to determine the variable cost per unit.

The advantage of knowing the fixed costs and variable cost per unit of a process is the ability to estimate costs given different levels of output of the process. Each additional unit of output should increase costs by the variable cost per unit until capacity constraints become a factor.

NUMERICAL EXAMPLE 3.8

Topper Restaurant is trying to estimate the cost of providing a meal using the account classification method. The manager estimates the following costs for serving 20,000 meals during the next year:

Food	$40,000
Service help	80,000
Supervisory help	60,000
Facility rental	50,000
Equipment	10,000

a. What are the fixed costs and the variable costs per unit?
b. What are the estimated costs if 30,000 meals are prepared?

■ **SOLUTION**

a. Supervisory help, facility rental, and equipment are all fixed costs. Service help may be fixed or variable and food is variable. If service help is fixed, fixed and variable costs would be calculated as follows:

Estimating Costs through the Identification of Variable and Fixed Costs

Fixed Costs:		Variable Costs:	
Service help	$ 80,000	Food	$40,000
Supervisory help	60,000		
Facility rental	50,000		
Equipment	10,000		
Total	$200,000	Total	$40,000

Variable costs/meal = $40,000/20,000 = $2/meal

b. The estimated costs if 30,000 meals are prepared include fixed costs of $200,000 and variable costs of ($2)(30,000), or total costs of $260,000.

SNAKE SKATEBOARDS—I (CONTINUED)

Jeff Williams decides to examine his product costs by trying to classify them as variable and fixed. He classifies the accounts in the following manner:

Support Function	Fixed/Variable	Amount
Administrative	Fixed	$ 90,000
Purchasing	Fixed	50,000
Production		
Plant manager salary	Fixed	25,000
Warehousing and handling	Fixed	15,500
Marketing	Fixed	100,000
Total fixed costs		$280,500
Production		
Cutting	Variable	$ 42,500
Gluing	Variable	8,750
Setting up molds	Variable	50,000
Painting	Variable	30,000
Assembling	Variable	38,250
Direct costs		
Materials	Variable	60,000
Labor	Variable	300,000
Total variable costs		$529,500

Jeff was uncertain about many of these categorizations. The cutting, gluing, setting up molds, painting, and assembling activities all would increase as more skateboards are produced. Therefore, they are classified as variable. Also, the direct costs, which include materials and labor, would increase as more skateboards are produced and thus are classified as variable. The remaining activities are not as likely to change with an increase in production, so they are categorized as fixed.

Given that Snake Skateboards plans to make 50,000 flat skateboards and 5,000 molded skateboards, or a total of 55,000 skateboards, Jeff estimates that the variable cost per skateboard is $529,500/55,000, or $9.627, and total fixed costs are $280,500. Using these variable cost per unit and fixed costs estimates, Jeff can estimate his costs for other levels of output. For example, if

Snake Skateboards makes 60,000 skateboards, the expected costs are (60,000)($9.627) + $280,500, or $858,120.

Jeff recognizes several problems with analyzing his product costs using fixed and variable costs. He knows that the molded skateboards cost more than the flat skateboards, but this method treats the two types of skateboards as identical. Also, by not differentiating the cost of the two types of skateboards, Jeff is not able to make product mix or pricing decisions. Jeff has estimated the costs of different processes, but he needs some method of tracing these costs to his different products.

Visually Fitting Historic Cost Date

Attempting to classify accounts as fixed or variable and estimating the future costs of each account requires considerable judgment, and errors are possible. Another method of estimating the variable and fixed costs is to look at the past costs of the process. The analysis of past costs will provide an approximation of estimated fixed and variable costs if the following conditions occur:

1. *Past costs reasonably approximate future costs.* If operational procedures and prices have not changed too much, then past costs should closely approximate future costs.
2. *Several periods of past cost data at different output levels exist.* If the process is new or recently developed, the analysis of past data will not work.
3. *The future output level is within the range of the past data.* If more units of output of the process are expected to be made in the future than in the past, the past data will not reveal potential capacity constraints.
4. *The costs of each process can be separately identified.* All the costs can be traced to the process.

If these conditions are satisfied, a graphical analysis of past costs and output levels will provide an estimate of the fixed and variable costs of the process. Figure 3.4 shows a graph of historical costs and the output level for many differ-

FIGURE 3.4

Estimating Fixed and Variable Costs

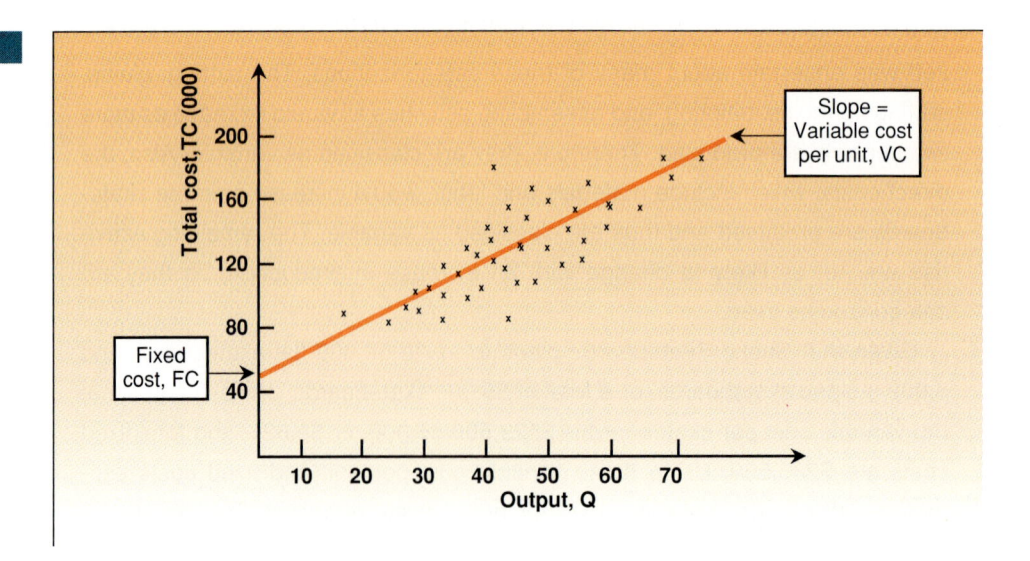

ent periods. A line is visually fitted through the plotted points. The objective is to draw a line that most closely represents the plotted points. This line approximates the fixed costs and the variable costs of the process. The fixed costs are represented by the intersection of the line with the vertical axis. In Figure 3.4, the fixed costs appear to be approximately $50,000. (Note: the vertical axis is in thousands.) The increasing costs due to increased output are variable costs. The variable cost per unit is the slope of the visually fitted line. The slope of the line can be estimated using two points on the line. The line in Figure 3.4 appears to go through the following points: (1) cost = $70,000, output = 10 and (2) cost = $130,000, output = 40. Taking the difference of the costs of the two points and dividing by the difference in the two levels of output yields the slope of the line, which is the variable cost per unit of output:

$$(\$130,000 - \$70,000)/(40 \text{ units} - 10 \text{ units}) = \$2,000 \text{ per unit of output}$$

The $50,000 estimate of fixed costs and the $2,000 estimate of variable costs per unit of output can be used to estimate process costs for other levels of output. For example, the estimated cost of the process with 60 units of output is:

$$\text{Total cost} = \$50,000 + (\$2,000/\text{unit})(60 \text{ units}) = \$170,000$$

The accuracy of process cost estimates using visually fitted historic costs depends on whether the economic and operating conditions of the past will continue into the future. There should also be concern in estimating costs outside the range of historic output. In Figure 3.4, the historic output level was between 18 and 69 units. The cost of making 80 units may be much higher than indicated by the line in Figure 3.4 because the capacity of the process may be 69 units of output and any further production would require additional capacity.

NUMERICAL EXAMPLE 3.9

Slugger Company makes wooden baseball bats. The company has used the same manufacturing procedure for years and the price of the wood and labor has remained relatively constant. The following data are historic costs of making the bats:

Year	Number of Bats Produced	Historical Costs
1989	10,000	$110,000
1990	13,000	120,000
1991	11,000	105,000
1992	15,000	125,000
1993	17,000	125,000
1994	13,000	115,000
1995	16,000	130,000

a. Estimate the variable cost per bat and the fixed costs using visual fitting.
b. Using the estimates of fixed and variable costs, estimate total costs if planned production is 14,000 bats.

■ **SOLUTION**
a. A plot of the data is provided in Figure 3.5.

FIGURE 3.5

Estimating Fixed and Variable Costs Slugger Company, 1989–1995

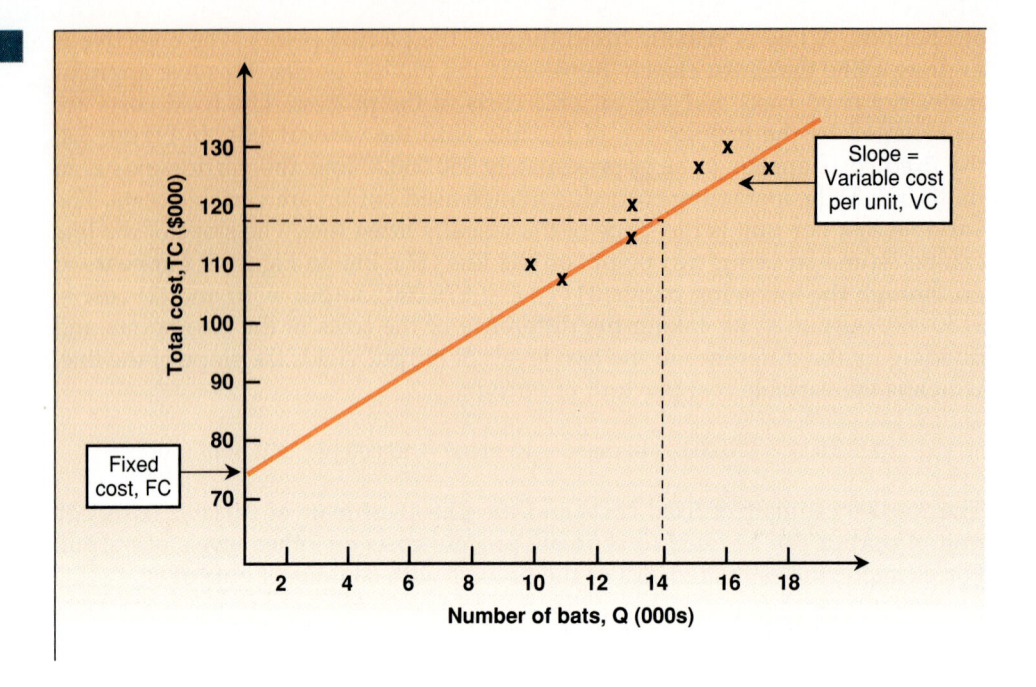

An examination of Figure 3.5 indicates that the fixed costs of making baseball bats is approximately $75,000. To find the variable cost per bat, the slope of the line must be determined. Two points on the line must be chosen to determine the slope. The line appears to go through the point representing 8,000 bats and $100,000 in costs and 18,000 bats and $130,000 in costs. The variable cost per bat is estimated by dividing the change in the vertical axis by the change in the horizontal axis:

$$\text{Variable cost per unit} = (\$130{,}000 - \$100{,}000)/(18{,}000 - 8{,}000)$$
$$= \$3/\text{bat}$$

b. The estimated costs of 14,000 bats are fixed costs of $75,000 plus variable costs of ($3/bat)(14,000 bats), or $42,000. Therefore, total estimated costs are $75,000 + $42,000, or $117,000.

SNAKE SKATEBOARDS (CONCLUDED)

Jeff Williams has historical cost data for making the skateboard, and the production process has remained constant. But Jeff Williams is not able to separate the indirect costs between the two products. In fact, Jeff is attempting to find a procedure that will trace indirect costs to the two types of skateboards. Therefore, fitting a line through historic costs will not be beneficial.

CONCEPT REVIEW

1. How is account classification used to estimate fixed and variable costs?
2. How is the visual fitting of past cost data used to estimate fixed and variable costs?

3.4 A Framework of Costs for Planning Purposes

This book introduces a number of different terms for costs for planning purposes. But if costs are to be used for planning purposes, they should represent opportunity costs. These opportunity costs are then compared with benefits to make decisions. The decisions may relate to customers, processes, departments, suppliers, or products. The first section of Table 3.1 describes possible cost objects and the decisions related to those cost objects.

The second section of Table 3.1 describes how costs are associated with the cost object. Costs related to a single cost object are easily identified with that cost object and are called *direct costs*. Costs associated with multiple cost objects are indirect and must be traced to cost objects through cost drivers.

The third section of Table 3.1 describes how costs vary with the rate of output. Fixed and variable costs can be used for estimating total opportunity costs. Marginal costs are more difficult to estimate and are commonly approximated by the variable cost when a process is operating in its relevant range.

The last section examines types of costs that make certain decisions simpler. For example, you only have to identify differential costs and benefits to make decisions between two alternatives. The terms *avoidable costs* and *incremental costs* will be introduced in Chapter 5.

TABLE 3.1 Types of Costs for Planning Decisions

The relevant cost for all planning decisions is the *opportunity cost*. The costs in this table help categorize and estimate opportunity costs. *Sunk costs* are irrelevant costs for planning purposes.

Costs Associated with Different Planning Decisions:

Cost Object	Planning Decisions
Product	Choice of product mix; pricing.
Customer	Choice of different customers through customer profitability; focus on type of customer.
Departmental activity/process	Eliminating the department; outsourcing. Choosing efficient processes; outsourcing; cost savings from non-value-added activities.
Supplier	Choice of supplier
Period	Reexamine organizational strategy; valuation by external markets.

Tracing of Costs to Different Cost Objects:

Type	Traceability
Direct	Costs that are easily identified with a single cost object.
Indirect	Costs that are associated with multiple cost objects and require cost drivers for tracing to cost objects.

Costs Associated with Rate of Output of a Process or Product:

Type	Association with Rate of Output
Variable	Costs increase proportionally with rate of output.
Fixed	Costs of starting process that don't change with rate of output.
Marginal	The cost of increasing output by one unit.

Costs Used to Simplify Planning Decisions:

Type	Definition
Differential	The costs that are different between two alternative choices.
Incremental (Ch. 5)	The additional costs of adding a process, department, customer, or product.
Avoidable (Ch. 5)	The cost savings of eliminating a process, department, customer, or product.

THE STORY OF MANAGERIAL ACCOUNTING

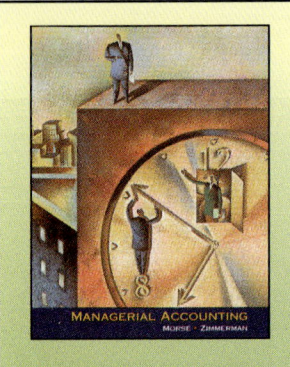

Team Decisions Regarding Planning

The *Managerial Acccounting* book team decided to develop a new management accounting book rather than change the existing book. One of the first issues facing the publication of this new book, *Managerial Accounting*, was timing. Heather, the marketing manager, noted that many of the best-selling textbooks in managerial accounting would come out with new editions in late 1996. Professors usually consider changing textbooks when new editions are published, so missing this window of opportunity could jeopardize the sales of *Managerial Accounting*. Irwin Publishing had only two years to develop this book to meet the 1996 target date. Peggy, the team accountant, had been asked to estimate the cost of missing the 1996 target date and publishing the book a year later. From which team members should she gather information and how should she analyze the data?

3.5 Summary

1. **Treat products as cost objects for the purpose of making product mix and pricing decisions.** Estimating the cost of a product allows managers to estimate the profitability of the product and whether to include that product in the product mix. The product cost can also serve as a guide for pricing by providing a lower boundary for the price.

2. **Identify outsourcing and cost-cutting opportunities by using processes as cost objects.** If the cost of a process is more than the cost of purchasing the process, the organization should consider outsourcing the process. The cost of non-value-added activities/processes offer cost-cutting opportunities.

3. **Make subunits of the organization cost objects for outsourcing decisions and evaluation of managers.** The cost of a subunit is often used to evaluate the manager of the subunit. The subunit's cost may also be compared with the cost of purchasing the processes performed by the subunit to make an outsourcing decision.

4. **Treat customers as cost objects to decide which customers to eliminate and to identify profitable types of customers.** The cost of a customer includes the cost of the product or service sold to the customer plus the cost of customer service, freight charges, and collection. These costs should be compared with the revenues from that customer to determine the customer profitability. Customer profitability can be used to identify preferable types of customers.

5. **Identify the low-cost supplier by making suppliers cost objects.** The cost of a supplier includes the cost of late delivery, inspections, unpacking, warehousing, purchasing, and quality. Suppliers should be chosen based on all of these costs.

6. **Calculate income for periods by treating periods of time as cost objects.** Period costs are used to calculate income for external reporting purposes. The net income is used to value the securities of an organization. The net income may also be used to evaluate the success of the organization's strategy.

7. **Identify direct and indirect costs to cost objects.** Direct costs are easily traced to cost objects, but indirect costs are associated with multiple cost objects, and cost drivers are used to trace indirect costs to cost objects.

8. **Estimate product or process costs through identification of variable and fixed costs.** If accounts can be identified with a process or product as either fixed or variable, then total fixed cost and the variable cost per unit can be estimated. If past costs approximate the opportunity cost of making a product or service, the past costs can be plotted with the level of output to estimate the fixed and variable product costs.

KEY TERMS

Cost driver The cause of the cost of an activity.

Cost object An item to be costed for decision-making purposes.

Cost of goods sold The historical cost of products sold as reported in the income statement.

Direct costs Costs that can be directly traced to a single cost object.

Indirect costs Costs that are associated with more than one cost object.

Outsourcing Choosing to have an outside supplier rather than an internal subunit of the organization provide a product or service.

Period costs Costs that are associated with periods of time rather than products for reporting to external parties.

Pricing decision The choice of a price for a product or service.

Product mix decision A decision on the types of proportions of products and services to offer.

Product or service cost The forgone opportunity of using resources to provide a product or service.

Target costing The process of designing a quality product at a sufficiently low cost to be able to sell the product at a competitive price and still yield a sufficient profit.

Value chain The activities related to a product or service that provide value to customers.

APPENDIX: USING REGRESSION TO ESTIMATE FIXED AND VARIABLE COSTS

Visually fitting a line through historical cost data is described in the chapter as a method of estimating the fixed and variable costs. Visually fitting a line requires some judgment and no two people are likely to draw the line exactly the same. There is a statistical method of drawing a line that is more objective. This method is called *regression* and is described in most statistics courses. Our purpose here is to illustrate how regression analysis can be used to estimate fixed and variable costs. Regression analysis identifies a line that minimizes the summation of the squared deviations of all the historical cost data points from the regression line.

The following data from Numerical Example 3.9 is used to demonstrate fitting a line with regression analysis.

Year	Number of Bats Produced	Historical Costs
1989	10,000	$110,000
1990	13,000	120,000
1991	11,000	105,000
1992	15,000	125,000
1993	17,000	125,000
1994	13,000	115,000
1995	16,000	130,000

This data must be inputted into a software package that performs regression analysis. The historical costs are the dependent variable, or the variable to be estimated. The number of bats is the independent variable, or the variable that will be used to estimate costs. The output of any regression software program looks like the following:

	Coefficient	Standard Error of Coefficient	t-Statistic
Constant	75,611	9,161	8.25
Number of bats	3.165	.6648	4.76

$R^2 = 78.3\%$

The estimate of the constant coefficient is an estimate of fixed costs equal to $75,611. The coefficient of the number of bats is the variable cost per bat equal to $3.165. The remaining information of the output indicates of how well the regression line represents the historical costs for different levels of output.

The R^2 is a measure of how well the number of bats explains the costs. If all the plotted points in Figure 3.4 were aligned in a straight line, knowing the number of bats would determine the costs. If the regression line closely represents the cost data, then the R^2 approaches 100%. The R^2 of 78.3% is quite high, indicating that the regression line is a close approximation of the historical cost data for different levels of output. An R^2 of 0% would indicate that there is no association between the number of bats and costs. An R^2 near zero indicates that the measures of the variable cost per unit and the fixed costs are not very accurate.

The standard errors of the coefficient indicate how confident we should be in the estimates of the fixed cost and variable cost per unit. In general, there is approximately a 95% chance that the true fixed cost estimate and the true variable cost per unit are within 2 standard errors of the estimates. Therefore, there is a 95% probability that true fixed cost is within the range of $75,611 + (2)($9,161), or $93,933, and $75,611 − (2)($9,161), or $57,289. The variable cost per unit is within $3.165 + (2)($.6648), or $4.4946, and $3.165 − (2)($.6648), or $1.8354.

T-statistics in excess of two indicate that the independent variable (fixed cost and variable cost per bat) is important in explaining total costs. Because both t-statistics are in excess of two, both fixed and variable costs are important components of total costs in this regression.

The estimated fixed cost and variable cost per unit allow for the estimation of costs given planned production. If planned production next year is 14,000 bats, the expected costs given the regression line are:

Fixed costs	$ 75,611
Variable costs ($3.165/bat)(14,000 bats)	44,310
Total estimated costs	$119,921

Although regression provides a more objective method of fitting historical cost data, it is susceptible to the same problems as the visually fitted line. In particular, regression assumes that the process that generated the historical costs is the same process that will be used in the estimation period.

Regression as well as visual curve fitting are only valid for estimating costs within production levels of the past. For example, the previous range of bats produced was 10,000 to 17,000. Estimates of costs of producing greater than 17,000 bats may be influenced by capacity constraints. Both methods, however, assume that variable costs per unit are constant at all levels of output, and they do not recognize capacity constraints. They assume that the relation between costs and levels of output is a straight line.

Because of these problems, regression analysis is not commonly used to estimate the fixed cost and the variable cost per unit. But regression could be used for other purposes. For example, regression could be used to identify cost drivers. In this case, the activity costs would be the dependent variable and different potential cost drivers could be tried as the independent variable. The cost driver with the closest association (highest R^2)

FIGURE 3.6 Total Costs of Hiring Personnel as a Function of Number of Personnel and Total Assets

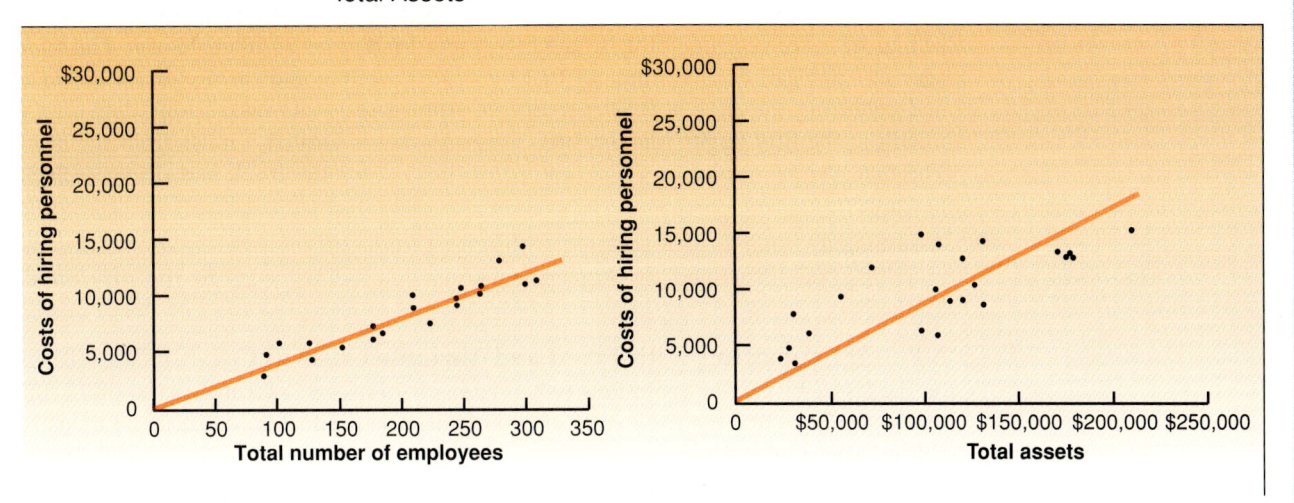

with the activity cost would be the cost driver used by the organization for that activity. For example, Figure 3.6 provides graphs describing the relation between the costs of hiring personnel and two different possible cost drivers: total number of employees and total assets. The total number of employees is more closely associated with the cost of hiring employees and has a higher adjusted R^2. Therefore, the total number of employees provides a more accurate cost driver for tracing the indirect costs of hiring personnel to different cost objects.

SELF-STUDY PROBLEM

Choosing Cost Objects for Planning Decisions   Becky Smith has just been hired by Acme Dental as the accountant. Acme Dental buys dental products from manufacturers and sells them to dental offices. Acme prides itself in immediate delivery of products. Acme operates a large warehouse for storage of products purchased from manufacturers. These products are delivered to the dental offices from the warehouse. The company has a number of salespeople who visit the dental offices and generate orders.

The present accounting system records costs in the following accounts:

Purchase of inventory	Utilities
Salaries	Warehouse rent
Freight charges	Entertainment and travel

The president tells Becky that he finds the accounting system useless for making decisions. He asks her to develop an accounting system that will help him make decisions.

What decisions might the president want to make and what cost objects should Becky choose to assist those decisions?

Solution

The president is likely to want to make decisions about product mix and prices, salespeople, suppliers, and customers. Product costs could help the president make decisions on which products to include in inventory and how to price those products. Determining the cost of having a salesperson (including their travel and entertainment costs) and comparing those costs with the revenue they generate could help the president decide on the effectiveness of each salesperson. The president may also want to determine the profit generated from each customer. Acme Dental also must make decisions about suppliers of raw materials. By making suppliers the cost object, the president can identify the best suppliers. Therefore, Becky should devise an accounting system that treats products, salespeople, suppliers and customers as cost objects.

NUMERICAL PROBLEMS

NP 3–1: Customer Profitability (LO 4; NE 4) Applegate Farms is currently selling 100 dozen eggs monthly to the Jiffy Super Market for $0.50 per dozen. The manager at Applegate Farms estimates that the cost of feeding and caring for the chickens and collecting the eggs is $0.30 per dozen. Applegate Farms makes four deliveries a month to the Jiffy Super Market. Jiffy Super Market is located 5 miles from the farm. The manager of Applegate Farms estimates the cost for the truck and driver is $0.50 per mile.

Assuming no other costs associated with selling to the Jiffy Super Market, what is the monthly profit generated by Applegate Farms from selling eggs to the Jiffy Super Market?

NP 3–2: Estimating with Fixed and Variable Costs (LO 8; NE 7) Based on the last few years of operations (when he made between 1,000 and 15,000 units), Bill Jones calculated that the fixed costs of making his sole product is $400,000 and the variable cost per unit is $200.

a. What is his expected cost in the next year using the fixed and variable costs if he expects to make 18,000 units?
b. What are two dangers of using the fixed and variable cost per unit as calculated to estimate next year's costs?

NP 3–3: Target Variable Costs (LO 1, 8; NE 1, 7) The Cover Company makes asphalt shingles for houses. The company has fixed costs of $2 million annually. The competitive market in shingles dictates a price of $10 per pack. The company expects to sell 400,000 packs.

In order to make $400,000 in profit, what variable costs per pack must the company attain?

NP 3–4: Pricing the Processing of Mortgages (LO 1; NE 2) Home Lending Inc. (HLI) is a mortgage application service company. It is a subsidiary of Relocation Realty, a large real estate sales firm. Real estate agents working for Relocation Realty refer their clients to HLI to arrange financing. Home buyers, instead of contacting several banks to compare mortgage rates, use HLI as an intermediary. HLI maintains a current list of all the various mortgage terms at all area banks (fixed and adjustable rates, terms, balloon payments, points, etc.). Home buyers in one place can then select the mortgage parameters that best fit their situation. Because all banks use a common mortgage application form, HLI can fill out and file the necessary application for their clients. Banks and HLI charge one point (1% of the requested loan amount) for filing the application if it is approved. (Applications denied by the banks are rare and the loan applicant is not charged any fee.) The consumer is indifferent between filing an application directly with the bank versus using HLI.

HLI employs mortgage processors who meet with the home buyers, go over the various loan options, file the applications, and represent the borrower when the loan is consummated. Each processor can file a maximum of 120 mortgages per year. HLI owns and maintains a mainframe computer system that automates the loan application process. In addition to the mortgage processors, secretaries function as receptionists, computer data entry clerks, and office supply managers. The president of HLI, Linda Jeter, oversees the office, hires (and fires) office staff, and helps with difficult loan applications. She reports to the owner of Relocation Realty.

The housing market is in a recession. Two years ago HLI processed 580 mortgages with an average mortgage of $80,000 and employed five processors and two secretaries. This year Jeter projects only 280 mortgage filings with an average mortgage of $70,000. She laid off two processors and a secretary last year.

The following data summarizes operations two years ago and the projections for this year:

	Two Years Ago	Projected for This Year
Number of mortgages	580	280
Average revenue per mortgage	$800	$700
Revenue	$464,000	$196,000
Mortgage processors	(135,000)	(90,000)
Secretaries	(34,000)	(17,000)
Computer maintenance	(30,000)	(30,000)
L. Jeter salary	(55,000)	(55,000)
Depreciation on computer	(40,000)	(40,000)
Office rent	(36,000)	(36,000)
Supplies, utilities, phones, etc.	(12,000)	(12,000)
Profit/loss	$122,000	$ (84,000)

HLI has noncancelable five-year contracts for office rent and computer maintenance, with one more year to run on each contract. The computer system and office equipment have no salvage values. Ms. Jeter has been told to cut the losses or else Relocation Realty will close the subsidiary. She is considering two possibilities: further layoffs of mortgage processors or cutting the price charged for mortgage processing to ¾ of 1%. She thinks such a price cut will not be met immediately by the competition and in the meantime will increase the quantity demanded by 30%.

Ignoring taxes, evaluate the various proposals and recommend a course of action Ms. Jeter should pursue. Justify your recommendation with a clearly presented financial analysis.

NP 3–5: Costs for Product Mix Decisions (LO 1; NE 1)

A farmer has an extra acre for growing vegetables. The farmer has the choice of planting carrots or onions. The acre would produce 500 pounds of carrots and 1,000 pounds of onions. The carrots sell for $0.17/pound and the onions sell for $0.11/pound. The carrot seeds cost $10 and the onion sets (similar to seeds) cost $40. Both carrots and onions require $50 of labor for tilling, weeding, and harvesting.

What should the farmer plant on the acre?

NP 3–6: Planning Decisions Related to Suppliers (LO 5)

A car manufacturer has decided to outsource car seats. The car manufacturer needs 20,000 seats. There are three manufacturers of car seats (Fast Co., Slow Co., and Steady Co.) who are asked to bid on the car seats. They have made the following bids:

	Fast Co.	Slow Co.	Steady Co.
Bid/Seat	$100	$90	$105

The car manufacturer has more information on the suppliers, who have been used previously. Each supplier has a different probability of having a late delivery and a defect. The car manufacturer uses just-in-time, so a late delivery causes the factory to shut down. The expected costs of each shutdown are $15,000. Defects are returned to the supplier, but the cost of dealing with the defect is $80 per defective seat. The number of defects and late deliveries expected from each manufacturer of the car seats for the 20,000-seat order are:

	Fast Co.	Slow Co.	Steady Co.
Number of defects	300	100	20
Number of late deliveries	10	25	0

Which supplier of car seats should the manufacturer use?

NP 3–7: Costs Associated with Periods (LO 6; NE 5) A new hardware store buys $340,000 of inventory during the year. The store sells all the items for 40% more than their costs. At the end of the year, the cost of inventory not yet sold was $40,000. The payments to the suppliers of the inventory are considered product costs, but all other costs are treated as period costs. Those costs include $15,000 for rent, $6,000 for utilities, and $60,000 for salaries.

What is the income for the period?

NP 3–8: Tracing Direct and Indirect Costs to Subunits (LO 3; NE 6)
The Triad Corporation is composed of a central headquarters and three divisions: Black, Red, and White. The central headquarters is responsible for planning and financing and is expected to have $12 million of costs in the coming year. A close examination of the costs of central headquarters indicates that its costs increase proportionally with the total assets of the divisions. In the coming year the three divisions are expected to have the following assets, revenues, and direct costs:

	Black	Red	White
Total assets	$10,000,000	$40,000,000	$50,000,000
Total revenues	$12,000,000	$35,000,000	$32,000,000
Total direct costs	$ 8,000,000	$25,000,000	$30,000,000

What is the income of each division after tracing the indirect costs of the central headquarters to the three divisions using total assets as the cost driver?

NP 3–9: Estimating Variable and Fixed Costs through Account Classification (LO 8; NE 8) Beadco Company sells necklaces of beads and is trying to determine the costs of working with each supplier. One supplier of ceramic beads operates in Kenya. During the year, the supplier is expected to sell Beadco 1,000,000 beads at a cost of $0.10/bead. The year's supply of beads is normally sent in a container, which costs $5,000 to ship to the company in New York. With 1,000,0000 beads, the container is only half full. There would be no additional freight charges if the container were full. To make the order with the Kenyan company, Beadco must send a purchasing agent to Kenya. The cost of the trip including the salary of the purchasing agent is $10,000. The processing of the purchase order also requires the use of 20 hours of personnel time, which includes time spent by the accountant and the treasurer. The average cost per hour for these personnel is $50. When the beads arrive, each bead must be inspected for quality and breakage. An inspector who is paid $20/hour can inspect 1,000 beads per hour.

a. What is the fixed cost per bead of working with the Kenyan supplier, if 1,000,000 beads are purchased?
b. What is the variable cost per bead purchased from the Kenyan supplier?
c. What would be the total costs of purchasing from the Kenyan supplier if 1,500,000 beads were purchased?

NP 3–10: Identifying Variable and Fixed Costs through Visual Fitting (LO 8; NE 9) A tennis ball manufacturer is noted for making all its tennis balls exactly the same. The manufacturer, however, is less certain about its costs. The manufacturer has not changed its operating methods in the last 10 years and the cost of labor and raw materials has remained about the same. The manufacturer has had the following costs and output during the last 10 years:

Year	Costs	Number of Balls
1987	$20,000,000	50,000,000
1988	25,000,000	75,000,000
1989	30,000,000	105,000,000
1990	28,000,000	100,000,000
1991	32,000,000	110,000,000
1992	23,000,000	80,000,000
1993	35,000,000	120,000,000
1994	31,000,000	115,000,000
1995	36,000,000	118,000,000
1996	22,000,000	90,000,000

Plot this data and visually fit a line through it.

a. What are the fixed costs of making tennis balls?
b. What are the variable costs per ball?
c. What are the expected costs in the coming year if the manufacturer expects to make 112,000,000 balls?
d. Why would it be more difficult to estimate the expected costs if the manufacturer expects to make 150,000,000 balls?

NP 3–11: Using Regression to Estimate Fixed and Variable Costs (LO 8) (Appendix)   Using the data in NP 3–10, use regression to estimate the fixed and variable costs per unit.

NP 3–12: Product Mix Decision (LO 1; NE 1)   Bob Jitters, owner of the Virtual Buzz Coffee House, is having a fit. Many customers have expressed disappointment that the Virtual Buzz does not serve espresso hot chocolate. Currently, Virtual Buzz serves both espresso and hot chocolate separately, but not together. The espresso sells for $0.75 per shot and costs $0.40 to make. The hot chocolate sells for $1.75 per mug and costs $0.50 to make. If Bob were to make espresso hot chocolate, he would sell it for $2.50, but it would cost $1.40 per mug to make. Monthly sales of espresso and hot chocolate are currently 3,000 shots and 300 mugs, respectively. Based on customer responses, Bob estimates that he could sell 500 mugs of the espresso hot chocolate per month, but his sales of hot chocolate would be cut in half. Bob does not feel that his other beverage sales will be affected.

Should Bob add espresso hot chocolate to his product mix?

NP 3–13: Costs and Revenues Related to Customers (LO 4; NE 4)
Home Town Bank has two types of individual customers who make demand deposits: college students and regular customers. The bank charges the students $0.10 per check. Regular customers get free checking service. The bank earns 10% on the deposits of the customers by lending the money but pays the customers 5% on deposits. Each type of customer costs the bank $20 per year in terms of accounting and mailing. Average college student deposits in Home Town Bank are $300, while regular customers have average deposits of $1,000. College students write an average of 100 checks a year.

Which type of customer is more profitable for the bank?

NP 3–14: Planning Decisions Related to Suppliers (LO 5)   After an extensive cost/benefit analysis, Mercy General Hospital has made a decision to outsource its ambulance operations to a private company. The administration has narrowed down its decision to two companies that meet the initial bid specifications. Hell's Bell's Company submitted a bid of $50,000 per year plus $30 per man hour of actual emergency service. Just In Time Company submitted a bid of $100,000 per year plus $25 per man hour of actual emergency service. Based on previous experience and trends, the administration expects between 12,500 and 15,000 hours of emergency service work during the next year.

a. What is the range of costs of the two ambulance services?
b. What other criteria should Mercy General consider in this decision?

NP 3–15: Planning Decisions Related to Subunits (LO 2, 3, 8; NE 3)

The Acme Corporation currently does its billing internally. The billing department currently occupies a 3,000-square-foot office that could be rented to another organization for $200,000 per year. In addition, the billing department also causes utilities costs of $20,000 a year, supply costs of $10,000 a year, postage costs of $290,000 a year, and has salary costs of $300,000 per year to issue 1,000,000 bills. All of the costs are fixed with respect to the number of bills except the postage costs. The Acme Corporation has recently received an offer from another company to do the billing for $1 per bill.

a. Should Acme Corporation outsource the billing process?
b. If Acme generates less sales, at what annual billing level should the company consider outsourcing the billing process?

NP 3–16: Relating Costs to Time Periods (LO 6; NE 5)

Master Artworks buys and sells paintings. During March the company had the following paintings (with their costs) in inventory. Some of the paintings have been sold and the sales price is also reported.

Painting	Cost	Sales Price
Van Goof	$30,000	$50,000
Rembranch	20,000	Not sold
Angelomichael	10,000	40,000
Gogone	25,000	Not sold
Monnay	13,000	10,000
Picatto	3,000	7,000

Master Artworks also has the following period costs during March: rent $3,000, salaries $10,000, utilities $1,000, and insurance $500.

What is the income for Master Artworks during March?

NP 3–17: Using Regression to Choose Cost Drivers (LO 8) (Appendix)

During the last 10 months, the Arcade Corporation has had the indirect costs shown in the following table. The Arcade Corporation is trying to determine a good cost driver for the indirect costs. The usage of two potential cost drivers, direct labor hours and machine hours, has also been recorded over the last 10 months.

Month	Indirect Costs	Direct Labor Hours	Machine Hours
1	$3,200,000	5,000	3,000
2	3,600,000	5,100	3,400
3	3,800,000	5,400	3,500
4	3,500,000	5,200	3,300
5	2,800,000	5,000	2,900
6	4,000,000	5,500	4,000
7	3,500,000	5,100	3,400
8	3,700,000	5,400	3,800
9	4,200,000	5,700	4,200
10	2,500,000	4,500	2,600

Which cost driver is most closely associated with the indirect costs?

DISCUSSION PROBLEMS

DP 3–1: Product Mix Decision (LO 1)

Jen and Barry's Ice Cream is a small company that makes its own ice cream and sells ice cream cones and cartons of ice cream in a retail space of the establishment. The company has been known for its 23 flavors of ice cream. The owner of the firm, however, is thinking of adding a 24th flavor: Chocolate Highway. Chocolate Highway is a mixture of chocolate ice cream, macadamia nuts, and chunks of white chocolate. The company currently makes chocolate ice cream, but none of its other products use macadamia nuts or white chocolate.

What costs should be considered in deciding whether to add Chocolate Highway to the product mix of Jen and Barry's?

DP 3–2: Target Costing and Product Mix (LO 1)   The Peter Paint Company makes water- and oil-based paints for houses. Recently, the company has been investigating other opportunities. One possibility is producing finger paints for children. Finger paints are considerably different than house paints because they must be designed to be easily washable. But the marketing people of the company feel there is an opportunity to enter this new market. They believe that the company could sell 1 million units of finger paints annually for $1 per unit.

How should the company use this information in making a decision to add finger paints to its product mix?

DP 3–3: Pricing Decision (LO 1)   Internetco offers a wireless connection to the Internet in Portland. The wireless connection is achieved with a remote modem that sends and receives signals through a network of antennas located throughout the city. The antenna network has already been established. The customer simply buys the remote modem from the company and then pays a monthly fee for the service. The company is attempting to decide what price to charge for the service.

What factors should the company consider in making the pricing decision?

DP 3–4: Direct and Indirect Costs (LO 7)   A copy shop has the following costs: copy machines, utilities, rent, paper, and labor related to copying, managing, and accounting.

a. Which of these costs are direct with respect to a particular customer's copying job?
b. Which of these costs are indirect with respect to a particular customer's copying job?

DP 3–5: Choosing Cost Objects (LO 1-6)   Identify the cost object for the following decisions:

a. Deciding how much to charge a customer for car repair work.
b. Deciding whether to build a new factory.
c. Deciding whether to buy a part rather than to continue to make it.
d. Deciding whether to provide additional credit to a customer.
e. Deciding whether to sell a division.
f. Deciding whether to have data processing done outside the organization.
g. Deciding which supplier to use.
h. Determining the annual profit.

DP 3–6: Value Chain (LO 2)   The FastBike Company manufactures bicycles and is trying to identify which overhead activities are value-added and which overhead activities are non-value-added. Describe each of the following activities as value-added or non-value-added:

Engineering and designing the bicycle.
Storing the finished bicycles.
Moving the raw materials from the warehouse to the assembly area.
Assembling wheels to the frame.
Providing customer service.

DP 3–7: Classifying Costs as Fixed and Variable (LO 8)   The city water department is responsible for supplying water to the city. Water is pumped from deep wells to reservoirs, chlorine is added, and the water is piped to the different customers in the city. The pumps only operate when the reservoirs decline to a certain level. The reservoirs are located on the highest part of the city so gravity can be used to establish water pressure for the city users. Pipes will frequently break due to age, so the city water department maintains a maintenance department. The water department has the following accounts to record costs:

Maintenance	Billing and collection
Power (for the pumps)	Salaries of top managers
Rent	Chemicals

If gallons of water consumed by the city is treated as the output of the water department, describe each of the accounts as either fixed or variable.

DP 3–8: Identifying Processes Performed by an Organization (LO 2)
The department of accounting of the University of New North Wales is responsible for teaching the accounting classes at the university. The accounting department is analyzing what it does. The purpose of the analysis is to operate more efficiently and allocate responsibilities among the professors. The accounting department is also thinking about hiring an administrator to perform certain activities that don't require the specific skills of the professors.

a. What are the general processes performed by an accounting department?
b. What processes could be performed by an administrator instead of a professor?
c. How could the costs of the different processes be measured?

DP 3–9: Tracing Costs to Subunits within a University (LO 3, 7)
The business school of Northwest Washington State College operates somewhat independently from the rest of the university. The business school accepts its own students and collects its own tuition. The business school also has its own external affairs officer who obtains donations from local businesses and alumni. The business school and its students, however, still use some of the services of the rest of the college. For example, the students and faculty of the business school use the college's library and athletic facilities. Also, business school students take classes outside the business school. The college feels that the business school should pay for this use of the college's facilities and services. This payment is to be based on costs traced to the business school.

How should the college's costs be traced to the business school?

DP 3–10: Making Planning Decisions with Customers (LO 4)
A bank spends considerable time evaluating loan applicants. People come to banks to request business loans or personal loans to purchase houses, cars, and so on. The loan officers must analyze these requests to decide which applicants should be granted a loan.

a. How does the process of evaluating a loan request relate to a cost/benefit analysis of customers?
b. Rather than just making a decision to deny or grant a loan application, what other options do loan officers have in dealing with loan applicants?

DP 3–11: Making Planning Decisions with Respect to Suppliers (LO 5)
In recent years, businesses have found that providing health insurance for employees is very costly. One procedure that has helped contain these costs is the use of a health maintenance organization (HMO). An HMO agrees to cover the health costs of the employees of an organization for payment of a premium of a certain amount per employee. The HMO then contracts with doctors to provide the health services. Choosing an HMO, however, has been a real dilemma for organizations. Some questionable suppliers have entered this market and have offered services, been paid the premiums, and then have not provided the health services. In these cases the organization still must cover the health expenses. Therefore, the HMO that provides the lowest bid is certainly not necessarily the lowest cost supplier of health services for employees.

a. What other factors should the organization consider in choosing an HMO other than the bid?
b. What are other ways of contracting with HMOs to ensure quality health service for employees?

Case

C 3–1: The Business School Game

James Madison has just graduated with a degree in business. He has not received any job offers, so he decided to become an entrepreneur. He has designed a board game based on the experiences of a student in business school. The game is composed of a board with various tracks to be followed by players, dice, pieces to mark a player's position, and paper money. Each game will also contain a set of instructions and will be packaged in a cardboard box. James has tested the game with many of his friends and they all seem impressed.

James is not sure what his next move should be. He recognizes that he must both produce and market the game. The production opportunities include (1) having another organization completely responsible for all the production, (2) having other organizations supply parts and doing the assembly himself, and (3) making all of the parts and assembling the game himself. James makes the following cost estimates with respect to these estimates.

1. **All production by outside organizations.** James has received bids from different organizations to make the business school game. The company in China has made a bid at $2 per game if fewer than 20,000 are ordered annually or $1.80 per game if 20,000 or more are ordered annually. Transportation costs to the United States from China would be $5,000 for a container that could hold as many as 40,000 games. Only one container a year would be necessary. An American company has made a bid of $3 per game, which would include transportation.

2. **Production of parts by outside organizations and assembly in-house.** The lowest bids including transportation for each of the parts are:

Board	$0.30/game
Pieces	$0.05/game
Dice	$0.05/game
Paper money	$0.20/game

    To assemble the games in-house, James will have to rent a building. Annual rent of the building would be $8,000 and utilities for the building would be an additional $2,000 per year. The labor required to assemble the parts of the game is six minutes per game. The cost of labor is $10 per hour.

3. **Total production of the game in-house.** After a careful analysis of costs of manufacturing, James has estimated the annual cost of production of the game in-house to be:

Number of Units	Total Costs
5,000	$20,000
10,000	35,000
15,000	42,000
20,000	48,000
25,000	53,000
30,000	56,000

There are also three different ways of marketing the business school game: (1) selling the game through the Internet, (2) selling the game through a toy catalogue, (3) or selling through a salesperson who would solicit retail stores. James estimates the following costs and expected sales of each of these marketing methods.

1. **Selling the game through the Internet.** James could advertise the game on the Internet by establishing a home page. A company has told James that they would set up a home page on the Internet for his business game for $2,000 annually. The home page would provide a telephone number and an e-mail address for buyers. The additional costs of taking orders are estimated to be $1 per game. James estimates that using this

method he could sell 5,000 games at a price of $10 per game and 10,000 games at a price of $8 per game.

2. **Selling the game through a toy catalogue.** The toy catalogue will agree to include James's business school game in the catalogue for $10,000 per year. The catalogue owner is responsible for taking orders. All James has to do is send the games to the catalogue owner. James estimates that he could sell 15,000 games annually through the catalogue if he charges $10 per game and 20,000 games if he charges $8 per game.

3. **Selling through a salesperson.** The salesperson would work only for a 30% commission on total sales. The salesperson can sell 25,000 games annually if the price is set at $10 per game and 30,000 games if the price is set at $8 per game.

Case Questions

a. What other factors should James consider in choosing a supplier?
b. If James chooses to ignore the other factors, which suppliers are the low-cost suppliers at different levels of units made?
c. What method of production, marketing, price, and quantity maximizes profit for James?

Chapter 4
Estimating Product Costs and Activity-Based Costing

LEARNING OBJECTIVES

1. Explain the relation between the product life cycle and the cost of a product.

2. Estimate direct product or service costs.

3. Classify indirect product costs as unit-, batch-, product-, and facility-level.

4. Trace indirect product costs using a single cost driver.

5. Identify problems with using a single cost driver to trace indirect product costs.

6. Use activity-based costing to estimate indirect product costs.

7. Identify the strengths and weaknesses of using activity-based costing to estimate indirect product costs.

Snake Skateboards—II

The owner of Snake Skateboards, Jeff Williams, is having a problem estimating the product cost of his company's two types of skateboards: flat and molded. The direct costs are fairly easy to estimate. These direct costs include the cost of materials (wood veneer, wheel assemblies, and plastic) and the labor of working on the skateboards. The current accounting records of Snake Skateboards have not separated the cost of materials ($60,000) and the cost of labor ($300,000) by type of skateboard. Jeff feels that a further analysis of the production process could identify the direct costs of the two types of skateboards.

The indirect costs of the two skateboards are more difficult to estimate. Snake Skateboards currently uses the following four accounts for indirect costs:

Administrative	$ 90,000
Purchasing	50,000
Production (excluding labor and materials)	210,000
Marketing	100,000
Total expected indirect costs	$450,000

An analysis of the indirect costs indicates that all the administrative costs ($90,000) include Jeff Williams' and his secretary's salaries. These costs are fixed and can't be traced to either product.

Purchasing costs ($50,000) are primarily indirect labor costs for purchasing agents and part-time accountants. The number of hours of indirect labor required for purchasing depends on the number of transactions with suppliers of raw materials.

The $210,000 in production costs are composed of (1) $50,000 for operating the plant and paying the plant manager's salary; (2) $90,000 related to setting up the presses and molds and moving each of the batches of skateboards when complete; and (3) $70,000 associated with the machine that cuts the wood veneer. The cost of setting up and moving each batch of 10 flat skateboards is the same as the cost of setting up and moving each batch of 5 molded skateboards. Each type of skateboard requires the same amount of cutting.

The marketing costs ($100,000) are primarily indirect labor and transportation costs for visits to customers. Because the customers are different for the two types of skateboards, the visits can be identified by product.

With this additional information, Jeff Williams plans to trace indirect costs to the two different types of skateboards. He will then be able to make informed decisions about which products to offer (product mix) and the prices to charge for them.

4.1 Product Life Cycle and Product Costs

The cost of the labor and materials are commonly identified as part of a product cost. But there is much more to the cost of providing a product or service. The **product life cycle** describes all the stages of supplying a product or service from its initial conception to the ultimate satisfaction of the last customer. The product life cycle recognizes that product costs are more than just the costs of making the product. An organization incurs considerable costs related to a product before the first unit is made. Additional costs are incurred after the product is sold because of delivery costs and customer service. These costs are incurred over the whole life of the product, which may be as short as a month or longer than 50 years. Computers and other electronic equipment tend to have very short product lives because new innovations quickly cause existing products to be outdated. Other products, such as corn flakes, have been around for many years and are still being produced.

Mall interviews with potential customers are a common step in the research and development phase of a consumer product. These interviews are used by an organization to design products that are desirable to customers. This is an important part of the product life cycle.

The product life cycle begins with the initial planning and proposal stage. Organizational activities at this stage include marketing surveys to determine customer demand, analysis of demographics to evaluate customer characteristics, an analysis of competitors, and an evaluation of the strengths and weaknesses of the organization.

When a proposal is accepted, the product or service is designed and engineered. During the design and engineering process, comparisons are made with leading competitors' products and services. This process of comparing an organization's products and activities with other organizations' products and activities is called **benchmarking.** The design stage is usually extremely important to the success of the product or service. Although the design and engineering activities themselves may not be very costly, the design and engineering stage predetermines most of the cost of providing the product or service. Once the design of the product or service is completed, most of the necessary raw materials, manufacturing activities, and labor requirements have been determined.

The production stage is the stage of manufacturing or of providing services. Most of the product and service costs are incurred at this stage. Activities during the production stage include acquiring resources, setting up machines to manufacture the product, assembling the product, and providing the service to the customer.

Once production begins, the organization must engage in distribution and customer service activities. An organization does not end its relationship with the customer at the time of the sale. Organizations should monitor customer satisfaction and obtain information on ways of improving the product or service. An organization should also support customers who are dissatisfied with the product or service through warranties and repairing faulty products.

Each of these stages contains activities that are costly to perform. If the product life cycle is likely to be very long, a useful exercise in analyzing the cost of a new product is to estimate the costs of the different stages over the life of the product. The costs of initiating the product and the costs of customer service are often forgotten in estimating the cost of a product. Table 4.1 is an example of this procedure.

The costs of the later stages are heavily influenced by the decisions made during the earlier stages. The planning and design stages commit the organization to most of the costs of providing a product or service. For example, the design stage determines the type of materials necessary to make the product. Unless the organization can find a cheaper supplier of materials, the cost of materials is committed at the time of designing the product. The cash outlays to buy the materials, however, are delayed until the production stage begins. Figure 4.1 provides a graph identifying the stages when product costs are committed and the stages when cash outlays are made. For example, once a product is designed, most of the costs have been committed, even though production has not been started and few of the costs have actually been incurred.

Because many product and service costs are predetermined during earlier stages of the product life cycle, management accountants should be involved in these earlier stages. If the management accountant only becomes involved during the production stage, the opportunities for the management accountant to influence the product or service cost through cost savings decisions are limited.

Typical decisions related to the product life cycle involve trade-offs among the different stages of the product life cycle. For example, more effort and cost at the

> **WHAT'S HAPPENING**
>
> Microsoft delayed the release of Windows 95, a computer software operating system, for further testing. How does that delay relate to the costs of different stages of the product life cycle?

TABLE 4.1

Costs of Different Stages in Different Years of the Product Life

Stage	1997	1998	1999	2000	2001	Totals
Design	$100,000	$ 50,000				$ 150,000
Marketing	20,000	50,000	$100,000			170,000
Engineering	80,000	100,000	10,000	$ 10,000		200,000
Production		100,000	800,000	700,000	$100,000	1,700,000
Customer service			30,000	40,000	50,000	120,000
Total product cost						$2,340,000

FIGURE 4.1

Product Life Cycle and Costs

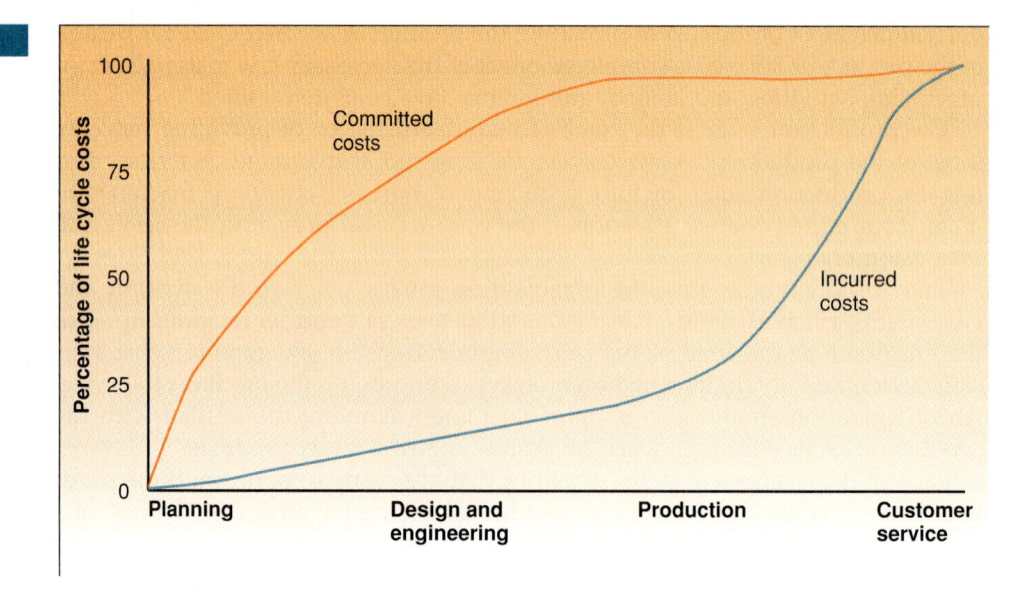

planning stage can reduce the customer service costs. A well-planned product is more likely to satisfy customer demand and less likely to cause customer complaints and returned merchandise. Also, design and engineering efforts can reduce production costs. Boeing has spent considerable time and effort using three-dimensional designs for their aircraft. These three-dimensional designs are costly to prepare but reduce production costs because potential problems in the production stage can be identified much more easily than with two-dimensional designs.

NUMERICAL EXAMPLE 4.1

FastSki is in the process of designing and engineering a new snow ski. Although the current design is acceptable, FastSki is considering further design and engineering efforts that would cost the company $100,000. The manager of design and engineering estimates that the extra design and engineering effort would reduce the cost of making a pair of skis by $22. FastSki expects to make and sell 10,000 pairs of this new ski in the coming year. Should FastSki spend the $100,000 to improve the design of the ski?

■ **SOLUTION** Spending $100,000 in the design stage will save ($22/pair)(10,000 pairs), or $220,000, in the production stage in the coming year. If production continues beyond the coming year, even greater production savings will occur. Therefore, the extra designing and engineering benefits FastSki.

Product Life Cycle and Product Costs | 105

This engineer is using computer-aided design (CAD) to manipulate a three-dimensional drawing of a part for a jet at Boeing. The design and engineering is an early stage in the product life cycle, but it is of critical importance in affecting the cost of the product.

SNAKE SKATEBOARDS—II (CONTINUED)

Jeff at Snake Skateboards is considering adding a skateboard with foot grips to his product mix. The foot grips make jumping on the skateboard easier. Jeff decides to look at the product life cycle to estimate the total product costs of the new skateboard. The expected life of the new skateboard is expected to be three years. The product life cycle of the new skateboard and the additional costs per year are estimated.

Stage	1997	1998	1999	Total
Design	$10,000			$ 10,000
Production	3,000	$100,000	$55,000	158,000
Marketing	5,000	10,000	5,000	20,000
Total costs	$18,000	$110,000	$60,000	$188,000

The total revenues from selling this new skateboard are estimated to be $165,000, which is less than the total product life cycle costs of $188,000. Therefore, Jeff decides not to add to his product mix.

CONCEPT REVIEW

1. Describe the various stages in a typical product life cycle.
2. At what stage of the product life cycle are most costs committed?

4.2 Estimating Direct Product Costs

Product costs should include both direct and indirect costs. Direct product costs are easily identifiable and traced to the product or service. The tracing of indirect product costs, also called **overhead costs** or **common costs,** is more difficult. Overhead is often only peripherally related to a product or service. For example, general research and development is often difficult to trace to a specific product. Methods of tracing indirect product and service costs are discussed later in this chapter.

Materials used to make a product are called **direct materials.** Direct materials may also be referred to as *raw materials*. The labor used to make the product or provide a service is also a direct cost of the product or service and is called **direct labor.** For example, the direct cost of making an oak chair includes the cost of direct materials (the cost of the oak and finish used to make the chair) and the cost of the direct labor (the cost of the labor used to cut, sand, assemble, and finish the chair). Most service organizations have direct labor costs but few direct material costs.

Although direct costs can be easily traced to the cost object, the management accountant still needs assistance in estimating direct costs. If the product or service has been provided previously, the historic cost usually is of some use in estimating future direct costs. But the management accountant should consult with engineers, suppliers, and personnel managers for information on estimating direct costs.

To determine the cost of direct materials, the management accountant must obtain a list of the required raw materials and parts necessary to make the product. Engineers are normally consulted for this information in a manufacturing plant. The management accountant must then obtain purchase prices for each material and part. Surveying suppliers and asking for bids for certain items allows the management accountant to estimate direct material prices. For example, to estimate the direct material costs of building a house, a contractor must identify all the materials

What's Happening

Fireman's Fund, an insurance company, has a difficult time keeping track of the direct labor costs of the different services the company offers. To solve this problem, the company periodically calls different employees and asks what they are working on at that point in time.[1] How would you estimate direct labor costs through this "snapshot" approach?

The construction of these houses requires numerous direct materials including lumber, cement, windows, doors, and shingles.

necessary to build the house. The contractor then goes to suppliers to determine the price of each item. The estimated direct material cost of the house is determined by multiplying the quantity of each piece of material in the house times its respective price.

To estimate the cost of direct labor, engineers and other experts are usually consulted to determine the hours of labor necessary to complete the product or provide the service. If the product or service is currently being offered, the labor time required can be directly measured. Adjustments should be made, however, for improvement through learning. Normally, the first time products are made or services provided, direct labor time will be longer. Once the employees have gained experience, the labor operations can be performed more efficiently. The cost of direct labor also requires estimates of labor rates, which may be provided by a personnel manager in a larger organization.

NUMERICAL EXAMPLE 4.2

To determine the direct cost of making a hamburger, the restaurant uses the following estimates:

Item	Quantity per Hamburger	Purchase Price
Meat	.25 lbs	$1.60/lb
Bun	1	$1.20/dozen
Catsup	.5 oz.	$.04/oz
Pickles	.5 oz.	$.06/oz
Labor	1 minute	$6/hour

Calculate the direct cost of making a hamburger.

■ **SOLUTION** The direct cost is determined by multiplying the quantity of the different items necessary to make a hamburger times its respective price. There is some question about whether the labor of the cook is a direct cost of making a hamburger. If the cook is also cooking other food at the same time, the labor would be an indirect cost to making a hamburger.

Item	Quantity per Hamburger	×	Purchase Price	=	Cost
Meat	.25 lbs.		$1.60/lb.		$.40
Bun	1		$1.20/dozen		.10
Catsup	.5 oz.		.04/oz.		.02
Pickles	.5 oz.		.06/oz.		.03
Labor	1 minute		$6/hour		.10

Total direct cost/hamburger = $.65

SNAKE SKATEBOARDS—II (CONTINUED)

Jeff Williams of Snake Skateboards estimates the direct materials and direct labor of the two types of skateboards. The direct materials include the thin sheets of wood veneer, glue, and the polyurethane wheels and axle assemblies. The molded skateboards also require a plastic sheet. To estimate the cost of these direct materials, Jeff goes to the various suppliers to obtain price information for the coming year. Each skateboard requires two sets of wheels and axles. The quantity of the remaining materials per skateboard is more difficult to estimate. Jeff examines usage of the sheets of wood veneer, sheets of plastic, and glue in the previous year. By cutting the veneer more carefully and using more experienced employees, Jeff figures he can reduce scrap and spoiled units. These improvements should reduce the quantity of materials per skateboard by 5%. Jeff decides that estimating glue costs per skateboard is too difficult and decides to treat cost of glue as part of production costs.

To estimate direct labor costs, Jeff uses the wage rates on the recently signed labor contract. To determine the amount of time necessary to make each type of skateboard, he uses a stopwatch to time workers. Assuming that learning will take place, Jeff estimates that the time to complete a skateboard in the coming year will be 7% less than his current observations.

The calculations for direct materials and labor after incorporating the improvements are:

Flat Skateboard

	Quantity	Price	Cost
Materials:			
Wood veneer	10 sq. ft./unit	$0.02/sq. ft.	$0.20/unit
Wheel assemblies	2/unit	$0.44 each	$0.88/unit
Total direct materials			$1.08/unit
Direct labor	0.5 hours/unit	$10/hr.	$5.00/unit
Total direct costs			$6.08/unit

Molded Skateboard

	Quantity	Price	Cost
Materials:			
Wood veneer	10 sq. ft./unit	$0.02/sq. ft.	$ 0.20/unit
Wheel assemblies	2/unit	$0.44 each	$ 0.88/unit
Plastic layer	1/unit	$0.12 each	$ 0.12/unit
Total direct materials			$ 1.20/unit
Direct labor	1 hour/unit	$10/hr.	$10.00/unit
Total direct costs			$11.20/unit

Jeff compares these direct costs with his competitors' prices of $15 for the flat skateboard and $25 for the molded skateboard. In both cases the direct costs are less than the competitors' prices, so there is no immediate indication that there is a need to drop a product and there may even be an opportunity to lower prices and still make a profit. But Jeff knows that the direct costs are only part of the picture. He must also estimate the indirect costs of his products.

CONCEPT REVIEW

1. How are direct product costs commonly classified?
2. Describe methods of estimating direct product and service costs.

4.3 Nature of Indirect Product Costs

Indirect product costs can't be traced directly to individual units of products or service. Resources used by multiple units of a product or service or by multiple products and services cause indirect product costs. Because indirect product costs can't be easily traced to specific units of products or services, the estimation of indirect product or service costs is likely to be more difficult and uncertain than estimating direct product and service costs.

Accounting reports to external parties cannot be relied on to estimate indirect product costs. They are based on generally accepted accounting principles (GAAP) and treat some indirect costs such as research and development and marketing costs as period costs rather than product costs. The rationale for treating research and development and marketing costs as period costs is the difficulty in measuring the future benefits of those activities. But research and development and marketing are part of the cost of developing and delivering a product to a customer. Also, the external accounting reports are based on historical costs, which may not be very good estimates of future indirect costs.

To estimate the indirect costs of products, the management accountant must have a good understanding of the operations of the organization. Knowing how different activities in the organization interact to create products allows the manager to more accurately trace indirect costs to products.

Unit-, Batch-, Product-, and Facility-Level Costs

Indirect product costs are costs that can't be directly traced to specific units of the product. Some indirect costs, however, can be traced to groups of specific units of the product or the product itself. In other words, some costs are common to more than one unit of a product and some costs are common to different types of products. For example, the cost of transporting a truckload of cattle is common to all the cattle on the truck. The cost of advertising a product is common to all units of the product. Indirect costs can be categorized by the level of common costs.

Unit-level costs are costs that vary with the number of units produced. Direct product costs, for example, can be traced to individual units of the product or service provided. Some costs that are traditionally treated as indirect costs may also be unit-level costs. Machine usage is an example of indirect unit-level costs. The cost of operating a machine increases with the number of units produced because of wear on the machine parts. These indirect costs are proportional to the number of units produced. Unit-level costs vary with the number of units produced and are equivalent to variable product costs.

Products are often provided in batches. A batch consists of multiple units of the same product that are processed together. Costs associated with batches are called **batch-level costs.** Batch-level costs are fixed with respect to the number of units in the batch but vary with the number of batches. Examples of batch-level costs include the cost of an airplane flight. Many costs of an airplane flight do not vary with the number of passengers. The cost of the flight crew and the plane are fixed with respect to the number of passengers up to the seating capacity of the plane. The cost of meals, however, is a unit-level cost because it varies with the number of passengers.

Manufacturing is frequently performed in batches to reduce the need to continually reset machines for different products. Once machines are set up for a batch run, multiple units can be manufactured without further set-up costs. The set-up cost to run the batch is common to all the units in the batch and is fixed with respect to the number of units in the batch.

Some indirect costs are related to all the units of a product or service. For example, engineering and design efforts are common to all units of a particular product. Costs that are common to all the units of a product are called **product-level costs.** Product-level costs are fixed with respect to the number of units and batches produced but vary with the number of products.

Other indirect costs can't be traced to a particular product. For example, the cost of a factory can't be traced to the many different products made within the factory. Also, the factory manager's salary is not associated with any particular

Nabisco makes these pastries in batches. After each batch the machinery must be cleaned and reset to make other pastries. The labor expense of cleaning and resetting the machinery constitutes batch-level costs.

unit, batch, or product of the organization. Costs that can't be identified with a particular unit, batch, product, or service are called **facility-level costs.** Facility-level costs are fixed with respect to the number of units, batches, and products or services produced. Facility-level costs are common to multiple products or services. Facility-level costs, however, vary with the size and number of facilities.

Recognizing whether an indirect cost is unit-, batch-, product-, or facility-level is important in understanding the relation between indirect costs and products and services. Activity-based costing, described later in this chapter, uses the level of indirect costs to trace indirect costs to products and services.

SNAKE SKATEBOARDS—II (CONTINUED)

Jeff Williams categorizes the indirect costs of Snake Skateboards as follows:

Support Function	Level	Amount
Administrative	Facility	$ 90,000
Purchasing	Batch	50,000
Production:		
Warehousing and handling	Batch	18,000
Cutting	Unit	50,000
Gluing	Unit	10,000
Setting-up molds	Batch	55,000
Painting	Unit	35,000
Assembly	Unit	42,000
Marketing	Product	100,000
Total		$450,000

This categorization indicates that the tracing of indirect costs to the two types of skateboards is complicated. Splitting the indirect costs between the flat and molded skateboards should recognize each of these levels of indirect costs.

CONCEPT REVIEW

1. What are indirect costs?
2. Explain how indirect costs are classified as unit-, batch-, product-, and facility-level.

4.4 Using Cost Drivers to Trace Indirect Costs to Products

Indirect product costs represent part of the opportunity cost of making a product or providing a service. But tracing indirect costs to products and services is a problem. In some cases the relation between the indirect costs and products is not clear. For example, the relation between the president's salary and the individual products is not obvious. In other cases, tracing indirect costs to different products or services can be very costly. Engineers and salespeople are usually able to identify when they are working on different products or services but recording and communicating that information is very time-consuming.

The lack of a well-specified relation between indirect costs and products and the cost of recording and communicating the relation between indirect costs and products lead management accountants to look for alternative methods of tracing indirect costs to products. One method of estimating the indirect cost of a product is to choose some characteristic of the different products that causes the indirect costs. As described in Chapter 3, that characteristic is called a *cost driver*. For example, if the indirect costs are caused by having more employees, the number of direct labor hours of a product could serve as a cost driver to trace indirect costs to the different products and services. Using direct labor hours as a cost driver presumes that products with more direct labor cause more of the indirect costs. If indirect costs are caused by setting up machines to run new batches, the number of batches could be used as a cost driver. The remainder of this section examines a method of tracing indirect product costs using a single cost driver.

Tracing Indirect Product Costs Using a Single Cost Driver

Tracing indirect costs to products and services using a single cost driver is quite common because it is simple and easy. The following four steps describe the tracing process:

1. **Identify and estimate all of the indirect product costs.** Before any indirect product costs can be traced, they must be identified and estimated. One way of identifying indirect product costs is to consider the life cycle of the various products and services. Each stage of the life cycle is composed of indirect costs. Another method of identifying and estimating indirect costs is to predict the costs of each of the support functions. In financial reporting to external parties some indirect costs, such as research and development and selling, are not traced to products and services. For making planning decisions, however, the opportunity cost of all indirect resources used by a product or service should be identified and estimated.

2. **Identify a cost driver to apply indirect costs and estimate the usage of the cost driver for all products and services.** Once the total indirect product costs are estimated, a cost driver must be chosen. The cost driver should reflect the cause of the indirect costs. This cost driver could be related to the process of making the product or providing the service. For example, the number of direct labor hours used on each product or service is a possible cost driver. Or some physical characteristic of the product or service could be used as a cost driver, such as number of parts. Usage of the cost driver should approximate the

opportunity cost of using the indirect resources. Identifying such a cost driver is difficult and requires a knowledge of the nature of the indirect costs and how they are associated with different products or services. The cost driver should be easily measurable because once chosen, the amount of the cost driver used by each product or service must be estimated. The total estimated cost driver usage is the sum of the estimated usage of the cost driver by each of the products and services of the organization. For example, if the number of machine hours is the cost driver, the number of machine hours used by all the products and services of the organization must be estimated.

3. Calculate the application rate by dividing estimated indirect opportunity costs by the estimated usage of the cost driver for all products and services. Once a cost driver is identified to trace indirect costs to different products or services, calculate the application rate by dividing the total estimated indirect costs by the total estimated usage of the cost driver across all products or services. For example, suppose the estimated indirect costs for a car repair shop are $50,000 for 2,500 repair jobs. The management accountant could apply them equally to each repair job by using an application rate of $50,000/2,500 repair jobs, or $20 per repair job. But that procedure would not recognize that some repair jobs are simple and the indirect cost of working on those cars is lower than the indirect cost of working on much more complex repair jobs. If the number of direct labor hours, cost of parts added, or number of hours in the shop are used as cost drivers to apply indirect costs, the indirect cost of working on a car may be more closely approximated. If direct labor hours are used to apply indirect costs and the 2,500 service jobs require an estimated 5,000 direct labor hours, the application rate would be $50,000/5,000 direct labor hours, or $10 per direct labor hour.

4. Apply indirect costs to the various products and services based on the expected usage of the cost driver for each product and service. Once the application rate is calculated, the estimated indirect costs are partitioned among the products and services based on the estimated usage of the cost driver by each of the products and services. In the car repair shop example, an application rate of $10 per direct labor hour is estimated. A repair job that requires 5 direct labor

Car repair shops typically use direct labor hours to apply overhead. The hourly rate a shop charges to repair your car consists of the hourly rate paid to the mechanic, plus the overhead rate, plus profits. Usually, the hourly overhead rate is larger than the hourly wage paid to the mechanic.

hours would have $10 per direct labor hour times 5 direct labor hours, or $50, of estimated indirect costs.

Each product or service will receive a portion of the indirect costs based on the estimated usage of the cost driver by that product or service. This procedure will partition all of the expected indirect costs to the products and service. In Chapter 9, actual usage of the cost driver is used to trace indirect costs to products. Because actual usage may be different than expected usage of the cost driver, not all of the estimated indirect costs will necessarily be traced to the products. In this chapter, however, we are concerned with estimating indirect product costs for making planning decisions before the product is made, so estimated usage of the cost driver is used to trace indirect costs.

NUMERICAL EXAMPLE 4.3

The Cascade Cleaning Service provides cleaning services for commercial buildings. The company cleans three different buildings:

	Square Feet	Estimated Hours of Cleaning Time
Anderson Office Building	100,000	8,000
Carla's Pizza	10,000	6,000
City Hall	90,000	6,000
Total	200,000	20,000

Cascade Cleaning Service has the following estimated indirect costs:

Supplies	$ 50,000
Administration	50,000
Total	$100,000

Apply these indirect costs to the different buildings using both square feet and estimated hours of cleaning time. Which application procedure is better?

■ **SOLUTION** If the square footage is used, the application rate is $100,000/200,000 square feet, or $0.50 per square foot. Using this application rate, the application of estimated indirect costs follows:

	Square Feet	Application rate	Estimated Indirect Costs
Anderson Office Bldg.	100,000	$0.50	$50,000
Carla's Pizza	10,000	0.50	5,000
City Hall	90,000	0.50	45,000
Total applied costs			$100,000

If estimated hours of cleaning are used, the application rate is $100,000/20,000 hours, or $5.00 per hour of cleaning. Using this application rate, the application of estimated indirect costs follows:

	Estimated Hours	Application Rate	Estimated Indirect Costs
Anderson Office Bldg.	8,000	$5.00	$40,000
Carla's Pizza	6,000	5.00	30,000
City Hall	6,000	5.00	30,000
Total applied costs			$100,000

There is insufficient evidence to determine which application procedure is better. The goal is to apply indirect costs to approximate the opportunity costs of using the indirect resources. The opportunity cost of using supplies is probably more closely associated with the hours of cleaning time. The administrative cost may be fixed and common to all the cleaning service jobs and does not represent an opportunity cost of providing a specific cleaning service job. The administrative costs would have to be analyzed more carefully to determine if they represent opportunity costs of individual cleaning service jobs. If not, the administrative costs should not be applied to the different cleaning service jobs to estimate indirect costs.

SNAKE SKATEBOARDS—II (CONTINUED)

Snake Skateboards could trace indirect costs by many different types of cost drivers. Two possible choices are by number of units and by number of direct labor hours. The total indirect costs are estimated to be $450,000. The number of units is estimated to be 50,000 flat boards and 5,000 molded boards, or a total of 55,000 units. Therefore, the application rate by number of units equals $450,000/55,000 units or about $8.181818 per unit. With this application rate, the indirect costs would be traced in the following manner:

	Number of Units	Application Rate	Traced Costs
Flat skateboards	50,000	$8.181818	$409,091
Molded skateboards	5,000	8.181818	40,909
Total traced costs			$450,000

Based on this tracing of indirect costs, the estimated cost per unit of the two types of skateboards is

	Direct Materials	Direct Labor	Indirect Costs	Cost/ Unit
Flat skateboards	$1.08	$ 5.00	$8.18	$14.26
Molded skateboards	$1.20	$10.00	$8.18	$19.38

Snake Skateboard could also apply indirect costs using the estimated number of direct labor hours. Each flat skateboard uses an estimated 0.5 hours of direct labor and each molded skateboard uses an estimated 1.0 hour of direct labor. A total of (0.5 hours/unit)(50,000 units), or 25,000 hours, are expected to be used for the flat skateboard and (1 hour/unit)(5,000 units), or 5,000 hours, are expected to be used for the molded skateboard. Therefore, a total of 25,000 hours + 5,000 hours, or 30,000, direct labor hours are expected to be used. The application rate would be $450,000/30,000 hours, or $15 per hour. Using this application rate, the indirect costs would be applied in the following manner:

	Units	Number of Hours	Application Rate	Traced Costs	Traced Costs per Unit
Flat skateboards	50,000	25,000	$15	$375,000	$ 7.50
Molded skateboards	5,000	5,000	15	75,000	15.00
Total traced costs				$450,000	

> Based on this tracing of indirect costs, the estimated cost per unit of the two types of skateboards is:
>
> | | Direct Materials | Direct Labor | Indirect Costs | Cost/ Unit |
> | --- | --- | --- | --- | --- |
> | Flat skateboards | $1.08 | $ 5.00 | $ 7.50 | $13.58 |
> | Molded skateboards | $1.20 | $10.00 | $15.00 | $26.20 |
>
> Jeff Williams is very confused by these results. Using the number of units to trace indirect costs, both the flat skateboard with a $15 sales price and the molded skateboard with a $25 sales price are profitable. When the number of direct labor hours is used to apply indirect costs, however, the flat skateboard is more profitable, and the molded skateboard has an estimated product cost greater than its sales price. After this analysis, Jeff is suspicious of using a single cost driver to trace indirect costs. He knows that the cost driver most closely associated with the indirect opportunity costs would yield the best estimate of the product cost of making a skateboard, but he isn't sure that either the number of units or direct labor hours are associated with the opportunity costs of using the indirect resources. In fact, his analysis of the unit-, batch-, product-, and facility-level costs indicate that a single cost driver will not trace indirect costs accurately.

Problems with Using a Single Cost Driver to Trace Indirect Costs

Indirect costs are traced to different products and services to estimate the opportunity cost of using indirect resources. The cost driver used to apply indirect costs, such as direct labor hours, should reflect the use of the indirect resources. The application procedure of using a single cost driver provides a good approximation of the use of indirect resources if the following two circumstances occur:

1. The indirect product costs are appropriately identified and estimated to approximate the opportunity cost of using indirect resources.
2. The usage of the cost driver is proportional to the cost of indirect resources used.

The first circumstance is the problem of identifying and estimating opportunity costs described in Chapter 2. The second circumstance occurs when the relation between the cost driver and the indirect product costs looks like Figure 4.2. With the cost driver proportional to the indirect costs, each product is assigned a cost that approximates the indirect cost of providing that product. For example, if machine hours is the cost driver used to apply indirect costs, each additional machine hour should correspond to the same additional indirect costs.

Generally, not all indirect costs are proportional to a single cost driver. Some indirect costs may be associated with one cost driver and other indirect costs may be associated with other cost drivers. For example, the costs of the personnel department may be related to the number of labor hours used by each product or service and the cost of the machines may be related to the hours of machine time used by each product or service.

Although a cost driver may be associated with the indirect costs, the relation is generally not proportional. Most likely a relation similar to Figure 4.3 occurs. This relation is the same relation proposed in Chapter 2 between total product

FIGURE 4.2

Graph of Indirect Costs When They Are Proportional to the Usage of the Cost Driver

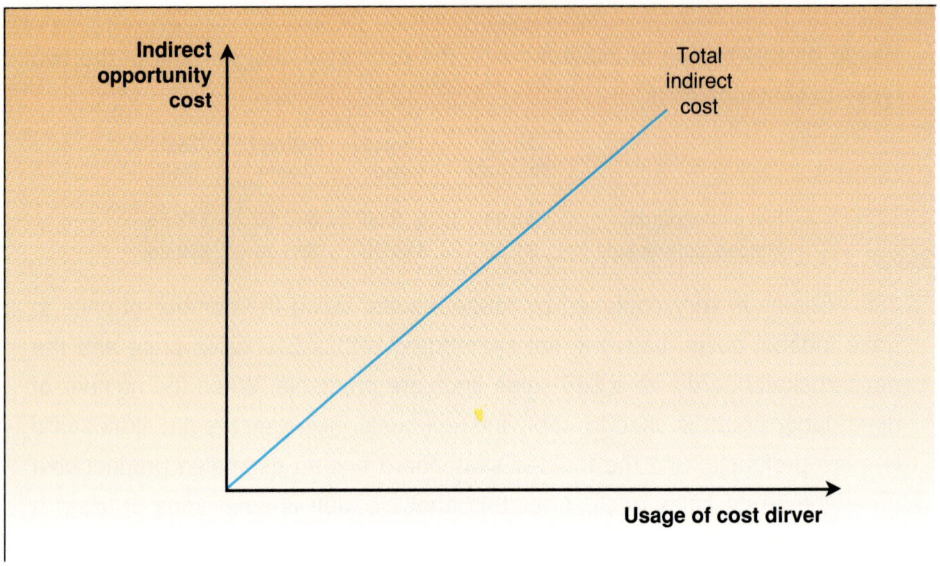
Indirect opportunity cost
Total indirect cost
Usage of cost dirver

FIGURE 4.3

The Usual Relation between an Indirect Cost and the Usage of Its Cost Driver

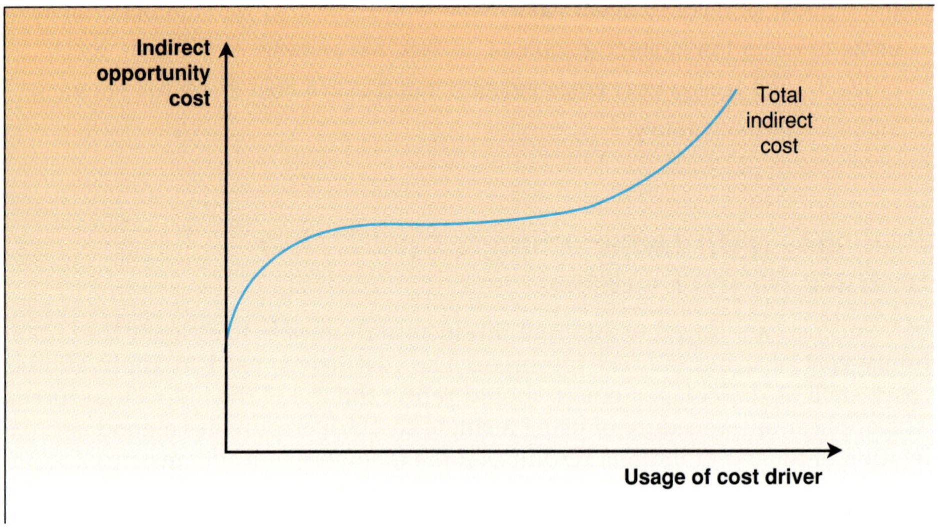
Indirect opportunity cost
Total indirect cost
Usage of cost driver

costs and the rate of output. Applying indirect costs using a single cost driver ignores the possibility of fixed indirect costs and capacity constraints. All indirect costs are treated as variable with respect to the cost driver.

Another problem with using a single cost driver to trace indirect costs among different products and services is that some indirect costs are at the batch-level and product-level. But cost drivers like labor hours and machine hours are related to the number of units produced. Therefore, more indirect costs would be traced to products and services with a large number of units (high-volume products or services) that require more labor and machine hours. But batch- and product-level costs increase with the number of batches and products, not with the number of units. For example, suppose each product causes the same engineering costs but engineering costs are applied to different products using direct labor hours. More engineering costs would be applied to the high-volume products than appropriate because more direct labor hours are necessary to make more units of the high-volume product.

NUMERICAL EXAMPLE 4.4

Minisoft is planning on opening a new division to develop software for accounting. One program will be developed to make financial statements for corporations and another program will be developed to balance checkbooks and make financial statements for individuals. Each program will require the same amount of research and development effort. Total research and development costs are estimated to be $5 million. Estimated sales and production for the corporate accounting program is 10,000 units. Estimated sales and production for the individual accounting program is 490,000 units.

a. What are research and development costs per unit of each program if the costs are applied equally to the corporate and individual programs?
b. What are research and development costs per unit of each program if the costs are applied based on estimated units made and sold of the corporate and individual programs?

■ SOLUTION

a. If the research and development costs are distributed equally between the corporate and individual programs, each program would receive $5 million/2, or $2.5 million. The cost per unit for each program is

$$\text{Corporate: } \$2.5 \text{ million}/10{,}000 \text{ units} = \$250/\text{unit}$$
$$\text{Individual: } \$2.5 \text{ million}/490{,}000 \text{ units} = \$5.10/\text{unit}$$

b. If the research and development costs are distributed by number of units, the research and development cost per unit for both types of programs would be $5 million/(10,000 units + 490,000 units), or $10/unit. The unit-level cost driver (number of units) shifts costs from the low-volume product (the corporate accounting program) to the high-volume product (the individual accounting program).

The next section describes a procedure to apply indirect costs to products. This procedure solves some but not all of the problems of applying indirect costs.

CONCEPT REVIEW

1. How are indirect costs applied to different products and services using a single cost driver?
2. What are some problems in applying indirect costs using a single cost driver?

4.5 Activity-Based Costing (ABC)

Most firms are finding that indirect costs are becoming a higher proportion of total product costs. Automation and computing systems have increased the indirect costs of many organizations and in many cases have replaced direct labor. As the proportion of indirect costs to direct costs increases, firms are taking a closer look at how indirect costs are related to the different products. Without an accurate tracing of indirect costs to products, organizations are likely to make poor product mix and pricing decisions.

Activity-based costing (ABC) is a procedure that attempts to provide more accurate product costs. ABC also has some control implications that are described in Chapter 11.

ABC begins with the identification of organizational activities that cause indirect costs. Indirect costs do not just happen. Something is being done to cause indirect costs and the management accountant must discover those activities. Some activities causing indirect costs provide value to the customer, such as engineering and marketing. These activities are on the value chain. Other activities, called *non-value-added activities,* provide little value to the customer, such as moving products within the organization and setting up machines.

Once the activities are identified, the indirect costs associated with each activity are estimated. If purchasing is identified as an organizational activity causing indirect costs, all the costs associated with the purchasing activity are identified and estimated.

After identifying the activities and estimating their costs, a cost driver is chosen for each activity. A cost driver causes, or "drives," the indirect costs of an activity. The choice of the cost driver should recognize whether the activity causes unit-level, batch-level, product-level, or facility-level costs. Ideally, cost driver usage is proportional to the indirect opportunity costs of the activity. Unit-level indirect costs should have cost drivers that vary with the number of units, batch-level indirect costs should have cost drivers that vary with the number of batches, and so on.

Cost driver usage by the different products is used as the basis for tracing costs from activities to products. Total cost driver usage by all the products must be estimated for each cost driver. To determine the application rate for each activity, the estimated costs of each activity are divided by the total estimated usage of their respective cost drivers.

Once an application rate is calculated for an activity, the activity costs are traced based on the usage of the cost driver by each of the products and services. This procedure is the same as the procedure with the single cost driver except in this case there are cost drivers and application rates for each of the activities.

NUMERICAL EXAMPLE 4.5

A tree nursery is considering a change in product mix in its inventory. The manager wants to estimate the effect of each type of tree on indirect costs. Indirect costs are identified and estimated for the following activities: watering, repotting (transferring trees to larger pots), and administration. Total estimated annual costs for each activity, the cost driver for each activity, and the expected annual usage of each cost driver are:

Activity	Estimated Costs	Cost Driver	Estimated Usage of Cost Driver
Watering	$100,000	Number of trees	500,000
Repotting	200,000	Number of repots	200,000
Administration	150,000	Number of different types of trees	500

a. What are the application rates for each of the activities?
b. At what levels is each activity given the choice of cost driver: unit, batch, product, or facility?
c. What are the indirect costs of 100 weeping birches, each of which require one repotting each year.

■ **SOLUTION**

a. The application rate for each activity is calculated by dividing estimated costs of the activity by the estimated usage of the respective cost driver:

Activity		Application Rate
Watering	$100,000/500,000	$0.20/tree
Repotting	$200,000/200,000	$1.00/repot
Administration	$150,000/500	$300/type of tree

b. Both watering and repotting are unit-level activities because their cost drivers vary with the number of units. The administration is treated as a product-level activity because each product receives the same indirect costs.

c. The indirect costs traced to the 100 weeping birches are:

Activity	Application Rate	Weeping Birch Usage	Weeping Birch Costs
Watering	$0.20/tree	100	$ 20.00
Repotting	$1.00/repot	100	100.00
Administration	$300/type of tree	1	300.00
Total annual indirect costs			$420.00

Advantages of ABC

ABC seeks to improve the tracing of indirect costs to products by recognizing the different levels of indirect costs. A single cost driver can't capture the complexity of the relation of indirect costs to products and services. Indirect costs that are batch-level or product-level can use cost drivers related to the number of batches and number of products, respectively.

ABC is most beneficial in deriving accurate product costs for organizations with specific characteristics. If a firm only has one product or service, there is no problem in tracing costs to different products or services. Therefore, ABC is more beneficial for firms with multiple products and services.

ABC is also more beneficial to firms that have products and services that use overhead activities in different ways. If some of an organization's products require considerable engineering time and others require considerable machine time, these products use overhead activities differently. Also, high- and low-volume activities tend to use overhead activities differently, especially if there are batch-level and product-level costs.

ABC is especially useful to organizations that have a high percentage of indirect product costs. Many organizations now have indirect product costs that are greater than 50% of total costs. When a large percentage of product costs are indirect, accurately tracing those costs to products becomes more important.

This combine is only one of the many different farm products made by John Deere. With multiple products using overhead sources, John Deere has turned to ABC to help determine the cost of the different products.

The usefulness of ABC in making planning decisions is not just limited to accurate product costs. ABC also assists managers in finding opportunities to reduce costs. The identification of activities that cause costs often reveals activities that are not value-added. These non-value-added activities are opportunities to reduce costs.

ABC also provides useful information on how the different overhead activities relate to the rest of the organization. **Activity-based management** is the process of managing the different activities to allow the organization to operate more efficiently. ABC is part of activity-based management. For example, AT&T managers had a problem in determining how operational decisions related to the bottom line (profit). By switching to activity-based management including ABC, AT&T managers were better able to estimate the cost of the outputs of the different activities and their relationship to profit.[2]

To install an ABC system in an organization requires considerable knowledge about how the different overhead activities are related to products. The process of implementing ABC forces members of the organization to analyze and understand their organization better. This knowledge will be beneficial in making other planning decisions.

Problems with ABC

Although ABC has many advantages over using a single cost driver to trace indirect costs to products, ABC is not without some problems and does not always achieve a particularly accurate estimate of the opportunity cost of making a product. As in the case of a single cost driver, the accuracy of the estimate depends on identifying and estimating the indirect costs of the activities and the relation of the cost driver to the costs of the activity. If cost driver usage is not proportional to the cost of the activity, inaccurate estimates will occur. Cost driver usage will not be proportional to activity costs if some of the activity costs are fixed with respect to the cost driver. For example, a company may decide to purchase an expensive testing machine to inspect different products. Inspection is an indirect cost activity and the number of inspections could be used as the cost driver. The cost of the machine, however, is fixed with respect to the number of inspections. The variable costs of inspection may be quite low.

ABC generally applies costs more accurately than a single cost driver because the different levels of indirect costs are recognized and the activity costs are more likely proportional to the usage of the cost driver. But if activity costs have a fixed component with respect to the cost driver, ABC usually ignores the difference between the fixed and variable costs of an activity. In this case, the application rate reflects both the fixed and variable costs of the activity and will not accurately reflect the opportunity cost of additional use of the activity.

ABC also can't resolve the problem of what to do with facility-level costs. Facility-level costs do not lend themselves to tracing to different products because they are common to more than one product.

ABC is more costly than using a single cost driver to trace indirect costs. More measurements and observations must be made to implement ABC. These additional measurements and observations, however, may also have control effects. For example, if engineering hours are used to trace engineering costs to products, engineering hours will be more carefully controlled. Therefore, both planning decision and control issues should be considered jointly in deciding whether to adopt ABC.

The planning decision reason for attempting to trace indirect costs to different products and services is to make more informed decisions such as pricing and product mix decisions. If these planning decisions are not sensitive to the accuracy of the estimate of indirect product costs, then the use of a single cost driver to trace indirect costs may yield sufficient accuracy. For example, organizations that have only a small percentage of indirect costs are unlikely to be concerned about the tracing of indirect costs to products and services. Large discount retail stores have very large direct costs in the form of costs of purchasing merchandise. The indirect costs tend to be relatively small when compared to the direct costs, so the method of applying indirect costs is not as important. Many professional services also have a cost structure that is dominated by direct costs. CPA firm costs are primarily for professional personnel whose work can be directly traced to a particular client or service. Once again, the relatively small proportion of indirect costs makes the application procedure less important.

SNAKE SKATEBOARDS—II (CONCLUDED)

Snake Skateboards would like to determine their product costs under ABC. The following indirect cost activities and cost drivers are identified, and activity costs, cost driver usage, and application rates are estimated:

Activity	Cost Driver	Costs	Cost Driver Usage	Application Rate
Administration	Direct labor hours	$ 90,000	30,000	$3/DLH
Purchasing	Number of orders	50,000	100	$500/order
Warehousing	Number of deliveries	18,000	150	$120/delivery
Cutting	Machine hours	50,000	5,000	$10/Machine hour
Gluing	Labor hours of gluing	10,000	5,000	$2/Gluing hour
Setting-up	Number of set-ups	55,000	6,000	$9.17/set-up
Painting	Gallons of paint	35,000	1,000	$35/gallon
Assembly	Hours to assemble	42,000	10,500	$4/hour
Marketing	Customer visits	100,000	80	$1,250/visit

The tracing of indirect costs to each product depends on the expected usage of the cost drivers by the two products. The tracing of indirect costs for each product are

Activity	Application Rate	Usage by Flat Skateboards	Applied to Flat Skateboards	Usage by Molded Skateboards	Applied to Molded Skateboards
Administration	$3/DLH	25,000	$ 75,000	5,000	$ 15,000
Purchasing	$500/Purchase	30	15,000	70	35,000
Warehousing	$120/Delivery	50	6,000	100	12,000
Cutting	$10/Machine hour	4,000	40,000	1,000	10,000
Gluing	$2/Gluing hour	4,500	9,000	500	1,000
Setting-up	$9.17/set-up	5,000	45,833	1,000	9,167
Painting	$35/gallon	500	17,500	500	17,500
Assembly	$4/hour	8,000	32,000	2,500	10,000
Marketing	$1,250/visit	40	50,000	40	50,000
Total			$290,333		$159,667

The indirect cost per unit using ABC with these cost drivers is

    Flat skateboards $290,333/50,000 units = $ 5.81/unit
    Molded skateboards $159,667/5,000 units = $31.93/unit

With direct costs, the estimated opportunity costs of making each product is

THE STORY OF MANAGERIAL ACCOUNTING

Team Decisions Regarding Production

The *Managerial Accounting* book team also had to decide on the type of book to produce. Books without color and pictures cost less to produce. Books with color and pictures, however, convey more information and maintain the interest of the reader. To make a decision, Peggy, the team accountant, must gather information about the direct and indirect costs of a black and white book with no pictures and the direct and indirect costs of a book with color and pictures. From which team members should Peggy gather this information and how should she analyze this information?

	Direct Materials	Direct Labor	Indirect Costs	Cost/ Unit
Flat skateboards	$1.08	$ 5.00	$ 5.81	$11.89
Molded skateboards	$1.20	$10.00	$31.93	$43.13

Using these product costs, the molded skateboard that sells for $25 looks like a big loser. Jeff Williams, however, should not eliminate the molded skateboards from the product without some further investigation. The ABC method applied facility-level costs that are common to both flat and molded skateboards and will not necessarily be avoided if no more molded skateboards are produced. The opportunity cost of making molded skateboards should consider the alternative use of the facilities if molded skateboards are no longer made. Also, some of the indirect costs may be sunk. In other words, they will be incurred whether or not molded skateboards are made. These sunk costs should be ignored in making the product mix decision.

CONCEPT REVIEW

1. What are the steps of performing activity-based costing?
2. What are the advantages and disadvantages of activity-based costing?

4.6 Summary

1. **Explain the relation between the product life cycle and the cost of a product.** The cost of a product includes costs from all stages of the product life cycle. Most product costs are committed during early stages, but most product costs are not incurred until the production stage.

2. **Estimate direct product or service costs.** Direct product and service costs are divided into direct labor and direct materials. Estimates of direct labor costs can be made by estimating the labor time required to make a product or service and multiplying that labor time by the estimated wage rate of workers. The direct material cost is estimated by determining the necessary parts and materials and multiplying by their respective prices. The labor rates and price of materials are intended to approximate the opportunity cost of using the labor and materials.

3. **Classify indirect product costs as unit-, batch-, product-, and facility-level.** Indirect product costs are unit-level if they vary by number of units, batch-level if they vary by number of batches, product-level if they vary by number of products, and facility-level costs if they vary by number of facilities.

4. **Trace indirect product costs using a single cost driver.** There are four steps to tracing indirect product costs: (1) identify and estimate all of the indirect product costs; (2) identify a cost driver to apply indirect costs and estimate the usage of the cost driver for all products and services; (3) calculate the application rate by dividing estimated indirect costs by the estimated usage of the cost driver for all products and services; and (4) trace indirect costs to the various products based on the estimated usage of the cost driver for each product.

5. **Identify problems with using a single cost driver to trace indirect product costs.** Not all indirect product costs are caused by a single cost driver. A single cost driver cannot capture the complexity of indirect costs caused by unit-, batch-, product-, and facility-level costs.

6. **Use activity-based costing to estimate indirect product costs.** Activity-based costing identifies activities that cause indirect costs and cost drivers that can be used to trace those activity costs to different products and services. An application rate is calculated for each cost driver to apply the indirect costs.

7. **Identify the strengths and weaknesses of using activity-based costing to estimate indirect product costs.** Activity-based costing recognizes that indirect costs vary with different levels of operations. Indirect costs also have different causes, and appropriate cost drivers are chosen to reflect these differences. Activity-based costing does not adjust for fixed opportunity costs and presumes that indirect costs vary with usage of the cost driver.

KEY TERMS

Activity-based costing A process of identifying activities that cause indirect costs and choosing cost drivers to apply those indirect costs to different products and services.

Activity-based management A process of managing the different overhead activities to allow the organization to operate more efficiently.

Batch-level costs Indirect costs that are associated with the number of batches of a particular product or service.

Benchmarking Comparison of an organization's products or services with the products or services of a top competitor.

Common costs Costs that are common to multiple cost objects.

Direct labor Labor costs that can be identified with a specific product or service.

Direct materials Parts and raw materials of a product.

Facility-level costs Indirect costs that are common to multiple products and services.

Overhead costs Indirect costs of products or services.

Product-level costs: Costs associated with a product but not with a particular unit or batch of the product.

Product life cycle The stages of developing, making, and delivering a product or service to a customer from its initial conception to serving the last customer.

Unit-level costs The costs associated with individual units of a product or service.

SELF-STUDY PROBLEM I

Estimating Direct and Indirect Costs The Pro Cycle Shop purchases bicycle parts for assembly and sales. The cost of each bicycle is estimated and used to determine the sales price. The Pro Shop purchases 100 wheels at a time. The cost of 100 wheels is $5,000. Bicycle frames are purchased in quantities of 50. The 50 frames cost $4,000. Miscellaneous parts including sprockets and seats are estimated to cost $30 per bicycle. Each bicycle requires two hours of labor to assemble. The Pro Cycle Shop pays employees $10 per hour. The Pro Cycle Shop estimates that the indirect costs of operating the shop will be $80,000. These costs include rent, utilities, and the manager's salary. Pro Cycle Shop expects to assemble and sell 2,000 bicycles during the year.

a. If direct labor hours is used as the cost driver for indirect costs, what is the product cost of a bicycle?
b. Why may the product cost estimated in "a" differ from the marginal opportunity cost of making another bicycle?

Solution

a. Direct costs:
    Direct materials
        Wheels: $5,000/100 wheels = $50/wheel
           ($50/wheel)(2 wheels) $100
        Frame: $4,000/50 frames = $80/frame   80
        Miscellaneous parts   30
    Direct labor
        ($10/hour)(2 hours) = $20   20
    Total direct costs $230

    Indirect costs:
      Total expected indirect costs = $80,000
      Total expected direct labor hours =
         (2,000 bicycles)(2 hours/bicycle) = 4,000 hours
      Application rate = $80,000/4,000 hours = $20/hour
      Indirect costs applied per bicycle =
         ($20/hour)(2 hours/bicycle) = $40   40
    Total Costs of Bicycle $270

b. The direct costs are probably a close approximation of the opportunity costs of the materials and labor required to make a bicycle. The applied indirect costs, however, may not be closely associated with the opportunity cost of making a bicycle at the Pro Shop. Most of the indirect costs appear to be fixed. If the shop is operating below capacity and there is no alternative use of the space, the marginal indirect opportunity costs are probably close to zero. If the shop is operating at capacity and there is an alternative use of the space, then the $40 of indirect costs applied to each bicycle may be representative of the opportunity cost of using the indirect resources.

SELF-STUDY PROBLEM II

Choosing the Appropriate Cost Driver Risley's Trucking provides freight services around the Phoenix metropolitan area. Jake Risley, the owner of Risley's Trucking, calculates its costs in ton-miles and charges its customers an additional 20 percent. A ton-mile is the shipping of one ton a distance of one mile.

Some deliveries are picked up and directly delivered, while other deliveries are sent to Risley's warehouse in Phoenix and stored in the warehouse for up to a week before delivery to their final destination. Jake offers this storage free as an incentive to increase business. To calculate the cost per ton-mile, Jake estimates all his costs for the next year and divides by the estimated ton-miles for the next year. This year he estimated the cost per ton-mile to be $5, so he has been charging his customers $6 per ton-mile.

Midway through the year, Jake realized that he is not making money. His warehouse is full and he has plenty of business for short-haul deliveries of small amounts, but his costs are higher than expected and his ton-miles are lower than expected.

Why is Jake having a problem and what is a potential solution?

Solution

Jake charges his customers by ton-miles but provides many other services free of charge. For example, there is no charge for loading and unloading the truck. There is no charge for storing loads for periods less than a week. Customers will naturally choose to use more of services that are underpriced (in this case they are free). Therefore, Jake is attracting customers that need temporary storage facilities, loading and unloading, and relatively light loads. Because Jake is charging for ton-miles, customers are reluctant to use him for heavy loads and longer distances.

Jake should recognize what is causing his costs and charge his customers accordingly. Most of his variable costs come from labor used to load, unload, and drive trucks. He also must pay several people to coordinate pickups and deliveries. His fixed costs are related to the storage facility and the trucks. The opportunity cost of using these trucks depends on alternative use, which could include their sale.

Because many of the costs are not related to the ton-mile cost driver, Jake should consider other cost drivers for costing and billing purposes. Potential cost drivers could include a cost for each pickup and delivery and a cost for storage. Some costs could still be applied based on ton-miles.

NUMERICAL PROBLEMS

NP 4–1: Estimating Direct Product Costs (LO 2; NE 2) The Wooden Chair Company makes maple and oak chairs. The cost of maple is $.80 per board-foot and the cost of oak $1.00 per board-foot. A board-foot is one foot square and an inch thick. The controller of the Wooden Chair Company estimates that both maple and oak chairs use 10 board-feet of wood. The cutting, assembling, and finishing of both maple and oak chairs require three direct labor hours. Labor costs are $8 per hour.

What are the direct product costs of maple and oak chairs?

NP 4–2: Estimating Direct Service Costs (LO 2; NE 2) A CPA firm is estimating the direct service costs of performing an audit. The firm estimates that the audit will require five partner hours, 20 manager hours, and 50 assistant hours. The estimated opportunity costs of using these people are $150 for partners, $80 for managers, and $40 for assistants.

What is the direct service cost of performing the audit?

NP 4–3: Estimating Direct Service Costs (LO 2; NE 2) Southwest Bank provides house loans for the region. Customers seeking a loan to buy a house initially talk to a loan officer who gathers the appropriate information about the customer. The bank then hires a local appraiser to evaluate the home being purchased. The customer and appraisal information is then sent to the vice president of the bank to make the final decision on the home loan. If both the bank and customer agree on the conditions of the home loan, the bank sends its lawyer to the closing on the sale of the house with the appropriate documents. Once the bank loan is implemented, a loan maintenance officer receives and records the monthly payments and sends the checks on to the treasurer, where they are deposited in the bank. The average time spent on a house loan by each of these employees and their hourly wages are:

Employee	Time (Hours)	Wage Rate/Hour
Loan officer	2.0*	$15
Appraiser	3.0*	40
Vice president	.5*	80
Lawyer	2.0*	70
Loan maintenance officer	4.0/year	20
Treasurer	1.0/year	30

*Only in the first year of the loan.

a. A decision to make the loan is made by the vice president. The loan office and appraisal work has already been completed. What is the cost of a loan application that has been turned down?
b. If the loan is accepted, the remaining labor costs are incurred. What is the average direct labor cost of an accepted loan the first year?
c. What is the average direct labor cost of an accepted loan the second year?

NP 4–4: Estimating Indirect Service Costs Using a Single Cost Driver
(LO 4; NE 3) A car repair shop applies overhead to different service jobs using direct labor hours. The manager estimates that total indirect costs will be $30,000 and total direct labor hours will be 2,000.

a. What is the application rate for indirect costs?
b. If a service job requires five direct labor hours, how much indirect service cost will be applied to that service job?
c. If direct labor costs $10 per hour, what would be the total service costs of a service job that requires six direct labor hours and requires $100 of parts?

NP 4–5: Estimating Application Rates (LO 4; NE 4)
Suppose engineering is identified as a product-level, indirect cost activity and the number of hours engineers devote to each product is used as a cost driver. Engineering costs are $100,000. Product A uses 700 hours and product B uses 300 hours for a total of 1,000 engineering hours. There are only two products.

What is the application rate for engineering costs and how is it applied to products A and B?

NP 4–6: Estimating Indirect Product Costs Using a Single Cost Driver
(LO 4; NE 3) A sheet metal wholesaler purchases sheet metal and cuts and bends the sheet metal to the specifications of its customers. The cutting and bending require the use of large, expensive machines. Because most of the indirect costs are related to these machines, the manager of the company decides to apply indirect costs based on the number of machine hours required to meet customer specifications. The manager estimates that total indirect costs for the next period will be $100,000 and the machines will be used a total of 2,000 hours.

a. What is the application rate for indirect costs?
b. What is the applied indirect cost of a job that requires four hours of machine time?

NP 4–7: Activity-Based Costing (LO 5; NE 5)
Collins Sheet Metal Shop is considering adding a metal dry box for rafts to its product mix. The metal box requires 20 square feet of ⅛ inch aluminum. The cost of the aluminum sheet metal is $5 per square foot. Direct labor on the box is estimated to be five hours at $10/hour. The following activities and their cost drivers and application rates are expected to be used in making the new box:

Activity	Cost Driver	Application Rate	Usage per Dry Box
Bending	Number of bends	$0.20/bend	20 bends
Drilling	Number of holes	$0.10/hole	30 holes
Welding	Number of inches	$0.30/inch	100 inches
Marketing	Number of products	$50/product	1 product
Accounting	Number of sales	$5/sale	Sold individually

Collins Sheet Metal is making 10 of these dry boxes.

What is the expected cost per dry box?

NP 4–8: Estimating Product Costs (LO 4; NE 3)
A tennis racquet manufacturer makes several kinds of tennis racquets. At the start of the year, the manufacturer estimates overhead to be equal to $4 million. The overhead is applied to tennis racquets based on direct labor dollars, which are estimated to be $2 million in the coming year. Direct material costs are estimated to be $3 million.

a. What is the application rate for the manufacturer?
b. What is the product cost of a batch of 1,000 racquets that uses 200 direct labor hours at $10 per hour and $5,000 of direct materials?

NP 4–9: Multiple Cost Drivers (LO 6; NE 5)
A manufacturing firm has the following expected overhead costs. cost drivers, and expected cost driver usage:

Overhead Item	Cost Driver	Expected Cost	Expected Cost Driver Usage
President's salary	Number of products	$100,000	100
Personnel Dept.	Direct labor hours	$ 80,000	8,000
Machine setups	Number of batches	$ 50,000	250

What is the indirect cost of a product that uses 100 direct labor hours and requires 5 batches to make 100 units?

NP 4–10: Cost of a Bank Service (LO 2; NE 3)
First Eastern Bank is a large, multibranch bank offering a wide variety of commercial and retail banking services. Eastern determines the cost of various services to provide information for a variety of decisions.

One set of services is a retail loan operation providing residential mortgages, car loans, and student college loans. All loan applications are filed by the applicant at a branch bank, where the branch manager fills out the loan application. From there, the loan application is sent to the loan processing department, where the applicant's prior credit history is checked and a recommendation is made regarding loan approval based on the applicant's credit history and current financial situation. This recommendation is forwarded to the loan committee of senior lending officers who review the file and make a final decision.

Thus, there are three stages to making a loan: application in a branch, the loan processing department, and the loan committee. Mr. and Mrs. Jones visit the West Street branch and file an application for a residential mortgage. Information about each stage of processing the Jones' loan application follows:

- *West Street Branch Bank.* The branch manager spends one hour taking the application. The branch manager spends 1,000 hours per year of her total time taking loan applications and the remainder of her time providing other direct services to customers. Total overhead in the West Street Branch is budgeted to be $259,000 excluding the manager's salary and is traced to direct customer services using the branch manager's time spent providing direct customer services. The branch manager's annual salary is $42,600.
- *Processing Department.* The processing department budgets its total overhead for the year to be $800,000, which is traced to loans processed using direct labor hours.

Budgeted direct labor hours for the year are 40,000 hours. Direct labor hours in the processing department cost $18 per direct labor hour. The Jones' loan requires five direct labor hours in the loan processing department.

- *Loan committee.* Ten senior bank executives constitute the loan committee. The loan committee meets 52 times per year, every Wednesday, all day, to approve all loans. The average salary and benefits of each member of the loan committee is $104,000. The loan committee spends 15 minutes reviewing the Jones' loan application before approving it.

For costing purposes, all employees are assumed to work eight-hour days, five days per week, 52 weeks per year.

Calculate the total cost of taking the application, processing, and approval for the Jones' mortgage.

NP 4–11: Exterior House Painters (LO 2; NE 2,4)   Your company, Day-Glo Painting, has just finished its first year of operation. During the first year of operation, you painted the exterior of 20 houses in pink with purple trim. Although the first few home owners were unsure about the colors and threatened to sue the company, the pink and purple houses are now becoming a fad and are quite popular. The income statement for the company during the first year is:

DAY-GLO PAINTING
Year of 1995

Revenues	$120,000
Direct labor ($20/hour)	(75,000)
Paint	(20,000)
Rental of painting equipment	(5,000)
General administration	(10,000)
Profit	$ 10,000

The direct labor of painting and cost of paint vary with the square feet of surface area painted. During the year, the company painted 400,000 square feet of surface. In addition, direct labor, but no significant paint, is used to paint the trim around doors and windows. Painting trim takes an hour per 20 feet of trim. During 1995 the company painted 40,000 feet of trim.

The second year is just beginning. The time and cost of labor and the cost of paint per gallon and the cost of rental and general administration are expected to be the same in the second year. Day-Glo Painting is bidding to paint a house that has 25,000 square feet of surface area and 3,000 feet of trim.

a. What is the cost of paint per square foot of surface?
b. What is the cost of direct labor per foot of trim?
c. What is the cost of direct labor per square foot of surface?
d. What is the rental and administration cost of painting the house?
e. What is the total cost of painting the house?

NP 4–12: Product Cost with Multiple Cost Drivers (LO 3,6; NE 5)
Neptune Corporation is planning on making 1,000 units of toy planets. The planets use $1 of raw materials per unit and 10 minutes of direct labor at $12 per hour. The manufacture of the 1,000 planets also use the following overhead cost drivers:

Cost Driver	Application Rate	Usage in Making Toy Planets
Machine hours	$20/machine hour	100 machine hours
Number of setups	$200/setup	3 setups
Raw material cost	$0.20/$1 of raw materials	$1,000 of raw materials
Number of products	$4,000/product	1 product

a. Describe each of the cost drivers as representing either unit-level, batch-level, product-level, or facility-level costs.

b. What is the average cost per nit for making toy planets?

NP 4–13: Trade-offs in the Product Life Cycle (LO 1; NE 1)

The Computer Chip Company has identified the following costs for each stage of a typical computer chip's life:

Design	$ 4,000,000
Manufacturing	$10,000,000
Customer service	$ 3,000,000

The controller and the manufacturing manager feel that there is an opportunity to reduce manufacturing costs by 10% if they are allowed to participate in the design process. Their participation in the design process will add $200,000 to the design costs.

Should the controller and manufacturing manager participate in the design process?

NP 4–14: Comparing Single Cost Drivers with ABC (LO 4,5,6; NE 3,4,5)

A road contractor has been using miles of road constructed as a cost driver. Based on last year's costs, he estimates that he can build a road for $3 million per mile. The county has recently asked him for an estimate to build 20 miles of road.

Before making his bid based on his $3 million per mile estimate, he goes to his accountant for advice. The accountant has analyzed last year's costs much differently. She has divided last year's costs into different activities, chosen a cost driver, and measured its usage last year. Her estimates follow:

Activity	Costs ($000,000)	Cost Driver	Cost Driver Usage
Surveying	10	Hours	200,000 hours
Excavating	200	Tons of earth moved	2,000,000 tons
Bridges	120	Number of bridges	60 bridges
Grading	80	Number of miles	200 miles
Gravel	30	Tons of gravel	750,000 tons
Paving	160	Number of miles	200 miles

The costs from the last year appear to be good estimates of costs in the coming year. The 20 miles of county road up for bid will require 30,000 hours of surveying, 300,000 tons of earth moved, 10 bridges, and 80,000 tons of gravel.

a. Allowing for a 10% profit what should be the road contractor's bid using the $3 million per mile cost driver?
b. What is wrong with using miles as a cost driver?
c. Allowing for a 10% profit, what should be the road contractor's bid using the multiple cost drivers suggested by the accountant?

DISCUSSION PROBLEMS

DP 4–1: Identifying Direct Costs of a Service Organization (LO 2)

Avant Airlines is attempting to estimate the direct cost of flying a passenger from Austin, Texas, to Los Angeles, California. The direct cost estimation is the initial step in determining a new pricing strategy for the airlines. A careful examination of operations, however, indicates that very few costs can be traced directly to a specific passenger on a flight.

Identify the direct costs of servicing an airline passenger and how they could be measured.

DP 4–2: Level of Indirect Costs (LO 3)

Describe the following activities as unit-level, batch-level, product-level, or facility-level.

a. Sending truckloads of products to customers.
b. Providing data processing services for the office.
c. Operating a machine to make products.
d. Setting up machines to make different products.
e. Applying for patents on products.
f. Accounting for sales transactions.

DP 4–3: Activity-Based Costing (LO 6)   True or False:

a. ABC is likely to benefit multiproduct firms more than single product firms.
b. A move from a single unit-based cost driver to ABC is likely to shift overhead from low-volume products to high-volume products.
c. ABC improves the tracing of direct costs to products.
d. With ABC all cost drivers should be correlated with the number of units of output.
e. The application rate per cost driver is normally calculated at the end of the period.

DP 4–4: Levels of Indirect Costs (LO 3)

A railroad company is trying to decide how to charge its customers for carrying freight. A manager suggests that multiplying the pounds times the miles traveled would be a good activity base for the price of transporting freight.

a. What types of customers will the railroad company tend to lose to other transport companies if the railroad company decides to charge customers based on pounds times the miles traveled?
b. Suggest a pricing system for freight based on the concept of activity-based costing.

DP 4–5: Cost Reduction (LO 3)

In a recent article in *The Wall Street Journal*, Thai Airlines announced that the company was reducing costs by reducing the different types of airplanes it flies from 15 to 5. The company was also reducing the number of different types of airplane engines it would use. The company, however, was not planning on reducing the number of airplanes in its fleet, only the composition of the fleet.[3]

a. How does the reduction in the different types of planes and engines lead to cost reductions?
b. How does this action relate to the different levels of indirect costs?

DP 4–6: Cost of Supporting Customers (LO 1)

In a recent *Wall Street Journal* article, the personal computer business was analyzed. The article noted that the sales of personal computers are climbing, but the sellers of personal computers are having problems providing support for the customers buying the computers. The companies can't keep up with customer complaints and requests for help. Most companies have had to increase their customer support staff.

How does this article relate to costs and the life cycle of making personal computers?

DP 4–7: Costs of Providing a Service (LO 2, 4)

The city of Progress is considering a reimbursement fee to recover costs of its fire department in cases where the parties responsible for the fire are found guilty of gross negligence by the local city court. If the program is successful, the city may extend the program to all emergency services and be able to reduce the local property tax levy. The city currently uses labor hours to trace costs to different services. The cost per labor hour is determined as follows:

Annual salaries and benefits (12,480 hours)	$225,000
Education and training	50,000
Property and liability insurance	40,000
Depreciation of building and equipment	65,000
Operating supplies	25,000
Utilities	20,000
Total annual costs	$425,000

Cost per labor hour = $425,000/12,480 = $34.05/labor hour

The fire department currently performs many services including: (1) fire fighting, (2) medical assistance, (3) hazardous waste removal, (4) rescuing pets, (5) search and rescue, (6) community service at local schools and the senior citizen center, (7) training, and (8) maintenance of equipment. The latter three activities account for over 80 percent of the annual labor hours.

Is the $34.05/labor hour fee an accurate measure of the cost of fighting fires due to gross negligence?

CASE

C 4–1: Pilot Plant The Bion Company has an R&D building which is shared by three wire and cable groups: High Voltage, Medium Voltage, and Low Voltage. Adjacent to the R&D building is a Pilot Plant, a small-scale production facility designed for limited runs of experimental and commercial products. The three groups rely on the pilot plant to produce samples of their formulations.

In the Pilot Plant, sample sizes vary from about 1,000 lbs. to 10,000 lbs. The R&D groups, including the pilot plant, are run as cost centers. The Pilot Plant also takes on special production runs for external customers that are too small for a regular plant. The Pilot Plant consists of three combination blending/extruding machines that produce pellets of compounded material. Unlike large commercial compounding machines that can operate 24 hours per day, these machines are run for approximately 1,000 hours a year. In the past, the Pilot Plant has costed its jobs based on direct materials, variable machine time, and allocated overhead. Overhead is allocated by machine time. A single plantwide machine rate is calculated pooling all three machines. The overhead pool includes plant fixed costs plus the labor cost of the department.

Approximately 20% of the machine technicians' time is spent performing general cleanup and maintenance. Machine time is calculated before each job by a computer program that outputs feed rate and setup parameters. Each product is scheduled to a specific machine based on its formulation. The cost schedule of each machine is shown below. Capacity represents the historic annual average capacity.

	Cleanup (hours/batch)	Capacity (lbs./yr.)	Variable Cost ($/hr.)	Operators
Machine 1	4	250,000	25	2
Machine 2	6	250,000	25	2
Machine 3	8	500,000	50	1

Fixed costs: $200,000/yr.
Labor costs:
 1 manager @ $ 45,000/yr.
 6 technicians @ $ 30,000/yr.

While formulations vary considerably, 90% of the blends are either resin or flame-retardant magnesium hydroxide. These bulky materials are normally ordered 1 to 2 weeks ahead of time and take up much of the floor space. The additives are quite standard and are kept in stock. Weigh-ups and general set-up are time-consuming and vary from job to job: a formulation that requires seven additives takes considerably more time to prepare than a similar run with two additives. In the past, time spent on set-up was not tracked, but it is a simple matter for the chief operator to include these numbers with the run report. One of the technicians is not assigned to a particular machine, but is responsible for arranging stock on the floor. The manager spends most of his time scheduling runs and attending to administrative work.

In a typical job, total weigh-up time is the amount of labor time required to locate, prepare, and mix the direct materials prior to inserting them in the machine.

Job #71302			
		Composition and Direct Cost	
Sample run 5,000 lbs:	90%	NCPE-0600, RESIN	$0.10/lb.
	8%	KISUMA, FLAME RETARDANT	$0.12/lb.
	2%	COMPOUND Z, ANTIOXIDANT	$0.14/lb.
RUN ON MACHINE 1		250 lbs. per hr. for 20 hours	
TOTAL WEIGH-UP TIME*		16 employee hours	

*Total weigh-up time is the amount of labor time required to locate, prepare, and mix the direct materials prior to inserting them in the machine.

Case Questions

a. Calculate the cost of the sample run as charged to the Low Voltage department.
b. What is wrong with this system? Construct an alternative costing system and describe its benefits.
c. Recalculate the cost of this run using this new system.

CHAPTER 5
Product Planning Decisions

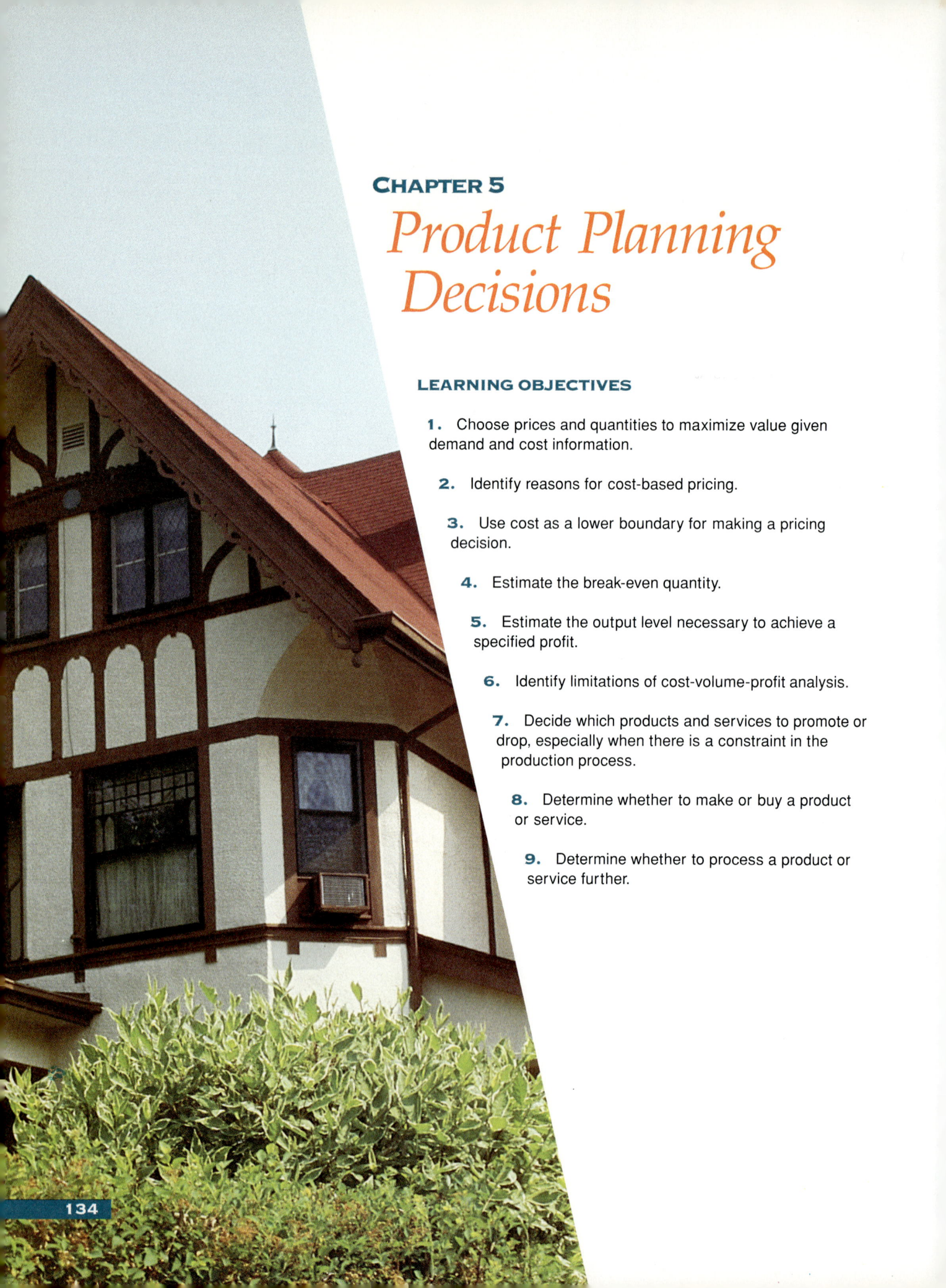

LEARNING OBJECTIVES

1. Choose prices and quantities to maximize value given demand and cost information.

2. Identify reasons for cost-based pricing.

3. Use cost as a lower boundary for making a pricing decision.

4. Estimate the break-even quantity.

5. Estimate the output level necessary to achieve a specified profit.

6. Identify limitations of cost-volume-profit analysis.

7. Decide which products and services to promote or drop, especially when there is a constraint in the production process.

8. Determine whether to make or buy a product or service.

9. Determine whether to process a product or service further.

Toad Hall Bed and Breakfast

Toad Hall was built by a wealthy Boston banker as a summer home in 1880 on the shore of a lake in the White Mountains of New Hampshire. Toad Hall, however, was not a small lake cottage. The main house had six bedrooms, and there was also a caretaker house on the property. Toad Hall had remained in the family for several generations, but the current generation could no longer afford the upkeep of such a large vacation house. They have put the property up for sale for $700,000.

Susan and Ed White live in New York City and have always dreamed of an escape to the country. When they saw the advertisement for Toad Hall, they rented a car and drove to New Hampshire to take a look. They were thrilled with the beautiful redwood interior and thought that Toad Hall would make a wonderful bed and breakfast inn. A local contractor was contacted to determine the cost of converting Toad Hall into a bed and breakfast. The contractor estimates that an additional $300,000 would be required to convert the main house into a bed and breakfast with six bedrooms with their own bathrooms. The Whites figure they could live in the caretaker house if they bought Toad Hall.

Before purchasing Toad Hall, the Whites make the following estimates of the costs of operating Toad Hall as a bed and breakfast inn. (The Whites would make a down payment of $200,000 on Toad Hall and the remodeling.)

Interest on mortgage of $800,000 at 10%	$80,000 per year
Insurance	$5,000 per year
Property taxes	$10,000 per year
Utilities and maintenance	$8,000 per year + $5 daily per rented room
Breakfast ($3/person, 2 people per room)	$6 daily per rented room
Maid service	$15 daily per rented room

After completing this list of costs, the Whites are unsure of how to use these costs to make a decision. They do realize, however, that they will need to determine a rental price for the rooms before they can complete the analysis.

5.1 Pricing Decisions

The pricing decision is one of the most important planning decisions that a manager makes. If the price of the organization's product or service is set too high, no one will purchase the product or service and the organization will fail. If the price is set too low, the organization will generate sales but will not be able to cover its costs and, once again, the organization will fail.

In some cases the price is determined by the competition, and an organization has little choice in setting prices. This is true if the product or service of an organization can't be differentiated from the products or services of its competitors and their prices are known to consumers. In most cases, however, an organization has some leeway in making pricing decisions because products and services differ from the competitors due to some unique characteristics.

Pricing to Maximize Value

A primary goal of a business organization is to maximize the ownership value. Therefore, identifying the price that will maximize the value of the business is important. To determine the price that maximizes value, a manager must know the quantity demanded for the product or service at different prices. Presumably the quantity demanded will rise if the price is lowered. On the other hand, fewer customers will purchase the product or service if the price is raised. The following schedule of quantities and prices for kayaks is a typical example of changing demand with changing prices:

Kayaks Sold	×	Price per Unit	=	Total Revenues
100		$900		$ 90,000
150		800		120,000
200		700		140,000
300		600		180,000
400		500		200,000
480		400		192,000
600		300		180,000

Notice that the number of units that can be sold increases with a decrease in price.

The maximum revenues are generated when a price of $500 per kayak is set and 400 kayaks are sold. But choosing the price that maximizes revenue does not necessarily maximize value. The product cost at different levels of output must also be estimated. If the variable cost per unit and fixed costs can be identified and measured, total costs at different levels of output are easy to estimate. In the kayak example, suppose that the fixed cost of making kayaks is $50,000 and the variable cost is $300 per kayak. Table 5.1 describes the total revenues, total costs, and value added from making and selling different numbers of kayaks.

Producing 300 kayaks and selling them at a price of $600 per unit creates the highest value added for the organization. The choice of making 300 kayaks can also be made using **incremental costs** and revenues. The incremental costs and revenues are the additional costs and revenues of making more units of a product or service. The incremental revenues of increasing production from 200 kayaks to 300 kayaks is $180,000 − $140,000, or $40,000, while the incremental costs are $140,000 − $110,000, or $30,000. Therefore, making 300 kayaks is preferred to making 200 kayaks. The incremental revenues of increasing production from 300 kayaks to 400 kayaks is $200,000 − $180,000, or $20,000, while the incremental

TABLE 5.1
Revenues, Costs, and Value Added

Kayaks Sold	Price	Total Revenues	− Total Costs	= Added Value
100	$900	$ 90,000	$ 80,000	$10,000
150	800	120,000	95,000	25,000
200	700	140,000	110,000	30,000
300	600	180,000	140,000	40,000
400	500	200,000	170,000	30,000
480	400	192,000	194,000	− 2,000
600	300	180,000	230,000	−50,000

Kayaks are expensive but popular for recreational use on rivers, lakes, and oceans. By lowering prices, manufacturers can sell more kayaks, but a price that is too low will of course cause losses. How does a manufacturer determine what price maximizes profit?

costs are $170,000 − $140,000, or $30,000. Therefore, moving beyond a price of $600 with production of 300 kayaks causes incremental costs to be greater than incremental revenues and is not preferred.

Economic theory states that the price and quantity should be chosen such that the marginal cost is equal to marginal revenue. To determine the marginal cost and marginal revenue, however, total revenues and total costs must be estimated at all levels of output. Estimating revenues requires an excellent knowledge of consumers and competitors. Estimates of revenues tend to be rough approximations and are not usually done on a unit-by-unit basis. In the kayak example, revenues and costs are estimated at price increments of $100 instead of on a unit-by-unit basis. Therefore, incremental costs and revenues are compared instead of marginal costs and revenues. Incremental costs are never equal to incremental revenues in the kayak example, but they are closest around the price of $600 and the output of 300 kayaks.

NUMERICAL EXAMPLE 5.1

Desert Coach Company converts buses into mobile homes. The purchase price of the bus plus the variable conversion costs are $100,000 per mobile home. The fixed costs of operating the factory are $1,000,000. The president of Desert Coach Company estimates the following levels of sales given different prices:

Price	Expected Sales
$150,000	50
175,000	44
200,000	30
225,000	20

What price per mobile home should be set by the president to maximize the value of the company?

■ **SOLUTION** The revenues and costs for the different levels of production are:

Price	Expected Sales	Total Revenues	Total Costs	Added Value
$150,000	50	$7,500,000	$6,000,000	$1,500,000
175,000	44	7,700,000	5,400,000	2,300,000
200,000	30	6,000,000	4,000,000	2,000,000
225,000	20	4,500,000	3,000,000	1,500,000

Making and selling 44 motor homes for $175,000 apiece is the preferred strategy.

TOAD HALL BED AND BREAKFAST (CONTINUED)

Susan and Ed White have no idea how to estimate the demand for rooms at the Toad Hall Bed and Breakfast. They have never operated a bed and breakfast, and Toad Hall has no history as a bed and breakfast inn. Susan and Ed White have checked with other local bed and breakfasts and found their prices to range from $75 to $150 per room. The Whites do recognize that the higher the price they charge for rooms, the fewer rooms they will rent.

Cost-Based Pricing

In spite of the obvious financial benefits of estimating demand with different prices and choosing prices that maximize the value added to the organization, many businesses use only costs to make pricing decisions. A 1982 survey found that 80% of the businesses in the United States use cost-based pricing.

Cost-based pricing generally uses the average product cost as the base. A percentage is added to the product cost to cover period costs not included in the average product cost and provide a profit. Some businesses such as grocery stores use very low percentage increases over the product cost. Other businesses such as fine jewelry stores choose prices two or more times greater than their product costs. The choice of the markup percentage is based on the relative size of nonproduct costs, the ability to sell the product quickly, and the pricing policy of competitors.

NUMERICAL EXAMPLE 5.2

A grocery store marks up all poultry items 10%. The cost of a 15-pound turkey is $20. At what price should the turkey be sold?

■ **SOLUTION** The turkey should be sold at $(1 + .10)(\$20)$, or $22.

Choosing prices based on the product cost without consideration of demand should cause businesses to be at a competitive disadvantage. An analysis of both product costs and the demand for products at different prices is necessary to maximize profit. The following reasons are often given for pricing based only on product costs: (1) difficulty in estimating customer demand at different prices, (2) contracts and regulations, (3) long-run customer goodwill, and (4) discouraging competition. Each of these reasons is discussed in the following sections.

Difficulty in Estimating Customer Demand

Many businesses have a difficult time estimating customer demand for their product or service. If the product or service is new, the marketing group can provide little insight on customer demand. The product or service may have numerous competitors whose reaction to a pricing decision is uncertain. A decision to lower prices may be followed by a similar decision by competitors and thus not lead to increased sales. These types of complications make demand estimation very difficult and point out the importance of knowing your customer and competitors well.

Philip Morris has recently attempted to increase its market share of cigarette smokers by lowering its price on its top products. This action was in response to the low prices of cigarettes being sold by discount producers. Philip Morris's action, however, triggered a reduction in prices by all the suppliers of cigarettes. With all the suppliers reducing prices, there has been no clear winner in terms of gains in market share. The suppliers, including Philip Morris, are simply selling their products at reduced prices causing lower profits. This example indicates the dilemma of estimating customer demand for a product at different prices.

Contracts and Regulations

Sometimes sales contracts are based on product costs. For example, a company may agree to build a hydroelectric dam for its costs plus 15%. Contracts with the defense department for complicated equipment commonly base price on product costs. Cost-based contracts are often used when the cost of the product is difficult to estimate before production begins. For example, estimating the costs of a new fighter jet is difficult because much of the technology is untested. By not determining the price until completion, the supplier of the product or service is not forced to bear the risk of uncertain costs. The purchaser of the product agrees to bear the risk by reimbursing the costs plus a certain amount for profit.

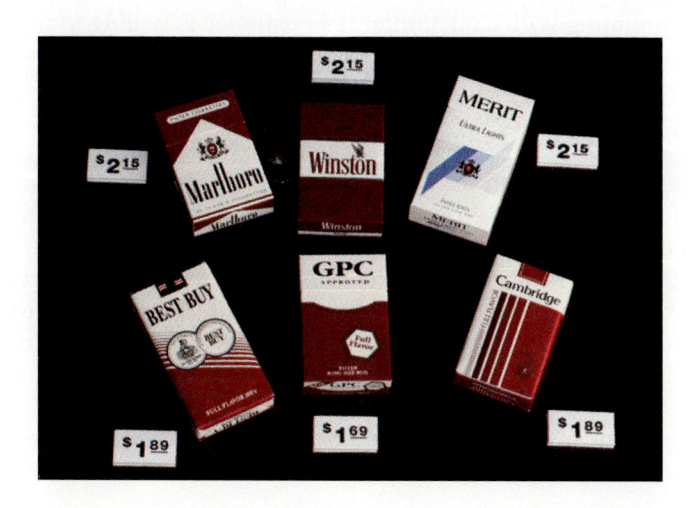

The pricing of cigarettes is a very sensitive issue. A price increase can cause a drop in demand because one brand of cigarette is a close substitute for other brands. A price decrease, on the other hand, may be duplicated by competitors.

Regulated industries such as utilities also use cost-based pricing. Utilities are often monopolies. Because monopolies have no competitors, they could set very high prices if not regulated. Regulatory boards allow these utilities to sell their service for a price that recovers the cost of the service and enough for a reasonable profit for the owners.

Long-Run Customer Goodwill

Temporary reductions in supply or increases in demand allow organizations to set a much higher price than normal. For example, a shortage of gasoline in the 1970s allowed retailers to set very high prices for gasoline. Increased demand for basketball tickets during a winning season allows the university to charge a higher price for the tickets. The organizations with these temporary opportunities do not always adjust their prices to take advantage of excess demand. They recognize that at least some customers will not return to a business that raised prices during a shortage. A long-run strategy that ignores short-run opportunities to raise prices may create the most value for the organization.

Discouraging Competition

An organization has more flexibility in pricing a unique product or service. Customers do not have the opportunity to shift to a similar product if the price is set too high. If organizations attempt to take advantage of the uniqueness of their product or service by setting a relatively high price, competitors will soon enter the market with similar products and services to share in the success. A lower price with only a small markup on the product cost, however, will discourage competitors from making similar products or services.

Cost as a Lower Boundary for Price

Pricing decisions should consider both demand and the costs of providing a product or service. But if demand is difficult to estimate, the product or service cost does offer a lower boundary in making the pricing decision. Pricing a product below its opportunity cost reduces the value of the organization. The two exceptions to this rule are **lead-loss pricing** and **predatory pricing.** Lead-loss pricing is a strategy of selling a particular product at a price below its cost to lure customers into a shop with the hope of selling other products. Predatory pricing is a strategy of selling a product at a price below its cost to drive out competition. Once competition is eliminated, the organization raises its prices to capture the benefits of being the sole supplier of the product. Predatory pricing is illegal in the United States. Organizations can't set prices below costs to eliminate competition.

Identifying the lower boundary for making a pricing decision is useful information in negotiating with a customer. If a customer is willing to pay some price above the product cost, then the organization should be willing to sell the product. The product cost should include estimates of the opportunity cost of using both direct and indirect resources to make the product.

The opportunity cost of a product depends on the forgone opportunity of using resources to make a product. These opportunity costs are commonly estimated by identifying the fixed costs and variable costs per unit. Once the fixed costs have been incurred to start production, the variable cost per unit is a good estimate of the opportunity cost of providing another unit of the product or service. The variable cost per unit is a good estimate until capacity is reached. Once capacity is reached, alternative uses of the capacity or the cost of increasing capacity should be considered in estimating the opportunity cost of making a product.

Using the variable cost as a lower boundary is only a short-run strategy when operating below capacity. Organizations must have sufficient revenues to cover fixed costs if they are to survive in the long run, but recognizing short-run opportunities is important. An example of a short-run opportunity is the receipt of a special, one-time order for additional units of a product already being manufactured. The customer offers to buy a certain number of units at a bargain price. If the offer is not accepted, the customer will go to another supplier. The organization must decide if the special order is a profitable opportunity. As long as the organization is below capacity, the organization can make additional units at the variable cost per unit. Therefore, a special order should be accepted if the bargain price is greater than the variable cost and there are no other long-term ramifications.

NUMERICAL EXAMPLE 5.3

The Living Seed Company makes packets of organic carrot seeds. The fixed costs of the company are $50,000 and the variable costs are $0.50 per pack. The company normally sells 200,000 packs for $1 per pack but has the capacity to make 300,000. A garden catalogue has just contacted the company and asked to buy 50,000 packs for $0.60 per pack. This purchase will not affect the company's other sales. Should the company accept the offer to buy 50,000 packs?

■ **SOLUTION** The offered price is greater than the variable cost per unit, so the company should accept the offer. This can be shown by comparing the profit with and without the sale. The profit without the sale is:

Revenues ($1/pack)(200,000 packs)	$ 200,000
Variable costs ($0.50/pack)(200,000 packs)	(100,000)
Fixed costs	(50,000)
Profit	$ 50,000

The profit with the sale is:

Revenues ($1/pack)(200,000 packs) + ($0.60/pack)(50,000 packs)	$ 230,000
Variable costs ($0.50/pack)(250,000 packs)	(125,000)
Fixed costs	(50,000)
Profit	$ 55,000

Why is the pricing of an airplane ticket so much more complicated than the pricing of a toaster oven? Why don't airlines just have one price for a ticket from Los Angeles to Chicago?

WHAT'S HAPPENING

American auto manufacturers recently claimed that Japanese auto manufacturers were dumping minivans in the United States. **Dumping** is defined as selling a portion of your inventory (usually in another country) below average cost. Are the Japanese auto manufacturers making poor business decisions if they are selling below average cost?

The airline industry expends considerable effort on the pricing decision. The variable cost of an additional passenger tends to be very small, usually the cost of the meal and luggage handling. Therefore, the airlines are willing to sell tickets at a discount to fill airplanes because the discounted ticket prices are well above the variable cost and provide a net benefit to the company. Pricing for airlines, however, is much more complicated than using the variable cost as a lower boundary. Airlines also attempt to sell higher priced tickets to passengers such as businesspeople and travelers making last-minute decisions who have little flexibility in traveling by other means. Offering free tickets to frequent fliers is also a pricing strategy to encourage repeated use of the airlines.

TOAD HALL BED AND BREAKFAST (CONTINUED)

Susan and Ed White estimate that their variable costs are $26 per room.:

Utilities and maintenance	$ 5
Breakfast ($3/person and 2 people per room)	6
Maid service	15
Total variable costs	$26/room

Ed is confused about using the variable cost to make a pricing decision. He asks Susan, "Do you mean that if a customer arrives late at night and we have empty rooms that will not be filled, we should be willing to rent a room for as low as $26? Nobody rents rooms for that low of a price. We'll lose money."

Susan replies, "The variable cost of renting one more room is $26. If we can rent it for $30, we make $4 more than if we don't rent it at all."

Ed is still not convinced. He provides another argument for not renting at such a low price: "What if we rent a room to someone earlier in the day for $100 and then rent a room for $30 to a late arrival. What happens if they have breakfast together and they discover the price difference? Won't the person paying the higher rent be upset?"

CONCEPT REVIEW

1. How should an organization make pricing decisions to maximize value?
2. Why is cost-based pricing used?
3. What is the lower boundary in making a pricing decision?

5.2 Cost-Volume-Profit Analysis

Cost-volume-profit (CVP) analysis is a method of estimating profit from an investment given different levels of output. The profit is defined as revenues less fixed and variable costs. The fixed and variable costs are approximations for opportunity costs over different levels of output. The profit equation using CVP is

$$\text{Profit} = \text{Revenues} - \text{Variable costs} - \text{Fixed costs}$$

The profit estimated from this procedure will not be exactly the same as the externally reported profit, which is based on historical cost numbers. Because CVP analysis is used for planning purposes, the costs in the equation should reflect estimated opportunity costs. One example of the difference between the expenses in externally reported profit and the costs used for CVP analysis is the use of cash. If the investment being considered involves the long-term use of cash, the planning decision should recognize that there is an opportunity cost of using cash. External accounting reports recognize any interest expense from borrowing money, but do not recognize the forgone opportunity of using cash to make part of the investment. Cash used to make the investment can no longer earn interest or other income for the organization. Therefore, CVP analysis should include the interest expense of borrowed cash plus the forgone opportunity of earning interest on the cash used to make the investment.

NUMERICAL EXAMPLE 5.4

Paul McDonald is thinking about buying a farm that costs $400,000. He can borrow $300,000 for the purchase at 10% interest but must use $100,000 of his own cash for the remaining part of the purchase. What is the annual cost of financing the investment in the farm?

■ **SOLUTION** External reports would only recognize the 10% interest on the loan (0.10)($300,000), or $30,000, annually. For CVP analysis, however, there is a forgone opportunity of using the $100,000 in cash to buy the farm. If the cash would have earned 10%, the cost of financing for CVP analysis is (0.10)($400,000), or $40,000, annually.

The profit equation for CVP analysis can be written as:

$$\text{Profit} = (P)(Q) - (VC)(Q) - FC$$

where:

P = Price per unit
Q = Quantity of units produced and sold
VC = Variable cost per unit
FC = Fixed costs

Rearranging the profit equation yields:

$$\text{Profit} = (P - VC)(Q) - FC$$

The price per unit minus the variable cost per unit is called the **contribution margin per unit.** The contribution margin per unit is the increase in profit caused by making and selling one more unit of the product or service. The fixed costs do not change as additional units are made. For example, if the contribution margin of making a car is $5,000, selling 100 more cars will increase profit by ($5,000)(100), or $500,000.

NUMERICAL EXAMPLE 5.5

Gravel is made by crushing stones. The variable cost of making gravel is estimated to be $10 per ton. The fixed costs of operating the facility per year are $100,000. The sales price of gravel is $25 per ton. What is the expected profit if 10,000 tons of gravel are crushed and sold? What would be the additional profit if 1,000 more tons are crushed and sold?

■ **SOLUTION** If 10,000 tons of gravel are crushed, the expected profit is

$$(P - VC)(Q) - FC = (\$25 - \$10)(10{,}000) - \$100{,}000 = \$50{,}000$$

The profit from making 11,000 tons of gravel is

$$(P - VC)(Q) - FC = (\$25 - \$10)(11{,}000) - \$100{,}000 = \$65{,}000$$

The additional profit from selling 1,000 more tons can also be estimated by multiplying the contribution margin per unit times the additional quantity:

$$(P - VC)(Q) = (\$25 - \$10)(1{,}000) = \$15{,}000$$

TOAD HALL BED AND BREAKFAST (CONTINUED)

Susan and Ed White have reevaluated their original cost numbers. They realize that the opportunity cost of purchasing and remodeling Toad Hall should include not only the interest payment on the mortgage but also the forgone interest earned on the $200,000 down payment. If that forgone interest is also at a 10% rate, the opportunity cost of investing $1,000,000 in Toad Hall is $100,000 per year. Therefore, the fixed costs per year of operating Toad Hall as a bed and breakfast are:

Opportunity cost of purchase and remodeling	$100,000
Insurance	5,000
Property taxes	10,000
Utilities and maintenance	8,000
Total fixed costs	$123,000

Variable costs per room rented per day or room-day are:

Utilities and maintenance	$ 5
Breakfast	6
Maid service	15
Variable cost per room-day	$26

As an initial estimate of profit, Susan and Ed assume that they can rent rooms at $80 per night and operate at half of the capacity of Toad Hall. Toad Hall's capacity would be (365 days per years)(6 rooms) or 2,190 room-days. Half of that capacity would be 2,190/2, or 1,095, room-days. With variable costs of $26 per room-day, there is an expected loss of:

$$(P - VC)Q - FC = (\$80 - \$26)(1{,}095) - \$123{,}000 = -\$63{,}870$$

This estimate is very discouraging for Susan and Ed.

Break-Even Analysis

In planning for an investment, information about the quantity of units that must be sold to break even or have zero profit is useful. If the organization cannot hope to sell enough units to break even, then the investment should not be made. **Break-even analysis** is the process of determining the number of units that must be sold to achieve zero profit. Break-even analysis using variable and fixed costs to approximate opportunity costs is achieved by solving for the quantity of units when profit is equal to zero:

$$0 = (P - VC)(Q) - FC$$
$$FC = (P - VC)(Q)$$
$$FC/(P - VC) = Q$$

The break-even quantity is simply the fixed costs divided by the contribution margin per unit.

NUMERICAL EXAMPLE 5.6

A hot dog vendor must pay $100 per day to rent her cart. She sells hot dogs for $1. The variable costs of making the hot dogs are $0.20 per hot dog. How many hot dogs must she sell per day to break even?

■ **SOLUTION** The break-even quantity is

$$FC/(P - VC) = \$100/(\$1 - \$0.20) = 125 \text{ hot dogs}$$

Break-even analysis can also be used to determine prices or target costs that are sufficient to cause zero profit. For example, the break-even equation can be solved for the price per unit.

$$0 = (P - VC)(Q) - FC$$
$$P = (FC/Q) + VC$$

NUMERICAL EXAMPLE 5.7

A company can build 20 manufactured homes a year with a fixed cost of $1 million and a variable cost per home of $50,000. At what price must the company sell the manufactured homes to break even?

■ **SOLUTION** The break-even price is

$$P = (FC/Q) + VC = (\$1{,}000{,}000/20) + \$50{,}000 = \$100{,}000/\text{home}$$

You can't sell 10 hot dogs a day and make a living. How many do you need to sell per day to pay the rent on the hot dog stand and make a reasonable living?

TOAD HALL BED AND BREAKFAST (CONTINUED)

Ed and Susan White were not thrilled with their initial profit estimate. So instead of estimating profit given an expected number of room rentals, they decide to estimate how many rooms they must rent to break even. They use their initial cost estimates of $123,000 of fixed costs and $26 of variable costs per room per day or room-day. They also assume that the daily room rental fee is $80 per room. The break-even quantity is

$$FC/(P - VC) = \$123,000/(\$80 - \$26) = 2,278 \text{ room-days}$$

This result is very discouraging because the break-even quantity is greater than the capacity of Toad Hall, which is 2,190 room-days (at 100% occupancy).

The Whites then decide to try to estimate a daily rental rate that will allow them to break even given a 50% occupancy rate (1,095 room-days).

$$P = (FC/Q) + VC$$
$$\text{Rental Rate} = (\$123,000/1,095) + \$26 = \$138 \text{ per room-day}$$

This rental rate is within the range of rental rates of competitor bed and breakfast inns, but that rental rate offers no profit for the Whites. The Whites decide to use $150 per room-day in their remaining calculations.

Achieving a Specified Profit

The profit equation with variable and fixed costs can also be used to determine the necessary quantity of a product or service that must be produced and sold to achieve a certain profit. Instead of being set at zero, the profit can be set at a specified amount and the profit equation can be used to solve for the necessary quantity of units produced and sold:

$$\text{Profit} = (P - VC)(Q) - FC$$
$$\text{Profit} + FC = (P - VC)(Q)$$
$$(\text{Profit} + FC)/(P - VC) = Q$$

The necessary quantity to achieve a specified profit is the sum of the profit and fixed costs divided by the contribution margin per unit.

CVP analysis can also be used to determine the necessary units that must be sold to achieve a specified profit after payment of an income tax. The appendix describes the equation to be used to calculate the necessary quantity to achieve a specified after-tax profit.

NUMERICAL EXAMPLE 5.8

Suppose the hot dog vendor who must pay $100 per day to rent her cart wants to make $60 profit a day. She sells hot dogs for $1 and the variable costs of making the hot dog are $0.20 per hot dog. How many hot dogs must she sell per day to have a profit of $60?

■ **SOLUTION** The necessary quantity to have a profit of $60 is

$$(\text{Profit} + FC)/(P - VC) = (\$60 + \$100)/(\$1 - \$0.20) = 200 \text{ hot dogs}$$

TOAD HALL BED AND BREAKFAST (CONTINUED)

Susan and Ed White realize they can't live on zero profit. To estimate an acceptable profit, the Whites examine their existing annual profit from working at their jobs in New York City. Presently their joint salaries are $100,000, but they pay $45,000 per year for their apartment. By living in the caretaker house at Toad Hall, they will not have to pay rent, so the net forgone profit of buying Toad Hall is $55,000. The Whites also value the intangibles of living in the country at $25,000 per year. Therefore, the Whites believe that they should obtain a profit of at least $30,000 annually from Toad Hall to make the investment comparable to their existing situation. The number of room-days that must be rented to achieve a $30,000 profit if a daily rental rate of $150 is used is

(Profit + FC)/(P − VC) = ($30,000 + $123,000)/($150 − $26) = 1,234 room-days

Although this number is still below the total capacity of 2,190, Susan and Ed White are not sure that they can rent that many rooms, especially at a daily rate of $150 per room.

Graph of CVP Analysis

CVP analysis can be easily represented by a graph. Figure 5.1 demonstrates the CVP problem for the hot dog vendor with fixed costs of $100, variable costs of $0.20 per hot dog, and a price of $1.00 per hot dog. The total cost line is the same form as the variable and fixed cost approximation of opportunity costs in Chapter 2. The fixed cost of $100 is the intercept of the vertical axis, and the variable

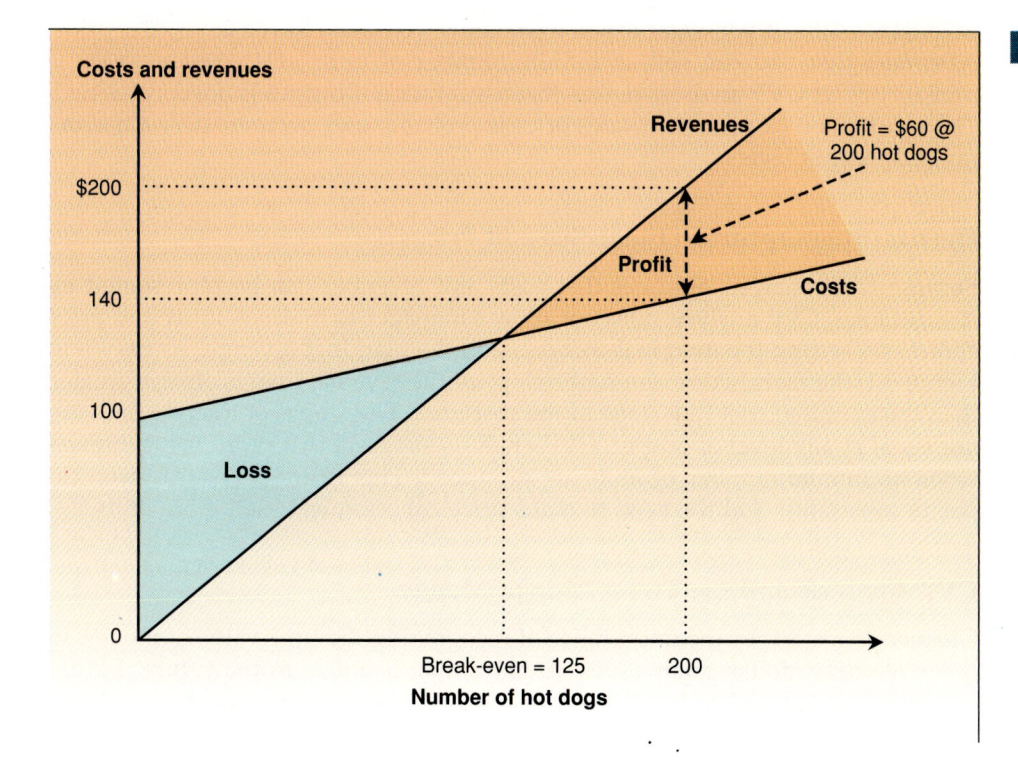

FIGURE 5.1

Cost Structure for a Hot Dog Vendor

cost per hot dog is the slope of the total cost line. The total revenue line is a straight line extending from the origin with a slope equal to the sales price per unit.

The break-even quantity occurs when total costs are equal to total revenues. Total costs equal total revenues at the point where the two lines intersect. The shaded area below the break-even quantity represents the expected loss if lower quantities are produced and sold. The shaded area above the break-even quantity represents the expected profit if higher quantities are produced and sold. From Numerical Example 5–6, we see that if 200 hot dogs are produced and sold, a $60 profit will be achieved.

Problems with CVP Analysis

CVP analysis is simple to use. Approximating opportunity costs with fixed and variable costs and assuming that the sales price and variable cost per unit are constant over all levels of output allows us to estimate profit by looking at the difference between the two straight lines in Figure 5.1. Most likely, however, costs and revenues are only reasonable approximations within a small range of output levels.

Approximating Opportunity Costs with Fixed and Variable Costs

Chapter 2 explains that fixed and variable costs only approximate opportunity costs in an intermediate range of outputs. That range was described as the relevant range. Opportunity costs are likely to be less than fixed costs plus variable costs at very low levels of output. Also, as an organization nears capacity, opportunity costs are likely to be higher than fixed plus variable costs. Therefore, CVP analysis should not be used at low levels of output or near capacity levels.

Assuming a Constant Sales Price

In most markets, if you want to sell more units, you must lower your sales price. Assuming that you can sell an infinite number of units at a constant price is unrealistic. Yet CVP analysis makes that assumption if output is not constrained. The assumption of a constant sales price is probably only accurate over a narrow range of output levels.

Determining Optimal Quantities and Prices

Because CVP analysis assumes that costs and revenues can be represented by straight lines, CVP analysis does not allow a manager to make quantity and price choices by setting the marginal cost equal to the marginal revenue. As drawn in Figure 5.1, the marginal revenue (the slope of the revenue line) is always greater than the marginal cost (the slope of the cost line). The slopes of the two lines are not equal at any level of output. CVP analysis suggests that profit is maximized when an infinite number of units are produced. This result is absurd given capacity constraints and the need to make price concessions to sell more units.

CVP Analysis and the Time Value of Money

Chapter 13 describes the importance of recognizing the time value of money. In other words, a dollar today is worth more than a dollar in the future. Future cash flows should be reduced to make them equivalent to present cash flows. CVP analysis does not recognize the time value of money.

The problems with CVP analysis described in this section indicate that CVP analysis should be used with care. CVP analysis has the advantage of being simple but should only be used as a rough planning tool. CVP analysis provides a manager with a low-cost approximation of the profit effect of an investment. Whether a manager wants to analyze the investment further depends on the cost of that analysis and the potential benefits of more accurate information.

CVP Analysis and Multiple Products

CVP analysis assumes that the fixed and variable costs of each product can be identified separately. An organization that provides multiple products, however, usually has costs that are common to multiple products. Under these circumstances, CVP analysis is not a very good planning tool unless the multiple products can be considered a "basket" of goods. The basket consists of all the different goods provided by the organization in proportion to their relative sales mix. In this way the basket would be treated as a single good. CVP analysis could then be used on the basket of goods. This procedure only works if the proportions of different products in the basket remain constant.

NUMERICAL EXAMPLE 5.9

A company is considering buying a factory that makes personal computers and laser printers. The factory is expected to make and sell twice as many personal computers as laser printers. The factory has annual fixed costs of $20 million that are not identified with either the personal computers or the laser printers. The sales price and variable cost per unit of the personal computer are $1,000 and $400, respectively. The sales price and variable cost per unit of the laser printer are $800 and $300, respectively. How many units of personal computers and laser printers must be sold to break even?

■ **SOLUTION** To solve this problem a basket of both goods must be established. Because the products are made and sold in a 2-to-1 proportion, the basket should contain two personal computers and one laser printer. The sales revenue of this basket is (2)($1,000/personal computer) + (1)($800/laser printer), or $2,800. The variable cost of this basket is (2)($400/personal computer) + (1)($300/laser printer), or $1,100. The break-even quantity of this basket is

$$\text{Quantity} = (\$20{,}000{,}000)/(\$2{,}800 - \$1{,}100) = 11{,}765 \text{ baskets}$$

The 11,765 baskets are equivalent to 23,530 (11,765 × 2) personal computers and 11,765 laser printers.

CONCEPT REVIEW

1. What is the basic profit equation for CVP analysis?
2. What is the purpose of performing break-even analysis?
3. What are the major assumptions of CVP analysis?
4. How does CVP analysis work with multiple products?

5.3 Product Mix Decisions

An important planning decision that the manager must make is the product mix. The product mix decision determines the types and quantities of products that an organization plans to sell. Important product mix decisions include (1) the decision to add a product or service, (2) the decision to drop a product or service, (3) the decision to make or buy a product or service, (4) the decision to

Football games are not the only use of football stadiums. As you know, football stadiums are often converted into baseball fields, rock concert arenas, and outdoor convention or meeting halls. The opportunity cost of using the stadium during football's off-season is generally quite low, making rental of the stadium usually very reasonable.

process a product further, and (5) the decision to promote a product or service. Each of these decisions is discussed in the following sections.

Decision to Add a Product or Service

When a product or service is added to an existing product mix, costs and revenues will both be affected. Costs will generally increase because additional inputs such as direct labor and direct material are necessary to make the new product or service. Indirect costs may also increase if additional indirect resources such as supervisory costs and utilities are used to make the new product or service.

Revenues will also be affected by an additional product. Revenues from selling the new product will be added to the revenues of the existing products. But revenues of the existing products may also be affected by the new product. A new product may be an accessory of an existing product and increase the sales of the existing product. For example, designing new software for an existing computer should increase sales for both the computer and the software. A new product may also be a substitute for an existing product and replace the sales of the existing product. For example, an improved laundry detergent would probably reduce the sales of existing laundry detergents.

The decision to add a new product should be based on a comparison of the incremental costs and incremental revenues. If incremental revenues are greater than incremental costs, the new product should be added. For example, if a hot dog vendor is considering the sale of soft drinks, she should only consider incremental costs such as the cost of a refrigeration unit and the cost of purchasing the soft drinks. Incremental revenues should not only include the sale of soft drinks but also the effect on hot dog sales. If incremental revenues are greater than incremental costs, the hot dog vendor should also sell soft drinks.

NUMERICAL EXAMPLE 5.10

The owner of a professional football team and a football stadium is considering renting the facility to a professional baseball team. The baseball team would need the stadium for 80 games and would be willing to pay rent of $20,000 per game. The football stadium, which originally cost $20 million to build, can be converted from football to baseball and baseball to football at a cost of $40,000 per conversion. The cost of cleaning and the maintenance due to each baseball game are estimated to be $15,000 per game. Because of the overlap of the football and baseball season, the stadium would have to be converted eight times each year. Should the owner of the professional football team rent the stadium to the baseball team?

■ **SOLUTION** The incremental revenues are (80)($20,000), or $1,600,0000. The incremental costs are (8 conversions)($40,000/conversion) + ($15,000/game)(80 games), or $1,520,000. The incremental revenues are greater than the incremental costs, so the football owner should rent to the baseball team. The cost to build the stadium is sunk and irrelevant.

TOAD HALL BED AND BREAKFAST (CONTINUED)

Ed and Susan White are considering adding a dinner service to the other services that they would offer at Toad Hall. This service would be available to guests and others. The kitchen and dining room are already available, so there would be no additional cost of using the facility. The incremental costs would include food and a cook. The incremental costs of providing 5,000 dinners annually are estimated to be $150,000. The average meal price is estimated to be $40. In addition, having a dinner service should increase room rentals (at $150 per room) by 200. Given this information, Sue and Ed calculate the additional profit the dinner service will generate:

Incremental revenues:	
Meals ($40)(5,000)	$200,000
Additional room rental revenues ($150)(200)	30,000
Total incremental revenues	$230,000
Incremental costs:	
Food and cook	$150,000
Variable room costs ($26)(200)	5,200
Total incremental costs	$155,200
Excess of incremental revenues over incremental costs:	$ 74,800

These additional estimated profits make the purchase of Toad Hall much more appealing.

Decision to Drop a Product or Service

Not all products and services are a success. Even previously successful products and services may lose their popularity with customers. At some point, management must decide when to drop these products or services. The product cost is the forgone opportunity of using the resources that make the product. When the product cost is estimated to be greater than the sales price of the product, the product should be dropped.

    The cost of making a product, however, is not always known and is often approximated using historical direct and indirect costs. The indirect costs are traced to the product through some cost driver. These indirect costs include overhead items, such as the supervisor's salary, that may not disappear if a product

WHAT'S HAPPENING

After dropping apparently unprofitable flights to certain cities, an airline company finds that its other flights are suddenly unprofitable. Why is this happening?

is dropped. In other words, not all of the estimated product costs may be avoidable if a product is dropped. A manager should attempt to identify the **avoidable product or service costs** in making a decision to drop a product or service. If avoidable costs are greater than the revenue of a product, the product should be dropped from the product mix.

NUMERICAL EXAMPLE 5.11

Based on the following information, a plastic pipe manufacturer is considering dropping from its product mix a pipe that can handle high pressure:

Revenues from high pressure pipe	$ 100,000
Costs from high pressure pipe:	
Direct material	(30,000)
Direct labor	(50,000)
Indirect costs	(30,000)
Loss from high pressure pipe	($ 10,000)

What factors should the manufacturer consider before dropping this product?

■ **SOLUTION** Direct costs are generally avoidable, but the indirect costs may not be avoidable. If only half of the indirect costs ($15,000) are avoidable, then revenues ($100,000) are greater than avoidable costs ($95,000). Another factor to consider is the possibility of an alternative use for the space, labor, and machines presently being used to make high pressure pipe. If there is an alternative use for those resources, managers should consider the forgone profit from those alternative uses as part of the opportunity cost of making high pressure pipe. Also, managers should consider the effect of dropping the high pressure pipe on the demand for its other products.

Decision to Make or Buy a Product or Service

Boeing Company is a producer of commercial airplanes. But most of the parts of airplanes produced by Boeing are made by other companies. Boeing imports these parts from all over the world and then assembles the airplanes in the United States (primarily near Seattle, Washington). Why doesn't Boeing make the various parts itself? Also, many companies have decided not to do their own data processing or tax accounting; they hire other companies to perform those functions. Why is there a reluctance to do their own data processing and tax accounting?

Organizations must decide what they can do themselves and what they should pay other organizations to do. This is the outsourcing decision described in Chapter 3. The basis for this decision should be a comparison of the opportunity costs of doing it themselves with the cost of purchasing the product. If the cost of purchasing the product is lower than the opportunity cost of providing the product themselves, the organization should purchase the product from the other organization.

The problem once again is identifying the opportunity costs. Estimated product costs are not always good approximations of the opportunity cost. Identification of avoidable costs if the product or service is currently provided in-house

Outsourcing at Sun Microsystems allows the company to focus on what it does best: designing. Identifying processes that can be done efficiently in-house and outsourcing other processes is an important decision for an organization.

is important. Traced overhead costs are not always avoidable if an organization decides to use an outside supplier. On the other hand, if the product is currently being provided by an outside supplier, the incremental costs of providing the product in-house should be identified if in-house production is being considered.

Other factors are also important with the make-or-buy decision. Using outside suppliers gives an organization less control over quality and timely delivery. But outside suppliers often have the expertise and machinery to provide the product at a relatively lower cost than the organization.

Some organizations have taken outsourcing (the use of outside suppliers) to an extreme. Sun Microsystems, a maker of computer workstations, concentrates on hardware and software design. Every other process is outsourced. The employees of the company never touch its top-selling products.[1]

TOAD HALL BED AND BREAKFAST (CONTINUED)

Susan and Ed White have thought of another way to make the Toad Hall Bed and Breakfast more profitable. Instead of making breakfast and dinner for guests, they could have the breakfast and dinners catered. By using a catering service, $100,000 in remodeling costs could be saved because the kitchen would not have to satisfy health code requirements. Also, a cook would not have to be hired. The breakfast costs of $3 per person would also be saved. A caterer would supply breakfasts for $5 each and dinners for $30 each. Dinners would still be sold for $40 each, and breakfast would be included as part of the rental of the room. The Whites assume that 2,500 breakfasts and 5,000 dinners would be served annually.

Incremental annual costs of providing breakfast and dinner (not catered):

Breakfasts ($3)(2,500)	$7,500
Dinners (food and cook)	150,000
Interest forgone in remodeling kitchen ($100,000)(10%)	10,000
Total incremental costs	$167,500
Catering costs	
Breakfasts ($5)(2,500)	$12,500
Dinners ($30)(5,000)	150,000
Total catering costs	$162,500

Catering the breakfasts and dinners will save $167,500 − $162,500, or $5,000 per year. The Whites are uncertain, however, if the catering company is reliable, so they decide not to use the catering service.

Decision to Process a Service or Product Further

Another decision related to the product mix is whether to process a product further and sell a more refined product. For example, wooden furniture may be sold without a stain or paint finish or already stained or painted. Also, a restaurant may choose to serve food as a buffet or deliver it directly to the table by a waiter or waitress. The decision to process further is based on a comparison of the incremental costs and incremental revenues of further processing. If the incremental revenues are greater than the incremental costs, the product should be processed further.

NUMERICAL EXAMPLE 5.12

A department store is deciding whether to sell bicycles assembled or unassembled. An unassembled bicycle is purchased by the department store for $100 and can be sold unassembled for $200. To assemble a bicycle requires a half hour of labor time. Labor costs $16 per hour. If the department store assembles the bicycle, it sells for $210. Should the bicycle be assembled by the department store or sold unassembled?

■ **SOLUTION** The incremental revenues are $210 − $200, or $10. The incremental costs are the cost of assembly or (1/2 hour)($16 per hour) or $8. The incremental revenues are greater than the incremental costs, so the bicycle should be assembled by the department store. Note that the department store's purchase cost of $100 is irrelevant in this decision. Once the department store purchases the unassembled bicycle, the $100 is a sunk cost.

Decision to Promote a Product or Service

The decision to promote a product or service is also based on a comparison of incremental costs and incremental revenues. In the case of advertising, the incremental revenues are the additional sales generated by the advertising. The incremental costs are the additional advertising costs and the additional costs of making more units. If the incremental revenues are greater than the incremental costs, the advertising campaign should proceed.

Another promotion decision for an organization is which one of its products to persuade a customer to buy. For example, which car on the lot of a new car dealership would the owner want the customer to buy? Which type of ticket does the manager of a baseball team want a fan to purchase? The organization wants to sell the product that generates the most profit. The contribution margin per unit is the profit from selling one more unit of a product if the organization is operating below capacity. The product with the highest contribution margin per unit is the product that will generate the most profit if sold. For most car manufacturers, the higher priced cars with more luxury options have the higher contribution margin per unit. Therefore, most car sales people will push customers to buy more expensive cars.

NUMERICAL EXAMPLE 5.13

A company manufactures three types of lawn tractors in separate divisions. Their costs and prices are:

Type of Tractor	Fixed Costs	Variable Cost per Unit	Price per Unit
MB-2000	$10,000,000	$500	$800
MB-2400	$30,000,000	700	1,300
MB-2800	$40,000,000	1,000	1,500

Assume all three divisions are operating below capacity. If a customer decided to buy one of these three tractors, which one should the company promote?

■ **SOLUTION** The contribution margins per unit of the three types of tractors are:

Type of Tractor	Contribution Margin per Unit
MB-2000	$300
MB-2400	600
MB-2800	500

The MB-2400 has the highest contribution margin per unit and is the tractor that the company prefers to sell. The fixed costs are irrelevant in this decision.

CONCEPT REVIEW

1. What types of costs should be considered in making a decision to add a product?
2. Why are avoidable costs used to make a decision to drop a product?
3. Why do some organizations decide to buy products rather than make them?
4. How should an organization decide whether to process a product further?
5. What types of products do organizations prefer to sell?

5.4 Product Mix Decisions with Constraints

If organizations are operating below capacity and the variable cost approximates the opportunity cost of making further units, the organization prefers to make and sell more of the product with the highest contribution margin per unit. If there is a capacity constraint that affects multiple products or services, however, the problem becomes more complex. For example, suppose a machine that is used to process more than one product is operating at capacity. If the organization has some flexibility in determining which product uses the machine more frequently, how should the organization make that decision?

Product Mix Decisions with a Single Constraint

The product with the highest contribution margin per unit is not necessarily the product that should have priority on a machine that is a constrained resource. Instead, the organization should determine which product yields the highest contribution margin per use of the machine. If a product with a high contribution margin per unit requires considerable machine time, the contribution margin per use of the machine would be low. Products with low contribution margins per unit that can be processed quickly on the machine will have high contribution margins per use of the machine. The following example demonstrates this relation (CM is the contribution margin):

Product	CM/Unit	Units/Machine Hour	CM/Machine Hour
A	$8	3	$24
B	$3	10	$30

In this example, using the machine on B, the low contribution margin product, produces a higher contribution margin per machine hour. Because the machine is the constraint in the production process for both products A and B, the organization wants to use the machine in the most profitable manner. Giving product B a higher priority in using the machine creates a higher profit for the organization.

NUMERICAL EXAMPLE 5.14

William Chang, CPA, is a sole proprietor. William does corporate, partnership, and individual tax returns. His major constraint and only cost is his time. On average, the revenues and time required for different types of tax returns are:

Type of Tax Return	Time in Hours	Revenues/ Tax Return
Corporate	20	$2,000
Partnership	10	1,200
Individual	5	400

Which type of tax return should William attempt to do if he has plenty of opportunities to do all three types of tax returns?

■ **SOLUTION** Because variable costs are zero (other than the opportunity cost of William's time), the contribution margin of doing each type of tax return is equal to the revenue. The contribution margin per use of scarce resource (hour of William's time) for each type of tax return is:

Tax Return	Contribution Margin/Hour
Corporate	$100/Hour
Partnership	$120/Hour
Individual	$80/Hour

The partnership tax return has the highest contribution margin per hour of William's time and is the preferred tax return to perform.

Identifying the product that yields the highest contribution margin per use of a scarce resource requires simple calculations. If there is more than one constraint (such as a constraint on both machine time and labor time), however, the problem is much more difficult to solve. Linear programming is a procedure that can be used to choose a product mix that maximizes the contribution margin given more than one constraint. This procedure is studied in operations classes and advanced cost accounting classes.

Theory of Constraints

Eliyahu Goldratt in a book called *The Goal* reinforces the importance of identifying constraints within an organization. This process of identifying and managing constraints is called the **theory of constraints.**

In describing opportunity costs and the rate of output, we noted that the marginal cost of making a product increases as capacity is reached. Not all processes within an organization, however, have the same capacity. For example, the steps to make plywood include debarking the logs, heating the logs, cutting logs into veneer (thin layers of wood), cutting the veneer into sheets, sorting the veneer, drying the veneer, layering and gluing the veneer, trimming the plywood, and sanding and patching the plywood. Each of these steps is likely to have a different capacity. In terms of tons of wood product processed per day, a particular plywood factory could have the following constraints:

Process	Tons of Wood Product per Day
Debarking log	300,000
Heating log	200,000
Cutting log into veneer	100,000
Cutting veneer	150,000
Sorting veneer	120,000
Drying veneer	130,000
Layering and gluing veneer	150,000
Trimming plywood	250,000
Sanding and patching plywood	300,000

The cutting of the log into veneer has the lowest capacity and is called the **bottleneck**. Bottlenecks can usually be identified even if the capacity of the different processes are unknown because work-in-process (unfinished inventory) accumulates prior to the bottleneck process. The bottleneck deserves the primary attention of management because the bottleneck inhibits the flow of a product being processed. Care should be taken that the bottleneck operates as many hours as possible. Maintenance of the bottleneck is extremely important and methods of increasing the capacity of the bottleneck should be considered. By increasing the capacity of the bottleneck, the organization can produce more units of its product or service. If those additional units can be sold at a price above the variable cost per unit, the organization can increase its profit.

Dealing with bottlenecks is a continuous process. Suppose that another lathe is purchased to cut logs into veneer in the plywood example. This additional

Chipboard is made by compressing wood chips with a glue mixture. In this picture the chipboard has just been compressed and is heading for the trimmer to cut the board into standard dimensions. The trimming can be done much faster than the compressing, so trimming is not a bottleneck.

> ### THE STORY OF MANAGERIAL ACCOUNTING
>
> ## Team Decisions Regarding Pricing
>
> Pricing is not an exact science in college textbook markets. Typically with new product introduction in other industries, pricing is one of the more crucial decisions facing the product team. In college textbook publishing, publishers do not have complete control over the price. Bookstores ultimately dictate the price for the final consumer, the student.
>
> Additionally, much if not all of the effort expended in marketing new products is aimed at the professor. Professors are increasingly concerned about the costs of learning materials, but seldom do they make a decision solely based on final cost to the student. The *Managerial Accounting* book team is planning on pricing *Managerial Accounting* like its key competitors. How could Peggy, the team accountant, provide additional information that might necessitate an alternative pricing strategy?

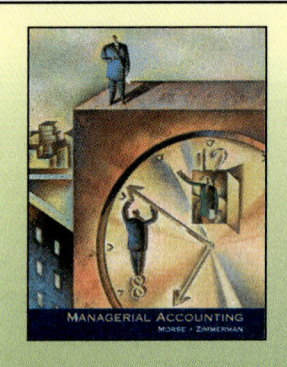

lathe increases the capacity of cutting logs to 200,000 tons per day, so cutting logs into veneer is no longer the bottleneck. Sorting veneer then becomes the bottleneck at 120,000 tons per day. The sorting of veneer then becomes the primary focus of management attention.

There are also control implications in the theory of constraints. Employees are often rewarded based on the output of the particular process they control. The more output they can produce, the more they are rewarded. In an organization with processes that have different capacities, this reward system can lead to dysfunctional behavior. The organization is not benefited by employees creating more output if they are operating a process that is not a bottleneck. Increasing the output of a nonbottleneck process simply increases work-in-process but does not lead to more finished units. More finished units can only be made by increasing the rate of the bottleneck. The excess work-in-process can actually be very costly to the organization because it can cause congestion and use resources. The just-in-time production method, described in Chapter 12, deals with the problem of excess work-in-process.

TOAD HALL BED AND BREAKFAST (CONCLUDED)

> The primary constraint in operating Toad Hall is space. Susan and Ed White could use one of the bedrooms as a private dining room. This choice should be based on the comparison of the contribution margins from alternative uses of the bedroom: room rental versus private dining room. The bedroom would be the last rented and the Whites estimate they can rent the room 100 days of the year with a contribution margin of $124 if rented at $150 per night. The total contribution margin from rental is (100)($124) or $12,400. The Whites estimate they can sell 1,100 more dinners in a private dining room with a contribution margin per dinner of $10 if catered. The total contribution margin from using the room as a private dining room is (1,100)($10) or $11,000. Therefore, the Whites decide not to use the bedroom as a private dining room.

> Following this analysis, the Whites decide to purchase Toad Hall. With the extra $74,800 in profit from adding the dinner service, the Whites can operate the remaining parts of the bed and breakfast at a loss of $44,800 and still achieve a total profit of $30,000. Also, if the bed and breakfast is financially unsuccessful, they assume they can sell Toad Hall to another overly enthusiastic couple wanting to leave the city.

5.5 Summary

1. **Choose prices and quantities to maximize value given demand and cost information.** Value is maximized when prices and quantity of output are chosen at the output level where the marginal cost is equal to the marginal revenue.

2. **Identify reasons for cost-based pricing.** Cost-based pricing is used when customer demand is difficult to estimate, contracts and price regulations are based on costs, and long-run customer goodwill and competition are factors.

3. **Use cost as a lower boundary for making a pricing decision.** The opportunity cost of providing a product or service should be the lower boundary for pricing the product or service unless a lead-loss strategy is being used.

4. **Estimate the break-even quantity.** The break-even quantity is the level of output that generates zero profit and can be estimated by dividing the fixed costs by the contribution margin per unit.

5. **Estimate the output level necessary to achieve a specified profit.** The output level necessary to achieve a specified profit is the sum of the profit and fixed costs divided by the contribution margin per unit.

6. **Identify limitations of cost-volume-profit analysis.** Cost-volume-profit analysis assumes opportunity costs can be approximated with fixed and variable costs, assumes a constant sales price, can't be used to determine optimal levels of output and price, and does not consider the time value of money.

7. **Decide which products and services to promote or drop, especially when there is a constraint in the production process.** Products or services should be added if the incremental revenues are greater than the incremental costs. Products and services should be dropped if the lost revenues are less than the avoidable costs. Managers who are maximizing profit prefer to sell products with higher contribution margins if the organization is operating below capacity. They will attempt to maximize profit by choosing to produce more of the product or service with the highest contribution margin per use of scarce resource.

8. **Determine whether to make or buy a product or service.** A product or service should be purchased instead of produced if the purchase price is greater than the opportunity cost of making the product or service.

9. **Determine whether to process a product or service further.** A product or service should be processed further if the incremental revenue is greater than the incremental costs.

KEY TERMS

Avoidable product and service costs Those costs that are no longer incurred if a product or service is dropped.

Bottleneck The process of an organization that has the least capacity.

Break-even analysis The process of identifying the number of units that must be sold to achieve zero profit.

Contribution margin per unit The sales price minus the variable cost per unit.

Cost-volume-profit (CVP) analysis The process of estimating profit assuming fixed and variable costs and a constant price over all rates of output.

Dumping Selling products below cost in another country.

Incremental costs The additional costs of making more units of a product.

Lead-loss pricing The selling of a product at a low price to attract customers to buy other products.

Predatory pricing Selling products at prices below cost to eliminate competition.

Theory of constraints A process of identifying and managing constraints in the making of products.

APPENDIX: ACHIEVING A SPECIFIED AFTER-TAX PROFIT

This appendix describes how to modify the cost-volume-profit formulas in the chapter to include taxes. Nonprofit organizations do not have to pay income taxes, but other organizations do. The amount of the tax paid depends on the taxable income and the income tax rates. The profit calculated using variable and fixed costs to approximate opportunity costs is not necessarily equal to taxable income. In Chapter 6, depreciation was also used to calculate taxable income. In this appendix, we assume that the profit determined by the variable and fixed costs is also the taxable income and a constant tax rate (t) is used to calculate taxes. Under these circumstances, the after-tax profit is

$$[(P - VC)(Q) - FC](1 - t)$$

To determine the quantity of units necessary to achieve a specified after-tax profit, the formula can be rearranged to solve for Q:

$$\text{After-tax profit}/(1 - t) = (P - VC)(Q) - FC$$
$$[\text{After-tax profit}/(1 - t)] + FC = (P - VC)(Q)$$
$$[(\text{After-tax profit}/(1 - t)) + FC/(P - VC)] = Q$$

The hot dog vendor example in the chapter had fixed costs of $100 per day, variable costs of $0.20 per hot dog, and a price of $1 per hot dog. If the vendor has a tax rate of 30% and wants to have a profit after taxes of $50 per day, how many hot dogs must she sell? Using the equation above:

$$[(\text{After-tax profit}/(1 - t)) + FC]/(P - VC) =$$
$$[(\$50/(1 - .3)) + \$100]/(\$1.00 - \$0.20) = 215 \text{ hot dogs}$$

How many hot dogs must she sell to break even (after-tax profit $0)?

$$[(\$0/(1 - .3)) + \$100]/(\$1.00 - \$0.20) = 125 \text{ hot dogs}$$

Notice that this is the same number of hot dogs when taxes are ignored. Taxes are only paid when there are profits. At break-even there are no profits, hence, no taxes.

SELF-STUDY PROBLEM

The Small Bike Company is the idea of Charles Johnson. Charles has designed a portable bicycle that can be disassembled easily and placed in a suitcase. He is thinking about implementing the idea and going into production. Charles estimates that the fixed costs of producing between 1,000 and 3,000 portable bicycles will be $50,000 annually. In addition, the variable cost per portable bicycle is estimated to be $40 per bicycle. Charles could outsource the suitcase production, which would reduce the fixed costs to $40,000 annually and the variable costs to $35 per bicycle. If the company makes less than 2,000 portable bicycles, there would be excess capacity that could be used to make 1,000 regular bicycles. There would be no additional fixed costs and the variable costs would be $60 per regular bicycle. There is no other use of the space.

a. Charles would like to make $60,000 annually on this venture. If Charles makes and sells 3,000 portable bicycles (with the suitcase), what price should Charles charge for each portable bicycle?
b. If Charles decides to charge $80 per portable bicycle while making the suitcase, what is the break-even number of portable bicycles?
c. If Charles makes 2,500 portable bicycles, should he consider buying the suitcases from an outside supplier if the supplier's price per suitcase is $10?
d. If Charles only makes and sells 2,000 portable bicycles because of limited demand, what is the minimum price that he should consider in selling 1,000 regular bicycles built with the excess capacity?

Solution

a. Profit = (Price per unit − Variable cost per unit)(Number of units) − Fixed cost
   $60,000 = (Price per unit − $40)(3,000) − $50,000
   Price per unit = $76.67
b. Break-even quantity = Fixed cost/(Price per unit − Variable cost per unit)
   Break-even quantity = $50,000/($80 − $40) = 1,250 portable bicycles
c. Avoidable costs if the suitcase is not made in-house:

Reduction in fixed costs ($50,000 − $40,000)	$10,000
Reduction in variable costs (2,500 units)($40 − $35)	7,500
Total avoidable costs	$17,500
Cost of purchasing suitcases ($10)(2,500)	$25,000

Therefore, the suitcases should be made in-house.

d. Because the regular bicycles do not add to the fixed costs, the variable cost per unit establishes the lower boundary for pricing the regular bicycles. As long as the price is greater than the variable cost, the company has a positive contribution margin from the regular bicycles.

NUMERICAL PROBLEMS

NP 5–1: Optimal Output Levels (LO 1)   Measer Enterprises produces standardized telephone keypads and operates in a highly competitive market in which the keypads are sold for $4.50 each. Because of the nature of the production technology, the firm can produce only between 10,000 and 13,000 units per month, in fixed increments of 1,000 units. Measer has the following cost structure:

Rate of Production and Sales (000 units)
($ in 000s)

	10,000	11,000	12,000	13,000
Factory cost, variable	$37,000	$40,800	$44,600	$48,400
Factory cost, fixed	9,000	9,000	9,000	9,000
Selling cost, variable	6,000	6,600	7,400	8,200
Administration, fixed	6,000	6,000	6,000	6,000
Total	$58,000	$62,400	$67,000	$71,600
Average unit cost	$5.80	$5.67	$5.58	$5.51

At what output level should the firm operate?

NP 5–2: Pricing (LO 1; NE 1) Four Stars Entertainment is trying to decide what price to charge customers to enter its new amusement park. The cost of operating the park is fixed at $300,000 per day. All rides are free with the price of admission. The expected daily attendance depends on the daily admission fee. Management makes the following estimates:

Individual Admission Fee	Expected Attendance
$10	20,000
$20	15,000
$30	12,000
$40	10,000
$50	7,000

a. What is the marginal cost of another individual attending the amusement park?
b. What price should Four Stars Entertainment charge for admission to maximize profit?

NP 5–3: Pricing (LO 2; NE 2) The Benson Shoe Company makes 100,000 pairs of shoes each year. The company has fixed costs of $200,000 per year and variable costs of $10 per pair of shoes. The company would like to have earnings 20% greater than total costs.

What price should the company charge?

NP 5–4: Break-Even Analysis (LO 4, 5; NE 6, 8) A taxi driver must pay $100 per day for taxi rental, insurance, and licenses. The taxi driver charges $0.50 per mile. The gas and maintenance costs are $0.15 per mile. The taxi driver travels 50 miles per day without customers.

a. Not counting tips, how many miles must the taxi driver carry customers to break even?
b. How many miles must the taxi driver carry customers to make $50 plus tips?

NP 5–5: Adding a New Service (LO 7; NE 10, 12) The Beechwood Paper Company presently sells large rolls of paper weighing 2,000 pounds to wholesalers for $1,000 apiece. The wholesalers cut the paper into letter-size paper and package it in 2-pound packages. These packages are sold to printers for $2 per package. There is no waste in the cutting process. The Beechwood Company currently produces 10 million pounds of paper annually at a fixed cost of $1 million and a variable cost of $0.30 per pound. If Beechwood bypassed the wholesalers and cut its own paper for sale directly to printers, Beechwood would have to add equipment and personnel such that the incremental fixed costs annually would be $3 million. Incremental variable costs would be $0.10 per pound.

Should Beechwood cut its own paper and bypass the wholesalers?

NP 5–6: Cost-Volume-Profit Analysis (LO 5; NE 8) You are considering starting a business selling in-line skates (including Rollerblades). You assume the price you'll charge is $100 per pair. You can purchase skates from a manufacturer in China for $20 per pair. Transportation costs to the U.S. are $5 per pair. Administration costs of operating are $1 million, regardless of the number of skates purchased or sold.

How many pairs of skates must be purchased and sold to make $100,000 in profit? (Ignore taxes.)

NP 5–7: Product Mix Decision (LO 7; NE 11, 13) A candy shop sells three types of candy: chocolate-filled, cream-filled, and caramel-filled. The candy shop manager is analyzing its product mix through the following product prices and costs:

	Chocolate-Filled	Cream-Filled	Caramel-Filled
Sales price/pound	$ 3.00	$ 2.00	$ 2.50
Direct costs/pound	(1.50)	(.50)	(1.00)
Variable overhead/pound	(.60)	(.50)	(1.00)
Fixed overhead/pound	(.25)	(.50)	(1.00)
Profit/pound	$ .65	$ .50	($.50)

The fixed costs are not avoidable and allocated to products based on number of pounds of candy produced. The candy shop has excess capacity.

a. Which product should the shop promote, if the promotion will result in the sale of 100 more pounds of the promoted type of candy?
b. Should the caramel-filled candy be dropped from the product mix? Explain.
c. How does the product mix problem change if the candy shop is operating at capacity?

NP 5–8: Cost-Volume-Profit Analysis (LO 4, 5; NE 6)(Appendix) With the possibility of the U.S. Congress relaxing restrictions on cutting old growth, a local lumber company is considering an expansion of its facilities. The company believes it can sell lumber for $0.18/board foot. A board foot is a measure of lumber. The tax rate for the company is 30%. The company has the following two opportunities:

Build Factory A with annual fixed costs of $20 million and variable costs of $0.10/board foot. This factory has an annual capacity of 500 million board feet.
Build Factory B with annual fixed costs of $10 million and variable costs of $0.12/board foot. This factory has an annual capacity of 300 million board feet.

a. What is the break-even point in board feet for Factory A?
b. If the company wants to generate an after-tax profit of $2 million with Factory B, how many board feet would the company have to process and sell?
c. If demand for lumber is uncertain, which factory is riskier?
d. At what level of board feet would the after-tax profit of the two factories be the same?

NP 5–9: Cost-Volume-Profit Analysis (LO 4, 5; NE 6, 8) Leslie Mittelberg is considering the wholesaling of leather handbags from Kenya. She must travel to Kenya to check on quality and transportation. The trip will cost $3,000. The cost of the handbag is $10 and shipping to the United States can occur through the postal system for $2 per handbag or through a freight company which will ship a container that can hold up to a 1,000 handbags at a cost of $1,000. The freight company will charge $1,000 even if less than 1,000 handbags are shipped. Leslie will try to sell the handbags to retailers for $20. Assume there are no other costs and benefits.

a. What is the break-even point if shipping is through the postal system?
b. How many units must be sold if Leslie uses the freight company and she wants to have a profit of $1,000?
c. At what output level would the two shipping methods yield the same profit?
d. Suppose a large discount store asks to buy an additional 1,000 handbags beyond normal sales. Which shipping method should be used and what is the minimum sales price Leslie should consider in selling those 1,000 handbags?

NP 5–10: Cost-Volume-Profit Analysis (LO 5; NE 6) The Rose Bowl sells tickets for $100 per person and has a capacity of 100,000 people. Each person buys an average of $20 worth of food and other trinkets. The cost of providing the food, trinkets, guards, ticket salespeople, and cleanup is estimated to be $10 per person. The fixed costs of renting the Rose Bowl and paying the teams is $10 million. Television pays $5 million for the right to broadcast the game.

How many tickets must be sold to have a profit of $3 million? (Assume no taxes.)

NP 5–11: Contribution Margin (LO 7; NE 5)

A firm makes telephones that sell for $50/unit and calculators that sell for $30/unit. The variable cost of making a telephone is $40/unit and the variable cost of making a calculator is $18/unit. The firm has additional manufacturing costs of $2 million.

a. If the firm sells 100 more units of the calculator, what is the additional profit to the firm?
b. If the firm could sell one more telephone or one more calculator, which product would the firm prefer to sell?
c. Under what conditions would the firm want to drop the telephones from the product mix?

NP 5–12: Cost-Volume-Profit Analysis (LO 4, 5; NE 6, 7, 8)

You are considering the purchase of a hotel with 20 rooms. If you buy the hotel, the fixed costs are expected to be $200,000 per year. The variable costs of renting a room for one night include $20 for maid service and $5 for utilities and other costs. Assume no taxes.

a. If you expect to rent the rooms for $90, how many rooms must you rent during the year to break even?
b. If you want to have a profit of $50,000 and expect to be at 70% of capacity for more than 365 days of the year, what price per room would you have to charge?

NP 5–13: Dropping Products or Increasing Output (LO 7; NE 5, 11)

You perform the following profitability analysis on the products you manufacture:

	Product A	Product B	Product C
Revenues	$300,000	$800,000	$100,000
Variable costs	200,000	500,000	40,000
Fixed costs	100,000	100,000	100,000
Profit	$ 0	$200,000	($ 40,000)
Number of units made and sold	1,000	10,000	100

Fixed costs are sunk and there is excess capacity.

a. Should Product C be dropped? Explain
b. Which product would provide the most profit if one more unit was sold?

NP 5–14: Contribution Margin and a Single Constraint (LO 7; NE 14)

The Warehouse Company makes three types of paper (A, B, and C) using the same paper machine. The fixed overhead costs are applied to the types of paper by machine hours. The following data is used to calculate the profitability of the three types of paper.

	A	B	C
Revenues	$900,000	$500,000	$100,000
Variable direct costs	600,000	300,000	50,000
Fixed costs	200,000	90,000	50,000
Profit	$100,000	$110,000	$ 0
Number of tons	4,000	3,000	500
Machine hours	1,000	450	250

a. If the paper machine is operating below capacity, which type of paper would produce more profit if an additional ton of the paper is made and sold?
b. If the paper machine is operating at capacity, which type of paper would the company prefer to make and sell?

NP 5–15: Contribution Margin (LO 7; NE 5)   Peluso Company, a manufacturer of snowmobiles, is operating at 70% of plant capacity. Peluso's plant manager is considering manufacturing headlights, which are now being purchased for $11 each (a price that is not expected to change in the near future). The Peluso plant has the equipment and labor force required to manufacture the headlights. The design engineer estimates that each headlight requires $4 of direct materials and $3 of direct labor. Peluso's plant overhead rate is 200% of direct labor dollars, and 40% of the overhead is fixed cost.

If Peluso Company manufactures the headlights, how much of a gain (loss) for each headlight will result?

(CMA adapted)

NP 5–16: Break-Even Quantity (LO 4; NE 6)   You are examining ways to expand an optometry practice and its earnings capacity. Optometrists perform eye exams, prescribe corrective lenses (eyeglasses and contact lenses), and sell corrective lenses. One alternative to expanding the practice being explored is to hire an additional optometrist to conduct additional eye exams. The annual cost of the optometrist, including salary, benefits, and payroll taxes, is $63,000. You estimate this individual can conduct two exams per hour at an average price to the patient of $45 per exam. The new optometrist will work 40-hour weeks for 48 weeks per year. However, because of scheduling conflicts, patient no-shows, training, and other downtime, the new optometrist will only be able to conduct, bill, and collect some fraction less than 100% of his/her available examination time.

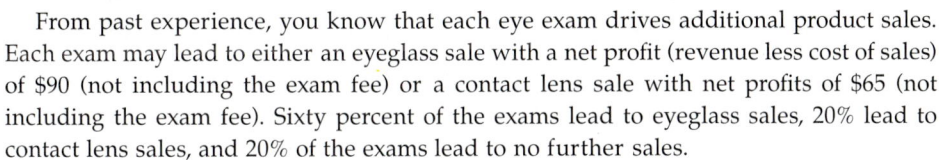

From past experience, you know that each eye exam drives additional product sales. Each exam may lead to either an eyeglass sale with a net profit (revenue less cost of sales) of $90 (not including the exam fee) or a contact lens sale with net profits of $65 (not including the exam fee). Sixty percent of the exams lead to eyeglass sales, 20% lead to contact lens sales, and 20% of the exams lead to no further sales.

Besides the salary of the optometrist, additional costs to support the new optometrist include:

Office occupancy costs	$ 1,200/year
Leased equipment	$ 330/year
Office staff	$23,000/year

In terms of the percentage of available time, what is the minimum level of examinations the new optometrist must perform to recover all the incremental costs from hiring the new optometrist?

NP 5–17: CVP Analysis with Multiple Products (LO 6; NE 9)   The Outdoor Flower Shop sells the following different types of flowers with their corresponding purchase and selling prices:

Type of Flower	Purchase Price per Dozen	Sales Price per Dozen
Roses	$8	$15
Daisies	1	3
Tulips	5	10

The shop tends to sell 50% roses, 20% daisies, and 30% tulips. The fixed costs of operating the shop are $30,000 annually.

How many dozens of each type of flower must be sold to break even?

NP 5–18: Make or Buy (LO 8)   The Neptune Car Company is considering opening a new plant to make cars. The plan is to make 10,000 cars annually at the plant. The size of the plant depends on what parts are going to be outsourced. If all parts are made within the plant, the fixed costs are expected to be $100 million and the variable costs are expected to be $4,000 per car. The company is considering outsourcing the engine, the drive shaft, and the dashboard. The reduction in fixed costs and the variable costs per car due to outsourcing each of those parts and the purchase price of those parts are:

Part	Reduction in Fixed Costs	Reduction in Variable Cost/Unit	Purchase Price
Engine	$20,000,000	$1,000	$1,200
Drive shaft	5,000,000	200	400
Dashboard	6,000,000	300	1,000

a. Which of the different parts should be outsourced based on the costs and prices?
b. What other factors should be considered in making the outsourcing decision?

NP 5–19: Constraints in the Advertising Budget (LO 7; NE 14)

The Promo Company has three different products: Ooze, Mud, and Goop. These products are used as facial creams and sold in bottles. Without advertising, these products are expected to have the following revenues and costs.

Product	Quantity Sold	Revenues	Variable Costs	Fixed Costs	Profit
Ooze	10,000	$100,000	$30,000	$40,000	$30,000
Mud	20,000	80,000	50,000	10,000	20,000
Goop	30,000	150,000	90,000	20,000	40,000

To attract customers to these wonderful products, the company has established an advertising budget of $10,000. The $10,000 is only sufficient to advertise one of the products. The marketing group feels that the $10,000 of advertising for a particular product will increase the quantity sold for Ooze, Mud, and Goop by 30%, 20%, and 10%, respectively. The company is presently well below capacity.

Which product should the Promo Company advertise?

NP 5–20: Maximizing Profit with Constraints (LO 7; NE 14)

The Judson Company makes widgets and wangles. Both widgets and wangles use a polishing machine as part of production. The widgets and wangles have the following price and cost characteristics:

	Widgets	Wangles
Annual capacity	1,000 units	2,000 units
Price per unit	$50	$100
Variable cost per unit	$20	$50
Annual fixed costs	$10,000	$10,000
Polishing machine hours per unit	1 hour	2 hours

The polishing machine can operate for a total of 3,000 hours during the year.

a. What product mix creates the greatest profit for the Judson Company given all the constraints?
b. If there were only machine hour constraints, what product mix would create the greatest profit mix for the Judson Company?

NP 5–21: Bottlenecks (LO 7)

A car manufacturing plant is responsible for assembling. The assembly line begins with the chassis. The following parts are added with the amount of time to assemble:

Part	Assembly Time
Engine	5 minutes
Drive train	4 minutes
Electrical system	10 minutes
Seats	6 minutes
Dashboard	3 minutes
Hood, trunk, and side panels	5 minutes
Doors	2 minutes

a. Under these circumstances, how fast can the assembly line move?
b. Where should the plant place additional effort to increase the speed of the assembly line?

DISCUSSION PROBLEMS

DP 5–1: Adding Services (LO 7)   Eastern University is considering adding 100 more undergraduate students, 25 in each entering class for the next four years. The university president argues that since there is excess capacity in existing classes, no additional faculty will be hired. Thus, the teaching cost of these 100 additional students is zero.

Comment on the president's decision.

DP 5–2: Pricing Services (LO 1)   The following story appeared in *The Wall Street Journal* on December 18, 1990.

> Big brokerage firms, responding to the deep slump in stock-trading volume, are hitting investors with a round of commission increases. Merrill Lynch & Co., the nation's biggest brokerage firm, will raise by 5% the commission rates it charges individuals to buy or sell stocks on any order over $5,000. . . . It is the firm's first commission boost in 4¼ years, and the first for trades over $10,000 in 12 years. (There will be no change in commissions for trades under $5,000.)
>
> Merrill also will boost its handling charges, which cover the cost of processing and mailing transactions statements, to $4.85 a transaction from $2.35. . . . John Steffens, Merrill's executive vice president in charge of private-client businesses, said the firm has been considering raising commissions and fees for some time. "We think [the increases] are justified based on a whole series of things, including postal-rate increases."
>
> "The deterioration in [trading] volumes has pressured a lot of firms to raise commissions to cover their infrastructure costs," said Dean Eberling, a securities industry analyst.
>
> Earlier this year other brokerage houses, including discount firms, raised commissions and fees.

Discuss the issues raised by this story.

DP 5–3: Cost Accounting Standards Board (LO 2)   The United States government often purchases items from suppliers using cost-plus contracts. The government would reimburse the suppliers for their costs and pay an additional percentage for profit. There were many problems associated with this procedure. Finally the government established the Cost Accounting Standards Board to identify acceptable accounting practices in determining the cost of a product.

a. Explain why the United States government uses cost-plus contracts.
b. Explain why the government was having problems with the cost-plus contracts.
c. How would the Cost Accounting Standards Board help these problems?

DP 5–4: Pricing Based on Cost (LO 3)   Your company makes mouse pads. The annual fixed costs of the mouse pads are $50,000 and the variable costs per unit are $1. The president has asked you to choose a price for the mouse pads. A careful study of the competition indicates that a price between $3 and $5 would be appropriate. The president, however, wants to use a cost-based pricing system. He suggests a price that is 100% greater than the average cost. You return to your office thinking that this type of pricing will be simple, but then you become confused in calculating the average cost and the corresponding price.

a. What information is missing to calculate the average cost?
b. What is the relationship between a price based on average cost and the quantity produced?
c. What is the danger of using any type of cost to determine the price?

DP 5–5: Break-Even Analysis with Uncertainty (LO 4)   A timber company is considering how large of a wood lot to purchase. The amount of timber on a wood lot is measured in board feet. The fixed cost of setting up to cut the timber is $20,000 and the variable cost is $0.20 per board foot. The selling price of the timber, however, keeps fluctuating and the timber company is uncertain what the selling price per board foot will be when the timber is cut and sold. The timber company estimates that the price will be between $0.60 per board foot and $1 per board foot. The expected price is $0.80 per board foot.

How can the company perform break-even analysis in terms of size of wood lot with uncertainty about the price of timber?

DP 5–6: Using Percentage Write-Up for CVP Analysis with Multiple Products (LO 3, 6)   A company is considering the purchase of a grocery store. The company would like to perform CVP analysis, but the store has 5,000 different products. There is also a common fixed cost of operating the grocery store. Each product has a different cost and price, so a basket of goods would be extremely difficult to calculate. The store, however, prices each product by writing up the variable cost of the product by 15%.

How could the company use CVP analysis on the grocery store even though there are multiple products?

DP 5–7: The Make-Or-Buy Decision (LO 8)   In a recent *Wall Street Journal* article,[2] the Fleer Corporation announced it will no longer make its own trading cards in house. The Fleer Corporation is primarily known for its sports cards, which are collected and traded by the young and not-so-young. The article stated that the company will focus on marketing, sales, and development. The outsourcing of production was expected to have a slightly positive impact on earnings.

a. How did Fleer make this decision to outsource the production of the trading cards?
b. When a company decides to outsource a process, would an immediate positive impact on earnings always be expected?

DP 5–8: Bottlenecks (LO 7)   An insurance company is primarily devoted to processing claims from insured customers. The processing of claims included an analysis of the claim form, a phone call to the claimant, a visual inspection of the damages, and the writing of a check to the claimant. The president of the company has just heard about the theory of constraints. He thought it was an interesting theory but only applicable for manufacturing companies. Therefore, he felt the theory of constraints was not relevant to his firm.

a. Can an insurance company like this one have bottlenecks?
b. How should the insurance company manage its process under the theory of constraints?

CASE

C 5–1: Promoting a Concert The Excellent Promotions Company promotes concerts. The company has three full-time employees who are responsible for contracting with bands, renting venues for the concert, and advertising the concert. The cost of operating the office including the salary of the three full-time employees (but not including advertising and specific concert payments) is $200,000 annually.

Temporary help is added the day of the concert to assist in security, ticket sales, and cleaning up. These employees are added based on the expected ticket sales of the concert. Usually by the day of the concert the company can estimate ticket sales quite well based on advanced ticket sales. These employees are paid $10 per hour and work for an average of five hours at each concert. The number of employees that must be hired include one security employee for each 100 tickets sold, one ticket seller for every 400 tickets sold, and one employee for cleaning up for every 200 tickets sold.

The promotions company is considering bringing a jazz band in for a concert. The jazz band wants $20,000 to come and perform. The promotions company can rent a local hall that holds 2,400 for the concert for $5,000. The sales price for a ticket to the concert is expected to be $20. A local food service company is willing to pay $500 to the promotions company to sell food and drinks at the concert. The advertising budget for the concert is expected to be $2,000.

Case Questions

a. How should the salaries of the three full-time employees of the company be treated in analyzing the profitability of the concert with the jazz band?
b. The success of this concert depends on the number of ticket sales. What is the break-even point in terms of ticket sales?
c. What is the maximum profit that this concert can generate?
d. Suppose that the promotions company decides to promote the concert and at the day of the concert there has been no advanced ticket sales and there is every indication of a disaster. If the sales price is reduced, the company estimates the following number of people will come:

Ticket Price	Attendees
$20	100
18	200
16	300
14	400
12	450
10	500

What is the ticket price that will provide the greatest profit for the company?

CHAPTER 6
Controlling Organizations

LEARNING OBJECTIVES

1. Identify control issues within an organization.

2. Link decision rights with individuals who have the specific knowledge to make the decision.

3. Recognize self-interest in motivating individuals within organizations.

4. Identify the costs and benefits of monitoring members of an organization.

5. Choose performance measures that reveal actions of members of an organization.

6. Design compensation contracts based on performance measures and decision rights assigned.

7. Balance the assignment of decision rights, the choice of performance measures, and the reward system.

8. Design internal control systems by separating the planning process from the control process.

Miller Department Store

Miller Department Store was built by Charles Miller in 1950. Charles Miller is still the owner of the store, but Robin Wheeler is presently the general manager and responsible for all the operating decisions related to the store. Miller Department Store is in a three-story building in the center of town. The store carries a wide variety of inventory and competes with specialty shops as well as with large discount retailers who have moved into malls in the suburban areas of the city. Miller Department Store attempts to compete through the quality of its inventory and customer service. The discount retail stores, however, have forced the store to compete also with lower prices. In recent years, Miller Department Store has recorded losses and Robin is thinking about reorganizing the store to improve managerial decisions and provide more motivation for employees.

The present organizational chart of the store has Robin at the top as general manager. Under Robin are managers representing the accounting department, the purchasing department, the receiving and warehouse department, the marketing department, the maintenance department, and the retail sales department. The accounting department is responsible for recording daily transactions, depositing cash in the bank, paying suppliers and employees, and providing monthly, quarterly, and annual financial statements. The purchasing department works with suppliers and makes all the inventory decisions for the store. The receiving and warehouse department is responsible for receiving and inspecting inventory arriving from suppliers. The receiving and warehouse department also stores the inventory until needed by the retail sales department. The marketing department is responsible for advertising and customer goodwill. The maintenance department is responsible for maintaining and cleaning the facility. The retail sales department is the biggest department, and the manager of the department is responsible for the hiring of salespeople and inventory display. Under the manager of retail sales are five assistant managers responsible for managing salespeople in each of the following sales departments: men's clothing, women's clothing, sporting goods, furniture, and toys. Prices of all products are 50% over their cost.

All employees are paid a fixed salary. There is considerable turnover among the salespeople reflecting boredom and low salaries. The managers tend to stay with the store for longer periods of time and appear to prefer the job security of working with Miller Department Store to other entrepreneurial endeavors.

Robin is not sure how to reorganize the department store and motivate the employees; but she knows that without a better system, Miller Department Store is unlikely to survive.

6.1 Control within an Organization

One role of management accounting is to supply information to assist managers in making better planning decisions. Planning decisions (described in Chapters 2–5) for products and services (mix and pricing decisions), activities and processes, subunits of the organization, customers, and suppliers can be improved with additional information.

The other role of management accounting is to assist in control. Control is the process of getting members of the organization to work toward the goals of the organization. Control is achieved through assigning duties to the members of an organization and motivating them to act in the best interests of the organization. Individuals owning and operating a business by themselves do not have to worry about control. Because the individual is both the owner and only employee, there are no assignment and motivation problems. As the business grows and the owner hires others to perform some of the functions of the organization, employees must be assigned duties and not all of the employees will naturally act in the best interest of the owners. Employees must be motivated through monetary and nonmonetary rewards to act in the owners' best interest. These control issues are faced by all organizations with more than one member.

Control within an organization is not achieved without a cost. Assigning decision rights and motivating, monitoring, and rewarding individuals within the organization require the use of resources such as time, money, and effort. An organization is only economically viable if the costs of control in an organization are less than the benefits of having an organization. If the costs of control exceed the benefits of having the organization, there is pressure for the organization to divide or disband. IBM and many other companies have recently downsized to a more manageable size. Part of the reason for downsizing is to alleviate control problems when the organization becomes involved in too many diverse activities.

Management accounting plays an important role in control. In particular, accounting is frequently used to measure performance. Performance measures are the basis for rewarding individuals within the organization. Budgeting (discussed in Chapter 8) is an important tool in communicating decision rights. Also, accountants within the organization play a major role in monitoring.

WHAT'S HAPPENING

The last decade has seen the collapse of communism in almost all of the countries in the world. Communism is an economic system that replaces a market system with central planning. Why is a central planning economic system so difficult to implement?

This chapter and the next focus on management accounting and control issues. Chapters 8–12 examine management accounting issues related to both planning decisions and control decisions.

CONCEPT REVIEW

1. What are the two internal roles of management accounting?
2. Why do larger organizations have greater control problems?

MILLER DEPARTMENT STORE (CONTINUED)

One option for Robin Wheeler, the general manager of Miller Department Store, is to eliminate most of the administrative departments and contract with outside parties to provide the services. For example, Robin could pay other organizations to do the accounting, marketing, maintenance, receiving, and warehousing. With these administrative operations in the hands of specialists in those fields, Robin could concentrate on what Miller Department Store does best: purchasing and selling. Robin would no longer have to worry about controlling managers and employees in those departments.

To successfully divest the department store of those administrative functions and have them performed by outside organizations, Robin will have to negotiate contracts with the supplying organizations that will satisfy both cost and quality considerations. For example, the cost of purchasing administrative services from other organizations should include the expected cost of resolving contract disputes. The quality of the purchased services should include timely delivery and flexibility. If the supplying organizations can supply administrative services at a lower cost without reducing the quality of service, Robin should consider disbanding some of her administrative departments and purchase administrative services from other organizations.

6.2 Knowledge and Decision Making within an Organization

The assignment of decision rights within an organization is a critical part of the structure of the organization. The assignment of decision rights determines who is responsible for different facets of the organization. Also, decision rights describe any limitations on decisions made by the different individuals within the organization. For example, a checkout clerk in a grocery store is responsible for collecting money for customers but can only accept checks below $20. The checkout clerk does not have the decision right to accept checks for an amount greater than $20 unless the store manager initials the check.

In the case of corporations, decision rights are assigned by the shareholders to a board of directors, who assign the vast majority of these rights to the chief executive officer (CEO). The board of directors retains the right to replace the CEO and set the CEO's pay. The CEO retains some rights and reassigns the rest to subordinates. This downward cascading of decision rights within an organization gives rise to the familiar pyramid shape of hierarchies. Centralization

This checkout clerk is assigned specific responsibilities. She can accept payment for items purchased, but she doesn't have the decision rights to purchase inventory for the store or to accept checks beyond a certain limit or without proper ID.

and decentralization revolve around the question of partitioning decision rights between higher versus lower levels of the organization. Centralized organizations tend to leave most of the decision rights with the leaders of the organization. Decentralized organizations allow lower level managers and employees to make more decisions.

Throughout the remainder of the book, we describe the importance of assigning decision rights to various subunits and people within the organization. Who or what group of individuals within the organization have the decision rights to set the price, to hire workers, to accept a new order, to sell an asset? One of the key decisions of managers is whether to retain the right to make a particular decision or to delegate the right to someone else. The question of whether the firm is centrally managed or is decentralized is an issue of decision right assignment. "Worker empowerment" is a term that is frequently used to assign more decision rights to workers (i.e., decentralization).

An important issue in the assignment of decision rights is the distribution of knowledge throughout the organization. Individuals have limited capacities to gather and process knowledge. Knowledge is costly to acquire, store, and process. Individuals choose to acquire different types of knowledge, allowing some individuals to make better decisions in one setting and other individuals to make better decisions in another setting. For example, a computer scientist has specialized knowledge to make informed decisions on the operation of computers. The purchasing agent has specialized knowledge about suppliers to make more informed decisions in purchasing items.

One solution to the problem of assigning decision rights within an organization is to distribute them to the individuals with the best knowledge for that particular decision. This solution links knowledge and decision rights. Linking occurs when knowledge and decision rights related to that knowledge reside with the same individual.

Ideally, knowledge and decision rights should be linked, and such linkage should lead to improved decision making. In some cases, however, an organization may intentionally separate knowledge and decision rights because the improved decision making that results from linking may come at too high of a cost to the organization. A manager with the best knowledge of a particular facet of the organization will not necessarily make the decision that is best for the organization. For example, in many firms, salespeople do not have the decision rights to negotiate prices directly with the customer, even though they have specialized knowledge of the customer's demand. Rather, pricing is determined centrally. Organizations that don't give salespeople the decision rights to make pricing decisions are concerned that the salesperson will choose a price that is too low in order to facilitate the sale.

The divergence of individual and organizational goals is the primary reason for not linking decision rights to the individual with the primary knowledge related to the decision. An individual with the specialized knowledge for the decision will not always make decisions consistent with the organization's goals.

If the individual with the specialized knowledge is given the decision right, then costly control procedures must be added to motivate the individual to make the decision consistent with the goals of the organization.

An alternative to having the person with the specialized knowledge making the decision is to have that individual transfer the knowledge to someone else with the decision rights to make the decision. For example, the president of an organization may want to retain the decision rights for long-term investment decisions but recognizes that other members of the organization have better knowledge about customer demand and technical production issues. If the individuals within the organization with that specialized information on customer demand and production transfer the knowledge to the president, the president can make an informed decision. If all the relevant knowledge can be transferred to the president, the decision rights and knowledge are once again linked.

One of the key factors in determining the assignment of decision rights is how the knowledge related to a decision is generated in the firm and how difficult or easy it is to transfer that knowledge. Linking knowledge and decision rights is easier to achieve if knowledge can be easily transferred. For example, prices and quantities can be transferred at a low cost. In these cases, the knowledge is transferred to the person with the rights to make the decision. Other knowledge is difficult to transfer. Technical knowledge, such as how to design a computer chip, is costly to transfer. Knowledge that changes quickly, such as whether a machine is idle for the next hour, is costly to transfer in time to utilize the knowledge. Therefore, the decision right to schedule the machine is usually transferred to the person with the knowledge, and again, the knowledge and decision rights are linked. Likewise, those with technical knowledge often have the decision rights.

Figure 6.1 demonstrates the relation between decision rights and knowledge and the role of accounting. In section A of Figure 6.1, the manager transfers decision rights to the knowledgeable individual but also creates a control system to

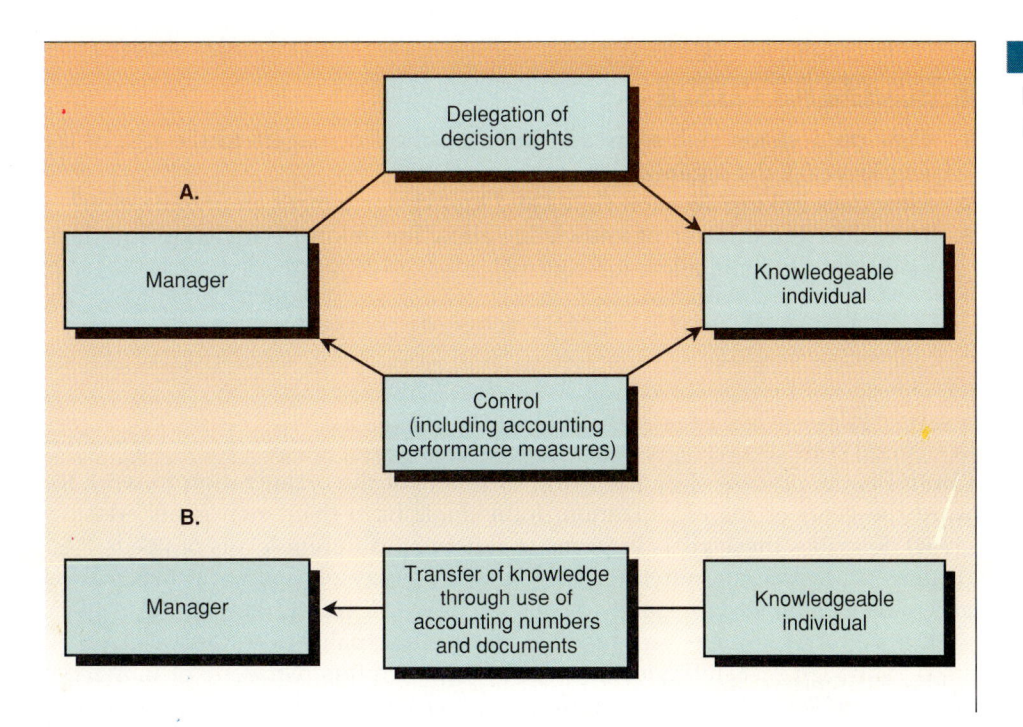

FIGURE 6.1

Knowledge and Decision Rights

motivate and monitor the knowledgeable individual making decisions. Management accounting is used to measure the performance of the individual with the decision rights and is important in the control process. In section B of Figure 6.1 the knowledgeable individual transfers the specialized knowledge to the manager who retains the decision rights. Knowledge is frequently transferred in the form of accounting numbers and documents.

Within all organizations, decision rights must be assigned and knowledge transfer systems developed. Ultimately, the goal is to link decision rights and knowledge. As we will see, accounting systems, especially budgets (Chapter 8) and standard costs (Chapter 14), are important devices for transferring knowledge to individuals with the decision rights or giving the decision rights to the individuals with the knowledge.

MILLER DEPARTMENT STORE (CONTINUED)

The manager of retail sales at Miller Department Store has recently been complaining that he can't sell the merchandise that the purchasing department is buying. For example, the purchasing department has been purchasing conservative clothing for middle-aged women. But the clientele of the store has changed to a younger crowd who are interested in brighter colors and newer fashions. The manager of retail sales also is complaining about the marketing department, which is always advertising items that are currently out of stock.

Robin Wheeler realizes that she must consider knowledge and decision rights when she reorganizes the store. One solution is to make the manager of retail sales in charge of purchasing and marketing given his knowledge of customer demand and the present inventory of the store.

CONCEPT REVIEW

1. How do decision rights cascade from top-level managers to the rest of the employees of the organization?
2. How does linking decision rights and knowledge benefit an organization?
3. How does the transfer of knowledge allow for linking knowledge and decision rights and still allow for control?

6.3 Motivating Individuals toward the Goals of an Organization

Control is the process of encouraging members of the organization to work toward the goals of the organization. Individuals have their own goals. Maslow (1954) describes these goals in terms of satisfying different levels of needs.[1] According to Maslow, an individual first seeks to satisfy physiological needs (food and shelter), followed by safety needs (security), love and belonging (a place within a group), esteem (self-respect), and self-actualization (creative expression). Although research questions the accuracy of this hierarchy of individual needs, there is no question that an individual joins an organization to satisfy some of these needs. Any decision made by an individual within an organization will be influenced by the personal desires of that individual. The problem of the organization is to motivate the individual members to achieve the goals of the organization.

Self-Interested Behavior

One of the fundamental tenets of economics is that individuals act in self-interest. In making a decision, an individual considers factors that cause personal pleasure or pain, such as consumption of resources, social interactions, effort, and recreation. Individuals make cost-benefit trade-offs to maximize personal pleasure and avoid pain. For example, a person must decide how hard to work. The opportunity cost of working is the effort required and the inability to do something else. But working also provides the individual with benefits such as cash and social status.

When an individual joins an organization, the individual perceives that the benefits of joining the organization are greater than the costs. The benefits of joining an organization may be monetary (salary) or nonmonetary (nice working conditions and feelings of power or adulation). The cost of joining an organization includes time and effort.

In accepting a new member, an organization must recognize that the individual is influenced by self-interest. The organization must devise a mechanism that motivates the new member to act in the best interest of the organization but still provides the new member with enough benefits to exceed the new member's costs.

Monitoring Costs

If the actions of an individual within an organization can be easily observed, then motivating the individual to act in the best interest of the organization is simple. The individual is assigned a particular duty (a decision right) and only receives benefits if the duty is performed. Because the individual can be observed performing the duty, there is no question whether the individual should be rewarded. For example, if an individual agrees to sweep floors in a grocery store, that individual can be easily observed sweeping the floors and is rewarded accordingly. The individual will accept and perform the duty if the benefits to the individual are greater than the cost of performing the duty.

But not all individuals can be easily observed when performing duties within an organization. For example, door-to-door salespeople normally operate alone and nobody else from the organization can observe their behavior. When an individual within an organization cannot be observed, there is some doubt if the individual has correctly performed the assigned job. The individual is influenced by self-interest and, therefore, may not act in the best interest of the organization. Salespeople may not exert themselves trying to make a sale.

One solution to this problem is to monitor members of the organization as they perform their duties. But monitoring individuals takes effort and is costly. **Monitoring costs** are a drain on the resources of an organization, but monitoring encourages the individuals of the organization to act in the best interest of the organization. Examples of monitoring include the use of supervisors, closed-circuit television, and random observations. In some cases, however, monitoring costs are very high. A traveling salesperson, for example, can be monitored if another person travels with the salesperson, but that would be very expensive. An indirect way of monitoring a salesperson is observing the person's daily, weekly, or monthly reported sales. The reported sales is an indirect observation of the performance of the salesperson. Another indirect method of monitoring the salesperson is to ask customers about the behavior of the salesperson. Many organizations survey their customers to get feedback on their interactions with salespeople.

This man is on the road selling products to customers. But who's watching the salesman to make sure he is doing his job appropriately? What keeps him from slipping away to a baseball game or his favorite fishing hole during working hours?

Accountants within organizations are often called on to monitor the actions of others within the organization. The role of internal auditors, for example, includes visits to different segments of the organization to verify that organizational policies are being followed.

The existence of self-interested behavior and monitoring costs requires organizations to create ways to motivate its members. To motivate members, organizations must design two systems: (1) performance measurement and (2) rewards. These two systems are described in the next two sections.

MILLER DEPARTMENT STORE (CONTINUED)

Robin Wheeler of Miller Department Store realizes that most of her time is spent on monitoring other individuals within the organization. She reviews most of the decisions made by the marketing and purchasing departments and spends several hours a day in the retail area of the department store watching salespeople and making sure the facility looks nice for customers. Robin would like to spend more time on planning decisions for the store, but she isn't confident that her managers will perform their duties to her liking if she doesn't keep her eye on them. She must think of some way to reduce these monitoring costs.

Performance Measurement

Performance measures describe how well an individual has performed a task. Although the individual may not be directly observed, performance measures can be used to evaluate and reward the performance of an individual within an organization. For example, a painter may be assigned to paint a house. Directly monitoring the actions of the painter is costly, but the performance of the painter can be evaluated by the quality of the paint job. If the paint job is deemed satisfactory, there is an assumption that the painter performed his duty as specified and should be rewarded. The quality of the paint job is the performance measure and is used as a basis for evaluating and rewarding the painter.

Similarly, instructors can't directly observe how much effort students are exerting on their studies. To provide incentive to study, professors assign grades based on student performance on examinations and assignments.

A good performance measure reveals how well an individual has performed his or her duties and motivates the individuals to achieve organizational goals. Good performance measures, however, are not always easy to find. Performance measures should reveal the actions of the individual being evaluated, but performance measures may also be affected by factors outside the control of the individual being evaluated. For example, salespeople are often evaluated based on the amount of sales. But sales are affected by both the efforts of the salespeople and other factors such as the economy and the potential of the sales district assigned to the salesperson. Salespeople could perform their duties exactly as expected by the organization and still do poorly in terms of number of sales.

Performance measures may not be able to isolate the performance of individuals. The performance measure may reflect the joint output of multiple individuals. If two people are carrying a large awkward box and it slips and falls, which worker do you blame? Did one of them let it go? Or, did it slip out of one worker's hands because the other worker tripped? If only team effort can be observed, team members have incentives to shirk their responsibilities. Team loyalty, pressure from other team members, and monitoring reduce this shirking but probably don't entirely eliminate it.

Accounting numbers are frequently used as performance measures. Shareholders use financial accounting reports to evaluate the chief executive officer (CEO). The CEO uses divisional accounting reports to evaluate presidents of the divisions. And presidents of divisions use internal accounting reports to evaluate managers. The quality of these performance measures depends on how closely they reveal the performance of the individual being evaluated.

Certain aspects of financial accounting systems exist today because of the demand for performance measures. Historical cost accounting systems are based on actual past transactions. By focusing on past transactions, the historical cost system may reveal the actions of the managers better than accounting systems based on market value or opportunity cost. Historical cost accounting systems exclude market value changes that are usually outside the control of the manager being evaluated.

Accounting numbers, however, are not always good performance measures. Accounting numbers are commonly affected by factors that are not under the control of the individuals being evaluated and, therefore, don't completely reveal the actions of the individuals.

A single performance measure seldom reveals all of the actions of an individual in an organization. Multiple performance measures will generally more accurately reveal individual actions. For example, professors use multiple performance measures (test scores, papers, and class participation) to evaluate students.

The key to choosing performance measures is their ability to reveal the actions of individuals within the organization. But because the performance measures are used to reward individuals, the individuals will act in such a way to positively influence the performance measures. If the performance measures are not aligned with the goals of the organization, or if they are easy to manipulate, then they will lead to dysfunctional behavior within the organization.

In a recent article in the *Harvard Business Review*, R. Kaplan and D. Norton suggest the importance of establishing goals and corresponding performance measures that provide a comprehensive view of the organization.[2] They call this set of measures the **balanced scorecard**. A balanced scorecard has performance measures related to the goals of the owners and to the satisfaction of customers. These measures also provide information about critical internal processes and

> **WHAT'S HAPPENING**
>
> During the basketball season just ended, a university's basketball team won 6 games and lost 21. The athletic director fires the basketball coach based on the losing record. Is the win/loss record of a basketball team a good performance measure of the coach?

Bausch and Lomb have excellent products, but customer service must still be promoted and rewarded within the organization. A satisfied and loyal customer will ultimately benefit shareholders through higher profits. Bausch and Lomb found that disgruntled customers are a high price to pay for short-term profit.

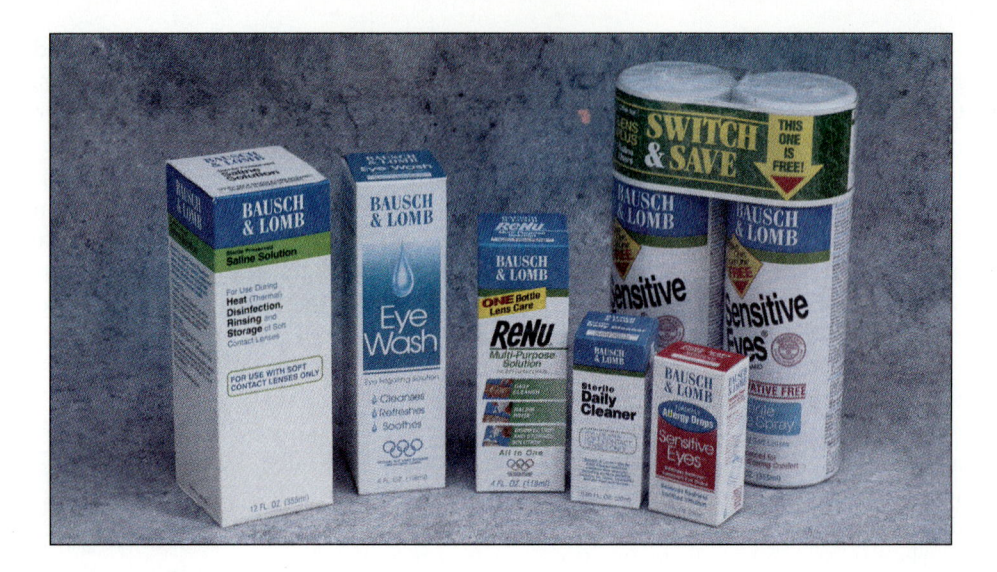

how the organization is learning and changing to take advantage of new opportunities.

An overemphasis on one performance measure can lead to an unbalanced scorecard. At Bausch and Lomb, a drug company and supplier of glasses and contact lenses, employees were under extreme pressure to improve earnings, which were being used as a performance measure. To achieve higher profits, some managers reportedly pressured customers, drugstores, and variety stores to accept excess shipments ($75 million) of sunglasses and contact lenses. Complaints from the customers alerted the board of directors to the problem. If Bausch and Lomb had a balanced scorecard with performance measures of customer satisfaction, the problem is less likely to have occurred.

Miller Department Store (continued)

In reorganizing Miller Department Store, Robin has not thought of performance measures. She knows that the owner, Charles Miller, expects her to operate the store at a profit, so a performance measure for her is profit. But she has not established any performance measures for her managers. What performance measures indicate that her managers have performed their duties as expected? Before choosing performance measures, she must reconsider what decision rights she has given each manager.

Robin makes the following table of decision rights and possible performance measures:

Manager	Decision Rights	Performance Measure
Accounting	Record transactions, make deposits, pay suppliers, make accounting reports	Timeliness of reports
Purchasing	Make inventory decisions	Sales and Inventory
Warehouse	Receive and store inventory	Inventory shrinkage
Marketing	Advertising and customer goodwill	Customer complaints
Maintenance	Maintaining and cleaning facility	Cleanliness of floors
Retail sales	Managing salespeople, inventory display	Sales

Rewarding Performance through Contracts

An individual joins an organization to achieve higher personal benefits relative to personal costs. Organizational benefits are distributed to individual members of the organization based on implicit or explicit contracts. A contract is an agreement between two parties to exchange products, services, or cash. Most employee contracts are agreements between an organization and an employee stating that the organization will pay the employee for services. A salary, bonus, company car, and an office are some of the payments or benefits employees can receive from the organization. An organization can be viewed as a set of contracts among its members that identify the assignment of decision rights, the performance measures to evaluate the members, and the method of sharing the benefits generated by the organization. Members of the organization who perform their specified duties and make good decisions as revealed by the performance measures will be rewarded.

If a performance measure is chosen to evaluate and reward an individual, the individual will perform in such a way as to influence the performance measure. In other words, what you measure is what you get. Therefore, the performance measure should not only reveal the action of the individual but should also be consistent with the goals of the organization. For example, a goal of a health care facility is to provide excellent health care. Health care facilities often use the number of patients seen as a performance measure for doctors. The performance measure reveals many of the actions of the doctors but encourages them to spend less time with individual patients to meet the standards of the performance measure. Less time with patients can lead to poorer health care, which is inconsistent with the goal of the organization.

To motivate members without incurring excessive monitoring costs, the organization must be careful in designing compensation contracts. Compensation by providing rewards is used as a motivational tool. If poor performance measures are chosen, however, individuals within the organization will not act in the best interest of the organization.

In a recent article, Chrysler Motors announced that executive compensation would be partially based on quality measures and customer satisfaction reports.[3] By rewarding these performance measures, the organization is telling the

The pressures to keep a car assembly line moving are enormous. If the line stops, workers are idled and nothing gets produced. Therefore, workers are reluctant to stop the process if small errors are found. If quality and customer service become performance measures, however, workers are more willing to stop the assembly line to make adjustments.

executives that quality and customer satisfaction are important to the company and are goals that the organization is trying to achieve.

MILLER DEPARTMENT STORE (CONTINUED)

Once Robin chooses performance measures for each manager of Miller Department Store, she looks at the reward system. Certainly the present fixed salaries offer little incentive for managers to perform. Robin decides to give each manager a bonus if he or she achieves a certain level in meeting the respective performance measures. But the bonus scheme does not work exactly as she expects. The accounting manager earns her bonus by issuing timely reports, but there are many errors in the reports. The purchasing department manager receives his bonus, but inventory in the store always seems very low. Inventory shrinkage is down and the warehouse manager receives his bonus, but inventory is slow getting from the warehouse to the sales floor. The marketing manager doesn't get her bonus and insists that customer complaints are due to low inventory and impolite salespeople. The maintenance manager gets his bonus by cleaning the floors hourly, but not much maintenance is performed; burned-out light bulbs are not changed promptly. The manager of retail sales doesn't get his bonus and once again complains about not being able to control inventory decisions. Robin realizes choosing performance measures and rewarding managers are more complex than she originally thought.

CONCEPT REVIEW

1. What are the costs and benefits to an individual of joining an organization?
2. Why should an organization incur monitoring costs?
3. What is the role of performance measures within an organization?
4. What characterizes a good performance measure?
5. How are rewards and performance measures related?

6.4 Organizational Structure and the Framework for Change Revisited

Chapter 1 proposes a framework for change within an organization. Figure 6.2 is a description of this initial proposal with more detail. This chapter focuses on the box in the figure related to the nature of the organizational structure. External forces such as technological innovation and global competition cause the firm to face different investment opportunities. To take advantage of these opportunities (and challenges), firms often require new organizational structures to provide their managers with incentives to make planning decisions that will increase organizational value. To be successful in change, an organization must integrate the following three types of systems that make up the organizational structure:

1. Systems that partition decision rights (centralization versus decentralization).
2. Systems that measure performance (accounting reports).
3. Systems that reward and punish performance (bonus plans).

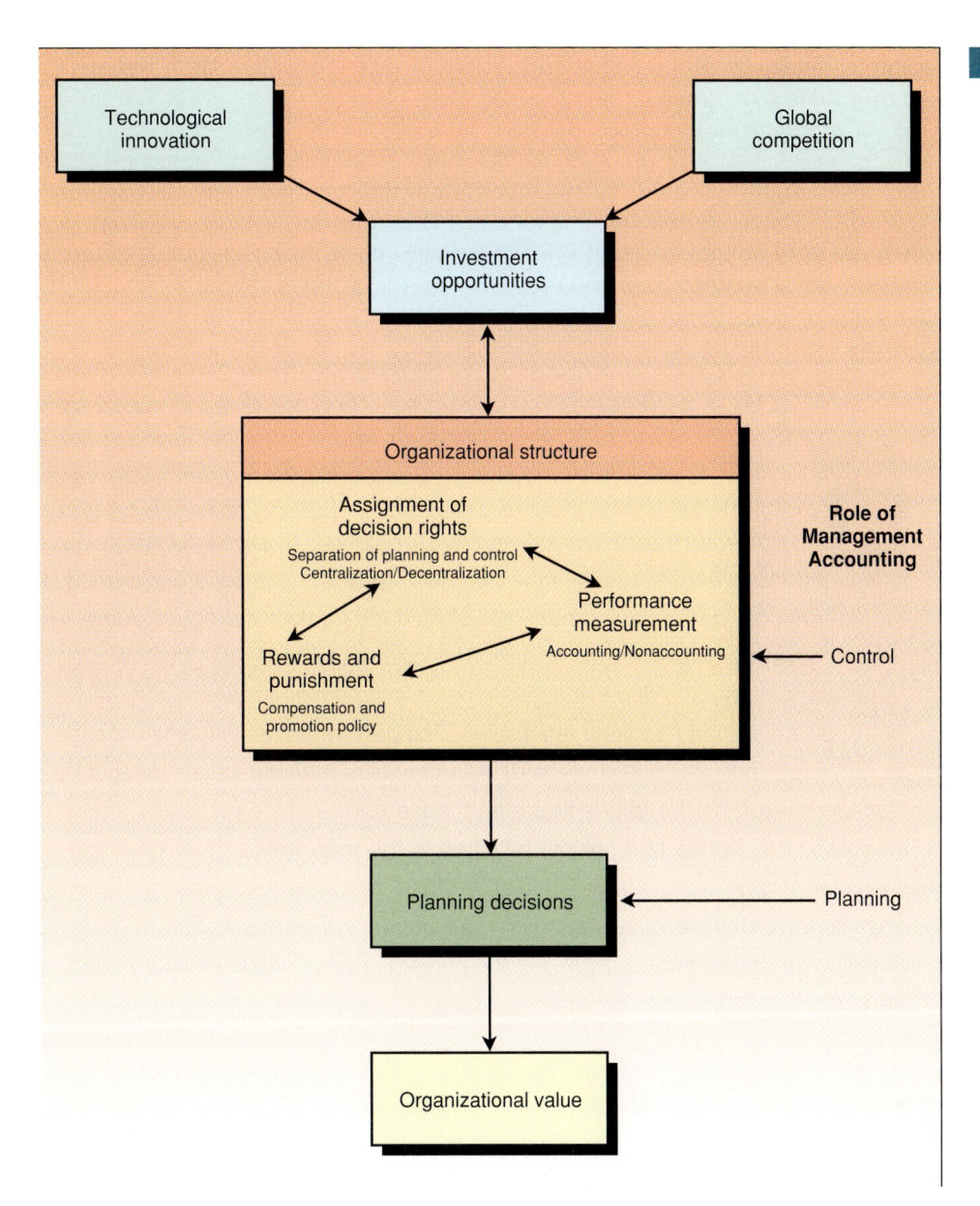

FIGURE 6.2
Framework for Organizational Change

These three systems are like the legs of a three-legged stool. For the stool to remain upright, all three legs must be matched to each other. Similarly, the three systems that compose the organization must be coordinated. The performance-measurement system must measure the manager's performance in areas over which the manager has been assigned the decision rights. Likewise, the reward system must be matched to those areas over which performance is being measured. Though this sounds obvious, what is not obvious is that changing one system requires changing the other two systems.

These systems will continue to change as the environment in which the business operates changes. Keeping the three systems balanced while changing each of them to meet new environmental demands is a problem for most organizations. Organizations must learn to manage change in the environment by making changes within the organization.

The internal accounting system is a significant part of the performance measurement system. Often changes are made in this system without regard to the impact of these changes on the reward and decision-partitioning systems. For example, managers proposing adopting activity-based costing (ABC) systems often find their recommendations rejected. ABC changes the reported accounting costs of products and services. Because these accounting costs are used to measure the performance of other managers, those managers with higher reported ABC costs might be afraid their compensation will be lower, and they will oppose ABC. Managers making changes to the accounting system are surprised when the stool no longer remains level because one of the legs is now a different length than the other two. Because the business environment is constantly changing, management accounting must continually adapt to organizational changes.

MILLER DEPARTMENT STORE (CONTINUED)

Robin's reorganization of Miller Department Store will have to consider the assignment of decision rights, the choice of performance measures, and the reward system jointly. Decision rights should be closely aligned with knowledge, performance measures should reflect decision rights, and rewards should be based on those performance measures. Presently, the purchasing and marketing departments are performing duties for which they have less knowledge than people in retail sales. The performance measures chosen by Robin only partially reflected the decision rights of the respective managers. Managers focus on the duties that affect those performance measures to get their bonuses. Duties that are not reflected in the performance measures are neglected. Some managers cannot affect their performance measures at all and are frustrated because they didn't get bonuses. Reorganization of Miller Department Store will be difficult, but the present organizational structure is not working.

CONCEPT REVIEW

1. What are the three systems of the organizational structure?
2. In which system does accounting play the biggest role?

6.5 Separating Planning Decision Process from Decision Control

Managers rarely are given all the decision rights to make a particular decision. Rather, there is an elaborate system of approvals and monitoring. Consider how a typical decision to hire a new employee works. First, a manager requests authorization to add a new position. This request is reviewed by higher level managers. Once the position is authorized, recruiting and interviewing occurs by the manager making the request and by higher level managers, and a new employee is hired. After being employed for awhile, the employee's performance is evaluated. In general, the following steps in the decision process occur: (1) initiation, (2) ratification, (3) implementation, and (4) monitoring.

Separating the planning decision process from the decision control process is an important method of maintaining control over the members of the organization. By assigning planning decisions to one set of individuals and control decisions to another set of individuals, there is less chance that individual decisions will stray from those desired by the organization. By separating responsibilities for planning decisions and control decisions, the members of the organization monitor each other.

Steps of Decision Process

Initiation is the first step in the decision process and is a planning decision process. Individuals identify potential areas of improvement within the organization such as new products or manufacturing processes. Other examples of initiation are the identification of profitable opportunities and new customers.

Ratification is a decision control process. Individuals with the decision right to ratify other individual's suggestions determine whether the suggestion is consistent with the goals of the organization. The ratification process is especially important if large sums of money are at issue. For example, large loan requests in banks or large investment decisions in manufacturing organizations must be ratified by a higher level manager.

Implementation is a planning decision process. Individuals are assigned responsibilities to carry out the plans of the organization. For example, investments are made and processes are revamped. Individuals are hired and fired. New products are manufactured by the organization.

Monitoring is a decision control process. Some individuals in the organization are responsible for monitoring other individuals to be sure that implementation happens as planned. Individuals and projects are evaluated to determine if they should be maintained or if adjustments must be made. The whole decision process is evaluated to determine if changes should be made in the future.

The fours steps of the decision process are described in Figure 6.3. Note that alternating steps are either a planning decision process or a control decision process. No single individual within the organization should handle sequential steps in the decision process. A different person is often responsible for each of the steps. If the organization is small, one person may be responsible for initiation and implementation and another person responsible for ratification and monitoring.

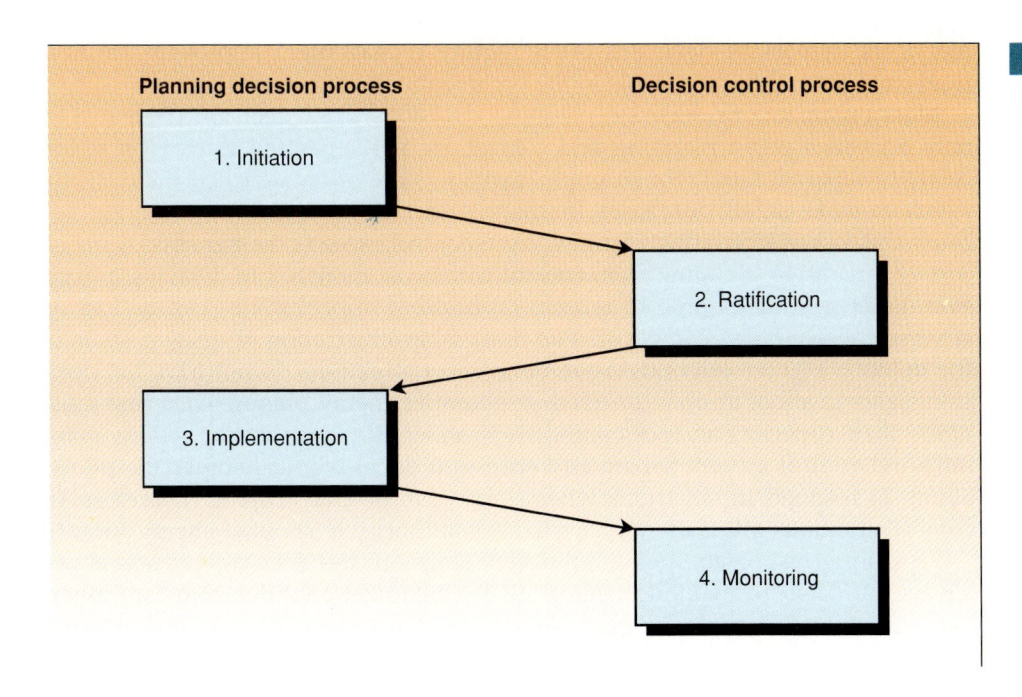

FIGURE 6.3

Separating Steps of Decision Process

Planning decision process	Decision control process
1. Initiation	
	2. Ratification
3. Implementation	
	4. Monitoring

THE STORY OF MANAGERIAL ACCOUNTING

Team Decisions Regarding Contracting

The *Managerial Accounting* book team contracted with Dale and Jerry in October of 1994 to write *Managerial Accounting*. In contracting with Dale and Jerry, the book team had two main goals: meet the late 1996 deadline and produce a high-quality management accounting textbook. To motivate Dale and Jerry to meet the 1996 deadline and reduce their golf outings, bonuses were paid to them upon the completion of each chapter.

To motivate Dale and Jerry to write a high-quality textbook, the team agreed to pay Dale and Jerry a percentage of the sales. A high-quality book would generate more sales, and Dale and Jerry would be paid more. In addition, the team contracted with another company to review and edit the manuscript. How does this other company affect the monitoring of Dale and Jerry, and what members of the *Managerial Accounting* book team are likely to participate in monitoring and rewarding Dale and Jerry?

Examples of Internal Control Systems

An individual manager does not generally have the authority to undertake all four steps in the above decision process. The manager requesting a new position does not have the decision rights to ratify (approve) the request. The separation of the planning decision process from the decision control process is part of the **internal control system.** The U.S. Constitution separates the powers of the various branches of government and operates as an internal control system. The executive branch makes a spending request that is approved by the legislature. The executive branch is then charged with making the expenditures. The judicial branch is the ultimate decision monitor of both the executive and legislative branches.

Hierarchies are another important mechanism for separating planning decisions from decision control. Most organizations are organized as hierarchies. Higher level managers have decision-control responsibilities over lower level managers. Important decisions often require management approvals (ratification) from several higher levels in the organization.

Most organizations separate planning decisions from decision control. The only occasions when planning and control are not separated is when it is too costly to separate them. For example, managers are often assigned the decision rights to make small purchases (perhaps under $500) without ratification because the cost of separating planning from control exceeds the benefits. A major cost of separating planning from control is the cost incurred in delaying a decision. Because it takes time to receive ratification, opportunities can be lost or adverse consequences can occur. The most vivid illustration of delay costs is in the military. Fighter pilots flying in noncombat situations do not have the decision rights to shoot at unauthorized or potential enemy planes. They first must notify their superiors and seek authority to shoot. But in combat situations, planning and control are not separated because to do so would hamper the pilots' ability to respond in situations when delays can be catastrophic. Therefore, in combat situations pilots do not have to seek authority to shoot at enemy aircraft.

Separating responsibilities for different stages of the decision process is not always sufficient to maintain control. Some organizational decisions are inherently difficult to control. For example, the purchasing agent for an organization can collude with suppliers to adversely affect the organizations. The purchasing agent can agree to purchase from a particular supplier based on a bribe. This bribe is called a *kickback*. Recently a real estate executive of Kmart was arrested for taking kickbacks from people selling land to Kmart.[4] Kmart has hired private investigators to examine the ties between employees and outside suppliers. Kmart has also changed its ethics codes to explicitly ban employees from accepting anything from suppliers.

MILLER DEPARTMENT STORE (CONCLUDED)

In assigning decision rights, Robin must think about separating planning decisions from decision control in Miller Department Store. This is especially true in the accounting area. For example, the person who writes the checks to pay the suppliers should not be the person who authorizes the payment of that bill. If the authorization and check-writing decision rights are given to the same individual, that person could potentially write checks to himself. The collection and deposit of cash should also be separated from the accounting for cash deposits. Accountants are generally in control positions and should not be in a position of making planning decisions.

Robin decides that the entire store must be reorganized to give the managers with the detailed knowledge of the customers' desires more decision authority over the merchandise sold in their area. The manager of the women's clothing department is on the floor every day talking to customers about what they are looking to buy. This manager acquires knowledge of the consumers' demands. Robin decides to link the decision rights over purchasing and pricing to the five sales departments. The toy sales department manager has the decision rights to purchase and price the toys; the furniture sales manager has the right to buy and price furniture; and so on. To provide incentives for these managers, each receives a fixed salary plus a percentage of the department's profits.

The five sales department managers still report to the retail sales manager, Julie Shepard, who is responsible for the profits of all five departments. While each of the five sales managers has the decision rights to make purchases and price them for their departments, Julie still retains the decision rights to ratify the purchasing and pricing decisions. This ratification ensures that common themes are captured and that the customer faces a consistent set of policies.

Marketing, receiving, and purchasing now report to Julie and their costs are deducted from the sales departments' profits. Most of the purchasing agents are reassigned to work directly under a retail sales department manager, such as the toy or furniture manager. Julie Shepard's compensation consists of a fixed wage plus a percentage of all the five sales departments' profits, less the costs of marketing, receiving, and purchasing.

Robin still retains the direct authority over the accounting and maintenance departments. Because accounting calculates the profits of the sales departments, accounting should be separated from the sales department. Also, maintenance works on the entire building, not just the part of the building used by the sales department.

188 Controlling Organizations

> **CONCEPT REVIEW**
>
> 1. What are the four steps of the decision process and how are they related to planning and decision control?
> 2. Why might an organization want to separate decision control from planning decisions?

6.6 Summary

1. **Identify control issues within an organization.** The purpose of control is to motivate individuals within the organization to act in the best interests of the organization.

2. **Link decision rights with individuals who have the specific knowledge to make the decision.** Ideally, decision rights within an organization should reside with the individual with the best information related to that decision or an individual in a position to receive that information. Either the decision rights are assigned to the person with the knowledge, or the knowledge is transferred to the person with the decision rights. The method chosen depends on the relative costs of transferring decision rights or transferring the knowledge.

3. **Recognize self-interest in motivating individuals within organizations.** Individuals join organizations and work within organizations to better their own welfare. The benefits each individual receives from joining the organization must exceed the costs the individual bears. Self-interested individuals do not automatically seek to further the organization's goals unless incentive systems motivate such behavior.

4. **Identify the costs and benefits of monitoring members of an organization.** Monitoring individuals within an organization to determine if they are properly performing their duties is costly. Someone must observe their behavior or measure the results of their actions. Without some monitoring, however, individuals will not always perform their duties to benefit the organization.

5. **Choose performance measures that reveal actions of members of an organization.** Performance measures should reveal the actions of the individuals being evaluated and be consistent with the goals of the organization. Also, the measures should not be easily manipulated by the individual being evaluated.

6. **Design compensation contracts based on performance measures and decision rights assigned.** Individuals within organizations should have compensation contracts that motivate the individual to act in the best interest of the organization. The performance rewards should be matched to and coordinated with the performance evaluation system and the decision rights assigned to the person. All three legs of the three-legged stool must match.

7. **Balance the assignment of decision rights, the choice of performance measures, and the reward system.** The assignment of decision rights, the choice of performance measures, and the reward system should be consistent with each other and change simultaneously when the organizational structure changes.

8. **Design internal control systems by separating the planning process from the control process.** Decision rights associated with making planning decisions such as initiation and implementation should be separated from decision rights for decision control such as ratification and monitoring.

KEY TERMS

Balanced scorecard A set of performance measures that provide a comprehensive view of the organization by recognizing the goals of shareholders and the satisfaction of customers.

Implementation The step in the decision process to carry out the plans of the organization.

Initiation The step in the decision process to identify areas of improvement within the organization.

Internal control system A system of checks and balances within the organization that help the organization achieve its goals.

Monitoring The step in the decision process to make sure that plans are implemented as planned.

Monitoring costs The cost of observing members of the organization directly or indirectly.

Performance measures A description of how well an individual has performed a task.

Ratification The step in the decision process to determine whether a proposal is consistent with the goals of the organization.

SELF-STUDY PROBLEM

Jennifer Whitsell had worked for men long enough. She never received recognition for her skills and was paid less than her male counterparts. Jennifer decided it was time to become her own boss, so she started her own advertising agency. Her agency's primary function was to match media companies with organizations that wanted to advertise. Her agency was paid a percentage of every advertising contract that her agency arranged.

Because she had such a difficult time as a woman working for men, Jennifer attempted to give women plenty of opportunities in her organization. But recently she had a problem. One of her female employees had just given birth and wanted a more flexible work schedule. Instead of working from nine to five, Monday through Friday, this woman wanted to work some evenings but take time off during the afternoons to be with her baby. She also wanted to work at home rather than in the office. Jennifer was not sure that allowing flexible work time would work in her company. Flexible time and working at home meant that Jennifer would not be able to control her employees very well because she would not be able to observe their activities. What if employees say they are going to work at home, but they end up playing with their children? On the other hand, she knows that flexible work time will improve morale and may even improve productivity.

How can Jennifer solve this problem?

Solution

Jennifer assumes that she can control her employees only by observing them. There are, however, many ways of controlling employees other than direct observation. For example, Jennifer could have employees work in teams. Members of teams tend to control each other. If performance measures are team-based, the other members will be sure that each does her fair share or they will complain.

Jennifer could also use employee output as a performance measure rather than the number of hours worked. In the case of the advertising agency, an employee that generates more advertising contracts contributes to the agency. The dollar amount of contracts written by an employee could be used as a performance measure. That performance measure would indirectly measure the effort and skill of the employee and is consistent with the goal of maximizing profit for the agency. Hours worked is not a very good performance measure because an employee could spend a lot of time in the office without contributing to the agency.

DISCUSSION PROBLEMS

DP 6–1: Monitoring (LO 4)   Long-haul (cross-country) moving company (e.g., Allied Van Lines) drivers are often independent contractors, whereas intracity movers are usually employees of the company.

Why are long-haul drivers often not employees of a company?

DP 6–2: Voluntary Disclosure of Performance Measures (LO 4)   Prior to the Securities Acts of 1933 and 1934, corporations with publicly traded stock were not required to issue financial statements. Yet many voluntarily issued income statements and balance sheets.

Discuss the advantages and disadvantages of such voluntary disclosures.

DP 6–3: Separation of Duties (LO 8)   In a bank, the employee interacting with someone seeking a loan does not have the authority to make the loan.

Why is the employee not given the decision rights to make the loan?

DP 6–4: Choosing Performance Measures (LO 1, 5)   Jen and Barry opened an ice cream shop in Eugene. It was a big success, so they decide to open ice cream shops in many cities, including Portland. They hire Dante to manage the shop in Portland. Jen and Barry are considering two different sets of performance measures for Dante. The first set would grade Dante based on the cleanliness of the restaurant and on customer service. The second set would use accounting numbers, including the profit of the shop in Portland.

What are the advantages and disadvantages of each set of performance measures?

DP 6–5: Compensation (LO 7)   Physicians practicing in Eastern University's hospital have the following compensation agreement. Each doctor bills the patient (or Blue Cross/Blue Shield) for his/her services. The doctor pays for all direct expenses incurred in the clinic, including nurses, medical malpractice insurance, secretaries, supplies, and equipment. Each doctor has a stated salary cap (e.g., $100,000). For patient fees collected over the salary cap, the doctor retains 30% of the additional fees less expenses. For example, if $150,000 is billed and collected from patients and expenses of $40,000 are paid, then the doctor retains $3,000 of the excess net fees [30% of ($150,000 − 40,000 − 100,000)] and Eastern University receives $7,000. If $120,000 of fees are collected and $40,000 of expenses are incurred, the physician's net cash flow is $80,000 and Eastern University receives none of the fees.

Critically evaluate the existing compensation plan and recommend any changes.

DP 6–6: Performance Measures (LO 5)   Donald Curtis, in the article "The Modern American Accounting System: Does It Really Measure Corporate Performance?" in *The Financial Executive* (January/February 1985), pp. 58–62, criticized corporate accounting systems by arguing:

> The SEC, the stock market, and the corporate compensation committees all seem to focus on accrual earnings as the only reliable and fair measure of corporate performance. . . . What's wrong is that the modern American accounting system is a very imperfect measure of corporate performance. (Whether publicly held or not). The plain fact is that it cannot *technically* do what we are asking it to do with anything like the precision we are expecting. A failure to adequately understand the system's limitations—combined with our penchant for treating things which seem to be quantifiable (such as profit) as more real than things which are difficult to quantify (such as quality of a company's [product])—has, in my view, contributed to serious mismanagement of American business during the last several years.

Critically evaluate.

DP 6–7: Identifying Control Issues (LO 1, 3)   Mary Sweet has just opened a candy store. The store is open from 10 A.M. to 8 P.M. each day, which means that Mary must work a minimum of 10 hours a day 7 days a week. In addition to sales, she must also spend time on purchasing, paying bills, and cleaning up. Mary quickly decides she needs to hire help. Her first hire is a person to operate the cash register for five days of the week. This person will also be responsible for closing the shop on those days so Mary can spend the evenings with her family. While Mary was operating the store by herself, she didn't have to worry about control issues. Now that she is hiring another person, she must consider mechanisms to control the new hire.

Describe some control problems that may arise and some mechanisms Mary could use to help control those problems.

DP 6–8: Linking Decision Rights and Knowledge (LO 2)
Professional football teams have both a coach and a general manager. The general manager is usually responsible for the general operations of the organization and maintains the decision rights for selecting personnel on the football team. The coach is responsible for the training of the football team and making decisions on game day. Many coaches have been unhappy with their relationship with the general manager and feel they should have more decision rights in choosing the players on the team. Some of the top coaches are now insisting on also being general managers.

What are the advantages and disadvantages of separating the duties of the coach and general manager with respect to selecting members of the football team?

DP 6–9: Monitoring Computer Use (LO 4)
Samson Company is an engineering firm. Many of the employees are engineers who are working individually on different projects. Most of the design work takes place on computers. The computers are connected by a network and employees can also "surf" the Internet through their desktop computers.

The president is concerned about productivity among his engineers. He has acquired software that allows him to monitor each engineer's computer work. At any time during the day, the president can observe on her screen exactly what the different engineers are working on. The engineers are quite unhappy with this monitoring process. They feel it is unethical for the president to be able to access what they are working on without their knowledge.

Describe the pros and cons of monitoring through observing the computer work of the engineers.

DP 6–10: Choosing Performance Measures (LO 5)
The president of the Canby Insurance Company has just read an article on the balanced scorecard. A company has a balanced scorecard when there is a set of performance measures that reflect the diverse interests and goals of all the stakeholders (shareholders, customers, employees, and society) of the organization. Presently, Canby Insurance Company has only one performance measure for the top executives: profit. The board of directors claims that profit as the sole performance measure is sufficient. If customers are satisfied and employees are productive, then the company will be profitable. Any other performance measure will detract from the basic goal of making a profit.

Explain the costs and benefits of only having profit as a performance measure.

DP 6–11: Performance Measures and Decision Rights (LO 6)
The new president of the Sawtooth Division of the Waterhouse Company is complaining about the limitations the CEO of Waterhouse company has placed on him. The Sawtooth Division is composed of several logging mills in the Pacific Northwest. These mills were designed to cut large "old growth" logs. Recent regulation has curtailed the cutting of almost all old growth forests and the mills are struggling to get a sufficient supply of logs to operate. The president is being evaluated based on the profit of the logging mills, and if things continue the way they are now, a loss is inevitable. The president's main complaint is that he doesn't have the right to change the logging mills to accommodate smaller logs or move into secondary wood products such as the making of wood trim or prefabricated houses.

Does the president of the Sawtooth Division have a reasonable complaint?

DP 6–12: Performance Measures and Teams (LO 3, 6, 7) Royal Motors is a car manufacturer. Until recently the company has operated as an assembly line. The chassis started at one end of the factory and as it moved through the factory, parts were added to the chassis until a completed car emerged at the other end of the factory. This assembly-line approach was developed by Henry Ford near the beginning of the twentieth century.

Royal Motors has recently decided to change to a cell manufacturing approach. A cell is composed of a team that completes a whole car in a relatively small area. Parts are brought to the cell for assembly. Workers have multiple skills that allow them to perform many different operations rather than a single operation on an assembly line.

On the assembly line, a worker was evaluated by how well the worker performed that single duty. The work performed by the individual workers of the team in a cell is not as easily identifiable.

How should Royal Motors change performance measures to accommodate cell manufacturing?

DP 6–13: Outcome versus Input Performance Measures (LO 5) The Travel Magazine executives are very unhappy with their photographer. She had been sent to Tahiti to take some pictures of sunny beaches to entice visitors to Tahiti. Unfortunately all the pictures taken by the photographer have a grayish tinge to them. The beaches appear to be rather ordinary in the pictures. The magazine executives are thinking about replacing the photographer. The photographer feels that it was not her fault that the photographs turned out so poorly. She worked extremely hard, but it rained almost every day she was in Tahiti.

Why has this conflict developed? Are there ways to resolve this conflict?

DP 6–14: Separation of Duties (LO 8) The local electric utility receives thousands of checks every day from its customers. The following processes occur in handling the checks: opening the letters, recording the amount of the check and the customer's account, filling in a deposit slip for the bank, and depositing the checks with the bank.

Describe methods of controlling these processes so checks are not misplaced or stolen.

DP 6–15: Target Costs as Benchmarks for Performance Measures (LO 6) The manufacturing division manager of a computer chip company had traditionally been evaluated based on costs. As long as he could produce computer chips more cheaply than the previous year, he received his bonus. The first year of manufacturing a new computer chip established the initial benchmark. But the company recognized that this type of reward system for the manufacturing manager would no longer work. First, the product life of the computer chips was becoming shorter and shorter. Some computer chips were made for only a year. Second, the company had switched to target costing. The company's customers would request a computer chip with certain characteristics and a price that the customer would be willing to pay for it. The engineers would then attempt to design a computer chip with all the appropriate features that the customer wanted that could be made cheaply enough to earn a profit. Once the engineers were satisfied that the computer chip had been appropriately designed, the company would sign the deal and turn the design over to the manufacturing division manager for production. The target cost based on the engineers' estimate became the benchmark on which the manufacturing manager's bonus was based. If he could produce the new chip at below the target cost, he would receive a bonus.

The manufacturing manager did not like this new bonus system. He felt that the target cost was imposed on him, and it did not consider the problems of producing new chips, especially the learning process.

How could the process of choosing a target cost and using it as a benchmark for the manufacturing division affect the manager's compensation?

CASE

C 6–1: Woodhaven Service Station Woodhaven Service is a small, independent filling station located in the Woodhaven section of Queens. The station has three gasoline pumps and two service bays. The repair facility specializes in automotive maintenance (oil changes, tune-ups, etc.) and minor repairs (mufflers, shock absorbers, etc.). Woodhaven generally refers customers who require major work (transmission rebuilds, electronics, etc.) to shops that are better equipped to handle such repairs. Major repairs are only done in-house when both the customer and mechanic agree that this would be the best course of action.

During the 20 years that he has owned Woodhaven Service, Harold Mateen's competence and fairness have built a loyal customer base of neighborhood residents. In fact, demand for his services has been more than he can reasonably meet, and yet the repair end of his business is not especially profitable. Most of his competitors earn the lion's share of their profits through repairs, but Harold is making almost all of his money by selling gasoline. If he could make more money on repairs, Woodhaven would be the most successful service station in the area. Harold believes that Woodhaven's weakness in repair profitability is due to the inefficiency of his mechanics. The mechanics are paid the industry average of $500 per week. While Harold does not think he overpays them, he feels he is not getting his money's worth.

Harold's son, Andrew, is a philosophy student at Humanities University, where he has learned the Socratic dictum of "to know the Good is to do the Good." Andrew provided his father with a classic text on employee morality, the Reverend Doctor Weisbrotten's *Work Hard on Thine Job and Follow the Righteous Way.* Every morning for two months, Harold, Andrew, and the mechanics devoted one hour to studying this text. Despite many lively and fascinating discussions on the rights and responsibilities of the employee, productivity did not improve one bit. Harold figured he would just have to go out and hire harder working mechanics.

The failure of the Weisbrotten method did not surprise Lisa, Harold's daughter. A student at Commerce College, she has the training to know that Andrew's methods were bunk. As anyone serious about business knows, the true science of productivity and management of human resources resides in Dr. von Drekken's masterful *Modifying Organizational Behavior through Commitment to a Happy Environment.* Yes, happiness leads to greater productivity! Harold followed the scientific methods to the letter. Yet, despite giving out gold stars, blowing up balloons, and wearing a smiley face button, Lisa's way proved no better than Andrew's.

Compensation Plans
Harold thinks that his neighbor, Jack Myers, owner of Honest Jack's Pre-Enjoyed Autorama, might be helpful. After all, one does not become as successful as Jack without a lot of practical knowledge. Or, maybe it is Jack's great radio jingle that does it. Jack says:

> It's not the jingle, you idiot! It's the way I pay my guys. Your mechanics make $500 a week no matter what. Why should they put out for you? Who cares about gold stars? My guys—my guys get paid straight commission and nothing more. They do good by me and I do good by them. Otherwise, let 'em starve.
>
> Look, it's real simple. Pay 'em a percent of the sales for the work they do. If you need to be a nice guy about it, fix that percent so that if sales are average, they make their usual 500 bucks. But if sales are better, they get that percent extra. This way they don't get hurt but have real reason to help you out.

Straight commission, however, seemed a little radical to Harold. What if sales were bad for a week? That would hurt the mechanics.

Harold figured that it would be better to pay each mechanic a guaranteed $300 a week plus a commission rate that would, given an average volume of business, pay them the extra $200 that would bring their wage back to $500. Under this system, the mechanics would be insulated from a bad week, would not be penalized for an average week, and would still have the incentive to attempt to improve sales. Yes, this seemed more fair.

On the other hand, maybe Jack only knows about the used car business, not about business in general. Harold figured that he should look for an incentive pay method more in line with the way things are done in the auto repair business. Perhaps he should pay his mechanics as he is paid by his customers—by the job. It is standard practice for service stations to charge customers a flat rate for the labor associated with any job. The number of labor hours for which the customer is charged is generally taken from a manual that outlines expected labor times for specific jobs on specific vehicles. The customer pays for these expected hours regardless of how many actual labor hours are expended on the job. Many shops also pay their mechanics by the job. Harold thinks that this approach makes theoretical sense because it links the mechanic's pay to the labor charges paid by the customer.

Case Questions

a. This question presents three popular approaches to motivating employees. Although certain aspects of each of these methods are consistent with the views presented in the text, none of these methods is likely to succeed. Discuss the similarities and differences between the ideas of the chapter and:

   1. Dr. Weisbrotten's approach
   2. Professor von Drekken's approach
   3. Harold Mateen's idea of hiring "harder working" mechanics.

b. Discuss the expected general effect at Woodhaven Service of the newly proposed incentive compensation plans. How might they help Woodhaven and, assuming that Harold wants his business to be successful for a long time to come, what major divergent behaviors would be expected under the new compensation proposals? How damaging would you expect these new behaviors to be on a business such as Woodhaven Service? Also, present a defense of the following propositions:

   1. Harold's plan offers less incentive for divergent behavior than Honest Jack's.
   2. Limiting a mechanic's pay by placing an upper bound of $750 per week on his earnings reduces incentive for divergent behavior.

c. Suppose that Harold owned a large auto repair franchise located in a department store in a popular suburban shopping mall. Suppose also that this department store is a heavily promoted, well-known national chain that is famous for its good values and easy credit. How should Harold's thinking on incentive compensation change? What if Harold did not own the franchise but was only the manager of a company-owned outlet?

d. In this case, it is assumed that knowledge and decision rights are linked. The mechanic who services the car decides what services are warranted. Discuss the costs and benefits of this fact for Woodhaven Service and the independently owned chain store repair shop.

CHAPTER 7
Role of Accounting within Decentralized Organizations

LEARNING OBJECTIVES

1. Use the controllability principle to choose performance measures for managers.

2. Identify responsibility centers based on the extent of each manager's decision rights.

3. Choose performance measures for cost, profit, and investment centers.

4. Identify the strengths and weaknesses of using the return on investment (ROI) and residual income as performance measures for investment centers.

5. Choose transfer prices to create performance measures that reflect the activities controlled by each manager.

6. Use opportunity costs to choose transfer prices that will lead to decentralized decision making that is best for the organization.

Shah Motors

Shah Motors is a new and used car dealership. Jeremy Shah is the owner and president of Shah Motors. Jeremy makes long-term strategic decisions for the company and supervises the three managers representing the new car sales, used car sales, and service departments.

The new car sales manager advises Jeremy on orders to the factory for new cars, makes the final pricing decision on sales, is responsible for customer satisfaction, and coordinates the new car sales staff. The sales staff is paid solely on a commission basis with the opportunity for a few bonuses such as free trips.

The used car sales manager operates out of a lot next to the new car dealership. The used car sales manager must accept from the new car dealership the used cars that are traded in to purchase a new car. The used car sales manager may also purchase inventory directly from wholesalers and people wanting to sell their used cars. The used car sales manager makes the final pricing decision and coordinates the used car sales staff, who are rewarded based on commissions from sales.

The service manager is in charge of the service department, which provides maintenance and repair services for cars. The service manager is responsible for maintaining a parts department and coordinating a service crew. The service crew is paid a fixed salary.

Like most car dealerships, Shah Motors' financial success has varied with the economy. When the economy is booming, the new and used car sales make the business very profitable. When the economy is weak, Shah Motors must rely on profits from the service department to survive. Jeremy Shah feels that his company should not be at the complete whim of the economy and is considering a new compensation scheme for the managers of Shah Motors. Presently, the managers receive a fixed salary, but Jeremy Shah feels that some type of bonus scheme might motivate the managers to work harder to achieve higher profits for the company.

7.1 Controllability Principle

The idea of holding managers responsible for only those decisions for which they are given authority is called the **controllability principle. Controllable costs** are costs that are affected by a manager's decisions. They are potential performance measures for the manager that controls them because by measuring them, superiors can evaluate the decisions the manager made. For example, the manager of a factory is held responsible for the costs of the factory because the factory manager makes decisions that affect factory costs.

A single manager generally does not have control over all the costs of an organization. Each manager has decision rights that are limited by the manager's job description, allowing the manager to control only certain costs. Some costs are also affected by the organization's environment and not controlled by any managers of the organization. For example, the price of raw materials is affected by the economic forces that a factory manager can't control. Uncontrollable costs generally don't reveal the actions of the manager and are poorer performance measures.

Costs can't generally be classified as either completely controllable or completely uncontrollable. Figure 7.1 demonstrates that costs are usually influenced by both managerial actions and uncontrollable environmental factors. For example, if a marina manager is not held accountable for damage done by hurricanes, the manager has less incentive to prepare the marina for severe storms. While managers cannot influence the likelihood of hurricanes, they can influence the costs incurred from the impact of severe storms. In these cases, the manager should be responsible for the portion of costs that can be controlled. Holding managers accountable for only those costs solely under their control does not give them incentives to take actions that can affect the consequences of an uncontrollable event. The feedback loop from the performance measures and rewards in Figure 7.1 demonstrate the influence of the performance measurement system and the reward system on the actions of the manager.

Managers generally don't want their rewards to be uncertain. To avoid uncertainty, managers want performance measures that are not affected by factors they cannot control. Therefore, controllable performance measures such as controllable costs are preferred as a performance measure by managers.

Some performance measures, however, are partially affected by factors not under the control of the manager. In the previous example, hurricanes were not controllable, but hurricanes affected costs. Managers would like to eliminate the uncontrollable portion of the costs as a factor in the performance measure.

One method of removing uncontrollable factors from a performance measure is to compare performance measures of different managers facing similar circumstances. With **relative performance measurement,** the performance of a manager is judged relative to how a selected comparable group performed. The comparison group helps control for random events that affect both the manager being evaluated and the managers in the comparison group. If the costs of the marina manager are compared with other marina managers adversely affected

FIGURE 7.1

Controllability of Costs

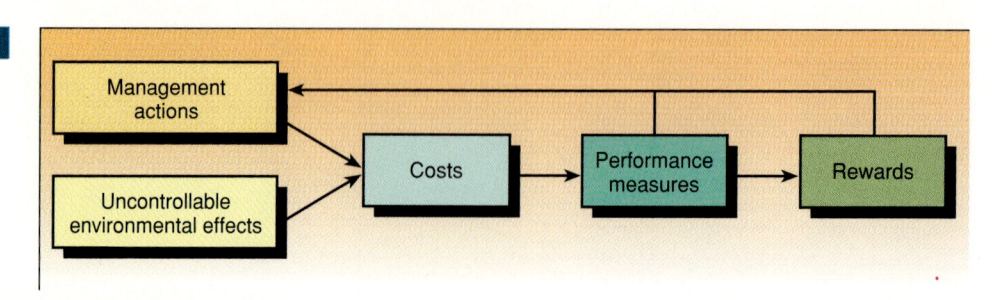

Who is responsible for this train wreck? When something goes wrong in an organization, the controllability principle is used to identify the responsible parties.

by the hurricane, the uncontrollable effects of the hurricane can be eliminated. Relative performance measurement is also used in assigning course grades. Many instructors "curve" the grades. Instead of awarding A's for scores of 94 to 100, the top 15% of the class receives A's. Curving the grades controls for unusually easy or hard exams and is a way of removing some of the risk from students.

Relative performance measures, however, do not recognize whether all the students or managers performed better or worse than some absolute standard. By comparing individual performances with the performance of others, approximately half of the individuals will always be graded better than average and half will always be graded worse than average. There is no possibility for all individuals to be rated above average even though all the individuals performed their duties as specified. Relative performance measures discourage cooperative effort across individuals because individuals recognize that they will be compared with the other individuals.

In summary, each manager of an organization is given certain decision rights. These decision rights define the limits of the manager's control. Within those boundaries is a part of the organization under the control of the manager. Ideally, managers are evaluated based on performance measures of activities controlled by the managers.

What's Happening

The success of an incumbent president getting reelected is closely tied to the strength of the economy. Why should the economy affect the chances of the incumbent president?

Shah Motors (continued)

To analyze his organization, Jeremy Shah outlines the decision rights he has given to his three managers. Before designing the performance measurement and reward system, Jeremy must determine what the various managers control.

Alice Dempster, new car sales manager:
  Controls: Product mix ordered from the factory, price, sales staff, and customer interactions

> Doesn't control: Size of new car inventory and showroom facility, and liabilities of the dealership
>
> Slick Thompson, used car sales manager:
> Controls: Purchasing and size of inventory, used car lot and office, sales staff, and prices of used cars
> Doesn't control: Acceptance of used cars from the new car center and liabilities of the dealership
>
> Grease Johnson, service department manager:
> Controls: Scheduling of maintenance, parts management, and service workers
> Doesn't control: Billing rates and price of parts, size of service shop, and liabilities of the dealership

CONCEPT REVIEW

1. Why is the controllability principle used in most organizations?
2. What are the advantages and disadvantages of using a relative performance measure?

7.2 Responsibility Centers and Performance Measures

Organizations are typically composed of subunits. For example, the firm might be organized into functional areas such as marketing, manufacturing, and distribution departments. Other organizations are divided into subunits by product or service offered. A university, for example, is divided into colleges that teach different topics. Each subunit is commonly subdivided into smaller subunits. For example, manufacturing may be further subdivided into parts manufacturing and assembly, and assembly organized by product assembled. Colleges are divided into departments and specialized groups within departments. Each of these subunits represents work groups with managers holding specific decision rights and responsibilities.

Responsibility accounting is the process of recognizing subunits within the organization, assigning decision rights to managers of those subunits, and evaluating the performance of those managers. These subunits of the organization are called *responsibility centers* and could be a single individual, a department, a functional area such as finance or marketing, or a division. The managers of each of these responsibility centers have different decision rights and, accordingly, different performance measures. In each case, decision rights should be linked with the specialized knowledge necessary to exercise the decision rights. Responsibility accounting then dictates that the performance measurement system is designed to measure the performance that results from the decision rights assigned to the managers. For example, if a manager is assigned decision rights to sell products to customers in New York, the performance measurement of this agent should not include sales to customers in Maine. The following sections and Table 7.1 describe different types of responsibility centers.

Cost Centers

The decision rights of a manager dictate the type of responsibility center and imply the appropriate performance measure for the manager. Some managers have more decision rights than others and thus generally make more complex decisions. Managers with less decision rights have less control over factors that affect the value of the organization. The decision rights or responsibilities of a

TABLE 7.1

Differences among Cost, Revenue, Profit, and Investment Centers

Type of Responsibility Center	Decision Rights	Performance Measurement
Cost center (type 1)*	Choose output for a given cost of inputs	Output (maximize given quality constraints)
Cost center (type 2)	Choose input mix to achieve a given output	Cost (minimize given quality constraints)
Profit center	Choose inputs and outputs with a fixed level of investment	Profit (maximize)
Investment center	Choose inputs, outputs, and level of investment	Return on investment, Residual income (maximize)

*If output is revenue, this type of center is often referred to as a *revenue center*.

manager are commonly described in terms of different types of responsibility centers.

Managers of **cost centers** tend to have the least decision rights within an organization. Cost center managers generally have control over a limited amount of assets but usually have no right to price those assets for sale or to acquire more assets. A manager of an internal service of an organization is typically a manager of a cost center. Managers of data processing, accounting, personnel, and research and development are usually cost center managers. Manufacturing managers are also usually classified as managers of cost centers.

There are two ways cost centers can operate. Some cost centers (labeled type 1 in Table 7.1) are given a fixed amount of resources (a budget) and told to produce as much output as they can for the given amount of fixed resources. For example, suppose the manager of the sales department has a fixed budget for sales staff and advertising. This manager is evaluated based on the amount of sales generated with the fixed budget. The cost center manager usually has authority to change the mix of inputs as long as the unit stays within the budget constraint. The sales manager can substitute between sales staff and advertising as long as the total cost stays within the budget.

The performance measure for the manager of a type 1 cost center is the amount and quality of the output. Producing a large number of units without controlling for quality is not in the best interest of the organization, so quality must be monitored. There is also the danger that an output performance measure will motivate the manager to overproduce. Overproduction can lead to the imposition of costs on other parts of the organization. For example, a

School districts are cost centers. Each school district receives a specified amount of cash for educational purposes. School district officials are responsible for choosing inputs (teachers, books, and buildings) that most efficiently educate the children of the district.

manufacturing manager of a bicycle factory who makes more bicycles than can be sold will impose costs on the part of the organization that is responsible for storing the finished inventory.

An alternative cost center arrangement (type 2 in Table 7.1) is to minimize costs while producing a fixed quantity of output. For example, the manager of a metal stamping department is told to produce 10,000 stampings per day of a fixed specification and quality. The manager is evaluated on meeting the production schedule and on reducing the cost of the 10,000 stampings without reducing quality. The performance measure is the total cost necessary to produce the required output. Once again, however, quality must be monitored because minimizing costs can lead to a lower quality of output.

Neither type of cost center manager has the decision rights to set the price or scale of operations. In both cases, the cost center manager has the decision rights to change how inputs are combined to produce the output. Performance measures include total costs, quantity produced, and quality of output.

Shah Motors (continued)

Jeremy Shah looks at his list of managers and what they control. Grease Johnson, the service manager, controls the input mix (service staff and parts) to repair a car but doesn't control the billing rate or the price of parts. At first glance, the service department appears to operate as a cost center. But Jeremy isn't sure how to choose the performance measure for the service department. Because output is limited to the cars needing repair, using the number of repairs as a performance measure doesn't appear to be appropriate. On the other hand, Jeremy was worried that using cost as a performance measure would encourage Grease to take shortcuts in making repairs. To circumvent this problem, Jeremy decided to use both costs and customer evaluations as performance measures for Grease.

Profit Centers

Some managers have more decision rights than controlling costs through the efficient use of resources. Managers of products typically are ultimately responsible for both the cost and pricing of the product. These product managers are described as managers of **profit centers** because they have some control over both revenues and expenses, which are the factors that lead to profit. Managers of restaurants and retail shops are also typically treated as managers of profit centers.

Profit center managers are given a fixed amount of assets and usually have the decision rights over the pricing and input mix decisions. They can decide what products to produce, their quality level (given some constraints), and how to market them. For example, the local branch of a chain of copy centers is treated as a profit center. The branch manager does not have the decision rights to increase the size of the building of the local branch or open other local branches. The branch manager, however, can change the mix of services offered by the store and is also responsible for the marketing of those services. The local branch manager has the decision right to price the various services offered because the branch manager has the knowledge of the local competition. If pricing decisions were not assigned to the branch manager, the company could not respond quickly to changes in competitor prices.

The primary performance measure for a profit center is the profit generated by the center. Because one of the goals of a profit organization is to generate profit, using profit as a performance measure will generally motivate the profit center manager to act in the best interest of the whole organization. But profit centers are not always independent of other profit centers within the same organization. For example, managers of restaurants belonging to the same chain can affect each others' profits. Customers who have a bad experience in one restaurant of the chain are unlikely to try other restaurants of the same chain. Therefore, other performance measures such as quality and customer satisfaction are commonly used in addition to profits to evaluate managers of profit centers.

Profit center managers have greater decision rights than cost center managers. In many cases, several cost centers are grouped together to form a profit center. The managers of the cost centers within the profit center are managed by and report to the manager of the profit center. For example, a manufacturing unit and a sales unit could be separate cost centers within a single profit center. The profit center manager tells the manufacturing manager what to produce and the sales manager how much cash is available to promote and generate sales. The manufacturing and sales managers can choose the mix of resources to accomplish their tasks, but pricing decision rights are held by the profit center manager. The manufacturing manager is evaluated on costs necessary to produce the required output. The sales manager is evaluated on sales generated from advertising and the efforts of the sales staff. The profit manager is evaluated on the profit of the combined efforts of manufacturing and sales.

> **WHAT'S HAPPENING**
>
> Sears was recently sued because some of its automotive service departments were performing unnecessary repairs. Sears had recently established a bonus system based on profit in these departments. Why would bonuses lead to inappropriate behavior?

SHAH MOTORS (CONTINUED)

Jeremy Shah believes that new car sales should be treated as a profit center. Alice Dempster, the manager, controls price and the product mix but not the size of the inventory or showroom. But using profit as a sole performance measure for Alice appears to be a little risky for both parties. Alice is worried that her performance will be affected by changes in the economy. Profits and, therefore, her reward will be depressed during economic downturns. Jeremy feels that using profits as a sole measure of performance is risky because he is not sure how long Alice will be working for Shah Motors. Some competitors have been trying to hire her. Jeremy is worried she will act in an unethical manner to entice customers to purchase cars without providing follow-up customer service to increase short-term profit. Jeremy decides to use a relative performance measure (profits compared to the industry average) in conjunction with customer surveys to evaluate Alice.

CONCEPT REVIEW

1. What are the two types of cost centers?
2. Why should quality performance measures be used in conjunction with cost as a performance measure for cost centers?
3. What type of decision rights do profit center managers typically have?

Movie directors normally operate on a limited budget and are evaluated as profit centers. Some directors with past successes, such as Kevin Costner, have more budgetary discretion and should be evaluated as investment centers. Costner was given considerable leeway for increasing the investment in Waterworld.

Investment Centers

Some managers have even more decision rights than the manager of a profit center. Managers of profit centers are limited to the use of a prespecified amount of assets. Managers of **investment centers** have all the decision rights of a profit center manager plus the decision right to expand or contract the size of operations. Division managers who control multiple product lines are normally considered investment center managers. Investment center managers can request more funds from the central administration to increase capacity, develop new products, and expand into new geographical areas. These requests are usually ratified by someone in the central administration. Even investment center managers have limited decision rights and some control is imposed.

Investment centers usually contain several profit centers. For example, local branches of a copy center organization are treated as profit centers and regional districts are treated as investment centers. The manager of a regional district is responsible for all the local branches (profit centers) within the district. In addition, the manager of a regional district has the responsibility of identifying and constructing new local branches. If existing local branches are not successful, the manager of the regional district also has the responsibility to liquidate those branches.

The choice of responsibility centers through the granting of decision rights reflects the hierarchy of the organization. The organization is composed of investment centers. Investment centers are composed of profit centers. And profit centers are composed of cost centers. This hierarchy of responsibility centers is demonstrated in Figure 7.2.

Performance measures for investment center managers are more difficult to identify because of the nature of the decision rights. Although investment managers have the opportunity to expand or contract their investment center, the investment center manager is generally not responsible for the financing of the

FIGURE 7.2   Hierarchy of Responsibility Centers

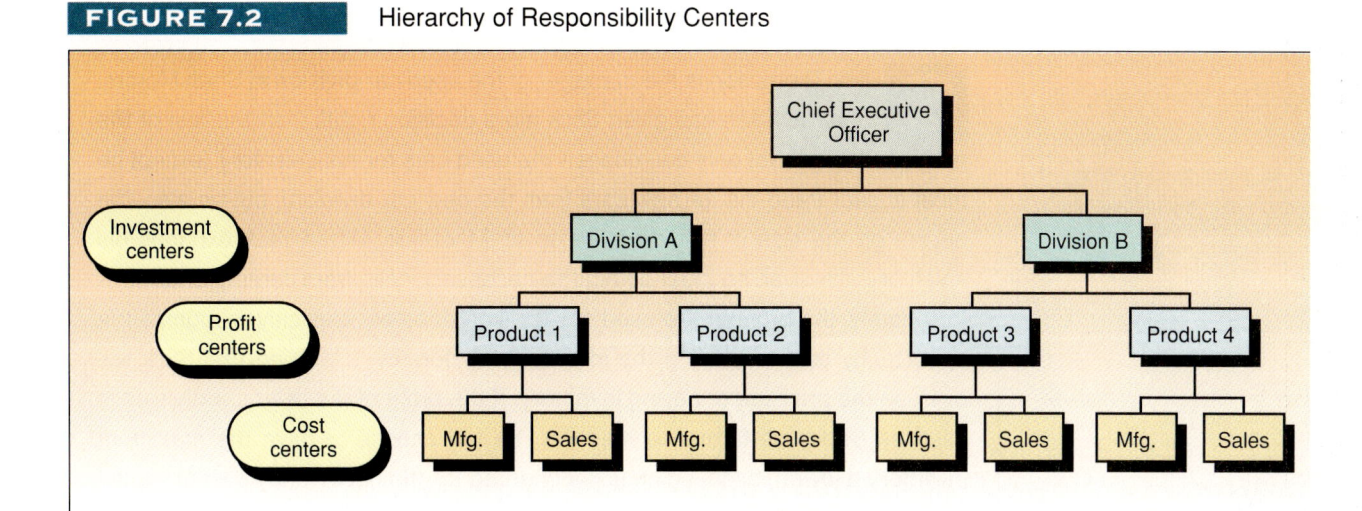

expansions. Cash infusions necessary for expansion usually come from the central administration, which is responsible for issuing debt and stock. The investment center manager generally only has control of assets and short-term liabilities such as accounts payable. The accounting reports of these investment centers have no interest expenses or dividend payments.

The absence of interest expenses in an investment center means that profit is not a very good performance measure for an investment center manager. Investment center managers can generally increase the profit from the assets by increasing the asset size. But increasing the size of the investment center without recognizing the opportunity cost of having more cash invested in assets (the **opportunity cost of capital**) can be harmful for the whole organization.

The opportunity cost of capital is represented by a percentage return that reflects the forgone opportunity of using the cash. The forgone opportunity could be placing the money in a bank account and earning interest or the cost of borrowing more money to fund other investment opportunities. The opportunity cost of capital in the former case is the interest rate earned in a bank account. The opportunity cost in the latter case is the interest rate paid to borrow money. Chapter 13 provides more of a description of the opportunity cost of capital. In this chapter, the opportunity cost of capital is provided. In finance, the opportunity cost of capital must be estimated.

NUMERICAL EXAMPLE 7.1

The television division of an electronics firm requests $100 million from central administration to develop, manufacture, and sell a new type of television. Central administration borrows the $100 million at a 10% interest rate and provides the cash to the television division. The television division invests the $100 million to generate annual profits of $6 million. What is the net effect of these transactions on the profit of the electronics firm?

■ **SOLUTION** The interest expense on the $100 million is $10 million annually. Therefore, the investment in the new television caused a $4 million loss ($6 million profit − $10 million interest expense) to the electronics firm.

SHAH MOTORS (CONTINUED)

Slick Thompson is the manager of the used car division at Shah Motors. Jeremy Shah has given Slick more decision rights than the rest of the managers. Slick not only can choose the used cars for his inventory (except he must accept trade-ins for new cars from the new car division), but he also can decide on the size of his inventory up to $1 million. When Slick expands his inventory, however, he must obtain the necessary cash from Jeremy Shah. Unfortunately, the profit of the used car division does not explicitly recognize the opportunity cost of holding the inventory, so Jeremy is worried that Slick will overuse the privilege of buying inventory. If the profit of the used car division is used as Slick's performance measure, he will choose to have the maximum inventory allowed, because he is not charged for the opportunity cost of capital tied up in inventory. More inventory will increase the opportunities for Slick to make a sale, but Slick would not be penalized for holding excess inventory. Jeremy must find a different performance measure for the used car division, which he recognizes as an investment center.

Return on Investment (ROI)

Because the profit (excluding the opportunity cost of capital) generated by an investment center is dependent on the size of the investment center, performance measures should reflect the size of the investment center. The larger the asset size of the investment center, the greater the opportunity cost of having cash wrapped up in the assets of the investment center. **Return on investment (ROI)** adjusts for size by dividing the profit excluding interest expense generated by the investment center by the total assets of the investment center.

The return on investment (ROI) is a measure to evaluate performance. How would you calculate the ROI of a bet on a horse race?

$$\text{Return on investment (ROI)} = \frac{\text{Earnings before interest}}{\text{Total assets of the investment}}$$

ROI is the most popular investment center performance measure and has intuitive appeal because ROI can be compared to the opportunity cost of capital (the interest rate of borrowing or the dividend rate of stock) to provide a benchmark for a division's performance.

If the ROI is greater than the opportunity cost of capital, the assets of the investment are increasing the value of the organization. An organization that can borrow $1,000 in cash for 10% for a year and turn around and invest the money in assets that generate a 14% annual return on the investment will increase the value of the organization. At the end of the year, the organization must repay the loan ($1,000) and the interest ($1,000)(.10), or a total of $1,100. But the organization has the investment ($1,000) and a return of ($1,000)(.14), or $1,140, for a net gain of $1,140 − 1,100, or $40.

NUMERICAL EXAMPLE 7.2

An investment center of an organization has the following investment opportunities:

Project	Required Investment	Annual Earnings before Interest
A	$500,000	$50,000
B	200,000	10,000
C	100,000	20,000

The opportunity cost of capital of the organization is 8%. What is the ROI of these investment opportunities and which investment would add value to the organization?

■ **SOLUTION** The ROI is the earnings divided by the investment.

Project	ROI
A	$50,000/$500,000 = .10, or 10%
B	$10,000/$200,000 = .05, or 5%
C	$20,000/$100,000 = .20, or 20%

Projects A and C would add value to the organization because the return on those investments is greater than the opportunity cost of capital of 8%.

Du Pont Company ROI Method

In the early 1900s, the E.I. Du Pont de Nemours Powder Company was the leading firm in the manufacturing of gun powder and high explosives with geographically dispersed operations and was later to grow into one of the world's largest chemical companies. To control and evaluate these operations Du Pont managers and Pierre Du Pont in particular developed the concept of return on investment.

The financial staff traced the cost and revenues for each product produced. This gave management accurate information of profits which provided a more precise way of evaluating financial performance. However, they found product-line profits to be an incomplete measure of performance because it did not indicate the rate of return on capital invested. One manager said, "The true test of whether the profit is too great or too small is the rate of return on the money invested in the business and not the percent of profit on the cost."

Developing a rate of return on each segment of business required accurate data on investment in fixed capital. Du Pont undertook a careful valuation of each of its plants, properties, and inventories by product line. These data along with profits allowed management to track ROI by product line. But in addition, they decomposed ROI (profits ÷ investment) into its component parts to account specifically for the underlying causes for changes in ROI. The Figure 7.3 illustrates this decomposition.

ROI is the product of sales turnover (sales ÷ total investment) and return on sales (earnings ÷ sales). Given these data, managers could determine the causes of a product's change in ROI. Du Pont managers used these data to evaluate new capital appropriations by establishing the policy that there "be no expenditures for additions to the earnings equipment if the same amount of money could be applied to some better purpose in another branch of the company's business."[1]

Problems with ROI

Although ROI has the advantage of controlling for the size of the investment center, there are problems with ROI as a performance measure. These problems include difficulty in measurement, not recognizing the risk of the projects, and incentives to underinvest.

ROI is not necessarily a measure of the division's percentage change in market value because accounting income (the numerator of the ROI) is not a measure of change in market value of the organization and investment (the denominator of the ROI) is not the market value of the division's investment. Traditionally the income and investment are measured using historical costs, which may differ from the market value. Accounting depreciation, which is deducted from accounting profits, does not necessarily reflect the change in market value of fixed assets. If ROI is used as a performance measure for an investment center, the manager of the investment center can make inappropriate decisions because of how the ROI is measured. For example, managers will be reluctant to buy new assets because the higher depreciation expenses cause lower profits (the numerator of ROI) and higher net assets (the denominator of ROI). The combined effect will reduce the short-term ROI even though there may be long-term benefits to purchasing the new assets.

The ROI of an investment center does not explicitly recognize the risk of the investment center. From finance theory, we know that higher returns are generally associated with assets that have higher risk. Therefore, a manager who gen-

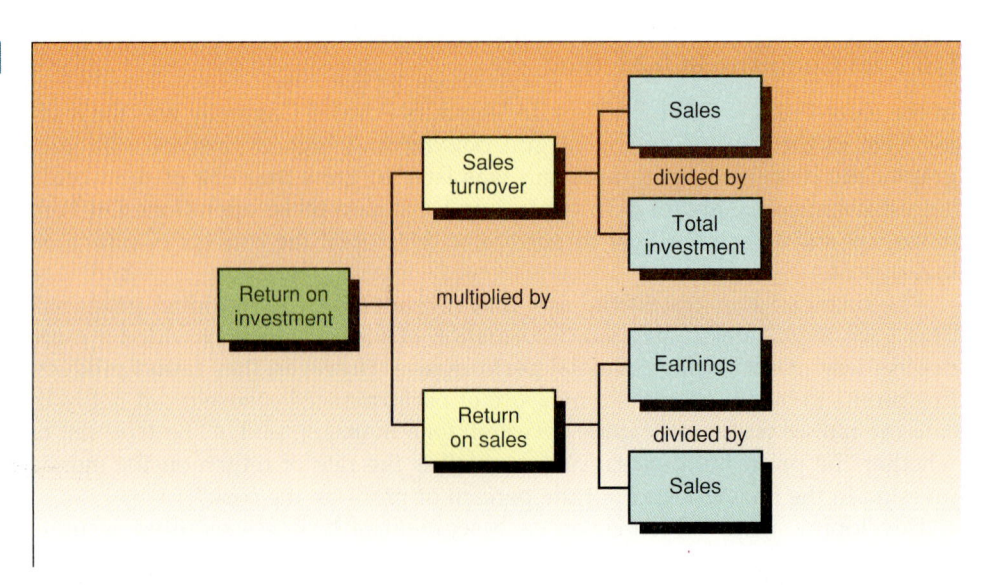

FIGURE 7.3

Decomposition of ROI

erates large ROI could be investing in riskier assets, which may not be consistent with the goals of the organization.

Using ROI as a performance measure of an investment center also leads to an underinvestment in assets. Managers will attempt to increase the ROI by only investing in assets that have very high returns. There is nothing wrong with investing in assets with high returns. As long as the return is greater than the opportunity cost of capital, the organization can increase its value. But by only investing in assets with very high returns, the manager may be forgoing the opportunity to invest in assets that have lower returns that are still greater than the opportunity cost of capital and will increase the value of the organization.

NUMERICAL EXAMPLE 7.3

An investment center manager is considering four possible investments. The required investment, annual profits (which are approximately equal to cash flows), and ROIs of each investment are:

Project	Required Investment	Annual Earnings	ROI
A	$400,000	$80,000	20%
B	200,000	10,000	5%
C	300,000	36,000	12%
D	100,000	15,000	15%

The investment center is currently generating an ROI of 18% based on $1,000,000 in assets and a profit of $180,000. The company can borrow cash at a 10% annual rate. Which projects will increase the ROI of the investment center? Which projects will increase the value of the organization?

■ **SOLUTION** Only project A will increase the ROI of the investment center:

$$(\$180{,}000 + \$80{,}000)/(\$1{,}000{,}000 + \$400{,}000) = 18.57\%$$

Projects C and D, however, will also increase the value of the whole organization because the additional interest expense from borrowing to invest in C [($300,000)(10%) = $30,000] and D [($100,000)(10%) = $10,000] is less than the profits generated by the investments.

Residual Income

To overcome the incentive problems of ROI such as underinvestment and lack of risk adjustment, some firms' use residual income to evaluate performance. **Residual income** is the difference between the investment center's profits and the opportunity cost of using the assets of the investment center. The opportunity cost of using the assets is the opportunity cost of capital times the market value of the assets. The residual income is also referred to as the *economic value added* The following equations define the relation between residual income and ROI.

WHAT'S HAPPENING

A new CEO of a firm wanted to improve the profitability by requiring that all new investments had projected ROIs of 30% or greater. Why did the profits and size of the firm decline as the ROI of the firm increased?

$$\text{Residual income} = \text{Profits} - (\text{Opportunity cost of capital})(\text{Total assets})$$
$$= \left(\frac{\text{Profits/Total}}{\text{assets}}\right)\left(\text{Total assets}\right) - \left(\text{Opportunity cost of capital}\right)\left(\text{Total assets}\right)$$
$$= (\text{ROI})\left(\text{Total assets}\right) - \left(\text{Opportunity cost of capital}\right)\left(\text{Total assets}\right)$$
$$= (\text{ROI} - \text{Opportunity cost of capital})(\text{Total assets})$$

Therefore, the residual income is positive if the ROI is greater than the opportunity cost of capital. A positive residual income number means that the investment center manager has added value to the organization by achieving a higher return on the assets than the cost of using the assets. If residual income is used as a performance measure, the investment manager invests in all assets that have a positive residual income and there is no underinvestment incentive.

Measuring residual income requires a measure of the opportunity cost of capital. The opportunity cost of capital should reflect the risk of the assets of the investment center. Banks are more reluctant to lend money to organizations that invest in higher risk projects. To compensate for the additional risk, banks charge a higher interest rate. This problem is discussed in Chapter 13 and finance texts. By choosing the opportunity cost of capital to reflect the risk of the assets, there will be no incentives to choose higher risk projects just to increase the ROI.

NUMERICAL EXAMPLE 7.4

A tractor division has profits of $20 million and investment (total assets) of $100 million. The division has an opportunity cost of capital of 15%. What is the residual income of the division?

■ **SOLUTION** The residual income is:

$$\$20 \text{ million} - (15\%)(\$100 \text{ million}) = \$5 \text{ million}$$

WHAT'S HAPPENING

A number of large companies including AT&T, Briggs & Stratton, Coca-Cola, CSX, Quaker Oats, and Whirlpool use economic value added (EVA) as a measure of performance. EVA is being widely heralded in the business press.[2] EVA is residual income. Besides adopting EVA, what other changes might you expect these corporations to be making?

The residual income is not without problems as a performance measure. As with ROI, the profits and total assets are commonly measured using the historical costs from the financial reporting system. If the accounting profits vary from changes in the market value of the assets and the book value of assets is not representative of the market value of the assets, then residual income will not function well as a performance measure. Managers will be trying to maximize accounting residual income, but the owners of the organization would prefer that managers increase the market value of the organization.

Another perceived problem is making performance evaluation comparisons across investment centers of different sizes using the residual income. The residual income is an absolute dollar number and is likely to be larger for larger investment centers. For example, consider the example in Table 7.2 of two investment centers, Divisions A and B:

Division A has a larger ROI, but Division B has a larger residual income because Division B is larger. Which division's manager is performing better? If both managers have control over the size of their divisions (they are investment centers), then the manager of Division B is performing better. Although the manager

TABLE 7.2
Comparison of Residual Income to ROI ($000)

	Division A	Division B
Net assets	$100	$1,000
Net income	30	250
Cost of capital (20%)	20	200
Residual income	$ 10	$ 50
ROI	30%	25%

of Division A is operating efficiently with a smaller amount of net assets, the manager of Division A is not able to find as many profitable opportunities as the manager of Division B. The manager of Division B adds more value to the organization and should be rewarded accordingly. The residual income is appropriate for evaluating managers of investment centers of different sizes because the manager has control of the size of the investment center. If the manager does not have control over size and the division is more like a profit center, then ROI is more appropriate as a relative performance measure of managers of different-sized divisions.

Multiple Performance Measures

As in the case of cost and profit centers, the manager of an investment center should not be evaluated by a single performance measure. An organization generally has multiple goals and a single performance measure will not motivate the manager to consider all of these goals. For example, investment center managers are usually constrained in terms of the quality of products they can sell and the market niches they can enter. The reason for these constraints is to prevent these investment center managers from debasing the firm's brand name capital (firm's reputation). For example, Eastman Kodak entered the consumer battery market by creating an investment center called Kodak Ultra Technologies. Kodak has a reputation for high-quality products. One way the managers of Ultra Technologies can meet their profit and return on investment targets is to lower costs by offering products of lower quality than expected by the consumer. Over time, consumers will come to learn of the lower-than-expected quality of the batteries. Ultra Technologies' managers may exceed their short-term target profits, but the market lowers its expectations of quality for all Kodak products. To control this problem, senior Kodak managers continually monitor the quality of the batteries produced to ensure they meet Kodak's quality standards.[3]

The U.S. president is evaluated by voters using multiple performance measures. Economic prosperity, moral leadership, and international peace are some of the performance measures used by voters when they cast their ballots.

SHAH MOTORS (CONTINUED)

Jeremy Shah is considering the use of ROI as a performance measure for Slick Thompson. Jeremy is not concerned with problems in measuring profit and net assets. Most of the assets of the used car division are in the form of used cars. These used cars are normally sold within four months of acquisition, so book value should not differ much from market value and the accounting profit of the used car division should be a close approximation of change in economic value. Jeremy is also not concerned about the risk of the used car division. The sale of used cars tends to be less sensitive to changes in the economy. Jeremy is concerned, however, about the underinvestment problem. He thinks that Slick Thompson may be able to increase ROI by only buying and selling foreign used cars, which generally have a higher profit margin than domestic cars. But good foreign used cars are hard to find and Slick would operate with a substantially reduced inventory. Jeremy feels that the domestic used car market is still profitable and doesn't want Slick to focus on

> foreign cars. Therefore, Jeremy feels that residual income is a better performance measure because it would encourage Slick to invest in all used cars that have ROIs greater than the opportunity cost of capital. Jeremy uses the interest rate on his debt to approximate the opportunity cost of capital.

Identifying Responsibility Centers

Although cost, profit, and investment centers are identified by the decision rights of the managers of those centers, not all managers fit exactly into one of those categories. For example, manufacturing managers are commonly treated as managers of cost centers, but the manufacturing managers typically influence revenues even though they don't have decision rights over pricing. Revenues are influenced by customer satisfaction due to timely delivery and quality. The manufacturing manager does influence timely delivery and quality, so the manufacturing manager is partially responsible for revenues.

Profit center managers seldom control all aspects of revenues and costs. Profit center managers, however, are usually able to make marginal adjustments to the asset size of the responsibility center. Investment center managers, on the other hand, seldom have unlimited authority to increase asset size.

Therefore, identifying the type of responsibility center is often difficult. But attempting to partition the organization into different types of responsibility centers is important for guiding the choice of performance measures. If the manager does not fit exactly into a particular category of a responsibility center, the traditional performance measures of cost, profit, and ROI can be used in conjunction with other nonfinancial performance measures that reflect the decision rights of the manager.

CONCEPT REVIEW

1. Why are performance measures of investment centers difficult to determine?
2. What are the benefits and problems in using ROI as a performance measure?
3. What are the benefits and problems in using residual income as a performance measure?
4. Why is it difficult to classify some responsibility centers?

7.3 *Transfer Pricing*

Most organizations contain multiple responsibility centers. Responsibility centers within the same organization can interact in many ways and can create adverse or favorable impacts on other responsibility centers. A manufacturing department's operating efficiency can be affected by the quantity and timing of the orders it receives from the marketing department. A purchasing department can affect the manufacturing department's operations by the timing and quality of the raw materials purchased. One responsibility center sharing a newly discovered, cost-saving idea or R&D development with other centers is an example of a favorable interaction. Managing these interactions (eliminating the negative ones and encouraging the positive ones) is critical to the successful partitioning of decision rights to the different managers of the organization. The firm's management accounting system can play a powerful role in improving these interactions.

Figure 7.4 presents a typical interaction, which is an internal transfer of a product or service. Division A within an organization purchases raw materials from an external supplier. Division A converts these raw materials into an inter-

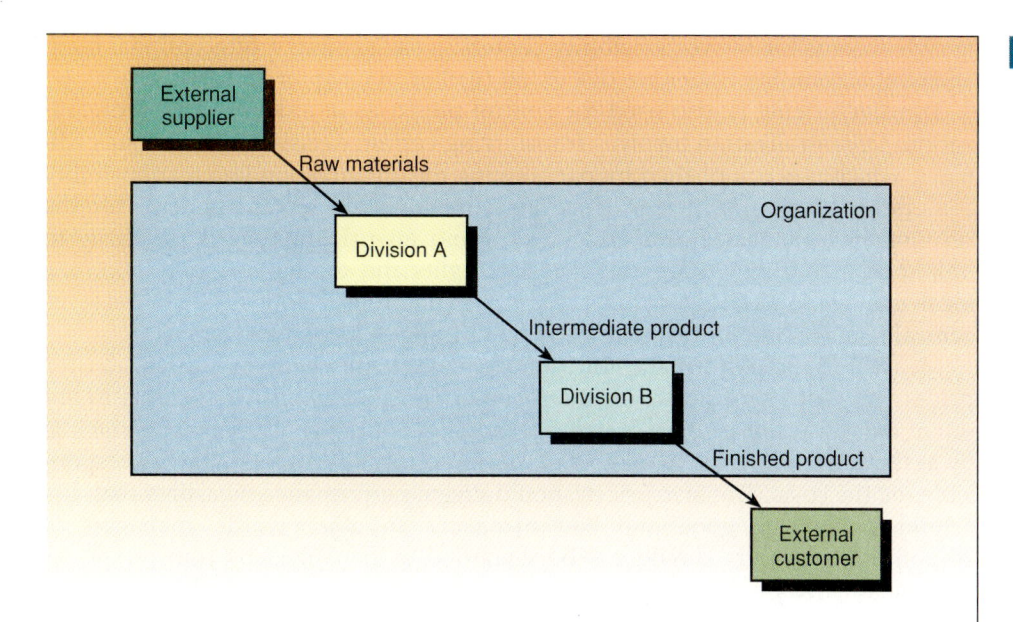

FIGURE 7.4

The External and Internal Transfer of Products

mediate product that is used by Division B. Division B converts the intermediate product into a finished product for sale to an external customer. The purchase price of the raw materials and the sales price of the finished product are determined by external market forces. The price of the intermediate product that is transferred between divisions within the organization is not directly affected by external market forces and there is some flexibility in setting that internal price.

The management accounting system recognizes the interactions of different responsibility centers through **transfer pricing.** When goods or services are transferred from one responsibility center to another, an internal price or transfer price is attached to the units transferred. For example, Chevrolet manufactures an engine that is installed in a Buick. The transfer price in this case is the internal charge the Buick Division of General Motors pays to the Chevrolet Division of General Motors. The transfer payment may not involve any cash flows between the two divisions, but an accounting entry is made to reflect a cost to the Buick Division and a corresponding revenue to the Chevrolet Division.

Transfer prices are much more prevalent in organizations than most managers realize. Consider the charge that the advertising department receives from the maintenance department for janitorial service, or the monthly charge for telephones, security services, data processing, or legal and personnel services. Most firms distribute costs of services to departments using the services as a method of charging internal users for goods or services received from another part of the organization. These cost distributions are internal transfer prices.

There are three main reasons for transfer pricing within firms: international issues, control (incentives and performance measures), and planning decisions. A multinational organization may have interacting responsibility centers in different countries. The responsibility centers are taxed in their respective countries, so transfer prices are necessary to calculate

Weyerhaeuser Corporation owns wood lots to supply wood fiber for its paper plants. Should the wood lots be treated as cost, profit, or investment centers?

taxable income for the responsibility centers in each country. International management accounting issues are discussed further in Chapter 15.

Transfer pricing is also used for control purposes in a decentralized organization. Decentralization involves transferring certain decision rights to subordinates, which is accomplished by partitioning the organization into responsibility centers and designing performance measurement and reward systems for the responsibility centers. Firms create profit and investment centers primarily to link specialized knowledge and decision rights and to increase motivation for local managers, although profit centers also improve response time, conserve central management's time, and facilitate training of local managers.

Measuring the performance of profit or investment centers requires transfer prices when one profit or investment center transfers goods or services to another unit. Transfer-pricing systems should reflect the controllability principle by assigning costs to the managers of the responsibility centers who are responsible for the costs. Transfer prices should create performance measures that discriminate between good and bad managers. In other words, managers of responsibility centers should not be rewarded or penalized by transfer prices that are affected by the performance of managers of other responsibility centers. For example, the manager of an engineering department should not be able to charge the manager of the production department for cost overruns due to mistakes made by the engineering department.

NUMERICAL EXAMPLE 7.5

The parts division of an organization sells parts to the assembly division of the same organization. The cost to the parts division of providing the parts is $10 per unit. The assembly division, at a cost of $4 per unit, assembles the parts purchased from the parts division and sells the assembled product to another organization for $23 per unit.

a. What is the profit per unit of the two divisions if the transfer price is $12 per unit?
b. What is the profit per unit of the two divisions if the cost of the parts department of $10 per unit is used as the transfer price?
c. If the parts department operates inefficiently, causing the cost of parts to rise to $11 per unit and that cost is used as the transfer price, what is the profit of the two divisions?
d. What is wrong with the solution in part c?

■ **SOLUTION**

a. If the transfer price is $12 per unit, the profit per unit of the two divisions is:

Parts Division		Assembly Division	
Revenue per unit	$12	Revenue per unit	$23
Cost per unit	10	Parts cost per unit	12
Profit per unit	$ 2	Assembly costs	4
		Profit per unit	$ 7

b. If the transfer price is $10 per unit, the profit of the two divisions is:

Parts Division		Assembly Division	
Revenue per unit	$10	Revenue per unit	$23
Cost per unit	10	Parts cost per unit	10
Profit per unit	$ 0	Assembly costs	4
		Profit per unit	$ 9

Notice that the larger transfer price shifts profit from the assembly division to the parts division. With each transfer price, the total profit of both divisions is $9 per unit.

c. If the transfer price is $11 cost per unit due to inefficiencies in the parts division, the profit of the two divisions is:

	Parts Division		Assembly Division	
	Revenue per unit	$11	Revenue per unit	$23
	Cost per unit	11	Parts cost per unit	11
	Profit per unit	$ 0	Assembly costs	4
			Profit per unit	$ 8

d. The additional cost of $1 per unit due to inefficiencies in the Parts Division does not affect the profit of the Parts Division but adversely affects the profit of the Assembly Division. Because the Parts Division is responsible for the extra $1 per unit cost, the performance measure of the Parts Division, not the Assembly Division, should reflect that responsibility.

Managers also use transfer prices for decentralized planning purposes. In a decentralized organization, managers of responsibility centers are given decision rights to make certain input and output decisions. For some inputs and outputs, however, the managers may not have the decision rights to go outside the organization. For example, the manager of the Buick Division in General Motors is required to purchase engines from the Chevrolet Division. The manager of the Buick Division does not have the decision rights to go to Chrysler or Ford to purchase engines. Under these circumstances, a transfer price doesn't affect the choice of the supplier or buyer but will influence the level of output of both divisions. For example, if the transfer price is too high, the internal buyer will tend to purchase less of the internally supplied service or product than would be optimal for the whole organization. The problem is choosing a transfer price that leads to decentralized decisions consistent with the goals of the whole organization.

NUMERICAL EXAMPLE 7.6

A company making earthmoving machines has a parts division and an assembly division. The parts division supplies the assembly division with a set of parts that are assembled and sold. The sales price per machine declines as more machines are sold because the demand for the machine is sensitive to the price. The divisional costs and company revenues and profits for different levels of output are:

Output per Month	Parts Division Costs	Assembly Division Costs	Selling Price per Unit	Total Revenues	Company Profits
1	$100,000	$ 50,000	$200,000	$200,000	$50,000
2	180,000	100,000	170,000	340,000	60,000
3	240,000	150,000	160,000	480,000	90,000

What problems will the company encounter if it uses a transfer price of $100,000 per set of parts and allows the manager of the assembly division, who is evaluated based on the assembly division's profits, to make the choice of how many sets of parts to assemble?

■ **SOLUTION** With a transfer price of $100,000, the profits of the assembly division are:

Output per Month	Cost of Parts	Other Assembly Costs	Revenues	Assembly Division Profit
1	$100,000	$ 50,000	$200,000	$50,000
2	200,000	100,000	340,000	40,000
3	300,000	150,000	480,000	30,000

Assembly division profits are highest when assembling one set of parts per month. The manager of the assembly division, therefore, will choose to assemble one set of parts even though the company's profit would be maximized if three sets of parts were made and assembled.

Managers of some responsibility centers are given the decision rights to buy or sell outside the organization even though there is an internal supplier of the responsibility center's inputs or an internal buyer of the responsibility center's outputs. Allowing managers to go outside the organization forces the responsibility centers within the organization to compete with outside suppliers and buyers. Competitive markets provide the discipline to encourage the efficient operation of responsibility centers. Inefficient responsibility centers will not survive under these circumstances. Once again, the transfer pricing system should be designed to motivate managers to make input and output decisions that are consistent with the organization's goals.

To motivate managers to make decentralized input and output decisions (choices of quantity, supplier, and customer) consistent with maximizing the profit of the whole organization, the transfer price should be set equal to the opportunity cost of providing the product or service being transferred. The opportunity cost of providing the product or service is the opportunity cost of using raw materials, labor, and the facilities and the forgone profit of not being able to sell the product or service to an outside party. Cash outlays, alternative uses of the material, labor, and facilities, and forgone profit should be considered in establishing the transfer price. Because the opportunity cost of providing the product or service may be difficult to estimate, the following sections describe some useful approximations.

Existence of a Competitive Market for the Intermediate Product or Service

Suppose a competitive market exists for the product or service being transferred between the two responsibility centers. The responsibility center providing the product or service could sell it to someone outside the organization and the responsibility center using the product or service could purchase it from an outside supplier. The sale to an outside buyer or the purchase from an outside seller would occur at a market price determined by competitive forces.

The general rule of transfer pricing is to use the external market price of the intermediate product or service if a competitive market exists. The market price approximates the opportunity cost of providing the product or service. The market price is equal to the opportunity costs of making the product or service plus the forgone profit of not selling the product or service to an outside party.

In some cases the external market price is not exactly equal to the opportunity cost of providing the intermediate product or service. Sometimes there are additional opportunity costs of dealing with external customers. For example, external customers may require more negotiating and accounting effort to complete the deal. Also, there may be additional transaction and customer service costs when dealing with an external customer. Therefore, the opportunity cost of selling to external customers is the market price less these additional costs, which should be reflected in a lower transfer price. A transfer price below the market price will encourage the internal customer to purchase the intermediate product and allow the company to avoid the costs of dealing with the external customer.

NUMERICAL EXAMPLE 7.7

The restaurant division of a hotel provides a catering service for the convention center of the hotel. The restaurant charges outside organizations $20 per person for catering. But to cater outside events the restaurant incurs additional costs of $1 per person. These additional costs include the cost of transporting and reheating the food. What transfer price should be used between the restaurant division and the convention center to encourage decentralized decision making that will maximize profit for the hotel?

■ **SOLUTION** The transfer price should be the market price of $20 less the additional transaction and contracting costs of $1, or $19 per person. The restaurant is indifferent at that transfer price between catering internally or externally. The $19 transfer price will encourage the convention center to buy from the restaurant division because the convention center would have to pay a price of about $20, reflecting additional costs, if it purchased from an outside supplier.

Producing internally (even though "cheaper" external markets exist) may also make sense if timeliness of supply and quality control is important. When these factors are included in the analysis, the external market may no longer be cheaper. The market price should be adjusted for these other factors to determine the transfer price.

Sometimes an internal supplier of a service or product can't compete with external suppliers even after adjusting for transportation costs, quality, and timely delivery. Under these circumstances, the internal supplier will be forced to improve efficiency or shift to providing other services or products.

NUMERICAL EXAMPLE 7.8

The Kali Company has two divisions. The paper division makes 10,000 tons of paper each year at a cost of $1,000 per ton. It can either sell all of the paper in the market for $1,500 per ton or transfer all of the paper to the printing division of Kali Company. The printing division converts the paper into gift wrap at an additional cost of $4,000 per ton. The gift wrap can be sold for $5,200 per ton.

a. What is the profit of the company if the paper is transferred to the printing division?
b. What is the profit of the company if the paper is sold in the market and the printing division is closed?
c. How does the use of the market price as the transfer price cause managers of the division to reach the solution that yields the highest profit for the company?

■ **SOLUTION**

a. The profit of the company if the paper is transferred to the printing division would be:

Revenues (10,000 tons)($5,200/ton)	$52,000,000
Paper costs (10,000 tons)($1,000/ton)	(10,000,000)
Printing costs (10,000 tons)($4,000/ton)	(40,000,000)
Profit	$ 2,000,000

b. The profit of the company if the paper is sold in the market and the printing division is closed would be:

Revenues (10,000 tons)($1,500/ton)	$15,000,000
Paper costs (10,000 tons)($1,000/ton)	(10,000,000)
Profit	$ 5,000,000

c. If the market price of $1,500 is used as the transfer price, the printing division's costs ($1,500/ton + $4,000/ton) will be greater than its revenues ($5,200/ton). Rather than operating at a loss, the manager can close the printing division or look for a more profitable opportunity. This example assumes that the costs of the two divisions are opportunity costs and reflect alternative uses of the inputs to the process.

No Competitive Market Exists for the Intermediate Product or Service

If no external market exists for the intermediate product or service, there is no alternative of selling the product or service to another buyer. The intermediate service or product can only be sold internally. There is no forgone profit opportunity, and the opportunity cost is limited to the opportunity cost of using the raw materials, labor, and facilities to supply the product or service. The opportunity cost of each input of the product or service should be considered in terms of cash outlays and alternative uses of the assets. For example, if the existing facilities have already been purchased and there is no alternative use of those facilities, the opportunity cost of using those facilities is limited to the incremental costs of operating within the facilities. Opportunity costs are approximated by the variable cost if the fixed costs are sunk. If fixed costs are sunk and included in the transfer price, the purchasing responsibility center will tend to purchase less of the intermediate product or service than is best for the whole organization.

NUMERICAL EXAMPLE 7.9

The CD-ROM division of a large computer company manufactures and sells CD players to the laptop division of the same firm. The variable cost to the CD-ROM division of providing the product is $100 per unit and the fixed, sunk cost is $50 per unit. The CD-ROM division has excess capacity and no alternative use of that capacity. The laptop division, at an additional variable cost of $60 per unit, modifies the product purchased from the CD-ROM division and sells the modified product to another computer company for $180 per unit. What is the contribution margin per unit for the organization if the transfer price is the variable cost? What happens if the full cost is used as the transfer price?

■ **SOLUTION** If the variable cost of the CD-ROM division ($100) is used as the transfer price, CD-ROM's contribution margin is $100 − $100, or $0, and the laptop division's contribution margin is $180 − $100 − $60, or $20, per unit. The contribution margin to the whole firm is $20 per unit. If the full cost of CD-ROM ($150) is used as the transfer price, CD-ROM's contribution margin is $150 − $100, or $50, but the laptop division's contribution margin is $180 − $150 − $60, or −$30. Under these circumstances, the manager of the laptop division can obtain a higher contribution margin ($0) by not selling modified CD-ROM players. The firm would then lose the chance of earning a $20 contribution margin per unit.

Numerical Example 7.9 makes an important point. Think of the firm's total profit as a pie. Choice among transfer pricing methods not only changes how the pie is divided among the profit or investment centers but also the size of the pie to be divided. Many managers think that changing transfer pricing methods merely shifts income among responsibility centers (as was illustrated in Numerical Example 7.5) and, except for relative performance evaluation, nothing else is affected. Unfortunately, this is not true. The level of the firm's output and overall firmwide profitability may change with different transfer prices.

One problem with using the variable cost as a transfer price is that the selling responsibility center does not recover its fixed costs. If *all* the selling division's output is transferred internally, the only revenue the seller receives is variable cost, and its fixed costs are not recovered. Thus, sellers show losses and appear to be losing money. One solution is to treat the selling division as a cost center or as part of the purchasing division.

Any transfer-pricing scheme that involves calculating variable costs creates incentives for selling division managers to classify costs as variable. Because classifying costs into variable and fixed is somewhat arbitrary, managers in the selling and buying divisions and senior managers waste resources debating the nature of costs. Moreover, the selling division manager has incentives to convert a dollar of fixed costs into more than a dollar of variable costs even though this reduces the value of the firm. For example, the selling division may choose to replace a $1 fixed machine cost with a $2 variable labor cost. The buying division pays the extra cost, not the selling division, and the selling division is relieved of the burden of the fixed cost.

To avoid these wasteful disputes that distract operating managers from operating and strategic decisions, managers often adopt simple, objective transfer-pricing rules such as full accounting cost. Since full cost is the sum of fixed and variable cost, full cost cannot be changed by simply reclassifying a fixed cost as variable cost. Using a full-cost transfer price results in better *control* by reducing the producer division's incentives to reclassify fixed costs as variable costs. But full-cost transfer pricing comes at a price: *decision making* is worse because the buying unit purchases too few units. Thus, the trade-off between making planning decisions and control is observed again.

> **WHAT'S HAPPENING**
>
> AT&T's research labs, Bellcore, established transfer prices on secretarial services. Whenever a research scientist or engineer wanted a paper or letter typed, a secretary prepared the document. The transfer price charged for typing included secretarial labor and administrative costs (rent, utilities, and taxes on the office space). After initiating the transfer pricing scheme, the highly paid researchers soon began typing their own papers because the transfer price per typed page had risen to $50. Much of the administrative costs and salaries are fixed. As users of the typing services started typing their own manuscripts, costs in the typing department did not fall proportionately, and the transfer price per page rose. What actions do you think Bellcore undertook to solve these problems?

To improve decentralized planning decisions, the transfer price should equal the opportunity cost of providing the intermediate product or service. If the selling responsibility center is operating at capacity and has alternative uses of that capacity, then the opportunity cost of providing a product or service should include the forgone profit of using the facility for some other purpose. Although the fixed cost of using the facility does not change with the number of units produced, the fixed cost may be a close approximation of the forgone profit of using the facility. Under these circumstances, the full cost (including variable and fixed costs) may be a reasonable approximation of the opportunity cost.

To summarize the discussion on transfer pricing, firms decentralize and form responsibility centers to take advantage of the divisional manager's specialized knowledge of local conditions. Responsibility center managers are given decision rights to make certain local decisions and are held responsible for the performance of the responsibility center. Transfer-price systems offer desirable mechanisms for permitting local managers to exploit specialized information that they possess about local opportunities.

Table 7.3 describes the appropriate transfer prices for decentralized planning decisions. In each case, the transfer price is intended to be equal to the opportunity cost of providing the intermediate product or service.

TABLE 7.3

Transfer Prices for Decentralized Planning Decisions

Circumstance	Transfer Price
Market price exists	Market price
No market price; supplying division has no alternative use of capacity	Variable cost
No market price; supplying division has alternative use of capacity	Full cost*

*The full cost is intended to be a rough approximation of the forgone opportunity of using the facilities of the supplying division to do something else.

Choosing Transfer Prices: Control and Making Planning Decisions

Accounting numbers are often used in setting internal transfer prices. The conflict between planning decisions and control discussed in Chapter 1 also applies to transfer prices. In setting the transfer price that maximizes firm value, one often must compromise between transfer pricing for planning decisions and control. The transfer price that most accurately measures the opportunity cost to the organization of transferring one more unit inside the organization might not be the transfer-pricing method that gives internal managers incentive to maximize the organization's value. For example, if the transfer-pricing method that most accurately measures the opportunity cost of units transferred also requires managers producing the units to reveal privately held and hard to verify knowledge of their costs, then these managers have much discretion over the transfer prices. If these prices are important in rewarding managers, the producing managers can distort the system to their benefit. Alternatively, a transfer-pricing scheme that less accurately measures opportunity cost but is less subject to managerial discretion might produce a higher firm value than a transfer-pricing scheme that more closely mimics opportunity costs.

Another control problem happens when actual opportunity costs are used as a transfer price. The selling responsibility center manager does not have an incentive to control costs because any increase in cost is passed on to the buying responsibility center through the transfer price. The manager of the buying responsibility center will be penalized for the inefficiencies of the selling responsibility center. To overcome this problem, an estimated cost should be used as the transfer price instead of the actual cost. Any variation of the actual cost from the estimated cost will be attributed to the manager of the selling responsibility center.

In some organizations, transfer prices are negotiated by the managers of the selling and buying responsibility centers. Negotiation, however, is time-consuming and leads to conflicts among responsibility centers. Division performance measurement becomes sensitive to the relative negotiating skills of the two division managers. Negotiated transfer prices are more successful when managers have a fallback position such as an external market for the intermediate product. In this case, the external market acts as a check on the managers behaving opportunistically.

Given the many different factors that influence the choice of transfer prices, it is not surprising that different organizations choose different transfer prices. Table 7.4 reports a survey of transfer-pricing methods used by Fortune 500 companies. Cost-based transfer pricing methods are more prevalent than market-based methods for domestic transfers, whereas market-based transfers are more

THE STORY OF MANAGERIAL ACCOUNTING

Team Decisions Regarding Performance Evaluation

The book team for *Managerial Accounting* is evaluated on three primary measures. First and foremost, the sales estimate for the product is established at the time of signing the contract with Dale and Jerry and still serves as the organizational goal for sales level. Complementing sales estimates are the cost parameters, which are also established at the time of signing and are constantly evaluated by Peggy and the book team throughout the product's development.

Finally, the importance of publishing the project along the time frame originally planned cannot be overstated. Are there additional elements you feel the book team, including Peggy, should consider for evaluation? What type of responsibility center is this book team?

TABLE 7.4

Comparison between the Transfer-Pricing Methods Used by Fortune 500 Companies in 1990

	Domestic Transfer Prices (% of total)	International Transfer Prices (% of total)
Pricing methods		
Cost-based transfer prices	46.2	41.4
Market-based transfer prices	36.7	45.9
Negotiated prices	16.6	12.7
Other	0.5	0.0
Total—all methods	100.0	100.0

Source: R. Tang, "Transfer Pricing in the 1990s," *Management Accounting*, February 1992, p. 25.

prevalent than cost-based transfers for international transactions. The higher use of market price as a transfer price for international transfers is presumably due to tax regulations in many countries that require the use of market price as a transfer price for calculating income taxes.

SHAH MOTORS (CONCLUDED)

In Shah Motors, the three divisions have considerable interactions. Both the new and used car divisions use the service department to make final preparations of a car sold to a customer. And all the divisions use the accounting services of the central administration. But the primary interaction that is causing problems at Shah Motors is the transfer of used cars from the new car division to the used car division. Alice Dempster, the new car sales manager, gives very generous trade-in allowances to buyers of new cars. She would like to pass these costs on to the used car division, but Slick Thompson claims that he would operate at a loss if he had to buy the used cars at their inflated trade-in price. Under present policy, Slick must buy all the used cars received by the new car division. To solve this problem, Jeremy decides to use published lists of used car prices as the transfer price. If Alice decides to give a trade-in allowance greater than the list price of the used car, she will have to bear the cost.

At the end of the year, Jeremy decides to calculate the profit of each of the three departments of his company. He distributes his central administration costs, which are mostly interest costs at 10% annually, to the three managers based on total sales. Transfers of trade-ins from the new car department to the used car department occur at a list price published by an outside source.

	New Car Sales	Used Car Sales	Service Dept.
Revenues	$ 8,000,000	$2,000,000	$1,500,000
Sale of trade-ins	1,000,000		
Total revenues	$ 9,000,000	$2,000,000	$1,500,000
Controllable costs	(5,000,000)	(700,000)	(1,200,000)
Cost of trade-ins		(1,000,000)	
Profit before distribution	$ 4,000,000	$ 300,000	$ 300,000
Distributed administration costs	(2,160,000)	(480,000)	(360,000)
Profit (loss)	$ 1,840,000	($180,000)	($60,000)
Average net assets	$20,000,000	$1,900,000	$ 300,000

Alice Dempster, the new car sales manager is most pleased with this segment reporting. She is evaluated based on profit, and the new car sales department shows a profit of $1,840,000.

Slick Thompson of the used car sales department is not happy with the profit analysis of the segments. Slick is supposed to be evaluated based on residual income. The profit calculated in the segment reports includes interest charges distributed from central administration. Slick argues that the residual income of his department is the profit before the distribution of administration costs less the opportunity cost of capital, or $300,000 − (10%)($1,900,000), or $110,000.

Grease Johnson is also unhappy with the analysis. He has provided good quality service at a low cost. He has no control over the pricing of his department's services. Also, the distributed administrative costs appear excessive given that they are mostly interest costs and the net assets of his department are relatively small.

Jeremy Shah agrees with most of his managers' arguments. He is still concerned, however, about the distribution of administration costs to the different departments. If he can't cover those administration costs with profits from the different departments, his business will incur a loss. Jeremy decides he better read Chapter 9 on distributing costs.

CONCEPT REVIEW

1. How should transfer pricing be used to improve decision control?
2. How should transfer prices be chosen to improve decentralized planning decisions?

7.4 Summary

1. **Use the controllability principle to choose performance measures for managers.** Managers should be evaluated based on the activities that they control. Performance measures should reflect those controllable activities.

2. **Identify responsibility centers based on the extent of each manager's decision rights.** Managers who have decision rights only over the input mix of their activities are managers of cost centers. Managers who have decision rights only over the input and output mix of their activities are managers of profit centers. Managers who have the additional decision rights to change the size of their responsibility center are managers of investment centers.

3. **Choose performance measures for cost, profit, and investment centers.** Managers should be evaluated by multiple performance measures to control for quality and other organizational goals, but the primary accounting performance measure for cost centers is cost, for profit centers is profit, and for investment centers is return on investment or residual income.

4. **Identify the strengths and weaknesses of using the return on investment (ROI) and residual income as performance measures for investment centers.** ROI provides a return measure that controls for size and is comparable to other return measures. The measurement of ROI, however, may be difficult and does not explicitly correct for differences in risk. The ROI also leads to underinvestment. The residual income measure, however, corrects for the underinvestment problem but requires an estimate of the opportunity cost of capital.

5. **Choose transfer prices to create performance measures that reflect the activities controlled by each manager.** Transfer prices are used to charge responsibility centers for products or services they receive from other responsibility centers within the same organization. The transfer price should be chosen so that each party of the internal transaction is rewarded or penalized for the activities each controls.

6. **Use opportunity costs to choose transfer prices that will lead to decentralized decision making that is best for the organization.** To allow decentralized managers to make the most profitable input and output decisions for the whole organization, the transfer price should reflect the opportunity cost. If a market price exists for the intermediate product or service, the market price adjusted for transaction and contracting costs is the appropriate transfer price. If no market exists for the intermediate product, the opportunity cost depends on alternative use of raw materials, labor, and facilities.

KEY TERMS

Controllable costs Costs that are affected by a particular manager's decisions.

Controllability principle Holding managers responsible for only those decisions for which they are given authority.

Cost centers Areas of responsibility within the organization where decision rights are limited to maximizing output given a certain level of cost or minimizing cost given a certain level of output.

Investment centers Areas of responsibility within the organization where decision rights include choices affecting costs, revenues, and the amount invested in the center.

Opportunity cost of capital The forgone opportunity of using cash for another purpose such as earning interest in a bank account.

Profit centers Areas of responsibility within the organization where decision rights include choices affecting costs and revenues but not size of investment.

Relative performance measure Performance is judged relative to how a selected comparable group performed.

Residual income A performance measure for investment centers that subtracts the opportunity cost of the investment from the income generated by the assets of the investment.

Responsibility accounting The process of recognizing subunits within the organization, assigning decision rights to managers in those subunits, and evaluating the performance of those managers.

Return on investment (ROI) A performance measure calculated by dividing the income from an investment by the size of the investment.

Transfer pricing A system of pricing of products and services transferred from one responsibility center to another within the same organization.

SELF-STUDY PROBLEM

Tam Burger has grown to over 200 stores within the past five years, 80% of which are franchised (independently owned). Two of the company-operated units, Northside and Southside, are among the fastest growing stores. Both are considering expanding their menus to include pizza. Installation of the necessary ovens and purchase of the necessary equipment would cost $180,000 per store. The current investment in the Northside store totals $890,000. Store revenues are $1,100,500 and expenses are $924,420. Expansion of Northside's menu should increase profits by $30,600. The current investment in the Southside store totals $1,740,000. The store's revenues are $1,760,800 and expenses are $1,496,680. Adding pizza to the menu should increase Southside's profits by $30,600.

Tam Burger evaluates their managers based on return on investment. Managers of individual stores have decision rights over the pizza expansion.

Required

a. Using current numbers, calculate the return on investment for both stores for the expansion project and for the stores after expansion.
b. Assuming a 14% cost of capital, calculate residual income for both stores before and after the potential expansion.
c. Will the Tam Burger stores choose to expand? How would the answer change if the stores were franchised units and owned by value-maximizing investors?

Solution

a. Return on investment before and after the pizza expansion.

	Northside	Southside
ROI before pizza:		
Revenue	$1,100,500	$1,760,800
Expenses	924,420	1,496,680
Net income	$ 176,080	$ 264,120
Assets	$ 890,000	$1,740,000
ROI	19.78%	15.18%
ROI of pizza only:		
Increased profits from pizza	$ 30,600	$ 30,600
Expansion cost	$ 180,000	$ 180,000
ROI of project	17.00%	17.00%
ROI after pizza:		
Total income	$ 206,680	$ 294,720
Total assets	$1,070,000	$1,920,000
Total ROI	19.32%	15.35%

b. Residual income before and after the pizza expansion.

	Northside	Southside
Cost of capital	14.00%	14.00%
Residual income before pizza:		
Net income	$ 176,080	$ 264,120
Assets × 14%	(124,600)	(243,600)
Residual income	$ 51,480	$ 20,520
Residual income of pizza only:		
Increased profits from pizza	$ 30,600	$ 30,600
Less: 14% × Expansion cost	(25,200)	(25,200)
Residual income	$ 5,400	$ 5,400
Residual income after pizza:		
Net income	$ 206,680	$ 294,720
Less: 14% × Assets	149,800	268,800
Residual income	$ 56,880	$ 25,920

c. The two units currently have different ROIs. The smaller Northside store is earning an ROI of just under 20%, while the larger Southside store is earning an ROI of just over 15%. Since the ROI of the project is 17%, adding the project to the Northside store lowers its average ROI, while adding the project to the Southside store raises its average ROI. The Northside manager will therefore not want to add pizza to the menu since the store's average ROI would drop as a result. The Southside manager however would want to add pizza since the store's ROI would subsequently rise.

If the stores were franchised units the owners would definitely expand. The ROI of the pizza is higher than the cost of capital. This assures a positive residual income for the project. As long as the residual income is positive, any franchise owner would jump at the opportunity. Franchise owners would not care if the store's average ROI dropped as long as the residual income increased.

NUMERICAL PROBLEMS

NP 7–1: ROI and Residual Income (LO 4; NE 2, 4) The following data summarizes the operating performance of your company's wholly owned Canadian subsidiary for 1994–1996. The opportunity cost of capital for this subsidiary is 10%.

	($ millions)		
	1994	1995	1996
Subsidiary net income	$14.0	$14.3	$14.4
Total assets in subsidiary	125	130	135

Calculate the ROI and residual income of the subsidiary for each year.

NP 7–2: ROI and Residual Income (LO 4; NE 3, 4) The following investment opportunities are available to an investment center manager:

Project	Initial Investment	Annual Earnings
A	$800,000	$90,000
B	100,000	20,000
C	300,000	25,000
D	400,000	60,000

a. If the investment manager is currently making a return on investment of 16%, which project(s) would the manager want to pursue?

b. If the cost of capital is 10% and the annual earnings approximate cash flows excluding finance charges, which project(s) should be chosen?

c. Suppose only one project can be chosen and the annual earnings approximate cash flows excluding finance charges. Which project should be chosen?

NP 7–3: ROI and Residual Income (LO 4; NE 3, 4) Suppose a division of a company is treated as an investment center. The division manager is currently getting an ROI of 15% from existing assets of $1 million. The cost of capital is 10%. The division manager has the option of choosing among the following projects, which are independent of existing operations and the other alternative projects.

Project	Investment	ROI
A	$100,000	14%
B	$400,000	20%
C	$200,000	14%
D	$300,000	12%
E	$500,000	8%

a. Given the current investment in existing assets, which additional projects should the division manager invest in if the objective is to maximize ROI?

b. Which projects increase the value of the company?

c. Which projects have a negative residual income?

d. Using this example, explain why underinvestment is a problem when using ROI for evaluation purposes.

NP 7–4: Transfer Prices (LO 6; NE 8, 9) The Alpha Division of the Carlson Company manufactures product X at a variable cost of $40 per unit. Alpha Division's fixed costs, which are sunk, are $20 per unit. The market price of X is $70 per unit. Beta Division of Carlson Company uses product X to make Y. The variable costs to convert X to Y are $20 per unit and the fixed costs, which are sunk, are $10 per unit. Alpha Division does not have sufficient capacity to satisfy both the external and internal market. Product Y sells for $80 per unit.

a. What transfer price of X causes divisional managers to make decentralized decisions that maximize Carlson Company's profit if each division is treated as a profit center?

b. Given the transfer price from part a, what should the manager of the Beta Division do?

c. Suppose there is no market price for product X. What transfer price should be used for decentralized decision making?

d. If there is no market for product X, is the Beta Division operation profitable?

NP 7–5: Dropping a Division (LO 6; NE 8) Scoff Division of World-Wide Paint is currently losing money, and senior management is considering selling or closing Scoff. Scoff's only product, an intermediate chemical called Binder, is used principally by the Latex Division of the firm. If Scoff is sold, Latex Division can purchase ample quantities of Binder in the market at sufficiently high quality levels to meet their requirements. World-Wide requires all of its divisions to supply product to other World-Wide Divisions before servicing the external market.

Scoff's statement of operations for the latest quarter is:

Scoff Division of World-Wide Paint
Profit/Loss Statement, Last Quarter
($000)

Revenues		
Inside	$200	
Outside	75	$275
Operating expenses		
Variable costs	$260	
Fixed costs	15	
Distributed corporate overhead	40	315
Net income (loss) before taxes		$ (40)

Notes:

1. World-Wide Paint has the policy of transferring all products internally at variable cost. In Scoff's case, variable cost is 80% of the market price.
2. All of Scoff's fixed costs are avoidable cash flows if Scoff is closed or sold.
3. Of the distributed corporate overhead, 10% is caused by the presence of Scoff and will be avoided if Scoff is closed or sold.

Should the Scoff Division be sold?

NP 7–6: ROI Using Market Values (LO 4; NE 2, 3)

Your firm uses ROI (return on investment) to evaluate investment centers and is considering changing the valuation basis of assets from historical cost to current value. The historical cost of the asset is updated using a price index to approximate replacement value. For example, a metal-fabrication press, which bends and shapes metal, was bought seven years ago for $522,000. The company will add 19% to this cost, representing the change in the wholesale price index over the seven years. This new, higher cost figure is depreciated using the straight-line method over the same 12-year assumed life (no salvage value).

a. Calculate depreciation expense and book value of the metal press first based on historical cost and then based on the change in the wholesale index.
b. In general, what is the effect on ROI of changing valuation bases from historical cost to current values?
c. The manager of the investment center with the metal press is considering replacing it as it is becoming obsolete. Will the manager's incentives to replace the metal press change if the firm shifts from historical cost valuation to the proposed price-level adjusted historical cost valuation?

(Contributed by L. Harrington, R. Lewis, P. Siviy, and S. Spector.)

NP 7–7: Transfer Price and Capacity (LO 6; NE 8, 9)

Microelectronics is a large electronics firm with multiple divisions. The Circuit Board Division manufactures circuit boards which it sells externally and internally. The Phone Division assembles cellular phones and sells them to external customers. Both divisions are evaluated as profit centers. The firm has the policy of transferring all internal products at market prices.

The selling price of cellular phones is $400 and the external market price for the cellular phone circuit board is $200. The outlay cost for the Phone Division to complete a phone (not including the cost of the circuit board) is $250. The variable cost of the circuit board is $130.

a. Will the Phone Division purchase the circuit boards from the Circuit Board Division? (Show calculations.)
b. Suppose the Circuit Board Division is currently manufacturing and selling externally 10,000 circuit boards per month and has capacity to manufacture 15,000 boards. From the standpoint of Microelectronics, should 3,000 additional boards be manufactured and transferred internally?
c. Discuss what transfer price should be set for part b above.
d. List the three most important assumptions underlying your analysis in parts b and c.

NP 7–8: Transfer Prices and Capacity (LO 6; NE 8, 9)

Jefferson Company has two divisions: Jefferson Bottles and Jefferson Juice. Jefferson Bottles makes glass containers, which it sells to Jefferson Juice and other companies. Jefferson Bottles has a capacity of 10 million bottles a year. Jefferson Juice currently has a capacity of 3 million bottles of juice per year. Jefferson Bottles has a fixed cost of $100,000 per year and a variable cost of $0.01/bottle. Jefferson Bottles can currently sell all of its output at $0.03/bottle.

a. What should Jefferson Bottles charge Jefferson Juice for bottles so that both divisions will make appropriate decentralized planning decisions?
b. If Jefferson Bottles can only sell 5 million bottles to outside buyers, what should Jefferson Bottles charge Jefferson Juice for bottles so that both divisions will make firm value-maximizing decentralized planning decisions?

NP 7–9: Transfer Prices and Divisional Profit (LO 5; NE 5) A chair manufacturer has two divisions: framing and upholstering. The framing costs are $100 per chair and the upholstering costs are $200 per chair. The company makes 5,000 chairs each year, which are sold for $500.

a. What is the profit of each division if the transfer price is $150?
b. What is the profit of each division if the transfer price is $200?

NP 7–10: Planning Decisions and Transfer Prices (LO 6; NE 6) A hotel company is divided into two divisions: construction and management. The construction division builds the hotels and the management division operates the hotels. The construction division borrows money to cover the cost of construction. The construction division charges the management division an annual price per room to use the hotel. The transfer price is used by the construction division to make the annual debt payments.

The estimated costs of both divisions and the estimated revenues for the management division for different sizes of hotels are given below:

Room Size	Construction Div. Annual Debt Costs	Management Div. Annual Costs	Management Div. Annual Revenues
150	$2,000,000	$10,000,000	$15,000,000
200	2,400,000	11,000,000	16,500,000
250	2,600,000	12,000,000	18,000,000
300	2,700,000	13,000,000	18,500,000

a. What room size of the new hotel maximizes the value of the company?
b. If the transfer price is set at $15,000 per year per room, what is the profit of each division?
c. What size of hotel will the management division choose if the transfer price is $15,000 per year per room?
d. Why is this transfer price not working for the company?

NP 7–11: ROI and Residual Income (LO 4; NE 2, 3, 4) The Alaskan Fishing Company operates five trawlers (fishing boats) out of Juneau, Alaska. The boats are of different sizes and incur different operating expenses during the year. The following table describes the operating data and value of each boat.

	Boats				
	A	B	C	D	E
Revenues	$5,500,000	$8,300,000	$10,400,000	$12,800,000	$20,400,000
Annual expenses	3,800,000	8,200,000	9,100,000	9,900,000	18,900,000
Income	$1,700,000	$ 100,000	$ 1,300,000	$ 2,900,000	$ 1,500,000
Book value	$ 0	$5,200,000	$ 6,100,000	$ 5,200,000	$ 8,300,000
Market value	$5,000,000	$6,200,000	$ 8,000,000	$10,000,000	$15,000,000

The cost of capital for the company is 10%.

a. What is the ROI of each boat using the book value of the investment in each boat?
b. What is the ROI of each boat using the market value of the investment in each boat?
c. What is the residual income of each boat using the book value of each boat?
d. What is the residual income of each boat using the market value of each boat?
e. Which trawler had the best year?

NP 7–12: Performance Measures for Cost Centers (LO 1, 2, 3) A soft drink company has three bottling plants throughout the country. Bottling occurs at the regional level because of the high cost of transporting bottled soft drinks. The parent company supplies each plant with the syrup. The bottling plants combine the syrup with carbonated soda to make and bottle the soft drinks. The bottled soft drinks are then sent to grocery stores.

The bottling plants are treated as costs centers. The managers of the bottling plants are evaluated based on minimizing the cost per soft drink bottled and delivered. Each bottling plant uses the same equipment, but some produce more bottles of soft drinks because of different demand. The costs and output for each bottling plant are:

	A	B	C
Units produced	10,000,000	20,000,000	30,000,000
Variable costs	$ 200,000	$ 450,000	$ 650,000
Fixed costs	$1,000,000	$1,000,000	$1,000,000

a. Estimate the average cost per unit for each plant.
b. Why would the manager of plant A be unhappy with using the average cost as the performance measure?
c. What is an alternative performance measure that would make the manager of plant A happier?
d. Under what circumstances might the average cost be a better performance measure?

NP 7–13: ROI and Residual Income (LO 4; NE 2, 3, 4)   Swan Systems developed and manufactures residential water filtration units that are installed under the sink. The filtration unit removes chlorine and other chemicals from drinking water. This Dutch company has successfully expanded sales of their units in the European market for the past 12 years. Six years ago Swan started a U.S. manufacturing and marketing division, and three years ago an Australian manufacturing and marketing division. Summary operating data for the last fiscal year are:

SWAN SYSTEMS
Summary of Operations
Last Fiscal Year
(millions of Dutch Guilders)

	Australia	Netherlands	U.S.	Total
Sales	50	55	75	180
Divisional expenses	38	33	58	129
Net income	12	22	17	51

Senior management is in the process of evaluating the relative performance of each division. While the Netherlands division is the largest and generates the most guilders of profits, this division also has the largest investment of assets as indicated by the following table:

SWAN SYSTEMS
Miscellaneous Operating Data
Last Fiscal Year
(millions of Dutch Guilders)

	Australia	Netherlands	U.S.	Total
Divisional net assets	80	195	131	406
Distributed corporate overhead*	4	4	6	14
Cost of capital	8.0%	8.0%	8.0%	

*Allocated based on divisional sales revenue.

After careful consideration, senior management decided to examine the relative performance of the three divisions using several alternative measures of performance: ROI (return on investment as measured by net assets, total assets less liabilities), residual income (net income less the cost of capital times net assets), and both of these measures after subtracting distributed corporate overhead from divisional income. The cost of capital in each division was estimated to be the same (8%). (Assume this 8% estimate is accurate.)

There was much debate about whether corporate overhead should be distributed to the divisions and subtracted from divisional income. It was decided to distribute back to each division that portion of corporate overhead that is incurred to support and manage the divisions. The distributed corporate overhead items include worldwide marketing, legal expense, and accounting and administration. Sales revenue was chosen as the cost driver because it is simple and best represents the cause-and-effect relationship between the divisions and the generation of corporate overhead.

a. Calculate ROI and residual income (1) before any corporate overhead is distributed and (2) after corporate overhead is distributed to each division.
b. Discuss the differences among the various performance measures.
c. Based on the data presented in the case, evaluate the relative performance of the three operating divisions. Which division do you think performed the best and which performed the worst?

DISCUSSION PROBLEMS

DP 7–1: Responsibility Centers (LO 1, 2, 3)   The Maple Way Golf Course is a private club that is owned by the members. It has the following managers and organizational structure:

Eric Olson: General manager responsible for all the operations of the golf course and other facilities (swimming pool, restaurant, golf shop).
Jennifer Jones: Manager of the golf course and responsible for its maintenance.
Edwin Moses: Manager of the restaurant.
Mabel Smith: Head golf professional and responsible for golf lessons, the golf shop, and reserving times for starting golfers on the course.
Wanda Itami: Manager of the swimming pool and family recreational activities.
Jake Reece: Manager of golf carts rented to golfers.

Describe each of the managers in terms of being responsible for a cost, profit, or investment center and possible performance measures for each manager.

DP 7–2: Transfer Prices (LO 5)   The Bookmark Company uses a cost-based transfer-price system to transfer books from the publication division to its bookstores. The transfer price is based on a budget established at the beginning of the year. At the end of the year, the publication division had a cost overrun, and the manager of the publication division wants to charge the bookstores for the extra costs. Under which of the following cases does the publication manager have a valid argument?

a. The cost overruns were due to equipment failure.
b. The cost overruns were due to rush orders from the bookstores.
c. The cost overruns were due to the return of defective books.
d. The cost overruns were due to lower demand for books than expected.

DP 7–3: Evaluating a New Product with ROI (LO 4)   A Canadian wholesaler of Mexican crafts is considering the importing of rugs. The rugs are handwoven in southern Mexico and use natural dyes. The rugs cost an average of $250 Canadian including transportation and handling, and the wholesaler plans to sell them in Canada for $300 Canadian. Therefore, the profit per rug should be $50 Canadian. The wholesaler's cost of capital is 10% annually. The wholesaler estimates an ROI on the project of $50/$250, or 20%. The residual income is estimated to be $50 − (10%)($250), or $25, Canadian per rug.

What is wrong with the use of ROI and residual income in this analysis?

DP 7–4: Responsibility Centers (LO 2)   News Inc owns five newspaper stands. Each stand has a manager who is responsible for ordering newspapers each day. News Inc purchases the newspapers for each stand. Any newspapers not sold at the end of the day are thrown away.

Describe how the newspaper stands might operate as cost centers, profit centers, and investment centers and the advantages and disadvantages of each type of responsibility center.

DP 7–5: Salespeople as Profit Centers (LO 2)   Memories Company sells cosmetics door-to-door. The company has traditionally paid its salespeople a commission based on total sales. The company is considering making each salesperson a profit center.

How would making each salesperson a profit center affect the behavior of the salespeople?

DP 7–6: Influencing the ROI (LO 4)   The president of a company is trying to improve the ROI of his company. He asks a consultant for assistance. The consultant tells the president that he either must increase his profit margin (income/sales) or sales turnover (Sales/Assets). The president complains that every time he tries to increase his profit margin, the sales turnover goes down.

Evaluate the consultant's advice and the president's complaint.

DP 7–7: ROI and Throughput (LO 4)   A popular book claims that manufacturing managers should always work to improve throughput (the time from starting the manufacturing to the time of sale).

How is this philosophy related to ROI?

DP 7–8: Transfer Prices (LO 6)   Peaceful Valley Company owns both hotels and manufacturing companies. One hotel has a convention center which is leased to various groups. The manufacturing companies want to use the convention center for a training session.

What conditions should affect the choice of the transfer price?

DP 7–9: Transfer Prices and Changing from a Cost to a Profit Center (LO 2, 5)   Northern Blue Company has manufacturing plants and retail shops. The retail shops purchase products from the manufacturing plants. Currently, the manufacturing plants are operated as cost centers and only supply the retail shops within the company. The transfer price is cost-based and the retail shops operate as profit centers. The president of the company is considering an increase in manufacturing capacity that will allow sales to customers outside the organization. The president plans to make the manufacturing plants profit centers.

Why are the managers of the retail shops unhappy with these new plans?

DP 7–10: ROI and Other Performance Measures (LO 4)   Brownside Company is very decentralized. The divisions can issue their own debt, but they must pay their own interest. The manager of the Park Division of Brownside Company is evaluated based on ROI. He has borrowed a considerable amount of money from the bank to expand the Park Division. A large interest expense on that debt is lowering the income of the division. The president of Brownside Company calculates the ROI of the Park Division by using the net income that includes the interest expense and dividing by the total assets of the division.

Why does the manager of the Park Division feel this measure of ROI is inappropriate? Suggest alternative performance measures for Park Division.

DP 7–11: Transfer Price (LO 6)   U.S. Pumps is a multidivisional firm that manufactures and installs chemical piping and pump systems. The Valve Division makes a single standardized valve. Two divisions, the Valve Division and the Installation Division, are currently involved in a transfer-pricing dispute. Last year half of the Valve Division's output was sold to the Installation Division for $40 per pump and the remaining half was sold to outsiders for $60 per pump.

The existing transfer price has been set at $40 per pump through a process of negotiation between the two divisions and also with the involvement of senior management.

The Installation Division has received a bid from an outside valve manufacturer to supply it with an equivalent valve for $35 each.

The manager of the Valve Division has argued that if it is forced to meet the external price of $35, it will lose money on selling internally.

The operating data for last year for the Valve Division are:

Valve Division
Operating Statement
Last Year

	To Installation Division		To Outside	
Sales	20,000 @ $40	$ 800,000	20,000 @ $60	$1,200,000
Variable costs	@ $30	(600,000)		(600,000)
Fixed costs		(135,000)		(135,000)
Gross margin		$ 65,000		$ 465,000

Analyze the situation and recommend a course of action. What should Installation Division managers do? What should Valve Division managers do? And, what should U.S. Pumps senior managers do?

DP 7–12: Transfer Prices (LO 5, 6)

Lewis is a large manufacturer of office equipment, including copiers. The Electronics Division of Lewis is a cost center. Currently, Electronics sells circuit boards to other divisions exclusively. Lewis has a policy that internal transfers are to be priced at full cost (fixed + variable). Thirty percent of the cost of a board is considered fixed.

The Electronics Division is currently operating at 75% of capacity. Because there is excess capacity, Electronics is seeking opportunities to sell boards to non-Lewis firms. The Lewis policy on outside sales states that each job must cover full cost and a minimum 10% profit. Electronics Division management will be measured on their ability to make the minimum profit on any outside contracts that are accepted.

Copy Products is another Lewis Division. Copy Products has recently reached an agreement with Siviy, a non-Lewis firm, for the assembly of subsystems for a copier. Copy Products has selected Siviy because of Siviy's low labor cost. The subsystem that Siviy will assemble requires circuit boards. Copy Products has stipulated that Siviy must purchase the circuit boards from the Electronics Division because of Electronics' high quality and dependability. Electronics is anxious to accept this new work from Copy because it will increase Electronics Division's workload by 15%.

In negotiating a contract price with Siviy, Copy Products needs to take into account the cost of the circuit boards from Electronics. The financial analyst from Copy Products assumes that Electronics will sell the circuit boards to Siviy at full cost (the same as the internal transfer price). Electronics is considering adding the minimum 10% profit margin to their full cost and transferring at that price to Siviy.

Copy Products is preparing to negotiate their contract with Siviy.

Develop and discuss at least three options that may be used in establishing the transfer price between the Electronics Division and Siviy. Discuss the advantages and disadvantages of each.

DP 7–13: Transfer Prices and Contracts (LO 5)

To induce utilities to award contracts to Westinghouse Electric to build nuclear reactors, Westinghouse contracted to supply uranium to these utilities at an average price of $9.50 over a 20-year period. In 1966, Westinghouse disclosed in its annual report:

> Westinghouse Electric Corporation has entered into a number of long-term contractual agreements to sell up to 80 million tons of uranium to utility companies to encourage nuclear reactor construction and to secure sales of uranium. The contracts are optional to the purchasers at a fixed price. The average contract price is approximately $9.50 per pound, and the current market price is $8.00 per pound. We cannot reasonably estimate the amount of purchases that will be made under these agreements because of the optional nature of the contracts.

By 1976, the market price of uranium was over $40 per pound. Westinghouse was unable to meet its commitments and was faced with a potential loss of $2.275 billion, which was over six times the company's net income in 1976.

In 1976, a new manager of the Westinghouse Uranium Supply Division (USD) was hired. This division is responsible for the acquisition and sales of uranium to utilities, both those that have Westinghouse reactors and those with competitor reactors. USD purchases raw uranium in world markets and then processes it into nuclear reactor fuel cells. This division is evaluated as a profit center. The new manager argues that because a number of long-term supply agreements were signed before he joined Westinghouse, USD's revenues on these old contracts should be measured using current market price rather than the original contract price.

a. How should the performance of the Uranium Supply Division be measured?
b. Public utilities, including those with nuclear power generating plants, are regulated by state commissions. State regulatory commissions set the utilities' prices for electricity based on cost plus a "fair return on capital." Cost is based on transaction prices. Given the facts in the problem, how should managers of public utilities with Westinghouse Electric contracts behave given the difference in the contract price of $9.50 per pound of uranium and a current market price of $44.50?

DP 7–14: Transfer Price from Shared Service (LO 6)

Susan Willard, the CEO of Troy Industrial Designs (TID), has called a meeting to evaluate the present method of charging the two offices at Washington and Rochester for the shared services of the Creative Design Group (CDG). She wants to discuss the present cost distribution system and suggest a better one.

TID is a reputable firm in the industrial design sector. They bid for design contracts from different firms. If successful, they either make prototypes based on the client's blueprints, design new products out of existing designs, or draw designs for a product the client has in mind. TID charges clients a fixed figure upon completion of the job and 1% of sales accruing to the client every year for the first seven years, for the use of TID designs or products designed by TID.

The two offices of TID are independently run by different managers and are profit centers. Each manager assigns account executives to individual accounts. The account executives are paid a fixed salary, but a large part of their compensation is their bonus which is based on the revenues accruing from the jobs they manage. On receiving a job, the account executive informs George Scott, the head of CDG. They meet with the client and decide on a plan, detailing the job, expected time to complete the job, and other factors specific to the job. The account executive then waits for the final design before informing the client and discussing the design with him. As soon as the job for a client is finished, the account executive makes a detailed report explaining the work done, the number of designers employed for the job, the number of hours worked on it, the amount billed to the client, and any follow-up needed. Designing is a one-time job and it is rare that additional time is needed to follow up on the same job. Account executives are responsible for any follow-up on the jobs done by them. If the client comes back with another project, it is treated as a separate job.

TID centralized the design departments of the two offices to take advantage of the specialized knowledge of the designers. Though CDG is only five years old, it employs the best talent and uses the latest technology. This has had a positive impact on customers, and because of this TID has grown rapidly in the past few years. The two offices have a lot of confidence in the Creative Design Group and use it for all their design needs. The rapid growth has caused top management to rethink the cost procedures and other organizational aspects of the business.

CDG is totally responsible for the designing part of the job. They only interact with the client at the design stage; all other aspects of the job are done by the account executive. CDG works in small teams. Each team is lead by a supervisor who reports to Scott on a day-to-day basis. Scott is evaluated on the excess of revenues collected from the two offices over the costs of his department. The cost charged to each office is decided before the designing job is taken by CDG. Before the client is brought in for the discussion, the account executive and Scott decide what fees CDG would charge the office for the services. Revenues for CDG come from the predetermined fees charged to the two offices.

Susan Willard suggests that the CDG should provide its services free of charge. Under this proposal, Scott would receive a fixed salary and a bonus based on overall firm profits (i.e., a percentage of the combined profits of the two offices). She thinks that, as the cost of the department is finally consolidated with the costs of the firm, there should be no distribution of costs for the department. Removal of the transfer price will help reduce the work of the accounts department and help streamline the accounts department to cope with the rapid growth of the firm. Willard says that the firm is committed to designing the best products and that cost allocations really do not matter.

Will the resources of the Creative Design Group (CDG) be efficiently utilized under the new plan? Why? What are the merits and demerits of the existing plan? Is the proposed plan better than the existing one? Why?

DP 7–15: Transfer Prices in a Competitive Market (LO 6)

Celtex is a large, very successful, decentralized specialty chemical producer organized into five independent investment centers. Each of the five investment centers is free to buy products either inside or outside the firm and is judged based on residual income. Most of each division's sales are to external customers. Celtex has the general reputation of being one of the top two or three companies in each of its markets.

Don Horigan, president of Synthetic Chemicals (Synchem) Division, and Paul Juris, president of Consumer Products Division, are embroiled in a dispute. It all began two years ago when Juris asked Horigan to modify a synthetic chemical for a new household cleaner. In return, Synthetic Chemicals would be reimbursed for out-of-pocket costs. After spending considerable time perfecting the chemical, Juris solicited competitive bids from Horigan and some outside firms and awarded the contract to an outside firm who was the low bidder. This angered Horigan who expected his bid to receive special consideration because he developed the new chemical at cost and the outside vendors took advantage of his R&D.

The current conflict has to do with Synchem producing chemical Q47, a standard product, for Consumer Products. Because of an economic slowdown, all synthetic chemical producers have excess capacity. Synchem was asked to bid on supplying Q47 for Consumer Products. Consumer Products is moving into a new, experimental product line and Q47 is one of the key ingredients. While the magnitude of the order is small relative to Synchem's total business, the price of Q47 is very important in determining the profitability of the experimental line. Horigan bid $3.20 per gallon. Meas Chemicals, an outside firm, bid $3. Juris is mad because he knows that Horigan's bid contains a substantial amount of fixed overhead and profit. Synchem buys the base raw material, Q4, from the Organic Chemicals division of Celtex for $1 per gallon. Organic Chemical's out-of-pocket costs (i.e., variable costs) are 80% of the selling price. Synchem then further processes Q4 into Q47 and incurs additional variable costs of $1.75 per gallon. Distributed fixed overhead adds another $0.30 per gallon.

Horigan argues that he has $3.05 of cost in each gallon of Q47. If he turned around and sold the product for anything less than $3.20 he would be undermining his recent attempts to get his salespeople to stop cutting their bids and start quoting full-cost prices. Horigan has been trying to enhance the quality of the business he is getting and he fears that if he is forced to make Q47 for Consumer Products, all of his effort the last few months would be for naught. He argues that he already gave away the store once to Consumer Products and he won't do it again. He questions, "How can senior managers expect me to return a positive residual income if I am forced to put in bids that don't recover full cost?"

Juris, in a chance meeting at the airport with Debra Donak, senior vice president of Celtex, described the situation and asked Donak to intervene. Juris believed Horigan was trying to get even after their earlier clash. Juris argued that the success of his new product venture depended on being able to secure a stable, high-quality supply of Q47 at low cost.

a. Prepare a statement outlining the cash flows to Celtex of the two alternative sources of supply for Q47.
b. What advice would you give Debra Donak?

DP 7–16: Identifying Responsibility Centers (LO 1, 2)
In a recent *Wall Street Journal* article, General Motors announced a reorganization to "designate individuals who will be accountable for the development of new cars and light trucks."[4] The newly created post of vehicle-line manager was established to "make sure new products get to market quickly and efficiently." Also, the position of brand manager was established for "making sure each individual model has a consistent and well-defined image in consumers' eyes."

a. Based on their responsibilities, would you classify the vehicle-line manager and the brand manager as managers of cost, profit, or investment centers?
b. What are possible performance measures for these two types of managers?

CASES

C 7–1: IBM Data Center for Eastman Kodak
In 1989, IBM and Kodak entered into an agreement whereby IBM would build and operate a data processing center in Rochester, N.Y., that consolidates five Kodak data centers into one. Of the five original data centers, three were at separate sites in Rochester, one was in Colorado, and the fifth was in Canada.

Over 300 data processing Kodak employees became IBM employees. Original, Kodak-owned IBM computer equipment was purchased by IBM and moved into the IBM data center. IBM augmented this equipment with a significant amount of new equipment (both IBM and non-IBM products).

Kodak pays an annual fee to IBM based on the amount of computing services they receive (e.g., lines printed, amount of disk space). The IBM data center pays all labor costs, occupancy costs, and the costs of all software and hardware acquired. The IBM data center is evaluated based on profits and the satisfaction of Kodak consumers.

Prior to the IBM-Kodak agreement, excess capacity in the mainframe business had increased price competition. A third-party vendor made a bid to operate Kodak's five data centers at a substantial cost savings to Kodak. One source of the savings came from the vendor's use of less expensive computers that are plug-compatible with IBM's machines. IBM made a competitive counteroffer, which they won, to keep the Kodak account and run the data center.

Kodak views this contract as being very important because it allows them to get out of the business of operating computers and focus their management's attention on more strategic issues such as the design and maintenance of their applications software directed at their core businesses. These application computer programs run at the data center and include billing, payroll, accounts payable and receivable, cost accounting, and manufacturing production control and scheduling.

IBM considers the data center an important test case for their other large corporate clients looking to move away from IBM hardware to plug-compatible mainframe clones. If IBM can successfully operate this data center for Kodak, it opens an important market of other large Fortune 100 companies. IBM has the expertise in centralizing and standardizing different data centers into one using a common set of operating standards. There are economies of scale in corporate computing. Also, operating data centers allows IBM to learn about large corporate-client computing, to develop new software and hardware, and to test new products before they are released.

One key issue that arises is the internal transfer price the IBM data center pays for the IBM hardware and software they "purchase" from other IBM divisions. This transfer price does not affect the price Kodak pays to IBM. Suppose a hypothetical IBM mainframe numbered A606 that sells for $3 million is installed in the Kodak data center. The variable cost of this machine is $1 million and its full manufactured cost, including fixed and variable costs, is $1.6 million. Moreover, IBM's total selling, general, and administrative (SG&A) costs are 30% of revenue, of which half (15%) varies directly with revenue. The comparable plug-compatible machine to the A606 sells for $1.9 million. The other IBM divisions providing goods and services to the data center have profit responsibilities.

Case Questions

a. What factors should IBM consider when developing the transfer pricing rule used to charge the data center for IBM products installed in the data center?
b. Given the limited information in the case, what transfer price rule would you suggest that IBM adopt for IBM products installed in the data center? Using your transfer price rule, what price should be charged for the hypothetical A606 mainframe example?

C 7–2: PortCo Products   PortCo Products is a divisionalized furniture manufacturer. The divisions are autonomous segments, with each division being responsible for its own sales, costs of operations, working capital management, and equipment acquisition. Each division serves a different market in the furniture industry. Because the markets and products of the divisions are so different, there have never been any transfers between divisions.

The Commercial Division manufactures equipment and furniture that is purchased by the restaurant industry. The division plans to introduce a new line of counter and chair units that feature a cushioned seat for the counter chairs. John Kline, the Commercial Division manager, has discussed the manufacturing of the cushioned seat with Russ Fiegel of the Office Division. They both believe a cushioned seat currently made by the Office Division for use on its deluxe office stool could be modified for use on the new counter chair. Consequently, Kline has asked Russ Fiegel for a price for 100-unit lots of the cushioned seat. The following conversation took place about the price to be charged for the cushioned seats.

Fiegel: "John, we can make the necessary modifications to the cushioned seat easily. The raw materials used in your seat are slightly different and should cost about 10% more than those used in our deluxe office stool. However, the labor time should be the same because the seat fabrication operation basically is the same. I would price the seat at our regular rate—full cost plus 30% markup."
Kline: "That's higher than I expected, Russ. I was thinking that a good price would be your variable manufacturing costs. After all, your capacity costs will be incurred regardless of this job."
Fiegel: "John, I'm at capacity. By making the cushioned seats for you, I'll have to cut my production of deluxe office stools. Of course, I can increase my production of economy office stools. The labor time freed by not having to fabricate the frame or assemble the deluxe stool can be shifted to the frame fabrication and assembly of the economy office stool. And you will save the cost of the framing raw materials. However, I am constrained in terms of the number of hours I have for cushion fabrication. Fortunately, I can switch my labor force between these two models of stools without any loss of efficiency. As you know, overtime is not a feasible alternative in our community. I'd like to sell it to you at variable cost, but I have excess demand for both products. I don't mind changing my product mix to the economy model if I get a good return on the seats I make for you. Here are my budgeted costs for the two stools and a schedule of my manufacturing overhead." [See Exhibits 1 and 2 for budgeted costs and overhead schedule.]

EXHIBIT 1
Office Division—Budgeted Costs and Prices

	Deluxe Office Stool		Economy Office Stool
Raw materials			
Framing	$ 8.15		$ 9.76
Cushioned seat			
Padding	2.40		—
Vinyl	4.00		—
Molded seat (purchased)	—		6.00
Direct labor			
Frame fabrication (0.5 × $7.50/DLH)	3.75	(0.5 × $7.50/DLH)	3.75
Cushion fabrication (0.5 × $7.50/DLH)	3.75		—
Assembly* (0.5 × $7.50/DLH)	3.75	(0.3 × $7.50/DLH)	2.25
Manufacturing			
Overhead (1.5 DLH† × $12.80/DLH)	19.20	(0.8DLH × $12.80/DLH)	10.24
Total standard cost	$45.00		$32.00
Selling price (30% markup)	$58.50		$41.60

*Attaching seats to frames and attaching rubber feet.
†DLH stands for direct labor hours.

EXHIBIT 2
Office Division—Manufacturing Overhead Budget

Overhead Item	Nature	Amount
Supplies	Variable—at current market prices	$ 420,000
Indirect labor	Variable	375,000
Supervision	Nonvariable	250,000
Power	Use varies with activity; rates are fixed	180,000
Heat and light	Nonvariable—light is fixed regardless of production while heat/air conditioning varies with fuel charges	140,000
Property taxes and insurance	Nonvariable—any change in amounts/rates is independent of production	200,000
Depreciation	Fixed dollar total	1,700,000
Employee benefits	20% of supervision, direct and indirect labor	575,000
Total overhead		$3,840,000
Capacity in DLH		300,000
Overhead rate/DLH ($3,840,000/300,000)		$12.80

Kline: "I guess I see your point, Russ, but I don't want to price myself out of the market. Maybe we should talk to corporate to see if they can give us any guidance."

Case Questions

a. John Kline and Russ Fiegel did ask PortCo corporate management for guidance on an appropriate transfer price. Corporate management suggested they consider using a transfer price based on opportunity cost. Calculate a transfer price for the cushioned seat based on variable manufacturing cost plus forgone profits.

b. Which alternative transfer-price system—full cost, variable manufacturing cost, or opportunity cost—would be better as the underlying concept for an intracompany transfer-price policy? Explain your answer.

(CMA adapted)

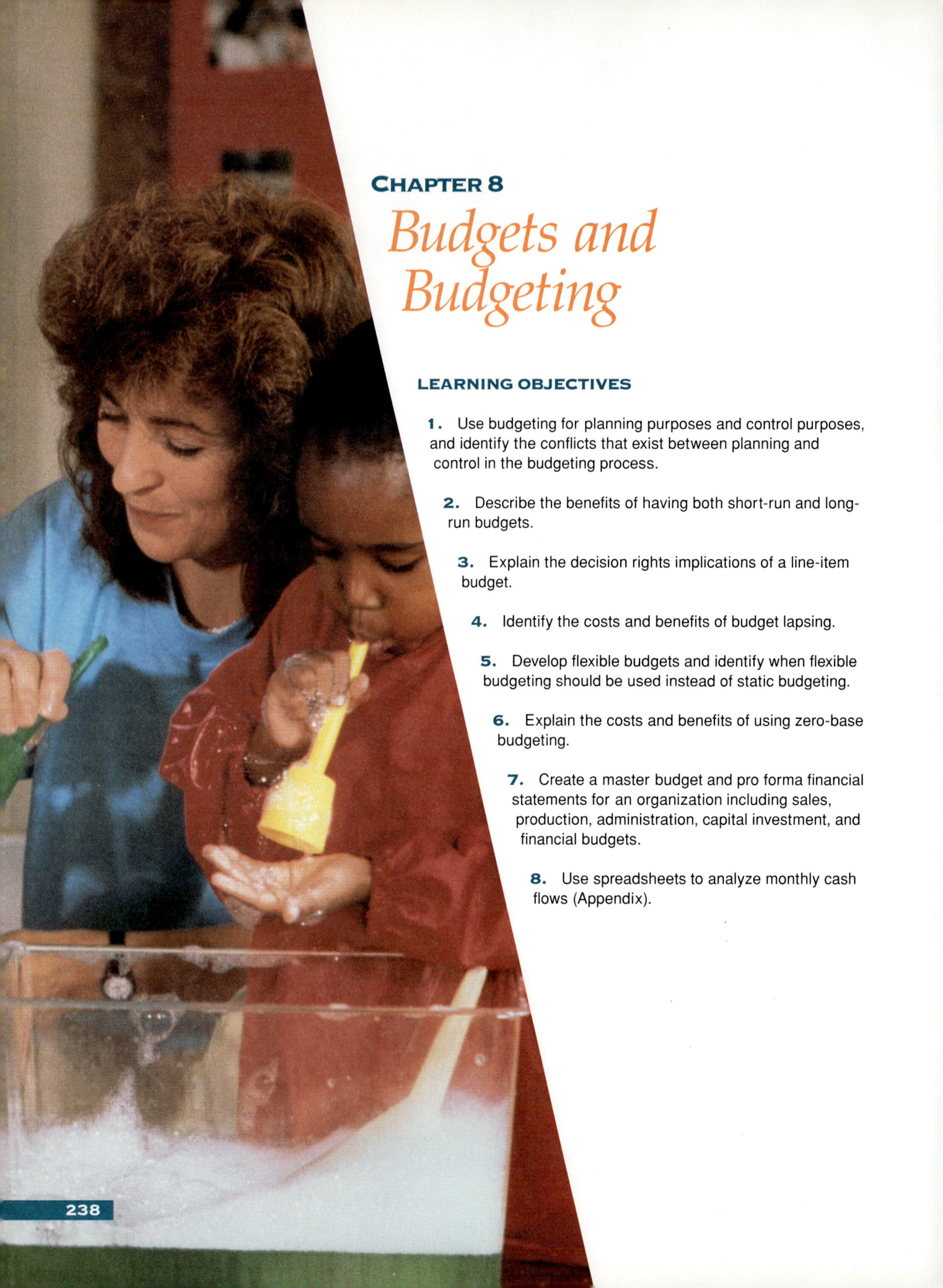

Chapter 8

Budgets and Budgeting

LEARNING OBJECTIVES

1. Use budgeting for planning purposes and control purposes, and identify the conflicts that exist between planning and control in the budgeting process.

2. Describe the benefits of having both short-run and long-run budgets.

3. Explain the decision rights implications of a line-item budget.

4. Identify the costs and benefits of budget lapsing.

5. Develop flexible budgets and identify when flexible budgeting should be used instead of static budgeting.

6. Explain the costs and benefits of using zero-base budgeting.

7. Create a master budget and pro forma financial statements for an organization including sales, production, administration, capital investment, and financial budgets.

8. Use spreadsheets to analyze monthly cash flows (Appendix).

Mapledale Child Center

Mapledale Child Center (MCC) is a not-for-profit organization that provides day care and kindergarten education to the children of the Mapledale housing subdivision of the city of Tucson. MCC rents space in a neighborhood building where both the day care and nursery school programs are housed along with MCC's administrative offices.

The day care program is for children between six months and five years of age. MCC charges $500 per month per child for day care for eight hours every weekday. MCC day care is open 12 months of the year. A licensed staff of counselors provides a structured set of activities gauged to the age of the children. One counselor is necessary for every five children. The day care center has a capacity of 50 children.

The kindergarten is four hours per day, either morning or afternoon, for nine months. Each session has a capacity of 75 children and costs $360 per month per child. MCC needs one kindergarten teacher for every 10 children. A nurse is always on staff for both the day care and kindergarten program.

MCC is supervised by a 10-member board of directors, who oversee the operations of MCC. The board of directors hires the manager of the day care center, the manager of the kindergarten program, and the office manager. The managers of the day care and kindergarten programs hire their staffs, plan their programs, and are responsible for the financial operations of their programs. The office manager has a secretary and bookkeeper, who prepare the monthly bills for the users of the facility, monthly financial reports for the board of directors, purchase supplies, and are responsible for collecting and disbursing funds.

The fiscal year of MCC is from July 1 through June 30. Prior to the beginning of the fiscal year, the office manager asks the day care and kindergarten managers to prepare budgets to plan for the coming fiscal year. MCC cannot spend more than its revenue, so the budgeting process is very important for planning for the new school year.

8.1 The Purpose of Budgets

Budgets are forecasts of future revenues and expenditures. **Budgeting** is the process of gathering information to assist in making those forecasts. Budgeting is a very costly process. Managers often spend up to 20% of their time on budgeting. The popularity of budgeting, however, indicates that the perceived benefits of budgeting are greater than the costs.

The benefits of budgeting are apparent in making planning decisions and for control. For planning purposes, the budgeting process generates and communicates information to improve coordination between departments and divisions within a company. The budgeting process is the starting process for initiating change in an organization. The control benefits of budgets include assigning decision rights and scarce resources, providing a goal to motivate managers, and establishing performance measures to reward managers.

Budgeting for Planning Decisions

Budgets play an integral role in making planning decisions. One purpose of budgeting is to transfer information to the individuals making decisions within the organization. Managers near the top of an organization's hierarchy must make major, long-term planning decisions. Yet some of the information necessary to make those decisions is located with managers near the bottom of the hierarchy. To improve major, long-term decisions, the information located near the bottom of the hierarchy must filter up to the top-level management. The budgeting process attempts to fulfill this role by encouraging the "bottom-up" flow of information. An example of this bottom-up flow in the budgeting process is the collection of expenditure requests by the central administration of a university from the various departments. The head of each department knows the needs of that department and those needs are communicated to the central administration through the budgeting process.

Although the earth itself may be a remnant of a "big bang," these earth replicas are produced through careful planning. The budgeting process gathers and communicates information to help managers meet the demand for globes and produce them efficiently.

Lower level managers of the organization also must make decisions. To improve their decisions, lower level managers could use information located with top-level managers. Top-level managers have aggregated information from the various parts of the organization and the outside environment. To allow lower level managers to make more informed decisions and decisions that are coordinated with other managers within the organization, the top-level managers must communicate their information and plans from the "top-down." For example, the top managers of a bottle-manufacturing firm must communicate production requirements to the managers of the different manufacturing facilities. The top-level managers have information on global demand for bottles and use this information to determine production requirements for each of the manufacturing facilities.

Budgeting for Control

Budgets also play an important role in control. The budget is often used to assign decision rights by allocating resources to different managers. Giving a manager an advertising budget of $800,000 authorizes that manager to consume $800,000 of firm resources on advertising. The level of decision rights given to the manager determines how the $800,000 on advertising can be spent. If the advertising manager has the confidence of the top-level managers and specialized knowledge on advertising, the budget may give the advertising manager the flexibility to choose how to spend the $800,000. If the advertising manager is new and does not have specialized knowledge, the budget may also specify how the $800,000 is to be spent. For example, $500,000 is to be spent on radio advertisements and $300,000 on newspaper advertisements. The more constraints that the budget imposes on the manager the less decision rights given to the manager.

> **WHAT'S HAPPENING**
>
> Firms complying with environmental regulations often must install equipment to clean waste water and air emissions. Such environmental projects can be costly and thus require careful financial planning, including detailed budgets. Why do most large firms develop detailed budgets for environmental projects?

The numbers in the budget are also used as goals to motivate members of the organization. Budgeted numbers become targets for the managers of the organization. For example, the manager of a factory making tennis racquets is allocated $700,000 to make 10,000 racquets. The 10,000 racquets is a goal for the manager of the factory. The manager is expected to work hard and manage well to achieve the goal of making 10,000 racquets with the $700,000.

Once the budget is set, it becomes the target by which performance is evaluated and rewarded. In setting the budget, some experts argue the budget should be tight but achievable. If budgets are too easily achieved, they provide little incentive to expend extra effort. If budgets are unachievable, they provide little motivation. The motivation to achieve budgeted numbers is through rewards. If budgeted numbers are achieved, the manager is rewarded through bonuses or other privileges. The manager of the tennis racquet factory works hard to achieve the goal of manufacturing 10,000 racquets for $700,000 because the manager knows that rewards are based on achieving the budget.

The difference between a budgeted performance measure and an actual performance measure is called the **variance.** An **unfavorable variance** occurs when actual costs are greater than the budgeted costs or actual revenues are less than budgeted revenues. A **favorable variance** occurs when actual costs are less than the budgeted costs or actual revenues are greater than budgeted revenues. Variances are commonly calculated in monthly reports to identify how successfully an organization is achieving its goals. Large favorable or unfavorable variances are commonly investigated to determine the reason for the variance and to correct any problems that may exist.

NUMERICAL EXAMPLE 8.1

The Ayala Company has the following budgeted and actual results for the month of July.

AYALA COMPANY
July Income
Budgeted and Actual Results

	Budgeted	Actual
Revenues	$450,000	$453,000
Cost of goods sold	(235,000)	(248,000)
General administration	(80,000)	(132,000)
Selling expenses	(100,000)	(90,000)
Profit	$ 35,000	($ 17,000)

Calculate the variances for each of the items in the monthly report and describe them as favorable or unfavorable. What item appears to warrant some investigation?

■ **SOLUTION** The variances are the difference between the budgeted and actual amounts:

AYALA COMPANY
July Income
Budgeted and Actual Amounts

	Budgeted	Actual	Variance
Revenues	$450,000	$453,000	$ 3,000 F
Cost of goods sold	(235,000)	(248,000)	13,000 U
General administration	(80,000)	(132,000)	52,000 U
Selling expenses	(100,000)	(90,000)	10,000 F
Profit	$ 35,000	($ 17,000)	$52,000 U

The actual general administration expense account is much different than expected and has the largest variance. Large unfavorable variances are generally the focus of an investigation if the cause of the problem is unknown. The other accounts have smaller variances but may also be investigated.

WHAT'S HAPPENING

A number of Japanese car companies such as Toyota and Daihatsu use an elaborate system of continuous cost improvement called *Kaizen costing*. Monthly budgets document differences between actual and budgeted cost reductions, and managers in each department are held responsible for the variances. Why would Japanese automakers be especially interested in lowering their costs?

Organizations should modify the budgeting process to meet their special planning and control needs. The Hon Company, the nation's largest maker of midpriced office furniture, operates in a very volatile industry. Annual budgets for the company do not provide meaningful targets because of changing demand for its product. To accommodate a rapidly changing environment, the Hon Company makes new budgets every three months. By continuously updating budgets every three months, the company is able to meet its two strategic objectives of ongoing new product and service development and rapid continuous improvement.[1]

In the rapidly changing business environment of office furniture, these Hon Company employees must meet frequently and update budgets based on new information.

MAPLEDALE CHILD CENTER (CONTINUED)

Budgeting is extremely important for the Mapledale Child Center (MCC). The budget is used to estimate the total enrollment and revenues available to MCC. Based on estimated enrollment and revenues, MCC determines how many teachers and counselors to hire. The budget also specifies how much the managers of the day care and kindergarten programs and the office manager can spend on educational and office supplies. A larger budget for educational and office supplies gives the managers more decision rights. There are no bonuses based on the budget, but having greater resources for teaching makes teaching easier and more rewarding.

8.2 Conflict between Planning and Control

Budgeting systems serve two principal purposes, planning and control. In making planning decisions, budgets communicate specialized knowledge from one part of the organization to another. For control, budgets serve as performance measurement systems. Because budgets serve several purposes, trade-offs must be made when designing or changing a budgeting system. The budget becomes the benchmark against which to judge actual performance. If too much emphasis is placed on the budget as a performance benchmark, managers with the specialized knowledge will stop disclosing accurate forecasts of future events for planning decisions. Managers will tend to report budget figures to make benchmarks easier to achieve.

The problem of trading off the making of planning decisions and control is particularly severe in marketing. Salespeople usually have specialized knowledge of future sales. This information is important in setting future production plans such as how many units to manufacture. But if budgeted sales are used to evaluate salespeople at the end of the year, then salespeople have an incentive to underforecast future sales, thus improving their performance evaluation.

However, production plans will then be too low and the firm will be unable to plan the most efficient production schedules.

To manage the trade-off between making planning decisions and control, many organizations put the chief executive officer in charge of the budgeting process. While the actual collection of data and preparation of the budget is the formal responsibility of the chief financial officer or controller, the president or chief executive officer has the final decision rights. There are several reasons for the chief executive to have immediate control. First, it signals the importance of the budgeting process. Second, resolving disagreements among departments requires making trade-offs and the chief executive, who has the overall view of the whole firm, is best able to make these trade-offs.

In addition to placing the chief executive in charge of the budgeting process, many firms also use a budget committee. Such a committee consists of the major functional executives (vice presidents of sales, manufacturing, finance, and personnel) with the chief executive as chairman. The purpose of such a committee is to facilitate the exchange of specialized knowledge and to reach consensus in establishing a budget.

The budget is an informal set of contracts between the various units of the organization. By accepting the budget, managers of the organization agree to perform the actions and abide by the limitations specified by the budget.

Most budgets are set in a negotiation process involving lower and higher level managers. Lower level managers have incentives to set easier targets to guarantee they will meet the budget and be favorably rewarded, whereas higher level managers have incentives to set the target to motivate the lower level managers to exert additional effort. The conflict between making planning decisions and control is often viewed as a trade-off between bottom-up budgeting versus top-down budgeting. Bottom-up budgets are those submitted by lower levels of the organization to higher levels and usually imply better information for planning decisions. An example of a bottom-up budget is the field sales offices' submission of their forecasts for next year to the marketing department. A top-down budget would be the central marketing department's use of aggregate data on sales trends to forecast sales for the entire firm and then the disaggregation of this firmwide budget into field office targets. This top-down budget provides greater control.

A bottom-up budget, in which the person ultimately being held responsible for meeting the target makes the initial budget forecast, is called **participative budgeting.** Participation enhances the motivation of the lower level participants by getting them to accept the targets.

The extent to which a budget is bottom-up or top-down ultimately depends on where the knowledge is located. If the knowledge is with the field salespeople, the decision right to set the budget should be linked with the knowledge and placed in the field. If the central marketing organization has better knowledge, a topdown budget is likely to prove better. Which budgeting scheme provides better motivation ultimately depends on how the performance measurement and reward systems are designed.

In a survey of 98 large U.S. companies, firms indicated that they used participative budgeting more frequently when lower level managers have specialized knowledge.[2] Moreover, participative budgeting is more frequently observed when managers' rewards are based on their performance against the budget. This evidence is consistent with budgets and performance reward systems being designed to link decision rights and specialized knowledge.

> **WHAT'S HAPPENING**
>
> A study of large U.S. companies and hospitals reports that boards of directors, chairmen of the board, presidents, and executive vice presidents of the organization are frequently involved in budget approval. Why do most organizations require several levels to approve the budget?

MAPLEDALE CHILD CENTER (CONTINUED)

> The managers of the child care and kindergarten programs are responsible for estimating how many children will be attending their programs next year. The managers are closer than the board of directors to the parents of the children and, therefore, have the specialized knowledge to make that estimate. But the program managers have a dilemma. They know that their estimated enrollment numbers will be used to allocate space, teachers and supplies to their respective programs. The higher the estimated enrollment, the greater the resources they will receive. On the other hand, if the program managers estimate too high of an enrollment, they will look bad based on their primary performance measure, which is to maintain a capacity number of students in their respective programs. Recognizing this conflict, the board of directors decided to do their own survey of the community to verify the estimates of the program managers.

CONCEPT REVIEW

1. What are the planning benefits of budgeting?
2. What are the control benefits of budgeting?
3. How do planning and control issues lead to conflict in the budgeting process?

8.3 How Budgeting Helps Resolve Organizational Problems

Budgeting systems are an administrative device used to resolve organizational problems. In particular, these systems help (1) link knowledge with the decision rights to make planning decisions and (2) distribute decision rights and measure and reward performance for control. This section further describes the economics of various budgeting devices, such as short-run versus long-run budgets, line-item budgets, budget lapsing, flexible budgets, and incremental versus zero-base budgets.

Short-Run versus Long-Run Budgets

Most organizations have annual budgeting processes. Starting in the prior year, organizations develop detailed plans of how many units of each product they expect to sell, at what prices, the cost of such sales, and the financing necessary for operations. These budgets then become the internal "contracts" for each responsibility center (cost, profit, and investment) within the firm. These annual budgets are *short-run* in the sense that they only project one year at a time. But most firms also project 2, 5, and sometimes 10 years in advance. These are *long-run* budgets and are a key feature of the organization's strategic-planning process.

Strategic planning is the term used to describe the process whereby managers select the firm's overall objectives and the tactics to achieve those objectives. It involves deciding what markets to be in, what products to produce, and what price-quality combination to offer and anticipating the response of competitors. For example, Eastman Kodak is faced with the strategic question of how to respond to the electronic imaging market. Making this decision requires specialized knowledge of the various technologies Kodak and its competitors face, in addition to knowledge of the demand for various future products.

Long-run budgets, like short-run budgets, encourage managers with specialized knowledge to communicate their forecasts of future expected events. Such long-run budgets contain forecasts of large asset acquisitions (and financing plans) for the manufacturing and distribution systems required to implement the strategy. Research and development budgets are long-run plans of the multiyear spending required to acquire and develop the technologies to implement the strategies.

In short-run budgets, important estimates include quantities produced and sold and prices. All parts of the organization must accept those estimates. In long-run budgets, important assumptions involve the choice of markets and the technologies to be acquired.

A typical firm integrates the short-run and long-run budgeting process into a single process. As next year's budget is being developed, a five-year budget is also produced. Year one of the five-year plan is next year's budget. Years two and three are fairly detailed and year two becomes the base to establish next year's one-year budget. Years four and five are less detailed, but incorporate new market opportunities. Each year, the five-year budget is rolled forward one year and the process begins anew.

The short-run (annual) budget involves both planning and control functions and thus a trade-off arises between these two functions. Long-run budgets are hardly ever used as a control (performance evaluation) device. Rather, long-run budgets are used primarily for planning. Five- and ten-year budgets force managers to think about strategy and to communicate the specialized knowledge of their potential future markets and technologies. Thus, long-run budgets have much less conflict between planning and control because much less emphasis is placed on using the long-run budget as a performance measurement tool.

Long-run budgets also reduce managers' focus on short-term performance. Without long-term budgets, managers have an incentive to cut expenditures such as maintenance, advertising, and R&D in order to improve short-run performance or to balance short-term budgets at the expense of the long-term viability of the firm. Budgets that span five years make it more likely that top management and/or the board of directors are informed of the long-term trade-offs being taken to accomplish short-run goals.

Line-Item Budgets

Line-item budgets refer to budgets that authorize the manager to spend only up to the specified amount on each line item. In the budget shown in Table 8.1, the manager is authorized to spend $12,000 on office supplies for the year. If the supplies can be purchased for $11,000, the manager with a line-item budget is

TABLE 8.1

Line-Item Budget Example

Line Item	Amount
Salaries	$185,000
Office supplies	12,000
Office equipment	3,000
Postage	1,900
Maintenance	350
Utilities	1,200
Rent	900
Total	$204,350

Internal Revenue Service (IRS) workers are limited by a line-item budget. Congressional funding of the IRS occurs through bills that specify how much money can be spent on each activity.

not able to spend the $1,000 savings on any other category (such as additional office equipment). Because the manager cannot spend savings from one line item on another line item without prior approval, the manager has less incentive to look for savings. Moreover, if next year's line item is reduced by the amount of the savings, managers have even less incentive to search for savings.

The benefit of a line-item budget is the imposition of more control on the manager. Managers responsible for line-item budgets cannot reduce spending on one item and divert the savings to items that enhance their own welfare. By maintaining tighter control over how much is spent on particular items, the organization reduces the possibility of management action that is inconsistent with the organization's goals.

Line-item budgets are quite prevalent in government organizations such as city and state governments. They also are used in some corporations but with fewer restrictions. Line-item budgets provide an extreme form of control. The manager does not have the decision rights to substitute resources among line items as circumstances change. To make such changes during the year requires special approval from a higher level in the organization, such as the city council. The decision right to change actual expenditures from the budget does not reside with the operating manager.

Line-item budgets illustrate how the budgeting system partitions decision rights, thereby controlling behavior. In particular, a manager given the decision rights to spend up to $3,000 on office equipment does not have the decision rights to substitute office equipment for postage. A survey of 120 large publicly traded firms found that among units reporting directly to the CEO, 22% cannot substitute among line items, 24% can substitute if they receive authorization, and 26% can make substitutions within prespecified limits.[3] The remaining 28% can make substitutions if the unit's financial objective is improved. These findings suggest that even at fairly high levels in for-profit firms, line-item budgets are prevalent.

Budget Lapsing

Another common feature in budgeting is **budget lapsing.** If budgets lapse, funds that have not been spent at year-end do not carry over to the next year. Budget lapsing creates incentives for managers to spend all their budget. Not only do managers lose the benefits from the unspent funds, but next year's budget might be reduced by the amount of the underspending.

Project budgets lapse at the end of the project instead of the end of the year. For example, construction projects might span several fiscal years. Funds unspent in one year are automatically carried over to the next year. However, any unspent funds when the project is completed lapse.

Budgets that lapse provide tighter controls on managers than budgets that do not lapse. If budgets don't lapse, managers have the decision right to choose when to make expenditures. When budgets lapse, managers can only make the expenditure in the year of the budget.

Without budget lapsing, managers could build up substantial balances in their budgets. Toward the end of their careers with the firm, these managers would then be tempted to make very large expenditures on perquisites. For example, they could take their staff to Hawaii for a "training retreat." Budget lapsing also prevents risk-averse managers from "saving" their budget for a "rainy day." If it is optimum for a manager to spend a certain amount of money on a particular activity, then saving part of that amount as a contingency fund is not optimum. One way to prevent these control problems from occurring is for budgets to lapse.

The disadvantage of lapsing budgets is less efficient operations. Managers devote substantial time at the end of the year ensuring that their budget is fully expended, even if it means buying items that have lower value (and a higher cost) than they would purchase if they could carry the budget over to the next fiscal year. Often, these end-of-year purchases cause the firm to incur substantial warehousing costs to hold the extra purchases. In one example, a Navy ship's officer purchased an 18-month supply of paper in order to spend his remaining budget. The paper weighed so much that it had to be stored evenly around the ship to make sure the ship did not tilt to one side.

Managers cannot adjust to changing operating conditions during the year if budgets lapse. For example, if the manager has expended all of his/her budget authority and the opportunity to make a bargain purchase arises, the manager cannot borrow against next year's budget without getting special permission.

What's Happening

In planning future operations of its overseas branches, Bank of America develops budgeted foreign exchange rates that estimate the number of U.S. dollars a particular foreign currency such as a British pound will buy in the future. This budget rate is a key planning assumption and has multiple uses within the firm such as coverting foreign earnings into U.S. dollars and evaluating subsidiary performance. Budgeted exchange rates are static budgets that do not change with fluctuations in the actual conversion rates between two currencies. Why would Bank of America want to evaluate some of its managers using budgeted exchange rates?

Static versus Flexible Budgets

All of the examples in this chapter have described **static budgets.** A static budget is one that does not vary with volume. Each line item is a fixed amount. In contrast, a **flexible budget** is one that is stated as a function of some volume measure. Flexible budgets are adjusted for changes in volume. Flexible budgets provide different incentives than static budgets.

As an example of flexible budgeting, consider the case of a concert. A band is hired for $20,000 plus 15% of the gate receipts. The auditorium is rented for $5,000 plus 5% of the gate receipts. Security guards costing $80 apiece are hired, one for every 200 people. Advertising, insurance, and other fixed costs are $28,000. Ticket prices are $18 each. A flexible budget for the concert is presented in Table 8.2.

Each line item in the budget is stated in terms of how it varies with volume, ticket sales in this case. Then a budget is prepared at different volume levels. At ticket sales of 3,000, an $11,000 loss is projected. At sales of 4,000 and 5,000 tickets, $3,000 and $17,000 of profit are forecasted, respectively.

TABLE 8.2

Flexible Budget for Concert

	(Formula)	Ticket Sales 3,000	4,000	5,000
Revenues	$18N*	$54,000	$72,000	$90,000
Band	$20,000 + 0.15(18N)	(28,100)	(30,800)	(33,500)
Auditorium	$5,000 + 0.05(18N)	(7,700)	(8,600)	(9,500)
Security	$80(N/200)	(1,200)	(1,600)	(2,000)
Other costs	$28,000	(28,000)	(28,000)	(28,000)
Profit/(loss)		($11,000)	$ 3,000	$17,000

*N is the number of tickets sold.

The major reason for using flexible rather than static budgets is to improve evaluation of the actual performance of a person or venture after controlling for volume effects, assuming of course that the individual being evaluated is not responsible for the volume changes. For example, consider the following illustration. After the concert which 5,000 people attended, the actual cost of the auditorium was $9,900 instead of the $9,500 flexible budget. The additional $400 was for damage. The budget for the auditorium is automatically increased to $9,500 due to the 5,000 ticket sales and the manager is not held responsible for volume changes. However, the manager is held responsible for the $400 unfavorable variance between the actual charge of $9,900 and $9,500. In evaluating the manager's performance, the cause of the variance will be investigated. For example, would additional security guards have prevented this damage?

When should a firm or department use a static budget and when should they use a flexible budget? Static budgets do not adjust for volume effects. Volume fluctuations in static budgets are passed through and show up in the difference between actual and budgeted numbers. Thus, static budgets hold managers

"Woodstock 94" was a carefully organized rock concert. The organizers used flexible budgeting to estimate revenues and costs. How are costs and revenues likely to vary with the number of spectators?

responsible for volume fluctuations. If the manager has some control over volume or the consequences of volume, then static budgets should be used as the benchmark to evaluate performance. Flexible budgets adjust for volume effects. Volume fluctuations in flexible budgets are not passed through and do not show up in the difference between actual and budgeted numbers. Flexible budgets do not hold managers responsible for volume fluctuations. Therefore, if the manager does not have any control over volume, then flexible budgets should be used as the benchmark to evaluate performance. Flexible budgets reduce the risk of volume changes being borne by managers.

Forty-eight percent of 219 publicly traded U.S. firms indicated that they used flexible budgets for manufacturing costs but only 27% used flexible budgets for distribution, marketing, R&D, or general and administrative expenses.[4] These data suggest that flexible budgets are widely used in manufacturing where volume measures are readily available and many costs vary with volume.

NUMERICAL EXAMPLE 8.2

The Duffy Bicycle Company makes mountain bikes that it sells for $200 apiece. The company establishes a flexible annual budget. The fixed manufacturing costs are budgeted as $2 million; the variable manufacturing costs are budgeted as $80 per bike. Selling and administrative costs are expected to be fixed and are budgeted as $1 million. No beginning or ending inventory is expected.

a. Make a budget for income for the company assuming the manufacture and sale of 20,000 bikes, 30,000 bikes, and 40,000 bikes.
b. If 34,000 bikes are actually made and actual revenues are $6,500,000, actual variable costs are $2,500,000, actual fixed manufacturing costs are $2,100,000, and actual selling and administration costs are $950,000, what are the variances of each of these accounts and the profit variance?

SOLUTION

a.

DUFFY BICYCLE COMPANY
Budgeted Income

Number of Bicycles Manufactured and Sold

	20,000	30,000	40,000
Revenues (× $200)	$4,000,000	$6,000,000	$8,000,000
Variable costs (× $80)	(1,600,000)	(2,400,000)	(3,200,000)
Fixed manufacturing	(2,000,000)	(2,000,000)	(2,000,000)
Selling and admin.	(1,000,000)	(1,000,000)	(1,000,000)
Profit (loss)	($ 600,000)	$ 600,000	$1,800,000

b. The budgeted revenues and costs, actual revenues and costs, and variances if 34,000 bikes are made are:

	Budgeted	Actual	Variance
Revenues (34,000 × $200)	$6,800,000	$6,500,000	$300,000 U
Variable costs (34,000 × $80)	(2,720,000)	(2,500,000)	220,000 F
Fixed manufacturing	(2,000,000)	(2,100,000)	100,000 U
Selling and admin.	(1,000,000)	(950,000)	50,000 F
Budgeted profit	$1,080,000	$ 950,000	$130,000 U

The unfavorable variance is caused by lower than expected prices and higher than expected fixed manufacturing costs.

Incremental versus Zero-Base Budgets

Most organizations construct next year's budget by starting with the current year's budget and adjusting each line item for expected price and volume changes. Each manager submits a budget for next year by making incremental changes in each line item. For example, the line item in next year's budget for purchases is calculated by increasing last year's purchases for inflation and including any incremental purchases for volume changes and new programs. Only detailed explanations justifying the increments are submitted or reviewed. An **incremental budget** is reviewed and changed at higher levels in the organization, but usually only the incremental changes are examined in detail. The base/core budget (i.e., last year's base budget) is taken as given.

Under **zero-base budgeting,** senior management mandates that each line item in total must be justified and reviewed each year; each line item is reset to *zero* each year. Departments must defend the entire expenditure each year, not just the changes. In a zero-base budget review, the following questions are usually asked: Should this activity be provided? What will happen if the activity is eliminated? At what quality/quantity level should the activity be provided? Can the activity be provided in some alternative way, such as hiring an outside firm to provide the goods or service? How much are other, similar companies spending on this activity (benchmarking)?

In principle, zero-base budgeting (ZBB) causes managers to maximize firm value by identifying and eliminating those expenditures whose total cost exceeds total benefits. Under incremental budgeting, in which incremental changes are added to the base budget, incremental expenditures are deleted when their costs exceed their benefits. But inefficient base budgets can continue to exist.

> **WHAT'S HAPPENING**
>
> President Jimmy Carter brought the concept of ZBB to the federal government in 1976. Why were governmental units headed by political appointees more likely to use ZBB?

In practice, ZBB is infrequently used. Zero-base budgeting is supposed to overcome traditional, incremental budgeting, but ZBB also often deteriorates into incremental budgeting. Each year under ZBB, the same justifications as last year's are typically submitted and adjusted for incremental changes. Because the volume of detailed reports rising up the organization is substantially larger under ZBB than under incremental budgeting, higher level managers tend to focus on the changes from last year anyway. The focus on budgetary changes is especially true if managers have been with the organization for a number of years and already know the base level budgets.

ZBB is most useful and common with changes in top-level management. New managers from outside the organization don't have the specialized knowledge in the base level budgets. These new managers also bring changes in strategy. Prior budgets are no longer as relevant and each line item must be justified in light of the changing goals of the new managers. However, ZBB is substantially more costly to conduct and is unlikely to continue once the new managers have gained knowledge of operations and the budgets have encompassed their new goals.

MAPLEDALE CHILD CENTER (CONTINUED)

The board of directors of the Mapledale Child Center (MCC) is primarily concerned about the annual budget. The only long-term problem they are considering is the purchase of a building for MCC. This decision will be based primarily on demand for child care and kindergartens in the Mapledale area. Long-term demand for MCC day care and kindergarten is a function of the cost, perceived quality of care and instruction, competition from other day care providers, and the future demographics of the Mapledale subdivision. Information on these factors is located with the board of directors, who are responsible for making this decision. Therefore, the budgeting process is not necessary to communicate the information.

The directors of the day care and kindergarten programs are relatively new, so the board of directors has decided to use a line-item budget. The line item budget relieves the directors of the day care and kindergarten programs of the decision on how to spend the money allocated to the programs. The board of directors also uses a lapsing budget so the novice program directors need not make decisions on which periods to spend resources.

A static budget is used based on the original projection of enrollment. The program directors are responsible for the quality of their programs, which is the major factor determining whether parents keep their children at MCC. Any lost revenue due to dropouts during the year is the responsibility of the program directors, so flexible budgeting provides the wrong incentives.

The board of directors for MCC has had greater longevity than the program directors and has considerable experience in budgeting for MCC. In addition, the operational procedures of MCC have not changed much over the years, so the board of directors has budget and accounting data from past years that can be used to prepare the new budget. Therefore, MCC uses an incremental approach to budgeting.

CONCEPT REVIEW

1. How do short-run and long-run budgets relate to planning and control?
2. How do line-item budgets affect the decision rights of a manager?
3. What are the costs and benefits of budget lapsing?
4. How do the responsibilities of the manager influence the choice between static and flexible budgets?
5. Under what conditions would zero-base budgeting be useful?

8.4 Comprehensive Master Budget Illustration

The previous sections described the basic concepts that must be considered in budgeting. This section describes how to construct a **master budget.** A master budget integrates the estimates from each department to predict production requirements, financing, cash flows, and financial statements at the end of the period. The master budget serves as a guide and a benchmark for the whole organization.

To prevent the example from becoming overwhelming with respect to the amount of data, a simple firm, NaturApples, that processes apples is used. This example describes how various parts of the organization develop their budgets. It illustrates the importance of coordination among the different departments of the organization and how budgets are then combined for the firm as a whole.

Description of the Firm: NaturApples

NaturApples processes apples into two products: applesauce and apple pie filling. Apples are purchased from local growers. They are processed and packed in tin cans as either applesauce or pie filling. Principal markets are institutional buyers such as hospitals, public schools, military bases, and universities. NaturApples' market is regional and is serviced by four salespeople who make direct calls on customers in a four-state area.

The firm is organized into two departments, processing and marketing. Each is headed by a vice president who reports directly to the president. In addition, there is a vice president of finance, who is responsible for all financial aspects of the firm, including collecting data and preparing budgets. The three vice presidents and the president constitute NaturApples' executive committee, which oversees the budgeting process.

Apples are grown by independent farmers in the region. Once harvested, the apples are purchased through the efforts of the vice president of finance and stored either in coolers at NaturApples or in third-party warehouses until NaturApples can process them. The processing plant operates for nine months of the year. In October, the plant starts up after a three-month shutdown. Workers first thoroughly clean and inspect all the processing equipment. The apples begin arriving in the middle of October and by the end of November, all the apple harvest is in warehouses or started in production. By June, all the apples have been processed and the plant shuts down for July, August, and September. NaturApples has a fiscal year starting October 1 and ending September 30.

For both products, applesauce and pie filling, the production process begins with the inspection, washing, peeling, and coring of the apples. The apples are then either mashed for applesauce or diced for pie filling, combined with other ingredients such as spices and chemical stabilizers, and cooked in vats. Both products are immediately canned on a single canning line in five-pound tins and packed in cases of 12 cans per case. At this point, the product has a two-year shelf life and is stored until ordered by the customer.

Overview of the Budgeting Process

The budgeting process begins the first of December, 10 months before the start of the fiscal year. The president and the vice president of finance forecast the next year's crop harvest, which will determine the purchase cost of apples. The vice president of marketing begins forecasting sales of applesauce and pie filling next year. Likewise, the processing vice president forecasts production costs and capacity. Every 2 months for the next 10 months, these marketing, processing, and apple procurement forecasts and budgets are revised in light of new information, and all three vice presidents and the president meet for a morning to discuss their revisions. On the first of August, the final master budget for the next fiscal year, which begins October 1, is adopted by executive committee and then taken to the board of directors for final approval. The executive committee also meets weekly to review current-year operations as compared to the budget and to discuss other operational issues. Figure 8.1 is a schematic diagram that illustrates the relationships among the component budgets of NaturApples' master budget. The final product of the master budget is the budgeted income statement, budgeted balance sheet, and budgeted cash flows at the bottom of Figure 8.1. All the other budgets provide the supporting detail, including the various key planning assumptions underlying the master budget.

The budgeting process should yield budgets that are internally consistent. For example, the amount of apples purchased should be equated to the amount processed into sauce and pie filling. To maintain consistency, a sequential and simultaneous budgeting process similar to Figure 8.1 is commonly used. The

FIGURE 8.1

Budgeting Process for NaturApples

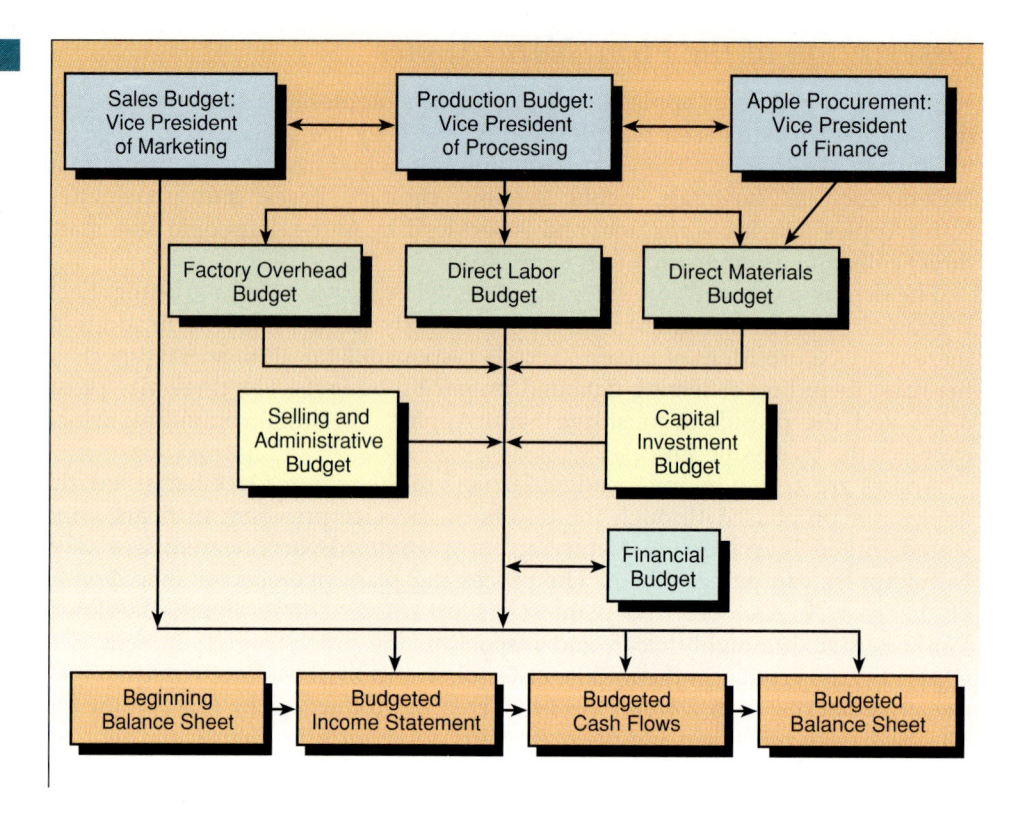

NaturApples purchases these apples and converts them into pie filling and applesauce.

budgeting process normally begins with a sales estimate, but the sales estimate depends on the price of the product. Sales quantities and prices should be chosen to maximize profits. The sales estimate must also consider production costs. Production costs depend on the availability and cost of raw materials (apples), direct labor, and overhead. Therefore, the sales budget, the production budget, and the procurement of apples should be considered together.

The production budget includes the raw materials, direct labor, and factory overhead budgets. These budgets jointly affect the estimated cost of goods sold. Not all expenditures are treated as part of the cost of goods sold. Selling and administrative expenditures are treated as expenses in financial reporting and are budgeted separately.

The production budget is also used to determine whether new property, plant, or equipment must be purchased to have sufficient capacity to meet production requirements. The capital investment budget reflects the estimated purchase of property, plant, and equipment for the next fiscal year.

Capital expenditures require cash. If cash is not available from operations, the firm may have to borrow to make large purchases. The financial budget is used to plan for borrowing, issuing stock, and making interest and dividend payments.

The individual budgets for sales, production, capital investments, and so forth are used to estimate financial statements at the end of the fiscal year. The estimated income statement and cash flow statement are used to adjust the beginning balance sheet to form an estimated ending balance sheet. The remainder of this section illustrates the preparation of these various component budgets and the estimated financial statements.

TABLE 8.3

NATURAPPLES
Expected Beginning Balance Sheet
10/1/1998

Assets
Cash		$ 100,000
Accounts receivable		200,000
Inventory		
Sauce (13,500 cases)($58/case)	783,000	
Pie filling (2,500 cases)($48/case)	120,000	903,000
Property, plant, and equipment (net)		2,300,000
		$3,503,000

Liabilities and Stockholders' Equity
Accounts payable	$ 100,000
Long-term debt	1,000,000
Stockholders' equity	2,403,000
	$3,503,000

Table 8.3 is the estimated balance sheet for the beginning of the fiscal year. The beginning balance sheet is estimated because the budget is determined before the end of the previous fiscal year. The beginning balance sheet represents the starting point for operations in the coming fiscal year.

Sales Budget

The sales (revenue) budget is generally created with the help of the marketing department. Employees of the marketing department usually have more information about the nature of potential customers and can provide insights on the relationship between the price and the quantity customers will purchase. The production department must also be involved with the sales budget because cost information is important in setting prices.

At NaturApples, the executive committee agrees on an estimate of next year's sales and prices based on information from the marketing and production departments. The sales budget for the next fiscal year is given in Table 8.4. The executive committee agrees that the firm should be able to sell 140,000 cases of sauce at $68 per case and 60,000 cases of pie filling at $53 per case. These quantities and prices were arrived at after months of exploring alternative price and quantity assumptions. In particular, the budgeted prices and quantities represent the managers' best judgment of the quantity at which marginal cost and marginal revenue are equal. Presumably, higher prices (and thus lower sales) or

TABLE 8.4

NATURAPPLES
Sales Budget
10/1/98–9/30/99

	Budgeted Cases	Budgeted Price/Case	Budgeted Revenue
Sauce	140,000	$68	$ 9,520,000
Pie filling	60,000	$53	$ 3,180,000
Total			$12,700,000

lower prices (and higher sales) will both result in lower profits than the combinations presented in Table 8.4.

Production Budget

The second major component of the master budget is the production budget. The production volume is chosen based on the following equation:

Beginning inventory + Production = Sales + Desired ending inventory

or

Production = Sales + Desired ending inventory − Beginning inventory

The total units in beginning inventory plus the units produced during the fiscal year must be either sold or in ending inventory.

NUMERICAL EXAMPLE 8.3

The BB Company manufactures baseballs. In the next year, the company expects to sell 20,000 baseballs. The company has 2,000 baseballs in the beginning inventory and wants to have 1,000 baseballs in ending inventory. How many baseballs should the company plan to manufacture?

SOLUTION

Production = Sales + Ending inventory − Beginning inventory
= 20,000 + 1,000 − 2,000 = 19,000

19,000 baseballs should be manufactured.

To solve for the number of units to produce at NaturApples, sales estimates from the sales budget in Table 8.4 are used. In addition, the beginning inventory from the expected beginning balance sheet in Table 8.3 must be estimated and a desired ending inventory position must be estimated. Table 8.5 describes the estimation of units to be produced given a desired ending inventory amount of 5,000 cases of sauce and 1,000 cases of pie filling. This ending inventory amount should cover expected sales in October before production begins for the next fiscal year.

The budgeted number of units to be produced during the year is used as a basis for estimating how much direct materials, direct labor, and factory overhead is necessary. This information is usually derived through discussions with the individual in charge of operations. For NaturApples, 50 pounds of apples and 0.60 hours of direct labor are necessary to make a case of sauce. To make a case of pie filling, 40 pounds of apples and 0.50 direct labor hours are necessary. The cost of apples is estimated to be $0.40 per pound and the cost of direct labor is estimated to be $10 per hour. Factory overhead is estimated to occur at $2 for every $1 of direct labor. Table 8.6 is the production budget for NaturApples and includes the raw materials, direct labor, and factory overhead budget.

TABLE 8.5
Number of Cases to Be Produced, 10/1/98–9/30/99

Product	Sales	+ Ending Inventory	− Beginning Inventory	= Production
Sauce	140,000	5,000	13,500	131,500
Pie filling	60,000	1,000	2,500	58,500

The production budget in Table 8.6 determines that 8,915,000 pounds of apples must be purchased to achieve the production target. If spoilage is a problem, then more apples must be purchased to cover expected spoilage. The production budget also provides an estimate of the direct labor requirements. To meet production targets, the company should plan on 108,150 hours of direct labor. The production budget also estimates the cost of apples, direct labor, and overhead. The overhead depreciation expense is identified separately because depreciation does not involve the use of cash. This is important to recognize for cash planning purposes.

The production budget in Table 8.6 is an annual budget. The company may also want to have monthly production budgets. Monthly production budgets are useful for planning cash flows and material and labor requirements, especially when production is uneven over time as in the case of NaturApples.

Selling and Administration Budget

Selling and administrative expenses are treated as period expenses for financial reporting purposes even though some of these costs can be traced to products. One of the functions of the budgeting process is to generate estimated financial

TABLE 8.6

NATURAPPLES
Production Budget
10/1/98–9/30/99

Raw Materials

Product	Pounds per Case	× Cases	= Pounds	× Cost per Pound	= Cost
Sauce	50	131,500	6,575,000	$0.40	$2,630,000
Pie filling	40	58,500	2,340,000	0.40	936,000
Total			8,915,000		$3,566,000

Direct Labor

Product	Hours per Case	× Cases	= Hours	× Cost per Hour	= Cost
Sauce	0.60	131,500	78,900	$10	$ 789,000
Pie filling	0.50	58,500	29,250	$10	292,500
Total			108,150		$1,081,500

Overhead

Product	Direct Labor Cost	× Overhead per Direct Labor Dollar	= Cost
Sauce	$789,000	$2	$1,578,000
Pie filling	292,500	$2	585,000
Total			$2,163,000*

*Includes $400,000 of depreciation expense

Product Costs

Product	Total Product Cost (Materials + Labor + Overhead)	/ Cases	= Cost per Case
Sauce	$4,997,000	131,500	$38
Pie filling	1,813,500	58,500	31
Total	$6,810,500		

TABLE 8.7

NATURAPPLES
Selling and Administration Budget
10/1/98–9/30/99

Selling and Administrative Areas	
Marketing	$ 470,000
Finance	160,000
Trucking	380,000
President's office	180,000
Total selling and administration	$1,190,000

statements at the end of the fiscal year, so selling and administrative expenses are commonly identified separately.

The selling and administration budget for NaturApples in Table 8.7 contains the remaining operating expenses, including the marketing department, finance, trucking costs, and the costs of the president's office. The total of all these administrative costs is $1.19 million.

Capital Investment Budget

The capital investment budget is used for major, planned purchases of property, plant, and equipment. These purchases generally appear as fixed assets in the balance sheet but could include a research and development effort on a new product that would be expensed.

In the process of establishing the production budget, the executive committee of NaturApples recognizes that an additional coring machine and dicing machine must be purchased to increase capacity. The expected purchase prices of the two machines are in the capital investment budget in Table 8.8.

Financial Budget

One reason for budgeting is to be sure that ample cash is available for operations and major purchases. If there are expected cash shortages, the organization must plan to borrow money to obtain additional cash. The financial budget is used to plan for the borrowing of cash. In addition, the financial budget is used to record planned interest expense, retirement of debt, issuance of stock, and the payment of dividends.

TABLE 8.8

NATURAPPLES
Capital Investment Budget
10/1/98–9/30/99

Capital Investment Project	Purchase Date	Cost
Coring machine	10/5/98	$ 40,000
Dicing machine	10/5/98	80,000
Total		$120,000

This robot moving ceramic material at Corning, Inc. is a capital investment. Cash flows for capital investments are estimated in the budgeting process.

NUMERICAL EXAMPLE 8.4

At the beginning of the month the Trevor Book Store has cash of $1,000 and accounts receivable of $4,000. This month, the manager of the bookstore plans to collect 80% of the beginning accounts receivable, make sales of $8,000 ($5,000 in cash and $3,000 on account due next month), and make payments of $12,000 to book publishers. How much must the bookstore borrow this month?

■ **SOLUTION**

Beginning cash balance	$ 1,000
Collection of receivables (.80 × $4,000)	3,200
Cash sales	5,000
Payments to publishers	(12,000)
Ending cash balance without financing	($ 2,800)

The manager must borrow at least $2,800 to cover the cash shortfall.

NaturApples must purchase both the coring machine and dicing machine early in the fiscal year. Given that the beginning cash balance is insufficient to cover this purchase, NaturApples must borrow an additional $100,000 from the bank. Near the end of the fiscal year, however, NaturApples should have enough cash to pay off that loan, retire an additional $200,000 of long-term debt, and pay shareholders $2,000,000 in dividends. In addition, the executive committee estimates that interest costs during the fiscal year will be $100,000. This information is provided in the financial budget in Table 8.9.

Budgeted Financial Statements

Budgeted financial statements are the end product of the budgeting process. For a profit organization, these statements include the budgeted income statement, the budgeted cash flow statement, and the budgeted balance sheet. These

TABLE 8.9

NATURAPPLES		
Financial Budget		
10/1/98–9/30/99		
Financial Transactions	**Date**	**Amount**
Loan from bank	10/5/98	$ 100,000
Repayment of bank loan	4/5/99	(100,000)
Retirement of long-term debt	6/1/99	(200,000)
Payment of interest	12/31/98	(50,000)
Payment of interest	6/30/99	(50,000)
Payment of dividends	9/30/99	(2,000,000)
Net cash flow from financial transactions		($2,300,000)

budgeted financial statements provide a picture of the financial condition of the organization at the end of the budget period if events happen according to plan.

Budgeted Income Statement

Most of the elements in the budgeted income statement come from parts of the prior budgets. The one part of the budgeted income statement that has not been estimated yet is the cost of goods sold. The estimation of the cost of goods sold depends on the accounting method used to record the flow of inventory costs. The first-in, first-out (FIFO) method assumes that the products sold are from the beginning inventory and early production and the products in ending inventory are those most recently made. Other inventory costing methods include last-in, first-out (LIFO) and average costing. These inventory costing methods are explained further in the appendix of Chapter 10 and in financial accounting textbooks.

NaturApples uses the FIFO method so the estimated cost of ending inventory is determined using the most recent product costs ($38 per case for sauce and $31 per case for pie filling).

Tax planning is also part of the budgeting process. For the next fiscal year NaturApples plans to pay 40% of net income in taxes. Table 8.10 contains the budgeted income statement for NaturApples. The numbers in the statement come from the previous budgets.

Budgeting for cash flows is an important process in all businesses, small and large. If these young entrepreneurs don't take in enough cash to purchase supplies for tomorrow's lemonade, they'll have to get a loan from dad or go out of business.

Budgeted Cash Flow Statement

Budgeting cash flows is extremely important to an organization. Running out of cash is very inconvenient and can lead to bankruptcy even though the organization is profitable. Therefore, monthly budgeted cash flow statements should be made to avoid shortfalls in cash.

Cash flow statements identify cash flows from operations, capital investments, and financial transactions. These transactions are captured in the sales, production, selling and administration, capital investment, and financial budgets.

In addition, cash flows are influenced by the collection of accounts receivables and the pay-

TABLE 8.10

NATURAPPLES
Budgeted Income Statement
10/1/98–9/30/99

Revenues (Sales budget)			$12,700,000
Cost of goods sold			
Beginning inventory (beg. balance sheet)		$ 903,000	
+ Production costs (production budget)		6,810,500	
− Ending inventory (production budget)			
Sauce ($38/case)(5,000 cases)	$190,000		
Pie filling ($31/case)(1,000 cases)	31,000	(221,000)	(7,492,500)
Gross margin			$ 5,207,500
Selling and administrative expenses (sell. and ad. budget)			(1,190,000)
Interest expense (financial budget)			(100,000)
Net income before taxes			$ 3,917,500
Income taxes ($3,917,500 × .40)			1,567,000
Net income			$ 2,350,500
Beginning stockholders' equity (Beg. balance sheet)			$ 2,403,000
+ Net income (from above)			2,350,500
− Dividends (financial budget)			(2,000,000)
Ending stockholders' equity			$ 2,753,500

ment of accounts payable. Hastening the collection of receivables and postponing the payment of payables can have a positive short-run effect on cash flows. But such behavior may not be consistent with the goals of the organization. For example, requiring customers to pay cash rather than billing them 30 days later may reduce total sales. For the purpose of annual budgeting, cash flow effects can be determined by estimating ending balances in the inventory, receivables, and payables accounts and calculating the change in those balances from the beginning of the year. Decreases in inventory and accounts receivable and increases in accounts payable means more cash available. Increases in inventory and accounts receivable and decreases in accounts payable means less cash available.

WHAT'S HAPPENING

Large companies such as Chevron have departments whose sole purpose is to make daily cash flow estimates. Given that Chevron can easily borrow money, why should Chevron be so concerned about daily cash balances?

NUMERICAL EXAMPLE 8.5

The Kreuger Corporation had beginning accounts receivable and accounts payable balances of $20,000 and $10,000, respectively. The corporation estimates that ending balances for accounts receivable and accounts payable will be $30,000 and $5,000, respectively. What are the cash flow implications?

■ **SOLUTION**

        Change in accounts receivable: $30,000 − $20,000 = $10,000

The increase of $10,000 implies a $10,000 decline in cash available.

        Change in accounts payable: $5,000 − $10,000 = ($5,000)

The decrease of $5,000 implies a $5,000 decline in cash available.

    The combined effect is a $15,000 decline in cash available.

The executive committee at NaturApples estimates that accounts receivable at the end of the next fiscal year will be $300,000 and accounts payable will be $150,000. The budgeted cash flow statement is portrayed in Table 8.11.

Budgeted Balance Sheet

The budgeting process begins with a beginning balance sheet. These beginning balances are adjusted for expected events during the coming fiscal year. The adjusted balances of each account constitute the budgeted balance sheet for the end of the fiscal year. The budgeted balance sheet for NaturApples is described in Table 8.12.

The budgeted financial statements (income, cash flow, and balance sheet) are called **pro forma financial statements.** Pro forma financial statements provide a prediction of how the financial statements will look in the future if the expected events occur. Because financial statements are used for performance measures, managers are very concerned about the pro forma financial statements. If the top managers of the organization do not like the pro forma financial statements that come out of the budgeting process, they will ask the organization to repeat the budgeting process using different strategies and assumptions until the pro forma

TABLE 8.11

NATURAPPLES
Budgeted Cash Flow Statement
10/1/98–9/30/99

Cash flows from operations:		
Income (income statement)		$2,350,500
Depreciation (income statement)		400,000
		$2,750,500
Change in accounts receivable:		
Ending accounts receivable (predicted)	$ 300,000	
Beginning accounts receivable (beg. bal. sht.)	(200,000)	(100,000)
Change in inventory:		
Ending inventory (predicted)	$ (221,000)	
Beginning inventory (beg. bal. sheet)	903,000	682,000
Change in accounts payable:		
Ending accounts payable (predicted)	$ 150,000	
Beginning accounts payable (beg. bal. sheet)	(100,000)	50,000
Total cash flows from operations		$3,382,500
Cash flows for capital investments (cap. inv. budget)		
Purchase of coring machine	($ 40,000)	
Purchase of dicing machine	(80,000)	(120,000)
Cash flows for financial transactions (financing budget)*		
Loan from bank	$ 100,000	
Repayment of bank loan	(100,000)	
Retirement of long-term debt	(200,000)	
Payment of dividends	(2,000,000)	(2,200,000)
Change in cash balance		$1,062,500
Beginning cash balance		100,000
Ending cash balance		$1,162,500

*The interest is already included in the net income.

THE STORY OF MANAGERIAL ACCOUNTING

Team Decisions Regarding Budgeting

Jeff, the team leader, and Heather, the marketing manager, begin the budgeting process for *Managerial Accounting* by estimating the number of books that will be sold. This estimate is based on the total market for managerial accounting textbooks, competitors' books, and the used book market. Kelly and Karen, the development and project editors, and Larry, the designer, estimate the costs of developing, designing, editing, proofreading, and indexing the book. These costs are fixed for the first edition. Dina, the production supervisor, provides cost estimates for manufacturing, which vary with the number of books produced. What is the role of Peggy, the accountant, in the budgeting process?

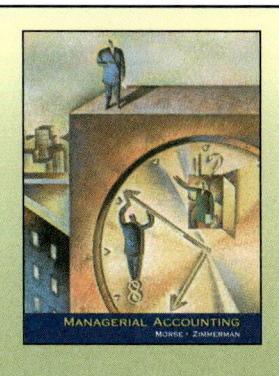

TABLE 8.12

NATURAPPLES
Budgeted Balance Sheet
9/30/99

Assets

Cash (cash flow statement)		$1,162,500
Accounts receivable (predicted)		300,000
Inventory (predicted):		
Sauce ($38/case)(5,000 cases)	$190,000	
Pie filling ($31/case)(1,000 cases)	31,000	221,000
Property, plant, and equipment (net):		
Beginning balance (beg. bal. sheet)	$2,300,000	
Capital investments (cap. inv. budget)	120,000	
Depreciation (income stmt.)	(400,000)	2,020,000
		$3,703,500

Liabilities and Stockholders' Equity

Accounts payable (predicted)		$ 150,000
Long-term debt:		
Beginning balance (beg. bal. sheet)	$1,000,000	
Retirement (financing budget)	(200,000)	800,000
Stockholders' equity (income statement)		2,753,500
		$3,703,500

financial statements are improved or they are convinced that there are no better alternative plans.

CONCEPT REVIEW

1. What is normally the first step in the master budget process?
2. How are estimated sales and inventory levels used to estimate production requirements?
3. Why is a financial budget necessary?
4. What are pro forma financial statements?

Mapledale Child Center (concluded)

The board of directors of Mapledale Child Center (MCC) has asked the two program directors to estimate the number of children that will attend their programs next year. The day care program director estimates an average of 40 children every month and the kindergarten program director estimates 60 children for the morning session and 50 children for the afternoon session. These estimates are consistent with the survey performed by the board of directors. The revenue budget for MCC is:

Revenue Budget

Program	Children	Price/Month	Months	Revenues
Day care	40	$500	12	$240,000
Kindergarten	110	360	9	356,400
Total revenues				$596,400

The production budget of Mapledale Child Center (MCC) encompasses the operations of the two programs of MCC. Given the enrollment estimates, the day care program director is given the right to hire eight full-time counselors and the kindergarten program director is given the right to hire five and a half full-time instructors (five for both the morning and afternoon and one for just the morning). The expected cost of hiring a counselor is $18,000 per year and the expected cost of hiring an instructor for kindergarten is $20,000 for nine months. Resources for educational supplies are also allotted to the two programs at $400 per child per year. The following budget also includes the program directors' salaries.

Production Budget

Child care program:		
Program director	$ 20,000	
Counselors (8 × $18,000)	144,000	
Educational supplies ($400 × 40)	16,000	
Total		$180,000
Kindergarten program:		
Program director	$ 20,000	
Instructors (5.5 × $20,000)	110,000	
Educational supplies ($400 × 110)	44,000	
Total		$174,000
Total program costs		$354,000

Mapledale Child Center also has a selling and administrative budget. This budget includes advertising, rent, insurance, and the salaries of the office manager, secretary, and bookkeeper.

Selling and Administrative Budget

Advertising	$ 10,000
Rent	100,000
Insurance	20,000
Salaries	50,000
Total	$180,000

> The Board of Directors of Mapledale Child Center (MCC) decides that the coming year is a good time to update the computer equipment in the office and the classrooms. The planned expenditure is $50,000. Mapledale Child Center (MCC) is a nonprofit organization. Nonprofit organizations typically don't have income statements. MCC operates strictly on a cash basis and does not record payables and receivables. Fixed assets such as computers are treated as cash expenditures and not recognized as assets. MCC is a service organization and has no inventory. Any leftover supplies from one period are considered immaterial. Therefore, MCC is only concerned about the cash flows and the beginning and ending cash balance. The Mapledale Child Center (MCC) has an estimated beginning cash balance of $10,000. The following cash flow statement is used to estimate the ending cash balance.
>
> | | |
> |---|---:|
> | Beginning cash balance | $ 10,000 |
> | Estimated revenues | 596,400 |
> | Program costs | (354,000) |
> | Selling and administrative costs | (180,000) |
> | Capital investments (computers) | (50,000) |
> | Ending cash balance | $ 22,400 |

8.5 Summary

1. **Use budgeting for planning purposes and control purposes, and identify the conflicts that exist between planning and control in the budgeting process.** Budgeting facilitates the flow of information from the bottom up for general planning and from the top down for coordination. The budget is used to allocate decision rights to different members of the organization and to establish performance measures, which are used to reward managers. The flow of information in the budgeting process may be inhibited or biased because the same information used for planning is also used to evaluate individuals.

2. **Describe the benefits of having both short-run and long-run budgets.** Long-run budgets are used for long-term planning. Short-term budgets are used for both planning and control.

3. **Explain the decision rights implications of a line-item budget.** Line-item budgets constrain decision rights by limiting the ability of managers to shift resources from one use to another.

4. **Identify the costs and benefits of budget lapsing.** Budget lapsing constrains the manager to expend resources in the budget period. This provides more control, but managers are not able to use their specialized information to make more efficient decisions and are often motivated to consume excess resources during the budgeted period.

5. **Develop flexible budgets and identify when flexible budgeting should be used instead of static budgeting.** Flexible budgeting adjusts for volume effects. If the manager cannot control volume, the flexible budget provides more appropriate numbers for evaluating the manager.

6. **Explain the costs and benefits of using zero-base budgeting.** Zero-base budgeting (ZBB) is costly because each line item in total must be justified. The benefit of ZBB is the additional flow of information that may be useful to new managers and may lead to more efficient use of resources.

7. **Create a master budget and pro forma financial statements for an organization including sales, production, administration, capital investment, and financial budgets.** The master budget is a plan for a certain period that includes expected sales, operating costs (production and administration), major investments, and methods financing those investments. The pro forma statements include the budgeted income statement, the budgeted cash flow statement, and budgeted balance sheet.

8. **Use spreadsheets to analyze monthly cash flows (Appendix).** Monthly cash flow analysis is extremely important to determine if there may be a cash shortage in any month. If a cash shortage is expected, the organization can plan to find some sort of financing to allow the organization to pay its bills and continue to operate. Spreadsheets offer a means of determining the sensitivity of the cash flows to different budget estimates.

Key Terms

Budget lapsing Budgets for one period cannot be used to make expenditures in subsequent periods.

Budgeting Process of gathering information to assist in making forecasts.

Budgets Forecasts of future revenues and expenditures.

Favorable variance The amount by which budgeted costs are greater than actual costs or budgeted revenues are less than actual revenues.

Flexible budget Budget that is adjusted for changes in volume.

Incremental budget Future budget based on current year's budgeted line-item amounts with adjustments for expected changes.

Master budget A document that integrates all the estimates from the different departments to establish guidelines and benchmarks for the whole organization.

Participative budgeting Eliciting opinions from affected managers in establishing a budget.

Pro forma financial statements Financial statements based on forecasted data.

Static budgets Budgets that don't adjust for volume.

Strategic planning The process whereby managers select the firm's overall objectives and the tactics to achieve those objectives.

Unfavorable variance The amount by which budgeted costs are less than actual costs or budgeted revenues are greater than actual revenues.

Variance The difference between a budgeted and an actual number.

Zero-base budgeting A budgeting process whereby each line item in total must be justified and reviewed each year.

Appendix: Monthly Cash Flow Estimates and Spreadsheets

One of the most important aspects of budgeting is to be sure that the organization has sufficient cash. Many organizations that are growing tend to underestimate the amount of cash that is needed by the organization. Cash is obviously needed for the purchase of long-term assets and production purposes. But cash is also needed because of increases in inventory and other current assets. Accounts receivable, for example, tend to increase as sales increase. The organization must wait to be paid cash for sales made on credit. Sometimes, the organization never gets paid by the customer.

An organization must be careful to estimate future cash flows because if the cash balance becomes negative, the organization will not be able to pay its own bills. An organization can be forced into bankruptcy because of a cash shortfall even though it is making a profit. Therefore, a monthly budget predicting cash flows is extremely important to avert an unexpected shortfall in cash. If an organization can predict a shortfall in cash early enough, plans can be altered to conserve cash or the organization can plan to borrow cash.

Most of the events affecting future cash flows are not completely predictable. Sales, collection of accounts receivable, and production costs are all difficult to predict. But unpredictability does not mean budgets for cash flows should not be made. Instead of making a single cash flow budget, the organization should make multiple cash flow budgets given different scenarios. These different scenarios would reflect different estimates about sales and other events affecting cash flows. For example, cash flows could be estimated assuming a monthly increase in sales of 1% per month and then assuming a monthly increase in sales of 2% per month. By changing the estimate of the monthly growth in sales, a manager can look at the sensitivity of cash flows to sales estimates. A manager can obtain a range of plausible cash flow estimates by varying the estimates of the different events affecting cash flows.

Analyzing the sensitivity of cash flows to different estimates can be very costly if a manager must go through all the procedures of the master budget by hand for each different estimate. Spreadsheets offer a means of quickly analyzing data that have specific relationships. Once a spreadsheet is set up with the raw data and the functional relationships, it is quite simple to change some of the parameters and get a new solution. In the case of cash flows, the relationships among the different events have been described in the master budget and can be easily placed in the form of a spreadsheet for analysis. The spreadsheet can provide cash flow estimates for multiple scenarios very simply. The spreadsheets also allow for simple updates of future monthly cash flows as the outcomes of earlier months become known.

The example in Table 8.13 illustrates the functional relationships that can be captured through spreadsheet analysis. The monthly cash budgeting process begins with estimates of monthly sales. The purchase of inventory sold occurs two months prior to the sales month, but the bills for those purchases are paid in the month prior to the sale. There is a 30% profit margin on sales. Other costs are estimated and paid in the month incurred. Large cash investments are identified separately. Sales are assumed to be composed of 20% cash sales, 50% credit sales that are collected in the following month, and 30% credit sales that are collected in the second month following the sales transaction. Only sales, purchases, and the accounts affecting cash flows and cash balances are reported in this example. A typical spreadsheet analysis would include multiple interrelated worksheets that could generate all of the pro forma financial statements. The subscripts on the functional relationships represent the month relative to month t.

The monthly cash flow analysis in Table 8.13 indicates that the organization will have cash problems in June primarily because of a large cash investment of $20,000 in fixed assets in May and increased inventory purchases in May and June. If these estimates are accurate, the organization will have to borrow money in June or reconsider the large cash investment in fixed assets.

The numbers in Table 8.13 are estimates or functions of estimates. There is no certainty that these estimates will actually occur. Suppose that there is a possibility of an additional larger sale of $25,000 that could occur in April.

TABLE 8.13 Monthly Cash Flow Budget

Account	Functional Relation	January	February	March	April	May	June
Sales	Estimated	$10,000	$20,000	$25,000	$15,000	$10,000	$20,000
Purchases	$(.70)(Sales_{t+2})$	17,500	10,500	7,000	14,000	21,000	15,000
Cash Flow Effects							
Cash sales	$(.20)(Sales_t)$	$2,000	$4,000	$5,000	$3,000	$2,000	$4,000
Collection of credit sales	$(.50)(Sales_{t-1}) +$ $(.30)(Sales_{t-2})$	10,000	10,000	13,000	18,500	15,000	9,500
Inventory payment	$Purchases_{t-1}$	(14,000)	(17,500)	(10,500)	(7,000)	(14,000)	(21,000)
Other costs	Estimated	(2,000)	(3,000)	(2,000)	(1,500)	(3,000)	(2,000)
Large cash investments	Estimated					(20,000)	
Net cash flows	$Cash\ sales_t +$ $Collections_t - Payments_t -$ $Other\ costs_t - Investments_t$	(4,000)	(6,500)	5,500	13,000	(20,000)	(9,500)
Beg. cash balance	End. cash balance$_{t-1}$	20,000	16,000	9,500	15,000	28,000	8,000
End. cash balance	Beg. cash balance$_t$ + Net cash flows$_t$	16,000	9,500	15,000	28,000	8,000	(1,500)

TABLE 8.14 Monthly Cash Flow Budget with Additional April Sale

Account	Functional Relation	January	February	March	April	May	June
Sales	Estimated	$10,000	$20,000	$25,000	**$40,000**	$10,000	$20,000
Purchases	$(.70)(Sales_{t+2})$	17,500	**28,000**	7,000	14,000	21,000	15,000
Cash Flow Effects							
Cash sales	$(.20)(Sales_t)$	$2,000	$4,000	$5,000	**$8,000**	$2,000	$4,000
Collection of credit sales	$(.50)(Sales_{t-1}) +$ $(.30)(Sales_{t-2})$	10,000	10,000	13,000	18,500	**27,500**	**17,000**
Inventory payment	$Purchases_{t-1}$	(14,000)	(17,500)	**(28,000)**	(7,000)	(14,000)	(21,000)
Other costs	Estimated	(2,000)	(3,000)	(2,000)	(1,500)	(3,000)	(2,000)
Large cash investments	Estimated					(20,000)	
Net cash flows	$Cash\ sales_t +$ $Collections_t - Payments_t -$ $Other\ costs_t - Investments_t$	(4,000)	(6,500)	**(12,000)**	18,000	**(7,500)**	**(2,000)**
Beg. cash balance	End. cash balance$_{t-1}$	20,000	16,000	9,500	**(2,500)**	**15,500**	8,000
End. cash balance	Beg. cash balance$_t$ + Net cash flows$_t$	16,000	9,500	**(2,500)**	**15,500**	8,000	**6,000**

Spreadsheet analysis can easily accommodate this adjustment by simply increasing the sales estimate in April of $15,000 by $25,000 to $40,000. Table 8.14 reveals the effects of this change on other accounts in bold print.

The additional sale in Figure 8.14 actually causes a shortage of cash during an earlier month (March). The organization will be forced to borrow money in March. This occurs because the organization must purchase the inventory before it sells the inventory. The additional sale, however, provides sufficient cash flows in May and June to allow for the $20,000 large cash investment.

SELF-STUDY PROBLEM

Joseph Chang, president of Changware Company, has developed a software program for accounting for drugstores. In the first year, sales were far greater than expected and Joseph has had to hire additional marketing and customer service personnel. In addition,

Joseph must keep up with the competition, so he has hired more software engineers and programmers to create new software. This hiring increase has caused Joseph to rent bigger facilities. Although Changware appears to be successful, Joseph has cash flow problems with all the expansion activities. Joseph believes it's time to make a budget.

a. Describe the planning and control implications of the budgeting process for Changware.
b. Should Changware emphasize short- or long-term budgets? Explain.
c. Should Changware use line-item budgets, budget lapsing, flexible budgets, or zero-base budgets? Explain.

Solution

a. Changware needs a budget for two reasons: planning and control. Changware is in a state of growth and change. The growth is requiring the use of additional cash and Joseph Chang must plan to make sure that the company has sufficient cash. He must estimate cash inflows from sales and the collection of accounts receivables to determine if there is sufficient cash to fund the expansion. If there are insufficient cash inflows from operations, Joseph will have to investigate alternative methods of financing such as bank loans or issuing stock.

  The growth in Changware also means that the company will become more decentralized and require more control efforts. Joseph Chang will not be able to make all the decisions. The budget will serve as a means to communicate with other members of the organization and establish expectations for performance. The budget could also be used as a benchmark for rewarding individuals within the organization.

b. Changware's budget should probably emphasize short-run planning and control. The change in the organization and the volatile nature of the software industry makes long-term budgets less valuable.

c. Ordinarily the addition of many new employees would suggest the use of a line-item budget. But flexibility is extremely important in an industry with an average product life of about a year. A line-item budget might constrain the organization too much.

  Budget lapsing probably will not be appropriate because the development of new software may take more than a year. The company would not want to constrain funding to fiscal years. The company is more likely to budget for a project rather than a period of time.

  Flexible budgets are appropriate if the responsible parties can't control the volume of sales. The manufacturing unit of the software is unlikely to have much control over volume, so flexible budgeting would be appropriate for that unit.

  Zero-base budgeting is likely to be appropriate for the company especially given that this is the first budget. Even subsequent budgets are not likely to be incremental because of the volatile nature of the business and the continual cycle of new products.

NUMERICAL PROBLEMS

NP 8–1: Estimating Production (LO 1; NE 3)   The Shocker Company's sales budget shows quarterly sales for the next year as follows:

	Quarter 1	10,000 units
	Quarter 2	8,000 units
	Quarter 3	12,000 units
	Quarter 4	14,000 units

Company policy is to have a finished goods inventory at the end of each quarter equal to 20% of the next quarter's sales.

Compute budgeted production for the second quarter of the next year.

(CMA adapted)

NP 8–2: Estimating Cash Payments for Inventory (LO 1; NE 5)   The annual cost of goods sold for a company is expected to be $82,000. The beginning inventory balance is $25,000. The ending inventory balance is expected to be $21,000. All purchases are on credit. The beginning and ending balances for accounts payable are expected to be $11,000 and $8,000, respectively.

How much cash must the company pay its suppliers this year?

NP 8–3: Computing Budgeted Manufacturing Costs (LO 1; NE 3) Candice Candy Company expects to sell 100,000 cases of chocolate bars during the next year. Budgeted costs per case are $150 for direct materials, $120 for direct labor, and $75 for manufacturing overhead (all variable). Candice Company begins the year with 40,000 cases of finished goods on hand and wants to end the year with 10,000 cases of finished goods on hand.

Compute the budgeted manufacturing costs of the Candice Candy Company for the next year.

NP 8–4: Flexible Budget (LO 5; NE 2) The Topper Restaurant uses a flexible budget to estimate profit in each month. The restaurant expects to charge $15 per meal on average. Some costs are assumed to vary with the number of meals served. The restaurant estimates a variable cost of $5 per meal served. The restaurant also has monthly fixed costs of $10,000.

Make a flexible budget of total revenue, costs, and profit for the month given 1,000 meals served, 1,500 meals served, and 2,000 meals served.

NP 8–5: Estimating Production Costs (LO 1; NE 3) The Fancy Umbrella Company makes beach umbrellas. The production process requires three square meters of plastic sheeting and a metal pole. The plastic sheeting costs $0.50 per square meter and each metal pole costs $1. At the beginning of the month, the company has 5,000 square feet of plastic and 1,000 poles in raw materials inventory. The preferred raw material amount at the end of the month is 3,000 square feet of plastic sheeting and 600 poles. The company has 300 finished umbrellas in inventory at the beginning of the month and plans to have 200 finished umbrellas at the end of the month. Sales in the coming month are expected to be 5,000 umbrellas.

a. How many umbrellas must the company produce to meet demand and have sufficient ending inventory?
b. What is the cost of materials that must be purchased?

NP 8–6: Flexible Budgets (LO 5) A chair manufacturer has established the following flexible budget for the month.

	Units Produced and Sold		
	1,000	1,500	2,000
Sales	$10,000	$15,000	$20,000
Variable costs	(5,000)	(7,500)	(10,000)
Fixed costs	(2,000)	(2,000)	(2,000)
Profit	$ 3,000	$ 5,500	$ 8,000

a. What is the sales price per chair?
b. What is the expected profit if 1,600 chairs are made?

NP 8–7: Flexible Budget (LO 5) Tubbs Company has established the following flexible budget for the coming month.

Units produced	10,000	11,000	12,000
Total costs	$30,000	$32,000	$34,000

a. What is the variable cost per unit?
b. What is the fixed cost?

NP 8–8: Estimating Cash Requirements (LO 8; NE 4) Humdrum Company is worried about cash flows. The company has $1,000 in cash at the start of the month. Sales are 30% cash sales and 70% account sales collected in the following month. January's total sales were $20,000 and total sales in February are expected to be $30,000.

Production costs in February are expected to be $25,000, all of which must be paid during February. The company would also like to buy equipment that costs $10,000.

How much will the company have to borrow to have $800 in cash at the end of February?

NP 8–9: Production Requirements (LO 1; NE 3)   The Birdie Company makes badminton rackets. Beginning inventory for the coming year is 1,000 rackets. During the year the company expects to sell 10,000 rackets and wants to have 800 rackets in inventory at the end of the year.

How many rackets must the company produce during the year to meet demand and have a sufficient inventory at the end of the year?

NP 8–10: Estimating Cash Collections and Accounts Receivable (LO 8)
Wolski Company expects sales in July to be $100,000. Of total sales, 20% are cash and the remaining are collected in August. Accounts receivable at the beginning of July are $70,000, which will be collected in July.

a. How much cash is expected to be collected in July from accounts receivable and cash sales?
b. What is the expected ending balance in July of accounts receivable?

NP 8–11: Pro Forma Financial Statements (LO 7)   The Gold Bay Hotel is in the process of developing a master budget and pro forma financial statements for 1999. The beginning balance sheet for the fiscal year 1999 is estimated to be:

GOLD BAY HOTEL
Estimated Balance Sheet
1/1/99

Cash	$ 20,000	Accounts payable	$ 20,000
Accounts receivable	30,000	Notes payable	500,000
Facilities	3,010,000	Capital stock	100,000
Accumulated dep.	(1,100,000)	Retained earnings	1,340,000
Total assets	$1,960,000	Total equities	$1,960,000

During the year the hotel expects to rent 30,000 rooms. Rooms rent for an average of $90 per night. The hotel expects to sell 40,000 meals during the year at an average price of $20 per meal. The variable cost per room rented is $30 and the variable cost per meal is $8. The fixed costs not including depreciation are expected to be $2,000,000. Depreciation is expected to be $500,000. The hotel also expects to refurbish the kitchen at a cost of $200,000, which is capitalized (included in the facilities account). Interest on the note payable is expected to be $50,000, and $100,000 of the note payable will be retired during the year. The ending accounts receivable amount is expected to be $40,000, and the ending accounts payable is expected to be $30,000.

Prepare pro forma financial statements for the end of the year.

NP 8–12: Estimating Direct Materials Purchase (LO 1; NE 3)   The Jung Corporation's budget calls for the following production:

Quarter 1	45,000 units
Quarter 2	38,000 units
Quarter 3	34,000 units
Quarter 4	48,000 units

Each unit of product requires three pounds of direct material. The company's policy is to begin each quarter with an inventory of direct materials equal to 30% of that quarter's direct material requirements.

Compute budgeted direct materials purchases for the third quarter.

(CMA adapted)

NP 8–13: Variance Analysis (LO 1)   August Company's budget for the current month called for producing and selling 5,000 units at $8 each. Actual units produced and sold were 5,200, yielding revenue of $42,120. Variable costs per unit are budgeted at $3, and fixed costs are budgeted at $2 per unit. Actual variable costs were $3.30 and fixed costs were $12,000.

a. Prepare a variance report for the current month's operation comparing actual and budgeted revenues and costs.
b. Write a short memo analyzing the current month's performance.

NP 8–14: Monthly Estimates of Cash Flows (LO 8) (Appendix) The Corner Hardware Store is developing a budget to estimate monthly cash balances in the near future. At the end of December, the cash balance is $6,000 and the accounts payable balance is $30,000 (reflecting December's purchases of inventory). The Corner Hardware Store expects $40,000 in sales in January and an increase in sales of 2% per month over the next 6 months. All sales are in cash. Inventory purchases are expected to rise at the same rate as sales and are paid in the month following the purchase. Other monthly cash outflows are expected to be $10,000 a month.

a. How much money will the store have to borrow to pay $20,000 for a new computer system in May?
b. How much will the store have to borrow to pay $20,000 for a new computer system in May if sales and purchases are expected to increase 5% a month?

NP 8–15: Monthly Estimates of Cash Flows (LO 8) (Appendix) The Quality Auto Parts Wholesaler maintains an inventory of car parts to supply local car repair shops. The company is making cash flow estimates for the coming year. The monthly purchases of inventory sufficient to cover sales two months later are made, but the bills for those purchases are paid in the month prior to their sale. There is a 20% profit margin on sales. Other costs are $2,000 a month, paid in the month incurred. Sales are assumed to be composed of 10% cash sales, 70% credit sales that are collected in the following month, and 20% credit sales that are collected in the second month following the sales transaction. The cash balance at the beginning of March is $5,000. Expected sales by month are:

Account	January	February	March	April	May	June	July	August
Sales	$10,000	$12,000	$10,000	$20,000	$25,000	$15,000	$10,000	$20,000

a. What will be the cash balances for the end of months March, April, May, and June?
b. Will the company have to borrow money during the months March–June?
c. Would the company have to borrow if June sales are expected to be $50,000 instead of $15,000?

NP 8–16: Master Budget and Pro Forma Statements (LO 7) The Eye Company makes reading glasses. The expected beginning balance sheet for the Eye Company on 1/1/98 is:

THE EYE COMPANY
Expected Beginning Balance Sheet
1/1/1998

Assets

Cash	$ 80,000
Accounts receivable	50,000
Inventory (6,000 units at $6/unit)	36,000
Property, plant, and equipment (net)	100,000
	$266,000

Liabilities and Stockholders' Equity

Accounts payable	$100,000
Long-term debt	100,000
Stockholders' equity	66,000
	$266,000

During 1998, the company expects to sell 100,000 units (reading glasses) for $12 apiece. The reading glasses are sold on account and the accounts receivable are expected to be $100,000 on 12/31/98. The company expects to have 10,000 reading glasses in inventory on 12/31/98.

By purchasing raw materials only when immediately needed for the assembly of reading glasses, the company does not maintain a raw materials inventory. The cost of the materials is $6/unit. The raw materials are bought on account and the company expects the accounts payable on 12/31/98 to be $120,000.

Labor and overhead are treated as period expenses. The average direct labor cost for each pair of reading glasses is expected to be $2. The overhead is fixed and expected to be $200,000 for the year. Of that overhead, $20,000 is depreciation. The remaining overhead requires cash payments.

The company plans to buy $50,000 in property, plant, and equipment during 1998 and issue $20,000 more long-term debt during 1998. The interest on the long-term debt for 1998 is expected to be $12,000. The company expects to pay $10,000 in dividends during 1998.

Construct a master budget for the Eye Company and pro forma statements for 12/31/98.

NP 8–17: Flexible Budgets (LO 5; NE 8 1, 2)   Adrian Power manufactures small power supplies for car stereos. The company uses flexible budgeting techniques in order to deal with the seasonal and cyclical nature of the business. The accounting department provided the following data on budgeted manufacturing costs for the month of January 1996:

ADRIAN POWER
Planned Level of Production
For January 1996

Budgeted production (in units)	14,000
Variable costs (vary with production):	
Direct materials	$140,000
Direct labor	224,000
Indirect labor	21,000
Indirect materials	10,500
Maintenance	6,300
Fixed costs:	
Supervision	24,700
Other (depreciation, taxes, etc.)	83,500
Total plant costs	$510,000

In January 1996, actual operations are summarized below:

ADRIAN POWER
Actual Operations
For January 1996

Actual production (in units)	15,400
Actual costs incurred:	
Direct materials	$142,400
Direct labor	259,800
Indirect labor	27,900
Indirect materials	12,200
Maintenance	9,800
Supervision	28,000
Other costs (depreciation, taxes, etc.)	83,500
Total plant costs	$563,600

a. Prepare a report comparing the actual operating results to the flexible budget at actual production.
b. Write a short memorandum analyzing the report prepared in part a above. What likely managerial implications do you draw from this report? (What are the numbers telling you?)

NP 8–18: Budgeting for a Takeover (LO 1)

You are working for a firm that specializes in mergers and takeovers and your job is to analyze potential acquisitions. You are assigned the task to evaluate a possible merger between NE and Upstate Airlines. These two carriers are competing in the upstate-downstate New York markets of Rochester, Albany, Syracuse, and New York City. There is currently excess capacity in these two airlines and your boss believes that a merger of the two airlines, accompanied by canceling some redundant flights and raising some fares, could create the synergy necessary to make a positive return on the acquisition. Your boss asks you to provide her with an estimate of the first-year cost savings that would result from a combination of NE and Upstate Airlines. You assemble the following operating data on the two airlines:

	NE Airlines	Upstate Airlines
Passenger miles flown	72 million	80 million
Average price per passenger mile	25¢	25¢
Number of jets	3	4
Operating labor costs	$5 million	$6 million
Corporate office expense	$2 million	$2 million
Landing and parking fees*	$0.75 million	$1 million

*These fees are proportional to the number of jets in the fleet

Both airlines are using the same type of jets. The annual operating cost and lease payment (including fuel, maintenance, licenses, and insurance) is $3 million per jet. After an analysis of the various markets served, you determine that a combination of the two airlines would result in the following operating characteristics: average price can be increased 10%, some duplicate flights can be canceled, and combined corporate office expense can be cut by $1 million. The combination of the higher prices and reduced frequency of flights is expected to cut demand by 6%. The existing flights have enough excess capacity to support a reduction in the fleet size of the combined airline by one jet.

Each firm's operating labor costs are proportional to the number of jets in the fleet. You assume that the combined firm will have operating labor costs per jet equal to that currently being incurred by NE. However, Upstate Airlines has a labor union contract with their employees that specifies that employees with five years or more service with the company cannot be laid off in the event of a merger. Therefore, some but not all the labor cost savings that could have been achieved by reducing the fleet to six jets will be achieved. An additional half million dollars of labor cost will be incurred as a result of the existing Upstate labor contract.

Prepare an analysis comparing the current profitability of the two airlines as independent firms and of a combined firm using the planning assumptions stated above.

NP 8–19: Flexible Budgets (LO 5)

Golf World is a 1,000-room luxury resort with swimming pools, tennis courts, three golf courses, and many other resort amenities.

The head golf course superintendent, Sandy Green, is responsible for all golf course maintenance and conditioning. Sandy also has the final say as to whether a particular course is open or closed due to weather conditions and whether players can rent motorized riding golf carts for use on a particular course. If the course is very wet, the golf carts will damage the turf, which Green's maintenance crew will have to repair. Since

Sandy is out on the course every morning supervising the maintenance crews, she knows the condition of the course.

Wiley Grimes is in charge of the golf cart rentals. His crew maintains the golf cart fleet of over 200 carts, cleans them, puts oil and gas in them, and repairs minor damage. He also is responsible for leasing the carts from the manufacturer, including the terms of the lease, the number of carts to lease, and the choice of the cart vendor. When guests arrive at the golf course to play, they pay greens fees to play and a cart fee if they wish to use a cart. If they do not wish to rent a cart, they pay only the greens fee and walk the course.

Grimes and Green manage separate profit centers. The golf cart profit center's revenue is composed of the fees collected from the carts. The golf course profit center's revenue is from the greens fees collected. In reviewing the results from April, golf cart operating profits were only 49% of budget. Wiley argued that the poor results were due to the unusually heavy rains in April. He complained that there were several days when the course was closed to golf carts even though only a few areas of the course were wet because the grounds crew was too busy to rope off these areas from carts, so that the entire course was closed to carts.

To better analyze the performance of the golf cart profit center, the controller's office has implemented a flexible budget based on the number of cart rentals:

GOLF WORLD
Golf Cart Profit Center
Operating Results
April

	Static Budget	Actual Results	Variance from Static Budget	Flexible Budget	Variance from Flexible Budget
Number of cart rentals	6000	4000	2000	4000	0
Revenues (@ $25/car)	$150,000	$100,000	$50,000 U	$100,000	$ 0
Labor (fixed cost)	7,000	7,200	200 U	7,000	200 U
Gas & oil (@ $1/rental)	6,000	4,900	1,100 F	4,000	900 U
Cart lease (fixed cost)	40,000	40,000	0	40,000	0
Operating profit	$ 97,000	$ 47,900	$49,100 U	$ 49,000	$1,100 U

a. Evaluate the performance of the golf cart profit center for the month of April.
b. What are the advantages and disadvantages of the controller's new budgeting system?
c. What additional recommendations would you make regarding the operations of Golf World?

NP 8–20: Flexible Budgeting (LO 5)

Wielson Company employs flexible budgeting techniques to evaluate the performance of several of its activities. The selling expense flexible budgets for three representative monthly activity levels are shown below.

Representative Monthly Flexible Budgets for Selling Expenses

Activity measures:			
Unit sales volume	400,000	425,000	450,000
Dollar sales volume	$10,000,000	$10,625,000	$11,250,000
Number of orders	4,000	4,250	4,500
Number of salespersons	75	75	75

Monthly expenses:			
Advertising and promotion	$1,200,000	$1,200,000	$1,200,000
Administrative salaries	57,000	57,000	57,000
Sales salaries	75,000	75,000	75,000
Sales commissions	200,000	212,500	225,000
Salesperson travel	170,000	175,000	180,000
Total selling expenses	$1,702,000	$1,719,500	$1,737,000

The following assumptions were used to develop the selling expense flexible budgets:

- The average size of Wielson's sales force during the year was planned to be 75 people.
- Salespersons are paid a monthly salary plus commissions on gross dollar sales.
- The travel costs are best characterized as a step-variable cost. The fixed portion is related to the number of salespersons, while the variable portion fluctuates with gross dollar sales.

A sales force of 80 persons generated a total of 4,300 orders resulting in a sales volume of 420,000 units during November. The gross dollar sales amounted to $10.9 million. The selling expenses incurred for November were as follows:

Advertising and promotion	$1,350,000
Administrative salaries	57,000
Sales salaries	80,000
Sales commissions	218,000
Salesperson travel	185,000
Total	$1,890,000

Prepare a selling expense report for November that Wielson Company can use to evaluate its control over selling expenses. The report should have a line for each selling expense item showing the appropriate budgeted amount, the actual selling expense, and the monthly dollar variation.

(CMA adapted)

NP 8–21: Flexible Budgets (LO 5)   The coating department of a parts manufacturing department coats various parts with an antirust zinc-based material. The parts to be processed are loaded into baskets and the baskets passed through a coating machine that sprays the zinc material onto the parts. Then the machine heats the parts to ensure the coating bonds properly. All parts being coated are assigned a cost for the coating department based on the number of hours the parts spend in a coating machine. Prior to the beginning of the year, cost categories are accumulated by department (including the coating department). These cost categories are classified as being either fixed or variable and then a flexible budget for the department is constructed. Given an estimate of machine hours for the next year, the coating department projected cost per machine hour is computed.

Data for the last three operating years is given below. Expected coating machine hours for 1995 are 16,000 hours.

Coating Department—Operating Data

	1992	1993	1994
Machine hours	12,500	8,400	15,200
Coating materials	$ 51,375	$ 34,440	$ 62,624
Engineering support	27,962	34,295	31,300
Maintenance	35,850	35,930	36,200
Occupancy costs (square footage)	27,502	28,904	27,105
Operator labor	115,750	78,372	147,288
Supervision	46,500	47,430	49,327
Utilities	12,875	8,820	16,112
Total costs	$317,814	$268,191	$369,956

a. Estimate the coating department's flexible budget for 1995. Explicitly state and justify the assumptions used in deriving your estimates.
b. Calculate the coating department's cost per machine hour for 1995.

DISCUSSION PROBLEMS

DP 8–1: Budget Lapsing (LO 4) Professors at Southeastern University are given a $1,000 budget per year to use for travel and research purposes. Presently the university allows the professors to carry over unused balances from one year to the next. The university is considering a new policy of having the $1,000 lapse from year to year.

What are the advantages and disadvantages of having the travel and research budget lapse?

DP 8–2: Different Types of Budgets (LO 2, 3, 4, 5, 6) The Sticky Company makes a glue that is used to glue the layers of wood veneer together to make plywood. The process for making the glue has been used for many years and the customers are satisfied with the product. The Sticky Company has had very low turnover of personnel and the president and the managers have all been with the company for many years. Although the company appears very stable today, plywood prices are rising and the construction industry is beginning to switch to a cheaper product called chipboard. Chipboard uses a different glue than the glue made by the Sticky Company.

Given the present condition of Sticky Company, which of the following budgeting techniques should the company use: long-term budgets, line-item budgets, budget lapsing, flexible budgets, zero-base budgeting?

DP 8–3: Long-Term Budgets (LO 2) The sales manager of the T Corporation is complaining about the budget process. He notes, "Each year the central administration asks for expected sales in each of the next three years. The first year's budget is used to determine production amounts and establish benchmarks for measuring performance and rewarding employees. The second- and third-year budgets, however, seem to be forgotten. Next year they ask us again for expected sales in each of the next three years. Why don't they use last year's forecast or only ask us to make sales forecasts for one year ahead?"

Does the sales manager have a legitimate complaint?

DP 8–4: Budgeting and Performance Evaluation (LO 1)

"I've given a good deal of thought to this issue of how companies . . . go about negotiating objectives with their different business units. The typical process in such cases is that once the parent negotiates a budget with a unit, the budget then becomes the basis for the bonus. And they are also typically structured such that the bonus kicks in when, say, 80% of the budgeted performance is achieved; and the maximum bonus is earned when management reaches, say, 120% of the budgeted level. There is thus virtually no downside and very limited upside.

Now, because the budget is negotiated between management and headquarters, there is a circularity about the whole process that makes the resulting standards almost meaningless. Because the budget is intended to reflect what management thinks it can accomplish—presumably without extraordinary effort and major changes in the status quo—the adoption of the budget as a standard is unlikely to motivate exceptional performance, especially since the upside is so limited. Instead it is likely to produce cautious budgets and mediocre performance.

So, because of the perverse incentives built into the budgeting process itself, I think it's important for a company to break the connection between the budget and planning process on the one hand and the bonus systems on the other hand. The bonuses should be based upon absolute performance standards that are not subject to negotiation."

(Source: G. Bennett Stewart, III, "CEO Roundtable on Corporate Structure and Management Incentives," *Journal of Applied Corporate Finance,* Fall 1990, p. 27.)

Critically evaluate the preceding quotation.

DP 8–5: Zero-Base Budgeting (LO 6)

Rogers Petersen and Cabots are two of the five largest investment banks in the United States. Last year there was a major scandal at Cabots involving manipulation of some auctions for government bonds. A number of senior partners at Cabots were charged with price fixing in the government bond market. The ensuing investigation led four of the eight managing directors (the highest ranking officials at Cabots) to resign. A new senior managing director was brought in from outside to run the firm. This individual recruited three outside managing directors to replace the ones who resigned. There was then a thorough housecleaning. In the following six months, 15 additional partners and over 40 senior managers left Cabots and were replaced, usually with people from outside the firm.

Rogers Petersen has had no such scandal and almost all of its senior executives have been with the firm for all of their careers.

a. Describe zero-base budgeting.
b. Which firm, Rogers Petersen or Cabots, is most likely to be using ZBB and why?

DP 8–6: Problems with Budgets (LO 1)

A June 4, 1990, *Fortune* magazine article with the title, "Why Budgets Are Bad for Business," included the following statements:

> Budgets, say experts, control the wrong things, like head count, and miss the right ones, such as quality, customer service—and even profits. Worse, they erect walls between the various parts of the company and between a company and its customers.
>
> When you're controlled by a budget, you're not controlling the business.
>
> Reliance on budgets is the fundamental flaw in American management. That's because they assume that everything important can be translated into this quarter's or this year's dollars, and that you can manage the business by managing the money. Wrong. Just because a budget was not overspent doesn't mean it was well spent.
>
> For tracking where the money goes, budgets are dandy. They become iniquitous when they are made to do more—when the budget becomes management's main tool to gauge performance. Managers do incredibly stupid things to make budget, especially if incentive pay is at stake. They woo marginal customers. They cut prices too deeply.
>
> The worst failure of budgets is what they don't measure. Budgets show what you spend on customer service, but not what value customers put on it.

Critically evaluate the article.

DP 8–7: Responsibility for an Unusual Event (LO 1)

In March, a devastating ice storm struck Monroe County causing millions of dollars of damage. Mathews & Peat (M&P), a large horticultural nursery, was hard hit. As a result of the storm, $653,000 of additional labor and maintenance costs were incurred to clean up the nursery, remove and replace damaged plants, repair fencing, and replace glass broken when nearby tree limbs fell on some of the greenhouses.

Mathews and Peat is a wholly owned subsidiary of Agro Inc., an international agricultural conglomerate. The manager of Mathews and Peat, Rick Dye, is reviewing the operating performance of the subsidiary for the year which included the ice storm. The results for the year as compared to budget are:

MATHEWS & PEAT
Summary of Operating Results for the Year 1996
($000)

	Actual Results	Budgeted Results	Actual as % of Budget
Revenues	$32,149	$31,682	101%
Less:			
Labor	13,152	12,621	104%
Materials	8,631	8,139	106%
Occupancy costs*	4,234	4,236	100%
Depreciation	2,687	2,675	100%
Interest	1,875	1,895	99%
Total expenses	30,579	29,566	103%
Operating profits	$ 1,570	$ 2,116	74%

*Includes property taxes, utilities, maintenance and repairs of buildings, etc.

After thinking about how to present the performance of M&P for the year, Dye decides to break out the costs of the ice storm from the individual items affected by the storm and report the storm separately. The total cost of the ice storm of $653,000 consists of additional labor costs of $320,000, additional materials of $220,000, and additional occupancy costs of $113,000. These amounts are net of the insurance payments received due to the storm. The alternative performance statement is given below:

MATHEWS & PEAT
Summary of Operating Results for the Year 1996
($000)

	Actual Results	Budgeted Results	Actual as % of Budget
Revenues	$32,149	$31,682	101%
Less:			
Labor	12,832	12,621	102%
Materials	8,411	8,139	103%
Occupancy costs*	4,121	4,236	97%
Depreciation	2,687	2,675	100%
Interest	1,875	1,895	99%
Total expenses	29,926	29,566	101%
Operating profits before ice storm costs	2,223	2,116	105%
Ice storm costs	653	0	
Operating profits after ice storm costs	$ 1,570	$ 2,116	74%

a. Put yourself in Dye's position and write a short, concise cover memo for the second operating statement which summarizes the essential points you want to communicate to your superiors.
b. Critically evaluate the differences between the two performance reports as presented.

DP 8–8: Lapsing and Multiyear Budgets (LO 2, 4)

Robin Jones, manager of market planning for Viral Products of the IDP Pharmaceutical Co., is responsible for advertising a class of products. She has designed a three-year marketing plan to increase the market share of her product class. Her plan involves a major increase in magazine advertising. She has met with an advertising agency that has designed a three-year ad campaign involving 12 separate ads that build on a common theme. Each ad will run in three consecutive monthly medical magazines and then be followed with the next ad in the sequence. Up to five different medical journals will carry the ad campaign. Direct mail campaigns and direct sales promotional material will be designed to follow the theme of the ad currently appearing at the time. The data below summarize the cost of the campaign:

	Year 1	Year 2	Year 3	Total
Number of ads	4	4	4	12
Number of magazines	5	5	4	
Cost per ad	$ 6,000	$ 6,200	$ 6,500	
Advertising cost	$120,000	$124,000	$104,000	$348,000

The firm's normal policy is to budget each year as a separate entity without carrying forward unspent funds. Jones is requesting that, instead of just approving the budget for next year (labeled "Year 1" above), the entire three-year project be budgeted. This would allow her to move forward with her campaign and give her the freedom to apply any unspent funds in one year to the next year or to use them in another part of the campaign. She argues that the ad campaign is an integrated project stretching over three years and should either be approved or rejected in its entirety.

Critically evaluate Ms. Jones's request and make a recommendation as to whether a three-year budget should be approved per her proposal. For purposes of your answer, assume that the advertising campaign is expected to be a profitable (positive net present value) project.

DP 8–9: Budget Effects of Purchasing Patterns (LO 1, 4)

You are working in the office of the vice president of administration at International Telecon (IT) as a senior financial planner. IT is a Fortune 500 firm with sales approaching $1 billion. IT provides long-distance satellite communications around the world. Deregulation of telecommunications in Europe has intensified worldwide competition and has increased pressures inside IT to reduce costs in order to allow lower prices without cutting profit margins.

IT is divided into several profit and cost centers. Each profit center is further organized as a series of cost centers. Each profit and cost center follows IT policy regarding submitting budgets to IT's vice president of administration and then is held responsible for meeting the budget. The vice president of administration described IT's financial control, budgeting, and reporting system as, "pretty much a standard, state-of-the-art approach where we hold our people accountable for producing what they forecast."

Your boss has assigned to you the task of analyzing firmwide supplies expenditures, with the goal of reducing waste and lowering expenditures. Supplies include all consumables ranging from pencils and paper to electronic subcomponents and parts that cost less than $1,000. Long-lived assets that cost under $1,000 (or the equivalent dollar amount in the domestic currency for foreign purchases) are **not** capitalized (and then depreciated) but rather categorized as supplies and written off as an expense in the month purchased.

You first gather the last 36 months of operating data for both supplies and payroll. The supplies and payroll data are for the entire firm. The payroll data is used to help you benchmark the supplies data. You divide each month's payroll and supplies amount by revenues in that month to control for volume and seasonal fluctuations. The following graph plots the two data series, monthly payroll and supply expenses.

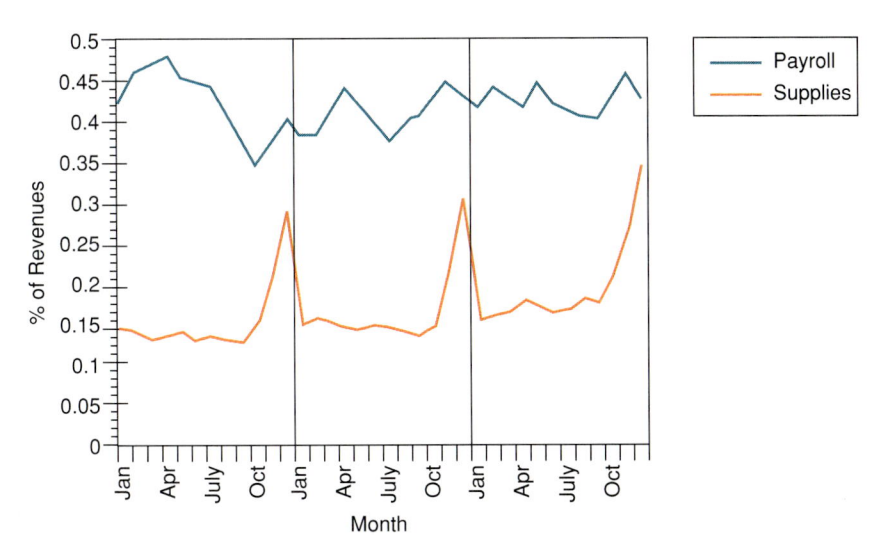

Payroll fluctuates between 35% and 48% of sales, and supplies fluctuate between 13% and 34% of sales. The above graph contains the last three years of supplies and payroll, where the vertical lines in the graph divide the fiscal years. For financial and budgeting purposes, IT is on a calendar year (January–December) fiscal year.

Besides focusing on consolidated firmwide spending, you prepare disaggregated graphs like the one above, but at the cost and profit center levels. The general patterns observed in the consolidated graphs are repeated in general in the disaggregated graphs.

a. Analyze the behavior over time of supplies expenditures for IT. What is the likely reason for the observed patterns in supplies?
b. Given your analysis in part a above, what corrective action might you consider proposing and what are its costs and benefits?

DP 8–10: Adjusting Budgets and Effect on Behavior (LO 1, 4)   Panarude Airfreight is an international air-freight hauler with over 75 jet aircraft operating in the United States and Pacific rim. The firm is headquartered in Melbourne, Australia, and is organized into five geographic areas: Australia, Japan, Taiwan, United States, and Korea. Supporting these areas are several centralized, corporate function services (cost centers): personnel, data processing, fleet acquisition and maintenance, telecommunications. Each responsibility center has a budget, negotiated at the beginning of the year with the vice president of finance. Any unspent funds at the end of the year do not carry over to the next fiscal year. The firm is on a January to December fiscal year.

After reviewing the month-to-month variances, Panarude senior management became concerned about the large spending patterns occurring in the last three months of each fiscal year. In particular, in the first nine months of the year, expenditure accounts typically show favorable variances (actual spending is less than budget) and in the last three months, unfavorable variances are the norm. In an attempt to smooth out these spending patterns, each responsibility center is reviewed at the end of each calendar quarter and any unspent funds can be deleted from the budget for the remainder of the year. For example, the budget and actual spending in the telecommunications department for the first quarter of 1995 is:

PANARUDE AIRFREIGHT
Telecommunications Department
1995 First Quarter Budget and Actual Spending
(Australian Dollars)

	Monthly Budget	Cumulative Budget	Actual Spending	Cumulative Spending	Monthly Variance	Cumulative Variance
Jan.	$110,000	$110,000	$104,000	$104,000	$6,000 F	$6,000 F
Feb.	95,000	205,000	97,000	201,000	2,000 U	4,000 F
Mar.	115,000	320,000	112,000	313,000	3,000 F	7,000 F

At the end of the first quarter, Telecommunications' total annual budget for 1995 can be reduced by $7,000, the total budget underrun in the first quarter. The remaining nine monthly budgets for Telecommunications is reduced by $778 ($7,000÷9). If at the end of the second quarter, Telecommunications' budget shows an unfavorable variance of say $8,000 (after reducing the original budget for the first quarter underrun), management of Telecommunications is held responsible for the entire $8,000 unfavorable variance. The first quarter underrun is **not** restored. If the second quarter budget variance is also favorable, the remaining six monthly budgets are again reduced by one-sixth of the second quarter favorable budget variance.

a. What behaviors would this budgeting scheme engender in the responsibility center managers?
b. Compare the advantages and disadvantages of the previous budget regime where any end-of-year budget surpluses do not carry over to the next fiscal year to the system of quarterly budget adjustments described above.

DP 8–11: Analyzing Variances (LO 1, 5)

Old Rosebud is a Kentucky horse farm that specializes in boarding thoroughbred breeding mares and their foals. Customers bring their breeding mares to Old Rosebud for delivery of their foals and after-birth care of the mare and foal. Recently there was a substantial decline in thoroughbred breeding brought about by changes in the tax laws. As a result of changes in the market for thoroughbred boarding, profits declined in this industry.

Old Rosebud prepared a master budget for 1996 by splitting costs into variable costs and fixed costs. The budget for 1996 was prepared before the extent of the downturn was fully recognized. Exhibit 1 compares actual to budget for 1996.

EXHIBIT 1
OLD ROSEBUD FARMS
Income Statement
For Year Ended 12/31/96

	Budget Formula (per mare per day)	Actual	Master Budget	Variance
Number of mares		52	60	8
Number of boarding days		18,980	21,900	2,920
Revenues	$25.00	$379,600	$547,500	$167,900 U
Less variable expenses:				
Feed and supplies	5.00	104,390	109,500	5,110 F
Veterinary fees	3.00	58,838	65,700	6,862 F
Blacksmith fees	.30	6,074	6,570	496 F
Total variable expenses	8.30	169,302	181,770	12,468 F
Contribution margin	16.70	210,298	365,730	155,432 U
Less fixed expenses:				
Depreciation and insurance		56,000	56,000	0
Utilities		12,000	14,000	2,000 F
Repairs and maintenance		10,000	11,000	1,000 F
Labor		88,000	96,000	8,000 F
Total fixed expenses		166,000	177,000	11,000 F
Net income		$ 44,298	$188,730	$144,432 U

Evaluate the operating performance of Rosebud Farms based on the variances in the table.

DP 8–12: Budgets and Cost Centers (LO 1)

Eastern University publishes and distributes over 100,000 copies of its "Official Bulletin on Undergraduate Studies" to prospective students, high school guidance counselors, faculty and staff of the university, and other interested parties. This 250-page catalogue with color pictures is one of the primary marketing devices for the university's undergraduate programs. High school seniors expressing interest in attending the university receive the bulletin along with other information about the university. It lists the various programs of studies, course offerings, and requirements. Each year it is revised and reprinted as courses and programs change and the photographs are updated, to improve it as a recruiting tool. The annual cost of preparing and printing the bulletin is about $1 million, which includes the cost of photographers, nonuniversity graphic designers, typesetting, and printing but excludes the cost of university employees who rewrite the text, proofread the galleys, and manage the entire process.

The responsibility of preparing the catalogue is shared by the admissions office and public relations. The admissions office coordinates the collection of the basic data on course and program changes. Many of these are not known until May, after the various faculties have met and approved academic program and course changes. These changes are edited and the overall content of the publication is determined based on the admissions office's experience with high school applicants. Admissions then sends a draft copy of the brochure to public relations. Public relations is responsible for the overall image and publicity of the university and for ensuring that the university publications present a consistent image. Public relations, using outside graphic designers, marketing specialists, typesetters, and printers whom they have come to know, take the changes and produce an attractive, high-quality brochure.

Admissions reports to the dean of the undergraduate college, who reports to the president. Public relations reports to the vice president of external affairs, who reports to the president. The admissions office affects the cost of the brochure in terms of the quantity of text to be included and how many bulletins must be ordered to satisfy their distribution plan. Public relations affects the cost by using more color photographs, more expensive paper and cover materials, and elaborate layouts. Both admissions and public relations affect the cost by not meeting timely production schedules. If copy is returned late or the design is not completed on time, additional charges are incurred by typesetters and printers working overtime to meet the publication schedule. It is critically important to the admissions process that the bulletin be available for distribution in September to high school seniors beginning their college search process.

Admissions and public relations are both cost centers. They have been arguing over whether the cost of the bulletin should be in the admissions office budget or the public relations department budget.

a. Discuss the advantages and disadvantages of placing the budget for the bulletin into the public relations versus the admissions office budget.
b. What are some other alternative ways of handling the bulletin's budget?
c. Based on your analysis, what recommendation would you make?

CASE

C 8–1: Master Budget   The Eugene Brewing Company is budgeting for the next year. The beginning balance sheet of the company is shown in Exhibit 1.

The company expects to collect the accounts receivable at the beginning of the year in January. In general, 30% of the company's sales are for cash. Of the sales on credit, 40% are paid in the following month and 60% are paid in the second month after the sale.

The accounts payable at the beginning of the year must be paid in January. All materials are purchased on credit and paid for the following month.

The long-term debt has monthly interest payments of 1% of the principal. The long-term debt is not due for another five years.

EXHIBIT 1

EUGENE BREWING COMPANY
Balance Sheet
As of 1/1/98

Assets		Liabilities and Equities	
Cash	$ 10,000	Accounts payable	$ 3,000
Accounts receivable	20,000	Long-term debt	50,000
Inventory	30,000		
Total current assets	$ 60,000	Total liabilities	$ 53,000
Fixed assets	200,000	Common stock at par	$ 10,000
Accumulated depreciation	(90,000)	Additional paid-in	20,000
		Retained earnings	87,000
Total assets	$170,000	Total liabilities and equities	$170,000

Eugene Brewing Company makes two different types of beer: an ale and a porter. The ale is a lighter beer requiring less ingredients than the darker and heavier porter. The input requirements for a case of beer for each type of beer are described below:

For making ale:

Material	Quantity/Case	Cost
Hops	5 lbs.	$.30/lb
Yeast	1 oz.	$.10/oz
Sugar	.5 lbs.	$.40/lb
Bottles	24	$.05/bottle

For making porter:

Material	Quantity/Case	Cost
Hops	10 lbs.	$.30/lb
Yeast	1 oz.	$.10/oz
Sugar	.8 lbs.	$.40/lb
Bottles	24	$.05/bottle

The labor to make a case of beer is the same for each type of beer: 0.20 hours at $10/hour. Labor is paid in the month earned.

Monthly overhead expenses are paid in the month incurred and are expected to be:

Electricity	$ 2,000
Indirect labor	20,000
Rent	5,000
Depreciation	2,000

Ale sells for $10/case and porter sells for $12/case. Estimated sales in cases for Eugene Brewing are:

	Ale	Porter
January	3,000	4,000
February	3,000	5,000
March	4,000	3,000
April	2,000	2,000

The beginning inventory includes 2,000 cases of ale and 3,000 cases of porter. The company prefers to have inventory at the end of each month equal to the expected sales in the next month. A first-in, first-out (FIFO) method of costing inventory is used.

Eugene Brewing Company must buy a new bottling machine for $20,000 at the end of January.

Case Questions

a. Estimate cash flows in each of the months.
b. Does the company need to borrow money any of the months?
c. Make a balance sheet as of the end of March and an income statement for the first three months. Assume that the company borrows cash at 1% a month to make up any shortage of cash.

Chapter 9
Cost Allocations

LEARNING OBJECTIVES

1. Describe the relationship among common resources, indirect costs, and cost objects.

2. Explain the role of allocating indirect costs for external financial reports, income tax reports, and cost reimbursement.

3. Identify reasons for cost allocation for planning purposes.

4. Identify reasons for cost allocation for control purposes.

5. Describe how the various reasons for cost allocation can cause trade-offs within the organization.

6. Allocate indirect costs using five basic steps.

7. Create segment reports for the organization.

8. Use direct, step-down, and reciprocal methods to allocate reciprocal service department costs. (Appendix)

Valley Clinic

Valley Clinic is composed of a group of family practitioner doctors who provide health services to different types of patients. Patients are categorized by the method of payment for services. Some patients come to Valley Clinic through an agreement with a local health maintenance organization (HMO). The HMO has agreed to cover all the employee medical costs of some of the larger area businesses for a fixed fee. The HMO then contracts with Valley Clinic to provide certain basic health services and act as a referral service if the patient needs the attention of a specialist or hospital. The HMO pays Valley Clinic $150 per year for each patient covered by the HMO who identifies a doctor at Valley Clinic as the primary care giver.

Other patients are covered by Medicare and other insurance plans, which pay Valley Clinic based on diagnostic related groups (DRGs). A DRG is a specified treatment given to the patient, such as setting a fractured bone or providing an annual physical examination. Medicare and insurance companies pay Valley Clinic a certain amount for each DRG provided to a patient covered by those plans.

Finally, another group of patients pay their own medical costs. These patients are charged an amount based on the cost of services provided.

The owners of Valley Clinic are 12 doctors, who are paid based on the profit they individually generate. The doctors have hired a director for the clinic, who is responsible for its general operations and management. The director is assisted by an accountant, a bookkeeper, a procurement manager, and a secretary. The costs related to this group are treated as general administration costs. The following departments assist the doctors in performing their duties: X-ray, nurses, and receptionists. In addition, the clinic incurs costs related to the building such as rent and utilities. Laboratory tests are performed by an outside agency and billed separately.

The primary problem facing the accountant of Valley Clinic is determining the cost of services provided by the doctors and determining the profit generated by each doctor. How should the accountant treat the general administration costs, the building costs, and the costs related to the departments that support the doctors?

9.1 Allocating Indirect Costs

Cost allocation is the process of assigning indirect costs to cost objects. **Cost objects** include products, activities, subunits of the organization, customers, suppliers, and time periods. Each of these cost objects has direct and indirect costs associated with them. Direct costs occur when resources are only used for one cost object. For example, raw materials are used by a specific product and are considered direct costs of the product, which is a cost object. Indirect costs, however, result from the use of resources by multiple cost objects. A machine that is used by many products is an indirect cost to those products. The allocation of indirect costs to cost objects is the subject of this chapter.

In Chapters 3 and 4, the allocation of indirect costs was performed for planning purposes. A manager who is making a planning decision related to a cost object would like to know the opportunity cost of that cost object to the organization. Opportunity costs are caused by the use of both direct and indirect resources. Direct costs are obviously related to the cost object, but indirect costs must be traced to cost objects through the use of cost drivers. The cost drivers are chosen to reflect the cause of the indirect costs. If the cost object uses the cost driver, indirect costs are traced to the cost object. Ideally the tracing of indirect costs through cost drivers will reflect the opportunity cost of using indirect resources.

Choosing cost drivers to trace indirect costs is appropriate if the purpose is to make a planning decision with respect to the cost object. But there are reasons for allocating indirect costs to cost objects other than making planning decisions. In this chapter, the allocation of indirect costs for control and external reporting purposes is also examined. Allocating indirect costs through cost drivers is not necessarily best for the organization when control and external reporting issues are considered. Other indirect cost allocation mechanisms may prove more beneficial in motivating managers or influencing users of external accounting reports.

The choice of the cost allocation method is subjective, and ethical considerations must be made. Cost allocations for control purposes can adversely affect certain managers and benefit others. Cost allocation methods for external re-

These quality engineers are checking the settings on the machinery in a soap factory. The salaries of these people are allocated to cost objects, in this case to the various soaps produced in the plant.

porting may be chosen to provide more profit for the organization to the disadvantage of external parties such as customers or the taxing authority.

The subjective nature of indirect cost allocations makes the process one of the most controversial in accounting. Inappropriate cost allocation mechanisms can lead to poor planning decisions, demoralized managers, and unhappy customers. In spite of the potential problems associated with cost allocation that are identified in this chapter, cost allocation is prevalent among organizations. For example, personnel department costs are an indirect cost to other departments and are commonly allocated to those departments. Hospitals allocate the indirect costs of shared medical equipment among departments using the equipment. Computer center costs are allocated among the computer users within the organization. Depreciation on the factory building is allocated among the products manufactured in the factory.

This prevalent use of cost allocation implies that there are also many benefits of allocating costs. But an organization should clearly identify why costs are being allocated and the effect of those cost allocations on the behavior of managers. Each cost allocation has planning, control, and external reporting implications, and an organization must often make trade-offs in choosing a cost allocation method.

VALLEY CLINIC (CONTINUED)

In Valley Clinic, the general administration, building, and departments (X-ray, nurses, receptionists) supporting the doctors are all indirect resources for the doctors. These indirect resources are used by all the doctors and many of the patients. The doctors and the patients are the cost objects or recipients of the allocated indirect costs from the indirect resources. A method must be chosen to allocate these indirect costs.

CONCEPT REVIEW

1. What are some examples of cost allocation?
2. What is the relationship between common resources and cost objects?

9.2 Reasons for Allocating Indirect Costs

Most organizations use cost allocation, but the allocation of indirect costs is not without controversy. One example is the allocation of indirect costs to responsibility centers controlled by managers. The controllability principle based on responsibility accounting suggests that managers should be responsible only for costs they can control. Yet the allocation of indirect costs is often a distribution of costs to managers who have little or no control over those costs. Managers in many organizations complain bitterly about the allocation of certain indirect costs. While managers do not usually have complete control of indirect costs, they often partially affect the use of the indirect resource. For example, if a production department expands its number of workers, greater demands are placed on the personnel department, which ultimately must expand or else provide less service to the other departments.

The allocation of some indirect costs to products is also controversial. In Chapter 5, the pricing decision that maximized profits was determined through the use of marginal costs. A product cost that includes allocated fixed costs does not appear to be a likely representation of the marginal cost of making a product.

The allocation of overhead has received more attention than any other cost accounting topic and has been a hotly debated problem since accountants have been recording indirect expenses. One commentator writing in 1916 described the situation as follows:

> Indirect expense is one of the most important of all the accounts appearing on the books of the manufacturer. Methods of handling its [allocation] have given rise to more arguments than the problem of the descent of man. It is the rock upon which many a ship of industry has been wrecked.[1]

Given the contentious nature of the allocation of indirect costs, there must be some benefits to allocating indirect costs. These benefits fall into three categories: (1) satisfaction of external requirements, (2) planning purposes, and (3) control purposes. These benefits are discussed in the following sections.

Satisfying External Requirements

Not all management accounting decisions are based on internal demand for information for making planning decisions and control. Organizations often have responsibilities to outside parties to provide certain information. Shareholders have the right to receive financial reports from the corporations they own. Profit organizations must file tax returns to governmental bodies and nonprofit organizations file informational returns. And some contracts between different organizations specify that costs of one organization will be reimbursed by the other organization. Therefore, cost information must be communicated from one organization to the other.

Allocated indirect costs play an important role in each of these settings. In some cases, the method of dealing with indirect costs is specified. In other cases, the allocation of indirect costs offers opportunities for an organization to achieve some financial objective such as reducing taxes. Each setting with its corresponding cost allocation requirements and opportunities is described in the following sections.

Financial Reports to Shareholders

The compilation of financial reports to shareholders is based on regulations from bodies such as the Financial Accounting Standards Board (FASB), the Securities and Exchange Commission (SEC), and other authoritative professional bodies such as the American Institute of Certified Public Accountants (AICPA). Rules from the FASB, SEC, and others do not cover all aspects of financial reporting. When rules from the regulatory bodies do not specify the appropriate accounting method, past accounting practices are used as a guideline. Rules from the regulatory bodies and guidelines based on past accounting practices make up generally accepted accounting principles (GAAP).

The allocation of indirect manufacturing costs to products is a financial accounting method that has become part of GAAP because of its use in the past. Traditionally, indirect manufacturing costs, but not indirect selling and administrative overhead costs, are allocated to products. In most wholesale, retail, and service organizations, no indirect costs are allocated to the product or service for financial reporting purposes.

The method used to allocate indirect manufacturing costs to products affects the calculation of profit. Indirect manufacturing costs that are allocated to products become part of the inventory cost and remain an asset until the product is sold. The allocation of indirect manufacturing costs to products that remain in inventory at the end of the period affects financially reported profits this period.

NUMERICAL EXAMPLE 9.1

A sports equipment manufacturer makes two types of balls: soccer balls and basketballs. There is no beginning inventory; during the year, the manufacturer made 20,000 soccer balls and 40,000 basketballs. Indirect manufacturing costs for the year were $100,000. All the soccer balls and 30,000 of the basketballs were sold during the year. The company is considering two possible methods of allocating indirect manufacturing costs. The first method allocates $80,000 to the soccer balls and $20,000 to the basketballs. The second method allocates $40,000 to the soccer balls and $60,000 to the basketballs. Which method causes a higher reported profit this period?

■ **SOLUTION** Because 10,000/40,000, or 25%, of the basketballs were not sold this period, indirect manufacturing costs associated with the unsold basketballs remain an asset and are not a deduction from income. Under the first method, 25% of $20,000, or $5,000, of manufacturing overhead is not deducted from income this period. Under the second method 25% of $60,000, or $15,000, is not deducted. Therefore, the second method causes reported profits to be $15,000 − $5,000, or $10,000, higher.

The pressure to allocate indirect costs to influence externally reported income will occur if a manager's compensation is based on that income number. Top-level managers frequently have bonuses tied to externally reported income, so they are concerned about how indirect manufacturing costs are allocated. There are constraints, however, in the allocation of costs for external reports. The allocation method must be part of GAAP, and managers cannot change the method of allocation without agreement from their external auditors.[2]

Reporting of Taxable Income

Tax accounting rules require that inventory be stated at cost, including an appropriate amount for indirect manufacturing costs. For example, inventory includes not only direct labor and direct material but also a fraction of factory depreciation, property taxes, and the salaries of security guards at the factory. As in the case of external financial reports, the allocation of these indirect manufacturing costs among products can influence the calculation of taxable income.

The owners of an organization would like to allocate costs in a manner that reduces taxable income. The lower the taxable income, the lower the tax payments. The methods of allocating indirect costs, however, are constrained by the rulings of the taxing authority.

Cost Reimbursement Contracts

Cost reimbursement is another reason for cost allocations. Government cost-based contracts and medical reimbursements for cost give rise to cost allocations. The United States Department of Defense purchases billions of dollars a year under cost-plus contracts. A cost-plus contract states that the consumer will compensate the supplier for the cost of the product or service plus some amount or percentage to allow the supplier to have a profit. For example, a weapons system contract may state that the supplier of the system will be paid for the cost of the weapons system plus a 10% markup to allow the supplier to make a profit.

Cost reimbursement contracts are frequently used when the product or service is unique and the cost of making the product or providing the service is very uncertain. With uncertain costs, suppliers may be unwilling to offer the product or service. By promising to reimburse costs, the customer

> **WHAT'S HAPPENING**
>
> During the 1960s and 1970s, hospitals had costs reimbursed by insurance companies. How did this cost reimbursement scheme affect the cost of hospital care?

removes the risk of uncertain costs from the supplier. The customer, however, must worry about incentives for the supplier to control costs. If the supplier knows that all costs will be reimbursed, the supplier will not be as careful in controlling costs.

Indirect cost allocation is a controversial part of cost reimbursement. If a supplier makes multiple products and some are sold on a cost reimbursement basis, the supplier would like to allocate as many indirect costs as possible to the products that are reimbursed based on cost. More indirect costs being allocated to products with cost reimbursement means greater revenues for the organization.

NUMERICAL EXAMPLE 9.2

An auditing firm has two types of clients: those that request a cost-plus 20% contract and those that request a fixed fee of $20,000 for auditing services. The auditing firm completes 50 audits of each type during the year. The average direct costs of each audit are $10,000. Indirect costs for the accounting firm are $500,000. The first method of allocating indirect costs assigns $200,000 to the cost-plus audits and $300,000 to the fixed-fee audits. The second method allocates $400,000 to cost-plus audits and $100,000 to fixed-fee audits. Which method provides a higher profit for the auditing firm?

■ **SOLUTION** The reported cost for the cost-plus audits under the first method is:

Direct costs (50)($10,000)	$500,000
Indirect costs	200,000
Total	$700,000

The total profit of both the cost-plus and fixed-fee contracts using the first method of allocating indirect costs:

Revenues	
Cost-plus ($700,000)(120%)	$ 840,000
Fixed-fee (50)($20,000)	1,000,000
Total	$1,840,000
Costs	
Direct (100)($10,000)	1,000,000
Indirect	500,000
Net Income	$ 340,000

The reported cost for the cost-plus audits under the second method is:

Direct costs (50)($10,000)	$500,000
Indirect costs	400,000
Total	$900,000

The total income of both the cost-plus and fixed-fee contracts using the second method of allocating indirect costs is:

Revenues	
Cost-plus ($900,000)(120%)	$1,080,000
Fixed-fee (50)($20,000)	1,000,000
Total	$2,080,000
Costs	
Direct (100)($10,000)	1,000,000
Indirect	500,000
Net Income	$ 580,000

The second method causes a higher income because more reimbursable indirect costs are allocated to the cost-plus audits.

The cost of operating this nuclear power plant is included in the rate consumers pay for electricity. A controversial question arises as to whether the cost of closing this plant should be included in future rates. That is, should consumers or stockholders pay for the eventual closing of the plant?

Because the allocation of indirect costs is such a critical aspect of cost reimbursement contracts, the contracts should specify the allowable cost allocation methods. To help regulate the cost allocations by suppliers of government agencies, the federal government established the Cost Accounting Standards Board (CASB) to issue standards covering the broad areas of cost measurement, cost assignment to accounting periods, and cost allocation within an accounting period. Suppliers of government agencies with cost-plus contracts must follow the accounting procedures specified by the CASB.

In addition to defense contractors, public utilities such as electric and gas companies have their revenues tied to reported costs. Public utilities are often granted exclusive monopolies over service territories by their states. In return for the monopoly, the state regulates the prices the utility can charge their customers. In many cases, the regulated prices are based on reported costs, including allocated costs. In public utility regulation, the major issue is deciding how to allocate the indirect costs of capacity, such as the electricity generating plant, among the different classes of users (residential versus business customers). In many public utility rate-setting cases, cost allocation is the preeminent issue.

VALLEY CLINIC (CONTINUED)

Valley Clinic is not a manufacturing concern with inventory, so there are no cost allocation problems in terms of manufactured products for financial reporting or income tax reporting. Valley Clinic, however, does charge the self-paying patients based on the cost of services provided. In this case, the patient is the ultimate cost object, and general administration and other service costs are allocated to the different patients. Given that the revenues generated from other patients are either fixed (HMO patients) or based on predetermined rates for the services provided (Medicare and insurance companies), Valley Clinic would like to allocate as many indirect costs to the self-paying patients as is ethically possible. The self-paying patients, however, are not restricted to

> coming to Valley Clinic, so there are other limits on what can be charged to these patients. For example, should self-paying patients be charged for the cost of supplying services to individuals who don't pay their medical bills? In choosing cost allocation methods for patients, Valley Clinic must offset the cost of disgruntled, self-paying patients and the benefit of additional short-run revenue. A strategy of increasing revenue in the short run by charging self-paying patients more can lead to a long-run loss in revenue if those patients decide to go to other clinics.

Different Accounting Systems for External and Internal Purposes

Using a single cost allocation method for external financial reports, tax reporting, and cost reimbursement can lead to trade-offs. Management may want to choose cost allocation methods that increase present income to receive bonuses, while owners may want to choose cost allocation methods that reduce present income for tax purposes. In addition, increasing revenues through cost reimbursement may lead to a different cost allocation scheme. One solution is to have different accounting systems for each purpose.

In a similar fashion, the cost allocation schemes used for external reports need not affect the choice of cost allocation schemes for internal purposes. The primary motivation for using a single accounting system is to reduce bookkeeping costs. Having multiple accounting systems is more costly than having a single accounting system for all purposes. The disadvantage of having a single accounting system is the trade-off that may arise from using the system for different purposes. These trade-offs in external reporting can lead to lost revenues and greater income taxes. Losses from using a single accounting system within the organization occur because of the conflict between planning and control. These issues are discussed in the next two sections.

CONCEPT REVIEW

1. How is cost allocation used with external financial and tax reporting?
2. How do cost reimbursement contracts influence cost allocations?

Cost Allocation for Planning Purposes

Information for planning purposes is used to make better decisions through more knowledge of the problem. The allocation of indirect costs can provide managers with information that allows them to make better decisions. In some cases the allocation of indirect costs provides a better measure of the opportunity cost of providing a product or service. The allocation of indirect costs also serves as a communication mechanism to let managers know how their actions are affecting costs in the rest of the organization.

Estimation of the Opportunity Cost of Products and Services

Managers must make planning decisions with respect to the products and services the organization offers. Managers with appropriate decision rights make pricing and product mix decisions. These planning decisions should be made based on the opportunity cost of providing those products. The allocation of indirect costs to products will improve planning decisions to the extent the indirect costs represent the opportunity costs of providing those products.

Indirect product costs occur because resources are used to produce more than one product. For example, a machine may be used to make different products. The use of that machine by a particular product has an opportunity cost if there are alternative uses of the machine. By not using the machine for one product, another product could be manufactured or the machine could be sold. Under these circumstances, some portion of the indirect costs should be allocated to the product to represent the opportunity cost of providing the product.

The allocated indirect costs do not necessarily equate to the opportunity cost of using a resource. For external reporting purposes, all indirect manufacturing costs are allocated to products. But the use of some indirect manufacturing resources does not constitute an opportunity cost. For example, the opportunity cost of using a machine may be approximately zero if there is no alternative use of the machine and the machine has a low salvage value. A clear understanding of how a product or service uses an indirect resource and of alternative uses of the indirect resource is important in estimating the opportunity cost of using the indirect resource.

Communication of Costs to Improve Planning Decisions

The allocated indirect costs also serve as a communication device to inform managers of the cost of their actions to the whole organization. When managers use internal resources or services, they impose costs on other parts of the organization. For example, most universities offer advising services to all the students. The cost of these advising services is allocated to the different schools within the university by the number of students in each school. The allocated cost is intended to represent the opportunity cost of advising more students. If a school accepts more students, more students will use the advising services and the advising office must hire more advisors. By allocating the cost of advising services to the different schools, the university is communicating to the deans of the schools the opportunity cost of providing advising services. With this additional information, the deans can make better decisions on admitting students.

Managers are not always aware of some of the costs (or benefits) they impose on other parts of the organization. In many cases, these costs or benefits are imposed on others without their consent or without direct compensation. These costs or benefits are called **externalities.** Externalities are usually considered in a social context. For example, pollution is a negative externality or cost imposed on others. Automobile exhaust pollutes the air, yet car drivers do not pay for the costs they impose on others by their pollution (except via gasoline taxes). The consumers of polluted air are not paid directly for the polluted air they breathe. Education contains a positive externality because people derive benefits from having more educated citizens with whom to interact. Well-manicured lawns of private homes create positive externalities as people pass and enjoy the sight and by increasing the property values of neighboring homes.

Externalities pervade organizations. Improvements in tracking materials in the supply room provide positive externalities to the manufacturing department because requisitions for material can be met more quickly. Hiring another salesperson imposes negative externalities on the personnel department and other departments that provide services to employees. Adding a new product or service can impose either positive or negative externalities on other products or services of the same organization. Communicating the costs or benefits of externalities through the allocation of indirect costs allows managers to make more

Air pollution is a classic example of an externality. Except for taxes on gasoline, motorists do not pay for the costs they impose on others by driving their cars and producing additional congestion and smog.

informed decisions. The problem with externalities, however, is that they are difficult to identify and measure. Therefore, the allocated costs that are intended to represent the externality may not accurately reflect opportunity costs.

VALLEY CLINIC (CONTINUED)

The doctors of Valley Clinic have little discretion in terms of pricing their services (except for the self-paying patients) but do have some discretion in determining what services to provide patients. In particular, the doctors can choose the number and types of X rays to be performed. The choice to use X rays will be, in part, due to the costs allocated from that service to the doctors. If the allocated costs reflect the opportunity cost of using X rays, the doctors can make better decisions on their use.

CONCEPT REVIEW

1. What type of cost should cost allocations approximate if used for planning purposes?
2. How are cost allocations used to resolve externality issues?

Cost Allocation for Control Reasons

Motivation and control are likely explanations for the prevalence of cost allocations within organizations. Cost allocations control managers through the allocation of decision rights and the effect of cost allocations on performance measures. Cost allocations also allow managers to monitor each other. The way indirect costs are allocated affects managers' behavior. Therefore, the choice of the allocation method is a tool for controlling managers.

Cost Allocations and the Allocation of Decision Rights

The allocation of costs in some organizations coincides with the allocation of resources. For example, universities may shift resources from one college to another by allocating more general administrative costs to one college than another. The allocated costs are like a tax that is imposed on each college. The university president constrains the deans of the colleges by allocating costs to them and forcing them to pay a higher tax. Funds are distributed to the deans after the allocated general administration costs are deducted. The deans have less resources and, therefore, less decision rights available.

Cost Allocations and Performance Measures

Responsibility centers are at least partially evaluated based on accounting numbers. Costs, profit, and ROI are common performance measures to evaluate managers. These accounting numbers are influenced by the allocation of indirect costs from resources used by multiple responsibility centers. For example, marketing department costs may be allocated to the various responsibility centers that benefit from marketing. These marketing department costs become part of the performance measures of the managers of the other responsibility centers.

As discussed in Chapter 6, performance measures ideally should reveal the actions of the manager being evaluated. The controllability principle is based on the theory that managers should only be evaluated on costs that they can control. Therefore, the allocation of indirect costs to responsibility centers for the purpose of measuring performance should only occur if the manager has some control over the cause of the indirect costs or how the indirect costs are allocated to the responsibility center. For example, if general administrative costs over which a manager has no control are arbitrarily allocated to that manager, the manager's performance measures will be affected and the manager will be rightfully upset.

An organization may choose to allocate uncontrollable indirect costs through methods that can be affected by managers. In doing so, the organization can motivate managers to achieve certain goals of the organization. For example, suppose an organization would like to reduce the number of employees within the organization. The president of the organization chooses to allocate the uncontrollable general administrative costs based on the number of employees in each responsibility center. To reduce the amount of general administrative costs allocated to their responsibility center, the managers of these centers reduce the number of employees in their responsibility center. Therefore, the allocation of general administrative costs motivates managers to achieve the goals of the organization even though general administrative costs may not be affected by a reduction in employees.

The cost allocations act like a tax system. In the previous case, the organization uses the allocation of general administrative costs to tax the number of employees. As in any tax system, individuals modify their behavior to reduce the taxes that are imposed on them. If a characteristic of the responsibility center such as the number of employees is used to allocate indirect costs, the characteristic is taxed and the manager will choose to use less of that characteristic. If multiple characteristics are used to allocate indirect costs, the manager of the responsibility center will use less of the characteristics that are taxed heavily and more of the characteristics that are taxed less or not at all.

> **WHAT'S HAPPENING**
>
> During the 1980s and early 1990s, IBM had the policy of allocating costs from one line of business to another. Managers in those lines of business constantly argued that some of their overhead should be carried by other IBM businesses. The cost allocation system masked the true profitability of many IBM businesses for years. IBM claimed it was making money in its PC business. But in 1991, "as IBM began to move away from its funny allocation system, IBM disclosed that its PC business was unprofitable."[3] What do you think IBM did?

NUMERICAL EXAMPLE 9.3

A department of a tennis racket factory is responsible for stringing the rackets. The rackets can be either strung by hand or strung by a machine. Both methods provide the same quality of stringing. The direct labor cost of stringing by hand is $2 per racket and the direct machine cost of stringing by machine is $3 per racket. Other costs are the same. What method of stringing rackets would the manager of that department use if the performance measure is cost? If factory administration costs are allocated to departments at a rate of $1 per dollar of direct labor, what method of stringing rackets would the manager use?

■ **SOLUTION** With no allocation of factory administration costs, the manager would choose to string rackets by hand because the $2 direct labor cost is less than the $3 machine cost. The allocation of $1 of administration costs per dollar of direct labor costs, however, increases the total reported cost of the manual method to $4 per racket and makes the machine method less costly, as measured by accounting costs.

Cost allocations change behavior within organizations. By imposing taxes on certain characteristics used to allocate costs, the organization is motivating managers to reduce those characteristics. The organization should recognize, however, that taxing certain characteristics may achieve short-term goals but may in the long run lead to perverse decisions on the parts of managers. For example, Tektronix, an electronics manufacturer, used direct labor to allocate indirect costs. Engineers were encouraged to reduce the cost of the products, so they reduced the amount of direct labor required to make new products. Eventually the factory was almost fully automated, but total costs were even higher.

To avoid such perverse behavior, an organization should continually evaluate its cost allocation methods. If the costs of an indirect resource are being allocated at a rate different than the opportunity cost of using that indirect resource, managers will have an incentive to use too much or too little of that indirect resource. In the case of Tektronix, direct labor was taxed at a rate higher than the opportunity cost of using direct labor. This led to an excessive use of other factors such as machines and a correspondingly higher cost of production.

Mutual Monitoring Incentives

The usual method of monitoring behavior within firms is for superiors to monitor subordinates. But monitoring can occur among managers at the same level of the organization, which is called **mutual monitoring.** Cost allocations from one responsibility center to another can result in mutual monitoring. Suppose the costs from a computer services department are allocated to other departments. These allocated costs are like transfer prices, which represent the cost of services provided. If the allocated costs of the computer service department become too high, managers of the other departments will complain and urge the computer services department to cut costs. If managers have the decision rights to seek computer services from other organizations, these managers will force the computer services department to lower their costs or the managers will seek other options. If costs from the computer services department are not allocated to other departments, the other department managers will not be concerned about controlling costs in the computer services department. There will be less mutual monitoring. The discipline to control costs in the computer services department will have to be imposed by higher level management.

Valley Clinic (continued)

Cost allocation at Valley Clinic plays an important role in determining the performance measures and rewards of the doctors. Doctors are rewarded based on the profit they generate for the clinic. Costs that are allocated to the doctors, who are the cost objects under this system, affect the profit associated with each doctor. General administration and other service department costs are allocated to the doctors to determine the profits generated by each doctor. Valley Clinic must be careful in allocating costs to the doctors. Doctors may have an incentive to under- or overuse a service department if costs are allocated by certain methods. Valley Clinic is very concerned about its reputation as a place that offers top quality medical service, and the clinic doesn't want the cost allocation scheme leading doctors to make decisions that could harm that reputation.

CONCEPT REVIEW

1. How can cost allocations affect decision rights?
2. How can cost allocations influence the behavior of managers?
3. What is mutual monitoring and how is it influenced by cost allocations?

9.3 Basic Steps of Cost Allocation

All indirect cost allocation methods are composed of the same series of steps. In Chapters 3 and 4, the steps leading to the application of indirect costs through cost drivers to cost objects was discussed. The steps described in this section are the same except the term **allocation base** is used instead of cost driver. An allocation base is a characteristic of the cost object that is used to allocate costs. Cost drivers are a type of allocation base that reflects the cause of the indirect costs being allocated. Cost drivers are important for estimating the cost of a product or other cost object. Allocation bases, however, may be chosen for other reasons than estimating costs, such as control. As described in the previous section, cost allocations can motivate managers to make certain decisions.

The five steps for cost allocation are: (1) defining the cost objects, (2) accumulating indirect costs in cost pools, (3) choosing an allocation base, (4) estimating an application rate, and (5) allocating indirect costs based on use of the allocation base. Each of these steps is described in the following sections.

Defining the Cost Objects

The organization must decide what departments, products, customers, suppliers, or processes should receive the indirect costs. For example, users of the computer center may be defined as cost objects. Or the computer center itself may be chosen as a cost object. The cost object can be a subunit of the organization, such as a cost or profit center. Services and products generated by an organization are treated as cost objects as described in Chapter 4. In each case the choice of a cost object is based on the desire to obtain cost information about the cost object that is useful for planning purposes or to influence the decisions of managers for control purposes.

> **VALLEY CLINIC (CONTINUED)**
>
> Valley Clinic has two cost objects: doctors and patients. For the remaining part of this chapter, allocation of costs to doctors to determine their share of the profit is analyzed. This allocation of costs will also influence their decisions to use common resources. A similar type of analysis, but with a different goal (cost reimbursement), would have to be performed to allocate costs to patients.

Accumulating the Indirect Costs in Cost Pools

The indirect costs being allocated are caused by the common use of a resource such as a machine, building, administrative service, or a production or service department. Costs associated with these resources are accumulated in **cost pools.** The size of the cost pool depends on how resources are aggregated. For example, each machine could have a separate cost pool or the costs associated with all the machines could be placed in a single cost pool.

Indirect costs associated with a resource include all the costs that can be traced to the resource. For example, the indirect cost pool associated with the computer department would include direct costs to the department such as the cost of the hardware, the labor costs of individuals working in the computer department, and computer paper, tapes, and other supplies.

In addition, a cost pool may contain costs that are only indirectly associated with the resource. These indirect costs are allocated to the cost pool from other cost pools that represent commonly shared resources. For example, the maintenance department is a resource that is used by many other departments. If the computing department uses the maintenance department, the computing department cost pool should contain allocated costs from the maintenance department cost pool.

Multistage cost allocation occurs when costs are allocated through a series of cost pools. Figure 9.1 is an example of a two-stage allocation procedure. Internal service department costs are allocated to production departments that use the internal service departments. Internal service departments include departments such as personnel, accounting, maintenance, and computer services. Production department costs are then allocated to the different products that use the differ-

FIGURE 9.1

Two-Stage Allocation Procedure

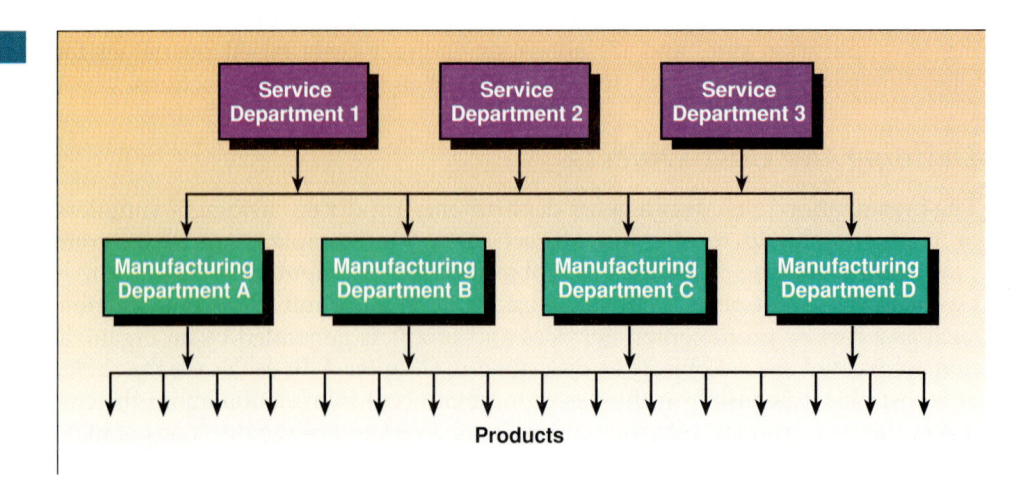

Large companies like Sears and Xerox have internal transportation departments with fleets of trucks to move supplies and both intermediate and final products. The costs of the internal transportation department are allocated to other divisions within the firm.

ent production departments. Production departments, such as assembly departments, are departments that are directly associated with the product or service that the organization sells. In this case, the production departments are the intermediate cost objects and the products are the final cost objects.

VALLEY CLINIC (CONTINUED)

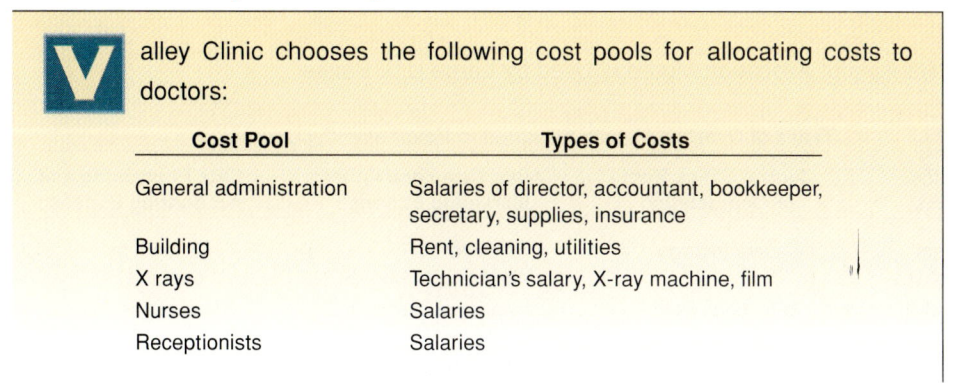

Valley Clinic chooses the following cost pools for allocating costs to doctors:

Cost Pool	Types of Costs
General administration	Salaries of director, accountant, bookkeeper, secretary, supplies, insurance
Building	Rent, cleaning, utilities
X rays	Technician's salary, X-ray machine, film
Nurses	Salaries
Receptionists	Salaries

Choosing an Allocation Base

An allocation base is a measurement of a characteristic used to distribute indirect costs of a cost pool to cost objects. Each cost pool may have a different allocation base. Cost drivers used in activity-based costing (ABC), described in Chapter 4, are allocation bases that distribute costs from overhead activity cost pools to different responsibility centers and products. The cost driver chosen through ABC is intended to reflect the usage of the overhead activity. An allocation base, however, need not even be associated with the costs in the cost pools. For example, a company may choose an allocation base to reduce a particular characteristic of the organization. If the number of defects is chosen as the allocation base for general administration costs, managers would be motivated to reduce the number of defects so less costs are allocated to their responsibility center. The number of defects may not be associated with general administrative costs. Instead the allocation base is chosen to achieve an organizational goal to reduce defects. Here, the cost allocation acts like a tax on defects.

The choice of the allocation base depends on the goals of the organization. Because cost allocations are used internally for two primary purposes (making planning decisions and control), there is no single choice of an allocation base that is always right or always wrong. Table 9.1 shows the choice of allocation bases made by 49 U.S. banks to allocate certain indirect costs (executive salaries, central office rent or depreciation, advertising and marketing expenses, and data processing and accounting expenses) to responsibility centers. The allocation bases are listed from the most important to the least important method. In general, the cost allocation bases chosen are those that have the greatest association with the cost being allocated. For example, the most important method for allocating executive salaries is time spent by executives on the responsibility center. Rent is allocated most frequently based on square footage. Advertising and data processing are usually allocated using the time spent on the responsibility center. Allocating advertising and marketing expense commonly uses the time spent by marketing personnel on the center as the allocation base.

Table 9.1 also indicates there is some diversity in the selection of allocation bases. This diversity may be due to different goals within the sample of banks. Another factor in the choice of allocation bases is the ease of measurement. A particular allocation base may be closely associated with an indirect cost but could be very difficult and costly to measure. For example, in Table 9.1 the most popular allocation base for executive salaries is the time spent by executives in each responsibility center. To measure this time, however, is a nuisance and some organizations may choose an easier allocation base to measure.

TABLE 9.1 Ranking of Allocation Methods Used by Large U.S. Banks

Level of Importance*	Executive Salaries	Central Office Rent or Depreciation	Advertising and Other Marketing Expense	Data Processing and Accounting Expense
1	Time spent by executives	Square footage	Time spent by marketing personnel	Time spent by accountants, etc.,
2	Personnel costs	Personnel costs	Number of customers served by the center	Transactions volume
3	Transactions volume	Transactions volume	Other (including "no allocation")	Personnel costs
4	Other (including "no allocation")	Number of customers served by the center	Transactions volume	Other (including "no allocation")
5	Number of customers served by the center	Interest costs	Personnel costs	Number of customers served by the center
6	Interest costs	Other (including "no allocation")	Interest costs	Interest costs
7	Square footage	(Not reported)	Square footage	Square footage

*1 = Most important; 7 = Least important.

Source: M Gardner and L Lammers, "Cost Accounting in Large Banks," *Management Accounting*, April 1988, Table 3.

VALLEY CLINIC (CONTINUED)

In choosing the allocation bases for the cost pools, Valley Clinic wants to motivate the doctors to use common resources efficiently but also provide good service to patients. The following choices are made with those goals in mind:

Cost Pool	Allocation Base
General administration	Number of patients
Building	Number of examination rooms
X rays	Number of X-ray patients
Nurses	Hours used
Receptionists	Number of patients

These choices are based partly on recognizing the opportunity cost of using common resources and partly to achieve the goal of good patient care. For example, insurance is a major general administration cost and closely related to the number of patients seen by the doctor. The number of examination rooms is used as an allocation base to discourage doctors from tying up too many examination rooms while patients wait for the doctor. Each doctor has the choice of how many examination rooms to reserve for his or her patients. The number of X-ray patients rather than the number of X rays is used as an allocation base for the X-ray department because of the fixed cost of getting the patient prepared for a series of X-rays and not wanting the doctor to skimp on the number of X rays. Under this system, the incremental cost of another X ray to the doctor is zero, so doctors will tend to have too many X rays taken on a particular patient. The use of staff, nurses and receptionists, is a problem in the clinic. The allocation bases tend to encourage doctors to use the reception staff more and use the nurses less because the allocated costs of using nurses increase by hour of use. But under this system, there is no incremental cost to the doctors of using receptionists to perform another task. Given that the salary of a nurse is greater than the salary of a receptionist, the clinic prefers substituting receptionists for nurses for some work.

Estimating an Application Rate

Once the allocation base for a cost pool is chosen, an application rate is calculated. The application rate is normally determined at the beginning of the year prior to the actual incurrence of the indirect cost. A predetermined application rate allows for the allocation of costs during the period before indirect costs are completely measured. The allocated cost information is more timely with predetermined application rates but may not reflect actual costs incurred. The sum of all indirect costs allocated to cost objects with a predetermined application rate may not be equal to the actual indirect costs incurred. This problem is discussed in Chapter 10. In this section we assume that management can make

The cost of operating this material testing lab at Du Pont does not vary with the number of units produced. Rather, costs in this lab vary with the number and complexity of the tests performed.

accurate estimates of indirect costs and allocation bases and there is no difference between allocated indirect costs and actual indirect costs.

The application rate for an allocation base is commonly estimated with the following ratio:

$$\frac{\text{Estimated dollars in the cost pool}}{\text{Estimated total usage of the allocation base}}$$

As an example, suppose that the estimated cost pool of the computer service department for the next period is $400,000. The number of hours computer service personnel work on projects for different responsibility centers is used as an allocation base. The managers of the responsibility centers estimate they will use 5,000 hours of computer service personnel time. Therefore, the application rate is $400,000/5,000 hours, or $80/hour.

There are several problems with this application rate. Cost allocation for planning decisions should be performed to obtain estimates of the opportunity cost of using the common resource. Some of the estimated computer costs may be sunk if they are estimated through a historical cost system. For example, the cost pool may contain historical cost depreciation rather than the change in market value of a fixed asset, which is often referred to as *economic depreciation.*

Even if only opportunity costs are identified in the cost pool, the cost pool may contain fixed costs with respect to the allocation base. For example, some of the costs of the computer service department may not vary with the number of hours personnel work for other departments. The opportunity cost of using some of the hardware is likely to be fixed with respect to the number of hours that computer service personnel work. All the computer service costs, however, are allocated as if they vary with the number of hours that computer service personnel work. After the fixed costs have been incurred, the application rate, which includes both fixed and variable costs, exceeds the variable costs of operating the computer service department. This relation is shown in Figure 9.2 with the cost application curve being steeper than the total cost line. If allocated costs

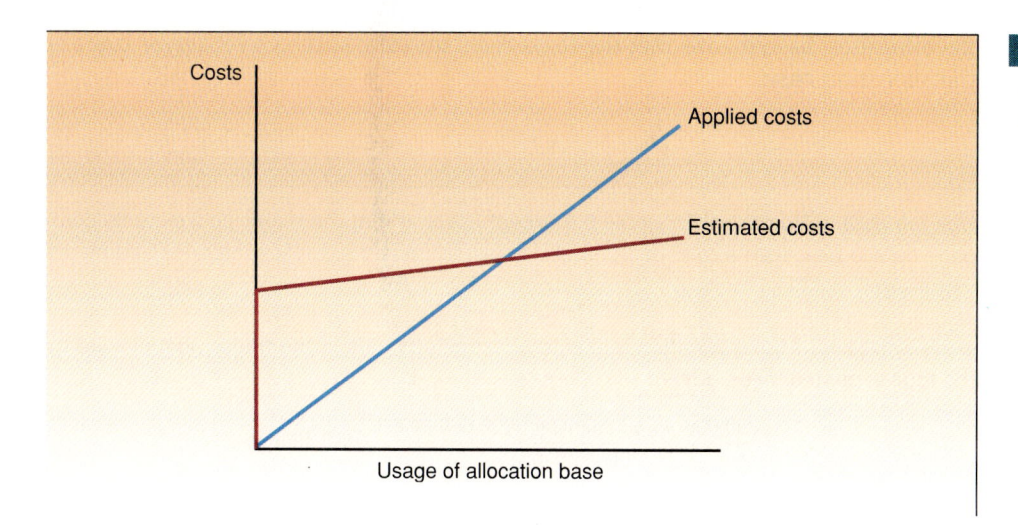

FIGURE 9.2

Applied and Estimated Costs

are higher than the incremental costs of operating the computer service department, managers will tend to use less of the computer service department than they should.

NUMERICAL EXAMPLE 9.4

A motor pool allocates costs to other departments of the same organization based on number of miles driven in company cars. The motor pool expects to incur annual fixed costs of $200,000 and variable costs of $0.20 per mile driven. The motor pool expects company cars to be driven a total of 800,000 miles. What is the application rate used by the motor pool and how may that application rate lead to underuse of the motor pool and costly behavior by other departments?

■ **SOLUTION** The application rate is total expected costs in the motor pool divided by the total expected miles driven:

$$\frac{\$200,000 + (\$0.20/\text{mile})(800,000 \text{ miles})}{800,000 \text{ miles}} = \$0.45/\text{mile}$$

This application rate, however, is higher than the incremental cost of operating an automobile, which is $0.20/mile. Because the application rate is like a transfer price, managers in other departments will choose to use means of transportation other than the motor pool if the cost per mile of alternative transportation is less than the application rate of $0.45/mile. The whole organization would benefit, however, if the motor pool is used anytime the alternative means of transportation cost more than $0.20/mile.

Fixed costs in the cost pool also mean that the application rate is affected by total estimated usage of the allocation base. If the cost pool contained only variable costs, a 10% increase in the estimated usage of the allocation base causes a 10% increase in the size of the cost pool. If there are fixed costs in the cost pool, however, the size of the cost pool will increase proportionally less than the usage of the allocation base. Therefore, greater estimated usage of the allocation base causes the application rate to be smaller. If the estimated usage of the allocation base declines, the application rate becomes larger. In other words, a reduction in the allocation base means that the fixed costs must be spread over fewer units of the allocation base.

NUMERICAL EXAMPLE 9.5

Use the data in Numerical Example 9.4 except assume that the motor pool expects company cars to be driven a total of 1,000,000 miles. What is the application rate used by the motor pool?

■ **SOLUTION** The application rate is total expected costs in the motor pool divided by the total expected miles driven:

$$\frac{\$200,000 + (\$0.20/\text{mile})(1,000,000 \text{ miles})}{1,000,000 \text{ miles}} = \$0.40/\text{mile}$$

This is less than the application rate when assuming 800,000 miles will be driven.

With fixed costs in the cost pool, one responsibility center can affect the application rate used to allocate costs to other responsibility centers. In other words, if one department decides not to use an internal service represented by a cost pool, the application rate increases and the service becomes more costly for other departments. Managers affecting the cost allocations to other managers violates the controllability principle. Managers prefer application rates that are insulated from the effects of other managers. Calculating application rates by the total estimated usage of the allocation base does not insulate managers if there are fixed costs in the cost pool being allocated.

NUMERICAL EXAMPLE 9.6

Use the data in Numerical Example 9.4. Suppose that one department decides not to use the motor pool because of alternative transportation opportunities, and the total expected miles to be driven is reduced to 600,000 miles. What is the effect on the application rate?

■ **SOLUTION** The new application rate is:

$$\frac{\$200,000 + (\$0.20/\text{mile})(600,000 \text{ miles})}{600,000 \text{ miles}} = \$0.53/\text{mile}$$

The reason the application rate is higher than the $0.45/mile in Numerical Example 9.4 is because the remaining users of the motor pool must pay a higher share of the fixed costs of operating the motor pool. The fixed costs must be spread over fewer users.

VALLEY CLINIC (CONTINUED)

The following table is used to calculate application rates at Valley Clinic:

Cost Pool	Expected Costs	Expected Allocation Base	Application Rate
General administration	$500,000	25,000 patients	$20/patient
Building	$100,000	20 exam. rooms	$5,000/exam. room
X rays	$ 50,000	500 X-ray patients	$100/X-ray patient
Nurses	$200,000	12,500 hours	$16/hour
Receptionists	$ 75,000	25,000 patients	$3/patient

Distributing Indirect Costs Based on Usage of the Allocation Base

Once the application rate for the allocation base is estimated, indirect costs are allocated to cost objects as the cost objects use the allocation base. For example, if hours of maintenance is the allocation base of the maintenance department cost pool, maintenance costs are allocated to cost objects when hours of maintenance are incurred by the cost object.

NUMERICAL EXAMPLE 9.7

The application rate for maintenance department costs is $20 per hour of service. The use of the maintenance department by other departments is:

Department	Hours
Accounting	50
Sales	80
Manufacturing	200

How much of the maintenance department costs are allocated to these departments?

■ SOLUTION

Department	Hours	Application Rate	Allocated Costs
Accounting	50	$20	$1,000
Sales	80	20	1,600
Manufacturing	200	20	4,000
Total costs allocated			$6,600

In summary, the cost allocation procedure allows for the flow of costs from a cost pool to cost objects. Cost objects are identified, costs are accumulated in cost pools, allocation bases are chosen, application rates are calculated, and indirect costs are allocated. These steps may be repeated several times as costs flow through an organization. A more difficult cost allocation problem exists, however, when different cost pools are the cost objects of each other. For example, suppose the maintenance department and the accounting department represent different cost pools and each department uses the other department. In other words, the accounting department uses the maintenance department and the maintenance department uses the accounting department. The interaction of service departments leads to a special cost allocation problem that is discussed in the appendix of this chapter.

VALLEY CLINIC (CONCLUDED)

Each doctor in the clinic acts as a profit center and is evaluated and rewarded based on the profit he or she generates. Dr. Kim is a doctor at Valley Clinic. She has 4,000 patients that generated total revenues of $400,000 during the year. Forty of her patients used X rays. Dr. Kim used two examination rooms and 3,000 hours of nurse time. The profit associated with Dr. Kim is:

Revenues			$400,000
Costs			

Cost Pool	Application Rate	Usage	Costs Allocated
General administration	$20/patient	4,000 patients	$ 80,000
Building	$5,000/exam. room	2 exam. rooms	10,000
X rays	$100/X-ray patient	40 X-ray patients	4,000
Nurses	$16/hour	3,000 hours	48,000
Receptionists	$3/patient	4,000 patients	12,000
Total costs			$154,000
Profit			$246,000

The $246,000 profit generated by Dr. Kim is her share of the total profit of the clinic. Notice, the $246,000 profit represents Dr. Kim's profit share and is compensation for her medical services.

CONCEPT REVIEW

1. How are cost objects chosen?
2. What is a cost pool?
3. What is the purpose of an allocation base?
4. How is an application rate calculated?
5. How are common costs allocated to multiple cost objects?
6. What is the difference between a cost driver and an allocation base?

9.4 Segment Reporting

WHAT'S HAPPENING

After an analysis of profits by the various individual rail lines constituting British Rail, management concluded that certain short lines were unprofitable after allocating all costs. Unprofitable lines were closed. Careful review of the facts revealed that labor was being charged to each rail line based on the amount of labor cost used on each line. But labor was a fixed, common cost. Labor union contracts prevented management from laying off workers when rail lines were closed. These workers were reassigned. What happened to profits when lines were closed?

Segment reporting is the process of developing accounting reports for the separate units of the organization. The income of each unit is measured to evaluate the performance of that unit and its managers. The ability to identify profitable and unprofitable segments of the business allows the president of an organization to add or withdraw resources from the segments and reward the managers of the segments. To calculate the income of each unit, the management accountant must use transfer prices if there are internal transfers among the units. The profit of each unit or segment should reflect the sales to other segments within the organization as well as sales to external customers.

The income of each segment also includes costs of resources that are used by multiple segments and, therefore, must be allocated to the segments. The internal purposes for allocating costs to segments are (1) to communicate information to managers of the different segments and (2) to motivate those managers to make decisions consistent with the goals of the organization.

Segment reporting is also used in external reports. Corporations are required to report the profit of segments of the company that correspond to different lines of business and different geographic segments. For example, DuPont reports the profit of the following lines of business: chemicals, fibers, polymers, petroleum, and diversified business. Each line of business is a cost object and a recipient of costs allocated from organizational resources used by the lines of business. Each line of business is also a profit center with both internal and external sales recognized.

Companies also have to report profit from different geographical areas. DuPont, for example, reports profit for its United States, European, and other geographical areas separately. This process also involves transfer pricing and the allocation of costs.

The reason external reports include segment reporting is to provide external users such as investors with more information about the profitability of the different components of the organization. If segment reports were not included in external reports, investors would not be able to discern if a highly profitable segment is offsetting an unprofitable segment.

Quaker paid a high price for the then successful Snapple Beverage Corporation in late 1994, but under Quaker, Snapple lost money ($75 million in 1995). Segment reporting allows managers to identify which segments are profitable and which are not. (Source of statistics: Business Week, February 5, 1996.)

NUMERICAL EXAMPLE 9.8

The Green Corporation makes two products: Chemex and Citrol. The corporation is divided into divisions by product line with managers in charge of each division. The Chemex Division sells 50 tons of Chemex on the open market for $10,000 per ton. Also, 20 tons of Chemex are transferred to the Citrol Division. The Citrol Division sells 100 tons of Citrol on the open market for $20,000 per ton. The Chemex Division has variable costs of $5,000 per ton and fixed costs of $200,000. The Citrol Division has variable costs of $8,000 per ton not counting the cost of Chemex. The fixed costs of the Citrol Division are $400,000. The central administration allocates $100,000 of fixed costs to the Chemex Division and $500,000 of fixed costs to the Citrol Division. Calculate the profits of the two divisions using the market price as the transfer price of Chemex.

■ **SOLUTION**

	Chemex Division	Citrol Division
Revenues		
Open market sales	$500,000	$2,000,000
Internal sales of Chemex	200,000	
Variable costs		
Internal purchase of Chemex		(200,000)
Other variable costs	(350,000)	(800,000)
Contribution margin	$350,000	$1,000,000
Fixed costs	(200,000)	(400,000)
Profit before allocated costs	$150,000	$ 600,000
Allocated costs	(100,000)	(500,000)
Divisional profit	$ 50,000	$ 100,000

If all the central administration costs have been allocated, the profit of Green Corporation is the sum of the profit of the two divisions, or $150,000.

> ### THE STORY OF MANAGERIAL ACCOUNTING
>
> # Team Decisions Regarding Internal Services
>
> As *Managerial Accounting* approached publication, the book team was contemplating an innovative supplement to enhance the value of the textbook. The book team realized the importance of technology and its implications for teaching and learning the topic of managerial accounting.
>
> The book team is convinced that a significant percentage of students have access to the CD-ROM technology and the World Wide Web, and they feel the risk of a new CD-ROM product entitled "Virtual Manager" is justified. To assist in making this CD-ROM, the book team would have to use the services of computer software division of Irwin Publishing. How will the allocation of costs from the computer software division affect the decision on making the "Virtual Manager"?

In the segment reports of the two divisions in Numerical Example 9.8, allocated costs, fixed costs, and internal sales are reported separately. These costs and sales are highlighted to allow managers to extract information from the reports to make certain decisions. For example, allocated costs may be eliminated for performance evaluation purposes if the allocated costs are not controlled by or affect the behavior of the manager of the division. The reporting of the contribution margin of each division allows a manager to ignore fixed costs to make incremental planning decisions. And internal sales should be highlighted to identify interactions among the divisions. These interactions provide important information when considering the elimination or changes in one of the divisions.

Segment reporting is just one of the end products of the transfer pricing and cost allocation. Product costs are also an end product of transfer pricing and cost allocations. The next chapter describes different methods of allocating costs to products.

CONCEPT REVIEW

1. What is the purpose of segment reporting?
2. How do transactions with other units of the organization affect segment reports?

9.5 Summary

1. Describe the relationship among common resources, indirect costs, and cost objects. Common resources are resources that are used by more than one subunit or product of the organization. Common resources generate indirect costs, which may be allocated to the users of the common resource. The recipients of allocated indirect costs are called *cost objects*.

2. Explain the role of allocating indirect costs for external financial reports, income tax reports, and cost reimbursement. For external financial reporting and income tax reports, manufacturing overhead is traditionally allocated to products. Costs allocated to products sold on a cost reimbursement contract provide additional revenues for the organization.

3. **Identify reasons for cost allocation for planning purposes.** If allocated costs provide better estimates of the opportunity cost of providing a product or service, they are valuable for planning purposes. In this case, cost allocations communicate information to managers about the opportunity cost of using common resources.

4. **Identify reasons for cost allocation for control purposes.** Indirect cost allocation is a method of allocating scarce resources in some organizations. Cost allocation is also used for external reporting, cost reimbursement, and motivating managers to use common resources in a manner consistent with the goals of the organization. Cost allocation can also be used for mutual monitoring.

5. **Describe how the various reasons for cost allocation can cause trade-offs within the organization.** Costs are allocated for external reporting, planning decisions, and control purposes. A single cost allocation system will lead to trade-offs because each reason for cost allocation may imply a different method of allocating costs.

6. **Allocate indirect costs using five basic steps.** Indirect costs are allocated by (1) defining the cost objects, (2) accumulating indirect costs in cost pools, (3) choosing an allocation base, (4) estimating an application rate, and (5) allocating indirect costs based on the use of the allocation base by the cost objects.

7. **Create segment reports for the organization.** Segment reports disclose the profit of subunits of the organization. The profit of the subunits reflects transfer prices and cost allocation.

8. **Use direct, step-down, and reciprocal methods to allocate costs of service departments that interact. (Appendix)** The direct method ignores any interaction of service departments. The step-down method allocates service department costs in sequence and ignores half of the interaction of service departments. The reciprocal method solves simultaneous equations (one for each service department) to account for all interactions of service departments.

KEY TERMS

Allocation base A characteristic of the cost object used to distribute indirect costs.

Cost allocations The distribution of indirect costs among cost objects.

Cost objects The subject of interest in determining the cost.

Cost pools The accumulation of costs related to an indirect activity.

Direct method (Appendix) A method of allocating service department costs that ignores any interaction of the service departments.

Economic designation The change in the market value of a fixed asset.

Externalities The effects of a decision on parties other than the contracting parties.

Multistage cost allocation The process of allocating costs to cost objects followed by the allocation of costs from those cost objects to other cost objects.

Mutual monitoring A process of having members of an organization control each other.

Reciprocal method (Appendix) A method of allocating service department costs that recognizes all interactions among the service departments.

Segment reporting The process of developing accounting reports for the separate units of the organization.

Step-down method (Appendix) A method of allocating service department costs that sequentially allocates the costs of the service departments.

Appendix: Allocating Costs of Service Departments with Interactions

In this chapter, cost allocations flow from the cost pools of indirect costs to cost objects. This flow of allocated costs could occur in multiple stages as in Figure 9.1, but costs do not flow back to any cost pools after the costs of that cost pool are allocated. In other words, costs could be allocated from the computer service department to the accounting department, but accounting costs could not then be allocated back to the computer service department. In many organizations, however, service departments, represented by different cost pools, provide services to each other. The cost pool of each department is the cost object of the other. This interaction leads to a special cost allocation problem. How can you allocate costs from one service department to another and then back again?

To allocate reciprocal service department costs, the ultimate cost objects must be identified and be different than the service departments with the reciprocal services. In the example in Table 9A.1, the ultimate cost objects are two operating divisions, A and B, which use two service departments, telecommunications and data processing. Both service departments use hours of their respective services as an allocation base.

Table 9A.1 provides the usage of the service departments by each other as well as the two operating divisions. Telecommunications consumes 100 hours of its own service internally and 200 hours of data processing. Data processing consumes 300 hours of its own service internally and 400 hours of telecommunications. The goal is to assign the costs of the service departments (telecommunications and data processing) to the operating divisions (A and B). Divisions A and B make the final products and the cost of those products should include the telecommunications and data processing costs.

Suppose the following total costs of the two service departments are to be allocated to divisions A and B:

Telecommunications	$200,000
Data processing	$150,000
Total costs	$350,000

There are several ways to allocate the service department costs to the operating divisions: direct allocation, step-down allocation, and reciprocal allocation. This appendix uses the data in Table 9A.1 to illustrate the computations of the various methods and to discuss the advantages and disadvantages of each method.

Direct Allocation Method

The first method for allocating service department costs is direct allocation. The **direct method** ignores all the internal and interactive usage of the service departments. Only the usage of the service departments by the two operating divisions is used to allocate the costs of the two service departments.

TABLE 9A.1 Hours of Use of Service Departments

	Tele-communications	Data Processing	Division A	Division B	Total
Telecommunications	100	400	400	100	1,000
Data processing	200	300	600	900	2,000

If only usage by the two operating divisions is considered, the application rates are determined by dividing each service department's costs by its total hours of service supplied to the two operating divisions. These application rates are calculated in the first section of Table 9.3. Once the application rates are estimated, the service department costs are allocated in the second section of Table 9A.2.

Table 9A.2 demonstrates that the total service department costs are allocated to the two operating divisions. Division A receives a total of $160,000 + $60,000, or $220,000, and Division B receives a total of $40,000 + $90,000, or $130,000, from the two service departments.

The direct method of allocating service department costs is very simple to perform, but ignoring the interaction of services by the service departments can lead to poor decisions being made by the managers of the organization. In particular, ignoring the reciprocal services means that the application rate will not reflect the opportunity cost of using the service department. Managers of the operating divisions will tend to over- or underuse the service departments depending on whether the application rate is lower or higher than the opportunity cost of the service department.

Another problem with direct cost allocation is that each service department will overuse the other service departments. Because each service department's costs are only allocated to the operating departments, the other service departments that use the service department view that service department as free. They are not charged for other service departments and, therefore, have no monetary incentive to limit their use of the other service departments. Accordingly, other control methods must be used to control the utilization of each service department by the other service departments. Such controls could include a priority system in providing services or a constraint in the budget limiting the number of hours that can be used among service departments.

Step-Down Allocation Method

The **step-down method** recognizes some of the interaction of service departments but not all of the reciprocal uses. The procedure begins by choosing a service department and allocating all of its costs to the remaining service and operating departments. Then, a second service department is chosen and all of

TABLE 9A.2

Direct Allocation Method

Calculation of the Application Rates

	Service Department Costs	Total Hours Used by Divisions A and B	Application Rate per Hour
Telecommunications	$200,000	400 + 100 = 500	$200,000/500 = $400
Data processing	$150,000	600 + 900 = 1,500	$150,000/1,500 = $100

Allocation of Service Department Costs to Divisions A and B

	Telecommunications			Data Processing		
	Hours Used	Application Rate	Costs Allocated	Hours Used	Application Rate	Costs Allocated
Division A	400	$400/hour	$160,000	600	$100/hour	$ 60,000
Division B	100	$400/hour	40,000	900	$100/hour	90,000
Total costs			$200,000			$150,000

its costs (including its allocated costs from the first service department) are allocated to the remaining service and operating departments. This process continues until all service department costs are allocated. In this way, all service department costs cascade down through the service organizations and eventually are allocated to the operating departments.

Figure 9A.1 describes the flow of costs through service departments and operating departments. Computing costs are allocated to the remaining service departments (accounting and purchasing) and the two operating departments (cutting and assembly). Accounting costs, which now include some allocated computing costs, are allocated to purchasing, cutting, and assembly. Then purchasing costs, which include some computing and accounting costs, are allocated to cutting and assembly. In this manner, all of the costs of the service department get allocated to the operating departments. The cost pools of cutting and assembly, which included allocated costs from the internal service departments, are then allocated to the different products to determine product costs.

Using the example in Table 9A.1, assume that the first service department costs to be allocated are telecommunications. Telecommunications' costs are allocated to data processing and Divisions A and B in the first step-down. In the second step, data processing costs plus data processing's share of telecommunication costs are allocated to Divisions A and B. The step-down method recognizes the use of telecommunications by data processing, but not the use of data processing by telecommunications. Internal use of each service department's own services is also ignored. The step-down allocation method is demonstrated in Table 9A.3.

The total costs allocated to Divisions A and B ($183,445 + $165,555, or $350,000) are equal to the original service department costs to be allocated. The costs allocated to each division using the step-down method are considerably different than the costs allocated by the direct method. The difference occurs because some of the interactions are considered.

The step-down method also has some problems. One problem is deciding the order of service departments to be allocated. The order of the service departments will ultimately affect the total costs that are allocated to the final cost objects. For example, if data processing was allocated first, the total service department costs allocated to Divisions A and B, respectively, would be approximately $227,062 and $122,941.

The order of the service departments also affects the application rates of the service departments. Service departments that are allocated early have lower

FIGURE 9A.1

Flow of Costs Using the Step-Down Method

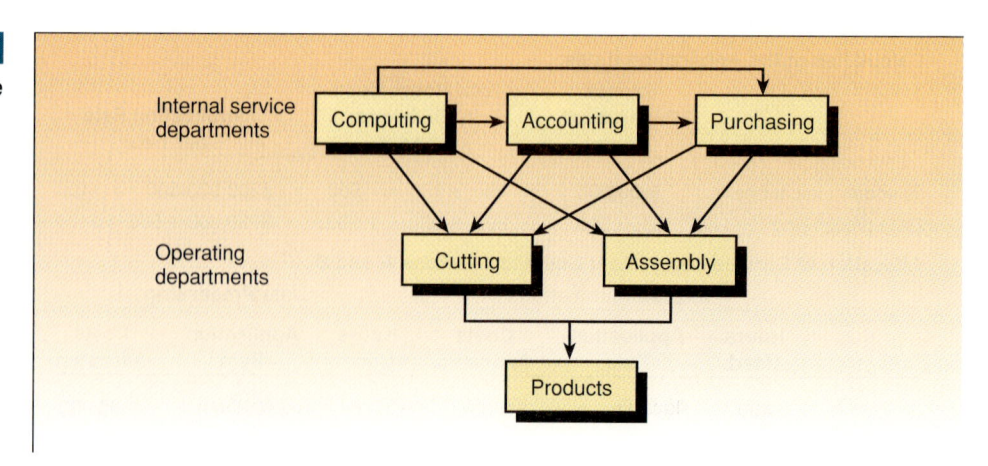

application rates than under the direct method and service departments that are allocated late have higher application rates than under the direct method. For example, the application rates under the direct and step-down methods are:

	Telecommunications	Data Processing
Direct method	$400.00	$100.00
Step-down method		
Telecommunications first	222.22	159.26
Data processing first	435.29	88.24

If these application rates are different from the opportunity costs of using the service departments, managers will tend to use too much or too little of the services offered by the service departments. The ordering of the service departments, however, allows the organization to weight certain allocation bases more than others. By allocating a service department's costs last under the step-down method, the organization is taxing the allocation base of that service department more heavily and discouraging its use.

The Reciprocal Method

The **reciprocal method** of allocating service department costs recognizes all the interactions among service departments. The reciprocal method begins with establishing an equation for each service department that includes the cost of the service department and the proportional use of the service department by other service departments and itself. In the example demonstrated in Table 9A.1, telecommunications (TEL) uses 100/1,000, or 0.100, of its own services and 200/2,000, or 0.10, of data processing. Data processing (DP) uses 300/2,000, or 0.15,

TABLE 9A.3
Cost Allocation by the Step-Down Method

Allocation of Telecommunications to Data Processing and Divisions A and B:
Application rate = $200,000/(400 + 400 + 100 hours) = $222.222/hour

To data processing ($222.222/hour)(400 hours) =	$ 88,889
To Division A ($222.222/hour)(400 hours) =	88,889
To Division B ($222.222/hour)(100 hours) =	22,222
Total costs allocated from telecommunications	$200,000

Allocation of Data Processing to Division A and Division B:

Costs to be allocated	
Original costs	$150,000
Costs from telecommunications	88,889
Total costs of data processing	$238,889

Application rate = $238,889/(600 + 900 hours) = $159.2593

To Division A ($159.2593)(600 hours) =	$ 95,556
To Division B ($159.2593)(900 hours) =	143,333
Total data processing costs allocated	$238,889

Total Service Department Costs Allocated to Divisions A and B:

	To Division A	To Division B
From telecommunications	$ 88,889	$ 22,222
From data processing	95,556	143,333
Total costs allocated	$183,445	$165,555

of its own services and 400/1,000, or 0.40, of telecommunications. These proportions are used to establish the following equations which represent the total cost of operating the service departments. The total cost is equal to each service department's costs plus a proportion of its own and other service department costs based on its use of the allocation base:

$$TEL = \$200{,}000 + 0.10(TEL) + 0.10(DP)$$
$$DP = \$150{,}000 + 0.15(DP) + 0.40(TEL)$$

These two equations have two unknown variables, the cost of telecommunications (TEL) and the cost of data processing (DP). By substituting one equation into the other, TEL and DP can be calculated as $255,172 and $296,552, respectively. These costs are considerably higher than the original costs of the two service departments but represent costs to be allocated to each other as well as the ultimate cost objects, Divisions A and B. To allocate costs to Divisions A and B, the proportion of divisional usage of the service department to total usage of the service department is multiplied by either TEL or DP. Table 9A.4 demonstrates this allocation.

The total allocated costs to Divisions A and B ($191,035 + $158,965, or $350,000) are equal to the original costs of the two service departments, so the reciprocal method is consistent with complete cost allocation. The reciprocal method also recognizes the interaction of service departments and will provide a cost allocation equal to the opportunity cost of using the service department if the costs being allocated are opportunity costs of operating the service departments and vary with the allocation base. If costs other than opportunity costs are being allocated, then users of the service departments are likely to misuse the service department no matter which method is used for cost allocation. Also, if fixed and variable costs of operating the service department are allocated together, no method of cost allocation will approximate the incremental cost of using the service department. To take full advantage of the reciprocal method's ability to estimate opportunity costs, only the variable costs in each service department should be allocated using the system of equations. The fixed costs in each service department should either not be allocated or be allocated based on another allocation base such as each operating division's planned use of the service department's capacity.

Although the reciprocal method has advantages over the direct and step-down method, the reciprocal method is more difficult to use. If there are 20 service departments, the solution requires the solving of 20 equations with 20 unknown variables. This calculation requires a computer. Before computers, organizations had to use the direct or step-down method and the popularity of those methods is still evident today.

TABLE 9A.4

The Reciprocal Method

To Division A	
From telecommunications ($255,172)(400/1,000)	$102,069
From data processing ($296,552)(600/2,000)	88,966
Total allocated costs to Division A	$191,035
To Division B	
From telecommunications ($255,172)(100/1,000)	$ 25,517
From data processing ($296,552)(900/2,000)	133,448
Total allocated costs to Division B	$158,965

SELF-STUDY PROBLEM

Incentives Created by Overhead Allocations

Reed Park, Inc., is a bottler/supplier of bottled spring water to both commercial and residential customers. Reed Park's corporate headquarters is located in Clearwater Springs, Colorado, and operates distribution centers (DCs) in three territories throughout the metro Clearwater Springs area. Customers pay a one-time subscription fee of $100 and then $11 per bottle. The company began by selling to residential areas and small businesses in the region. In recent years, its sales have moved toward larger businesses. The Metro center was the first DC established and is the oldest of the three. The newest center, Metro West, was established four years ago and continues to show great growth potential.

Bottling and distribution operations are treated as separate entities and the costs associated with each are easily tracked and charged to the appropriate division. There have been no problems related to the accounting systems between the two divisions. However, the managers in the distribution division have recently begun raising some questions regarding the accounting systems in place within their division.

Distribution center operations are relatively straightforward. Bottled water shipments are taken from the main bottling plant and stored at the DCs for delivery to customers at later dates. Most subscribing customers take delivery once every two weeks. Expenses associated with DC operations can be seen in the quarterly income statement found in Exhibit 1. DC overhead includes lease, building maintenance, security, and other costs related to running the warehouse facility. Staff and administrative expenses include salaries of sales and support staff as well as the cost of materials used in running the office (office supplies, forms, pens, etc.).

Each distribution center has its own sales staff. The corporate office handles the subscription process and provides to the drivers/delivery employees the information regarding delivery type and schedule. The majority of corporate overhead allocated to distribution centers results from the processing and maintenance of subscriptions and schedules. Reed Park allocates these overhead costs based upon the proportion of the book value of trucks at each DC facility to the total book value of the entire Reed Park delivery fleet. This allocation scheme was implemented at the time the company was founded to relate costs to the most significant cost item. Each DC is treated as a profit

EXHIBIT 1

REED PARK
Quarterly Income Statement
Three Distribution Centers
(dollars in thousands)

	Metro		Metro East		Metro West	
Revenues		$865.0		$928.0		$766.4
Expenses:						
Delivery wages	$ 34.2		$ 40.0		$ 33.6	
Overtime wages	4.2		3.2		4.4	
Staff and administrative	150.0		120.0		125.0	
DC overhead	75.0		80.0		90.0	
Fuel	24.0		28.1		26.0	
Truck maintenance	105.0		65.0		75.0	
Corporate overhead	235.7	(628.1)	283.0	(619.3)	391.3	(745.3)
Net income		$236.9		$308.7		$ 21.1

center and DC management is evaluated based upon its territory's net income performance.

Trucks are requested by distribution centers and purchased by the corporate offices under a corporate fleet contract with a major truck manufacturer. Like interest, the truck lease expense is shown as a separate corporate level expense and is not allocated to the DCs. (See Exhibit 2 for relevant data.)

The bottled water industry is experiencing strong growth, as is Reed Park. While Reed Park's business seems to be profitable, all is not well within the ranks of the organization. Corporate has been pressuring DCs to expand their territories and increase delivery volume, but DCs have been reluctant to meet this request. Some DC managers are beginning to question the amount of overhead being charged to them. They complain that increased deliveries will only cause overhead costs to rise. DC drivers are also unhappy; they complain about being overburdened by their ever-expanding routes and the pressure to meet difficult delivery schedules.

Steve Austin, assistant to the controller, has been assigned the task of examining the situation and developing alternatives if, indeed, a solution is needed.

a. Describe the problems, if any, at Reed Park. Specifically, discuss items related to decision making, cost allocation, and incentives.
b. Describe some alternative ways to allocate corporate overhead.
c. Which allocation system would you choose and what effects do you feel it would have upon Reed Park's distribution operations?
d. Calculate net incomes for the three DCs under the system you have chosen and compare these results with those found under the present system.
e. How does total profit of the three DCs compare across the original allocation and your proposed allocation scheme?

(Contributed by D. Lonczak, R. Bingham, M. Eisenstadt, and B. Sayers.)

Solution

a. The current overhead allocation system at Reed Park is creating tremendous incentive problems with distribution center managers. Because corporate overhead is allocated based on the book value of delivery trucks, an internal tax is created when new trucks are acquired by the distribution centers. This provides incentives for DC

EXHIBIT 2
Data for Reed Park Analysis

	Metro	Metro East	Metro West
Delivery employees	80	70	50
Delivery employee wages (per hour)	$8	$8	$8
Total subscriptions	8,533	7,200	5,040
Deliveries per quarter	51,198	43,200	30,240
Bottles delivered per quarter	75,000	78,000	62,400
Average miles driven per delivery	4	4.5	5.2
New subscriptions this quarter	400	700	900
Trucks based at distribution center	70	65	60
Truck dollar value	$700,000	$690,000	$670,000
Accumulated depreciation	350,000	270,000	90,000
Allocation base	350,000	420,000	580,000
Overhead allocation percentage	26%	31%	43%

Additional notes:
- Trucks average 15 mpg
- Fuel cost $1.20 per gallon
- Delivery charge $11 per bottle delivered
- Subscription fee $100 per subscription

managers to attempt to make more and more deliveries with their current number of trucks. In addition, these managers have incentives to keep older, less reliable trucks in their delivery fleet. These problems are evidenced by the increasing complaints among drivers and the high percentage of overtime pay found in the respective income statements.

Other problems in the accounting system include the fact that the cost of bottled water and the cost of trucks are not being charged to the distribution centers. Since both of these are "free" (except for corporate overhead being allocated based on the depreciated cost of trucks), DC managers are likely making the wrong decisions.

b. **Equal overhead allocation** Since corporate overhead results from functions that are necessary for the survival of each distribution center, this expense could be equally allocated among the three centers.

Allocation based on profits To take into account the profitability levels of each of the centers, corporate overhead could be allocated based on the net profits of each DC. This would provide a noninsulating allocation scheme and lead to some degree of monitoring and cooperation among the centers.

Allocation based on total subscriptions Since most of the corporate overhead expense results from the maintenance of subscriptions, corporate overhead can be tied to the total number of subscriptions held by each distribution center.

c. Reed Park should allocate corporate overhead based on total subscriptions. Since much of corporate expense results from the processing and maintenance of subscriptions, this allocation scheme ties the distribution of these costs to a more accurate cost driver. This method removes the disincentive for DC managers to request additional trucks, use older trucks for deliveries, and force drivers to work overtime. While this method imposes an "internal tax" on the sale of subscriptions, the new allocation encourages distribution centers to sell subscriptions to customers who buy larger quantities.

d. Exhibit 3 shows income statements for the three distribution centers under the proposed allocation scheme. Under the current allocation, Metro West is being unfairly

EXHIBIT 3

REED PARK
Quarterly Income Statements
Three Distribution Centers
Under Proposed Allocation Scheme
(dollars in thousands)

	Metro		Metro East		Metro West	
Revenues		$865.0		$928.0		$766.4
Expenses:						
Delivery wages	$ 34.2		$ 40.0		$ 33.6	
Overtime wages	4.2		3.2		4.4	
Staff and administrative	150.0		120.0		125.0	
DC overhead	75.0		80.0		90.0	
Fuel	24.0		28.1		26.0	
Truck maintenance	105.0		65.0		75.0	
Corporate overhead	373.1	(765.5)	315.8	(652.1)	221.1	(575.1)
Net income		$ 99.5		$275.9		$191.3

*Corporate overhead allocated based on subscriptions.

Supporting notes:

	Metro	Metro East	Metro West
Total subscriptions	8,533	7,200	5,040
Percentage of total	41.0%	34.7%	24.3%

penalized because of the high book value of their newer trucks. On the other hand, the Metro center, with lower truck book values, appears more profitable due to the fact that they are not receiving a large enough portion of the corporate overhead expense. The proposed allocation method provides each distribution center with improved incentives for growth and profitability.

However, such a change substantially alters the relative profitability of the three divisions. Metro is the big loser and Metro West the big winner.

e. Total profit of the three DCs is the same ($566.7) for both allocation methods. The reason is that the total corporate overhead cost of $910 does not vary with the allocation method used. The same number of dollars are being allocated, and thus the total profit of the three DCs is invariant to the allocation method. The allocation method affects how the total pie is distributed to the DCs, not the size of the pie.

NUMERICAL PROBLEMS

NP 9–1: Effect of Allocation Base Choice on Profit (LO 6; NE 2)
Beach Chair Corporation makes two types of beach chairs: reclining and straight-back. The direct costs per unit of the two chairs are:

	Reclining	Straight-Back
Direct materials	$3	$5
Direct labor	$5	$2

The company has no beginning inventory. During the year the company plans and makes 10,000 reclining chairs and 20,000 straight-back chairs. The company sells all of the reclining chairs for $20 each but only half of the straight-back chairs for $18 each during the year. Budgeted and actual manufacturing overhead costs during the year are $150,000.

a. Calculate the operating profit using direct material dollars as the allocation base for the manufacturing overhead.
b. Calculate the operating profit using direct labor dollars as the allocation base for the manufacturing overhead.

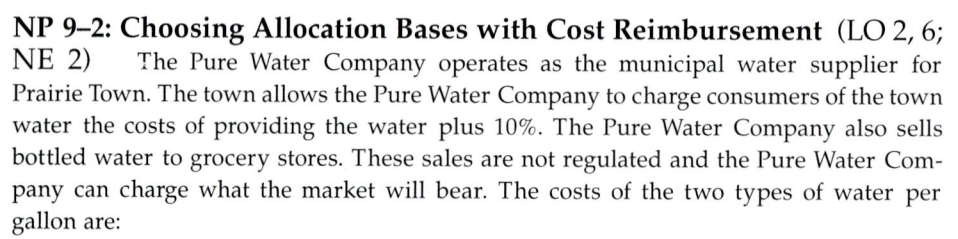

NP 9–2: Choosing Allocation Bases with Cost Reimbursement (LO 2, 6; NE 2)
The Pure Water Company operates as the municipal water supplier for Prairie Town. The town allows the Pure Water Company to charge consumers of the town water the costs of providing the water plus 10%. The Pure Water Company also sells bottled water to grocery stores. These sales are not regulated and the Pure Water Company can charge what the market will bear. The costs of the two types of water per gallon are:

	Municipal Water	Bottled Water
Direct labor	$0.001	$0.10
Direct materials	$0.001	$0.01

The overhead costs of providing water are $2 million per month. Each month the Pure Water Company sells 10 million gallons of water to its municipal customers and 10,000 gallons of bottled water for $1 gallon.

a. What is the profit of the company if overhead costs are allocated by direct labor dollars?
b. What is the profit of the company if overhead costs are allocated by direct material dollars?

NP 9–3: Allocation and External Reporting (LO 2, 6; NE 1, 8)   A building contractor started and finished a 20-unit condominium complex during the year. The direct costs per unit were $100,000 and the indirect costs per unit were $50,000. The indirect costs are manufacturing overhead and are considered product costs. By the end of the year, the contractor had sold 12 units for $200,000 apiece. The contractor had additional indirect expenses of $500,000 that were considered period expenses.

a. What is the income of the building contractor for the year?
b. What is the ending inventory of the contractor?
c. What is the income of the contractor if all indirect costs are considered period expenses?

NP 9–4: Cost Allocation and Contingency Fees (LO 2, 6; NE 2)   A lawyer allocates overhead costs based on his hours working with different clients. The lawyer expects to have $200,000 in overhead during the year and expects to work on clients' cases 2,000 hours during the year. In addition he wants to pay himself $50 per hour for working with clients. The lawyer, however, does not bill all of his clients based on covering overhead costs and his own salary. Some clients pay him contingency fees. If the lawyer works with a client on a contingency fee basis, the lawyer receives half of any settlement for his client. During the year the lawyer works 1,200 hours that are billable to clients. The remaining hours are worked on a contingency basis. The lawyer wins $300,000 in settlements for his clients, of which he receives half. Actual overhead was $210,000.

What does the lawyer earn during the year after expenses?

NP 9–5: Cost Reimbursement and Cost Allocation (LO 2, 6; NE 2)
A consultant has an agreement with Worldwide Foods that all her costs while working on their project would be reimbursed in addition to her being paid $100 per hour. Other clients pay her a fee of $150 per hour with no cost reimbursement. During the year, she expects to have overhead costs of $150,000 and expects to work 2,000 hours for clients. Of those 2,000 hours, 400 hours are expected to be on the project with Worldwide Foods. The overhead costs are the only expected costs and are allocated based on hours worked for clients.

What does the consultant expect to earn during the year?

NP 9–6: Cost Allocations and Performance Measures (LO 4; NE 3)
The Harrison Corporation allocates indirect costs to different products using the following allocation bases and application rates:

Allocation Base	Application Rate
Direct labor hours (DLH)	$10/DLH
Machine hours (MH)	$20/MH

Jim Ellers is responsible for manufacturing toy trucks at the lowest possible cost. The direct material costs of making toy trucks are $4 per unit. Jim Ellers has no control over the cost of the direct materials. But he can influence how the toy trucks are made. The toy trucks could be made using 10 minutes of direct labor and 20 minutes of machine time. Another option is to use 30 minutes of direct labor and 5 minutes of machine time. The direct cost of labor is $12 per hour.

Which method of manufacturing the toy trucks will minimize the total cost of the toy trucks?

NP 9–7: Fixed Costs and Allocated Costs (LO 6; NE 4, 6)   The maintenance department's costs are allocated to other departments based on the number of hours of maintenance used by each department. The maintenance department has fixed costs of $500,000 and variable costs of $30 per hour of maintenance provided. The variable costs include the salaries of the maintenance workers. More maintenance workers can be added if greater maintenance is demanded by the other departments without affecting the fixed costs of the maintenance department. The maintenance department expects to provide 10,000 hours of maintenance.

a. What is the application rate for the maintenance department?
b. What is the additional cost to the maintenance department of providing another hour of maintenance?
c. What problem exists if the managers of other departments can choose how much maintenance to be performed?
d. What problem exists if the other departments are allowed to go outside the organization to buy maintenance services?

NP 9–8: Fixed Costs and Cost Allocation (LO 4, 6; NE 4, 6)   The personnel department's costs are allocated to the other departments based on the number of direct labor hours. The personnel's expected fixed costs are $400,000 and its variable costs are $0.25 per direct labor hour. The personnel department has sufficient capacity such that fixed costs will not change with increased direct labor. The expected annual usage of direct labor by other departments is:

	A	B	C	D
Direct labor hours	100,000	500,000	250,000	150,000

a. What is the application rate for the personnel department's costs?
b. What would the application rate be if Department B was closed?
c. Why would the managers of Departments A, C, and D be upset with the closure of Department B?

NP 9–9: Cost Allocation and Dropping a Unit (LO 3; NE 6)   Cosmo operates two retail novelty stores: the Mall Store and the Town Store. Condensed monthly operating income data for Cosmo Inc. for November is presented below. Additional information regarding Cosmo's operations follows the statement.

	Total	Mall Store	Town Store
Sales	$200,000	$80,000	$120,000
Less variable costs	116,000	32,000	84,000
Contribution margin	$ 84,000	$48,000	$ 36,000
Less direct fixed expenses	60,000	20,000	40,000
Store segment margin	$ 24,000	$28,000	$ (4,000)
Less indirect fixed expenses	10,000	4,000	6,000
Operating income	$ 14,000	$24,000	$ (10,000)

- One-fourth of each store's direct fixed expenses would continue through December of next year if either store were closed.
- Cosmo allocates indirect fixed expenses to each store on the basis of sales dollars.
- Management estimates that closing the Town Store would result in a 10% decrease in Mall Store sales, while closing the Mall Store would not affect Town Store sales.
- The operating results for November are representative of all months.

a. A decision by Cosmo Inc. to close the Town Store would result in a monthly increase (decrease) in Cosmo's operating income during next year of how much?
b. Cosmo is considering a promotional campaign at the Town Store that would not affect the Mall Store. Increasing monthly promotional expenses at the Town Store by $5,000 in order to increase Town Store sales by 10% would result in a monthly increase (decrease) in Cosmo's operating income during next year of how much?

c. One-half of Town Store's dollar sales are from items sold at variable cost to attract customers to the store. Cosmo is considering the deletion of these items, a move that would reduce the Town Store's direct fixed expenses by 15% and result in the loss of 20% of the remaining Town Store's sales volume. This change would not affect the Mall Store. A decision by Cosmo to eliminate items sold at cost would result in a monthly increase (decrease) in Cosmo's operating income during next year of how much?

(CMA adapted)

NP 9–10: Direct and Indirect Costs (LO 3, 6)   Nixon & Ross, a law firm, is about to install a new accounting system that allows the firm to track more of the overhead costs to individual cases. Prior to the introduction of this new system, overhead was allocated to individual client cases based on billable professional staff salaries. Attorneys working on client cases charge their time to "billable professional staff salaries." Attorney time spent in training, law firm administrative meetings, and the like is charged to an overhead account titled "unbilled staff salaries." Overhead is allocated to clients based on billable professional hours.

A summary of the costs for 1995 is given below:

Billable professional staff salaries	$ 4,000,000
Overhead	$ 8,000,000
Total costs	$12,000,000

The overhead costs were as follows:

Secretarial costs	$1,500,000
Staff benefits	$2,750,000
Office rent	$1,250,000
Telephone and mailing costs	$1,500,000
Unbilled staff salaries	$1,000,000
Total costs	$8,000,000

Under the new accounting system, the firm will be able to trace secretarial costs, staff benefits, and telephone and mailing costs to their clients.

The following are the costs incurred on the Lawson Company case:

Billable professional staff salaries	$150,000
Secretarial costs	$ 25,000
Staff benefits	$ 13,500
Telephone and mailing costs	$ 8,000
Total costs	$196,500

a. Calculate the 1995 overhead application rate under the old cost accounting system.
b. How would this application rate change if the secretarial costs, staff benefits, and telephone and mailing costs were reclassified as direct costs instead of overhead, and overhead was assigned based on direct costs (instead of staff salaries)? Direct costs are defined as billable staff salaries plus secretarial costs, staff benefits, and telephone and mailing costs.
c. Use the overhead application rates from (a) and (b) above to compute the cost of the Lawson case.
d. Nixon & Ross bill clients 150% of the total costs of the job. What would be the total billings to the Lawson Company if the old overhead application scheme is replaced with the new overhead scheme?
e. Steve Nixon, managing partner, has commented that replacing the old allocation system with the direct charge method of the new accounting system will result in more accurate costing and pricing of cases. Critically evaluate the new system.

NP 9–11: Allocation of Central Corporate Overhead (LO 6, 7; NE 8)

American Wood Products is the world's largest integrated timber grower and wood processor. The Forest Group manages and harvests timber from company-owned and public forests. The Lumber Group buys cut trees from either the Forest Group or other timber companies and processes the trees into a full line of wood products including plywood, lumber, and veneers. The Building Products Group buys wood products (from the Lumber Group and other companies) as well as other building supplies such as dry wall and roofing products and distributes these products worldwide to retailers. The senior managers in each group receive a bonus based on their group's profit before taxes.

Central corporate overhead is allocated to each group on the basis of actual sales revenues in each division. The current year's corporate overhead allocated to the three groups is:

Corporate salaries and other	$ 50,000,000
Research and development	600,000,000
Interest	850,000,000
Corporate overhead	$1,500,000,000

Operating data for the last fiscal year are (in millions of dollars):

	Forest Group	Lumber Group	Building Products Group	Total
Revenues	$5,000	$8,000	$12,000	$25,000
Operating expenses	3,500	7,000	11,500	22,000
Gross margin	$1,500	$1,000	$ 500	$ 3,000
Corporate overhead	300	480	720	1,500
Profit (loss) before taxes	$1,200	$ 520	($220)	$ 1,500
Group assets	$5,000	$2,000	$ 1,000	$ 8,000

Instead of allocating $1.5 billion of overhead to the groups on the basis of revenues, the controller is proposing that each of the overhead categories be allocated using a different allocation base. In particular:

Overhead Category	Allocation Base
Corporate salaries and other	Sales revenue
Research and development	Gross margin
Interest	Group assets

a. Calculate each group's profits before taxes using the controller's proposed allocation scheme.
b. What are the pros and cons of allocating corporate overhead to operating divisions?
c. What are the advantages and disadvantages of the controller's proposed change relative to the existing method?

NP 9–12: Allocating Service Department Costs (LO 8) (Appendix)

A company has two service departments (power and maintenance) and two production departments (parts and assembly). The following table indicates costs, the allocation bases, and usage of the allocation bases (budgeted = actual) of the two service departments by each other and the production departments.

Service Department	Cost	Allocation Base	Power	Maintenance	Parts	Assembly
Power	$30,000	KWH	5,000	8,000	15,000	20,000
Maintenance	$40,000	Square Feet	5,000	10,000	80,000	40,000

a. Use the direct method to allocate service department costs to the parts and assembly production departments.
b. Use the step-down method beginning with the power department to allocate service department costs to the parts and assembly production departments.
c. Use the reciprocal method to allocate service department costs to the parts and assembly production departments.

NP 9–13: Estimating Application Rates (LO 3, 4, 5, 6)

Mutual Fund Company (MFC) is considering centralizing its overnight mail function. Five departments within MFC use overnight mail service: Trades Processing, Trades Verifications, Securities Processing, Accounts Control, and Customer Service. Although these departments send different types of packages (weight and content), often different departments send packages to the same destinations. Currently, each of these departments independently contracts for overnight mail service. The present rates of the five departments are:

Present Rates per Package

	\multicolumn{5}{c	}{Number of Pounds in Package}
	1	2	3	4	5
Department:					
Trades Processing	$ 7.25	$ 8.50	$ 9.75	$11.00	$12.25
Trades Verifications	7.75	8.75	9.75	10.75	11.75
Securities Processing	8.00	9.50	11.00	12.50	14.00
Accounts Control	10.00	12.00	14.00	15.50	16.50
Customer Service	16.00	18.00	20.00	22.00	24.00

MFC has requested each of the five departments to submit an estimate of its overnight mail for the coming year. The departments' estimates are as follows:

Estimated Usage

	Packages per Day	Annual Number of Packages*	Avg. Weight per Package	Pounds per Year
Trades Processing	100	25,000	5 lbs.	125,000
Trades Verifications	100	25,000	3 lbs.	75,000
Securities Processing	100	25,000	2 lbs.	50,000
Accounts Control	50	12,500	5 lbs.	62,500
Customer Service	10	2,500	1 lb.	2,500
Total	360	90,000		315,000

*Based on 250 days per year.

Using these volume estimates, MFC was able to negotiate the following corporate rates with EXP Overnight Express:

Corporate Rates per Package

Weight (pounds)	Rate
1	$ 7.75
2	8.70
3	9.65
4	10.65
5	11.60
6	12.55
7	13.55
8	14.50
9	15.45
10	16.45

The centralized overnight mail unit would be run as a cost center. All expenses will be charged back to the five departments. The charge-backs would comprise two components:

1. The corporate rate per package charged by EXP (based on weight).
2. An overhead allocation per package.

MFC plans to use a "prospective" overhead rate. Pounds per package will be used as the allocation base. As each package comes in, overhead is charged. The rate is set at the beginning of the year. This allows the overnight mail service costs to be allocated as service is provided. The indirect costs that constitute overhead are labor, supervision, and other expenses, as follows:

Overhead Expenses	
Three employees @ $11,000 per person, per year	$33,000
One supervisor @ $18,000 per year	$18,000
Other costs (rent, utilities, etc.)	$24,000
Total overhead	$75,000

At this time, there is much controversy and skepticism about the centralization of the overnight mail function. The managers of Trades Processing and Trades Verifications are the two managers who are most opposed to the proposed system. They claim that this proposed system is not only unfair, but also that the annual cost savings created by this centralized system do not justify a change.

a. Calculate the overhead allocation rate that would be used with the centralized system.
b. Calculate the estimated cost overall and per department of MFC's overnight mail service under both the present system and the proposed centralized system.
c. Discuss why the managers of the Trades Processing and Trades Verifications are opposed to the proposed centralized system. Do you agree with their criticisms?
d. Evaluate the proposed method of allocating overhead under the centralized system. Is there a better method to allocate cost? If so, how?
e. Do you think the proposed centralized system can be improved? If so, how?

[Contributed by A. DiGabriele, M. Perez, N. Rivera, C. Tolomeo, and J. Twombly.]

NP 9–14: Developing Application Rates (LO 3, 4, 5, 6)

Marfrank Corporation is a manufacturing company with six functional departments—Finance, Marketing, Personnel, Production, Research Development (R&D), and Information Systems—each administered by a vice president. The Information Systems Department (ISD) was established two years ago, in 1993, when Marfrank decided to acquire a new mainframe computer and develop a new information system.

While systems development and implementation is an ongoing process at Marfrank, many of the basic systems needed by each of the functional departments were operational at the end of 1994. Thus, calendar year 1995 is the first year when the ISD costs can be estimated with a high degree of accuracy. Marfrank's president wants the other five functional departments to be aware of the magnitude of the ISD costs in the reports and statements prepared at the end of the first quarter of 1995. The allocation of ISD costs to each of the departments was based on their actual use of ISD services.

Jon Werner, vice president of ISD, suggested that the actual costs of ISD be allocated on the basis of the pages of actual computer output. This allocation base was suggested because reports are what all of the departments use in evaluating their operations and making decisions. The use of this basis resulted in the allocation presented below.

Department	Percentage	Allocated Cost
Finance	50	$112,500
Marketing	30	67,500
Personnel	9	20,250
Production	6	13,500
R&D	5	11,250
Total	100	$225,000

After the quarterly reports detailing the allocated costs were distributed, the Finance and Marketing Departments objected to this allocation method. Both departments recognized that they were responsible for most of the output in terms of reports, but they believed that these output costs might be the smallest of ISD costs and requested that a more equitable allocation basis be developed.

After meeting with Werner, Elaine Jergens, Marfrank's controller, concluded that ISD provided three distinct services—systems development, computer processing represented by central processing unit (CPU) time, and report generation. She recommended that a predetermined rate be developed for each of these services from budgeted annual activity and costs. The ISD costs would then be assigned to the other functional departments using the predetermined rate times the actual service provided. Any difference between actual costs incurred by ISD and costs allocated to the other departments would be absorbed by ISD.

Jergens and Werner concluded that systems development could be charged based on hours devoted to systems development and programming, computer processing based on CPU time used for operations (exclusive of database development and maintenance), and report generation based on pages of output. The only cost that should not be included in any of the predetermined rates would be purchased software; these packages were usually acquired for a specific department's use. Thus, Jergens concluded that purchased software would be charged at cost to the department for which it was purchased. In order to revise the first quarter allocation, Jergens gathered the information on ISD costs and services shown below.

Information Systems Department Costs

	Estimated Annual Costs	Actual First Quarter Costs	Systems Development	Computer Processing	Report Generation
Wages and benefits					
Administration	$100,000	$ 25,000	60%	20%	20%
Computer operators	55,000	13,000		20	80
Analysts/programmers	165,000	43,500	100		
Maintenance					
Hardware	24,000	6,000		75	25
Software	20,000	5,000		100	
Output supplies	50,000	11,500			100
Purchased software	45,000	16,000*	—	—	—
Utilities	28,000	6,250		100	
Depreciation					
Mainframe computer	325,000	81,250		100	
Printing equipment	60,000	15,000			100
Building improvements	10,000	2,500		100	
Total department costs	$882,000	$225,000			

*Note: All software purchased during the first quarter of 1995 was for the benefit of the Production Department.

Information Systems Department Services

	Annual Capacity	Systems Development (4,500 hours)	Computer Operations (CPU) (360 CPU hours)	Report Generation (5,000,000 pages)
Actual usage during first quarter—1995:				
Finance		100 hours	8 CPU hours	600,000 pages
Marketing		250	12	360,000
Personnel		200	12	108,000
Production		400	32	72,000
R & D		50	16	60,000
Total usage		1,000 hours	80 CPU hours	1,200,000 pages

a. (1) Develop predetermined rates for each of the service categories of ISD, i.e., systems development, computer processing, and report generation.

(2) Using the predetermined rates developed in requirement a(1), determine the amount each of the other five functional departments would be charged for services provided by ISD during the first quarter of 1995.

b. With the method proposed by Elaine Jergens for charging the ISD costs to the other five functional departments, there may be a difference between ISD's actual costs incurred and the costs assigned to the five user departments.

(1) Explain the nature of this difference.
(2) Discuss whether this proposal by Jergens will improve cost control in ISD.
(3) Explain whether Jergens's proposed method of charging user departments for ISD costs will improve planning and control in the user departments.

(CMA adapted)

NP 9–15: Allocating Service Department Costs (LO 8) (Appendix)

Donovan Steel has two profit centers: Ingots and Stainless Steel. These profit centers rely on services supplied by two service departments: Electricity and Water. Ingots' and Stainless's consumption of the service departments' outputs (in millions) is given in the following table:

	Service Departments		Profit Centers		
Service Departments	Electricity	Water	Ingots	Stainless Steel	Total
Electricity	2,500 kwh	2,500 kwh	3,000 kwh	2,000 kwh	10,000 kwh
Water	1,000 gal	800 gal	1,000 gal	2,000 gal	4,800 gal

The total operating costs of the two service departments are:

Electricity	$ 80 million
Water	60 million
Total cost	$140 million

Required

a. Service department costs are allocated to profit centers using the step-down method. Water is the first service department allocated. Compute the cost of electricity per kilowatt-hour using the step-down allocation method.

b. Critically evaluate this allocation method.

NP 9–16: Allocating Corporate Overhead to Sales Districts (LO 3, 7)

World Imports buys products from around the world for importing into the United States. The firm is organized into a number of separate regional sales districts that sell the imported goods to retail stores. The Eastern Sales District is responsible for selling the imports in the northeastern region of the country. Sales districts are evaluated as profit centers and have authority over what products they wish to sell and the price they charge the retailers. Each sales district employs a full-time direct sales force. Salespersons are paid a fixed salary plus a commission of 20% of revenues on what they sell to the retailers.

The Eastern District sales manager, J. Krupsak, is considering selling an Australian T-shirt that the firm can import. Krupsak has prepared the following table of his estimated unit sales at various prices and costs. The cost data of the imported T-shirts was provided by World Imports corporate offices.

WORLD IMPORTS
Eastern Sales District
Proposed Australian T-Shirt
Estimated Demand and Cost Schedules

Quantity (000s)	Wholesale Price	T-Shirt Imported Cost
10	$6.50	$2.00
20	5.50	2.20
30	5.00	2.50
40	4.75	3.00

The unit cost of the imported shirts rises because the Australian manufacturer has limited capacity and will have to add overtime shifts to produce higher volumes.

Corporate headquarters of World Imports is considering allocating corporate expenses (advertising, legal, interest, taxes, and administrative salaries) back to the regional sales districts based on the sales commissions paid in the districts. They estimate that the corporate overhead allocation rate will be 30% of the commissions (or for every $1 of commissions paid in the districts, $0.30 of corporate overhead will be allocated). District sales managers receive a bonus based on net profits in their district. Net profits are revenues less costs of imports sold, sales commissions, other costs of operating the districts, and corporate overhead allocations.

The corporate controller, who is proposing that headquarters costs be allocated to the sales regions and included in bonus calculations, argues that all of these costs must ultimately be covered by the profits of the sales districts. Therefore, the districts should be aware of these costs and must price their products to cover the corporate overhead.

a. Before the corporate expenses are allocated to the sales districts, what wholesale price will Krupsak pick for the Australian T-shirts and how many T-shirts will Krupsak sell? Show how you derived these numbers.
b. Does the imposition of a corporate overhead allocation affect Krupsak's pricing decision on the Australian T-shirts? If so, how? Show calculations.
c. What are the arguments for and against the controller's specific proposal for allocating corporate overhead to the sales districts?

NP 9–17: Incentives of Make-Buy Decisions in Cost-Plus Contracts

(LO 2)   BFR is a ship-building firm that has just won a government contract to build 10 high-speed patrol boats for the Coast Guard for drug interdiction and surveillance. Besides building ships for the government, BFR has a commercial vessel division that designs and manufactures commercial fishing and commuting ships. The commercial division and government division are the only two divisions of BFR, and the Coast Guard contract is the only work in the government division.

The Coast Guard contract is a cost-plus contract. BFR will be paid its costs plus 5% of total costs to cover profits. Total costs include all direct materials, direct labor, purchased subassemblies (engines, radar, radios, etc.), and overhead. Overhead is allocated to the Coast Guard contract based on the ratio of direct labor expense on the contract to firm-wide direct labor.

BFR can either purchase the engines from an outside source or build the engines internally. The following table describes the costs of the Commercial Division and the Coast Guard contract if the engines are built by BFR versus purchased outside.

Cost Allocations

BFR
Cost Structure
($ millions)

	Commercial Division	Coast Guard Contract—Engines Manufactured Internally	Coast Guard Contract—Engines Purchased Externally
Direct labor	$14.6	$22.8	$18.2
Direct material		32.9	25.9
Purchased engines		0.0	17.0

Overhead for BFR is $83.5 million and does not vary if the engines are purchased outside or manufactured inside BFR. Overhead consists of corporate-level salaries, building depreciation, property taxes, insurance, and factory administration costs.

a. How much overhead is allocated to the Coast Guard contract if
   (1) The engines are manufactured internally.
   (2) The engines are purchased outside.
b. Based on the total contract payment to BFR, will the Coast Guard prefer BFR manufacture or purchase the engines?
c. What is the difference in net cash flows to BFR of manufacturing versus purchasing the engines?
d. Explain how cost-plus reimbursement contracts affect the make-or-buy decision for subassemblies.

NP 9–18: Allocating the Cost of Shared Resources and Incentives
(LO 4) Grove City Broadcasting owns and operates a radio and a television station in Grove City. Both stations are located in the same building and are operated as separate profit centers with separate managers who are evaluated based on station profits. Revenues of both the radio and television station are from advertising spots. The price of a standard 30-second ad is based on audience size which is measured by an independent outside agency. The radio station sells a 30-second ad for $100. (Assume that all 30-second ads sell for $100 irrespective of the time of day the ad is aired.) The $100 price is based on an expected audience size of 20,000 listeners. If the listener audience is doubled, the 30-second ad would sell for $200. Or, each radio listener is worth $0.005 ($100 ÷ 20,000) of advertising revenue per 30-second ad. Television viewers are worth $0.008 per 30-second ad.

The radio station sells 3,550 30-second ads per month and the TV station sells 3,200 30-second ads per month.

The Sports Wire has approached both the radio and television managers about subscribing to their service which brings all sports scores, sports news, and sports analyses to the station via an on-line computer system over standard telephone lines. The radio or TV station's sports announcers could download scores and news directly into their sports announcing scripts that can be read over the air. Sports Wire is more comprehensive and contains more sports stories than the current general news wires that Grove City is receiving. If one of the two stations bought the Sports Wire, the price would be $30,000 per month. For an extra $5,000 per month, both the radio and TV stations can utilize the Sports Wire. If both stations use the Sports Wire, the $5,000 additional fee includes an extra computer terminal that allows two users to be on the system at the same time without interfering with each other.

The Sports Wire will not increase the number of ads each month, just the revenue per ad. The Grove City radio manager believes that purchasing the Sports Wire would allow him to increase his audience by 1,500 listeners per ad. The television manager believes her audience size would increase by 500 viewers per ad.

a. If the two managers did not cooperate but rather made their decisions assuming each was the sole user of the system, would either buy the Sports Wire? Support your answer with detailed calculations.

b. If the owner of Grove City Broadcasting had all the facts available to the two managers, would the owner buy the Sports Wire?
c. The cost of the current wire services Grove City purchases are allocated to the two stations based on the number of stories aired each month from the wire service. The owner of Grove City Broadcasting decides to purchase the Sports Wire for both stations and to allocate its $35,000 cost based on the number of Sports Wire stories aired each month. At the end of the first month, the radio station used 826 Sports Wire stories and TV used 574. Allocate the Sports Wire cost to the radio and TV stations.
d. What is the allocated cost per Sports Wire story in the first month?
e. Given the allocation of the Sports Wire cost, what behaviors can you predict will occur from the radio and TV station managers?
f. Design an alternative allocation scheme that avoids the problems identified in part (e). Discuss the advantages and disadvantages of your allocation scheme.

NP 9–19: Segment Reporting (LO 7; NE 8)   The Morris Corporation has two divisions: Engineering and Consulting. Both divisions charge customers by the hour of work performed. Engineering charges $100 per hour and Consulting charges $200 per hour. Engineering bills 10,000 hours during the year to outside customers and 2,000 hours to the Consulting Division of Morris Corporation. Consulting bills 5,000 hours to outside customers. Engineering's variable costs are $40 per billable hour and annual fixed costs are $500,000. Consulting has variable costs of $60 per billable hour not counting the services purchased from Engineering and annual fixed costs of $400,000. Engineering services are transferred to Consulting based on the market rate. Central administration allocates $200,000 to each division.

Calculate the profit of each division using transfer prices and allocated costs.

DISCUSSION PROBLEMS

DP 9–1: Choosing Allocation Bases for Levying Taxes (LO 2)   The town of Seaside has decided to construct a new sea aquarium to attract tourists. The cost of the construction is to be paid by a special tax. Although most of the townspeople believe the sea aquarium is a good idea, there is disagreement about how the tax should be levied.

Suggest three different methods of levying the tax and the advantages and disadvantages of each.

DP 9–2: Methods of Applying Overhead (LO 3)   Rose Bach has recently been hired as Controller of Empco Inc., a sheet metal manufacturer. Empco has been in the sheet metal business for many years and is currently investigating ways to modernize its manufacturing process. At the first staff meeting Bach attended, Bob Kelley, chief engineer, presented a proposal for automating the Drilling Department. Kelley recommended that Empco purchase two robots that would have the capability of replacing the eight direct labor workers in the department. The cost savings outlined in Kelley's proposal included the elimination of direct labor cost in the Drilling Department plus a reduction of manufacturing overhead cost in the department to zero because Empco charges manufacturing overhead on the basis of direct labor dollars using a plantwide rate.

The president of Empco was puzzled by Kelley's explanation of the cost savings, believing it made no sense. Bach agreed, explaining that as firms become more automated, they should rethink their manufacturing overhead systems. The president then asked Bach to look into the matter and prepare a report for the next staff meeting.

To refresh her knowledge, Bach reviewed articles on manufacturing overhead allocation for an automated factory and discussed the matter with some of her peers. She also gathered the historical data presented below on the manufacturing overhead rates experienced by Empco over the years. Bach also wanted to have some departmental data to present at the meeting and, using Empco's accounting records, was able to estimate the annual averages presented below for each manufacturing department in the 1980s.

Historical Data

Date	Average Annual Direct Labor Cost	Average Annual Manufacturing Overhead Cost	Average Manufacturing Overhead Application Rate
1940s	$1,000,000	$ 1,000,000	100%
1950s	1,200,000	3,000,000	250
1960s	2,000,000	7,000,000	350
1970s	3,000,000	12,000,000	400
1980s	4,000,000	20,000,000	500

Annual Averages

	Cutting Department	Grinding Department	Drilling Department
Direct labor	$ 2,000,000	$1,750,000	$ 250,000
Manufacturing overhead	11,000,000	7,000,000	2,000,000

a. Disregarding the proposed use of robots in the Drilling Department, describe the shortcomings of the system for applying overhead that is currently used by Empco Inc.

b. Do you agree with Bob Kelley's statement that the manufacturing overhead cost in the Drilling Department would be reduced to zero if the automation proposal was implemented? Explain.

c. Recommend ways to improve Empco Inc.'s method for applying overhead by describing how it should revise its overhead accounting system
   (1) In the Cutting and Grinding Departments.
   (2) To accommodate the automation of the Drilling Department.

(CMA adapted)

DP 9–3: Cost Reduction in Service Departments (LO 4)   Increased global competition has spurred most firms to take a hard look at their costs and become "lean and mean." Rochco, a large industrial complex, has seen offshore competition erode its market share. This industrial site of over 100 functional departments, some cost centers and others profit centers, has over the past few years undergone several restructuring and labor reduction programs to make the firm more cost competitive.

Five years ago, the many service groups supporting Rochco's manufacturing operations were broken up into well-defined business centers. Top management encouraged all divisions to take over more decentralized decision making and mandated that the service groups provide value to the firm over outside contractors or be shut down. Dennis Flynn, manager of Building Services Department (BSD), was asked by Jim Corrado, general manager of Rochco operations, to describe how he would take his unit from its then dismal position vis-à-vis outside cleaning contractors to being the cleaning service of choice for its customers. An aggressive five-year plan was developed with breakeven to be achieved in the third year. This was not an easy task considering that when benchmarked against outside cleaners, BSD's costs exceeded their competitors' prices by 53%.

The majority of Rochco properties are cleaned daily by BSD, which runs as a cost center allocating its expenses at full cost based on the man-hours of service consumed by site customers. Over 80% of BSD's cost is labor, not uncommon for a cleaning service. However, BSD's wage rates have historically been higher than their competitors due to Rochco's policy of paying in the upper bracket of local industry to attract good people. Mr. Flynn's operating budget two years ago was $17 million.

Labor turnover is higher in BSD than the Rochco average (20% vs. 5% annually). The primary reason is that BSD is one of the few departments to hire labor from outside the company. The manufacturing departments tend to recruit personnel from BSD before looking externally, for two reasons: BSD provides basic safety training and Rochco culture orientation to their people, and BSD people represent "screened" employees to the hiring departments, inspiring greater confidence that the employee is a good, reliable worker.

The manufacturing departments also use BSD workers to fill in when normal production workers are on vacation.

Last year, BSD reduced its full costs to less than 29% over market prices, ahead of the forecast of 37%. BSD's costs are now $15 million annually. There is more pressure than ever on all Rochco managers to reduce costs. In June, J. William Laurri, a manufacturing manager and one of BSD's largest customers, told Mr. Flynn that he was seriously considering going outside for cleaning services based on price. Laurri manages another cost center with challenging cost reduction goals and represents 50% of BSD's customer base. Mr. Flynn is concerned that the loss of Laurri will irreparably damage BSD's progress toward its five-year break-even goal and raise costs to other department to such an extent that most of his customers will switch to contract cleaners. Although BSD is still uncompetitive at full cost, it is almost competitive (within 2%) on a direct cost basis.

a. Describe the cost accounting and control issues in this situation that are driving Mr. Flynn, Mr. Corrado, and Mr. Laurri.
b. Dennis Flynn is confident that his cost-cutting program will succeed by the target date if BSD keeps its current accounts. Should he discount BSD's services in order to keep Mr. Laurri?
c. Should Jim Corrado insist that managers of the operating units continue to use BSD's services (what are the pros and cons of such an order)?

(Contributed by S. Usiatynski, H. Merkel, and M. J. Joyce.)

DP 9–4: Cost Allocation of Tuition Benefits in Universities (LO 3, 4, 5)

Eastern University prides itself on providing faculty and staff a competitive compensation package. One aspect of this package is a faculty and staff child tuition benefit of $4,000 per child per year for up to four years to offset the cost of college education. The faculty or staff member's child can attend any college or university, including Eastern University, and receive the tuition benefit. If a staff member has three children in college one year, then the staff member receives a $12,000 tuition benefit. This money is not taxed to the individual staff or faculty member.

Eastern University pays the benefit directly to the other university where the staff/faculty member's child is enrolled (or reduces the amount of tuition owed by the faculty/staff if the student is attending Eastern University) and then charges this payment to a benefits account. This benefits account is then allocated back to the various colleges and departments based on total salaries in the college or department.

Critically evaluate the pros and cons of the present university accounting for tuition benefits. What changes would you recommend making?

DP 9–5: Effect of Allocation Bases on Behavior (LO 4)

Portable Phones, Inc., manufactures and sells portable, wireless telephones for residential and commercial use. Portable Phones' plant is organized by product line, five phone-assembly departments in total. Each of these five phone-assembly departments is responsible for the complete production of a particular phone line including manufacturing some parts, purchasing other parts, and assembling the unit.

Each of the five phone-assembly department managers reports to a product-line manager who has profit responsibility for his/her product. These five product-line managers have authority over pricing, marketing, distribution, and production of their product. The five phone-assembly departments are each cost centers within their respective product-line profit centers.

A key component of each phone is the circuit board(s) containing the integrated circuit chips. Each phone assembly department purchases from outside vendors the basic boards and chips to be attached to its board(s). The Board Department of the plant receives the boards and chips in kits from each phone-assembly department and assembles them into completed boards ready for assembly into the phones. The Board Department (with a cost structure that is 80% fixed and 20% variable) uses a single, highly automated assembly line of robotic insertion machines to precisely position each chip on the board and soldering machines to solder the chips onto the board. The Board Department is a common resource for the plant; all five of the phone assembly departments use the Board Department to assemble some or all of their boards. Since the Board Department has a single assembly line, it can only assemble boards for one type of phone at a time. The assembly departments have authority to seek the most competitive supplier for all their parts and services, including circuit board assembly.

The Board Department's assembly schedule is determined at the beginning of each month. The five assembly departments request a time during the month when they plan to deliver particular kits to the Board Department and the number of boards to be assembled. The manager of the Board Department then takes these requests and tries to satisfy the assembly departments' requests. However, the Board Department manager finds she has a peak load problem; the assembly departments tend to want their boards assembled at the same time. The only way to satisfy these requests is to work overtime shifts during these peak periods even though the Board Department has excess capacity at other times of the month.

The total monthly costs of the Board Department (equipment depreciation, maintenance, direct labor, supervision, and engineering support) are assigned to the phone-assembly departments based on an hourly rate. The Board Department's total monthly costs are divided by the number of hours of capacity in the month (e.g., if a particular month has 22 working days, this is equivalent to 352 hours or 22 days $\times$ 2 shifts $\times$ 8 hours per shift) to arrive at a charge per hour. To give the phone-assembly departments incentives to have their kits (boards and chips) delivered to the Board Department in a timely manner, the phone-assembly department is charged for the time from when the last job (a batch of boards assembled for a phone-assembly department) was finished by the Board Department until the time the next job is finished. For example, suppose Phone Assembly Department A's phones were finished at 9:00 A.M., Department B delivered their kits at 1:00 P.M., and they were completed at 7:00 P.M. the same day. Department B would be charged for 10 hours of the Board Department's costs even though the Board Department was idle for 4 of the 10 hours.

When first installed, the Board Department was expected to be operating at full capacity, two shifts per day, six days per week. But due to overseas outsourcing of some models and increased competition, the Board Department is now operating at about 70% of the initial planned capacity.

a. If you manage a phone-assembly department, everything else being held constant, when during the month would you tend to request your phone circuit boards be assembled by the Board Department? Explain why.
b. Identify various dysfunctional behaviors likely to be occurring among the phone-assembly departments and the Board Department.
c. What management changes would you suggest? In particular (but not limited to), what changes would you make in the accounting system? Explain why each change should be made and what you hope to accomplish by the change.

CASE

C 9–1: Allocating Computer Costs The Independent Underwriters Insurance Co. (IUI) established a Systems Department two years ago to implement and operate its own data processing systems. IUI believed that its own system would be more cost effective than the service bureau it had been using.

IUI's three departments—Claims, Records, and Finance—have different requirements with respect to hardware and other capacity-related resources and operating resources. The system was designed to recognize these differing demands. In addition, the system was designed to meet IUI's long-term capacity. The excess capacity designed into the system would be sold to outside users until needed by IUI. The estimated resource requirements used to design and implement the system are shown in the following schedule.

	Hardware and Other Capacity-Related Resources	Operating Resources
Records	30%	60%
Claims	50%	20%
Finance	15%	15%
Expansion (outside use)	5%	5%
Total	100%	100%

IUI currently sells the equivalent of its expansion capacity to a few outside clients.

At the time the system became operational, management decided to redistribute total expenses of the Systems Department to the user departments based on actual computer time used. The actual costs for the first quarter of the current fiscal year were distributed to the user departments as follows:

Department	Percentage Utilization	Amount
Records	60%	$330,000
Claims	20	110,000
Finance	15	82,500
Outside	5	27,500
Total	100%	$550,000

The three user departments have complained about the cost distribution since the Systems Department was established. The Records Department's monthly costs have been as much as three times the costs experienced with the service bureau. The Finance Department is concerned about the costs distributed to the outside user category because these allocated costs form the basis for the fees billed to the outside clients.

James Dale, IUI's controller, decided to review the distribution method by which the Systems Department's costs have been allocated for the past two years. The additional information he gathered for his review is reported in Tables 1, 2, and 3.

Dale has concluded that the method of cost distribution should be changed to reflect more directly the actual benefits received by the departments. He believes that the hardware and capacity-related costs should be allocated to the user departments in proportion to the planned, long-term needs. Any difference between actual and budgeted hardware costs would not be allocated to the departments but remain with the Systems Department.

The remaining costs for software development and operations would be charged to the user departments based on actual hours used. A predetermined hourly rate based on the annual budget data would be used. The hourly rates that would be used for the current fiscal year are as follows.

Function	Hourly Rate
Software development	$ 30
Operations	
Computer related	$200
Input/output related	$ 10

Dale plans to use first quarter activity and cost data to illustrate his recommendations (see Tables 1, 2, and 3). These recommendations will be presented to the Systems Department and the user departments for their comments and reactions. He then expects to present his recommendations to management for approval.

Case Questions

a. Prepare a schedule to show how the actual first quarter costs of the Systems Department would be charged to the users if James Dale's recommended method was adopted.

b. Explain whether James Dale's recommended system for charging costs to the user departments will
   1. Improve cost control in the Systems Department.
   2. Improve planning and cost control in the user departments.
   3. Be a more equitable basis for charging costs to user departments.

(CMA adapted)

TABLE 1
Systems Department Costs and Activity Levels

	Annual Budget		First Quarter Budget		First Quarter Actual	
	Hours	Dollars	Hours	Dollars	Hours	Dollars
Hardware and other capacity-related costs	—	$600,000	—	$150,000	—	$155,000
Software development	18,750	562,500	4,725	141,750	4,250	130,000
Operations:						
Computer related	3,750	750,000	945	189,000	920	187,000
Input/output related	30,000	300,000	7,560	75,600	7,900	78,000
Total		$2,212,500		$556,350		$550,000

TABLE 2
Historical Utilization by Users

	Hardware and Other Capacity Needs	Software Development Range	Software Development Average	Operations Computer Range	Operations Computer Average	Operations Input/Output Range	Operations Input/Output Average
Records	30%	0–30%	12%	55–65%	60%	10–30%	20%
Claims	50	15–60	35	10–25	20	60–80	70
Finance	15	25–75	45	10–25	15	3–10	6
Outside	5	0–25	8	3–8	5	3–10	4
	100%		100%		100%		100%

TABLE 3
Utilization of Systems Department's Services (in hours)—First Quarter

	Software Development	Operations Computer-Related	Input/Output
Records	425	552	1,580
Claims	1,700	184	5,530
Finance	1,700	138	395
Outside	425	46	395
Total	4,250	920	7,900

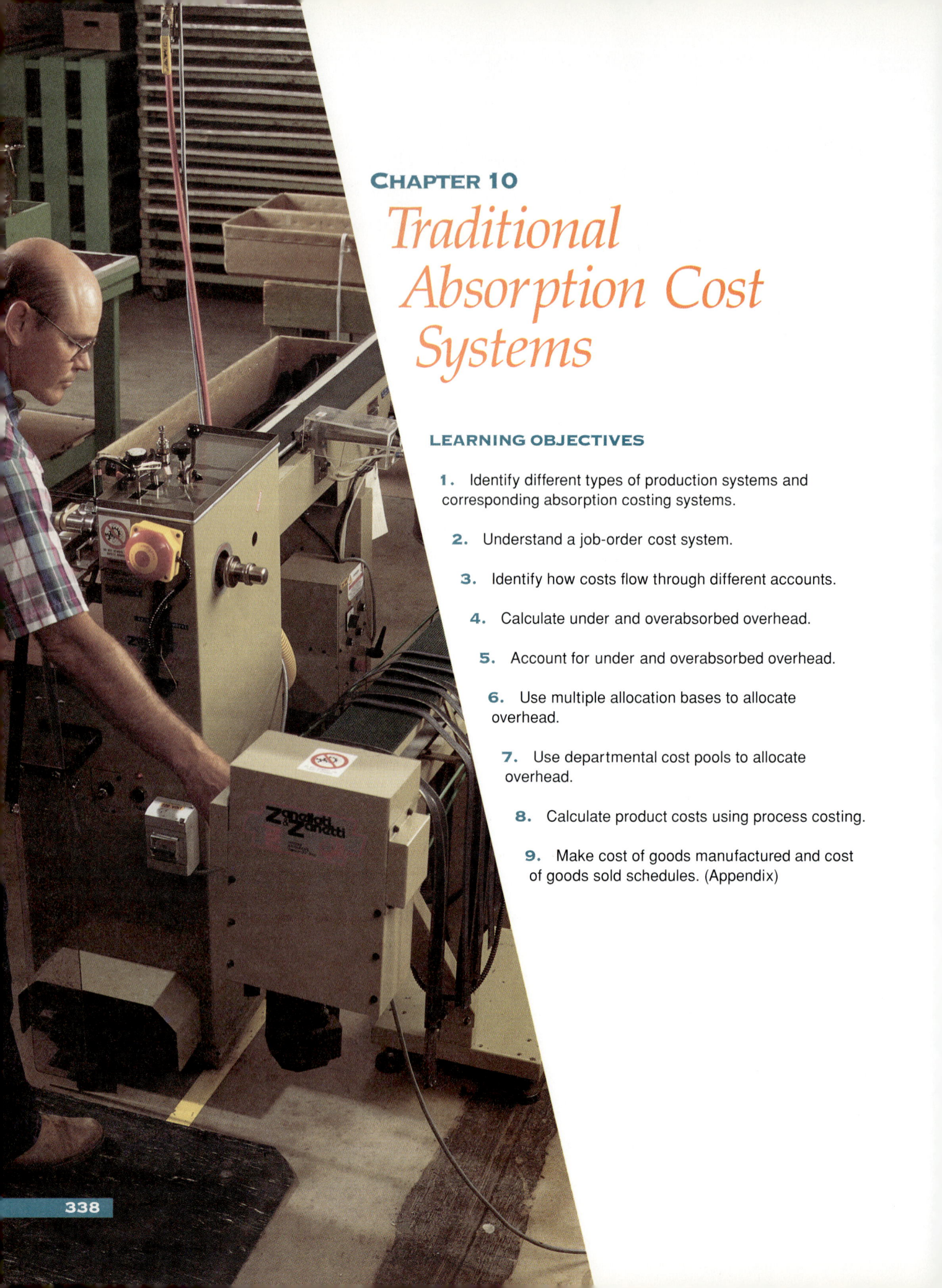

Chapter 10
Traditional Absorption Cost Systems

LEARNING OBJECTIVES

1. Identify different types of production systems and corresponding absorption costing systems.

2. Understand a job-order cost system.

3. Identify how costs flow through different accounts.

4. Calculate under and overabsorbed overhead.

5. Account for under and overabsorbed overhead.

6. Use multiple allocation bases to allocate overhead.

7. Use departmental cost pools to allocate overhead.

8. Calculate product costs using process costing.

9. Make cost of goods manufactured and cost of goods sold schedules. (Appendix)

Santa Fe Belts

Santa Fe Belts is a manufacturer of leather belts. Although belts can be made from pigskin, lambskin, and exotic animals such as crocodiles and sharks, the primary material used by Santa Fe Belts and most belt manufacturers is cowhide. The cowhide is composed of two layers: the top grain, which is the outer layer, and the split leather, which is the inner layer. The top grain is the preferred material for belts because it is the most durable and beautiful. The split leather does not have a natural grain although a grain may be embossed on the split leather to more closely resemble top grain.

The construction of a belt begins with the purchase of dyed cowhides. Santa Fe Belts buys both top grain for the production of expensive belts and split leather for making cheaper belts. The first process in making a belt is the cutting of the leather into strips equal to the length and width of the desired belt size. Cutting is performed to minimize waste and avoid bruises or brands on the leather.

Most belts have two layers: an outside layer of leather and an inside liner to help the belts maintain shape. Naturally, the nicest leather is used for the outside layer. Some belts use top grain on the outside and split leather as a liner. The second process of making the belt includes laminating and combining the two layers with glue. In addition, the edges of the leather strips are beveled and dyed. This process is referred to as *combining*.

The third process of belt making is the punching of holes and making the loop. Belts typically have five to seven holes with an additional hole for the buckle.

The fourth and final process includes adding the buckle, stitching the belt, and stamping the belt with the company logo and the size. Buckles are typically made of silverplated zinc, but brass, steel, copper, nickel and aluminum are also used. The fourth process is referred to as *finishing*.

Santa Fe belts has two factories. The first factory makes belts to order. These belts tend to use top grain leather and are more expensive. The factory receives the design specifications from the customer and makes the belts accordingly. Machines and procedures must be modified for each order. The manager of the factory is responsible for negotiating a price for these special orders.

The second factory makes a split-leather standard belt that is sold to department and discount stores. All the machines in this factory are dedicated to making the standard belt. Purchases from these stores tend to be large and unpredictable, so the factory maintains a relatively large inventory to meet customer demand.

Each factory is divided into the four processes described above: cutting, combining, punching, and finishing. Each factory also identifies direct material, direct labor, and overhead costs. Direct labor and overhead can also be identified with each process. Costs are used for planning (pricing and product mix decisions) and control (motivating, evaluating and rewarding managers).

10.1 Absorption Costing in Organizations

The last chapter described the general process of allocating costs to cost objects. This chapter describes a particular, widely used cost allocation system called **absorption costing.** Absorption costing is the process of allocating variable and fixed overhead costs to products, which are the cost objects. This chapter applies many of the concepts introduced last chapter to describe absorption costing. In manufacturing facilities, all manufacturing (variable and fixed) overhead is commonly allocated to the products generated by the facility. If it costs $32 million to operate a factory and 28,000 units are manufactured (including units still in inventory), then an absorption cost system allocates the $32 million among the 28,000 units. Absorption cost systems lead to the same trade-offs between making planning decisions and control as other accounting method choices, but most of the discussion of this trade-off is deferred to Chapter 11; this chapter focuses on the mechanics of these cost systems.

Absorption cost systems are widely used in financial reporting for determining inventory valuation and cost of goods manufactured. These systems have been developed in manufacturing firms, which is the setting used in this chapter to describe these systems. However, the same concepts can be applied to the service sector, including financial institutions, as well as professional services firms such as law firms, advertising agencies, and public accounting firms. To keep the chapter focused and readable, absorption cost systems in service industries are not described, although several problems at the end of this chapter and in other chapters illustrate absorption costing in nonmanufacturing settings. Nonmanufacturing settings tend to have simpler absorption costing systems because they do not have tangible work-in-process and finished goods inventories.

There are two basic types of absorption systems: **job order systems** and **process cost systems.** Job order costing is used in departments that produce output in distinct jobs (job order production) or batches (batch manufacturing). A job might consist of a single unit, such as the construction of an office building, or a batch of units, such as 200 windshield wiper motors for automobiles. (In a service organization, a job might be handling a client's lawsuit or processing a loan application at a bank.) The cost of each job is tracked separately, and job order cost systems accumulate costs by jobs.

Alternatively, in some assembly processes and continuous flow production processes, process cost systems are used. Production in these settings is continuous (e.g., an oil refinery), and distinct batches do not usually exist. Under process costing, manufacturing overhead is allocated equally to all the units produced.

In practice, there is great diversity in how firms' accounting systems allocate costs to products, jobs, or activities. Even within batch manufacturing, no two systems are exactly the same. Many plants use hybrids of job order and process costing. Each accounting system is tailored to the peculiarities of the department or plant. However, there are similarities across all these systems that are addressed in this chapter. The central problem addressed in cost systems is how to allocate indirect costs to products, jobs, or services.

CONCEPT REVIEW

1. What are the two different types of production processes?
2. What types of absorption cost systems are appropriate for different production processes?

SANTA FE BELTS (CONTINUED)

> Although both Santa Fe Belt factories make belts and have the same processes and machines, their methods of operating are much different. The first factory makes belts as ordered from customers. Each order specifies the design and amount of belts that are required. The factory treats each order as a batch. Each batch goes through the same four processes but may require different types of material, amounts of direct labor, and machine time. Given the nature of the operations of this factory, the management has decided to use job-order costing as a method of identifying the direct costs of each batch and allocating overhead costs to those batches.
>
> The second factory processes belts as a continuous flow. The factory only makes the standard belt and batches are not distinguishable as they move through the factory. This factory uses process costing to determine the cost of the belts.

10.2 Job-Order Costing

Job-order costing is the process of recording and accumulating the cost of making an identifiable product or batch of the same or similar products. A plant that manufactures different types of metal boxes in batches is used to illustrate job-order costing. Each box is produced in a batch requiring several different raw material inputs and several different classes of direct labor. Moreover, the boxes utilize various combinations of common resources such as machines, supervisors, shipping docks, factory space, and so on. Each batch is referred to as a job. Every job passes through a common machining process. The time spent in this machining center is recorded for each job, and this time is used to allocate overhead costs to the job. In other words, machine hours is used as an allocation base. Each job in the factory has a job-order cost sheet that records the costs associated with the products manufactured in the batch and the number of machine hours spent processing the job. A typical job-order cost sheet is in Table 10.1.

Job #5167 in Table 10.1 was started on 3/13 and completed on 5/23. The job sheet records all direct materials issued for the job, including the date, the type of materials (represented by codes), the cost of the materials, and the quantity of materials. Direct labor related to job #5167 is also recorded on the job order sheet. This information is either obtained from time cards of the workers or directly recorded on the job sheet by the worker. Notice that different types of

TABLE 10.1
Job-Order Cost Sheet

Job Number 5167   **Date Started** 3/13
    Date Completed 5/23

Date	Raw Materials Type	Cost	Qty.	Amount	Machine Hours	Direct Labor Type	Rate	Hrs.	Amount
3/13	103a	$30	205	$ 6,150	13	a65	$18	15	$ 270
3/14	214	50	106	5,300	111	a68	30	20	600
4/1	217	15	52	780	45	b73	10	81	810
4/23	878	5	229	1,145	28	c89	20	368	7,360
5/23					16	c89	20	419	8,380
Totals				$13,375	213				$17,420

Total direct materials	$13,375
Total direct labor	17,420
Overhead (213 machine hours @ $25/hour)	5,325
Total job cost	**$36,120**
Divided by: Number of units in batch	1,560
Average cost per unit produced	$23.15

This pressman is making final settings before starting a two-color print run. All the costs associated with this print run—including paper, ink, overhead, and the pressman's wages—are charged to this job.

labor (represented by codes) with different labor rates worked on the job. Job #5167 accumulated $13,375 of direct materials costs and $17,420 of direct labor costs. Also recorded on the job sheet is the number of machine hours used by the job. In this plant, machine hours are used to allocate overhead costs at the rate of $25 per machine hour. The $25 per machine hour is a predetermined application rate. Chapter 9 discussed the calculation of application rates. Job #5167 used 213 hours of machinery. Multiplying 213 machine hours times $25 per machine hour yields $5,325 of overhead costs charged to this job. The total costs for this job are $36,120. With 1,560 units produced in this batch, the average cost is $23.15 per unit.

Machine hours are used as the allocation base for indirect manufacturing costs accumulated in the overhead account. It should be remembered from Chapter 9 that using machine hours as the allocation base is similar to a tax on machine hours and creates incentives to economize on machine hours. The example of job #5167 illustrates several important features of job order costing:

- All direct costs of manufacturing the job are traced directly to the job.
- Each job is charged for some manufacturing overhead.
- At least one allocation base such as machine hours is used to distribute overhead costs to jobs.
- The application rate for overhead (here, the rate per machine hour) is set at the beginning of the year, before the first jobs are started. This overhead rate is based on an estimate of what factory overhead costs and machine hours will be for the year.
- Reported product costs are average, not variable nor marginal, costs. Each job is assigned a portion of the overhead. Since overhead contains some fixed costs, overhead distributed to jobs contains some of the fixed costs.

In the 1870s, Andrew Carnegie built the Edgar Thompson Steel Works in Pittsburgh, which was later to become part of U.S. Steel. One of Carnegie's many management innovations—and his obsession—was a detailed cost accounting system. Each department in the steel works listed the amount and cost of labor and materials used by each order as it passed through the department. Carnegie received daily reports showing the direct costs of the products produced and would repeat, "Watch the costs, and the profits will take care of themselves."

Carnegie's cost sheets were called the marvel of ingenuity and careful accounting. He required his people to explain the most minute change in unit costs. Carnegie and his managers used these data to evaluate the performance of his people, maintain the quality and mix of raw materials, evaluate improvements in process and product, and price products. New orders would not be accepted until there had been a careful checking of the costs.[1]

NUMERICAL EXAMPLE 10.1

A customer orders a special tool (job number 676) that requires 5 units of part 103 at a cost of $40/unit, 4 units of part 244 at a cost of $20/unit, and 1 unit of part 566 at a cost of $100/unit. The tool also requires 5 hours of direct labor at $18/hour. Overhead is allocated to the part at a rate of $15/direct labor hour. The job is started and finished on May 6. Prepare a job-order sheet for the tool.

SOLUTION

Job Number 676

Date Started 5/6
Date Completed 5/6

	Raw Materials				Direct Labor		
Date	Type	Cost	Qty.	Amount	Rate	Hours	Amount
5/6	103	$ 40	5	$200	$18	5	$90
	244	20	4	80			
	566	100	1	100			
				$380			

Total direct materials	$380
Total direct labor	90
Overhead (5 direct labor hours @ $15/hour)	75
Total Job Cost	**$545**

CONCEPT REVIEW

1. What costs are recorded on a job-order cost sheet?
2. How are overhead costs added to the job-order cost sheet?

SANTA FE BELTS (CONTINUED)

In developing its job-order cost system, the first factory of Santa Fe Belts must design a job cost sheet, train employees to make appropriate entries on the job cost sheet, and decide how to allocate overhead to the different batches. To keep their accounting system simple, Santa Fe Belts decides to accumulate overhead in a single cost pool and allocate costs by direct labor hours. The application rate for the year is determined by dividing the estimated overhead costs ($800,000) for the year by the estimated direct labor hours (80,000 hours) for the year. Therefore, an application rate of $800,000/80,000 hours or $10/hour is used. The overhead costs include supplies such as dye, thread, hangers, and labels.

An example of a completed job-order cost sheet for Santa Fe Belts is:

Job-Order Cost Sheet

Job Number 543
Job Description:
  1,000 belts using design #456G
Date Started 6/30
Date Completed 7/5

Direct Material Costs

Date	Process	Part	Quantity	Unit Cost	Total
6/30	Cutting	Top grain leather	750 sq. ft.	$3.30/sq. ft.	$2,475
7/5	Finishing	Buckle (#356)	1,000	$.80/buckle	800
Total Direct Materials Cost					$3,275

Direct Labor Costs

Date	Process	Hours	Cost/Hour	Total
6/30	Cutting	10	$10/hour	$100
7/2	Combining	15	$ 8/hour	120
7/3	Punching	5	$12/hour	60
7/5	Finishing	15	$12/hour	180
Totals		45		$460

Total Cost of Job

Direct materials	$3,275
Direct labor	460
Overhead (45 hours)($10/hour)	450
Total costs	$4,185
Number of units	1,000
Manufacturing cost per belt	$4.185

10.3 Cost Flows through the Accounts

The job sheet illustrated in Table 10.1 is the underlying source document in the job-order cost system. For many years, manufacturing firms maintained job-order cost sheets manually with paper and ink. Today, job-order cost sheets are often electronic records in computer systems. Costs are commonly recorded through the use of bar codes and hand-held computers.

Table 10.1 illustrates the job-order cost sheet for one job. Modern factories can have hundreds or even thousands of jobs in various stages of completion on the factory floor at any one time. The accounting system keeps track of the costs charged to each job. As costs are charged to individual jobs, the costs are simultaneously entered in a work-in-process inventory account, which contains all of the costs of all unfinished jobs in the organization. Each job cost sheet can be thought of as a subsidiary account for the work-in-process account. The sum of the costs on the job cost sheets is equal to the balance of the work-in-process account.

Figure 10.1 diagrams the flow of costs from the original documents to the job-order cost sheet (as represented by work-in-process), to finished goods, and finally to cost of goods sold. Labor costs are recorded based on the amount of time the employee works times a labor rate, which includes unemployment taxes, social security, and pension expenses. When an employee works on a job, the employee records the time spent on the job and his or her labor rate on the job cost sheet. At the same time, labor costs are reduced by the same

FIGURE 10.1 Schematic of a Job Order Cost System

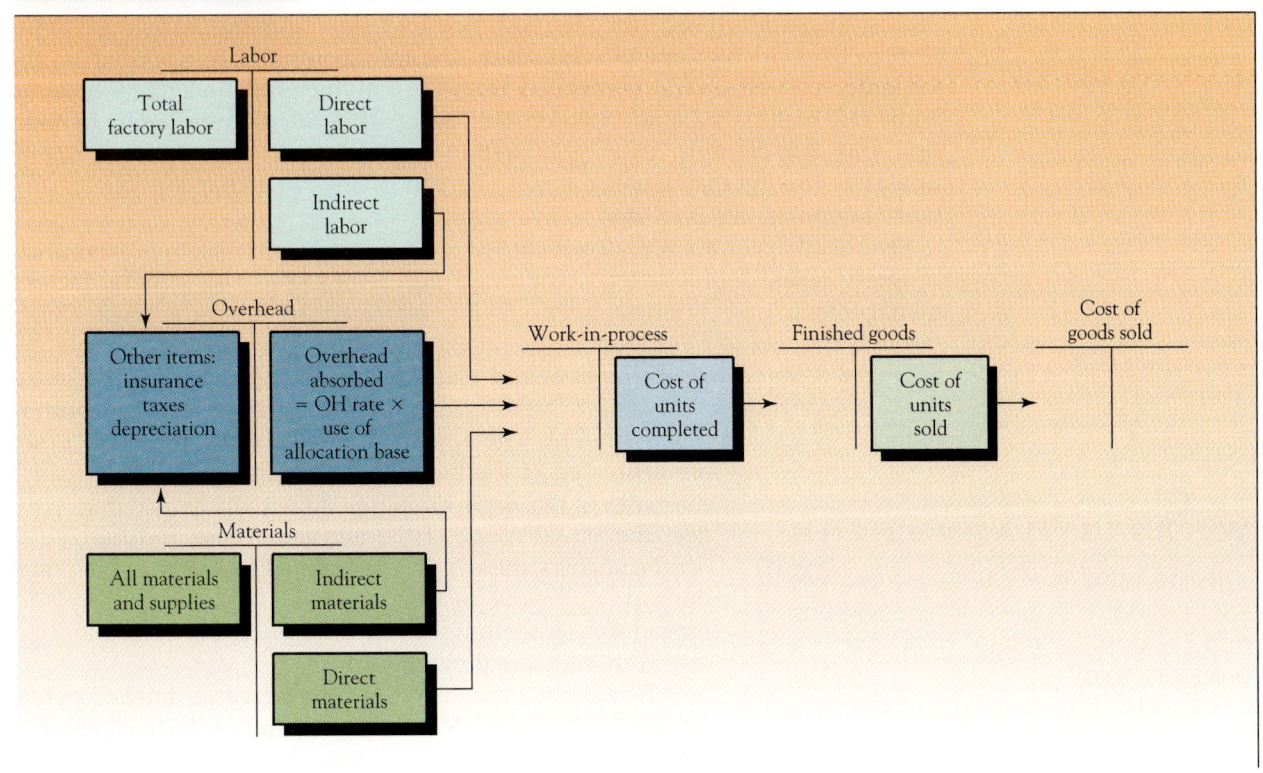

Physically managing the large number of different jobs in this factory often requires sophisticated material handling systems. How does the accounting system keep track of the different jobs and parts?

amount. Not all labor costs will eventually appear on job cost sheets. Employees have downtime when they are not working on any job but are still getting paid. Also, some employees do not work directly on jobs. Any labor costs that do not end up on job cost sheets become part of the overhead account.

Material costs are initially recorded at the time of purchase as raw materials. Raw materials are controlled by the manager of the inventory warehouse and requisition slips are necessary to move raw materials from the warehouse to the factory floor. At the time of requisition, the raw materials are recorded on the job-order cost sheet and eliminated from the raw materials inventory account. Some raw materials are not used directly on jobs but are used indirectly by multiple jobs. For example, a steel rod used in a lathe to check the machine's operation after routine maintenance is not charged to any particular job. The cost of those raw materials is treated as overhead.

Overhead accounts are also recorded in other accounts (such as insurance, property taxes, depreciation, accounting, purchasing, security, general factory management, and utilities) before being allocated to job-order cost sheets through the use of allocation bases. In Figure 10.1 the overhead accounts are aggregated into a single cost pool and allocated by a single allocation base. At the time overhead is allocated to a job-order cost sheet, the overhead account is reduced by an equivalent amount. The application rates of the allocation bases are estimated at the beginning of the time period. Because estimates of the application rate do not always accurately reflect the actual usage of the allocation base and the actual overhead costs, the overhead allocated to jobs may not equal the costs in the overhead account. The next section explains procedures to account for any differences between allocated overhead and actual overhead.

When a job is finished and transferred to finished goods inventory, the total job cost from the job-order cost sheet is transferred out of the work-in-process account and into the finished goods account. Similarly, when the goods are sold, the costs flow out of the finished goods account and into the cost of goods sold account.

WHAT'S HAPPENING

Why do retail and wholesale organizations not use job order systems and seldom allocate overhead to products sold?

These Japanese textile workers are inspecting the finished cloth before transferring it to the finished goods inventory.

In a typical manufacturing plant, direct labor is about 30% of total factory costs, direct material is another 30% of total factory costs, and overhead is 40% of total costs.[2] These percentages can vary widely, however. In some cases, direct labor can be as low as 1%–5% of total manufacturing costs and overhead as high as 80%.

NUMERICAL EXAMPLE 10.2

The job cost sheet for a special product is:

Job Number 711

Date Started 5/26
Date Completed 6/15

	Raw Materials				Direct Labor		
Date	Type	Cost	Qty.	Amount	Cost	Hours	Amount
5/26	130	$30	6	$180	$18	5	$ 90
6/15	248	10	20	200	15	10	150
				$380		15	240

Total direct materials	$380
Total direct labor	240
Overhead (15 direct labor hours @ $10/hour)	150
Total Job Cost	**$770**

Overhead is allocated based on direct labor hours (DLH). The parts were in the raw materials inventory before being used on job 711. The product is sold on 7/10. Identify the cost flows on each of these dates: 5/26, 6/15, and 7/10.

■ **SOLUTION** Cost flows:
On 5/26: $180 from Raw Materials Inventory to Work-in-Process
$90 from Labor to Work-in-Process
$50 from Overhead to Work-in-Process for overhead related to direct labor hours (5 DLH × $10/DLH)

On 6/15: $200 from Raw Materials Inventory to Work-in-Process
$150 from Labor to Work-in-Process
$100 from Overhead to Work-in-Process for overhead related to direct labor hours (10 DLH × $10/DLH)

When finished:
$770 from Work-in-Process to Finished Goods

On 7/10: $770 from Finished Goods to Cost of Goods Sold

CONCEPT REVIEW

1. When production begins, which account receives costs?
2. When production ends, which account receives costs?
3. Which account reflects the production costs of a product that is sold?

SANTA FE BELTS (CONTINUED)

Santa Fe Belts has an inventory of leather and buckles. When an order arrives, the manager of the cutting process requisitions the leather necessary to make the belts. Similarly, the manager of the finishing process requisitions the buckles when the partially completed belts arrive in the finishing department. The manager of the raw materials inventory uses the requisition slips to verify the reduction in raw materials and their cost. The recipients record the cost and amount of raw materials used in their division on the job cost sheet. When the raw materials are recorded on the job cost sheet, they become part of the cost of work-in-process. In a similar fashion, direct labor and overhead become part of work-in-process when recorded on the job cost sheet. Upon completing the batch of belts, the total cost of the batch is recorded as part of finished inventory. When delivered to the customer, the cost of the batch is recorded as cost of goods sold.

Santa Fe Belts has a fiscal year ending 6/30. Job order number 543 (described on page 344) is the only partially completed batch in the first factory. The work-in-process as of 6/30 is:

Direct materials	$2,475
Direct labor	100
Overhead (10 hours)($10/hour)	100
Total work-in-process	**$2,675**

10.4 Allocating Overhead to Jobs

In Chapter 9, the following steps were described for allocating overhead (indirect product) costs: (1) defining the cost objects, (2) accumulating indirect costs in cost pools, (3) choosing an allocation base, (4) estimating an application rate, and (5) allocating indirect costs based on use of the allocation base. In this section the cost objects are jobs, which include individual products or batches of products. The accumulation of indirect costs includes costs that are both fixed and variable with respect to the allocation base. The allocation base is some input into the production process such as direct labor hours, machine hours, or material costs. As described in Chapter 9, the allocation base is chosen for making planning decisions and for control reasons. The application rate is predetermined based on budgeted overhead costs and predicted use of the allocation base. The predetermined application rate allows for the allocation of overhead costs to jobs throughout the period based on usage of the allocation base.

These steps create an absorption cost system in that all manufacturing costs are absorbed by the jobs if budgeted overhead costs and usage of the allocation base in the application rate are accurate predictions of the actual overhead costs and the actual allocation base usage. But the predictions may not be accurate and allocated overhead costs may not equal actual overhead costs. In this section we examine reasons why the application rate may not allocate all overhead costs, why we should be concerned about having applied overhead different from actual overhead, and how to account for differences between actual overhead costs and overhead costs allocated to jobs. This section also looks at the use of multiple allocation bases for allocating overhead to jobs.

Over- and Underabsorbed Overhead

The application rate is a ratio of predicted overhead costs to predicted usage of the allocation bases. As long as the actual overhead costs divided by the actual usage of the allocation base (the actual application rate) is equal to the predicted application rate, the allocated overhead costs will equal the actual overhead costs. In reality, however, the estimated application rate is unlikely to equal the actual application rate. Therefore, the applied overhead will not equal the actual overhead. If allocated overhead costs are greater than actual overhead costs, the difference is called **overabsorbed overhead**. If allocated overhead costs are less than actual overhead costs, the difference is called **underabsorbed overhead**.

NUMERICAL EXAMPLE 10.3

A tool manufacturer uses machine hours (MH) to allocate overhead costs. The company expects to use 1,000 machine hours during the month, and overhead costs are expected to be $100,000. Therefore, the application rate of $100,000/1,000 MH, or $100/MH, is used.

a. If during the month the actual overhead costs are $90,000 and actual machine hours are 900, what is the difference between applied and actual overhead?

b. If during the month the actual overhead costs are $98,000 and actual machine hours are 950, what is the difference between applied and actual overhead?

■ **SOLUTION**

a.
Actual overhead costs	$90,000
Applied overhead costs ($100/MH)(900 MH)	90,000
Difference	$ 0

There is no difference between applied and actual costs because the actual application rate ($90,000/900 MH = $100/MH) is equal to the estimated application rate.

b.
Actual overhead costs	$98,000
Applied overhead costs ($100/MH)(950 MH)	95,000
Difference (underabsorbed)	$ 3,000

The actual application rate ($98,000/950 MH = $103.16/MH) is greater than the estimated application rate ($100/MH) causing the overhead to be underabsorbed.

FIGURE 10.2
Cost Allocation with Fixed Costs

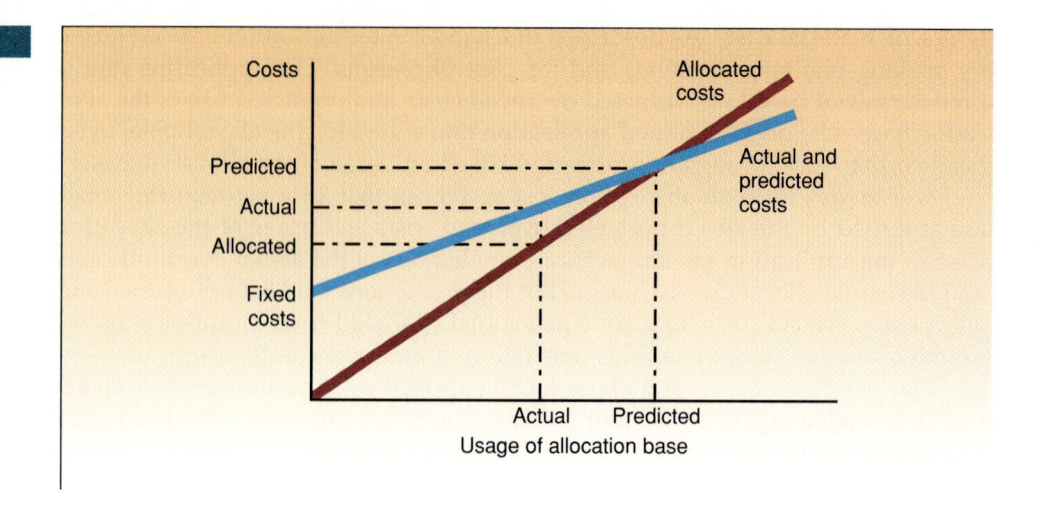

There are many reasons why the actual application rate may be different than the predicted application rate and lead to a difference between actual and allocated overhead costs. One example is in Figure 10.2. The predicted and actual overhead cost functions are assumed to have a fixed cost component. The allocated overhead costs, however, are applied through the usage of an allocation base. If the allocation base is not used, no overhead costs are allocated, so the allocated cost function goes through the origin. The application rate is estimated by dividing the predicted overhead costs by the predicted usage of the allocation base. Therefore, the allocated cost line in Figure 10.2 goes through the point where the predicted overhead costs and the predicted usage of the allocation base meet and has a slope equal to the application rate. If the actual usage of the allocation base turns out to be less than predicted, less overhead costs are allocated than the predicted amount. Actual costs, however, do not decrease as rapidly and will be greater than the allocated costs. This relation can be seen on the vertical axis of Figure 10.2. Even though the actual and predicted cost functions are the same, the incorrect estimate of the usage of the allocation base causes underabsorbed overhead. Under the same conditions, overabsorbed overhead would occur if the actual usage of the allocation base is greater than the predicted usage of the allocation base.

NUMERICAL EXAMPLE 10.4

A bicycle manufacturer estimates that the company will use 3,000 direct labor hours (DLH). Direct labor hours are used to allocate overhead. The company estimates that fixed overhead costs will be $30,000 and variable costs will be $20/direct labor hour. At the end of the year, the company finds that it estimated overhead costs correctly, but used 4,000 direct labor hours. What is the relation between actual overhead costs and allocated overhead costs?

■ **SOLUTION** The company estimates the following overhead costs:

Fixed costs	$30,000
Variable costs ($20/DLH)(3,000 DLH)	60,000
Total estimated overhead costs	$90,000

The application rate is $90,000/3,000 DLH or $30/DLH. The company actually uses 4,000 DLH, so (4,000 DLH)($30/DLH), or $120,000, of overhead is allocated to the products. The actual overhead, however, is:

Fixed costs	$ 30,000
Variable costs ($20/DLH)(4,000 DLH)	80,000
Total actual overhead costs	$110,000

Therefore, the allocated overhead costs are $120,000 − $110,000, or $10,000, greater than the actual overhead costs. The overhead costs are overabsorbed.

Why Worry about Over- and Underabsorbed Overhead?

Differences between allocated and actual overhead exist because expectations about costs and cost driver usage are not accurate. One option is to ignore the differences, but there are planning, control, and external reporting reasons for adjusting product costs for over- and underabsorbed overhead.

Because many of the products are sold by the time over- and underabsorbed overhead is identified at the end of the period, there is little opportunity to adjust prices of the products already manufactured. The organization, however, can use product costs adjusted for over- and underabsorbed overhead to make future pricing and product mix decisions. If the over- and underabsorbed overhead occurred because of mistakes in estimates, then these mistakes should be corrected before making subsequent planning decisions. If the over- and underabsorbed overhead is due to a one-period aberration, then adjustments to product costs based on initial overhead cost allocations are unnecessary for planning purposes.

Over- and underabsorbed overhead costs also have control implications. Because allocated costs are used as performance measures, there are incentives to influence the allocation of overhead costs. One way of affecting allocated overhead costs is to influence the calculation of the application rate. If the application rate is calculated with biased estimates of overhead costs and allocation base usage, managers can avoid the allocation of some overhead costs. Unless the allocated overhead is adjusted for underabsorbed overhead, managers will be tempted to

WHAT'S HAPPENING

A study of 32 plants in the electronics, machinery, and automobile-components industries reports that manufacturing overhead costs are, on average, three times the direct labor cost. For example, in electronics overhead is 26% of total manufacturing costs whereas direct labor is 8%. Direct material is the remainder (66%).[3] Why is direct labor so low in electronic plants?

Robots in an auto plant weld car bodies. The costs of the robots are classified as overhead. In this department, there is very little direct labor.

influence application rates with biased estimates. These biased estimates will not only affect control but will also harm planning efforts.

External reports are based on actual costs not on estimated costs. Allocated overhead costs reflect estimates of actual overhead costs. Ultimately, however, these estimates must be replaced by actual overhead costs for external reporting purposes. Therefore, some adjustment for under- and overabsorbed overhead must be made to the external reports. Also, cost reimbursement contracts are frequently based on actual costs not estimated costs. Therefore, adjustments for under- and overabsorbed overhead are commonly made to determine the final bill for a cost reimbursement contract.

When allocated overhead costs are different than actual overhead costs, some decision must be made on accounting for the difference. The next section describes different procedures for dealing with the difference between allocated and actual overhead costs.

Accounting for Over- and Underabsorbed Overhead

At the end of the accounting period, an accounting adjustment must be made to eliminate any over- or underabsorbed overhead for the reasons stated in the previous section. There are three methods of accounting for over- and underabsorbed overhead: (1) adjust cost of goods sold, (2) prorate among work-in-process, finished goods, and cost of goods sold, or (3) recalculate the application rate and apply to all the jobs during the year. Each of these methods has a different impact on current earnings. If net income is used as a performance measure for some managers, they will be concerned about the method of accounting for over- and underabsorbed overhead. Managers are not usually free to select any of the three methods. In general, if the over- or underabsorbed overhead is quite high, managers can't use the first method of simply adjusting the cost of goods sold.

The choice of the methods also depends on how the allocated over- and underabsorbed costs are being used. If the purpose of the allocation is to communicate costs for planning purposes, the method that most closely approximates the opportunity cost of using indirect resources should be used. If the purpose of the allocation is to control managers, then the over- and underabsorbed overhead allocation should reflect controllability by the managers. The superiority of any of the following methods depends on the circumstances surrounding the allocation.

Adjusting Cost of Goods Sold

The simplest method of accounting for over- or underabsorbed overhead is to adjust cost of goods sold. If overhead is overabsorbed, the cost of goods sold is reduced by the amount of overabsorption. If overhead is underabsorbed, the cost of goods sold is increased. No adjustments are made to the work-in-process or finished goods inventory at the end of the period. This method, however, cannot be used for external reporting if the over- and underabsorbed overhead is significantly different than zero.

Prorating

Through **proration,** the over- or underabsorbed overhead is allocated to the work-in-process, finished goods, and cost of goods sold proportional to the size of those accounts at the end of the period. For example, if the ending balances of work-in-process, finished goods, and cost of goods sold are $10,000, $15,000, and $25,000, respectively, 20% of the over- or underabsorbed overhead would be allocated to work-in-process, 30% allocated to finished goods, and 50% to cost of goods sold.

Recalculation of the Application Rate

Recalculating the application rate and reallocating overhead to all the products manufactured during the year is the most costly in terms of accounting efforts. The actual application rate is calculated and used to reallocate all the overhead to the products. Recalculating the application rate and reallocating overhead may be required in some cost reimbursement contracts.

NUMERICAL EXAMPLE 10.5

At the end of the accounting period, a window manufacturer has the following account balances:

	Direct Costs	Allocated Overhead	Balance
Work-in-process	$ 10,000	$ 2,000	$ 12,000
Finished goods	25,000	5,000	30,000
Cost of goods sold	85,000	13,000	98,000
Total	$120,000	$20,000	$140,000

The amount of overhead allocated to these accounts during the period was $20,000 based on an application rate of $5/direct labor hour (DLH), but actual overhead costs were $25,000.

a. What adjustments are made to the account balances if the underabsorbed overhead is completely allocated to cost of goods sold?
b. What adjustments are made to the account balances if the underabsorbed overhead is prorated?
c. What are the new balances if the application rate is recalculated?

■ SOLUTION

a. The underabsorbed overhead is $25,000 − $20,000, or $5,000. If all the underabsorbed overhead is allocated to the cost of goods sold, the adjusted account balances would be:

	Original	Allocation	Adjusted
Work-in-process	$ 12,000	0	$ 12,000
Finished goods	30,000	0	30,000
Cost of goods sold	98,000	$5,000	103,000
Total	$140,000	$5,000	$145,000

b. If all the underabsorbed overhead is prorated, the adjusted account balances would be:

	Original	Percentage	Allocation	Adjusted
Work-in-process	$ 12,000	8.57%	$ 428	$ 12,428
Finished goods	30,000	21.43%	1,072	31,072
Cost of goods sold	98,000	70.00%	3,500	101,500
Total	$140,000	100.00%	$5,000	$145,000

c. The actual number of direct labor hours to produce the items in each balance can be calculated by dividing the allocated overhead by the application rate of $5/DLH:

Work-in-process $2,000/($5/DLH)	400 DLH
Finished goods $5,000/($5/DLH)	1,000 DLH
Cost of goods sold $13,000/($5/DLH)	2,600 DLH
Total	4,000 DLH

The actual application rate is $25,000/4,000 DLH, or $6.25/DLH. The overhead allocated in the following table is calculated by multiplying the actual application rate times the actual number of direct labor hours:

	Direct Costs	Allocated Overhead	Balance
Work-in-process	$ 10,000	$ 2,500	$ 12,500
Finished goods	25,000	6,250	31,250
Cost of goods sold	85,000	16,250	101,250
Total	$120,000	$25,000	$145,000

SANTA FE BELTS (CONTINUED)

The first factory of Santa Fe Belts predicted that overhead costs would be $800,000 and the number of direct labor hours would be 80,000 hours. The predetermined application rate is $800,000/80,000 hours, or $10/hour. The actual overhead costs, however, are $765,000 and actual direct labor hours are 75,000 hours. The underabsorbed overhead is:

Actual overhead	$765,000
Allocated overhead ($10/hour)(75,000 hours)	750,000
Underabsorbed overhead	$ 15,000

The actual overhead application rate is $765,000/75,000 hours, or $10.20/hour. Santa Fe Belts could use this actual application rate to recalculate the overhead allocated to each batch of belts, but Santa Fe Belts decides that this would be a costly procedure without obvious benefits given they can't recapture any costs from their customers. Instead, the cost of goods sold is increased by $15,000 to account for the underabsorbed overhead.

Multiple Allocation Bases

In the previous discussion in this chapter, all of the overhead costs are first accumulated in a single overhead account and then allocated to products using a single overhead rate. Figure 10.3 describes this overhead allocation procedure. When a single overhead rate is used, all of the overhead is accumulated in a single cost pool. A cost pool is a collection of accounts accumulated for the purpose of allocating the costs in the pool to other cost objects such as departments, processes, or products.

An alternative, more complicated way to allocate overhead costs is to use multiple allocation bases. In this case, there are multiple overhead cost pools, each

FIGURE 10.3
Single Overhead Cost Pool and Application Rate

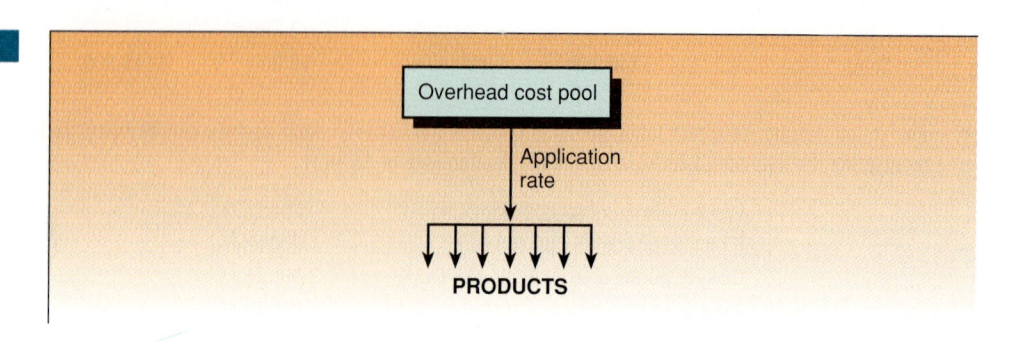

FIGURE 10.4
Multiple Overhead Cost Pools and Application Rates

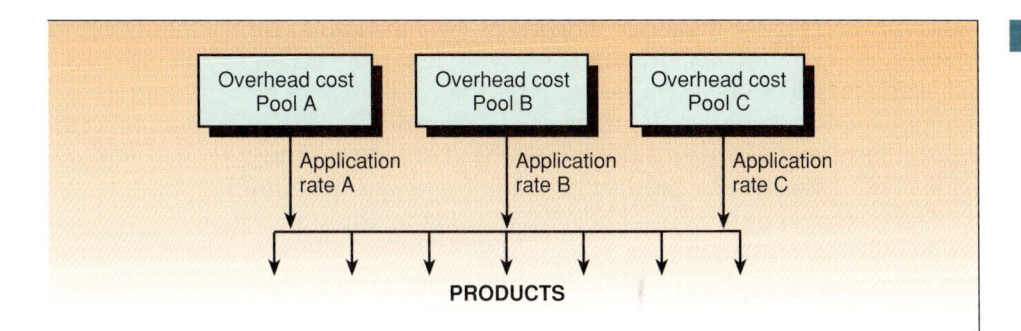

having its own allocation base and application rate. Figure 10.4 illustrates this method.

The advantages of using multiple cost pools and allocation bases include improved planning and control. Improved planning occurs because multiple allocation bases are more likely to capture the different ways overhead resources are being used by the cost objects. Each allocation base should be proportional to the opportunity costs of using the overhead cost pool.

Using multiple allocation bases will not always lead to more accurate product costs. If only one product is being made in the factory, then all factory overhead will be allocated to the same product no matter how many allocation bases are used. Process costing, discussed in the next section, is more appropriate when a factory only makes one product.

Also, multiple allocation bases will yield the same overhead cost allocations as a single allocation base if all the products use the multiple allocation bases in the same proportion. For example, if a company makes two different hockey skates and one type of skate uses 70% of all the allocation bases and the other type of skate uses 30% of all the allocation bases, then one of the allocation bases could be used to allocate all of the overhead.

In general, however, different products tend to use allocation bases with different intensities. Some products use a higher proportion of direct labor and

At the Dan Post Boot factory in El Paso, Texas, direct labor of bootmakers is a large component of the boot's manufacturing costs.

other products use a higher proportion of machine hours. Under these circumstances, using multiple allocation bases will yield more accurate product costs if allocation bases can be identified to reflect the opportunity cost of using the different overhead resources. Using multiple allocation bases that do not reflect the opportunity cost of using different overhead resources, however, will not provide better estimates for product costs to be used for planning purposes.

There are also some control benefits of using multiple allocation bases. When using only one allocation base, managers will overuse all the overhead resources not associated with the allocation base. By using more than one allocation base, the organization can tax the use of more than one overhead resource. With multiple allocation bases, managers would have to make trade-offs in using overhead resources.

Improved control also can occur if an organization has multiple goals. With multiple goals, an organization can use multiple allocation bases more effectively in achieving those goals. For example, if an organization is trying to both decrease defects and the use of direct labor, both the number of defects and the number of direct labor hours can be used as allocation bases for different cost pools. Because allocation bases are taxed through the allocation of overhead, managers will be motivated to reduce defects and reduce direct labor.

Activity-based costing (ABC) is a cost allocation method that uses multiple allocation bases. With ABC the allocation bases are cost drivers, which reflect the cause of the costs in the overhead cost pools. A cost driver is chosen for each overhead activity cost pool. By using multiple cost drivers, ABC can be an effective method of allocating costs for planning purposes as described in Chapter 4. ABC also has control implications, which are discussed in Chapter 11.

NUMERICAL EXAMPLE 10.6

A bicycle manufacturer has the following three overhead cost pools:

Indirect labor	$ 750,000
Utilities	650,000
All other costs	1,100,000
Total overhead	$2,500,000

Costs from each of these cost pools are then allocated to jobs by using separate allocation bases. For example:

Overhead Item	Allocation Base	Expected Usage
Indirect labor	Direct labor dollars	3 million direct labor dollars
Utilities	Machine hours	100,000 hours
All other costs	Direct material dollars	4 million direct material dollars

How much overhead is allocated to mountain bikes that use 1 million direct labor dollars (DL$), 20,000 machine hours (MH), and 2 million direct material dollars (DM$)?

■ **SOLUTION** The application rates are:

Indirect Labor: $750,000/3,000,000 DL$	$ .25/DL$
Utilities: $650,000/100,000 MH	$6.50/MH
All other costs: $1,100,000/4,000,000 DM$	$ .275/DM$

Allocated to mountain bikes:	
Indirect Labor: ($.25/DL$)(1,000,000 DL$)	$250,000
Utilities: ($6.50/MH)(20,000 MH)	130,000
All other costs: ($.275/DM$)(2,000,000 DM$)	550,000
Total allocated costs:	$930,000

Allocation of Overhead by Departments

Another method of accumulating overhead cost pools and allocating them to products involves developing different overhead application rates by departments. This is a two-stage allocation process. The first stage is to accumulate costs in departmental cost pools. These costs include direct costs of the department and indirect costs allocated to the department from general overhead accounts and service departments. The second stage is to choose separate allocation bases and application rates for each department. The departmental costs are then allocated to products. Figure 10.5 illustrates this two-stage allocation process.

The allocation bases and application rates used to allocate costs from the departments to the products are specific to that department. One department may use machine hours and another department may use number of engineering hours to allocate the departmental overhead costs. Or the allocation base for each department could be direct labor hours specific to that department. For example, a factory contains three departments: machining, painting, and assembly. The $2,500,000 of total overhead costs are broken down into three different departments and allocated to products by the number of direct labor hours used in each department:

Department	Expected Dept. Costs	Expected Dept. Direct Labor Hours	Application Rate
Machining	$ 900,000	10,000	$90/DLH
Painting	750,000	150,000	$ 5/DLH
Assembly	850,000	85,000	$10/DLH
Total overhead	$2,500,000		

Each department could also use different allocation bases. The choice of the allocation base once again depends on its use for planning decisions or control. Whether managers use a single allocation base or multiple allocation bases (using departmental cost pools or other types of cost pools) depends on the organizational structure and the incentive systems in place, management's demand for more accurate cost data for decision making, and the cost of using more complex cost systems.

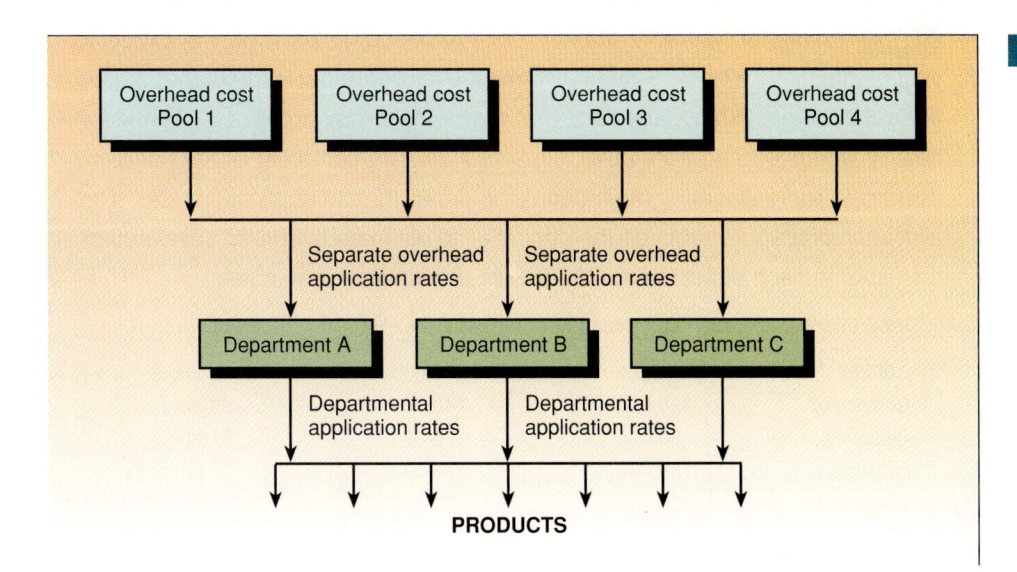

FIGURE 10.5

Two-Stage Cost Allocation with Departmental Application Rates

Traditional Absorption Cost Systems

In a small, random sample of U.S. manufacturing plants, a survey of the frequency of types of overhead schemes was conducted. The following results were reported:[4]

Single plantwide overhead rate (Figure 10.3)	30% of respondents
Multiple overhead rates (Figure 10.4)	18% of respondents
Separate departmental overhead rates (Figure 10.5)	52% of respondents

In another study involving Korean, Japanese, and U.S. firms, the following data were reported:[5]

Allocation Scheme	Korea	Japan	U.S.
Single rate for entire plant	43%	18%	31%
Rate for groups of work centers	29%	68%	31%
Rate for each work center	24%	15%	38%
Rate for each machine	9%	3%	7%

One must be careful in reading too much into the differences across countries because different survey techniques and different response rates exist. However, these findings suggest that substantial variation exists in the practice of treating overhead costs. A large number of firms in each country use a single plantwide application rate and a few firms calculate application rates by machine. The purpose of providing these data is to illustrate that overhead allocation practices differ from plant to plant.

CONCEPT REVIEW

1. Why do actual overhead costs generally not equal overhead allocated based on a predetermined application rate?
2. Why should an organization be concerned about over- and underabsorbed overhead?
3. What three methods can be used to deal with under- and overabsorbed overhead?
4. Under what conditions will multiple allocation bases yield more accurate product costs than a single allocation base?

SANTA FE BELTS (CONTINUED)

Santa Fe Belts is under pressure to change their cost allocation system. Pricing of specially ordered belts is based, in part, on the expected cost of making the belts. Some customers who order special belts that require a great deal of finishing labor feel that the product they order is burdened too heavily with overhead from other departments. The controller of the company decides to try reallocating overhead using departmental application rates. This allocation procedure requires the controller to estimate overhead costs and direct labor in each department. She makes the following estimates:

Department	Overhead Costs	Direct Labor Hours	Application Rate
Cutting	$250,000	10,000	$25/hour
Combining	320,000	40,000	$8/hour
Punching	50,000	5,000	$10/hour
Finishing	180,000	25,000	$7.20/hour
Totals	$800,000	80,000	

> She decides to test the departmental allocation method on job number 543 (on page 344). The following cost allocation occurs:
>
> | Department | Direct Labor Hours | Application Rate | Allocated Overhead |
> |---|---|---|---|
> | Cutting | 10 | $25.00/hour | $250 |
> | Combining | 15 | $ 8.00/hour | 120 |
> | Punching | 5 | $10.00/hour | 50 |
> | Finishing | 15 | $ 7.20/hour | 108 |
> | Total allocated overhead | | | $528 |
>
> When using only one cost pool, the overhead allocation to job number 543 is $450. The difference of $78 appears to be large enough to warrant further testing. If sufficiently large differences do exist across different orders, the company will have to consider changing to cost allocation by department.

10.5 Process Costing

Job-order cost systems are built around distinct jobs or batches in the factory. But some manufacturing processes have continuous flow production. For example, a car manufacturer dedicated to making a single model is designed to operate as an assembly line with cars being processed continually. A vegetable canning company operates a continuous process of cleaning, chopping, cooking, and canning vegetables. A cement manufacturer continuously mixes the ingredients of cement and packages the mix. Each of these companies is devoted to making a single product (at least for a period of time) in a continuous process.

Because the production process is a continuous flow operation, discrete batches do not exist. In process costing, costs are assigned to identical products that are produced in a continuous flow through a series of manufacturing steps or *processes*. These processes are usually organized as separate cost centers for control purposes.

For product-costing purposes, all the costs are associated with the same product. The cost allocation is not among different products but among units still in work-in-process inventory and units transferred out of the plant to finished

This oil refinery is an example of a continuous flow production process that uses process costing.

goods inventory or cost of goods sold. Because work-in-process and finished goods are assets and cost of goods sold is an expense, the allocation will affect the profit of the organization.

Process costing is inherently simpler and less costly to maintain than job-order costing because one does not have to account for separate batches. On the other hand, the information provided is far more aggregate and less useful for decision making. In particular, costs for individual batches are not available and hence cannot be used to evaluate cost trends across different jobs of similar products.

The simplest example of process costing can be obtained by dividing total manufacturing costs (including indirect and direct costs) during a period by the number of units produced. For example, if the car manufacturer makes 5,000 cars during a month and incurs $50,000,000 of manufacturing costs, the average cost per car is $50,000,000/5,000 cars, or $10,000/car. The $10,000 is an average cost containing both variable and fixed costs. Therefore, the average cost provides no information about the incremental cost of making additional cars. The $10,000 average cost, however, can be used in external financial reports indicating the cost of inventory and the cost of goods sold.

The process costing problem becomes more difficult when work-in-process exists at the end of the accounting period. If there is work-in-process at the end of the accounting period, there are some units that have been partially processed but not finished. Partially completed units have consumed some of the period's manufacturing costs. Dividing total manufacturing costs during the period by the number of units finished during the period ignores the resources used to partially complete units.

To recognize the partial completion of some units at the end of the period, the concept of **equivalent units** is used. An equivalent unit is a measure of production during a period of time. An equivalent unit uses the percentage of completion to determine the equivalence of finished units completed during the period. For example, completing 40% of the work of making 50 cars is equivalent to completing (.40)(50), or 20, cars. By recognizing the percentage of completion of ending work-in-process, the work performed during the period can be described in terms of equivalent units.

NUMERICAL EXAMPLE 10.7

A tractor manufacturer began and completed 500 tractors during the period. In addition, another 50 tractors were worked on during the period and on average were 60% completed. There was no beginning work-in-process. Manufacturing costs during the period were $5,000,000. How many equivalent units of work were performed during the period? What was the average cost of a tractor?

■ **SOLUTION** The total equivalent units completed during the period were:

Units 100% completed	500
Partially completed units (.60)(50)	30
Total equivalent units	530

The average cost per tractor is $5,000,000/530, or $9,434.

Once the average cost per unit is determined, the average cost can be used to partition the period's production costs into costs associated with goods that are finished and goods that are still in work-in-process. In the case of the tractors in

Numerical Example 10.7, the cost of the tractors that are finished is (500 tractors)($9,434/tractor) or $4,717,000. The cost of the tractors in work-in-process at the end of the period is (30 tractors)($9,434/tractor), or approximately $283,000. The original $5,000,000 in manufacturing costs are allocated to finished goods and work-in-process. Costs allocated to finished goods are transferred to cost of goods sold when the product is sold.

Additional complications in process costing arise when there is beginning work-in-process. With beginning work-in-process, the equivalent units of work performed during the period must also include the work necessary to complete the beginning work-in-process. The number of equivalent units of work performed during the period would include three components: (1) work to complete beginning work-in-process, (2) work on units that are both started and completed during the period, and (3) work on units that are started during the period but not completed (ending work-in-process).

NUMERICAL EXAMPLE 10.8

A manufacturer of televisions had 1,000 units in beginning work-in-process that were 30% completed last year. This year the remaining 70% of the work on the 1,000 units was completed and 10,000 more units were started and completed. In addition, 500 more units were started this period but were only 60% completed. Manufacturing costs during the period were $2,000,000. What was the cost per equivalent unit during the period?

■ **SOLUTION** The number of equivalent units of work performed during the period was:

Work to complete beginning work-in-process (.70)(1000)	700
Work on units started and completed	10,000
Work on ending work-in-process (.60)(500)	300
Total equivalent units	11,000

The cost per equivalent unit is $2,000,000/11,000, or $181.82.

Allocating costs between units that are finished and units still in work-in-process is complicated with the existence of beginning work-in-process. The cost of the beginning work-in-process due to work performed in the previous period must also be allocated. The cost allocation procedure depends on the accounting cost flow assumption. The FIFO, weighted-average cost, and LIFO procedures lead to different cost allocations. Those procedures are explained briefly in the appendix and in detail in financial accounting and cost accounting textbooks.

Process costing yields cost numbers for work-in-process, finished goods, and cost of goods sold for external financial reporting. The use of process costs for planning purposes is limited if process costs do not approximate opportunity costs. Because process costs are fully absorbed, they include fixed and variable costs. Dividing total process costs by the number of equivalent units produced yields an average cost. In general, an average cost does not represent the opportunity cost of making one more unit of the product.

Process costing is used for control because externally reported accounting numbers are frequently used to evaluate managers. Using process costing for performance evaluation, however, will lead to management making decisions to minimize average cost per unit. But minimizing average cost per unit and maximizing profit are not necessarily consistent. Minimizing the average cost can lead to production greater than the units that can be sold and excess inventory costs. Problems related to absorption costing systems such as job-order or process costing systems are described in Chapter 11.

> **CONCEPT REVIEW**
>
> 1. What is the primary purpose of process costing?
> 2. How does the concept of equivalent units enable the calculation of the average cost per unit?

SANTA FE BELTS (CONCLUDED)

The second factory of Santa Fe Belts uses a process costing system because the standard belt is its only product with no distinguishable batches. Instead of keeping track of the cost of each belt as it is processed, the second factory only tracks total manufacturing costs as they occur. At the end of each month, the total manufacturing costs are divided by the number of belts produced to determine the average cost per belt. For example, in January total manufacturing costs are $40,000 and the number of standard belts manufactured during January is 10,000. The average cost per belt in January is $40,000/10,000 belts, or $4/belt.

The president of Santa Fe Belts uses the $4/belt cost to make pricing decisions for standard belts and evaluate and reward managers at the second factory, but problems are arising in both areas. The $4/belt cost is an average cost and includes fixed costs. The president would like to know the marginal cost of making standard belts, but the process costing system does not reveal any information about marginal costs. The president also is noticing an increase in inventory at the second factory and wonders if rewarding the manufacturer based on reducing the average cost of making the belt is affecting inventory decisions. The president decides to read the next chapter on problems with absorption costing systems.

10.6 Summary

1. **Identify different types of production systems and corresponding absorption costing systems.** Job shops and batch manufacturers tend to use job cost systems. Assembly processes and continuous flow processes tend to use process costing.

2. **Understand a job-order cost system.** A job-order cost system is used to record the direct labor, direct material, and overhead costs related to a particular product or batch of products. Costs are separately accumulated on the job cost sheet while work is being performed on the product or batch.

3. **Identify how costs flow through different accounts.** Costs flow from raw materials, labor, and overhead accounts to work-in-process accounts during production, to finished goods accounts upon completion of production, and to cost of goods sold when sold.

4. **Calculate under- and overabsorbed overhead.** Under- and overabsorbed overhead occurs when the actual overhead costs are different than the applied overhead costs.

5. **Account for under- and overabsorbed overhead.** Under- and overabsorbed overhead can be (1) placed directly in cost of goods sold, (2) prorated among work-in-process, finished goods, and cost of goods sold, or (3) eliminated by recalculating the application rate using the actual overhead costs and allocation base usage.

6. **Use multiple allocation bases to allocate overhead.** Overhead is divided into different cost pools and allocated to different products using different allocation bases and application rates for each cost pool.

7. **Use departmental cost pools to allocate overhead.** Overhead is divided into departmental cost pools and allocated to products based on usage of the department's allocation base.

8. **Calculate product costs using process costing.** With process costing, the production costs are divided by the number of units to determine an average cost per unit. If there is partial completion of units during the period, equivalent units are used to divide into production costs to calculate average cost per unit.

9. **Make cost of goods manufactured and cost of goods sold schedules. (Appendix)** The cost of goods manufactured schedule includes raw material used (beginning raw materials + purchases − ending raw materials), direct labor, and manufacturing overhead to determine total manufacturing costs. The cost of goods manufactured is equal to the total manufacturing costs plus beginning work-in-process less ending work-in-process. The cost of goods sold is equal to the cost of goods manufactured plus the beginning finished goods inventory less the ending finished goods inventory.

Key Terms

Absorption costing The inclusion of variable and fixed overhead in the product cost.

Equivalent units A measure of production recognizing partial completion used in process costing to identify work performed during a period of time.

First-in, first-out (FIFO) An inventory flow that assumes that the oldest units in inventory are sold first.

Job order systems A system of recording costs for a particular job, which could be a single unit or a batch.

Last-in, first-out (LIFO) An inventory flow that assumes that the newest units in inventory are sold first.

Overabsorbed overhead The amount of overhead applied greater than actual overhead cost incurred.

Process cost systems A system of determining product costs by dividing total costs by the number of equivalent units produced.

Proration The process of dividing over- or underabsorbed overhead into finished goods inventory, cost of goods sold, and work-in-process.

Specific identification inventory valuation An inventory flow that uses the historical costs of the actual units transferred out of an inventory account.

Underabsorbed overhead The amount of overhead applied less than actual overhead cost incurred.

Weighted-average cost A per unit product cost determined by taking the weighted average of the cost of all units in inventory.

Appendix: Cost of Goods Manufactured and the Cost of Goods Sold and Alternative Cost Flow Methods for Inventory

This appendix examines the flow of costs for a particular job from raw materials, work-in-process, finished goods inventory, and cost of goods sold. The jobs are specifically identified, and their manufacturing costs move from account to account as that particular job is being manufactured, finished, and sold. This flow of costs determines the cost of the goods manufactured and the cost of goods sold, which in turn affect net income. These relations are captured in two schedules: cost of goods manufactured and cost of goods sold.

The cost of goods manufactured is a schedule that identifies the resources used for manufacturing to determine the total cost of goods manufactured during the period. Table 10A.1 provides an example of a cost of goods manufactured schedule. In this schedule the raw materials used is calculated indirectly by using beginning and ending raw material balances and the purchases during the period:

$$\text{Raw materials used} = \text{Beginning raw materials} + \text{Purchases} - \text{Ending raw materials}$$

In a similar manner, the cost of goods manufactured is calculated indirectly using beginning and ending work-in-process and total manufacturing costs of the period:

$$\text{Cost of goods manufactured} = \text{Beginning work-in-process} + \text{Total manufacturing costs} - \text{Ending work-in-process}$$

The cost of goods manufactured in Table 10A.1 represents the cost of finished units transferred to the finished goods inventory. The cost of goods sold schedule in Table 10A.2 uses the $245,000 cost of goods manufactured to calculate the

TABLE 10A.1

WESTERN COMPANY
Schedule of Cost of Goods Manufactured
Month of May 1998

Direct material		
Raw Material Inventory, May 1	$ 40,000	
May purchases of raw materials	100,000	
Available raw materials	140,000	
Raw material inventory, May 31	(50,000)	
Raw materials used in May		$ 90,000
Direct labor		100,000
Manufacturing overhead		
Indirect labor	$ 30,000	
Utilities	10,000	
Depreciation	5,000	
General administration	15,000	
Total		60,000
Total manufacturing costs		250,000
Work-in-process, May 1		10,000
Work-in-process, May 31		(15,000)
Cost of goods manufactured		$245,000

Appendix: Cost of Goods Manufactured and the Cost of Goods Sold and Alternative Cost Flow Methods for Inventory

TABLE 10A.2

WESTERN COMPANY Schedule of Cost of Goods Sold Month of May 1998	
Finished goods inventory, May 1	$180,000
Cost of goods manufactured (from Table 10.2)	245,000
Cost of goods available for sale	425,000
Finished goods inventory, May 31	(150,000)
Cost of goods sold	$275,000

cost of goods sold. The cost of goods sold is calculated indirectly by using the beginning and ending finished goods inventory and the cost of goods manufactured during the month:

$$\text{Cost of goods sold} = \text{Beginning finished goods inventory} + \text{Cost of goods manufactured} - \text{Ending finished goods inventory}$$

The cost of goods sold in Table 10.3 is then used to calculate the net income for the period.

In the cost of goods manufactured and cost of goods sold schedules, the cost of the ending inventories of the raw materials, work-in-process, and finished goods are used in determining the cost of goods sold. There are several external reporting methods that are acceptable in calculating the cost of those ending inventories. Under the **specific identification inventory valuation method,** the ending inventory is determined by identifying the specific units of the raw materials, work-in-process, and finished goods and their respective historical costs. This procedure has implicitly been used in this textbook. The specific identification method, however, may be costly to implement because management must keep track of the batches from which each item came.

Accountants have other alternatives in measuring the cost of ending inventory and the cost of goods sold. Under **first-in, first-out (FIFO),** the ending inventory is assumed to be the items produced most recently and is valued based on the cost of producing the most recent batches. The cost of goods sold, therefore, is based on the costs of the beginning inventory and items produced earlier in the period. Under **last-in, first-out (LIFO),** the ending inventory is assumed to be composed of items produced initially. The valuation of ending inventory under LIFO is based on the costs of items produced at the beginning of the accounting period and the costs of the beginning inventory. Therefore, the cost of goods sold is based on the cost of items most recently produced. The **weighted-average cost method** uses a weighted average of the cost of beginning inventory items and the cost of items produced during the accounting period to determine the cost of ending inventory and cost of goods sold. These methods are described in more detail in financial accounting texts.

Different inventory costing methods only provide different accounting numbers when there is an ending inventory and inventory costs (either manufacturing or wholesale) are changing over time. During periods of stable costs, the inventory costing method will have no effect on accounting reports. If prices are changing rapidly, however, the inventory costing method can have a big effect on the valuation of inventory and the earnings reported by the organization. The choice of an inventory cost method is important because it affects external financial statements, taxes, and contracts based on the external financial statements.

During periods of rising costs, the FIFO method generally causes the ending inventory cost to be higher. If an inventory costing method makes the cost of the ending inventory higher, the cost of goods sold is lower, and the net income is higher. During periods of rising costs, the LIFO method generally causes the cost of the ending inventory to be lower, the cost of goods sold to be higher, and the net income to be lower. A lower net income is advantageous to reduce taxes, so LIFO is popular for tax reporting.

If external financial statements are used for performance evaluation, the inventory costing method will also affect internal decision making and control. For the remainder of this text, we assume that organizations use the specific identification inventory valuation method, but the use of other inventory costing methods should be recognized.

NUMERICAL EXAMPLE 10.9

The Portland Company makes cement. The company had the following bimonthly manufacturing output during 1998:

Month	Output in Tons	Manufacturing Costs	Cost per Ton
January/February	3,000	$ 60,000	$20.00
March/April	3,500	71,750	20.50
May/June	2,500	52,500	21.00
July/August	3,000	63,000	21.00
September/October	3,200	67,200	21.00
November/December	3,300	72,600	22.00
Total	18,500	$387,050	Average: $20.92

Beginning inventory = 5,000 tons at $20.00 per pound, or a total of $100,000
Ending inventory = 6,000 tons

a. What is the cost of the ending inventory under the FIFO, LIFO, and weighted-average cost methods?
b. What is the cost of goods sold under each of the methods?

■ SOLUTION

a. FIFO: The last 6,000 tons manufactured include 3,300 from November/December and 2,700 from September/October. These tons of cement cost (3,300 tons)($22/ton) + (2,700 tons)($21/ton), or $129,300.

LIFO: The last 6,000 tons include 5,000 units from beginning inventory and 1,000 units from January/February. These tons of cement cost (5,000 tons)($20/ton) + (1,000 tons)($20/ton) or $120,000.

Weighted-average cost: The average cost per ton including beginning inventory and manufacturing this year is ($100,000 + $387,050)/(5,000 + 18,500) or $20.72553/ton. The cost of the 6,000 tons of cement in ending inventory is ($20.72553/ton)(6,000 tons) or $124,353.

b. FIFO:

	Beginning inventory, 1/1/98	$100,000
	Manufacturing costs	387,050
	Ending inventory, 12/31/98	(129,300)
	Cost of goods sold	$357,750

LIFO:

	Beginning inventory, 1/1/98	$100,000
	Manufacturing costs	387,050
	Ending inventory, 12/31/98	(120,000)
	Cost of goods sold	$367,050

Weighted-average cost:

Beginning inventory, 1/1/98	$100,000
Manufacturing costs	387,050
Ending inventory, 12/31/98	(124,353)
Cost of goods sold	$362,697

CONCEPT REVIEW

1. How does the schedule for cost of goods manufactured relate to the cost of goods sold?
2. How do FIFO, LIFO, and the weighted-average cost methods affect the cost of ending inventory and cost of goods sold?

SELF-STUDY PROBLEM

Over- and Underabsorbed Overhead   IPX is a specialized packaging company that packages other manufacturers' products. Other manufacturers ship their products to IPX in bulk. IPX then packages the products using high-speed, state-of-the-art packaging machines and ships the packaged products to wholesalers. A typical order involves packaging small toys in see-through, plastic, and cardboard packaging.

IPX uses a flexible budget to forecast annual plantwide overhead which is then allocated to jobs based on machine hours. The annual overhead budget is forecasted to be $6 million of fixed costs and $120 per machine hour. The expected number of machine hours for the year is 20,000. The application rate is estimated using total costs.

At the end of the year, 21,000 machine hours were used and actual overhead incurred was $9.14 million.

a. Calculate the application rate set at the beginning of the year.
b. Calculate the amount of over-/underabsorbed overhead for the year.
c. The company policy is to write off any over-/underabsorbed overhead to cost of goods sold. Will net income rise or fall this year when the over-/underabsorbed overhead is written off to cost of goods sold?

Solution

a. The application rate equals the forecasted overhead divided by the forecasted usage of the allocation base, machine hours (MH):

$$[\$6,000,000 + (\$120/MH)(20,000\ MH)]/20,000\ MH = \$420/MH$$

b.
Actual overhead	$9,140,000
Absorbed overhead ($420/MH)(21,000 MH)	−8,820,000
Underabsorbed overhead	$ 320,000

c. The underabsorbed overhead will increase the cost of goods sold and decrease net income.

NUMERICAL PROBLEMS

NP 10–1: Job-Order Cost Sheet (LO 2; NE 1)   The Talbott Company has received an order (#324) for 100 widgets. On January 20, the shop foreman requisitioned 100 units of part 503 at a cost of $5 per unit and 500 units part 456 at a cost of $3 per unit to begin work on the 100 widgets. On the same day, 20 hours of direct labor at $20 per hour are used to work on the widgets. On January 21, 200 units of part 543 at $6 per unit are requisitioned and 10 hours of direct labor at $15 per hour are performed on the 100 units of widgets to complete the job. Overhead is allocated to the job based on $5 per direct labor hour.

Make a job-order cost sheet for the 100 widgets.

NP 10–2: Job-Order Cost Sheet (LO 2; NE 1) BPA Accounting is performing an audit for the Chadwick Company. BPA Accounting uses a cost sheet to record the cost of each audit. Only professional services (by associates, managers, and partners) and overhead are recorded on the cost sheet. The cost sheets are then compared with the bid price of the audit to determine if the audit was profitable and to improve future bids on audits. BPA Accounting had bid $10,000 to do the Chadwick Company audit. During the month of January, the following work was performed on the Chadwick Company audit: 10 hours of associate work at $30 per hour, 4 hours of manager work at $50 per hour, and 1 hour of partner time at $100 per hour. During February, the following work was performed at the same rates as in January to finish the audit: 100 hours of associate time, 50 hours of manager time, and 8 hours of partner time. Overhead is allocated at $20 per professional service hour provided.

a. Make a cost sheet for the Chadwick Company audit.
b. Was the Chadwick Company audit profitable for BPA Accounting?

NP 10–3: Job Cost Flows (LO 2, 3; NE 2) The job cost sheet for 1,000 units of toy trucks is:

Job Number 555
Date Started 4/13
Date Completed 6/18

Date	Type	Raw Materials Cost	Qty.	Amount	Direct Labor Cost	Hours	Amount
4/13	565	$3	1,000	$3,000	$18	20	$ 360
5/24	889	1	4,000	4,000	12	10	120
6/18	248	2	1,000	2,000	15	100	1,500
				$9,000		130	$1,980

Total direct materials	$ 9,000
Total direct labor	1,980
Overhead (130 direct labor hours @ $10/hour)	1,300
Total job cost	**$12,280**

All of the materials for the job were purchased on 4/10. The batch of 1,000 toy trucks is sold on 7/10.

What are the costs of this job order in the raw materials account, the work-in-process account, the finished goods account, and the cost of goods sold account on 4/30, 5/31, 6/30 and 7/31?

NP 10–4: Job Cost Flows (LO 2, 3; NE 2) The Tip Tap Company receives an order for 10,000 units of taps (a tool used to make threads in a block of steel). The taps require considerable machining on a blank (Part #14). Blanks are sometimes ruined in the machining process, but the cost of the ruined blanks is treated as a part of the cost of the job. Direct labor hours are used to allocate overhead. Each blank, spoiled or good, requires the same amount of direct labor hours. The job-order cost sheet for the order is:

Job Number 43
Date Started 4/20
Date Completed 6/20

Date	Type	Raw Materials Cost	Qty.	Amount	Direct Labor Cost	Hours	Amount
4/20	14	$1	3,500	$ 3,500	$18	200	$ 3,600
5/14	14	1	4,000	4,000	18	220	3,960
6/20	14	1	3,300	3,300	18	200	3,600
			10,800	$10,800		620	$11,160

Total units worked on	10,800	
Good units	10,000	
Spoiled units	800	
Total direct materials		$10,800
Total direct labor		11,160
Overhead (620 direct labor hours @ $10/hour)		6,200
Total job cost		**$28,160**

All of the blanks for the job were purchased on 3/10. The batch of 10,000 taps is sold on 7/15.

What are the costs of this job order in the raw materials account, the work-in-process account, the finished goods account, and the cost of goods sold account on 3/31, 4/30, 5/31, 6/30 and 7/31?

NP 10–5: Estimated, Actual, and Allocated Overhead (LO 4; NE 3,4)

The Philbrick Company makes recreational equipment. Overhead is allocated to the different products based on machine hours. At the beginning of the year, the company estimates that overhead will be $4 million and machine hours will be 200,000. During the year, the company actually has $4.3 million of overhead and 190,000 machine hours.

a. How much overhead is allocated?
b. What is the over-/underabsorbed overhead?

NP 10–6: Estimated, Actual, and Allocated Overhead (LO 4; NE 3,4)

The Dinkleberry law firm allocates overhead to different clients based on hours of work performed by Mr. Dinkleberry. At the start of the year, Mr. Dinkleberry estimates that the total overhead of the coming year will be $100,000. He also estimates that he will perform 2,000 hours of work for clients. During the year he works 2,100 hours for clients and incurs $110,000 of overhead.

a. How much overhead is allocated?
b. What is the over-/underabsorbed overhead?

NP 10–7: Over-/Underabsorbed Overhead (LO 4; NE 3,4)

The Alphonse Company allocates fixed overhead costs by machine hours and variable overhead costs by direct labor hours. At the beginning of the year, the company expects fixed overhead costs to be $600,000 and variable costs to be $800,000. The expected machine hours are 6,000 and the expected direct labor hours are 80,000. The actual fixed overhead costs are $700,000 and the actual variable overhead costs are $750,000. The actual machine hours during the year are 5,500 and the actual direct labor hours are 90,000.

a. How much overhead is allocated?
b. What is the over-/underabsorbed overhead?

NP 10–8: Prorating Over-/Underabsorbed Overhead (LO 5; NE 5)

A computer manufacturer has the following account balances at the end of the year.

Work-in-process	$ 100,000
Finished goods	800,000
Cost of goods sold	2,000,000
Total	$2,900,000

These accounts contain $500,000 of allocated overhead. Actual overhead, however, is $600,000.

What are the account balances after prorating the underabsorbed overhead?

NP 10–9: Allocating Over-/Underabsorbed Overhead (LO 5; NE 5)

A chair manufacturer uses direct labor to allocate overhead. At the end of the year, the company had the following account balances with and without allocated overhead.

Account	Direct Costs	Direct Labor Hours	Allocated Overhead	Ending Balance
Work-in-process	$ 10,000	100	$ 5,000	$ 15,000
Finished goods	40,000	300	15,000	55,000
Cost of goods sold	200,000	1,600	80,000	280,000
Total	$250,000	2,000	$100,000	$350,000

Actual overhead during the year was $90,000. Estimated and actual direct labor hours are equal.

a. What are the ending account balances if the cost of goods sold is adjusted for the over-/underabsorbed overhead?
b. What are the ending account balances if the over-/underabsorbed overhead is prorated?
c. What are the ending account balances if the application rate is recalculated to reflect actual overhead costs?

NP 10–10: Multiple Overhead Rates (LO 6; NE 6)

A building contractor for houses has the following three overhead cost pools:

General administration	$ 500,000
Utilities	100,000
Equipment	1,000,000
Total overhead	$1,600,000

Costs from each of these cost pools are then allocated to housing contracts by using separate allocation bases:

Overhead Item	Allocation Base	Expected Usage
General administration	Direct labor dollars	$2,000,000 in direct labor
Utilities	Number of houses	40 houses
Equipment	Cost of house	$16,000,000 in total costs

How much overhead is allocated to a house that uses $20,000 of direct labor and has a total cost of $300,000?

NP 10–11: Allocation of Overhead by Departments (LO 7; NE 6)

The Puzzle Company makes jigsaw puzzles. In the manufacturing process, each type of jigsaw puzzle must go through the gluing, cutting, and boxing departments. The overhead costs in each of these departments are allocated by direct labor hours. Expected overhead costs and direct labor hours used to choose an application rate are:

Department	Expected Dept. Costs	Expected Dept. Direct Labor Hours
Gluing	$ 90,000	10,000
Cutting	200,000	40,000
Boxing	110,000	50,000
Total overhead	$400,000	100,000

A job of 5,000 jigsaw puzzles requires 10 hours of gluing, 15 hours of cutting, and 12 hours of boxing.

a. How much overhead is allocated to the job if overhead is allocated by department?
b. How much overhead is allocated to the job if overhead is allocated by a single companywide application rate?

NP 10–12: Equivalent Units (LO 8; NE 7)

The White Flour Company mills wheat into flour. The equivalent units are measured in terms of tons of flour produced.

At the beginning of the year, the mill contained 20 tons of flour that was 30% milled. During the year, another 500 tons of flour is completely milled. At the end of the year, the company has 40 tons of flour 80% milled.

How many equivalent tons of flour are milled by the White Flour Company during the year?

NP 10–13: Cost per Equivalent Unit (LO 8; NE 8)

A computer manufacturer has an assembly line for making computers. At the beginning of the year, the company had 300 computers on the assembly line that were 40% complete on average. The computer company started and completed another 5,000 computers. At the end of the year, another 500 computers were still on the assembly line and 30% complete on average. During the year, the computer manufacturer had costs of $2 million.

a. How many equivalent units were produced during the year?
b. What is the cost per equivalent unit of computers worked on during the year?

NP 10–14: Equivalent Units (LO 8; NE 8)

Department 100 is the first step in the firm's manufacturing process. Data for the current quarter's operations are:

	Units
Beginning work-in-process (70% complete)	30,000
Units started this quarter	580,000
Units completed this quarter and transferred out	550,000
Ending work-in-process (60% complete)	60,000

How many equivalent units were completed during the current quarter in Department 100?

NP 10–15: Recalculating Overhead Allocation with the Actual Application Rate (LO 5; NE 5)

Jackson Industries makes an assortment of aircraft parts. The company allocates overhead based on direct labor costs (DL$). At the beginning of the year, the company estimated that overhead costs would be $400,000 and direct labor costs would be $250,000. The application rate was estimated to be $400,000/$250,000, or $1.60/DL$. The actual overhead costs were $420,000 and the actual direct labor costs $210,000. A batch of parts that used $10,000 of direct labor was completed during the year and sold based on a contract of actual costs plus 20%. The original bill was sent using the estimated application rate.

How much greater would the bill have been using actual overhead and direct labor costs?

NP 10–16: Over-/Underabsorbed Overhead (LO 2, 4; NE 3, 4)

The Rosen Company has two manufacturing departments, production and assembly. Each department has separate application rates. The following estimates were made by the Rosen Company for its production and assembly departments for the calendar year 1998:

	Production	Assembly
Factory overhead	$ 300,000	$100,000
Direct labor cost	1,000,000	500,000
Machine hours	1,500	6,250
Direct labor hours	5,000	10,000

The company uses a budgeted application rate for the application of overheads to orders. Machine hours are used to allocate overhead in the production department and direct labor hours are used to allocate overhead in the assembly department.

a. What is the application rate for each department?
b. What are overhead costs for job 77? A summary of job 77 is given below:

	Production	Assembly
Direct materials used	$3,000	$2,000
Direct labor costs	7,000	2,500
Machine hours	100	250
Direct labor hours	500	750

c. Actual operating results for January 1998 are:

	Production	Assembly
Factory overhead	$325,000	$ 65,000
Direct labor cost	900,000	600,000
Machine hours	1,550	6,250
Direct labor hours	5,000	7,500

Calculate the over-/underabsorbed overhead for each department.

NP 10–17: Work-in-Process, Finished Goods, and Cost of Goods Sold (LO 3; NE 2) Ware Paper Box manufactures corrugated paper boxes for use in the produce industry. It uses a job-order costing system. Operating data for February and March are:

Job	Date Started	Date Finished	Date Sold	Total Mfg. Cost as of 2/28	Total Mfg. Cost in March*
613	1/28	2/5	2/15	$12,500	
614	2/5	2/17	2/20	17,200	
615	2/20	2/27	3/5	18,500	
616	2/25	3/10	3/20	10,100	$13,400
734	2/21	3/15	4/1	4,300	8,200
735	2/27	4/1	4/9	9,100	2,400
736	3/2	3/22	4/19		16,300
617	3/15	3/20	3/26		19,200
618	3/22	4/5	4/15		14,400

*Manufacturing costs incurred only in March. Does not include any manufacturing costs incurred in prior months.

Calculate the following amounts:

a. Work-in-process inventory as of 2/28
b. Work-in-process inventory as of 3/31
c. Finished goods inventory as of 2/28
d. Finished goods inventory as of 3/31
e. Cost of goods sold for February
f. Cost of goods sold for March

NP 10–18: Cost per Equivalent Unit (LO 8; NE 7) DeJure Scents manufactures an after-shave. In May, they started 15,000 gallons. There was no beginning inventory. May's ending inventory of work-in-process was 2,000 gallons which were 50% complete.

In May, manufacturing costs were $73,000.

a. Calculate the equivalent units.
b. Calculate the cost per equivalent unit.
c. Calculate the cost of the ending inventory and the cost transferred to finished goods inventory.

NP 10–19: Equivalent Units (LO 8; NE 8) Chemtrex is an agricultural chemical producer. Process costing is used in their mixing department. At the beginning of

July, they had 700,000 gallons 70% complete in work-in-process. During July, they started another 4,000,000 gallons and they finished 3,700,000 gallons. One million gallons of ending work-in-process were 60% complete at the end of July.

Calculate the number of equivalent units of conversion work performed during July.

NP 10–20: Job Cost of a Loan Application (LO 2; NE 1)

First Eastern Bank is a large, multibranch bank offering a wide variety of commercial and retail banking services. Eastern uses an absorption costing system to monitor the cost of various services and to provide information for a variety of decisions.

One set of services is a retail loan operation providing residential mortgages, car loans, and student college loans. All loan applications are filed by the applicant at a branch bank, where the branch manager fills out the loan application. From there, the loan application is sent to the loan processing department, where the applicant's prior credit history is checked, and a recommendation is made regarding loan approval based on the applicant's credit history and current financial situation. This recommendation is forwarded to the loan committee of senior lending officers who review the file and make a final decision.

Thus, there are three stages to making a loan: application in a branch, the loan processing department, and the loan committee. Mr. and Mrs. Jones visit the West Street branch and file an application for a residential mortgage. Information about each stage of processing the Jones' loan application follows.

- West Street Branch Bank. The branch manager spends one hour taking the application. The branch manager spends 1,000 hours per year of her total time taking loan applications and the remainder of her time providing other direct services to customers. Total overhead in the West Street Branch is budgeted to be $259,000, excluding the manager's salary, and is allocated to direct customer services using the branch manager's time spent providing direct customer services. The branch manager's annual salary is $42,600.
- Processing department. The processing department budgets its total overhead for the year to be $800,000, which is allocated to loans processed using direct labor hours. Budgeted direct labor hours for the year are 40,000 hours. Direct labor hours in the processing department cost $18 per direct labor hour. The Joneses' loan requires five direct labor hours in the loan processing department.
- Loan committee. Ten senior bank executives constitute the loan committee. The loan committee meets 52 times per year, every Wednesday, all day, to approve all loans. The average salary and benefits of each member of the loan committee is $104,000. The loan committee spends 15 minutes reviewing the Joneses' loan application before approving it.

For costing purposes, all employees are assumed to work eight-hour days, five days per week, 52 weeks per year.

Calculate the total cost of taking the application, processing, and approval for the Joneses' mortgage.

NP 10–21: Work-in-Process and Prorating Over-/Underabsorbed Overhead (LO 2, 4, 5; NE 5)

The following figures were taken from the records of Wellington Co. for the year 1998. At the end of the year, two jobs were still in process. Details about the two jobs are given below:

	Job A	Job B
Direct labor	$10,000	$28,000
Direct materials	$32,000	$22,000
Machine hours	2,000	3,500
Direct labor hours	1,000	2,000

Wellington Co. applies overhead at a budgeted rate, calculated at the beginning of the year. The budgeted rate is the ratio of budgeted overhead to budgeted direct labor costs. Budgeted figures for 1998 were as follows:

Budgeted direct labor costs	$250,000
Budgeted overhead	187,500

Actual figures for 1998 were:

Direct labor	$350,000
Overhead	192,500
Finished goods inventory	75,000
Cost of goods sold	550,000

There were no opening inventories. It is the practice of the company to prorate any over-/underabsorption of overheads to finished goods inventory, work-in-process, and cost of goods sold based on the total dollars in these categories.

a. Compute the cost of work-in-process before prorating over-/underapplied overheads.
b. Prepare a schedule of finished goods inventory, work-in-process and cost of goods sold after prorating over-/underapplied overheads.
c. What is the difference in the operating income if the over-/underapplied overhead is charged to cost of goods sold instead of being prorated to finished goods inventory, work-in-process, and cost of goods sold?

NP 10–22: Use of Multiple Application Rates (LO 6; NE 6) Frames, Inc., manufactures two types of metal frames, large and small. Steel angle iron is first cut to the appropriate sizes, and the pieces are then welded together to form the frames. The process involves a high degree of automation. There is considerable indirect labor by skilled technicians and engineers who maintain the automated equipment. There are two manufacturing departments, cutting and welding. The following reports detail the actual costs of production for the year:

FRAMES, INC.
Year Ending 12/31

Direct Costs

Frame Type	Units Produced	Direct Labor	Direct Materials
Large	10,000	$ 480,000	$950,000
Small	30,000	1,140,000	800,000

Overhead Costs by Department

Overhead Costs	Cutting	Welding	Total
Utilities	$58,000	$174,000	$ 232,000
Indirect labor	430,000	480,000	910,000
General factory costs			150,000
Total overhead costs			$1,292,000

Kilowatt Hours (000s)

Frame Type	Cutting	Welding	Total
Large	530	1,040	1,570
Small	910	1,200	2,110
Total kilowatt hours	1,440	2,240	3,680

a. Compute the unit costs of large frames and small frames for the year using a single, factorywide overhead rate. The factorywide overhead allocation base is direct labor cost.

b. Compute the unit costs of large frames and small frames for the year using different overhead rates for utilities, indirect labor, and general factory costs. Utility costs and indirect labor costs are allocated to frames using kilowatt hours. General factory costs are allocated to frames using direct costs (the sum of direct labor and direct materials).
c. Compute the unit costs of large frames and small frames for the year using departmental overhead rates for the cutting and welding departments. General factory overhead costs are evenly divided between the two departments before departmental overhead is allocated to the frames. Cutting department overhead costs are allocated based on the amount of direct materials costs, and welding department overhead costs are allocated based on kilowatt hours in the welding department.
d. Analyze why different unit costs result from the different methods of allocating overhead costs to the products. Which method is best?

NP 10–23: Departmental Rates to Allocate Overhead (LO 7; NE 6)

MumsDay Corporation manufactures a complete line of fiberglass attaché cases and suitcases. MumsDay has three manufacturing departments (molding, component, and assembly) and two service departments (power and maintenance).

The sides of the cases are manufactured in the molding department. The frames, hinges, locks, etc., are manufactured in the component department. The cases are completed in the assembly department. Varying amounts of materials, time, and effort are required for each of the various cases. The power department and maintenance department provide services to the three manufacturing departments.

MumsDay has always used a plantwide overhead rate. Direct labor hours are used to assign the overhead to its product. The predetermined rate is calculated by dividing the company's total estimated overhead by the total estimated direct labor hours to be worked in the three manufacturing departments.

Whit Portlock, manager of cost accounting, has recommended that MumsDay use departmental overhead rates. The planned operating costs and expected levels of activity for the coming year have been developed by Portlock and are presented by department in the schedules (000 omitted) below.

	Manufacturing Departments		
	Molding	Component	Assembly
Departmental activity measures			
Direct labor hours	500	2,000	1,500
Machine hours	875	125	–0–
Departmental costs			
Raw materials	$12,400	$30,000	$ 1,250
Direct labor	3,500	20,000	12,000
Variable overhead	3,500	10,000	16,500
Fixed overhead	17,500	6,200	6,100
Total departmental costs	$36,900	$66,200	$35,850
Use of service departments			
Maintenance			
Estimated usage in labor hours for coming year	90	25	10
Power (in kilowatt hours)			
Estimated usage for coming year	360	320	120
Maximum allotted long-term capacity (in kilowatt-hours)	500	350	150

	Service Departments	
	Power	Maintenance
Departmental activity measures		
Maximum capacity	1,000 KWH	Adjustable
Estimated usage in coming year	800 KWH	125 hours
Departmental costs		
Materials and supplies	$ 5,000	$1,500
Variable labor	1,400	2,250
Fixed overhead	12,000	250
Total service department costs	$18,400	$4,000

a. Calculate the plantwide overhead rate for MumsDay Corporation for the coming year using the same method as used in the past.

b. Whit Portlock has been asked to develop departmental overhead rates for comparison with the plantwide rate. The following steps are to be followed in developing the departmental rates.

1.) The maintenance department costs should be allocated to the three manufacturing departments using labor hours.

2.) The fixed costs in the power department should be allocated to the three manufacturing departments according to long-term capacity and the variable costs according to planned usage.

3.) Calculate departmental overhead rates for the three manufacturing departments using a machine-hour base for the molding department and a direct-labor-hour base for the component and assembly departments.

c. Should MumsDay Corporation use a plantwide rate or departmental rates to assign overhead to its products? Explain your answer.

(CMA adapted)

NP 10–24: Multiple Cost Drivers (LO 6; NE 6)

Astin Car Stereos manufactures and distributes four different car stereos. The following table summarizes the unit sales, selling prices, and manufacturing costs of each stereo.

ASTIN CAR STEREOS
Summary of Operations
Fiscal Year 1998

	A90	B200	B300	Z7
Sales price	$100	$120	$140	$180
Manufacturing cost (all variable)	$ 80	$ 90	$100	$120
Units sold	15,000	13,000	12,000	9,000

Selling and distribution (S&D) expenses are $1,270,000. They are treated as a period cost and written off to the income statement. To assess relative profitability of each product, S&D expenses are allocated to each product based on sales revenue.

On further investigation of the S&D expenses, one-half of them are for marketing and advertising. Each product has its own advertising and marketing budget, which is administered by one of four marketing managers. Z7 is the premier product which is advertised heavily. Forty percent of the marketing and advertising budget goes towards Z7, 30 percent to B300, 20 percent to B200, and 10 percent to A90.

The other half of the S&D expenses are composed of distribution and administration costs (25%) and selling costs (25%). The distribution and administration department is responsible for arranging shipping and billing customers. (Customers pay transportation charges directly to the common carrier.) It also handles federal licensing of the car radios.

Upon analysis of the work in the distribution and administration department, each of the four products places even demands on the department and each consumes about the same resources as the others. Selling costs consist primarily of commissions paid to independent sales people. The commissions are based on gross margin on the product (sales revenue less manufacturing cost).

a. Allocate all S&D expenses based only on sales revenue. Identify the most and least profitable products.
b. Allocate all S&D expenses based only on the advertising and marketing budget. Identify the most and least profitable products.
c. Allocate all S&D expenses using the advertising and marketing budget for advertising and marketing costs, the distribution and administration costs using the demand for these resources by the products, and the selling costs based on commissions. Identify the most and least profitable products.
d. Discuss the managerial implications of the various schemes. Which products are the most/least profitable under each of the three allocation schemes? Why do the different schemes result in different product line profits? Which product is really the most/least profitable?

NP 10–25: Cost of Goods Manufactured and Cost of Goods Sold (LO 9; NE 9)

The Williams Company manufactures garage door openers. At the beginning of November, the company had the following inventory accounts:

Raw materials	$20,000
Work-in-process	$15,000
Finished goods	$30,000

At the end of November, the company had the following inventory accounts:

Raw materials	$10,000
Work-in-process	$25,000
Finished goods	$50,000

During the month of November, the company made purchases of raw materials equal to $100,000. The company also incurred direct labor costs of $200,000 and overhead of $50,000.

a. Make a schedule calculating the cost of goods manufactured during November.
b. Make a schedule calculating the cost of goods sold during November.

NP 10–26: Cost of Goods Manufactured and Cost of Goods Sold (LO 9; NE 9)

The Smith Company has the following inventory balances at the beginning of 1999:

Raw materials	$ 50,000
Work-in-process	$ 75,000
Finished goods	$100,000

At the end of 1999, the controller calculates the cost of goods sold to be $700,000 and the cost of goods manufactured as $750,000. Ending work-in-process for 1999 was estimated to be $95,000. During 1999, the company purchased $200,000 of raw materials and used $190,000 of raw materials. Manufacturing overhead during 1999 was $300,000.

a. What was the ending raw materials balance in 1999?
b. What amount of direct labor was paid during 1999?
c. What was the ending balance of finished goods in 1999?

NP 10–27: Cost of Goods Sold and Different Cost Flow Methods for Inventory (LO 9; NE 9)   The City Gravel Company has the following outputs, costs, and ending inventory for its five years of operation:

Year	Output in Tons	Manufacturing Costs	Cost per Ton	Ending Inventory (Tons)
1995	300,000	$ 300,000	$1.00	20,000
1996	400,000	500,000	1.25	30,000
1997	500,000	750,000	1.50	50,000
1998	400,000	600,000	1.50	70,000
1999	800,000	1,400,000	1.75	80,000

a. What is the cost of goods sold in each of the years using FIFO?
b. What is the cost of goods sold in each of the years using LIFO?
c. What is the cost of goods sold in each of the years using weighted-average cost?

DISCUSSION PROBLEMS

DP 10–1: Using Job-Order Cost Sheets (LO 2)   The shop foreman is complaining to the controller about all the time his workers are wasting in filling out job-order costs sheets. He estimates that 10% of his employees' time is spent recording labor hours spent on different jobs. Given that the direct labor costs of the factory are $2 million per year, the foreman estimates that the company is losing $200,000 a year filling out job-order cost sheets.

What alternatives are there to using time for filling out job order cost sheets?

DP 10–2: Job-Order and Process Costing (LO 1)   A management accounting professor was trying to explain the difference between job-order costing and process costing to the class. He pointed out that the job-order costing system is generally used when distinct batches, or jobs, can be identified. Process costing, on the other hand, is used for the continual processing of homogenous products. A student pointed out another difference between job-order and process costing. She noted that job-order costs are determined at the time the job is being performed by using predetermined overhead rates. Process costs, on the other hand, are normally determined at the end of the period based on the number of equivalent units produced and actual overhead costs.

What does the timing difference between job-order costing and process costing say about how job-order costs and process costs are used for planning purposes?

DP 10–3: Modified Job-Order and Process Costing (LO 1, 2, 8)   The Trophy Company makes medallions for the Olympic Festival. All of the medallions are exactly the same except for the type of metal that is stamped into the medallion. The company makes gold, silver, and bronze medallions. Each of these medallions goes through the same steps of cutting, stamping, polishing, and packaging. The controller is uncertain whether to use a job-order system or a process costing system to determine the costs of the different types of medallions.

Provide arguments for the use of both types of costing systems and suggest a hybrid costing system.

DP 10–4: Application Rates for Departments (LO 7)   The Glass Eye Company manufactures hand-blown glass pieces. The company has three glassblowing departments (A, B, and C) that revolve around three different furnaces. The work performed in each of these departments can be replicated by any of the other departments, but department C has newer and more expensive equipment that has a higher depreciation expense. Overhead costs are allocated to the different batches of glassware based on the direct labor hours. Each of the glassblowing departments has its own application rate, with department C being the largest. The company prices its product based on absorbed costs, so customers have been asking that their special orders be performed in departments A or B. As a result, department C with the best equipment is being used least.

What is wrong and what are some remedies for this problem?

DP 10–5: Underabsorbed Overhead (LO 5)   The end of the year has arrived and it's bonus time for the successful managers of Crescent Company. Each division manager is evaluated by the profit of his or her division after costs are allocated from headquarters. One of the costs that is allocated from headquarters is the cost of data processing, which is performed centrally for all of the divisions. The data processing costs are allocated to the divisions based on the number of transactions processed. The application rate was calculated at the beginning of the year based on estimated data processing costs and the estimated transactions to be processed by all of the divisions. Near the start of the year, however, one of the divisions was unexpectedly sold to another company and did not use very much data processing before being sold. At the end of the year, not all of the data processing costs were allocated. The president of the company decided to allocate the underabsorbed data processing costs to the remaining divisions based on how much data processing they used during the year. In allocating the underabsorbed overhead to the divisions, some division managers were not able to achieve their profit goals and didn't receive their bonuses.

Is this type of cost allocation appropriate?

DP 10–6: Process Costing and Underabsorbed Overhead (LO 8)   Process costing can be performed with estimated cost and production data and actual cost and production data. A company estimated total manufacturing costs to be $4,000,000 and estimated equivalent units to be 20,000. Therefore, the estimated cost per equivalent unit was $200. Inventory costs were adjusted for completed units based on this $200 estimated cost per equivalent unit. At the end of the year, the actual manufacturing costs were $5,000,000 and the equivalent units produced were actually 22,000.

How would you determine the underabsorbed overhead, and how would you account for the underabsorbed overhead?

DP 10–7: Application Rates and Depreciation Methods (LO 2)   The frame-welding department of a large automotive company welds car frames as they pass down the assembly line. Four computer-controlled robots make the welds on each frame simultaneously. When installed last year, each robot was expected to have a five-year useful life before being made obsolete and being replaced by newer, faster models with more advanced electronics. Over its life, each robot is expected to make 100 million welds. The robots cost $8 million apiece and have no salvage value at the end of their useful lives after taking into consideration the cost of dismantling and removing the robots.

The firm has a traditional absorption costing system that costs each frame as it is produced. The accounting system supports decision making and control. Straight-line depreciation is used for both internal and external reporting and accelerated depreciation is used for taxes. As frames move through the welding stations, they are charged based on the number of welds made on each frame. Different car frames require different numbers of welds, with some frame models requiring up to 1,000 welds. Welds cost $0.11 each. This charge is set at the beginning of the year by estimating the fixed and variable costs in the welding department. The expected number of welds projected for the year is determined by taking the forecasted number of frames times the number of welds per frame. The expected number of welds is used to estimate total costs in the welding department. The cost per weld is then the ratio of the projected welding costs and the expected number of welds. Seventy-two million welds were projected for the current year.

The following statement illustrates the computation of the charge per weld:

FRAME WELDING DEPARTMENT
Charge per Weld
Current Year

	Variable Costs (at 72 million welds)	Fixed Costs	Total Costs
Depreciation*		$6,400,000	$6,400,000
Welding rods	$ 700,000		700,000
Engineering services	300,000	200,000	500,000
Electricity	180,000		180,000
Factory overhead	85,000	55,000	140,000
Total	$1,265,000	$6,655,000	$7,920,000
÷ Expected number of welds	72,000,000	72,000,000	72,000,000
Cost per weld	$ 0.0176	$ 0.0924	$ 0.1100

*Depreciation per year = (4 robots × $8 million per robot)/5-year life

After reviewing the above statement, Amy Miller, manager of the body fabricating division, which includes the welding department, made the following remarks:

> I know we use straight-line depreciation to calculate the depreciation component of the cost per weld now. But it would seem to make a lot of sense to compute robot depreciation using units-of-production depreciation. Each robot cost $8 million and was expected to perform 100 million welds over its useful life. That comes to eight cents per weld. Thus, we should charge each weld at eight cents plus the remaining fixed and variable costs as calculated on this statement. If I back out the $6.4 million depreciation from the above figures and recompute the fixed costs per weld at 72 million welds, I get $255,000 divided by 72 million, or $0.00354. Add this to the variable cost per weld of $0.0176 plus the 8 cents depreciation and our cost per weld is $0.1011 per weld, not the 11 cents now. This reduces our costs on our complicated frames by as much as $10.
>
> The real advantage of using units-of-production depreciation, in my opinion, is that depreciation is no longer a fixed cost but becomes a variable cost. This has real advantages because when you lower your fixed costs your break-even point is lower. Operating leverage is lower and thus the overall risk of the company is reduced.
>
> I think we should go to the plant controller and see if we can convince him to use a more realistic basis for calculating depreciation costs of the robots.

Evaluate Amy Miller's proposal.

CASE

C 10–1: Flow of Costs and Under-/Overabsorbed Overhead
Targon Inc. manufactures lawn equipment. A job-order system is used because the products are manufactured on a batch rather than a continuous basis. Targon employs a full-

absorption accounting method for cost accumulation. The balances in selected accounts for the eleven-month period ended August 31, 1996, are presented below.

Stores inventory	$ 32,000
Work-in-process inventory	1,200,000
Finished goods inventory	2,785,000
Factory overhead	2,260,000
Cost of goods sold	14,200,000

The work-in-process inventory consists of two jobs:

Job. No.	Units	Items	Accumulated Cost
3005-5	50,000	Estate sprinklers	$ 700,000
3006-4	40,000	Economy sprinklers	500,000
			$1,200,000

The finished goods inventory consists of five items:

Items	Quantity and Unit Cost	Accumulated Cost
Estate sprinklers	5,000 units @ $22 each	$ 110,000
Deluxe sprinklers	115,000 units @ $17 each	1,955,000
Brass nozzles	10,000 gross @ $14 per gross	140,000
Rainmaker nozzles	5,000 gross @ $16 per gross	80,000
Connectors	100,000 gross @ $ 5 per gross	500,000
		$2,785,000

The factory cost budget prepared for the 1995–96 fiscal year is presented below. The company applied factory overhead on the basis of direct labor hours.

The activities during the first 11 months of the year were quite close to budget. A total of 367,000 direct labor hours have been worked through August 31, 1996.

Factory Cost Annual Budget
For the Year Ending September 30, 1996

Direct materials	$ 3,800,000
Purchased parts	6,000,000
Direct labor (400,000 hours)	4,000,000
Overhead:	
Supplies	190,000
Indirect labor	700,000
Supervision	250,000
Depreciation	950,000
Utilities	200,000
Insurance	10,000
Property taxes	40,000
Miscellaneous	60,000
Total factory costs	$16,200,000

The September 1996 transactions are summarized below.

1. All direct materials, purchased parts, and supplies are charged to stores inventory. The September purchases were as follows:

Materials	$410,000
Purchased parts	285,000
Supplies	13,000

2. The direct materials, purchased parts, and supplies were requisitioned from stores inventory as shown in the table below.

	Purchased Parts	Materials	Supplies	Total Requisitions
3005-5	$110,000	$100,000	$ —	$210,000
3006-4	—	6,000	—	6,000
4001-3 (30,000 gross rainmaker nozzles)	—	181,000	—	181,000
4002-1 (10,000 deluxe sprinklers)	—	92,000	—	92,000
4003-5 (50,000 ring sprinklers)	163,000	—	—	163,000
Supplies	—	—	20,000	20,000
	$273,000	$379,000	$20,000	$672,000

3. The payroll summary for September is as follows:

	Hours	Cost
3005-5	6,000	$ 62,000
3006-4	2,500	26,000
4001-3	18,000	182,000
4002-1	500	5,000
4003-5	5,000	52,000
Indirect	8,000	60,000
Supervision	—	24,000
Sales and administration	—	120,000
		$531,000

4. Other factory costs incurred during September were:

Depreciation	$62,500
Utilities	15,000
Insurance	1,000
Property taxes	3,500
Miscellaneous	5,000
	$87,000

5. Jobs completed during September and the actual output were:

Job. No.	Quantity	Items
3005-5	48,000 units	Estate sprinklers
3006-4	39,000 units	Economy sprinklers
4001-3	29,500 gross	Rainmaker nozzles
4003-5	49,000 units	Ring sprinklers

6. The following finished products were shipped to customers during September:

Items	Quantity
Estate sprinklers	16,000 units
Deluxe sprinklers	32,000 units
Economy sprinklers	20,000 units
Ring sprinklers	22,000 units
Brass nozzles	5,000 gross
Rainmaker nozzles	10,000 gross
Connectors	26,000 gross

Case Questions

a. Calculate the over- or underapplied overhead for the year ended September 30, 1996. Be sure to indicate whether the overhead is over- or underapplied.
b. Calculate the dollar balance in the work-in-process inventory account as of September 30, 1996.
c. Calculate the dollar balance in the finished goods inventory as of September 30, 1996, for the estate sprinklers using a FIFO basis.

(CMA adapted)

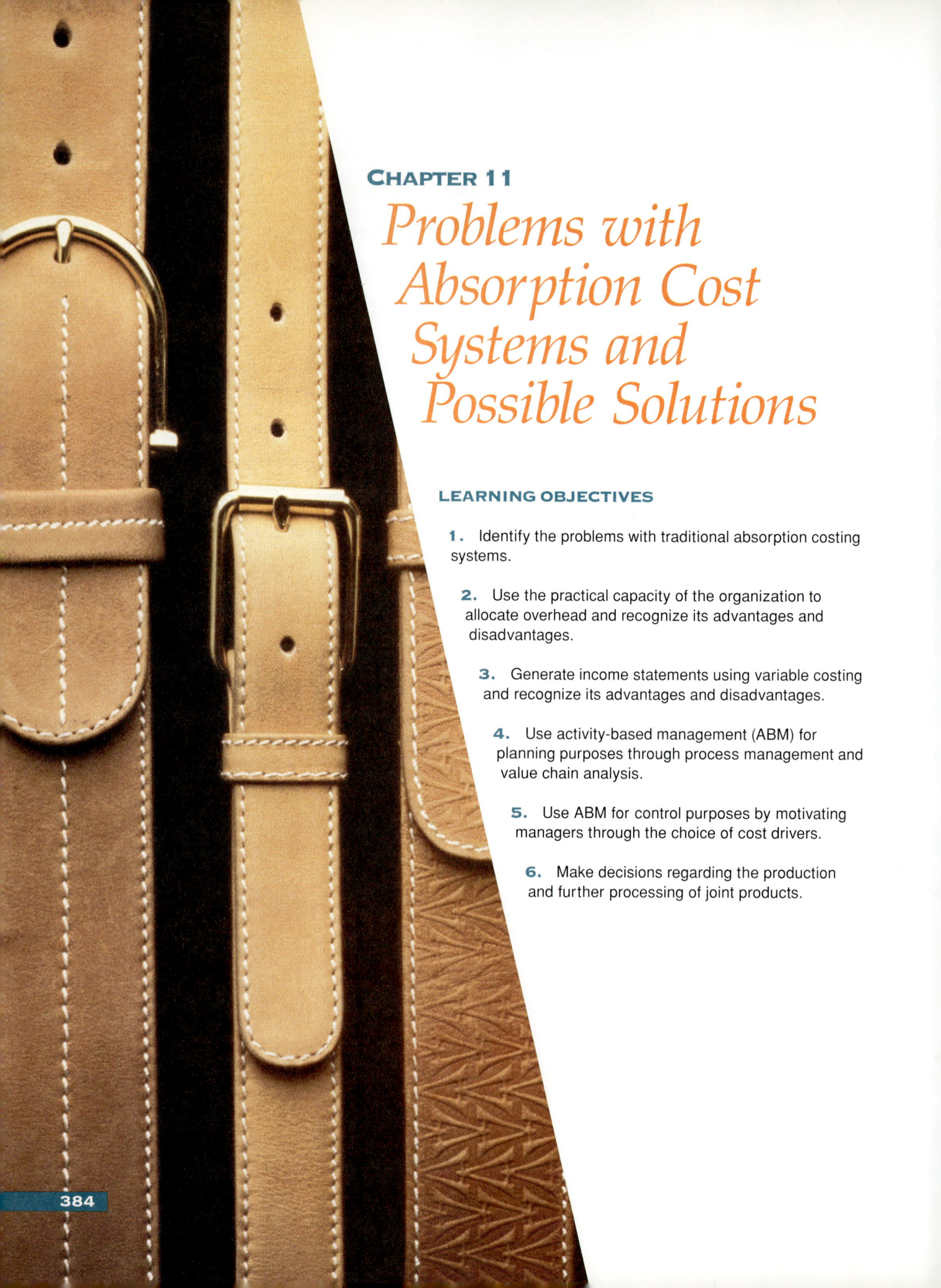

CHAPTER 11
Problems with Absorption Cost Systems and Possible Solutions

LEARNING OBJECTIVES

1. Identify the problems with traditional absorption costing systems.

2. Use the practical capacity of the organization to allocate overhead and recognize its advantages and disadvantages.

3. Generate income statements using variable costing and recognize its advantages and disadvantages.

4. Use activity-based management (ABM) for planning purposes through process management and value chain analysis.

5. Use ABM for control purposes by motivating managers through the choice of cost drivers.

6. Make decisions regarding the production and further processing of joint products.

Santa Fe Belts—II

Roberto Gomez, the owner and president of Santa Fe Belts, is considering several changes to the company. The first change is related to the accounting system used to calculate income for both of the factories. Cynthia McDonald is the manager of the belt factory that makes special belts to order. Her factory uses a job-order system and allocates overhead using direct labor hours as the allocation base. Richard Scott is the manager of the factory that mass produces standard belts and uses process costing to determine product costs. Each manager is responsible for sales and costs and is evaluated based on the profit generated by his or her respective factory. Roberto is especially concerned about pricing decisions made by each of the managers based on existing cost systems. In some cases, belts manufactured by Santa Fe Belts appear to be overpriced and in other cases they appear to be underpriced. Santa Fe Belts is also having a difficult time attracting large customers and both factories are operating below capacity. The factory operated by Richard Scott is also building a considerable inventory of unsold belts.

Roberto has also decided to open a leather-processing operation. The leather-processing operation would buy cowhides directly from meat-processing plants. The cowhides would be tanned, skived (split), embossed, and dyed. The top grain will be used by the factory making special belts, and the split leather will be used by the factory making standard belts. Any excess leather will be sold on the open market.

11.1 Criticisms of Absorption Cost Systems

Chapter 10 describes traditional absorption cost systems. These systems have been widely used for 60 years. Some elements of these systems have been traced back to the industrial revolution. For as long as these systems have been used, they have been criticized for producing misleading information and creating incentives that are inconsistent with maximizing the value of the firm. Despite these criticisms, absorption cost systems are the predominant systems in use in manufacturing firms today. This section analyzes absorption cost systems by examining some common complaints. The following three sections offer alternatives to traditional absorption cost systems: allocating overhead based on practical capacity, variable costing, and activity-based costing. The final section describes a particularly intractable cost allocation problem: joint costs.

As described in Chapter 1, cost systems serve numerous functions, including making planning decisions, control, and external reporting. No single system can satisfy all the requirements of each function. Trade-offs among the requirements for each function must be made. Costing systems are constantly being revised and updated as technology and firms' organizational structures change. Examining the well-known problems in absorption cost systems and the alternative costing systems provides a greater appreciation of how to implement such systems. Also, one must be careful not to reject a particular type of cost system (e.g., absorption costing versus variable costing) just because a particular firm or industry implements it poorly.

Incentive to Overproduce

In absorption cost systems, both variable and fixed costs are included in the product cost. The average cost of the product is determined by dividing the variable and fixed costs of making a product by the number of units produced. This procedure occurs in both job-order and process costing.

The average product cost, however, exhibits some strange qualities that are not necessarily consistent with the opportunity costs of making the product. For example, as long as the variable cost per unit is constant, the average cost per unit decreases as more units are produced. This decrease is due to fixed costs being "spread" over more units. For example, if the fixed costs of operating a hotel are $100,000 per month, the fixed cost per room rented will decline as more rooms are rented. If 5,000 rooms are rented during the month, the fixed cost per

The used car dealer must decide on how many pre-owned cars to carry in inventory. The more used cars, the greater the chance of a sale, because customers are more likely to find what they want. However, the larger inventory must be financed at the bank and a larger lot must be rented.

room rented is $100,000/5,000 or $20/room. If 8,000 rooms are rented during the month, the fixed cost per room rented is $100,000/8,000, or $12.50/room. The decline in fixed costs per unit as the number of units increases has nothing to do with changing costs. It simply reflects the increase in the number of units.

Managers who are evaluated based on the average cost per unit produced, therefore, have an easy way of reducing the average cost per unit. They simply increase the number of units produced as long as there are no capacity constraints. Increasing the number of units produced is not necessarily bad for the organization. As long as all the units are sold and the contribution margin of each unit is positive, the organization should encourage greater production.

A problem arises, however, if not all the units produced can be sold. Excess units in inventory can lead to increased storage and handling costs. There is also the opportunity cost of capital invested in the inventory. Inventory that is held requires a cash investment that could be used elsewhere in the organization to generate profit or eliminate debt. This opportunity cost of holding inventory is not specifically identified in historical accounting systems. Without recognizing the opportunity cost of capital, the net income number will increase as more units are produced and added to the inventory. In Numerical Example 11.1, inventory handling costs are recognized but not the opportunity cost of holding inventory.

NUMERICAL EXAMPLE 11.1

A plant with $1 million of fixed overhead costs makes decks of playing cards with a variable cost per deck of $1.00. The plant only makes playing cards and allocates all the fixed costs to the product by number of decks produced. The firm can sell 200,000 decks a year for $10.00 each. There is no beginning inventory. The plant manager has the opportunity to make 200,000 decks, 220,000 decks, or 240,000 decks. Handling excess inventory costs $.10/deck. Handling costs are expensed in the year they are incurred. Which production level causes the highest reported income for the year?

■ **SOLUTION**

	Production Levels		
	200,000	220,000	240,000
Fixed costs	$1,000,000	$1,000,000	$1,000,000
Variable costs ($1/unit)	200,000	220,000	240,000
Total costs	$1,200,000	$1,220,000	$1,240,000
Average cost per deck	$6/deck	$5.55/deck	$5.17/deck
Revenues (200,000 decks)($10/deck)	$2,000,000	$2,000,000	$2,000,000
Cost of goods sold			
(200,000 decks)($6/deck)	(1,200,000)		
(200,000 decks)($5.55/deck)		(1,110,000)	
(200,000 decks)($5.17/deck)			(1,034,000)
Excess inventory handling costs	0		
(220,000 − 200,000)($.10/deck)		(2,000)	
(240,000 − 200,000)($.10/deck)			(4,000)
Net income	$ 800,000	$ 888,000	$ 962,000

Producing 240,000 decks causes the net income to be higher. Increased production, however, harms the organization because handling costs ($4,000 for the 40,000 decks if 240,000 are made) and opportunity costs of using cash (not reported) are incurred.

The cost of goods sold is lower with excess production because some of the fixed costs are left in the ending inventory account and not treated as an expense. If 240,000 decks of cards are made in Numerical Example 11.1, the average cost of a deck is $5.17, of which $4.17 is a fixed cost. Therefore, the ending inventory contains ($4.17/deck)(240,000 − 200,000 decks), or $166,800 of fixed costs. The cost of the ending inventory including the fixed cost portion won't become an expense until sold in the future. At the time of sale of the inventory in the future, the fixed costs in inventory will become part of the cost of goods sold and will reduce that future income.

Numerical Example 11.1 demonstrates that managers can increase short-term income and harm the organization at the same time. In the long run, income will be lower because the higher inventory costs are passed on to subsequent years, but not all managers will remain with the organization long enough to bear the costs of the earlier overproduction. As long as managers are evaluated based on short-term income and have the potential to leave the organization, there is an incentive to overproduce with absorption costing. Managers who are evaluated based on long-term performance and are committed to the organization for the long run have less incentives to overproduce.

Overproduction is another example of the trade-off that exists between planning and control. The organization would like the manager to use resources efficiently and not overproduce. But because short-term net income is commonly used to evaluate the manager, the manager has an incentive to overproduce.

There are several ways to mitigate the incentive to overproduce. The first is to charge managers large amounts for holding inventory. The net income reported in financial statements does not explicitly consider the opportunity cost of using cash to hold inventory. By "taxing" managers for extra inventory, the incentive to overproduce is reduced.

A second method is a strict senior management policy against adding to or building inventories. Compensation plans can contain a clause that bonuses tied to net income will not be paid if inventories exceed a certain amount. However, such strict constraints are cumbersome and costly to monitor. And in some circumstances, such as new product introduction and unexpected orders, higher inventory levels are preferred by the organization.

A third approach is to choose performance measures other than short-term net income to evaluate managers. Long-term profit, the stock price change, total

Toy companies planning for Christmas inventory levels have difficult decisions to make. People scramble for a successful product like Power Rangers or the latest Barbies when inventory isn't sufficient to meet demand. Other, unsuccessful products languish on store shelves or in warehouses.

sales, or percentage of defects could also be used as performance measures of the manager.

A fourth possibility is to use just-in-time (JIT) production systems to reduce inventory levels. In a JIT system, manufacturing does not typically begin until the part or final product is ordered by a customer. Intermediate products flow immediately from one stage of production to another without waiting in work-in-process inventories. If the production schedule is determined by demand, then the plant manager or product line manager does not have the discretion to set production levels in excess of demand. In essence, a JIT system removes the decision rights from managers to set production levels. These decision rights are replaced by demand-driven market orders. Typically, JIT systems reduce inventories and thus the incentive to overproduce to increase reported profits. JIT systems and their accounting implications are discussed in Chapter 12.

A final option is to change the costing system. Variable costing systems, discussed later in this chapter, reduce the incentive to overproduce.

Santa Fe Belts—II (continued)

Roberto Gomez realizes that some of his problems at Santa Fe Belts are due to the existing management accounting systems. In particular, the increase in the size of ending inventory at the standard belt factory appears to be due to Richard Scott's incentive pay and the way the income is calculated. Richard Scott receives a bonus if the factory generates profit greater than $200,000. This profit number has been more difficult to achieve in recent years, but Richard has managed to make the benchmark each year and receive the bonus. But each year the unsold inventory at the end of the year has increased. The increase in inventory has added some storage costs to the factory but has also allowed more fixed costs to be recorded as part of inventory rather than as an expense. Richard appears to make just enough excess inventory to raise income sufficiently to make his bonus. Roberto decides that Richard has performed the rest of his duties well and doesn't deserve to be fired for this sleight of hand (pen?). In the future, however, Roberto decides to constrain Richard's decision rights by limiting the amount of ending inventory Richard's factory is allowed to hold.

Underuse of Allocation Base Used to Allocate Fixed Costs

In absorption costing systems, fixed and variable overhead costs are allocated to products through an allocation base. The allocation of overhead costs simulates a tax on the allocation base. Managers who are evaluated based on product costs will use less of the allocation base because allocated costs increase product costs and act as a tax on the manager.

The organization, however, may not benefit from the reduced usage of the allocation base. Cost allocations lead to good planning decisions if the allocated costs approximate the opportunity costs of using the allocation base. Fixed cost allocations to products through the usage of allocation bases are unlikely to approximate the opportunity costs of using the indirect resources. By definition, fixed costs of the indirect resource do not change with the usage of the allocation base. For example, the computing center may use the number of computer network terminals as an allocation base for allocating computer center costs to other departments. The computing center costs, however, contain fixed costs that do not change with the number of terminals. Yet those fixed costs are allocated to departments by the number of terminals. Therefore, the allocated cost of having another terminal is greater than the opportunity cost of having the computing center purchase and support another terminal. If the allocated cost is too high, departments will compromise their operations by having too few computer network terminals. The following numerical example demonstrates this problem.

NUMERICAL EXAMPLE 11.2

The expected fixed costs of operating the computing center are $1,000,000 per year. The computer center has excess capacity. The expected variable costs, which reflect the opportunity costs of additional terminals, are $5,000 per terminal. The number of terminals in each department is used to allocate the computing center costs. The application rate, based on expected usage of 200 terminals, is [$1,000,000 + (200)($5,000)]/200, or $10,000 per terminal. The engineering department estimates the following benefits of having terminals in the engineering department:

Number of Terminals	Expected Benefits	Marginal Benefits
1	$15,000	$15,000
2	27,000	12,000
3	35,000	8,000
4	41,000	6,000
5	44,000	3,000

What number of terminals would the engineering department choose if the allocation rate of $10,000 per terminal is used? What is the net loss to the organization of using $10,000 per terminal as the application rate instead of the opportunity cost per terminal?

■ **SOLUTION** The engineering department will only use 2 terminals because the marginal benefit of using the third terminal is $8,000, which is less than the allocated cost. To maximize the profit of the organization, the engineering department should be using 4 terminals because the marginal benefit of using the fourth terminal ($6,000) is still greater than the opportunity cost ($5,000). The additional benefit of having the third and fourth terminals in the engineering department is $41,000 − $27,000, or $14,000. The additional opportunity cost of having 2 additional terminals is ($5,000)(2), or $10,000. The net loss of not having the additional 2 terminals is $14,000 − $10,000, or $4,000.

Misleading Product Costs

If the allocation of fixed costs does not represent the opportunity costs of using the allocation base, product costs calculated by the absorption costing system will not approximate the opportunity cost of making the products. If product costs from the accounting system do not represent opportunity costs, managers using those reported product costs are likely to misprice products and choose inappropriate product mixes.

A common example of misusing product costs from full absorption cost systems is the death spiral. The **death spiral** occurs when an organization begins to drop products because the full cost of the product is greater than its price. Once the product is dropped, the fixed overhead that was previously allocated to the dropped product is redistributed to the remaining products. This redistribution may lead to other products appearing to be unprofitable because of the increased overhead the products must bear. When these products are dropped, more overhead is again allocated to the remaining products. And so the cycle continues until the organization has no profitable products left. Numerical Example 11.2 describes the death spiral.

NUMERICAL EXAMPLE 11.3

A company makes two types of refrigerators—compact and full size. Fixed overhead costs are allocated based on direct labor dollars. The product profitability of each product is:

	Compact	Full Size
Revenues	$500,000	$1,000,000
Direct costs	(300,000)	(450,000)
Fixed costs	(240,000)	(360,000)
Profit	($ 40,000)	$ 190,000

Management decides to drop the compact model because it is unprofitable. What is the impact on the profitability of the full-size model?

■ **SOLUTION** By dropping the compact model, all the fixed overhead is shifted to the full-size refrigerator. Its profitability is now:

	Full Size
Revenues	$1,000,000
Direct costs	(450,000)
Fixed costs	(600,000)
Profit	($ 50,000)

Absorption costing systems do not necessarily lead to calculated product costs that differ from the opportunity costs of making the product. The allocation of fixed costs could approximate opportunity costs if there is a forgone opportunity of using the resource generating fixed costs. For example, a facility that causes fixed costs could have an alternative use. If the facility is operating at capacity, there is the possibility that there are alternative uses of the facility that are profitable and have not been utilized because of limited space. In this case, the allocation of the fixed costs could lead to more accurate product costs by representing the opportunity cost of not being able to use the facility for an alternative purpose.

Alternatives to Traditional Absorption Costing Systems

Because of many of the previously described criticisms of absorption costing systems, alternative procedures have been suggested and are becoming increasingly popular. These procedures have been developed to overcome specific problems in making planning and control decisions. In some cases, however, designing a system to improve planning decisions can have an adverse effect on control decisions and vice versa. The next three sections of the chapter describe three alternatives to the traditional costing systems: (1) allocating overhead based on practical capacity, (2) variable costing, and (3) activity-based costing.

CONCEPT REVIEW

1. Why is there an incentive to overproduce with a traditional absorption costing system?

2. What alternatives are available to discourage overproduction?
3. Why does the allocation of fixed costs lead to underuse of its allocation base?
4. What causes the death spiral?

SANTA FE BELTS—II (CONTINUED)

> Pricing products has been a difficult problem at the factory making specialized belts. In general, Cynthia McDonald makes bids 20% above fixed and variable costs. The direct material costs of the leather and the buckle have been fairly easy to estimate. The direct labor costs are less clear because some of the labor requirements on new designs are difficult to estimate. The overhead costs are the real problem, however. Presently, overhead is added to the product cost based on the estimated number of direct labor hours. But the different belts tend to use different overhead resources, so using a single allocation base appears to be questionable. Cynthia is winning very few bids on belts that require considerable direct labor relative to other resources.
>
> Also, managers within the factory tend to be reluctant to hire more workers. Instead, the managers are clamoring for more machines to take the place of workers. These machines, however, are very expensive. Cynthia feels that direct labor is more cost effective than machines.

11.2 Allocating Overhead Based on Practical Capacity

In Chapter 10 the predetermined application rate for overhead is calculated by dividing the expected overhead costs by the expected usage of the allocation base. By using the expected usage of the allocation base, the total overhead allocated to products should approximate the total actual overhead.

An alternative to a full absorption costing system is a partial absorption costing system. Under this system, all variable overhead is allocated to products, but only the fixed cost of overhead resources used are allocated to products. The fixed costs of unused overhead resources (excess capacity) are treated as expenses of the period and do not become part of the product costs. Allocating overhead based on capacity used is achieved by calculating a fixed cost application rate by dividing the expected fixed overhead costs by the practical capacity of the allocation base. The **practical capacity** is the maximum level of operations that can be achieved without increasing costs due to congestion. For example, the practical capacity of a paper mill operating 24 hours a day is estimated to be 2,000 tons per week. The paper mill could produce 2,300 tons per week by increasing the speed of the machines, but that would lead to much higher maintenance and replacement costs.

The practical capacity of the allocation base occurs when general operations are at practical capacity. For example, if the allocation base for fixed overhead costs is direct labor hours, the application rate would be calculated by dividing the expected fixed overhead costs by the number of direct labor hours that would occur if the factory were operating at practical capacity.

Allocating fixed overhead costs by an application rate using the practical capacity of the allocation base will generally cause fixed overhead costs to be

Allocating Overhead Based on Practical Capacity 393

The practical capacity of this Golden Gate ferry depends on weather conditions and length of trip. The same ferry can carry more passengers for short hauls in calm waters. In open seas, however, fewer passengers can be carried and more safety equipment is needed. Increasing capacity requires either a larger ferry or more ferries.

underabsorbed. The capacity level of the allocation base is generally larger than the expected level, so the application rate will be smaller. A smaller application rate leads to less overhead being allocated. The proportion of fixed costs allocated to products to expected fixed costs is equal to the proportion of actual usage of the allocation base to the practical capacity of the allocation base. This relationship can be seen in the following equations:

$$\frac{\text{Application}}{\text{rate}} = \frac{\text{Expected fixed overhead}}{\text{Practical capacity of allocation base}}$$

$$\frac{\text{Allocated}}{\text{fixed costs}} = \left(\frac{\text{Application}}{\text{rate}}\right) \times \left(\frac{\text{Actual usage of}}{\text{allocation base}}\right)$$

Combining these two equations and rearranging:

$$\frac{\text{Allocated fixed costs}}{\text{Expected fixed overhead}} = \frac{\text{Actual usage of allocation base}}{\text{Practical capacity of allocation base}}$$

This equation indicates that the proportion of allocated fixed costs equals the proportion of practical capacity used. Any fixed cost that is not allocated is the cost of having excess capacity. The unallocated overhead is not allocated to the products but treated as a separate period expense item.

NUMERICAL EXAMPLE 11.4

The fixed costs of operating a furniture factory are primarily due to the cost of the facility. The expected and actual annual cost of the facility is $200,000. The fixed cost of the facility of 20,000 square feet is allocated to the manufacture of chairs and tables based on the square footage used to make and assemble those products. The manufacture of chairs uses 10,000 square feet. The manufacture of tables uses 4,000 square feet. And 6,000 square feet is unoccupied. What is the application rate using capacity square footage? How much of the fixed costs are allocated to chairs and tables and how much is treated as the cost of excess capacity?

■ **SOLUTION** The application rate is:

$200,000/20,000 square feet = $10/square foot

Cost Object	Usage of Square Footage	Application Rate	Allocation
Chairs	10,000 sq. ft.	$10/sq. ft.	$100,000
Tables	4,000 sq. ft.	$10/sq. ft.	40,000
Excess capacity	6,000 sq. ft.	$10/sq. ft.	60,000
Totals	20,000 sq. ft.		$200,000

The $60,000 allocated to unused capacity is a period expense.

Using the practical capacity of the allocation base to determine the application rate has several advantages. The product costs generated from this system are probably closer to the opportunity cost than the traditional system because the cost of having excess capacity, which is not an opportunity cost of making the products, is not assigned to the products. Some fixed costs are still allocated to the products, however, and those allocated fixed costs may not represent opportunity costs of making the product.

A second advantage is that fixed costs allocated to products will not change much with different levels of operations. The denominator of the application rate is the capacity of the allocation base, which will not change unless the capacity is changed. A decision to drop one product would not affect fixed costs allocated to another product. The organization should not fall victim to the death spiral if the capacity is used as a basis for allocating fixed costs.

A third advantage is having a measure of the cost of unused capacity. Under the traditional absorption costing system, the cost of unused capacity is included in the product cost and not easily identified. Knowledge about the cost of unused capacity is useful in making decisions to change capacity.

There are some disadvantages with using practical capacity to allocate fixed costs. This procedure does not alleviate the incentive to overproduce. By producing more units and using more of the allocation base, managers can shift costs allocated to unused capacity (which is an expense) to product costs, which become an asset if unsold during the period. Managers who are evaluated based on short-run profit will have incentives to increase income by overproducing.

Managers will also tend to underuse the allocation base even if only some fixed costs are being allocated. Once fixed overhead costs have been incurred to start operations, the usage of the allocation base is taxed at a higher rate than the opportunity cost of using the overhead resource. Allocation rates that are higher than the opportunity cost of using the indirect resource will cause managers to use the indirect resource less than they would if the opportunity cost of using the indirect resource were allocated. This problem was described in Numerical Example 11.2.

CONCEPT REVIEW

1. How are application rates calculated using practical capacity?
2. What portion of the fixed overhead is allocated to products when application rates are calculated using practical capacity?
3. What are the advantages and disadvantages of using practical capacity to allocate fixed costs?

Santa Fe Belts—II (continued)

Cynthia McDonald has another problem. As she loses business because certain bids are too high, she must reduce the number of workers. The fixed costs of the facility, however, are allocated based on the number of direct labor hours. Therefore, the application rate is rising, thereby raising the bids for new orders even higher. Cynthia is worried that she will continue to lose business and the application rate will become even higher. Roberto Gomez has suggested that she use the practical capacity of direct labor hours to calculate the application rate. This will prevent the application rate from rising if the level of operations is reduced. Alternatively, maybe Cynthia shouldn't base her bids on costs, or at least not on the fixed overhead costs.

11.3 Variable Costing

The cost of a product under **variable costing** only includes the variable costs of making the product. The variable costs include direct material, direct labor, and variable overhead. The fixed overhead costs are treated as period costs and expensed in the period incurred. Therefore, the difference between absorption costing and variable costing is the treatment of fixed manufacturing costs: fixed costs are included as part of product costs under absorption costing and written off as period expenses under variable costing.

There are many advantages to variable costing. The variable cost per unit approximates the opportunity cost of making another unit if the organization is operating below capacity. This information is useful in pricing and product mix decisions. Prices above the variable cost per unit provide a positive contribution margin. The contribution margin per unit (price less variable cost per unit) is also used to ration scarce resources among products. Organizations prefer to make and sell products with higher contribution margins per unit given constraints in the production process.

Variable costing also reduces the dysfunctional incentive to overproduce. With all fixed costs treated as period expenses, increased production will not spread the fixed costs across more units and allow fixed costs to reside in the inventory account at the end of the period. Additional inventory will have little effect on the profit. The incremental cost of making additional units will approximately equal the recorded inventory cost.

NUMERICAL EXAMPLE 11.5

A factory making electric fans has estimated and actual fixed costs of $50,000 and variable cost per unit of $6. The allocation base is the number of units produced. The factory sales price of the electric fan is $10 per unit. There is no beginning inventory. During the year the factory makes and sells 20,000 electric fans. The manager of the factory has the opportunity to make another 5,000 units the last month of the year, but those 5,000 units cannot be sold this year. What is the profit of the factory with and without the additional 5,000 units under the absorption and variable costing systems?

■ **Solution** Under the absorption costing system without the additional 5,000 units, the application rate is [$50,000 + ($6/unit)(20,000 units)]/20,000 units, or $8.50/unit. The profit is:

Sales ($10/unit)(20,000 units)	$200,000
Cost of goods sold ($8.50/unit)(20,000 units)	(170,000)
Profit	$ 30,000

Under the absorption costing system with the additional 5,000 units, the application rate is [$50,000 + ($6/unit)(25,000 units)]/25,000 units, or $8.00/unit. The profit is:

Sales ($10/unit)(20,000 units)	$200,000
Cost of goods sold ($8.00/unit)(20,000 units)	(160,000)
Profit	$ 40,000

The cost of the ending inventory of 5,000 units is ($8.00/unit)(5,000 units), or $40,000.

Under the variable costing system without the additional 5,000 units, the application rate is the variable cost of $6/unit and fixed costs are expensed. The profit is:

Sales ($10/unit)(20,000 units)	$200,000
Cost of goods sold ($6.00/unit)(20,000 units)	(120,000)
Fixed costs	(50,000)
Profit	$ 30,000

Under the variable costing system with the additional 5,000 units, the application rate is still the variable cost of $6/unit and fixed costs are expensed. The profit is still:

Sales ($10/unit)(20,000 units)	$200,000
Cost of goods sold ($6.00/unit)(20,000 units)	(120,000)
Fixed costs	(50,000)
Profit	$ 30,000

The cost of making the additional 5,000 units is ($6/unit)(5,000 units), or $30,000, which is recorded as the ending inventory cost.

Numerical Example 11.5 indicates that the profit under both absorption and variable costing is the same when there is no beginning or ending inventory. When ending inventory is added, the variable costing method still reports the same income, but the absorption costing system has a higher income because some of the fixed costs are allocated to the ending inventory cost. The fixed costs allocated to the ending inventory become cost of goods sold the next period. Absorption costing just postpones the expense. Therefore, absorption costing may cause a lower profit in the next period depending on the amount of ending inventory the next period.

A variable costing system will also not have fluctuating product costs as the output volume changes. The product costs are the variable costs, which should not vary with normal fluctuations in output. The absorption costing system, on the other hand, causes the product cost to be an average cost, which will decline with greater output as fixed costs are spread over more units.

The disadvantages of variable costing include misleading product costs if there is an opportunity cost of using fixed overhead resources. Overhead resources have positive opportunity costs if there are alternative uses of those resources and those opportunity costs should be included in the cost of the product. The allocation of fixed costs provides a method of representing the opportunity cost of using the fixed overhead resources. If, however, the cost of fixed overhead resources is sunk and without alternative use, then the variable cost more closely approximates the opportunity cost of making the product.

If managers are evaluated based on product costs and are not responsible for fixed overhead costs, managers will tend to overuse the overhead resources generating the fixed costs. Managers will avoid using variable overhead resources, which affect product costs, and attempt to use fixed overhead resources instead. This substitution will lead to dysfunctional behavior for the whole organization if there is an opportunity cost in using those fixed overhead resources. For example, facility costs are often considered fixed. If these fixed costs are not allocated to managers, managers will want to use more space because the space is free to them. But space is probably not free to the whole organization. Extra space could be rented or sold.

An implementation problem with variable costing is the choice of allocation base to allocate variable overhead costs. In Numerical Example 11.5, the allocation base is the output measure of number of units produced. If multiple products are made in the factory and common variable overhead resources are used, then some input measure such as direct labor hours is commonly used as an allocation base. As long as only one input variable is used as an allocation base, overhead can be classified as variable or fixed with respect to that allocation base. If multiple allocation bases are used, however, the definition of variable and fixed becomes less clear. For example, batch-level costs are fixed with respect to the number of units or other unit-level costs but vary with the number of batches and allocation bases such as number of set-ups. These definition problems become more obvious when different levels of commonality are recognized in activity-based costing, which is discussed in the next section.

Variable costing attracted much attention in the 1950s and 1960s. Some companies experimented with it, and some are still using it but only for internal reports. Absorption costing remains the predominant method of costing in manufacturing organizations, although all firms treat some overhead as a period expense rather than a product cost. For example, Allegheny Ludlum Steel Company writes off depreciation, plant insurance, property taxes, and factory management salaries to income. These fixed costs are not part of Allegheny Ludlum's product costs and are treated as period costs. Also, research and development costs must be treated as a period cost for external reporting purposes.

The preference for absorption costing implies that the benefits of switching to variable costing for some organizations are not as high as the costs. Most organizations have stayed with absorption costing even when potential problems with planning decisions and control exist. Today, however, many organizations are considering the change from a traditional absorption costing system to a different absorption costing system called *activity-based costing (ABC)*. The next section examines the advantages and disadvantages of using ABC for planning decisions and control.

CONCEPT REVIEW

1. How are fixed costs treated with variable costing?
2. What are the advantages of using variable costing?
3. Why is variable costing not more widely used?

SANTA FE BELTS—II (CONTINUED)

Cynthia McDonald feels that the shift to practical capacity to calculate the application rate isn't sufficient to deal with her pricing problem. The fixed costs of her facility are sunk and there are no alternative uses of the facility. Therefore, the relevant costs in making the pricing decision are the variable costs. By estimating product costs based on their variable costs, she can lower her bids and become more competitive. Any job that provides revenues

> greater than its variable costs has a positive contribution margin and should be pursued. The problem with variable costing in the specialty belts factory, however, is that the notion does not capture the diverse use of overhead resources used by the different types of belts made in the factories.

11.4 Activity-Based Costing/ Activity-Based Management

Activity-based costing (ABC) is introduced in Chapter 4 as a method of estimating product and service costs for planning purposes. To estimate product and service costs, activities that cause overhead costs are identified and cost pools accumulate the costs associated with each activity. Cost drivers are then chosen to reflect the cause of the cost of the overhead activity. An application rate is estimated for each cost driver and used to trace activity costs to the products or services.

ABC also recognizes that some overhead costs vary with number of units produced (unit-level), other overhead costs vary with the number of batches (batch-level), and another group of overhead costs vary with the number of different products (product-level). And some costs are fixed unless the size of the facility is changed (facility-level). The identification of overhead activities and the choice of cost drivers should recognize these different levels.

NUMERICAL EXAMPLE 11.6

The Color Company makes stained glass windows. The process begins with a design. Colored glass is then cut to the specifications of the design and soldered together. There are set-up costs of changing from making one type of window to another type. The expected costs of the company are:

Direct labor (cutting and soldering at $10/hour)	$100,000
Direct materials (glass and solder)	10,000
Set-ups	8,000
Design	30,000
Purchasing and inventory	20,000
Factory rental	50,000
Total	$218,000

Each stained glass window uses approximately two hours of direct labor and $2 of direct materials. Application rates for the other costs are:

Set-ups	$40/set-up
Design	$1,000/design
Purchasing and inventory	$2/direct material dollar (DM$)
Factory rental	$5/square footage dedicated to the product

What level is each of the four overhead accounts? What is the cost of 200 stained glass windows of a particular type that require 3 set-ups, 1 design, and 400 square feet?

■ **SOLUTION** The set-ups are batch level, the design is product level, the purchasing and inventory is unit level, and the factory rental appears to be facility level. The cost of the 200 units of the particular type of stained glass window is:

Direct labor ($10/hour)(2 DLH/unit)(200 units)	$4,000
Direct materials ($2/unit)(200 units)	400
Set-ups (3 set-ups)($40/set-up)	120
Design (1 design)($1,000/design)	1,000
Purchasing and inventory ($2/DM$)($400)	800
Factory rental ($5/DLH)(400 square feet)	2,000
Total	$8,320

The reason for using ABC in Numerical Example 11.6 is to obtain a more accurate estimate of the cost of making a product or supplying a service. But ABC has other planning and control implications. The control and planning implications of ABC are frequently described as **activity-based management (ABM)**. This section identifies the attributes of ABM that affect planning decisions and control.

Planning Decisions through Activity-Based Management

Many different planning decisions can be improved through ABM. In Chapter 4, improved product cost measurement through ABC allowed for superior pricing and product mix decisions. But there is more to ABM than just measuring product costs. ABM allows managers to have a much better understanding of the activities being performed in the organization. With a better understanding of the activities in an organization, managers can make changes to allow the organization to operate more efficiently. Improved efficiency and lower costs can occur through a better understanding of the relationship of activities within the organization and identifying activities that don't add value to the organization.

Understanding Complex Organizations with ABM

As organizations grow and provide more products and services, the nature of the organization becomes much more complex. Relationships among the different parts of the organization are less obvious. One manager's decision can have an unpredictable ripple effect throughout the organization. For example, an engineer's decision to alter the design of a product will have some effect on how materials are purchased and how the product is manufactured. As organizations become more complex, they become more difficult to manage because interdependencies become less obvious. One role of a management accounting system is to identify and communicate the "cause-and-effect" relations within an organization. In other words, if a manager makes a decision, what are the costs and benefits imposed on other parts of the organization? If these cause-and-effect relations can be identified and the cost allocation system reflects those relations, planning decisions can be improved. For example, if an engineer knows the purchasing and manufacturing costs of making a design change, the engineer could make a better decision by trading off different costs.

Improving a product design to make a cost-effective product is one example of using ABM to improve efficiency. ABM can also be used to evaluate suppliers and customers. Suppliers and customers affect the activities of the organization and create costs within the organization. A good ABM

This stained glass craftsman makes many different kinds of stained glass windows. How would you estimate the cost of each window?

system will identify the costs associated with specific suppliers and customers and allow managers to make better choices with respect to suppliers and customers.

ABM is also consistent with process management. **Process management** focuses on the activities performed by an organization. The organizational structure is designed around these processes. Process management emphasizes continuous improvement in the efficiency of operating processes.

To implement an ABM system, an understanding of the relationships within the organization is necessary. Activities that cause overhead costs and their corresponding cost drivers can only be identified with a careful analysis of the operations of the organization. Once in place, however, ABM not only allocates costs but also provides information about the consequences of different managerial decisions.

NUMERICAL EXAMPLE 11.7

An apple producer is considering the automation of the grading of apples. Apples are graded based on size, color, and bruises. Presently, the apples pass on a conveyor belt before four employees. The employees manually divert the apples to their proper destination. A scanning machine, however, can be rented for $70,000 per year and be operated by a single individual. Employees are paid $20,000 per year. If relationships with other organizational activities are ignored, should the grading process be automated? What other organizational activities are likely to be affected by automating the grading process?

■ **SOLUTION** By converting to the scanning machine, the organization can save by laying off three employees (one would have to remain to operate the machine). The costs savings would be (3)($20,000), or $60,000. These cost savings are less than the rental cost, so the company should not automate the grading process if other activities are ignored.

Other activities, however, are potentially affected by the change and should be considered. For example, the scanning machine might be able to operate faster and decrease the overall process time of the apples. The scanning machine may be more accurate and

ABC can be used to identify the value-added activities to manufacture this UPS electric car. Because new technology is required, research and development and engineering are important value-added activities.

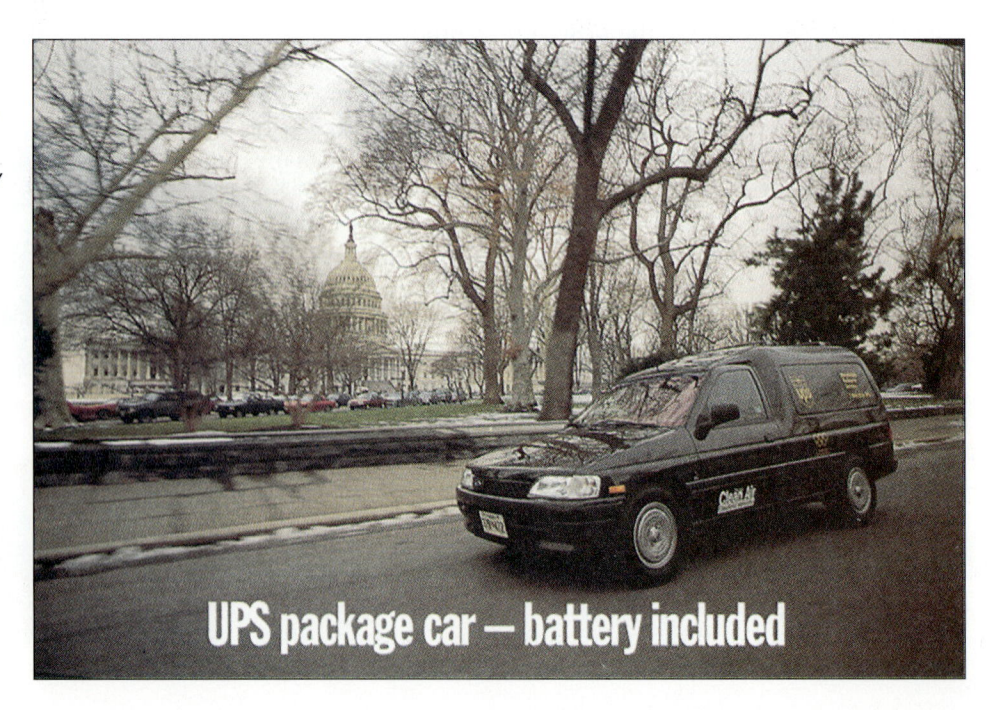

UPS package car — battery included

reduce the need for additional quality control. Space requirements should also be considered. The scanning machine would also affect maintenance activities and utility costs. Reduced employees could simplify work in the personnel office and floor management. All of these activities should be considered in this decision. ABM would allow for the measurement of the effect of automating the scanning process on other activities.

The Value Chain and ABM

The value chain of an organization is a sequence of activities that are necessary to satisfy the demands of the organization's customers. These critical activities add value to the product or service of the organization. Some value chains for common organizations are described in Figure 11.1.

The purpose of analyzing the value chain of an organization is to identify the key aspects of operations and eliminate unnecessary costs. Those activities that are in the value chain are called **value-added activities.** Value-added activities are critical to the success of the organization and should be enhanced.

Most organizations also have **non–value-added activities.** Non–value-added activities are activities that do not directly benefit the customer. Non–value-added activities include storing and moving inventory, security, downtime, and some meetings. Because non–value-added activities do not directly benefit customers, they should be seen as opportunities for cost savings.

ABM provides direction in analyzing the value chain and eliminating non–value-added activities. In setting up an ABM system, the value-added and non–value-added activities are identified. The ABM system allocates the cost of all of the activities to the different products and services through the use of cost drivers. To discourage non–value-added activities, large application rates can be established for the cost drivers of the non–value-added activities. The additional "tax" on the non–value-added activities motivates managers to discover methods of minimizing non–value-added activities and focusing on the value-added activities.

> **WHAT'S HAPPENING**
>
> An ABC system often identifies accounting as an overhead activity with its own cost pool and cost driver. Some claim that accounting is a non–value-added activity. What is accounting's claim to adding value?

Control Decisions through Activity-Based Management

Activity-based management (ABM) also has control implications. Although an ABM system is designed to reflect the "cause and effect" of costs of activities for better planning decisions, an ABM system will also affect management behavior if the ABM system is used for performance evaluation and rewards. The most direct control implication is through the choice of cost drivers described in the next section. An ABM system may also be misused by managers attempting to affect their performance evaluation. These control implications must also be considered in a decision to convert to ABM.

Manufacturing
Research and development → Engineering → Purchasing → Production → Marketing → Distribution → Customer service

Retail Store
Purchasing → Marketing and sales → Customer service

Health Services
Diagnosis → Treatment → Rehabilitation

Restaurants
Purchasing → Processing and cooking food → Customer service

FIGURE 11.1
Value Chains of Different Organizations

Choosing Cost Drivers and Motivating Managers with ABC

ABC systems are generally designed to achieve more accurate product costs. The cost drivers are chosen to reflect the cause of overhead activity costs. The use of a cost driver by a product or department results in an additional amount of overhead being allocated to that product or department. The allocation of overhead through a cost driver, therefore, implies an internal tax system. Managers responsible for a product must make choices about the use of overhead resources. If use of an overhead resource is tied to a particular cost driver, such as number of setups, managers will be more reluctant to use that particular overhead resource. Managers will generally attempt to shift their use of overhead resources to avoid more expensive cost drivers. Overhead resources that have no associated cost drivers will tend to be overused by managers.

The effect of choosing cost drivers on management behavior must be considered in the design of an ABM system. If organizations want to control managers' use of certain overhead resources, cost drivers related to the use of those overhead resources should be chosen. Ideally, the application rate for a particular cost driver should be equal to the opportunity cost of using the cost driver. If the application rate is lower than the opportunity cost, managers tend to use the cost driver too much. If the application rate is higher than the opportunity cost, managers tend to use the cost driver too little.

A comparison with traditional absorption costing systems indicates that an ABM system is more capable of equating application rates to opportunity costs. By using multiple cost pools and cost drivers and identifying unit, batch, product, and facility costs, an organization is more likely to find cost drivers that reflect the cause of the overhead cost pools.

An organization may intentionally choose cost drivers with application rates that differ from the opportunity cost of using the cost driver. Management may choose to overtax or undertax certain cost drivers to achieve other goals of the organization such as reducing product proliferation or the use of direct labor. If a company wants to encourage managers to automate processes, direct labor with a high application rate may be used as a cost driver to discourage the use of direct labor. The organization, however, must recognize that the overtaxing of direct labor will eventually lead to the underuse of direct labor and inefficient operations.

NUMERICAL EXAMPLE 11.8

A maker of circuit boards can insert parts on the circuit board by hand or by machine. Some parts require less direct costs if inserted by hand and other parts require less direct costs if inserted by machine. On average, manual insertion requires 5 seconds per part and machine insertion requires 0.1 seconds per part. The company presently uses both manual and machine insertion and encourages managers to use the method with the lowest direct cost. The company is now thinking about introducing an overhead allocation system that has both direct labor hours and machine hours as cost drivers and having managers make decisions based on full (direct and indirect) costs. What will happen if the following application rates are used: $20/direct labor hour and $100/machine hour?

■ **SOLUTION** The reported cost of inserting each part manually will increase by ($20/direct labor hour)(5 seconds/60 seconds)(1 minute/60 minutes) = $0.0278/part. The cost of inserting each part with a machine will increase by ($100/direct labor hour)(0.1 seconds/60 seconds)(1 minute/60 minutes) = $0.0028/part. The direct labor application rate makes manual insertion more costly on average and will encourage managers to use the machine insertion more frequently.

Average Costs, the Incentive to Overproduce, and ABC

In a traditional absorption costing system with a single, unit-level allocation base, variable costs are the costs that vary with the number of units produced and all other costs are considered fixed. The average cost is the sum of the variable and fixed costs divided by the number of units produced. As long as there is sufficient capacity and the variable cost per unit does not change as volume increases, the average cost per unit declines with the production of additional units. The decline in the average cost per unit is due to the fixed costs being spread over more units. As seen in this chapter, the decline in average cost with more units produced provides the manager with an incentive to overproduce.

ABC has the advantage over a traditional absorption costing system by identifying costs that vary by unit, batch, product, and facility. ABC gives the appearance that all costs are variable, so there is no need to worry about fixed costs. But facility costs are likely to be fixed in the short-run because new facilities are only added or eliminated infrequently. And product and batch costs, by definition, are also fixed with respect to the number of units produced. If an average cost is determined through adding unit, batch, product, and facility costs and dividing by the number of units produced, average costs can be reduced by making more units, especially if they are all in the same batch. Therefore, the incentive to overproduce can also occur under ABC.

NUMERICAL EXAMPLE 11.9

In Numerical Example 11.6, 200 units of a particular type of stained glass window cost:

Direct labor ($10/hour)(400 DLH)	$4,000
Direct materials ($2/unit)(200 units)	400
Set-ups (3 set-ups)($40/set-up)	120
Design (1 design)($1,000/design)	1,000
Purchasing and inventory ($2/DM$)($400)	800
Factory rental ($5/DLH)(400 square feet)	2,000
Total	$8,320

What is the average cost per window? What would be the average cost per window if 400 windows are made with no additional set-ups, designs, or usage of square feet? Instead of using average cost, how should the cost of making 200 additional windows be analyzed using ABC?

■ **SOLUTION** The average cost per window if 200 windows are made is $8,320/200, or $41.60/window. If 400 windows are made, the estimated costs for direct material, direct labor, and purchasing and inventory should double, but the other overhead costs should remain the same. The total costs of making 400 windows should be ($8,320 + $4,000 + $400 + $800), or $13,520. The average cost of 400 windows is $13,520/400, or $33.80/window. The lower average cost does not mean the manager of the product is performing better. The average cost naturally declines when some costs are not unit level. The advantage of ABC is the identification of different levels of overhead costs. The performance of the manager in making 200 additional units of the window should be based on a comparison of the estimated incremental unit-level costs with the actual incremental costs.

Acceptance of ABC

Activity-based costing systems are most likely adopted in plants producing multiple and diverse products with fixed factory overheads as a large fraction of product costs and increased pressure from competitors. Single-product plants have little trouble in computing product costs because all the costs are easily

Product diversity in this Mexican restaurant makes costing of individual entrees difficult. How can ABC help this restaurant remain competitive?

assigned to the single product. Product diversity can arise because of different production volumes (some products run in large numbers and others in small volumes). Product complexity involves some products being simple and others complicated to manufacture. In plants with different product volumes or manufacturing complexities, simple unit-based cost drivers cannot capture the diversity. If fixed factory overhead is a small fraction of total product cost, reallocating a small cost pool using more accurate cost drivers does not cause individual product costs to vary much. Finally, firms facing little competition are able to price their products well above cost and are less concerned about product costs. Having accurate average product costs is more critical if competition is driving prices down to or even below cost. This analysis predicts that activity-based costing systems are *not* expected to be adopted everywhere, nor is their value the same across all plants.

A 1995 study of the use of ABC by 60 executives in 25 manufacturing firms indicates considerable satisfaction with the change to ABC.[1] The 60 executives interviewed indicated a significant improvement in satisfaction with the cost management system after changing to ABC. These executives felt that ABC performed better than their prior system for product costing, cost control, and performance measures. Not all of these firms, however, used ABC as the sole accounting system. Many companies use ABC for supplemental analysis, but don't integrate ABC into the financial reporting system. In the 1995 study mentioned above, companies used ABC for the following purposes:

Process improvement	92%
Product pricing/mix	72%
Product/process designs	48%
Customer profitability	36%
Performance measures	28%
Outsourcing	24%

From this survey we see that most of the interest in activity-based costing is for more accurate product or process cost data for making planning decisions. A central tenet of activity-based costing is that more accurate product or process costs are always preferred to less accurate product or process costs. However, more accurate product cost knowledge can be *less* desirable if it leads to poorer control. Control reasons can cause firms to choose less accurate cost systems. Zytec simplified their cost system to just one cost driver: time to manufacture the product (cycle time). While such a single cost-driver system produces less accurate product costs when compared to multiple cost-driver ABC systems, senior management wanted to focus employee attention on what was believed to be the single most important cost reduction factor in the firm.

Only 28% of the firms using ABC use it for performance measurement. An organization should not change performance measures without changing the rest of the organizational structure (decision rights and rewards). Managers are often reluctant to make changes in the organizational structure because of the uncertain effect on management rewards.

Hitachi, a large Japanese electronics producer, manufactures VCRs in one of its plants. This plant is very heavily automated but continues to allocate overhead based on direct labor, even though the managers know that direct labor does not reflect the cause-and-effect relation between overhead and the overhead cost drivers. The Hitachi managers continue to use direct labor as the allocation base because they are committed to long-term aggressive automation. Taxing direct labor is a way to reduce direct labor and thereby lower production costs.

Hitachi is an example of sacrificing planning for control. The Hitachi managers are willing to accept less precise estimates of product costs for planning decisions because they achieve desirable incentives that further their automation goals.[2]

> **WHAT'S HAPPENING**
>
> The use of ABC is almost nonexistent in Japan. Japan's industry is distinguished by minimal non–value-added activities and cost centers associated with products rather than functions. Why is ABC used less in this economic environment?

CONCEPT REVIEW

1. Why may overproduction occur with ABC?
2. Why is ABC more difficult to implement than a traditional absorption costing system?
3. What is the advantage of identifying the value chain of an organization?
4. Why is ABC not universally accepted?

SANTA FE BELTS—II (CONTINUED)

Cynthia McDonald, the manager of the factory making specialized belts at Santa Fe Belts, feels that activity-based costing (ABC) will solve many of her problems. Her pricing decisions do not formally reflect the different uses of overhead resources by the different types of belts. Many of the overhead costs do not vary with direct labor hours, the current allocation base. To implement ABC, Cynthia must examine her factory in terms of activities. Her first step is to determine the value chain for making and selling the belts. The critical activities in making the belts are cutting, laminating, gluing, beveling edges, dyeing edges, punching holes, making loops, adding the buckle, stitching, and stamping the logo. These activities are followed by distribution and customer service. Cynthia notices that many of the costly activities in the factory are not on the value chain. For example, considerable effort is involved in resetting the machines for each new batch. Also, batches are continually being moved to and from inventory as they wait for the next step in processing. Most administrative costs are also not on the value chain. Cynthia views these non–value-added activities as ripe for cost savings.

To implement product costing through ABC, Cynthia chooses cost drivers for each of the identified activities. Direct labor hours still seem appropriate for some activities, but the costs of some of the machine-intensive activities appear to be more correlated with machine hours. Batch-level costs also exist in terms of setting up machines and customer service costs tend to be product-level costs. Cynthia believes this new ABC system will provide more accurate product costs but still worries about the sunk excess capacity costs. She decides not to allocate capacity-level costs for pricing purposes until the factory increases operations sufficiently to reach capacity.

Cynthia is still not sure about the control problems that may arise from a change to ABC. Some of the departmental managers are worried about the effect of the change in the accounting system on their evaluations. Cynthia decides the safest decision is to use ABC as a supplemental accounting system to aid in pricing. At a later time she can decide whether to replace the existing traditional absorption costing system with ABC for financial reporting.

11.5 Joint Costs

One of the primary reasons for allocating costs to products is to determine more accurate product costs for planning purposes. The ABC system is designed to trace costs from overhead activities to products through the use of cost drivers. The accuracy of the resultant product costs depends on how well the cost drivers capture the cause of the cost of the activity. In some cases, the cost allocations lead to reasonably good approximations of the product cost, and in other cases, less reliance is placed on the cost allocation. This section, however, deals with an extreme case in which the cost allocation is arbitrary and cost allocations should not be used for making planning decisions.

Joint products are produced from a single input. The input is generally some raw material that is split into joint products. For example, hamburger and liver are joint products of a butchered cow. In a mining operation, gold and silver are joint products of the processed ore. Usually, but not always, joint products are produced in fixed proportions, meaning that more gold cannot be produced by producing less silver. The production of joint products is demonstrated in Figure 11.2.

FIGURE 11.2
Production of Joint Products

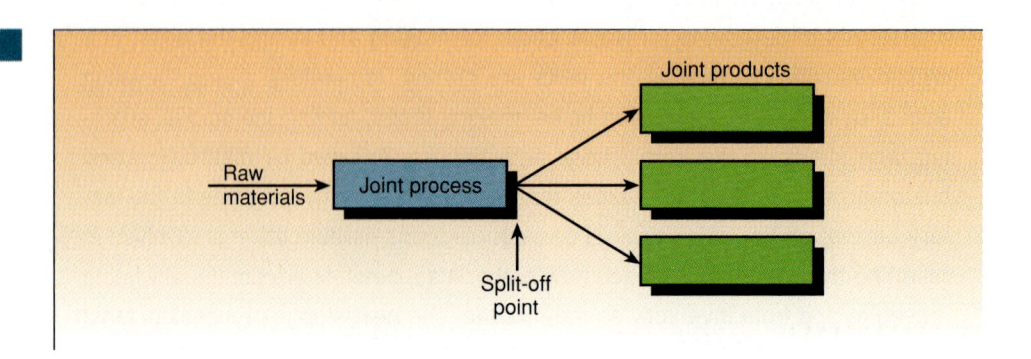

The cost of the input and the cost of processing the input to generate the joint products are called the **joint costs.** The cost of the petroleum and the refining are joint costs of making kerosene, gasoline, tar, and the other joint products that are separated through the distillation process. Joint costs are obviously part of the cost of making joint products, but there are no obvious ways of tracing joint costs to specific joint products. In other words, what part of the cost of a barrel of petroleum can be traced to the gasoline distilled from the petroleum? All of the joint costs are necessary to make each of the joint products. And any incremental joint costs produce all of the joint products.

The inability to trace joint costs to joint products does not mean that joint costs cannot be allocated to joint products. To the extent that joint costs are manufacturing costs, GAAP suggests that these joint costs should be allocated to the joint products for financial reporting purposes. Joint costs may also be allocated for cost reimbursement contracts.

There are many ways to allocate joint costs to joint products. For example, in an oil refinery, petroleum is split into numerous joint products including gasoline, kerosene, and asphalt. The cost of each barrel of petroleum can be allocated to the joint products based on physical measures (weight, volume, BTUs), relative sales value, or net realizable value. These methods are described in the appendix. The important point to remember is, however, that any joint cost allocated to a joint product is arbitrary and should not be used for pricing or product mix decisions.

Why are allocated joint costs arbitrary and useless for planning purposes? In Chapter 2, opportunity costs are identified as the critical costs for making planning decisions. The opportunity cost of making only gasoline from petroleum can't be separated from the opportunity cost of making the other joint products. the opportunity cost of the whole joint process, however, can be determined. In the case of distilling petroleum, the opportunity cost is the forgone benefit of not purchasing the petroleum and using the oil refinery for other purposes. Therefore, a cost/benefit analysis can be performed with respect to the whole joint

From a dairy cow's milk, cream and milk are joint products. Fertilizer is a by-product of the dairy operation.

process. The joint opportunity costs can be compared with the total sales value of the joint products. In other words, the opportunity cost of purchasing and using the oil refinery should be compared with the total revenues generated from selling the gasoline, kerosene, tar, and other joint products.

NUMERICAL EXAMPLE 11.10

Apples are purchased by a company making apple cider for $0.10/kilogram. The apples are crushed and pressed to make the apple cider. The processing costs $0.03/kilogram of apples. Every kilogram of apples generates 700 grams of apple cider and 300 grams of mash. The apple cider is sold for $0.18/kilogram and the mash is sold for $0.02/kilogram as fertilizer. Is the joint process profitable?

■ **SOLUTION** The joint costs are the sum of the raw materials and the processing: $0.10 + $0.03, or $0.13 per kilogram of apples. The benefits are the sum of the revenues generated from all the joint products. Each kilogram of apples creates the following sales value:

Apple cider: ($0.18/kilogram)(700 grams)	$0.126
Mash: ($0.02/kilogram)(300 grams)	0.006
Total sales value per kilogram of apples	$0.132

The sales value is greater than the cost, so the joint process is profitable. Note that this decision is made without the allocation of joint costs.

Opportunity costs can also be used to make decisions following the joint process. Once the joint products are split, there is often a decision of whether to process a joint product further or sell the joint product as it comes out of the joint process. For example, sawdust and lumber are joint products of a lumber company. The lumber company can sell the sawdust or process it further into particle board. The lumber can be sold or processed further into furniture.

The decision to process a joint product further is independent of the allocation of joint costs. At the time of making the decision, the joint costs are sunk. The joint products have already been divided and the joint costs have already been incurred. The decision to process a joint product further is once again based on opportunity costs. The opportunity cost of processing the joint product further is the forgone revenue from selling the unprocessed joint product. The opportunity cost of selling the unprocessed joint product is the net profit forgone of processing the joint product further and selling the processed joint product.

Another way of looking at the problem of processing a joint product further is to compare the incremental costs of further processing with the incremental revenues of selling the processed joint product over selling the unprocessed joint product. For example, the sales price of a ton of sawdust is $200 and the sales price of particle board made from a ton of sawdust is $2,500. The incremental cost of converting a ton of sawdust to particle board is $2,000. Therefore, the incremental revenue ($2,500 − $200 = $2,300) is greater than the incremental costs, so the sawdust should be processed further.

NUMERICAL EXAMPLE 11.11

A salmon processing plant purchases salmon for $1 per pound from a fishing fleet. The processing plant separates the salmon into fillets and "parts." A pound of salmon yields 70% fillets and 30% parts. The separation process costs $0.20/pound of salmon. The fillets an be sold directly after separation or processed further and canned. The parts can

THE STORY OF MANAGERIAL ACCOUNTING

Team Decisions Regarding Implementing ABC

Managerial Accounting is just one of many different book projects ongoing at Irwin Publishing. Many of the other book projects at Richard D. Irwin are specialty books with a much smaller expected demand than *Managerial Accounting*. Presently, overhead costs are allocated to book projects based on total revenues. Why is the *Managerial Accounting* book team pushing Irwin to change to ABC, which would recognize many of the product-level costs related to publishing?

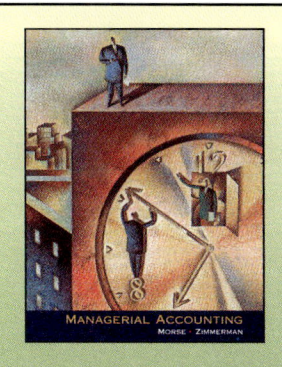

---

be sold directly as fertilizer or processed further into canned cat food. The sales prices and processing costs are:

	Unprocessed Sales Price	Further Process Costs	Processed Sales Price
Fillets	$2.50/lb	$0.50/lb	$4.00/lb
Parts	$0.10/lb	$0.30/lb	$0.35/lb

Which joint products should the salmon processing plant process further?

■ **SOLUTION** The decision should be made based on a comparison of incremental costs and incremental revenues:

	Incremental Costs	Incremental Revenues
Fillets	$0.50/lb	$4.00 − $2.50 = $1.50/lb
Parts	$0.30/lb	$0.35 − $0.10 = $0.25/lb

The fillets should be processed further because the incremental revenues are greater than the incremental costs. The parts should be sold for fertilizer because the incremental revenues of making cat food are less than the incremental costs. Note that the joint costs of buying and separating salmon is not relevant to the decisions regarding further processing.

Joint products are sometimes called **by-products.** By-products are joint products of relatively low value compared to other joint products. By-products may even have a negative value because there may be a cost in disposing of them. Delta Air Lines had considered its cargo operations as a by-product of its passenger service even though the cargo service produced $565 million in revenues.[3] To emphasize the importance of its cargo operations, Delta Airlines has reorganized and made its cargo operations a separate unit. Whether a joint product is called a by-product or joint product, however, should not affect the decisions described in this section. But specifying a joint product as a by-product will have an effect on the cost allocation methods discussed in the appendix.

CONCEPT REVIEW

1. What are joint products and joint costs?
2. Why are allocated joint costs irrelevant for planning decisions?
3. How should the decision to process a joint product further be made?

SANTA FE BELTS—II (CONCLUDED)

The decision to buy cowhides and do the tanning, skiving, and dyeing at Santa Fe Belts was treated positively by the managers of the two factories. Because their bonuses are based on profit, they felt that the cost of the leather used in the belts would be cheaper than purchasing the leather on the open market. Also, one factory used top grain leather and the other factory used split leather, so the two joint products could be used internally.

The problem was deciding how to allocate the joint costs of tanning and skiving the cowhide. Cynthia McDonald felt that using weight as an allocation base would be appropriate, but Richard Scott complained bitterly. He would receive half of the joint costs, but the split leather had a much lower value. Richard suggested the use of sales revenue as the allocation base, but Cynthia did not like that idea because her special belts had a much higher price than the standard belts.

Roberto Gomez decided to set up the tanning, skiving, and dyeing operation as a separate profit center. The new profit center would set a transfer price equal to the market price. Because leather has an active market, the opportunity cost of transferring the leather internally is approximately the market price (ignoring synergies and transaction costs). A transfer price equal to the market price would give all the profit center managers the appropriate incentives for decentralized decision making. Joint cost allocation would still be necessary for financial reporting, but the joint cost allocation would not be used for planning decisions or control.

11.6 Summary

1. **Identify the problems with traditional absorption costing systems.** Traditional absorption costing systems can cause overproduction, underuse of allocation bases, and misleading product costs.

2. **Use the practical capacity of the organization to allocate overhead and recognize its advantages and disadvantages.** The application rate is calculated by dividing fixed costs by the practical capacity of the allocation base. Product costs only include the cost of capacity used. Excess capacity costs are a period expense. Advantages include a product cost that is not affected by changes in levels of production and identifying the cost of unused capacity. Disadvantages include the incentive to overproduce and the underuse of the allocation base.

3. **Generate income statements using variable costing and recognize its advantages and disadvantages.** With variable costing, only variable costs are treated as part of the product cost. Fixed costs are expensed in the period incurred. Variable costing reduces the incentive to overproduce and provides product costs closer to the opportunity cost when there is excess capacity. The disadvantages include the excessive use of fixed overhead resources and the exclusion of fixed opportunity costs in the product cost.

4. **Use activity-based management (ABM) for planning purposes through process management and value chain analysis.** ABM uses an understanding of

the relationships of the various activities or processes that operate within an organization. Process management establishes an organizational structure based on these activities. The value chain is the sequence of activities critical to satisfying the demands of customers. Activities that are not on the value chain provide opportunities for cost savings.

5. **Use ABM for control purposes by motivating managers through the choice of cost drivers.** The choice of cost drivers has an effect on the behavior of managers. Managers who use cost drivers are "taxed" and, therefore, control their use of the cost drivers.

6. **Make decisions regarding the production and further processing of joint products.** A joint process that produces joint products is profitable if the joint costs are less than the sales value of all the joint products. A joint product should be processed further if the incremental revenues are greater than the incremental costs.

KEY TERMS

Activity-based management The use of activity-based costs to make planning decisions and for control.

By-products Joint products of relatively low value compared to other joint products.

Death spiral The process of dropping products without lowering overhead costs.

Joint costs The costs of the input and the processing of the input to generate joint products.

Joint products Products generated from the splitting of a single material input.

Net realizable value method (Appendix) A procedure of dividing joint costs based on the sales value less the finishing costs of the joint products.

Non–value-added activities Activities that do not provide value to the customer.

Physical measure method (Appendix) A procedure of dividing joint costs based on a physical characteristic of the joint products.

Practical capacity The highest rate at which an organization can operate without a rise in congestion.

Process management Creating an organizational structure around activities and attempting to continuously improve those processes.

Relative sales value method (Appendix) A procedure of dividing joint costs based on the gross sales value of the joint products.

Value-added activities Activities that provide value to the customer.

Variable costing Determining product costs based only on the variable cost of making the product.

Appendix: Allocating Joint Costs

Although allocated joint costs should not be used for making planning decisions, external reporting requirements may require joint costs to be allocated to joint products. For example, GAAP suggests allocating joint manufacturing costs to joint products. Also, customers paying for joint products on a cost reimbursement basis would lead to the allocation of joint costs.

The choice of allocation base is arbitrary because no allocation base is closely associated with the joint cost. The following allocation bases, however, are commonly used: physical measure, gross sales value at time of split-off, and net realizable value.

The **physical measure method** is convenient because physical measures such as weight or volume are easily observed. For example, if weight is used to allocate the joint costs of purchasing and butchering a cow, each of the joint products (steaks, roasts, hamburger, cowhide, entrails, and bones) receive joint costs proportional to their weight. One feature of allocating joint costs by physical measure is that joint products that have little value may receive the bulk of the joint costs. In the case of butchering a cow, the value of the bones is relatively small, but given their weight, the bones receive a high proportion of the joint costs. If the allocated joint costs are greater than the value of the bones, the bones will appear to be unprofitable. The profitability of the joint products after joint cost allocation, however, is not relevant in making product mix decisions. A meat-processing plant can't stop producing cow bones.

The **relative sales value method** allocates joint costs of joint products based on the sales value of each of the joint products at the time they are split into separate products. If the relative sales value method is used, the joint products with the higher sales value receive more of the joint costs. In the case of butchering a cow, the steaks receive a higher proportion of the joint cost because their relative sales value is higher. The gross sales value method is less likely than the physical measure method to cause some joint products to be profitable and other products to be unprofitable. On the other hand, market prices used to determine the sales value are often not easily determined and may change over time.

The **net realizable value method** uses the net realizable value of each joint product to allocate joint costs. The net realizable value is the difference between sales revenue and the additional costs required to process the product from the point at which the joint products are split off until they are sold. For example, the meat-processing plant may choose to tan the cowhide to make leather. The net realizable value of the leather is the sales value of the leather less the tanning costs. One feature of the net realizable value method is that all the processed joint products will be either profitable or unprofitable after the allocation of joint costs.

Designating a joint product as a by-product can also lead to different joint cost allocations. One method of treating by-products is to allocate no joint costs to the by-products. All of the joint costs would be allocated to the joint products that are not designated as by-products. For example, a meat-processing company might consider all nonmeat parts of the cow to be by-products. In this case only the steaks, roasts, hamburger, and other meat products receive joint costs by one of the methods previously mentioned. The cowhide, bones, and entrails receive no joint costs.

Another way of dealing with by-products is to allocate joint costs to by-products equal to the net realizable value of the by-products. By definition, the by-products would have a profitability equal to zero. The remaining joint costs would be allocated to the joint products not designated as by-products by one of the methods mentioned previously. Allocating joint costs equal to the by-product's net realizable value is commonly used if the by-product has a negative net realizable value. For example, a by-product of producing electric power from a nuclear plant is spent radioactive fuel rods. These fuel rods have a negative net realizable value because someone must be paid to dispose of them. Allocating joint costs equal to a negative net realizable means that joint costs are increased by the amount of the negative net realizable value. Therefore, the joint costs allocated to the electric power of a nuclear plant will include the cost of disposing of the spent fuel rods.

JOINT COST ALLOCATION EXAMPLE

A processor of chickens pays $1.60 for a three-pound chicken. The cost of killing and processing the chicken into parts is $0.40 per chicken. The processor treats the feathers and entrails as by-products. The feathers can be sold for $0.01 per chicken to a pillow manufacturer. The processor pays someone $.05 per chicken to dispose of the entrails. The remaining parts can be sold without further processing to a cat food manufacturer or cleaned, inspected, and packaged for human consumption. Table 11.1 provides sales prices and costs of the parts per chicken. Allocate the joint costs to the joint products by three methods: weight, the relative sales value method, and the net realizable value method. By-products should receive joint costs equal to their net realizable value.

TABLE 11.1

Sales Prices and Costs of Parts of a Chicken (per Chicken)

Part	Weight	Sales Price for Cat Food	Cost of Cleaning, Inspecting, and Packaging	Sales Price to Grocery Stores	Net Realizable Value
Back	6 oz	$0.10	$0.10	$0.22	$0.12
Fillets	16 oz	0.15	0.20	1.50	1.30
Drumsticks	12 oz	0.12	0.15	0.80	0.65
Wings	4 oz	0.03	0.10	0.30	0.20
Totals	38 oz*	$0.40	$0.55	$2.82	$2.27

*The entrails and the feathers make up the remaining weight

■ **SOLUTION** The incremental revenue from selling to grocery stores is greater than the incremental costs of processing the parts further for each part, so none of the chicken will be sold to the cat food manufacturer. Because the by-products receive joint costs equal to their net realizable value, the joint costs allocated to the remaining joint products are:

Cost of chicken	$1.60
Cost of killing and processing	0.40
Allocated to feathers	(0.01)
Allocated to entrails	0.05
Total	$2.04

Joint Cost Allocation Using Weight:

	Back	Fillets	Drumsticks	Wings
Weight	6 oz	16 oz	12 oz	4 oz
% of total weight (38 oz)	15.79%	42.10%	31.58%	10.53%
Allocated joint costs of $2.04	($0.32)	($0.86)	($0.64)	($0.22)
Further processing costs	(0.10)	(0.20)	(0.15)	(0.10)
Sales price	0.22	1.50	0.80	0.30
Profitability	($0.20)	$0.44	$0.01	($0.02)

Joint Allocation Using Relative Sales Value:

	Back	Fillets	Drumsticks	Wings
Sales value after split-up	$0.10	$0.15	$0.12	$0.03
% of sales value ($.40)	25.00%	37.50%	30.00%	7.50%
Allocated joint costs of $2.04	($0.51)	($0.77)	($0.61)	($0.15)
Further processing costs	(0.10)	(0.20)	(0.15)	(0.10)
Sales price	0.22	1.50	0.80	0.30
Profitability	($0.39)	$0.53	$0.04	$0.05

Joint Allocation Using Net Realizable Value:

	Back	Fillets	Drumsticks	Wings
Net realizable value (NRV)	$0.12	$1.30	$0.65	$0.20
% of total NRV ($2.27)	5.29%	57.27%	28.64%	8.81%
Allocated joint costs of $2.04	($0.11)	($1.17)	($0.58)	($0.18)
Further processing costs	(0.10)	(0.20)	(0.15)	(0.10)
Sales price	0.22	1.50	0.80	0.30
Profitability	$0.01	$0.13	$0.07	$0.02

Note that the net realizable method is the only joint cost allocation method that causes all the joint products to have a positive profit. In general, the net realizable method causes all the joint products to have a positive profit or all the joint products to have a negative profit.

SELF-STUDY PROBLEM

The Hampshire Textile Company makes two types of cloth—cotton and polyester. The company had no beginning inventory and manufactured 300,000 yards of cotton cloth and 500,000 yards of polyester. During the year, the company sold 250,000 yards of cotton cloth for $3/yard and 400,000 yards of polyester for $2/yard. The manufacturing costs during the year are:

Direct materials	
Cotton fiber	$ 250,000
Polyester fiber	200,000
Direct labor	
Cotton	100,000
Polyester	60,000
Weaving machine (capacity = 5,000 hours)	100,000
(3,000 hours for cotton; 1,000 hours for polyester)	
Utilities	50,000
Set-ups of weaving machine for new runs	400,000
Factory rental	200,000
Total	$1,360,000

The weaving machine costs and utilities vary with the number of machine hours. The set-up costs are fixed with respect to the number of units produced but vary with the number of set-ups: 30 for cotton and 50 for polyester. The factory rental costs are fixed with respect to number of units produced but vary with number of square feet dedicated to each product: 30,000 square feet for cotton, 70,000 square feet for polyester. There are no raw materials left over at the end of the year.

a. What is the profit of the company with absorption costing and machine hours used to allocate all overhead items?

b. What is the profit of the company using practical capacity costing if machine hours are used to allocate all overhead items and set-up and factory rental costs are considered fixed?

c. What is the profit of the company if variable costing is used and machine hours are used to allocate the weaving machine costs and the utility costs, but the set-ups and factory rental are considered fixed costs?

d. What is the profit of the company with ABC if machine hours are used to allocate the weaving machine costs and the utility costs, number of set-ups are used to allocate set-up costs, and factory rental costs are allocated based on square footage of space used?

e. What are the advantages and disadvantages of each method?

Solution to Self-Study Problem

a. Cotton uses 3,000 machine hours and polyester uses 1,000 machine hours, so cotton receives ¾ of all the overhead costs. The average costs per yard using absorption costing are:

	Cotton	Polyester
Direct materials	$250,000	$200,000
Direct labor	100,000	60,000
Machine costs (¾ cotton, ¼ polyester)	75,000	25,000
Utilities (¾ cotton, ¼ polyester)	37,500	12,500
Setups (¾ cotton, ¼ polyester)	300,000	100,000
Factory rental (¾ cotton, ¼ polyester)	150,000	50,000
Total	$912,500	$447,500
Number of yards manufactured	300,000	500,000
Average cost per yard	$3.04167/yard	$0.895/yard

The profit using absorption costing is:

Revenues		
Cotton (250,000 yards)($3/yard)		$750,000
Polyester (400,000 yards)($2/yard)		800,000
Cost of goods sold		
Cotton ($3.04167/yard)(250,000 yards)		(760,417)
Polyester ($0.895/yard)(400,000 yards)		(358,000)
Profit		$431,583

b. Capacity is 5,000 machine hours, but the machine is used only 4,000 hours. A fifth of the fixed costs are treated as period costs. The average costs per yard using capacity costing are:

	Cotton	Polyester
Direct materials	$250,000	$200,000
Direct labor	100,000	60,000
Machine costs (¾ cotton, ¼ polyester)	75,000	25,000
Utilities (¾ cotton, ¼ polyester)	37,500	12,500
Setups (⅗ cotton, ⅕ polyester)	240,000	80,000
Factory rental (⅗ cotton, ⅕ polyester)	120,000	40,000
Total	$822,500	$417,500
Number of yards manufactured	300,000	500,000
Average cost per yard	$2.74167/yard	$0.835/yard

The profit using capacity costing is:

Revenues		
Cotton (250,000 yards)($3/yard)		$750,000
Polyester (400,000 yards)($2/yard)		800,000
Cost of goods sold		
Cotton ($2.74167/yard)(250,000 yards)		(685,417)
Polyester ($0.835/yard)(400,000 yards)		(334,000)
Capacity costs (⅕)(400,000 + 200,000)		(120,000)
Profit		$410,583

c. The variable costs per yard are:

	Cotton	Polyester
Direct materials	$250,000	$200,000
Direct labor	100,000	60,000
Machine costs (¾ cotton, ¼ polyester)	75,000	25,000

Utilities (¾ cotton, ¼ polyester)	37,500	12,500
Total	$462,500	$297,500
Number of yards manufactured	300,000	500,000
Average cost per yard	$1.54167/yard	$0.595/yard

The profit using variable costing is:

Revenues	
Cotton (250,000 yards)($3/yard)	$750,000
Polyester (400,000 yards)($2/yard)	800,000
Cost of goods sold	
Cotton ($1.54167/yard)(250,000 yards)	(385,417)
Polyester ($0.595/yard)(400,000 yards)	(258,000)
Fixed costs (200,000 + 400,000)	(600,000)
Profit	$306,583

d. The average costs per yard using ABC are:

	Cotton	Polyester
Direct materials	$250,000	$200,000
Direct labor	100,000	60,000
Machine costs (¾ cotton, ¼ polyester)	75,000	25,000
Utilities (¾ cotton, ¼ polyester)	37,500	12,500
Setups (30/80 cotton, 50/80 polyester)	150,000	250,000
Factory rental (30,000/100,000 cotton, 70,000/100,000 polyester)	60,000	140,000
Total	$672,500	$687,500
Number of yards manufactured	300,000	500,000
Average cost per yard	$2.24167/yard	$1.375/yard

The profit using ABC is:

Revenues	
Cotton (250,000 yards)($3/yard)	$750,000
Polyester (400,000 yards)($2/yard)	800,000
Cost of goods sold	
Cotton ($2.24167/yard)(250,000 yards)	(560,417)
Polyester ($1.375/yard)(400,000 yards)	(550,000)
Profit	$439,583

e. The absorption costing method using a single allocation base has little advantage other than being simple and consistent with generally accepted accounting principles. Fixed and variable costs are mixed and the average cost gives little indication of the opportunity cost of making more units of either product. Machine hours are taxed higher than their opportunity costs and may be underused relative to other indirect resources. Fixed costs will reside in inventory and may encourage overproduction.

The capacity costing procedure has the advantage of identifying the cost of unused capacity. Some fixed costs, however, are still mixed with the variable costs leading to the same problems as absorption costing.

Variable costing provides a cost that should represent the cost of making additional units as long as no further setups or square feet are required. There is no incentive for overproduction, but all nonunit-level costs are treated as fixed.

ABC has the advantage of recognizing different levels of overhead costs and probably provides the product cost that most closely approximates opportunity cost of producing each product. The average cost that is calculated for ABC, however, does not represent the opportunity cost of making another unit. A better approximation of the opportunity cost of making another unit can be generated by also considering the impact on cost drivers of the overhead activities.

NUMERICAL PROBLEMS

NP 11–1: Cost Allocation and Overproduction (LO 1; NE 1)
The Scantron Company makes bar-code scanners for supermarkets. The sales staff estimates that the company will sell 500 units next year for $10,000 each. The production manager estimates that fixed costs of making the scanners are $2 million and the variable cost per unit is $4,000. Assume there are no storage costs for scanners that are not sold and the company uses absorption costing.

a. What is the profit of the company if the company actually makes and sells 500 units?
b. What is the profit of the company if the company makes 600 units but sells 500 units?

NP 11–2: Death Spiral (LO 1; NE 3)
An insurance company has the following profitability analysis of its services:

	Type of Insurance		
	Life	Auto	Home
Revenues	$5,000,000	$10,000,000	$3,000,000
Commissions	(1,000,000)	(2,000,000)	(600,000)
Payments	(3,000,000)	(7,300,000)	(2,000,000)
Fixed costs	(500,000)	(500,000)	(500,000)
Profit	$ 500,000	$ 200,000	$ (100,000)

The fixed costs are distributed equally among the services and are not avoidable if one of the services is dropped.

What is the profitability of the remaining services if all services with losses are dropped?

NP 11–3: Allocating Costs Using Practical Capacity and Variable Costing (LO 2, 3; NE 4, 5)
The Card Company makes playing cards and baseball cards. The primary cost of making the cards is the use of printing machines. Therefore, overhead is allocated based on machine hours. The Card Company has sufficient machines to operate 20,000 hours during the year. The fixed costs of making all types of cards are $2 million. The variable costs (including direct costs) of making a deck of playing cards are $0.10 per deck. The variable costs of making a pack of baseball cards are $0.30 per pack. The company makes 2 million decks of playing cards using 8,000 machine hours. The sales price of a deck of playing cards is $1.00 and the company sells 1.8 million decks. The company also makes 1 million packs of baseball cards using 7,000 machine hours. The sales price for a pack of baseball cards is $1.50 and the company sells 900,000 packs. There was no beginning inventory.

a. What is the profit of the company if the company uses practical capacity to allocate fixed costs?
b. What is the profit of the company if the company uses variable costing?

NP 11–4: Processing Further (LO 6; NE 11)
Walters Company produces 15,000 pounds of Product A and 30,000 pounds of Product B each week by incurring a joint cost of $400,000. These two products can be sold as is or processed further. Further processing of either product does not delay the production of subsequent batches of the joint product. Data regarding these two products are as follows:

	Product A	Product B
Selling price per pound without further processing	$12.00	$ 9.00
Selling price per pound with further processing	$15.00	$11.00
Total separate weekly variable costs of further processing	$50,000	$45,000

To maximize Walters Company's manufacturing contribution margin, how much total separate variable costs of further processing should be incurred each week?

NP 11–5: Variable and Absorption Costing (LO 1, 3; NE 1, 5)   Varilux manufactures a single product and sells it for $10 per unit. At the beginning of the year there were 1,000 units in inventory. On further investigation, you discover that units produced last year had $3 of fixed manufacturing cost and $2 of variable manufacturing cost. During the year Varilux produced 10,000 units of product. Each unit produced generated $3 of variable manufacturing cost. Total fixed manufacturing cost for the current year was $40,000. There were no inventories at the end of the year.

Prepare two income statements for the current year, one on a variable cost basis and the other on an absorption cost basis. Explain any difference between the two net income numbers and provide calculations supporting your explanation of the difference.

NP 11–6: Profit and Absorption Costing (LO 1; NE 1)   The MAPICS Company uses full absorption costing and has the following cost structure:

Variable costs per unit	$0.30
Fixed costs	$2.0 million
Normal production	1.0 million units
Selling price	$2.50/unit

In the first year of production, MAPICS produced 1.4 million units and sold 1.0 million units. In the second year, MAPICS sold 1.0 million units but produced .8 million units. There was no beginning inventory in year 1, and FIFO is used to value inventories.

a. Analyze the change in profitability between years 1 and 2.
b. What would profits have been if 0.6 million units were produced in the second year?

NP 11–7: Further Processing of Joint Products and Allocation of Joint Costs (LO 6; NE 11) (Appendix)   A production department produces two joint products, X and V, using a common input. These are produced in batches. The common input costs $8,000 per batch. To produce the final products (X and V), additional processing costs beyond the split-off point must be incurred. There are no beginning inventories. The following data summarize the operations.

	Products	
	X	V
Quantities produced per batch	200 lbs.	400 lbs.
Additional processing costs per batch beyond split-off	$1,800	$3,400
Unit selling prices of completely processed products	$40/lb.	$20/lb.
Ending inventory	2,000 lbs.	1,000 lbs.

a. Compute the full cost of the ending inventories using both the net realizable value and the pounds to allocate joint costs.
b. If the selling prices at the split-off point (before further processing) were $35 and $1.00 per pound of X and V, respectively, what should the firm do regarding further processing? Show calculations.

NP 11–8: Allocating Joint Costs and Processing Further (LO 6; NE 11) (Appendix)   Sonimad Sawmill manufactures two lumber products from a joint milling process. The two products developed are mine support braces (MSB) and unseasoned commercial building lumber (CBL). A standard production run incurs joint costs of $300,000 and results in 60,000 units of MSB and 90,000 units of CBL. Each unprocessed unit of MSB sells for $2 per unit and each unprocessed unit of CBL sells for $4 per unit.

If the CBL is processed further at a cost of $200,000 it can be sold at $10 per unit, but 10,000 units are unavoidably lost (with no discernible value). The MSB units can be coated with a preservative at a cost of $100,000 per production run and then sold for $3.50 each.

a. If no further work is done after the initial milling process, calculate the cost of CBL using physical quantities to allocate the joint cost.

b. If no further work is done after the initial milling process, calculate the cost of MSB using relative sales value to allocate the joint cost.
c. Should MSB and CBL be processed further or sold immediately after initial milling?
d. Given your decision in part c, prepare a schedule computing the completed cost assigned to each unit of MSB and CBL as charged to finished goods inventory using net realizable value for allocating joint costs.

(CMA adapted)

NP 11–9: Allocating Joint Costs (LO 6) (Appendix) Metro Blood Bank, a for-profit firm, collects whole blood from donors, tests it, and then separates it into two components: platelets and plasma. Three pints of whole blood yield two pints of platelets and one pint of plasma. The cost of collecting the three pints, testing them, and separating them is $300.

The platelets are sold for $165 per pint. But before they are sold they must be packaged, labeled, and frozen. The variable cost of this additional processing is $15 per pint. Plasma is sold for $115 per pint after incurring additional variable processing costs of $45 per pint.

The selling prices of the platelets and plasma are set by competitive market forces. The prices of platelets and plasma quoted above are the current market prices. But these prices vary widely depending on supply and demand conditions. Metro Blood Bank ships its products nationwide to maximize profits. It has three operating divisions: Blood Collection and Processing, Platelets, and Plasma. Collection and Processing is a cost center, and Platelets and Plasma are profit centers.

Neither platelets nor plasma have any commercial value without further processing.

a. Prepare two statements showing the profits per pint of platelets and plasma where the collection and processing costs are assigned to platelets and plasma using:
   (1) The number of pints of platelets and plasma produced from the whole blood.
   (2) The net realizable value of platelets and plasma.
b. Discuss the advantages and disadvantages of each of the methods in part a for assigning the collection and processing costs to the blood products.

NP 11–10: Allocating Joint Costs (LO 6) (Appendix) The Doe Company sells three products: sliced pineapples, crushed pineapples, and pineapple juice. The pineapple juice is a by-product of sliced pineapple, while crushed pineapples and sliced pineapples are produced simultaneously from the same pineapple.

The production process is:

a. 100,000 pounds of pineapples are processed at a cost of $120,000 in Department 1. Twenty percent of the pineapples' weight is scrap and discarded during processing. Twenty percent of the processed pineapple is crushed and is transferred to Department 2. The remaining is transferred to Department 3.
b. In Department 2, a further cost outlay of $15,000 is required to pack the crushed pineapple. Here a further 10% is lost while processing. The packed product is sold at $3 a pound.
c. In Department 3 the material is processed at a total additional cost of $40,000. Thirty percent of the processed pineapple turns into juice and is sold at $0.50 a pound after incurring $3,500 as selling costs. The remaining 70% is transferred to Department 4.
d. Department 4 is used to pack the sliced pineapples into tins. Costs incurred here total $25,500. The cans are then ready for sale at $4 a pound.

Prepare a schedule showing the allocation of the processing cost of $120,000 between crushed and sliced pineapple using the net realizable value method. The net realizable value of the juice is to be added to the sales value of the sliced pineapples.

NP 11–11: ABC and Average Cost in a Service Industry (LO 4; NE 9)
For many years the Honey Lake Summer Camp had used the number of campers per week to estimate weekly costs. The summer camp is open for 10 weeks during the summer with a different number of campers each week. July is busiest with June and the end

of August least busy. Costs from the last week of summer camp in 1998 are used to estimate costs for 1999 for pricing purposes. The following costs occurred during the last week of 1998 and the costs in each cost category are expected to be the same for 1999:

	Weekly Cost
Supervisor's salary	$ 400
Cook's salary	300
Camp counselor salaries (1 for each occupied cabin, each of which holds 10 campers) (5 counselors × $200/counselor)	1,000
Food (50 campers × $100/camper)	5,000
Supplies (50 campers × $20/camper)	1,000
Utilities (50 campers × $10/camper)	500
Insurance (50 campers × $20/camper)	1,000
Property tax ($10,000/10 weeks)	1,000
Weekly total	$10,200

Cost per camper: $10,200/50 campers = $204/camper

The Honey Lake Summer camp expects 75 campers during the second week of July.

a. What is the expected cost of that week using the average cost?
b. What is the expected cost of that week using ABC?

NP 11–12: Absorption Costing and Overproduction (LO 1; NE 1)

Zipp Cards buys baseball cards in bulk from the companies producing the cards. Zipp buys the cards in sheets of 48 cards. It then cuts the sheets into individual cards and sorts and packages them, usually by team. Zipp then sells the packages to large discount stores. The table below provides information regarding the results from operations for 1995 and 1996.

ZIPP CARDS
Summary of Operations
1995 and 1996
(one unit = 48 cards)

	1995	1996
Unit sales (of 48 cards)	50,000	48,000
Price	$5.00	$4.90
Production in units (budgeted = actual)	50,000	75,000
Variable cost	$1.00	$1.00
Fixed manufacturing overhead	$160,000	$160,000

Volume is measured in terms of 48-card sheets processed. Budgeted, and actual, production in 1995 was 50,000 units. There were no beginning inventories on January 1, 1995. In 1996, budgeted and actual production rose to 75,000 units.

After concluding the 1996 year, the owner of Zipp was pleasantly surprised when the accountant showed the president the income statement for the 1996 year. The president remarked, "I'm surprised we made more money in 1996 than 1995. We had to cut prices and we didn't sell as many units, but yet we still made more money. Well, you're the accountant and these numbers don't lie."

a. Prepare income statements for 1995 and 1996 using absorption costing.
b. Prepare a statement reconciling the change in net income from 1995 to 1996. Explain to the president why the firm made more money in 1996 than in 1995.

NP 11–13: Absorption Costing and Overproduction (LO 1; NE 1)

The Medford Mug Company is an old-line maker of ceramic coffee mugs. It imprints company logos and other sayings on mugs for both commercial and wholesale markets. The firm has the capacity to produce 50 million mugs per year, but the recession has cut production and sales in the current year to 15 million mugs. The operating statement for 1995 is:

MEDFORD MUG COMPANY
Income Statement
Year Ending 1995
(millions)

Sales (15 million @ $2)		$30.0
Less: Cost of goods sold		
Variable cost (15 million @ $0.50)	(7.5)	
Fixed cost	(20.0)	(27.5)
Gross margin		2.5
Less: Selling and administration		(4.0)
Operating profit		$(1.5)

At the end of 1995, there was no ending inventory of finished goods.

The board of directors is very concerned about the $1.5 million operating loss, and they hire an outside consultant who reports back that the firm suffers from two problems. First, the president of the company receives a fixed salary, and since she owns no stock, she has very little incentive to worry about company profits. The second problem is that the company has not aggressively marketed its product and has not kept up with changing markets. The current president is 64 and the board of directors makes her an offer to retire one year early so that they can hire a new chief operating manager to turn the firm around. The current president accepts the offer to retire and the board immediately hires a new president with a proven track record as a "turnaround" specialist.

The new president is hired with an employment contract that pays a fixed wage of $50,000 a year plus 15% of the firm's operating profits (if any). Operating profits are calculated using absorption costing. In 1996, the new president doubles the selling and administration budget to $8 million (which includes the president's salary of $50,000). He designs a new line of "politically correct" sayings to imprint on the mugs and expands inventory and the number of distributors handling the mugs. Production is increased to 45 million mugs and sales of mugs climb to 18 million mugs at $2 each. 1996 variable costs per mug remain at $0.50 and fixed costs at $20 million.

At the end of 1996, the president meets with the board of directors and announces he has accepted another job. He believes he has successfully gotten Medford Mug back on track and thanks the board for giving him the opportunity. His new job is helping to turn around another struggling company.

a. Calculate the president's bonus for 1996.
b. Evaluate the performance of the new president for 1996. Did he do as good a job as the "numbers" in part a suggest?

NP 11–14: Absorption and Variable Costing Using FIFO (LO 1, 3; NE 1, 5)

Smidt & Sons produces a single product and has the following operating data:

	1994	1995	1996
Units produced	22,000	16,000	15,000
Units sold	20,000	15,000	18,000
Fixed manufacturing overhead	$800,000	$880,000	$950,000
Variable manufacturing cost	$3.00	$3.10	$3.20
Variable selling costs	$0.25	$0.30	$0.35
Selling Price	$45.00	$50.00	$53.00

The firm uses FIFO inventory costing and there was no beginning inventory in 1994.

a. Calculate net income using absorption costing.

b. Calculate net income using variable costing.
c. Reconcile the annual differences between the two costing methods.

NP 11–15: Absorption and Variable Costing (LO 1, 3; NE 1, 5) BBG
Corporation is a manufacturer of a synthetic chemical. Gary Voss, president of the company, has been eager to get the operating results for the just-completed fiscal year. He was surprised when the income statement revealed that income before taxes had dropped to $885,500 from $900,000, even though sales volume had increased by 100,000 kg. The drop in net income occurred even though Voss had implemented two changes during the past 12 months to improve the profitability of the company:

- In response to a 10% increase in production costs, the sales price of the company's product was increased by 12%. This action took place on December 1, 1994, the first day of the 1995 fiscal year.
- The managers of the selling and administrative departments were given strict instructions to spend no more in fiscal 1995 than in fiscal 1994.

BBG's Accounting Department prepared and distributed to top management the comparative income statements presented below.

BBG CORPORATION
Statements of Operating Income
For the Years Ended November 30, 1994 and 1995
($000 omitted)

	1994	1995
Sales revenue	$9,000	$11,200
Cost of goods sold	$7,200	$ 8,320
Under(over)-absorbed overhead	(600)	495
Adjusted cost of goods sold	$6,600	$ 8,815
Gross margin	$2,400	$ 2,385
Selling and administrative expenses	1,500	1,500
Income before taxes	$ 900	$ 885

The accounting staff also prepared related financial information that is presented in the schedule below to assist management in evaluating the company's performance. BBG uses the FIFO inventory method for finished goods.

BBG CORPORATION
Selected Operating and Financial Data
For 1994 and 1995

	1994	1995
Sales price	$10.00/kg.	$11.20/kg.
Material cost	$ 1.50/kg.	$ 1.65/kg.
Direct labor cost	$ 2.50/kg.	$ 2.75/kg.
Variable overhead cost	$ 1.00/kg.	$ 1.10/kg.
Fixed overhead cost	$ 3.00/kg.	$ 3.30/kg.
Total fixed overhead costs	$3,000,000	$3,300,000
Normal production volume	1,000,000 kg.	1,000,000 kg.
Selling and administrative (all fixed)	$1,500,000	$1,500,000
Sales volume	900,000 kg.	1,000,000 kg.
Beginning inventory	300,000 kg.	600,000 kg.
Production	1,200,000 kg.	850,000 kg.

a. Explain to Gary Voss why BBG Corporation's net income decreased in the current fiscal year despite the sales price and sales volume increases.

b. A member of BBG's Accounting Department has suggested that the company adopt variable (direct) costing for internal reporting purposes.
   (1) Prepare an operating income statement through income before taxes for the year ended November 30, 1995, for BBG Corporation using the variable (direct) costing method.
   (2) Present a numerical reconciliation of the difference in income before taxes using the absorption costing method as currently employed by BBG and the proposed variable (direct) costing method.
c. Identify and discuss the advantages and disadvantages of using the variable (direct) costing method for internal reporting purposes.

(CMA adapted)

NP 11–16: Activity-Based Costing (LO 4; NE 6) Friendly Grocer has three departments in its store: beverages, dairy and meats, and canned and packaged foods. Each department is headed by a departmental manager. Operating results for the last month (in thousands) are given below.

	Beverages	Dairy and Meats	Canned and Packaged Foods	Totals
Sales	$250.00	$470.00	$620.00	$1,340.00
Direct costs:				
Cost of goods sold	200.00	329.00	527.00	1,056.00
Indirect costs:				
SG&A (20% of COGS)	40.00	65.80	105.40	211.20
Operating income	$ 10.00	$ 75.20	($ 12.40)	$ 72.80

The direct costs consist of the cost of goods sold. Indirect costs consist of selling, general, and administrative (SG&A) costs and are allocated to each department at the rate of 20% of cost of goods sold. Based on the preceding report, beverages had operating income of $10 thousand, dairy and meats had operating income of $75.2 thousand, and canned and packaged foods lost $12.4 thousand.

Senior management is concerned that the allocation of costs might be distorting the relative profitability of the three departments. Upon further analysis of the SG&A account, the following breakdown was obtained.

Shelf space costs	$ 90.00
Handling costs	20.00
Coupon costs	15.00
Shrinkage	28.00
Other indirect costs	58.20
Total	$211.20

Shelf space costs consist of store occupancy costs such as depreciation on the building and fixtures, utilities, store maintenance, property taxes, and insurance. Beverages constitute 25% of the shelf space, dairy and meats constitute 35% of the space, and canned and packaged foods constitute 40% of the shelf space.

Handling costs consist of the labor required to stock the shelves and remove outdated products. The beverage suppliers (Coca Cola, Pepsi, etc.) provide the labor to shelve their products (i.e., the beverage delivery people stock their products on the shelf). Dairy and meat labor costs for stocking are three quarters of the handling costs and canned and package foods' labor and handling costs are one quarter of the total.

Coupon costs consist of the labor costs to process the redeemed coupons. Dairy and meats do not have any coupons. Twenty per cent of the coupons redeemed are for beverages and 80% are for packaged and canned foods.

Shrinkage consists of the cost of products spoiled, broken, and stolen. The following table shows shrinkage by product category.

Beverages	$ 1
Dairy and meats	$21
Canned and packaged foods	$ 6

The remaining indirect costs are allocated based on cost of goods sold.

a. Construct an activity-based costing system and recalculate the operating income of the three departments.
b. Based on the statement you prepared in part a, write a short memo to management discussing the revised operating income of the three departments and which statement (yours or the one in the question) management should use.

DISCUSSION PROBLEMS

DP 11–1: Average Costs and Variable Costs as Performance Measures (LO 1, 3)   The manager of the manufacturing unit of a company is responsible for the costs of the manufacturing unit. The president is in the process of deciding whether to evaluate the manager of the manufacturing unit by the average cost per unit or the variable cost per unit. Quality and timely delivery would be used in conjunction with the cost measure to reward the manager.

What problems are associated with using the average cost per unit as a performance measure?

What problems are associated with using the variable cost per unit as a performance measure?

DP 11–2: Allocating Overhead Using Practical Capacity (LO 2)   The president of a printing company has decided to use the practical capacity of the printers of the company to determine the application rates per machine hour for overhead. She feels that the information on the cost of unused capacity would be valuable information. As the controller begins calculating application rates for the coming year, he is surprised to find that several more printers were purchased during the previous year even though there was considerable excess capacity.

How does the cost allocation system affect the behavior of managers?

DP 11–3: Reluctance to a Change to ABM (LO 4, 5)   Harry had been working as a shop foreman for Four Lakes Fabricating for 10 years. He had been responsible for all of the jobs that had been assigned to his job shop team and felt he had performed quite well. The management had evaluated him based on his ability to manufacture special projects at the lowest possible cost and had always rewarded him with a bonus at the end of the year. Harry felt he knew the processes of his shop better than anyone and could always find the most efficient method of making a new product. Management had recently proposed to Harry the idea of changing to an activity-based management (ABM) system.

Why is Harry confused and upset with management's interest in ABM?

DP 11–4: Using Allocated Joint Costs (LO 6)   The Green Packing Company has discovered an increasing demand for frozen boneless chicken fillets. The frozen chicken fillets can be thawed and cooked quickly and are becoming very popular with people who don't want to deal with the bones and other parts of the chicken that have less meat. The company was recently presented with an offer to buy frozen boneless chicken fillets for $1 per pound. The Green Packing Company, however, is not sure that the company can accept the new offer because the cost of chicken fillets is greater than $1 per pound (see below).

Joint costs purchasing and butchering a chicken	
Cost of a chicken	$0.30
Butchering costs per chicken	0.10
Cost of deboning, freezing, and packaging fillets per chicken (0.50 lb/chicken)	0.15
Cost of chicken fillets per chicken (0.50 lbs.)	$0.55
Cost of chicken fillets per pound (2 × $0.55)	$1.10

All of the joint costs of purchasing and butchering the chicken are allocated to the chicken fillets in this analysis because the chicken fillets are specially ordered.

How should the company analyze this special order for chicken fillets?

DP 11–5: Activity-Based Management for Planning and Control (LO 4, 5)

Jeff's Cabinetry Shop makes and installs kitchen cabinets. Jeff Schultz is the president and has five managers: Sheldon for customer relations, Janice for inventory and warehousing, Bill for shop manufacturing, Jack for installation, and Jane for administration. Each manager has identified the following overhead processes, expected costs and cost drivers in their areas:

Process

Sheldon:
- Advertising
- Designing
- Bidding
- Contracting
- Satisfying customers

Janice:
- Purchasing
- Delivery processing
- Storing
- Processing requisitions

Bill:
- Estimating and requisitioning material
- Scheduling
- Construction

Jack:
- Delivery to site
- Installation

Jane:
- Accounting
- Billing and collecting
- Payroll

a. Using the process of each manager, create a value chain for Jeff's Cabinetry Shop.
b. What processes appear to be non–value-added?
c. Sheldon is responsible for making bids on new jobs. What are the direct costs and how should they be estimated?
d. What are potential cost drivers for the processes of each manager that can be used in bidding for new jobs?
e. How does the choice of those cost drivers affect management behavior?

DP 11–6: Allocating the Cost of Scrap (LO 6)

ITI Technology designs and manufactures solid state computer chips. In one of their production departments, a six-inch circular wafer is fabricated by laying down successive layers of silicon and then etching the circuits into the layers. Each wafer contains 100 separate solid state computer chips. After a wafer is manufactured, the 100 chips are cut out of the wafer, initially tested, mounted into protective covers and electrical leads attached, and a final quality control test is performed.

The initial testing process consists of successive stages of heating and cooling the chips and testing how they work. If 99% of each chip's circuits work properly after the testing, they are classified as high-density (HD) chips. If between 75% and 99% of a chip's circuits work properly, it is classified as a low-density (LD) chip. If fewer than 75% of the circuits work, it is discarded. Twenty wafers are manufactured in a batch and 50% of each batch is HD, 20% is LD, and 30% are discarded. HD chips are sold to defense contractors and LD chips to consumer electronic firms. Chips sold to defense contractors require different types of mountings, packaging, and distribution channels than chips sold to consumer electronic firms. HD chips sell for $30 each and LD chips sell for $16 each.

Each batch of 20 wafers costs $29,100: $8,000 to produce, test, and sort and $21,100 for mounting, attaching leads, and final inspection and distribution costs ($14,500 for HD chips and $6,600 for LD chips). The $29,100 total cost per batch consists of direct labor, direct materials, and variable overhead.

The following report summarizes the operating data per batch:

ITI TECHNOLOGY
Operating Cost Summary for HD and LD Chips

	Total	HD Chips	LD Chips	Scrap
Percent of chips	100%	50%	20%	30%
Total costs	$29,100	$14,550	$5,820	$8,730
Revenue	$36,400	$30,000*	$6,400†	$0
Total costs	29,100	14,550	5,820	8,730
Profit per batch	$ 7,300	$15,450	$ 580	(8,730)

*$30,000 = 50% × 20 wafers × 100 chips per wafer × $30/chip.
†$6,400 = 20% × 20 wafers × 100 chips per wafer × $16/chip.

The cost of scrap is charged to a plantwide overhead account which is then allocated directly to the lines of business based on profits in the line of business.

a. Critically evaluate ITI's method of accounting for HD and LD chips.
b. What suggestions would you offer ITI's management?

DP 11–7: Variable Costing (LO 2) You are working as a loan officer at TransPacific Bank and are analyzing a loan request for a client when you come across the following footnote in the client's annual report:

> Inventories are priced at the lower of cost or market of materials plus other direct (variable) costs. Fixed overheads of $4.2 million this year and $3.0 million last year are excluded from inventories. Omitting such overhead resulted in a reduction in net income (after taxes) of $720,000 for this year. Our tax rate is 40%.

In preparation of presenting the loan application to the bank's loan committee, write a brief paragraph in nontechnical terms describing what this footnote means and how it affects the bank's decision regarding the evaluation of the financial condition of the borrower.

CASES

C 11–1: Overhead Costs in a New Factory Karsten is one of the premier carpet manufacturers in the world. They manufacture carpeting for both residential and commercial applications. Home sales and commercial sales each account for about 50% of total revenue. The firm is organized into three departments: manufacturing, residential sales, and commercial sales. Manufacturing is a cost center and the two sales departments are profit centers. The full cost of each roll of carpeting produced (including fully absorbed overhead) is transferred to the sales department ordering the carpet. The sales departments are evaluated as profit centers; the fully absorbed cost of each roll is the transfer price.

The current manufacturing plant is at capacity. A new plant is being built that will more than double capacity. Within two years, management believes that they can grow their businesses such that most of the excess capacity is eliminated. When the new plant comes on line, the plan is for one plant to produce exclusively commercial carpeting and the other to produce exclusively residential carpeting. This change will simplify scheduling, ordering, and inventory control in each plant and will allow some economies of scale to be created by producing longer mill runs. Nevertheless, it will take a couple of years before these economies of scale can be realized.

Each mill produces carpeting in 12-foot-wide rolls of up to 100 yards in length. The output of each mill is measured in terms of yards of 12-foot rolls produced. Overhead is assigned to carpet rolls using carpet yards produced in the mill. The cost structure of each plant is as follows:

	Old Plant	New Plant
Normal machine hours per year	6,000	5,000
Normal carpet yards per hour	1,000	1,400
Normal capacity	6 million yards	7 million yards
Annual manufacturing overhead costs excluding accounting depreciation	$15,000,000	$21,000,000
Accounting depreciation per year	$ 6,000,000	$21,000,000

Besides being able to run the new mill at higher speed and thereby producing more carpet yardage per hour, the new mill will use 15% less direct materials and direct labor because the new machines, being more automated, produce less scrap and require less direct labor per yard. A job sheet run at the old mill is:

Carpet no A6106: (100-yard roll)
Direct materials	$ 800
Direct labor	$ 600
Direct costs	$1,400

Although the new mill has lower direct costs of producing carpeting than the old mill, the higher overhead costs per yard at the new mill have the sales department managers worried. They are already lobbying senior management to have the old mill assigned to produce their products. The commercial sales department manager argues: "More of my customers are located closer to the old plant than are residential sales' customers. Therefore, to economize on transportation costs, my products should be produced in the old plant." The residential sales department manager counters with the argument, "Transportation costs are less than 1% of total revenues. The new plant should produce commercial products because we expect new commercial products to use more synthetic materials and the latest technology at the new mill is better able to adapt to the new synthetics." Senior management is worried about how to deal with the two sales department managers' reluctance to have their products produced at the new plant. One suggestion put forth is for each plant to produce about half of commercial sales products and about half of residential sales products. But this proposal would eliminate most of the economies of scale that would result from specializing production in each plant to one market segment.

Case Questions

a. Calculate the overhead rates for the new plant and the old plant, where overhead is assigned to carpet based on normal yards per year.
b. Calculate the expected total cost of carpet no. A6106 if run at the old mill and if run at the new mill.
c. Put forth two new possible solutions that overcome the desire of the residential and commercial sales department managers to have their products produced in the old plant. Discuss the pros and cons of your two solutions.

C 11–2: Overhead Costs and Dropping a Product with Joint Costs

Carlos Sanguine, Inc., makes premium wines and table wines. Grapes are crushed and the free-flowing juice and the first-pressing juice are made into the premium wines (bottles with corks). The second- and third-pressing juices are made into table wines (bottles with screw tops).

The data in Exhibit 1 summarize operations for the year:

EXHIBIT 1
Summary of Operations for the Year

| Tons of grapes | 10,000 |
| Average cost per ton | $190 |

	Premium Wines	Table Wines
Number of cases produced and sold	400,000	70,000
Selling price per case	$11.00	$7.00
Revenues	$4,400,000	$490,000
Grape costs[a]	1,650,000	250,000
Packaging costs	1,000,000	140,000
Labor	200,000	35,000
Selling and distribution[b]	400,000	35,000
Manufacturing overhead	400,000	87,500
Operating profit (loss)	$ 750,000	($ 57,500)

Note: A greater quantity of juice is required per case of premium wine than per case of table wine because there is more shrinkage in the premium wines than in table wines.

[a] Grape costs represent the cost of the juice placed into the two product categories and are calculated as:

	Gallons of Juice Used in Each Product	Amount of Grape Juice (%)	× Grape Costs	= Grape Cost per Product
Premium wines	13,200,000	86.84%	$1,900,000	$1,650,000
Table wines	2,000,000	13.16%	$1,900,000	250,000
Total	15,200,000	100%		$1,900,000

[b] Each product has its own selling and distribution (S&D) organization. Two-thirds of selling and distribution expenditures vary with cases produced and the remainder of the expenditures do not vary with output.

EXHIBIT 2
Manufacturing Overhead by Products

	Premium Wines	Table Wines	Total
General winery costs[a]	$212,800	$37,200	$250,000
Production facilities costs[b] (depreciation and maintenance)	187,200	50,300	237,500
Manufacturing overhead	$400,000	$87,500	$487,500

[a] General winery costs do not vary with the number of cases or number of product lines and are allocated based on cases produced.

[b] One-fourth of total production facilities costs varies with cases produced. The remainder are fixed costs previously incurred to provide the production capacity.

Exhibit 2 provides a breakdown of the manufacturing overhead expenses into general winery costs and production facilities costs.

Based on Exhibits 1 and 2, the accounting department prepared Exhibit 3.

Management was concerned that the table wines had such a low margin and some urged that these lines be dropped. Competition kept the price down at the $7.00/case level which caused some managers to question how the competition could afford to sell the wine at this price.

Before making a final decision, top management asked for an analysis of the fixed and variable costs by product line and their break-even points. When management saw Exhibit 4, the president remarked, "Well, this is the final nail in the coffin. We'd have to almost triple our sales of table wines just to break even. But we don't have that kind of capacity. We'd have to buy new tanks, thereby driving up our fixed costs and break-even points. This looks like a vicious circle. By next month, I want a detailed set of plans on what it'll cost us to shut down our table wines."

EXHIBIT 3
Product Line Cost Structure

	Cost Structure per Case			
	Premium Wines		Table Wines	
Net sales		$11.00		$7.00
Variable costs				
Grapes	$4.13		$3.57	
Packaging	2.50		2.00	
Labor	0.50		0.50	
Selling and distribution	1.00	8.13	0.50	6.57
Margin		$ 2.87		$0.43
Less manufacturing overhead		1.00		1.25
Operating profit (loss)		$ 1.87		($0.82)

EXHIBIT 4
Fixed and Variable Costs per Product and Product Break-Even Points

	Premium Wines		Table Wines	
Sales		$11.00		$7.00
Less variable costs				
Grapes	$4.13		$3.57	
Packaging	2.50		2.00	
Labor	0.50		0.50	
Selling and distribution	0.67		0.33	
Manufacturing overhead	0.13	7.93	0.13	6.53
Contribution margin		3.07		0.47
Less unitized fixed costs per unit				
Selling and distribution	0.33		0.17	
Manufacturing overhead	0.87	1.20	1.12	1.29
Profit (loss)		$ 1.87		($0.82)
Break-even:				
Fixed costs	(400,000 × $1.20)	$480,000	(70,000 × 1.29)	$90,300
Divided by contribution margin		$ 3.07		$0.47
Number of cases to break even		156,000		192,000

EXHIBIT 5
Effects of Discontinuing Table Wines

1. No effect on the sale of premium wines is expected.
2. The juice being used in the table wines can be sold to bulk purchasers to use in fruit juices for $150,000 per year.
3. The table wine production facilities (tanks, refrigeration units, etc.) have no use in premium wine production. These can be sold for $350,000, net of disposal costs.

Exhibit 5 summarizes the shutdown effects.

Case Question

Based on the data, what should management do?

C 11–3: Choosing Cost Drivers to Reflect Variable Cost of Overhead

Industry Background Ryetown Steel, Inc., is the nation's largest distributor of steel and fabricated steel products. Over the last two decades, the company's sales have grown substantially as most major metal users no longer purchase directly from the producing mills but purchase instead through service centers such as Ryetown Steel. Distributors process the steel products to customer specifications, mainly cutting the steel to nonstandard dimensions. Consequently, service centers have gained tremendous market share at the expense of the integrated mills. Searching for ways to improve cash flow, increase productivity, properly manage inventories, and reduce storage space, metal users increased their reliance on service centers. With pressures to become more internally efficient, end-users could no longer rely on the producer's erratic lead times and large minimum production quantities. As just-in-time deliveries become vogue, the steel service centers were positioned to expand their role in the market. From 1970 to 1989, the steel service center market grew from 15% of total metal purchased to over 40%.

Ryetown Background Ryetown is a full-line service center that carries nearly all grades produced and is considered the "supermarket" of the steel service center industry. Ryetown has 26 full-line service centers throughout the United States. Its largest warehouse and headquarters is in Chicago, the largest metal-consuming market in the United States. The 26 plants operate as investment centers, with the local plant manager having responsibility for market growth and return on investment. Each plant manager's R.O.I. standard is different. For instance, if one plant shipped heavily to another plant, its R.O.I. goal would be lower since the shipping plant incurred the investment and the variable cost, but was not credited for the profit revenue generated from the sale to the customer. For example, Chicago, a large export plant, has an R.O.I. goal of just 9%. Buffalo, a large importer of material, has an R.O.I. goal of 24%.

Ryetown considers one of its strategic advantages to be the ability of the various plant locations to service large original equipment manufacturers throughout the U.S. by positioning its inventory to cater to the specific grades of steel used in the local markets. Until the early 1980s, Ryetown stocked almost every grade at each location, minimizing the need for interplant transfers. In 1975, 10% of the metal sold by Ryetown was transferred between plants. The shipping plant was compensated for its service with a predetermined service charge to help cover the variable cost of the shipping plant. These service charges consisted of a standard item charge and a per hundredweight charge. The per hundredweight charge was the same across the company regardless of the processing time involved. In other words, whether an item was shipped unfabricated or was cut to a specific length, an identical charge was applied. See Exhibit 1 for a listing of charges.

By 1990, however, as Ryetown consolidated inventories to help preserve capital, it relied very heavily on interplant transfers, with almost 60% of the metal sold to customers transferred in from other plants. Furthermore, with an increasing number of customers demanding just-in-time deliveries, Ryetown fabricated more and more of its shipments in order to send the product directly to the customer's production assembly line.

In 1991, Ryetown's president, Jacqueline Koster, became concerned as to whether the service charges adequately reflected the marginal cost of the shipping plant. In September, Ms. Koster asked Mr. Russ Vack, senior industrial engineer, to evaluate the current service charge system and, if required, recommend a new system that would more accurately reflect the variable expense associated with interplant transfers. Mr. Vack's recommendations in October 1991 are outlined in Exhibit 2, with a summary in Exhibit 2A. Exhibit 3 lists hourly machine wage rates for a few selected commodity groups, and Exhibit 4 depicts a selected number of item transfers in the month of May 1991.

Case Questions

a. Compute the current and proposed charges using the sample data from May 1991 for the four commodity groups listed on Exhibit 4. Compute the total variance between these two alternatives.
b. Discuss the current system from the perspective of the Buffalo plant, the Chicago plant, and the company as a whole.
c. Will the new costing system affect the way local management operates?
d. What recommendations would you make to Ryetown's president? Why?

(Contributed by J. Engel, G. Niederpruem, and J. Stein)

EXHIBIT 1

Service Charges on Interplant Sales, Emergency Transfers, and Planned Transfers of Plant Materials

Department	Product	Service Charge	CWT Charge*
10	H.R. carbon bars and strip	$32.00	$ 0.90
10	C.F. carbon bars	32.00	1.10
10	Alloy bars	32.00	0.90
10	Stainless bars and tubes	32.00	1.20
10	Aluminum bars, shapes and tubes	32.00	1.40
10	Carbon and alloy tubing and pipe	43.00	2.50
10	Structural shapes and tubes	43.00	0.80

10	Carbon plate:
	   Cold saw and abrasive
	   Other cut
		43.00	1.30

10	Alloy plates and sheets
	   Cold saw and abrasive
	   Other cut
		43.00	1.60

10	Stainless plate:
	   Cost saw and abrasive
	   Burn
	   Shear and other cut
		43.00	4.90

10	Aluminum plates:
	   Saw cut
	   Other cut
		43.00	3.90

10	Pattern sheets	43.00	0.90
10	Production sheets	43.00	1.20
10	Stainless sheet and coils	43.00	5.40
10	Aluminum sheets	43.00	6.00

10	Steel coils:
	   Edge
	   Slit
	   Slit and cut-to-length
	   Slit and blank
	   Slit, cut-to-length and shear
	   Slit and edge
	   Cut-to-length
	   Cut-to-length, box and crate
	   Blanking
	   Cut-to-length and shear
	   Cut-to-length, shear and roll
	   Flatten:
	      Pickle
	      Pickle and slit
	      Pickle, slit and cut-to-length
	      Pickle, slit, cut-to-length and shear
	      Pickle and cut-to-length
	      Pickle, cut-to-length and shear
		43.00	0.40

10	Aluminum coils	43.00	1.60
10	Magnesium and titanium	43.00	16.80
10, 70	Miscellaneous products	43.00	2.80

*CWT denotes "hundred weight."

EXHIBIT 2
Recommendations

To: Ms. J. Koster
Plant: General Office
From: Mr. Russ Vack
Date: October 16, 1991
Subject: Transaction Variable Operating Expense

It is recommended that the transaction operating expense be based on two factors:

1. Item expense
2. Process expense

Item Expense

The expense of direct labor (DL) for the functions of receiving, assembly, crane, and loading, indirect labor (IDL), and other variable operating expense are more item-oriented than weight-oriented. Therefore, the dollar expense divided by operating items would generate an item charge to be applied to every item ordered, independent of the number of pieces in the order.

Exhibit 2A outlines the fixed item charges by various commodity groupings. The fixed item charge varies depending on whether the item is cut or uncut.

Process Expense

Processing expense is affected by many factors such as total weight, piece weight, commodity, complexity of cut, and so on. The current service charge plus hundredweight charge is valid for the average order only, whatever that may be. A more accurate reflection of process cost would be to use processing time multiplied by the average hourly rate. This cost would then be charged to the transaction.

Example

$$\text{Cost of Transaction} = I_{exp} + T(R)$$

where: I_{exp} = Item expense (per item ordered)
T = Standard time in hours
R = Average hourly rate

EXHIBIT 2A
Summary of Proposed Fixed Item Charges*

Charge per item by commodity groupings:

	Fixed Item Charge	
	Uncut	Cut
HR carbon bars and strip	$25	$35
CF carbon bars	$25	$35
Alloy bars	$25	$35
Nickel and stainless bars and tubes	$25	$35
Aluminum bars, shapes, and tubes	$25	$35
Carbon and alloy tubing and pipe	$35	$45
Structural shapes and tubes	$35	$45
Miscellaneous products	$35	$45
Carbon plate	$35	$60
Alloy plate and sheet	$35	$60
Nickel and stainless plate	$35	$60
Aluminum plate	$35	$60
Pattern sheets	$35	$50
Production sheets	$35	$50
Stainless sheets and coil	$35	$50
Aluminum sheets and coil	$35	$50
Steel coils	$35	$50
Nickel sheets	$35	$50

*Processing charges are computed using processing time multiplied by the average hourly rate for each commodity.

EXHIBIT 3
Machine Rates per Hour

Commodity	Hourly Rate
Structurals	$25.00
Plates	$28.00
Alloy bar	$27.00
Stainless bar	$30.00

EXHIBIT 4
Sample of Items Transferred in the Month of May 1991

Commodity	Gross Weight in Pounds	Assembly and Processing Time (hours)
Structural shapes and tubes		
200 pcs. 2" × 2" × ¼"—20' (Uncut)	12,760	.42
100 pcs. 6" @ 8.2#—Channel 2'0" long. (Cut)	1,640	1.17
10 pcs. 24" @ 150#—Wide flange Beams 14'0" Long. (Cut)	21,000	1.97
Carbon plates		
10 pcs. ¼" × 48" × 120" (Uncut)	4,080	0.25
28 pcs. 2" × 24" Dia. (Cut)	9,533	3.43
100 pcs. ¾" × 24" × 36" (Cut)	18,378	2.63
Alloy bars		
100 pcs. HR 4140—2" rd—12' long. (Uncut)	12,816	0.38
50 pcs. HR 4140—1" rd.—1'0" long. (Cut)	134	0.40
1200 pcs. HR 4140—7" rd.—0'2" long. (Cut)	26,180	129.40
Stainless bars		
10 pcs. 1" × 2" × 12' (Uncut)	816	0.15
25 pcs. 3½" rd. × 2'0" long. (Cut)	1,636	1.47
100 pcs. 4" rd. × 10'0" long. (Cut)	42,730	9.35

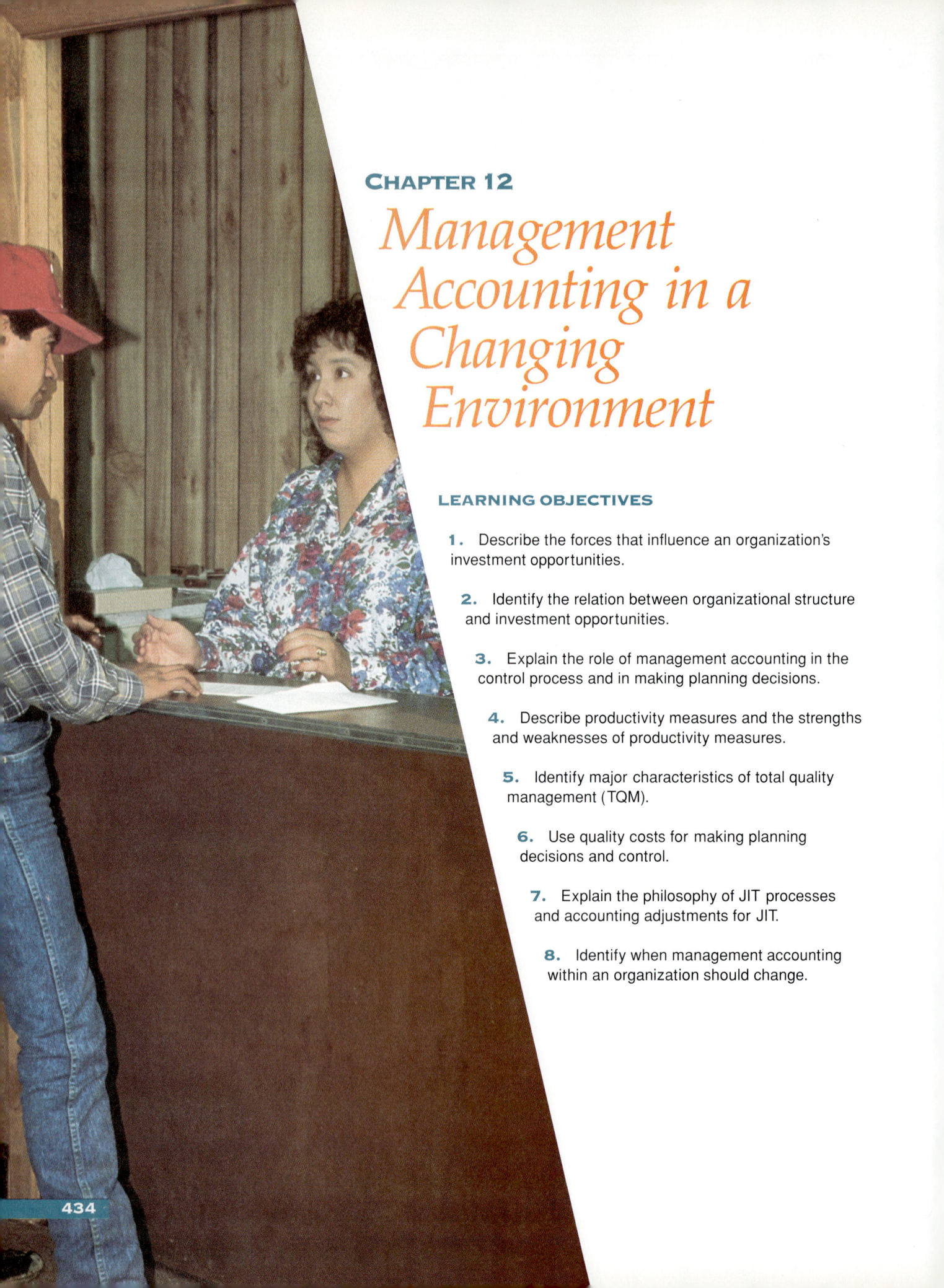

CHAPTER 12
Management Accounting in a Changing Environment

LEARNING OBJECTIVES

1. Describe the forces that influence an organization's investment opportunities.

2. Identify the relation between organizational structure and investment opportunities.

3. Explain the role of management accounting in the control process and in making planning decisions.

4. Describe productivity measures and the strengths and weaknesses of productivity measures.

5. Identify major characteristics of total quality management (TQM).

6. Use quality costs for making planning decisions and control.

7. Explain the philosophy of JIT processes and accounting adjustments for JIT.

8. Identify when management accounting within an organization should change.

Department of Motor Vehicles (DMV)

The Department of Motor Vehicles (DMV) is a division of the State Department of Transportation. The governor delegates the responsibility of operating the Department of Transportation to the Secretary of Transportation, who delegates responsibility for operating the DMV to a commissioner. The current commissioner of DMV is Melody Kim.

The DMV has three major responsibilities: (1) issuing drivers licenses, (2) registering and licensing motor vehicles that operate on public roads, and (3) maintaining and accessing records on those licenses. In addition to the central offices in the state capitol, the DMV has offices in all the major communities of the state.

When the Secretary of Transportation hired Melody to manage the DMV, he told her that things at the DMV must change. The citizens of the state complained incessantly about long lines and unfriendly service. The state police were also unhappy about slow response times when making inquiries about licenses. The DMV was one of the most visible state agencies, and the citizens were unhappy with what they saw. To show their displeasure with how the state was operating, the voters had recently passed a property tax limitation making the state government responsible for covering any shortages necessary to operate public schools. That left a diminishing amount of revenues available for other state services. Melody and the DMV would have to do a better job of serving the people and state police with less money.

12.1 An Integrative Framework for Change and Management Accounting

This book is based on the theme that environmental and competitive forces influence the investment opportunities of an organization. Organizations must adapt to these changing investment opportunities by changing their organizational structures. Organizational structures assign decisions rights, measure performance, and reward individuals within the organization. These control activities lead to decisions by members of the organization that affect the value of the organization. Management accounting has a role in assigning decision rights, measuring performance, and providing information for making planning decisions. That theme is described in Figure 12.1, which is a further extension of figures in Chapters 1 and 6.

Environmental and Competitive Forces Affecting Organizations

The top two boxes in Figure 12.1 indicate that the firm's investment opportunities depend on external forces including technological innovations and global competition. New technology such as fiber optics causes relative prices of competing

FIGURE 12.1
Framework for Organizational Change

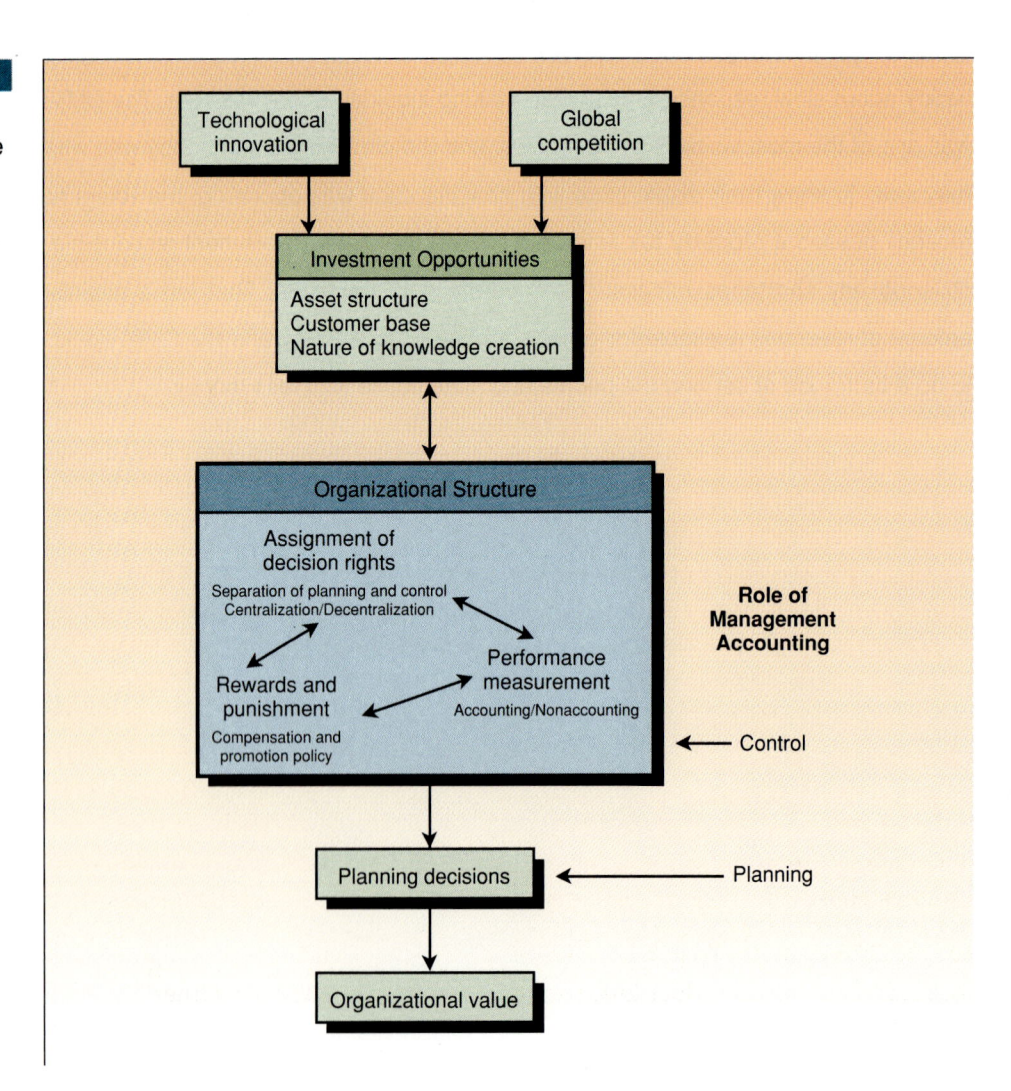

technologies to change, which in turn causes some investment opportunities to become more valuable and others less valuable. Technological change affects the costs of transmitting knowledge and monitoring performance. For example, manufacturing plants use beepers and cellular phones to monitor maintenance personnel. Technological change sets off a chain reaction that causes changes not only in the investment opportunities but also in the organization's knowledge base, asset structure, customer base, and organizational structure (including its internal accounting system).

A similar chain reaction is set off when market conditions change. Increased global competition has forced many organizations that once faced protected domestic markets to become more cost competitive. Instead of making products domestically, organizations now outsource parts and subcomponents globally, causing organizational changes. Market conditions change for a variety of reasons, including changes in government regulations and taxation policies. Changes in tax rates cause the profitability (after taxes) of investment opportunities to change, thus affecting which projects are accepted. The North American Free Trade Agreement (NAFTA) reduced tariffs between Canada, Mexico, and the United States. As a result of NAFTA, companies relocate production sites in search of lower costs. Not only does the flow of trade increase between the three countries, but the geographic dispersion of company operations changes. Emerging markets in the former Soviet Union also set off chain reactions within organizations seeking to expand into these markets. Their investment opportunities will change, prompting modifications in organizational structure.

Technological change affects the way farmers plant, irrigate, fertilize, and harvest their crops. Computer systems provide farmers with much better information for managing their crops.

Successful organizations (and managers) will be those who adapt quickly to changing markets and technologies to allow the organization to take advantage of new investment opportunities. New profitable investments will appear and some previously profitable investments will become unprofitable. Successfully implementing profitable projects requires organizational structures that link decision rights and knowledge and that create incentives for managers to use the knowledge to take actions that capture the value of the investments undertaken.

While this book has focused on the organization's management accounting system, it is important to understand the larger setting into which the accounting system fits. Figure 12.1 highlights how external shocks to the organization from technological innovation and global competition set into motion changes in organizational structure, including the choice of accounting systems. Senior managers are constantly trying to adapt to these external shocks by modifying the organizational structure.

Investment Opportunities

Each organization faces different **investment opportunities**.[1] Investment opportunities consist of those investment projects available to the organization both today and in the future. For example, some organizations, including consumer electronics firms, have large research and development (R&D) programs that spin off many new product ideas, some of which are profitable. Other organizations, such as utilities, have very few new investment projects. Regulatory agencies limit the types of businesses they can provide, and their investment

Nike's logo is recognized globally. The company has expanded from shoes to clothing based on the strength of its high brand-name capital. Why does Nike pay sports teams to put its "swoosh" on their uniforms?

opportunities consist of maintaining their power-generating capacity. Public utilities rely on increases in consumer demand for electricity and heat to grow the utility's business, and most of their value derives from their existing assets in place (power plants and distribution systems). Therefore, one way to characterize an organization's investment opportunities is according to the source of its future investments—its existing assets or growth opportunities.

A very important existing asset that generates future investment opportunities is the organization's brand-name capital. Brand-name capital provides the organization with consumer name recognition that lowers the information costs of introducing new products. "Pepsi" is recognized worldwide. And when Pepsi introduced Diet Pepsi, consumers already had an expectation of taste and quality before sampling the new product. Its existing brand-name capital gives Pepsi a cost advantage in introducing a new brand that new entrants do not have. Thus, brand-name capital affects the type of new investments a firm will undertake.

The investment opportunities of an organization are affected by the organization's asset structure, its customer base, and its method of creating and disseminating knowledge within the organization. Each of these factors can be modified over time. In the short run, however, managers of the organization are constrained by the organization's asset structure, customer base, and ability to create knowledge in taking advantage of investment opportunities.

Asset Structure

The **asset structure** of an organization is the nature of the assets held by the organization. Assets of some organizations are primarily short term and assets of other organizations are primarily long term. Some assets do not appear on the historical cost balance sheet such as human resources and past research and development. For example, pharmaceutical company assets are primarily in drug patents and brand-name drugs, whereas telephone company assets are primarily in telephone lines and switching equipment. The nature of the assets affects the organizational structure. For example, the use of certain assets such as inventory is quickly revealed in accounting statements through sales and cost of goods sold. Therefore, accounting numbers provide good performance measures in retail and wholesale companies where inventory is a major part of the asset structure. On the other hand, the value of some assets such as oil and gas reserves is difficult to measure and not closely represented by accounting numbers. Therefore, the performance measure of managers in oil and gas exploration firms are usually not accounting-based. Stock options and bonuses based on stock price appreciation or other performance measures are used.

Customer Base

The **customer base** describes the type of customer and the geographic dispersion of the customers. The nature of the customer base affects how the firm is organized to service customers. For example, franchised retail stores such as fast-food outlets are an alternative to company-owned stores when the customer base is geographically dispersed. The franchised store is operated by an independent owner who has more incentive to acquire specialized knowledge of the local market and to maximize profits than if the store were operated by an employee of the parent company. But to monitor the quality of the franchised local outlets, the franchiser must have a field organization to inspect local operations, which in turn dictates how the franchiser is organized (including the performance evaluation and reward systems for the field group).

Knowledge Creation

Knowledge creation is determined by the investment projects selected by the organization. If the organization is in very stable markets in which knowledge is not created quickly, a more centralized organizational structure can be adopted. Certain kinds of knowledge (like sales figures) can be converted to numerical representation and can be easily communicated to others in the firm. But other types of knowledge, such as customer preferences in particular markets, are more difficult to record and convey to others. Easily communicated knowledge allows decision rights to be vested higher in the organization, meaning that lower level performance evaluation and reward systems can be simpler.

As another example of how investment affects knowledge creation, consider the decision to invest in Europe. Suppose a U.S. sneaker company decides to sell its shoes in Germany, France, Italy, the Netherlands, and Spain. Separate companies are established in these five countries, each headed by a local national. Because of different languages, cultures and business practices in the five countries, each local company manager has country-specific knowledge. In this example, the decision to invest in Europe affects how knowledge needed to sell its sneakers is generated. Therefore, the investments chosen by the organization determine how and where knowledge is generated, which affects the assignment of decision rights.

Summary

In summary, investment opportunities through the long-term choice of asset structure, customer base, and knowledge creation affect the organizational structure. There is also a reciprocal effect of the organizational structure through the assignment of decision rights, performance measurement, and rewards on investment opportunities (notice the two-way arrow in Figure 12.1). Management incentives will potentially encourage managers to change the asset structure and customer base and create knowledge to expand or change the investment opportunities of the organization. For example, U.S. Steel changed its name to USX, sold many of its steel manufacturing plants, and motivated managers to seek investment opportunities in other industries.

Organizational Structure

The box Organizational Structure in Figure 12.1 outlines the three major elements of the three-legged stool described in Chapter 6. The first element, assignment of decision rights (responsibilities), should link knowledge and decision rights. Ideally decision rights should be transferred to the individual with the specialized knowledge relevant for making a planning decision. But individuals with specialized knowledge cannot always be relied on to make decisions consistent with the goals of the organization. Personal goals will influence their decisions.

One solution to this problem is to transfer the knowledge to the individual who is more likely to make decisions consistent with the goals of the organization. But information, like technical knowledge, is sometimes costly to transfer. Also, individuals are reluctant to transfer knowledge that may be used to evaluate themselves.

As described in Chapter 6, decision rights are commonly assigned to separate planning decisions from control decisions. This separation of making planning decisions and control leads to mutual monitoring. For example, the manager responsible for writing payroll checks is generally different from the person who makes the payroll list. Each individual monitors the other to assist the organization in achieving its goals.

The second component of the organizational structure in Figure 12.1 is the performance measurement system, which includes the accounting system. Besides using accounting-based measures of performance, organizations also develop nonaccounting-based measures such as the organization's stock price, customer complaints, quality, and percent of deliveries on time. Performance measures should be consistent with the assignment of decision rights. Responsibility centers within an organization are based on the decision rights of the manager, and performance measures of those managers should reflect controllability. The manager of a profit center, for example, has some control over revenues and costs and is evaluated, in part, by the profit of the profit center.

The third component of the organizational structure is the reward and punishment system. This consists of the organization's compensation and promotion policies. Rewards are based on performance measures, which should be consistent with the decision rights. The three components of the organizational structure should be balanced as a three-legged stool.

Making Planning Decisions and the Value of the Organization

Planning decisions are the means of achieving the goals of and adding value to the organization. Planning decisions include choosing organizational goals, selecting members of the organization, identifying competitive advantages, choosing a product mix and prices, and choosing processes for delivering products and services. Each of these planning decisions is made with the assistance of information. Accounting is one source of information that assists managers in making planning decisions.

By developing and selling services and products at prices in excess of their costs, the value of the organization is increased. Good planning decisions based on sound information allow the organization to accomplish its goals.

The Role of Management Accounting and Change

The role of management accounting in Figure 12.1 is to assist in control through the organizational structure and in making planning decisions. Management accounting plays an integral role in the organizational structure by assigning decision rights through the budgeting process and providing performance measures for managers. Management accounting also identifies the costs and benefits of different planning decisions, allowing managers to make choices that increase the value of the organization.

Because management accounting is closely related to the organizational structure, management accounting must evolve with the organizational structure. Figure 12.1 provides two important observations:

1. Changes in the accounting system rarely occur in a vacuum. Accounting system changes generally occur at the same time as changes in the organization's investment opportunities and other organizational changes. In particular, accounting changes occur contemporaneously with changes to the assignment of decision rights and the performance evaluation and reward systems.
2. Alterations in the organizational structure, including changes in the accounting system, are likely to occur in response to changes in the organization's investment opportunities caused by external shocks from technology and shifting market conditions.

Three significant managerial implications are derived from these two observations. First, before implementing an accounting or other organizational change, it is important to understand what is driving the change. Second, an accounting system should not be adopted merely because other organizations are doing so; they may have different external factors causing their previous systems to become obsolete. Third, accounting systems should not be changed without making concurrent, consistent changes in the way decision rights are assigned, performance measured, and rewards distributed. All three parts of the organization's structure must be internally consistent and coordinated.

U S West is a regional Bell telephone company based in Denver. In September of 1993, management announced the layoff of 9,000 employees (15% of its workforce), consolidating 560 service centers into 26 and streamlining the customer-order system. Also announced were plans to convert its network covering 14 states into a broadband system for high speed data transfer and video-on-demand. U S West invested $2.5 billion in Time Warner Entertainment. These moves were seen as U S West competing with cable companies and other carriers in the new telecommunications era.

In addition to announcing the strategy and organizational changes, U S West also announced it was changing from straight-line depreciation to accelerated depreciation. The one time accounting change reduced assets $3.2 billion. The reason for the change was that new technology causes telephone assets to be replaced more often. ". . . [telephone companies'] assets aren't lasting as long as they were thought to, and need to be replaced."[2]

These announcements by U S West in one day illustrate how accounting choices (depreciation methods), organizational structure (consolidating service centers), the opportunity set (video-on-demand), investment opportunities (providing broadband system), technology and competition are all intertwined.

This chapter identifies three innovations that have recently evolved in many organizations because of global competitive pressures and new technology. These innovations are productivity, total quality management, and just-in-time. Each of these innovations has implications for the management accounting process.

CONCEPT REVIEW

1. What environmental forces have affected organizations recently?
2. What are the major components of an organization's investment opportunities?
3. How does the organizational structure relate to the investment opportunities?
4. How do planning decisions affect organizational value?
5. What is the role of management accounting and how must it change?

DEPARTMENT OF MOTOR VEHICLES (DMV) (CONTINUED)

Melody Kim began her term as commissioner of the DMV by analyzing the decision rights available to her and the forces affecting the DMV. Melody has no control over revenues. The fees for licenses and the financial support provided by the state are determined by the legislature. Melody also has no control over the quantity of output. The number of registrants and requests from the state police are determined by the demographics of the state. Therefore, the DMV is a cost center with Melody responsible for the efficient use of inputs in providing quality service.

In providing quality service for her customers, Melody is facing two environmental changes that make her management situation different than her predecessors'. First, she must deal with declining resources. Competition from other state agencies and less state tax revenues dictate cost reductions. The state legislature has been unsympathetic and cries of a bloated bureaucracy have been heard on the floor of the senate. Some representatives are even suggesting privatizing the DMV.

Second, computer technology has changed considerably in the last few years. Not many years ago, all registration and license renewals had to be completely retyped, a process that required considerable labor time. Search requests by the state police required a person to go through a warehouse of file cabinets looking for the appropriate file. Cross-references based on make and year of a car could take days to complete.

Melody views advanced computer technology as an opportunity to make the DMV succeed even with reduced funds. Replacing state employees with computers, however, is not easy. Employees of the state civil service are a strong political force. Any layoffs would be determined by seniority. Melody would have to lay off the younger employees, who might have more experience in operating computers.

12.2 *Innovations and Management Accounting Systems*

As the goals and operations of an organization change, the original management accounting system will no longer provide the appropriate information for control and making planning decisions. Different information becomes more useful for decision making. Performance measures must be changed to provide incentives for managers to meet new goals. In this chapter, three new management innovations and the corresponding adjustments to the management accounting system are described: (1) productivity and productivity measures, (2) total quality management (TQM) and quality measures, and (3) just-in-time processes.

Productivity and Productivity Measures

Economists and managers have long recognized the importance of productivity in determining an organization's success. Productivity is the relation between the organization's output of goods and services and the inputs necessary to produce that output. If an organization is able to produce more output with the same inputs, we say it has improved its productivity. Likewise, if two organizations produce the same quantity of goods and service but one organization uses less input, that organization is called more productive. Countries keep statistics on productivity per worker, and these numbers are reported in the financial press as representing a measure of the competitiveness and/or well-being of that country.

The impetus for measuring productivity at the organizational level has come from global competition. Japanese manufacturing firms were reporting large outputs per worker and selling their products at lower prices. In an attempt to become more competitive, some U.S. organizations experimented with various productivity measures. By measuring productivity, organizations hope to motivate managers to make choices that will make the organization more profitable. In its most basic form, productivity is defined as

$$\text{Productivity} = \frac{\text{Output in units}}{\text{Input in units}}$$

If the organization uses a single input (steel) to produce a single homogeneous product (a horseshoe) that never changes over time, then a measure of productivity is the units of output per quantity of input, or the number of horseshoes per pound of steel. By reducing steel waste, more horseshoes can be produced

This automated ice cream factory increases the productivity of labor because fewer employees can now produce more output. However, the total productivity of the firm, taking into account the higher capital investment for the automation, may actually be lower.

with the same amount of steel. Productivity is the ratio of horseshoes to steel, in physical volume terms. But productivity is usually thought of as the amount of output per unit of labor. Most managers want to know the number of horseshoes produced per person, and how this number changes over time and compares to the competition. Steel is not the only input to making horseshoes.

Productivity is relatively easy to measure with a single input and a single output. If the organization produces several types of outputs (large and small horseshoes) and the mix of output varies over time, then the productivity measure must somehow combine the quantities of outputs into a single aggregate quantity. Likewise, several inputs (labor, overhead, and materials) must be combined to derive an aggregate input measure. Accountants traditionally combine multiple inputs and outputs through prices. Using prices per unit as the relative weights, the productivity measure with two outputs and three inputs becomes

$$\text{Productivity measure} = \frac{\text{Output}_1 \times \text{Price}_1 + \text{Output}_2 \times \text{Price}_2}{\text{Input}_1 \times \text{Cost}_1 + \text{Input}_2 \times \text{Cost}_2 + \text{Input}_3 \times \text{Cost}_3}$$

where price is the sales price of the output and cost is the purchase price of the input.

The numerator of the productivity measure is the output quantities times their respective prices per unit, which is equal to the total revenues. The denominator is the input quantities times their respective costs per unit, or total costs.

Using prices to combine multiple types of outputs and inputs has its problems. The productivity measure is affected by both quantity changes and price changes. If the productivity measure is used as a performance measure, it should reflect controllability. Managers, however, can't always control both quantities and prices, especially the purchase price of inputs. If prices are uncontrollable by managers, managers would like to eliminate the effect of prices on productivity measures.

To exclude uncontrollable price changes from the performance measure, yet still have a way to aggregate multiple inputs and outputs, constant prices could be used for comparing productivity measures over time. By specifying constant expected or past prices and costs as the method of aggregating different outputs and inputs, managers rewarded on the basis of the productivity measure will not have to worry about changing prices that can't be controlled.

NUMERICAL EXAMPLE 12.1

A manufacturer of horseshoes makes two types, large and small. There are two inputs, labor and steel. The following data summarize the operations for the last two years:

| | 1998 | Physical Quantities | |
Inputs/Outputs	Prices	1998	1999
Outputs:			
Small horseshoes	$4/unit	500 units	600 units
Large horseshoes	$6/unit	500 units	550 units
Inputs:			
Steel	$1/lb.	1,000 lbs.	1,200 lbs.
Labor	$12/hour	300 hrs.	320 hrs.

a. Calculate productivity measures for 1998 and 1999 using 1998 prices.
b. Calculate the percentage change in productivity.

■ **SOLUTION**

a. Using the 1998 prices, the productivity measures are calculated as:

how it was prepared and by whom, and what was cooked on the grill before your hamburger.

Quality may also be defined as having more options. A VCR that can be programmed for five programs is said to be of higher quality than one with only two programs. Similarly, Burger King tries to portray their hamburgers as being of higher quality than McDonald's because at Burger King the customer "can have it your way" (i.e., more options).

Meeting customer expectations is another way of defining quality. Customers have expectations with respect to all of a product's attributes: delivery schedules, operating characteristics, service, and so on. For example, a customer might expect a service technician to arrive on average within two hours of the call requesting service. If the service representative arrives in less than two hours, the organization has met the customer's expectation. Xerox, for example, defines quality as 100% customer satisfaction.

Joseph Juran, a noted quality expert, emphasizes that quality has multiple meanings, including product performance and satisfaction. He notes that product satisfaction causes customers to buy the product whereas customers complain about product deficiencies. To most quality experts, quality is defined as meeting customer expectations, which include expectations about opulence, conformity, reliability, and number of options.

The traditional approach to ensuring product quality was to "inspect-it-in." Inspection stations and quality assurance inspectors were added along the production line to weed out inferior products. Statistical sampling methods were used to draw random samples from a batch and reject the entire batch if a statistically large number of bad units were detected in the sample. Notice that the quality was defined by the organization as meeting a certain set of specifications, which may or may not be of interest to the consumer. Sections of the factory stored defects waiting to be reworked or scrapped. Organizations built into their operating budgets a normal allowance for scrap and rework. In some cases, if market demand exceeded production in a period, marginally defective products were released. Defective products reaching the market were corrected by the field service organization under warranty arrangements.

By the 1970s, two key factors combined to make the traditional approach to quality obsolete in many industries. First, the cost of detecting problems and monitoring production via computer instrumentation fell relative to the cost of maintaining quality via direct labor inspectors. The cost of labor (including health care benefits) made the cost of manually detecting and correcting errors very expensive relative to performing these tasks electronically. Second, worldwide competition expanded to include nonprice forms of competition such as quality. Once the Japanese automobile companies gained price competitiveness against the American companies, they turned their attention to achieving quality advantages. Both the lower cost of detecting defects and increased global competition fostered the concept of *zero defects*. The goal of zero defects, while never achievable, becomes the target. Each year, fewer defects than the year before becomes the standard.

To avoid defects reaching paying customers, some organizations test their products with a sampling of potential customers. Intel distributes its computer

Motorola seeks to produce fewer than 3.4 defects per million parts. The term "six sigma" is derived from plus or minus six standard deviations from the norm, or essentially 99.990% defect-free manufacturing. Should firms seek zero defects in their manufacturing process?

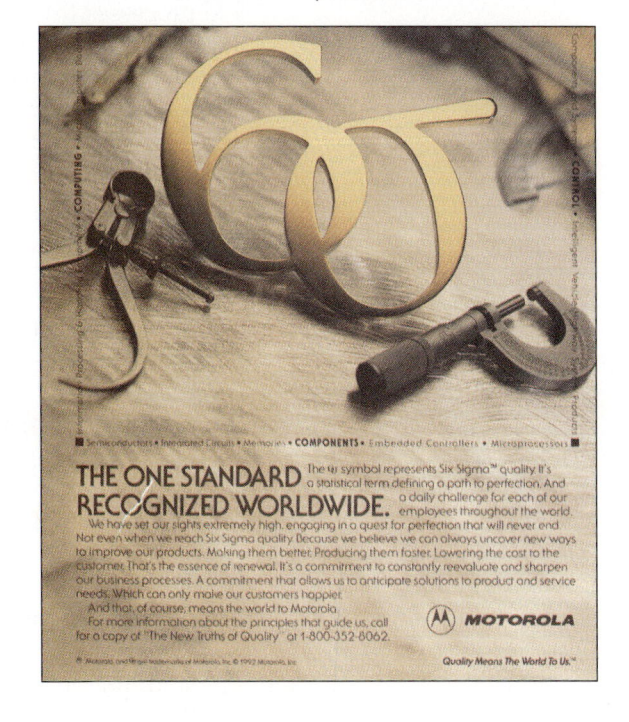

chips to sophisticated users to "stress" the chips and identify any potential defects. A flaw in the original Pentium chip was discovered by a sophisticated user and the company made corrections.

TQM Movement

The movement toward improved quality and customer satisfaction is called *total quality management (TQM)*. TQM is a method of managing that includes involved leadership, employee participation, empowerment, teamwork, customer satisfaction, and continual improvement.

Through TQM, companies redesign their products to require fewer different part numbers, making it easier to maintain tighter controls on the quality of their suppliers. Production processes are reengineered to reduce defects. Robots and more instrumentation are built into manufacturing to ensure more uniform production. In addition to the above changes, major changes in the organization's structure also occur, including modifying the performance evaluation and reward systems and the assignment of decision rights. Decision rights are pushed down lower in the firm where the knowledge of customer preferences reside.

In summary, most TQM programs contain the following elements:

- *Quality is a firmwide process.* Every employee from the senior manager to the janitor must understand the quality work processes. Quality links customers to suppliers. The pursuit of excellence is a prime motivator in the company.
- *Quality is defined by the customer.* Customer satisfaction is the primary goal of the organization. Customers expect reliability, conformity, timely delivery, and customer service.
- *Quality requires organizational changes.* The organization's structure (assignment of decision rights, performance measurement, and reward systems) must encourage mutual cooperation and create incentives to improve quality. Senior managers should develop hands-on, specialized knowledge of how to improve quality. Workers are empowered (i.e., given decision rights) to make changes that increase quality.
- *Quality is designed into the product.* Quality must be designed into the product and processes from the very beginning of manufacturing through delivery of a quality product to the consumer. Designers and engineers should work with manufacturers, marketers and accountants to design products that meet customers' needs, are simple to manufacture, and are not too costly. Once products are designed and engineered, many of the quality attributes are predetermined.

IBM recently redefined its business strategy as Market-Driven Quality. The goal is total customer satisfaction, guided by the following four market-driven principles:

- Understand our markets.
- Commit to leadership in the markets we choose to serve.
- Execute with excellence across our enterprise.
- Make customer satisfaction the final arbiter.

To implement these principles, the following initiatives are being undertaken:

- Research, understand, and segment total potential market needs. Commit to market leadership and deliver the right solutions at the right time.
- Remove defects in everything we do to achieve market-driven quality.
- Reduce the total time between customer wants/needs and fulfill those needs to the customer's total satisfaction.
- Give employees the authority and information they need to make timely decisions and carry out the activities necessary to ensure total customer satisfaction.

BMW combines quality systems techniques in production with meticulous final inspection to ensure that cars meet customers' quality standards.

- Establish achievable business targets with a particular focus on quality and customer satisfaction.

Measuring the Costs of Quality

If the goal of the organization is to achieve customer satisfaction, then some measures of quality are necessary to determine if the organization is achieving its goal and to motivate and reward managers. Many measures of quality are not part of the cost accounting system. Typical TQM quality measures include product design (number of new parts, number of parts), vendor rating systems (number of defects, on-time delivery), manufacturing (defect rates, scrap, rework, on-time delivery), and customer satisfaction (surveys, warranty expense).

Quality is also often measured in terms of defects. For example, a component part must be within 0.001 millimeters of standard or else it is termed *defective*. If changing the machine producing the part reduces the number of defects from five per thousand to three per thousand, then quality is said to have increased. This concept of quality is based on achieving certain specifications. One problem of defining quality in terms of defect rates is that opportunistic workers can appear to improve quality if they have the decision rights to redefine the standard used as the benchmark for determining defects. For example, suppose defects are defined as being in excess of 0.001 millimeters of a tolerance. If defects were redefined as being in excess of 0.0015 millimeters, fewer "defects" would result. Therefore, when installing quality improvement programs, management must ensure that the definition of defects is held constant.

The benefits and problems of measuring quality without the inclusion of costs are the same as occur with productivity measures. Defect rates, on-time delivery, and customer complaints are easy for managers to understand and easy to measure. Without a corresponding cost system, however, these diverse measures are difficult to aggregate. Managers do not know how to make trade-offs among quality decisions. For example, is it more costly to design and manufacture a product without defects or to focus on inspection and correcting defects from initial production? Is it cheaper to buy a scanning machine for more accurate inspections or stay with manual inspections? Managers need costs to make these comparisons for planning purposes.

Part of the TQM philosophy is that improved quality can actually be less costly to the organization. The opportunity cost of selling defective products and not satisfying customers can be very high. Errors must be corrected and disgruntled customers mollified. Customers will seek other suppliers of the service or product. A reputation for shoddy workmanship is often the death knell for organizations. Even if a defect is discovered before being sent to a customer, the cost of handling and fixing the problem can be quite high. In many cases, the defective product cannot be fixed and the defective product must be junked. The opportunity cost of not being able to sell a product because it is defective is equal to the costs of making the defective product plus the forgone profit.

If defects can be reduced through lower-cost prevention efforts, then organizations would no longer suffer the larger opportunity costs of fixing or throwing away defects. The philosophy of TQM is consistent with the adage "An ounce of prevention is worth a pound of cure." For example, a little extra effort to make sure the Hubble space telescope's mirror was correctly ground would have saved the huge cost of sending a space shuttle mission to correct the telescope.

Quality costs are typically categorized in four groups:

1. **Prevention costs** are incurred to eliminate defective units before they are produced. These costs include reengineering and design, high-quality parts, improved processes, and employee training.
2. **Appraisal costs** are incurred to eliminate defective units before they are shipped. These costs include inspecting and testing both raw material and work-in-process.
3. **Internal failure costs** are incurred when a defect is discovered before being sent to the customer. These costs include the costs of handling and fixing the product or the cost of disposing of the product. The opportunity cost of not being able to sell the disposed unit should also be included.
4. **External failure costs** are incurred when a customer receives a defective product. These costs include the cost of returns, warranty work, product liability claims, and the opportunity cost of lost sales from reputation effects.

The advantage of categorizing costs is to recognize trade-offs among different activities. A move to TQM is generally accompanied by an increase in prevention costs that is more than offset by lower failure costs. In Figure 12.2, the quality costs of a division of Texas Instruments are described over six years after

FIGURE 12.2

Change in Quality Cost Categories with TQM

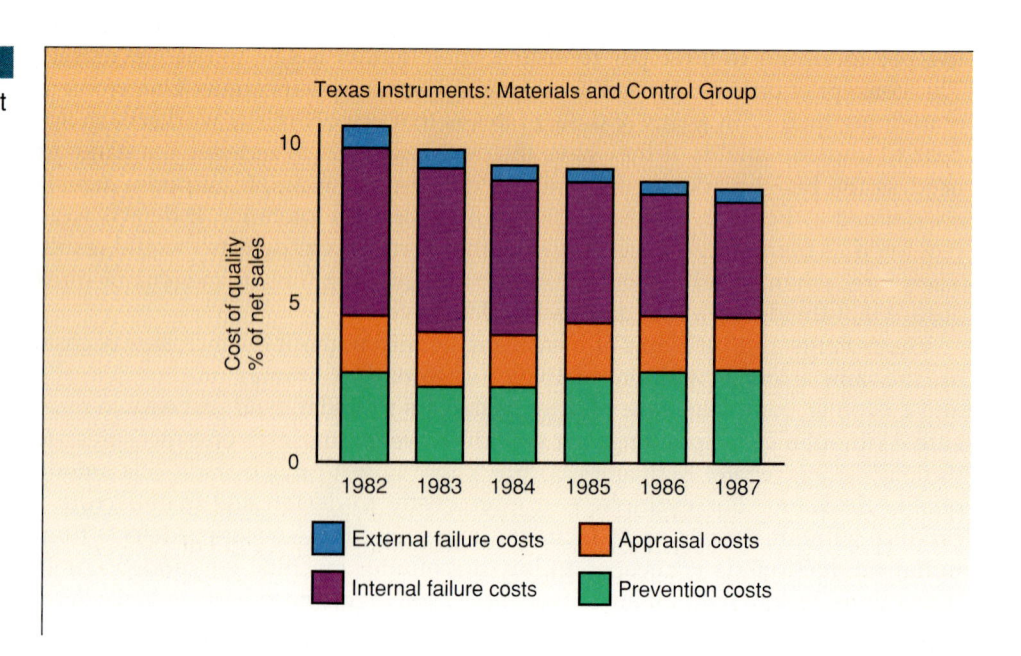

implementing TQM.[3] Notice that the failure costs have declined over this period. Although the prevention and appraisal costs remained about the same, the decline in failure costs indicate that resources were more effectively used. The net effect is higher quality at a reduced cost.

Most management accounting systems do not specifically identify quality costs. Many are imbedded in overhead accounts and the opportunity costs are commonly not reported at all. Therefore, a quality cost system must generally be constructed outside the traditional cost accounting system, which makes quality costs costly to identify and measure.

One of the benefits of measuring and identifying quality costs is to bring them to the attention of senior managers. Many companies have found their quality costs to be over 10% of sales. Total quality costs can often be reduced through increased prevention efforts and a corresponding decline in failure costs. The resulting cost savings of 5% to 10% are extremely important to an organization in a globally competitive market.

Another benefit of measuring quality costs is to measure improvement in quality performance. Total quality costs should decline as an organization engages in TQM. If total quality costs are not declining, then the organization should reexamine its TQM processes.

Quality costs are not commonly used explicitly for planning purposes. In principle, quality costs offer an opportunity to compare and trade off different quality efforts. Quality costs should be used to identify the optimal prevention and appraisal procedures. But organizations seem to lack confidence in the identification and measurement of quality costs. Also an understanding of the linkages between the cost categories is necessary. For example, how will an improved product design affect appraisal activities and reduce internal and external failure? Until senior management can clearly identify more uses of quality costs, they will be reluctant to bear the cost of measuring and identifying quality costs.

NUMERICAL EXAMPLE 12.2

The Compty Computer Company is having problems with the hard drive for its computer. A particular part fails about 2% of the time and costs $2,000 each time to replace the part and deal with customer dissatisfaction. The company could redesign the computer and leave out the part for $500,000 or perform extensive inspections on the part that would cost $20 per computer. What should the company do if it plans to make 30,000 computers during the coming year before the computer becomes obsolete?

■ **SOLUTION** The cost of not redesigning the computer or increasing inspections is (2%)(30,000 computers)($2,000/defect) = $1,200,000. The cost of increasing inspections is ($20/computer)(30,000 computers) = $600,000. The cost of changing the design ($500,000) is lower than the two other alternatives and is preferred.

Some companies are now incorporating the explicit quality-based criteria into their performance measurement schemes. Such changes in performance evaluation schemes, however, are not without their problems. There is no question that quality is important and should be improved. The problem is that quality is an elusive concept with many different dimensions. Not only is quality difficult to define precisely, it is difficult to measure objectively.

While there has been much attention to quality improvement programs in firms, many quality programs have failed to achieve their objectives. A 1992 *Newsweek* article reports that a number of companies, including McDonnell Douglas aircraft and Florida Power & Light, are abandoning their TQM programs.[4] Wallace Co. won a national quality award in 1990 and filed for bankruptcy in 1992. Although quality should be a primary goal of an organization, other goals can't be ignored. The balanced scorecard approach to evaluating performance discussed in Chapter 6 emphasizes the importance of having performance measures that motivate managers to recognize all of the stakeholders in the organization, not just the customer.

> **WHAT'S HAPPENING**
>
> The International Organization of Standards (ISO) is a European Community body that establishes quality standards. To become ISO 9000 certified, a manufacturer must document that they rely on written policies, procedures, and quality methods. Independent external registrars then visit the plant requesting ISO 9000 certification to ensure the applicant has the necessary documentation, quality manuals, and procedures in place. It certifies that policies exist that allow quality products to be manufactured. Does ISO 9000 certification guarantee that quality products are being manufactured?

Summary

To summarize, total quality management (TQM), if followed to the letter, is very much an attempt at restructuring the firm's organization. Decision rights must be linked with knowledge. As global competition increases, customers are able to find products more to their liking. Organizations must know what attributes of the product consumers most desire. Employees having day-to-day contact with customers usually possess the detailed knowledge of customer preferences. Somehow this detailed knowledge of what customers want must be transferred within the organization to the product planner and manufacturing managers. Alternatively, some of the decision rights over product design and distribution must be transferred to the lower level workers who have the detailed knowledge of customer preferences.

TQM programs attempt to do both. Multidisciplinary task forces are formed to conduct special studies and to improve quality. These task forces, composed of people from all levels of the organization, are an attempt to assemble the specialized knowledge concerning customer preferences. Sometimes these task forces are given decision rights to change the product or processes. Worker empowerment transfers decision rights to employees with specialized knowledge within the organization.

To successfully restructure the organization and assign decision rights to the people with the knowledge about customer preferences, the performance evaluation and performance reward systems must also be changed. Empowering workers with decision rights requires systems to evaluate and reward their performance. It is likely that firms that have tried to implement TQM but have not garnered the hoped-for benefits did not modify the performance measurement and reward systems to support the changes in decision rights.

Although TQM has not been universally accepted, some aspects of TQM have become a part of almost every organization. Organizations may not completely follow TQM with all of its ramifications, but almost every manager has heard of TQM and has become more aware of the benefits of satisfying customers.

DEPARTMENT OF MOTOR VEHICLES (DMV) (CONTINUED)

When productivity measures at the DMV led to quality problems, Melody Kim decided to attend a seminar on TQM. The leader of the TQM seminars focused on TQM in a manufacturing organization, but Melody was convinced that TQM could work for a service organization like the DMV. The product of the DMV is providing the public with the service of obtaining licenses and registrations and providing the state police and other legal authorities with information about registrants.

> Melody defined quality as friendly service. Employees were required to take training programs on interacting and reducing confrontation with customers. Supervisors were instructed to monitor the behavior of clerks dealing with customers. The TQM program appeared to be a success. Both the employees and the customers of the DMV were noticeably happier. As confrontations were reduced, the clerks were able to serve customers at a faster rate.
>
> To determine if the TQM program was saving the DMV money, Melody had the controller of the DMV estimate quality costs before and after the implementation of TQM. The controller defined quality costs as:
>
> Prevention costs: Employee training costs
> Appraisal costs: Supervisor salaries
> Internal failure costs: Clerk downtime while mistakes in service are corrected
> External failure costs: Time spent dealing with dissatisfied and irate customers
>
> After implementing the TQM program, prevention and appraisal costs went up, but internal and external failure costs went down by a greater amount. Therefore, TQM was cost effective.
>
> To verify that customers were satisfied with service at the DMV, Melody had customers fill out a survey. The survey indicated customers appreciated the smiling faces behind the counter, but still were unhappy with the long lines and time necessary to get their licenses and registrations. Melody realized that she may have defined quality incorrectly. Customers were more concerned with speed of service. Melody decided to attend a conference on just-in-time (JIT).

Just-in-Time (JIT) Processes

With just-in-time (JIT) processes, production and demand are synchronized by not starting production until an order is received. In this way, products are *pulled* through the plant rather than *pushed* through by a master production schedule designed to keep the plant operating at full capacity. The goal of a JIT plant manager is to reduce the time the product spends in the plant. If total production time decreases, costs will also decrease because fewer inventories have to be financed, stored, managed, and secured. To accomplish these goals, the plant is reorganized so that raw material and purchased parts are delivered to the factory right before they are entered into the production process, and there are no intermediate work-in-process inventories. Units flow from one production cell to another with no interruptions and all work is processed continually. Units only spend time in the factory when actual work is being expended on them. Of course, the preceding description is for an ideal JIT installation. Figure 12.3 compares a traditional system with a JIT system.

JIT systems seek to minimize a product's **throughput time,** which is the total time from the receipt of the order to the time of delivery to the customer. Throughput time is the sum of:

- Processing time.
- Time waiting to be moved or worked on.
- Time spent in transit.
- Inspection time.

FIGURE 12.3
Traditional Systems versus JIT Systems

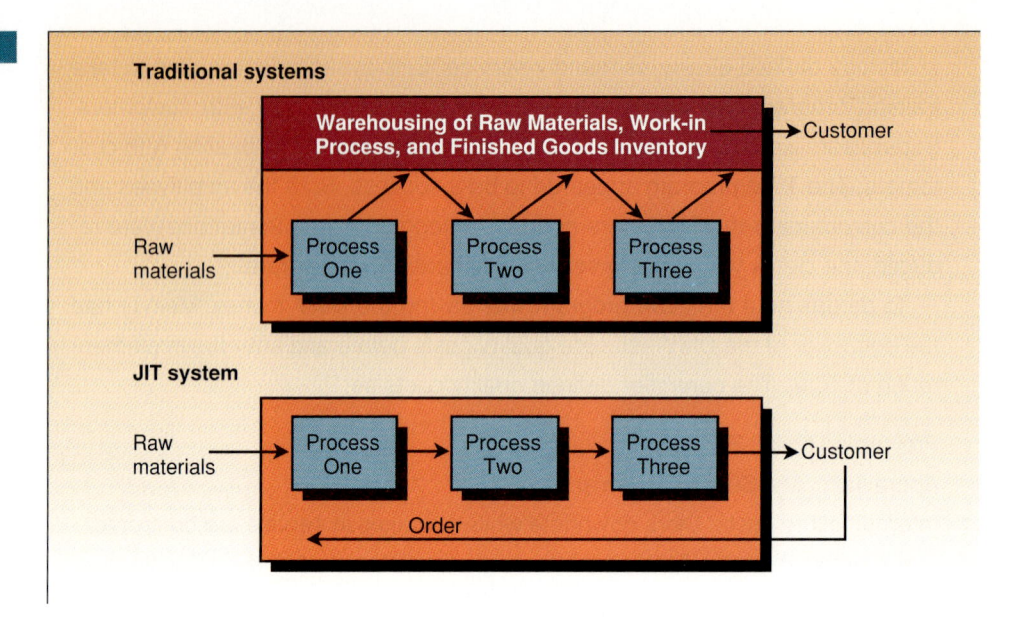

Traditional systems

Raw materials → [Process One] ↔ [Process Two] ↔ [Process Three]
↔ Warehousing of Raw Materials, Work-in Process, and Finished Goods Inventory → Customer

JIT system

Raw materials → [Process One] → [Process Two] → [Process Three] → Customer
← Order

In a JIT manufacturing environment, the goal is to drive the last three items (waiting, transit, and inspection time) to zero. The sum of the last three items is referred to as *wasted* or *non-value-added time.* The benefits of reducing throughput time include smaller in-process inventories, leading to:

- Lower capital costs of holding inventories.
- Factory and warehouse space and cost savings.
- Reduced overhead costs for material movers and expediters.
- Reduced risk of obsolescence.
- Faster response time to customers and reduced delivery times.

Factory Changes Caused by JIT

To accomplish the goal of reducing throughput time and to achieve the above benefits, the following changes must take place:

1. *Increase quality.* To prevent production downtime, the quality of raw materials and the quality of the manufacturing process must be improved. Increased material and process quality eliminate the need to stop processing because of defect.
2. *Reduce set-up times.* If machines can be set up for a new production run very quickly (or instantaneously), then parts do not have to wait for processing to begin. Moreover, inventories do not accumulate in front of the machine while it is being set up.
3. *Balance flow rates.* The rate of production in the various manufacturing cells must be the same or else work-in-process inventories will build up after the cells with the faster flow rates.
4. *Change factory layout.* Redesign the factory to reduce travel times. Machines that perform the same function are not all grouped in one department, but rather by how the products are sequenced through the machines. The factory becomes organized around dedicated JIT production lines producing a single type of product, sometimes called *dedicated flow lines.*

5. *Implement new performance measurement and reward systems.* No longer must employees be measured and rewarded on efficiency measures such as the number of units produced or keeping machines busy. Individual work cells are no longer rewarded for maximizing output. Such efficiency measures encourage workers to build inventories and to have inventories in front of their station as buffer stocks. The performance measure in a JIT system is throughput time divided by process time. The closer this ratio gets to one, the smaller the non-value-added time. Employees are encouraged to work as a team to achieve this goal.

One important aspect of JIT involves redesigning the firm's relationship with its suppliers. In the past, managers believed that having several suppliers of each input increased competition and kept prices down. Firms had policies of dividing total purchases among several sources, which required each input order to be inspected to ensure quality and made it more difficult to coordinate timely delivery of supplies. In a JIT environment, firms have drastically reduced the number of suppliers, often going to long-term, sole-sourcing contracts whereby a single supplier provides all of the firm's demand for a given input. The purchasing firm benefits from lower prices due to volume discounts, lower ordering costs since only a single-relationship contract is required, and higher quality assured by audits of the supplier's process rather than by inspecting each shipment. Even transportation costs are lower because suppliers can use long-term contracts with shippers. Buyers and sellers are integrating their computer systems so that orders are also received JIT. For example, "Motorola's Paging Product Group has won 60% global market share due partly to cooperation with suppliers that has brought significant advances in cost quality, cycle time, and technology."[5] Supply costs have fallen 8% to 10% annually for many years for Motorola.

Factors Driving JIT

The interest in JIT has arisen because of automation, information technology, and global competition. Factory automation allows organizations to produce small batches of different products because setting up computer-programmed robots is much simpler than traditional machinery. Robots are ready to produce a different product with the insertion of different software. With short setup times, organizations can produce a variety of products to meet varied demand in a short time period.

Information technology allows much better coordination among different departments and between suppliers and customers. Bar coding and scanning at the local supermarket is monitored by suppliers to allow for timely deliveries of products. Information technology in the form of programs such as **materials requirement planning (MRP)** allows organizations to quickly ascertain resource requirements to make a product. An MRP system is a computerized program that makes the necessary orders for raw materials and schedules the production to facilitate a short throughput time when an order arrives. MRP systems may also be tied to the organization's accounting system.

Global competition is another reason for the growing popularity of JIT. JIT can result in lower costs and greater customer satisfaction. Ideally, lower costs will occur because of reduced inventory holding and handling costs. But lower costs will not always result from a switch to JIT. Small batch runs and reconfiguring the factory layout may cause costs to increase.

Greater customer satisfaction should arise from more timely delivery of products. By reducing throughput time, the organization can often deliver goods

The sales clerk rings up a customer sale by scanning the bar code into the register. Not only does the computer look up the correct price of the item, but the inventory of that item is automatically updated. In some cases, the manufacturer's computer is informed that the item is sold, and it submits an order to the factory to produce another unit of inventory.

more quickly. But lower inventory levels can also have the opposite effect. If a problem develops during production, the organization does not have inventory on hand to satisfy immediate customer demand. As long as the organization faces shocks to either production or demand, such as labor strikes, weather-related interruptions in the flow of raw materials, or changing prices for its products, then satisfying customers with timely delivery can be a problem.

Accounting System Changes in Response to JIT

The accounting system has an altered role under JIT. For control purposes, performance measures should coincide with the goals of JIT. Reducing throughput time is a primary performance measure for JIT organizations. Traditional productivity measures to minimize input costs are inappropriate performance measures in a JIT system. Those types of productivity measures encourage inventory building. Instead, organizations with JIT want to encourage production sufficient to cover only demand. Also, team effort is important in JIT environments, so performance measures should reflect cooperative goals. Employees should be rewarded for achieving higher team performance measures rather than higher individual performance measures.

By not having a job cost sheet for each batch, throughput time can be shortened because employees do not need to spend time recording costs. Having line workers fill out job order sheets as they work on a product is non-value-added time. Firms that have adopted these JIT accounting systems have significantly reduced the number of accounting transactions. Some firms have reduced their journal entry volume twenty-fold because detailed payroll postings to jobs are eliminated and jobs are no longer tracked through the work-in-process accounts as they move from department to department.

Because inventory is in the form of work-in-process for such a short time, there is less need to worry about valuing partially completed products. The only time that an organization may want to value work-in-process is at the end of the accounting period for external reporting purposes. Balance sheets identify the assets of the organization at a particular point in time. Generally some

Motocycle maker Harley-Davidson almost went bankrupt. Now its motorcycles are in great demand. What accounts for this turnaround?

work-in-process exists at that point in time and its full cost must be determined.

Problems with JIT

JIT processes and accounting systems are not without their problems. Firms hold inventories to smooth out fluctuations in supply or demand. If there is a labor strike, or bad weather prevents delivery of raw materials, or there is an unexpected increase in demand, inventories allow the firm to avoid the opportunity costs of lost sales. Reorganizing the factory, improving product and process quality, and changing purchasing relationships with suppliers can smooth out some of the fluctuations in production but cannot eliminate all the shocks to the system. Those random fluctuations outside the control of management, such as weather-related and demand-related shocks, will cause the firm to carry some inventories as a buffer against losing sales. Few organizations have been able to completely eliminate raw materials inventory. For example after installing JIT at one Hewlett-Packard plant, raw material inventory ranged from a two-day to a five-day supply and finished inventory fell from a 2.8 months' supply to a 1.3 months' supply. But since production tripled, the actual dollar value of inventory on hand increased.

A JIT accounting system that does not track work-in-process requires other systems to keep track of inventory. At the Hewlett-Packard plant, the number of accounting entries was drastically reduced. However, the accounting system was no longer able to track inventory levels, which meant that physical counts of inventory (some every six weeks)

WHAT'S HAPPENING

Harley-Davidson has about 500 workers directly manufacturing motorcycles. Over the years, direct labor has shrunk to about 10% of a motorcycle's product cost. In the past, each worker had to keep track of every product worked on in the course of the day. For an average worker, this meant about 20 products. Each day the accounting system had to record 10,000 entries. However, management was not using this information for any decision making. After introducing JIT, Harley-Davidson changed the accounting system. Direct labor was no longer treated as a direct cost. Direct labor and overhead were treated as conversion costs. Conversion costs were assigned to individual products based on how many hours the product was in the manufacturing process. This change greatly simplified the accounting process because 10,000 individual labor transactions were no longer entered daily.[6] Why did managers closely track direct labor costs in the past?

were required to supply managers with information on specific inventory levels. Inconsistent with the basic JIT philosophy, these inventory counts are non-value-added activities disrupting the production process by forcing workers to stop producing and count the inventory.[7]

DEPARTMENT OF MOTOR VEHICLES (DMV) (CONCLUDED)

The JIT conference that Melody attended was very exciting. Once again the emphasis was on manufacturing firms, but Melody gained many insights that would work for the DMV. Melody defined throughput as the time a customer spent in the office of the DMV. She decided to evaluate the managers of the local offices by the average throughput time for a customer obtaining a license or registration. She gave the local managers the decision rights to change procedures to achieve a quicker throughput time. The local managers came up with the following ideas:

Prefilled forms, so customers would only have to sign the forms if the information was correct.

Flexible, multiskilled employees, so employees could supplement other overburdened employees.

Use of part-time labor during busy times.

Registration via mail.

Throughput time declined sharply and customers were happy. The main question was whether there was also cost savings. Melody was happy to find that the more efficient use of employees through JIT actually led to lower costs.

CONCEPT REVIEW

1. How is productivity generally measured?
2. What are some advantages and disadvantages of using productivity measures to evaluate employees?
3. Explain the philosophy of total quality management (TQM).
4. What are the four categories of quality costs?
5. What are the advantages of just-in-time (JIT)?

12.3 When Should Management Accounting Be Changed?

There is no such thing as an ideal management accounting system. Each organization has different circumstances that lead to different management accounting systems. Also, management accounting must continually deal with trade-offs among external users wanting information describing firm performance and internal users wanting information for making planning decisions and control decisions. Finally, each organization is continually changing to meet the demands of a changing environment. Because organizations are in a continual state of flux, management accounting must continually adapt.

THE STORY OF MANAGERIAL ACCOUNTING

Team Decisions Regarding Quality

All the members of the *Managerial Accounting* book team are concerned about quality. Jeff, the team leader, and Heather, the marketing manager, know that a poor quality book will not sell. Kelly and Karen, the development and project editors, and Larry, the designer, are responsible for correcting editorial, typesetting, and design problems in the manuscript and page proof. The book must be educationally superior and pleasing to the eye. Dina, the production supervisor, is responsible for ensuring that the book's design is brought to fruition through printing without defects. What is the role of Peggy, the accountant, with respect to quality?

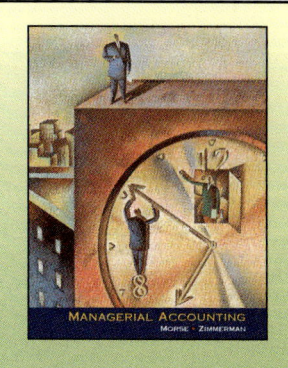

There are certain signs that indicate that the management accounting process is not working well. One sign is dysfunctional behavior on the part of managers because of poorly chosen performance measures. Managers will make decisions to positively influence performance measures. If those performance measures are not consistent with the goals of the organization, management will make decisions that don't coincide with the organization's goals. When managers of an organization are acting at cross-purposes with each other, the management accounting system is not working and should be changed.

Another sign of problems with the management accounting process is poor planning decisions. If product mix and pricing decisions based on management accounting are not adding to the organizational value, then the management accounting system may not be approximating opportunity costs very well. One indication of a poor management accounting system is the inability to win bids to sell products that are a company's specialty, but winning bids to sell products that the company has no comparative advantage in making. John Deere Component Works had this problem and realized the management accounting system was not allocating overhead properly.[8]

Organizations should not necessarily look to the latest management accounting fads to give them direction in changing their management accounting systems. Activity-based costing (ABC), for example, is only appropriate for certain types of organizations. Each organization must continually evaluate and improve their management accounting system to meet the challenges of a changing environment and a changing organization.

12.4 Summary

1. **Describe the forces that influence an organization's investment opportunities.** Technology in the form of automation and computer/information technology and global competition are recent factors that have influenced the investment opportunities of organizations.

2. **Identify the relation between organizational structure and investment opportunities.** The investment opportunities of an organization are determined by its assets, customers, and knowledge creation. These factors affect and are affected by the organization structure, which is composed of the assignment of decision rights, the performance evaluation system, and reward system.

3. **Explain the role of management accounting in the control process and in making planning decisions.** Management accounting, by means of budgets, is used to assign decision rights. Management accounting is also used to measure performance. Management accounting also assists in making planning decisions.

4. **Describe productivity measures and the strengths and weaknesses of productivity measures.** Productivity measures are calculated by dividing units of output by units of input. Productivity measures are easy to understand by employees and often reflect controllable variables. Productivity measures, however, may lead to overproduction and lower profits because they ignore relative price changes.

5. **Identify major characteristics of total quality management (TQM).** TQM is a philosophy that places customer satisfaction first. Continual improvement, involved leadership, employee participation, and employee empowerment are all part of TQM.

6. **Use quality costs for making planning decisions and control.** The comparison of quality costs over time provides a benchmark to determine if TQM efforts are successful. Quality costs should also be used to make planning decisions comparing different quality efforts.

7. **Explain the philosophy of JIT processes and accounting adjustments for JIT.** The philosophy of JIT is to produce to order rather than produce for inventory. To be successful, the organization must have a short throughput time to meet demand. Under JIT there are no job-order costs. Accounting performance measures should also be chosen to encourage faster throughput time and discourage increased inventory.

8. **Identify when management accounting within an organization should change.** Management accounting must continually adapt to changing environments and organizations. Signs of problems with the management accounting system are dysfunctional behavior by managers and poor planning decisions.

KEY TERMS

Appraisal costs Costs related to identifying defective units before they are shipped to customers.

Asset structure The nature of assets held by the organization.

Customer base The type and geographical location of customers.

External failure costs Costs incurred when a customer receives a defective product.

Internal failure costs Costs incurred when a defect is discovered before being received by a customer.

Investment opportunities The projects available to an organization today and in the future.

Material requirement planning (MRP) Programs that allow organizations to quickly ascertain resource requirements to make a product.

Prevention costs Costs incurred in the production process to reduce defects.

Throughput time The total time from receipt of an order to the time of delivery.

SELF-STUDY PROBLEM

Jose Morales operates a small sewing shop that makes dresses and pants. Jose receives orders for the dresses and pants from large clothing companies that contract with companies like Jose's to manufacture the clothing that is then sold to retailers. The clothing companies provide Jose with the pattern and specifications for the item. Any dresses and pants that don't meet specifications are returned to Jose. The business is extremely competitive. Jose is forced to operate on small margins because the clothing companies are threatening to send the manufacturing to other countries. Jose has managed to keep his business operating by promising a low number of defects and timely delivery. Jose has achieved a low number of defects by careful inspection of all clothing leaving the shop. Jose has been less successful in achieving timely delivery.

Jose hired 20 seamstresses to do the sewing. Prior to the sewing, however, the cloth must be cut. Once the sewing has been completed, buttons and snaps are added. The dresses and pants are then inspected, pressed, and packaged.

Required

Describe how Jose Morales might use productivity measures, TQM, and JIT and the advantages and disadvantages of each.

Solution to the Self-Study Problem

Jose can use productivity measures to evaluate each of his seamstresses individually and the overall business. A typical productivity measure for a seamstress would be the number of good units completed in an hour. By requiring only defect-free units to be included in the productivity measure, Jose can control for quality. On the other hand, he must have someone check the quality of each item to verify that it is without defect as it leaves the seamstresses.

Productivity for the whole business is a little more difficult to measure because of multiple inputs and outputs. One simple measure is to divide the value of all of the outputs by the cost of all of the inputs. That overall productivity measure, however, provides little direction for improvement if less than expected.

Jose must maintain the quality of his product to survive, so TQM appears to be relevant for Jose. TQM, however, suggests a different approach to achieving fewer defects. Instead of discovering defects at final inspection, Jose should attempt to reduce defects before they happen. More training of employees and better sewing machines could help reduce initial defects. With less initial defects, Jose can save on the cost of spoiled units discovered after completion. In the long run, TQM can save on costs, but in the short run, the training and new machines will be costly.

Jose has a problem delivering orders on schedule. JIT suggests that production should start after receipt of an order rather than producing for inventory. Jose has already been following this rule, but he needs to shorten his throughput. One method of shortening throughput is to have small groups of seamstresses work in teams with individuals doing the cutting, adding the snaps and buttons, pressing, and packaging. Work-in-process could be reduced, allowing defects to be identified and processes corrected more quickly. The team members could become multiskilled to assist each other when needed. All of these actions would increase throughput. Jose would have to change the organizational structure, however, to achieve JIT, and many employees might be temporarily resentful of moving to a new evaluation system.

NUMERICAL PROBLEMS

NP 12–1: Productivity Measure with a Single Input and Output (LO 4; NE 1)
A tax accountant is examining his productivity. In 1996 he did 300 tax returns in 1,400 hours. In 1997 he did 250 tax returns in 1,200 hours.

What was his percentage increase in productivity from 1996 to 1997?

NP 12–2: Productivity Measures with Multiple Inputs and Outputs (LO 4; NE 1)
A farmer grows two crops—lettuce and beans. The farmer uses three inputs—labor, seed, and fertilizer. The past prices and the quantities of each are given in the following tables:

	Past	Physical Quantities	
Inputs/Outputs	Prices	Last Year	This year
Outputs:			
Lettuce	$1500/ton	500 tons	600 tons
Beans	$1300/ton	200 tons	100 tons
Inputs:			
Labor	$10/hour	1,000 hrs.	1,200 hrs.
Seeds	$12/pound	300 lbs.	320 lbs.
Fertilizer	$500/ton	10 tons	12 tons

a. Calculate productivity measures for last year and this year using past prices.
b. Calculate the percentage change in productivity.

NP 12–3: Quality Costs (LO 6; NE 2)   A company has measured the following quality costs by categories for the last five years.

Category	1987	1988	1989	1990	1991
Prevention	$5000	$6000	$7000	$8000	$9000
Appraisal	5000	5000	6000	7000	8000
Internal Failure	9000	9000	7000	5000	3000
External Failure	9000	8000	7000	6000	5000

a. Given the above costs, is it likely that the company's defect rate has gone up or down? Explain.
b. If these costs reflect all the relevant quality costs, have the increased costs of prevention and appraisal yielded a net benefit to the company?

NP 12–4: An Inspection Decision with Quality Costs (LO 5; NE 2)
A company is considering additional final inspection costs of $1 per unit before delivery to customers. The additional inspection should reduce the defect rate from 3% to 1%. If a defective unit is found, it is scrapped at no additional cost. The manufacturing costs before the final inspection are $200 per unit. The management believes that the external failure costs are $40 per defective unit.

Should the management incur the additional inspection costs?

NP 12–5: Scrap Costs (LO 6)   O'Reilly Manufacturing produces three models of a product: Super, Supreme, and Ultra. These models are basically the same design, but different quality standards are applied in the production process. Frequent production line stops, adjustments, and start-ups cause a certain amount of scrap costs. Also, scrap occurs when inspectors reject a product for not meeting the specifications for that product. Once rejected, the product has no commercial value and is hauled away. All costs incurred to produce a scrapped product are charged to a scrap account, which is part of overhead. The budgeted operating statement for the firm, by product, is:

O'REILLY MANUFACTURING
Budgeted Operating Statement for 1998

	Super	Supreme	Ultra	Total
Unit volume	85,000	42,000	13,000	
Selling price	$ 205	$ 225	$ 235	
Revenue	$17,425,000	$9,450,000	$3,055,000	$29,930,000
Less:				
Raw materials	$ 8,500,000	$4,200,000	$1,300,000	14,000,000
Direct labor	5,312,500	3,150,000	975,000	9,437,500
Overhead	3,478,245	2,062,395	638,360	6,179,000
Total cost	$17,290,745	$9,412,395	$2,913,360	$29,616,500
Profits	$ 134,255	$ 37,605	$ 141,640	$ 313,500

Other information:

- Overhead costs are allocated to products based on direct labor dollars.
- Direct labor cost is $25 per hour.

Overheads consist of:

Depreciation	$3,500,000
Indirect labor	450,000
Scrap	1,679,000
Other	550,000
Total	$6,179,000

Additional data include:

	Super	Supreme	Ultra
Direct labor hours per unit	2.5 hours	3 hours	3 hours
Total scrap	$850,000	$504,000	$325,000
Profits per unit	$1.58	$0.90	$10.90

Management is concerned about the relatively low profit per unit on the Supreme line as compared to the Ultra line and is considering a variety of marketing strategies to increase the sales of Ultras since the profit margins are substantially higher.

Critically analyze management's conclusion that profits are substantially higher on Ultra. Present supporting figures to back up your analysis and conclusions.

NP 12–6: Becoming ISO 9000 Qualified (LO 5, 6; NE 2)

The Stowbridge Division is analyzing expanding their total quality management program. They already have a TQM program in place. But one of their customers, Amlan Equipment, is asking all their suppliers to become ISO 9000 qualified. ISO 9000 is a process that certifies that the firm meets various quality standards. Once their suppliers are ISO 9000 qualified, Amlan can reduce their inspection costs because they can depend on quality parts from their suppliers. Not all of their suppliers will be certified, and those that are will receive more business from Amlan.

Amlan purchases a stainless steel rotor from Stowbridge. To meet the ISO 9000 certification, Stowbridge estimates that it will have to incur the following annual incremental costs for as long as it wants to maintain its ISO 9000 certification:

Annual Incremental Costs to Be ISO 9000 Certified	
Training	$74,000
Inspection	96,000
Prevention	62,000
Direct materials	10%
Direct labor	15%

To manufacture the current quality of the rotors (before receiving ISO 9000 certification), the budgeted selling price and cost data per rotor is provided below:

Selling price	$14.00
Less:	
Direct materials	$ 4.30
Direct labor	2.40
Manufacturing overhead (all fixed)	2.05
Selling and administrative (all variable)	1.60
Unit cost	$10.35
Unit profit	$ 3.65

Unless Stowbridge receives ISO 9000 certification, they will lose Amlan's business of 120,000 units per year. In addition, management estimates that the higher quality of the rotor will allow Stowbridge to add 14,000 rotors to its existing sales from new and existing customers. Stowbridge is currently selling 480,000 rotors per year including the Amlan sales. The 480,000 current sales amounts to 63% of plant capacity. The additional 14,000 units sold can be manufactured without exceeding plant capacity. The higher quality process after receiving ISO 9000 certification would apply to all the rotors produced.

Should Stowbridge seek ISO 9000 certification? Support your recommendation with an analysis of the costs and benefits of ISO 9000 certification.

NP 12–7: Allocating Costs Based on Throughput Time (LO 7)   Toby Manufacturing produces three different products in the same plant and uses a job-order costing system to estimate product costs. A flexible budget is used to forecast overhead costs. Total budgeted fixed factory overhead is $450,000 and variable overhead is 120% of direct labor dollars. There is no beginning or ending inventory.

Projected volumes, selling prices, and direct costs for the three products for the next calendar year are given by:

	Product AAA	Product BBB	Product CCC
Projected number of units	6,000	3,000	1,000
Direct materials per unit	$22	$ 25	$ 30
Direct labor per unit	$11	$ 12	$ 16
Selling price	$98	$115	$140

The manufacturing process requires six operations. Between operations, intermediate products are moved and warehoused until the next production stage. The three products each require 10 days of processing time to complete all six operations. But the products have different throughput times because of different waiting times between operations. *Throughput time* is defined as the total time from ordering the raw materials for the product until the product is completed and shipped. Product AAA has the shortest throughput time (20 days) because the large volume allows more accurate forecasts and more continuous scheduling of production. Product BBB has a total throughput time of 40 days and Product CCC has a total throughput time of 50 days. Products BBB and CCC have longer warehousing times of work-in-process because of more frequent scheduling changes, and more frequent supplier delays.

Half of what is currently treated as fixed overhead cost is involved in the warehousing function.

a. Prepare a pro forma income statement by product line for the year based on full absorption costing. Product costs should include overhead assigned on direct labor cost.
b. Prepare a revised pro forma income statement by product line using throughput time to allocate fixed overhead related to warehousing.
c. Comment on the differences.

NP 12–8: Compensation and Quality (LO 5, 6; NE 2)   Tagway 4000 is a computer manufacturer based in Montana. One component of the computer is an internal battery that is used to keep track of the time and date while the computer is turned off. Tagway produces the batteries in house. The division, which produces 1,000,000 batteries each year, is treated as a cost center. The manager of the division is compensated based on her ability to keep total costs low as well as meet quality control measures of number of defects and delivery time. She has a base salary of $144,000. She is eligible for a $34,000 bonus if total costs are less than or equal to $2,000,000 without including her compensation. She is eligible for a $40,000 bonus if there are 32 or fewer defects per 1,000,000 units produced. Finally, she is eligible for a $22,000 bonus if batteries are delivered on time. On time is defined as averaging two days between the order from the assembly department and delivery to the assembly department.

The basic cost of producing a battery is $1.55. However, current methods have an inherent defect rate of 1,032 defects per 1,000,000. The cost of improving the defect rate involves using higher quality materials and more experienced labor. Based on currently available inputs, improving the defect rate below 32 per 1,000,000 is impossible. From 1,032 defects to 32 defects per 1,000,000, the cost of removing each defect is $450. In other words, the cost to reduce defects to the desired level of 32 per 1,000,000 is $450,000. This production method also delivers the batteries in an average of 4 days. The cost of overtime necessary to lower the average to 3 days is $90,000. The cost of speeding up delivery another day is $95,000, making the cumulative cost of lowering the average to two days $185,000. The marginal cost of reducing the average delivery a third day is $115,000 making the total cost of reducing the average delivery time to 1 day $300,000.

a. Create a table showing the production costs related to defect rates of 1,032, 500, 100, 50, and 32 per 1,000,000 and average delivery times of 1 to 4 days. Do not include the manager's salary. Note the minimum cost.
b. Create a table showing the manager's compensation related to defect rates of 1,032, 500, 100, 50, and 32 and average delivery times of 1 to 4 days. Note the maximum compensation level.
c. Comment on the ideal number of defects and delivery times necessary to achieve the minimum costs and the maximum compensation level.

NP 12–9: Productivity Measures (LO 4; NE 1)   The Productivity Company produces two outputs, A and B, using only two inputs, labor and material. There are no fixed costs, inventories, or overhead (indirect labor and materials, taxes, etc.). There is no inflation. The company sells everything it produces and uses a productivity measurement system.

The following table summarizes operations in the base year, 1993, and the current year, 1996:

	Outputs				Inputs			
	A		B		Labor		Materials	
	Price	Units	Price	Units	Wage	Hours	Price	Pounds
1993	$1.00	10,000	$2.00	10,000	$15.00	850	$5.00	2650
1996	$0.90	11,000	$2.10	9,000	$14.94	870	$7.41	1862

a. Compute the change in productivity from the base year, 1993, to 1996 using 1993 prices.
b. Compute the change in productivity from the base year, 1993, to 1996 using prices of the respective years.
c. What additional information do productivity measurements provide beyond the information in a traditional cost accounting system?

DISCUSSION PROBLEMS

DP 12–1: Choosing TQM (LO 1, 5)   The Wonderful Toy Company is celebrating its 100th anniversary this year. The company has been successful in designing and making educational toys for department stores and smaller hobby stores. The sales manager has recently returned from a national convention and heard that many other toy manufacturers are implementing TQM. The president of the company, the great grandchild of the founder of the company, does not think that the company needs TQM. He states, "We have been in business for 100 years and this company has been very profitable. Our customers must be happy with us because they are still buying our products. Why should we change the way we do business?"

Evaluate the president's statement.

DP12-2: Acquisition of a Life Insurance Company (LO 2)

A company with a chain of department stores across the country is trying to decide how to use some excess cash. The company is thinking about acquiring another company, but is wary of making the same mistake as last year when the company bought a casino in Nevada. The casino was not a financial success, and the company had serious problems in managing the new venture. This year the company is considering the purchase of a life insurance company.

Describe the investment in a life insurance company in terms of the asset structure of the department store chain, the customer base, and the knowledge acquisition.

DP 12-3: JIT and the Role of Accounting (LO 3)

The president of Kelly Windows is an avid believer in JIT. Kelly Windows manufactures bay windows. The president wants no inventory or work-in-process on the floor at the end of each day. Windows are only manufactured after being ordered, and throughput time is quick enough to complete most orders during the day of the order. The president is also trying to eliminate all non–value-added activities. She considers accounting to be non-value-added and would like to reduce accounting activities sharply if not completely.

As the controller, how can you defend the accounting activities performed by your department?

DP 12-4: Productivity Measures and Inflation (LO 4)

The China Truck Company manufactures trucks in China that are primarily purchased by domestic customers. Parts are purchased from suppliers that are also in China. The company tends to have large inventories and uses FIFO for calculating profit. The company also calculates productivity measures for the factory by dividing the revenue of the company (sales price × quantity sold) by the cost of the trucks sold. The cost of trucks sold is also determined using FIFO, so the truck costs are based on manufacturing costs from a time period earlier than the time of sale. A large growth rate and other factors have led to a 25% inflation rate during the last year. A 25% inflation rate means that the truck prices and the manufacturing costs are each rising approximately 25% each year.

How does the combination of an inflation rate and FIFO affect productivity measures?

DP 12-5: Measuring Quality Costs (LO 5)

The president of Precision Machines wants to convert to TQM. The industrial machinery produced by Precision Machines is critical to the customers. If defective machinery is sold to customers, very high costs are incurred by the customer. Precision Machines usually has to pay those costs because of warranties or lawsuits. The president feels that TQM will help the organization satisfy its customers. As part of the change to TQM, the president has asked you, the controller, to devise a system for measuring the different categories of quality cost: prevention, appraisal, internal failure, or external failure.

Describe the costs in each of these categories and which categories will be the most difficult in making cost estimates.

DP 12-6: JIT and Stock-Out Costs (LO 7)

James Industries is considering a shift to JIT. The president feels that considerable costs can be saved by reducing inventory. The marketing manager is worried, however. She recognizes that the inventory holding costs such as storage and the opportunity cost of cash used to hold inventory are high and will be reduced if the company changes to JIT. But she is worried that the president has forgotten about stock-out costs. Stock-out costs occur when customers want to purchase an item, but the item is not immediately available so the customer goes elsewhere to make the purchase.

How should the company measure stock-out costs? What can be done to minimize stock-out costs?

CASE

C12–1: Quality Costs Software Development Inc. (SDI) produces and markets software for personal computers, including spreadsheet, word processing, desktop publishing, and database management programs. SDI has annual sales of $800 million.

Producing software is a time-consuming, labor-intensive process. Software quality is an extremely important aspect of success in computer software markets. One aspect of quality is program reliability. Does the software perform as expected? Does it work with other software in terms of data transfer and interfaces? Does it terminate abnormally? In spite of extensive testing of the software, programs always contain some bugs. Once the software is released, SDI stands behind the product with phone-in customer service consultants who answer questions and help the customer work around problems in the software. SDI's software maintenance group fixes bugs and sends out revised versions of the programs to customers.

SDI tracks the relation between quality costs and quality. The quality measure it uses is the number of documented bugs in a software package. These bugs are counted when a customer calls in with a complaint and the SDI customer service representative determines this is a new problem. The software maintenance programmers then attempt to fix the program and eliminate the bug. To manage quality, SDI tracks quality costs. It has released 38 new packages or major revisions in existing packages in the last three years. Exhibit 1 reports the number of defects (bugs) documented in the first six months following release. Also listed in the table are total product cost and quality cost per software package release.

Product costs include all the costs incurred to produce and market the software, excluding the quality costs in the table. Quality costs consist of three components—training, prevention, and software maintenance and customer service costs. Training costs are expenditures for educating the programmers and updating their training. Better educated programmers produce fewer bugs. Prevention costs include expenditures for testing the software before it is released. Maintenance and customer service costs are those of the programmer charged with finding the bugs and reissuing the revised software and the customer service representatives answering phone questions. The training and prevention costs are measured over the period the software was being developed. The number of defects and maintenance and service costs are measured in the first six months following release.

All the numbers in the table have been divided by lines of computer code in the particular program release. Programs with more lines of code cost more and also have more bugs. Prior studies find that lines of code is an acceptable way to control for program complexity. Thus, the numbers in the table are stated in terms of defects and cost per 100,000 lines of code.

Exhibit 2 plots the relationship between total quality cost and number of defects. The vice president of quality of SDI likes to use it to emphasize that costs and quality are inversely related. She is fond of saying, "Quality pays! Our total costs are a function of the number of defects. The more we spend on quality, the lower our costs."

Case Question

Critically evaluate the vice president's analysis.

EXHIBIT 1
SDI Defects and Quality Costs by Program Release*

Program Release	Number of Defects	Product Cost	Training Cost	Prevention Cost	Software Maintenance and Customer Service Cost	Total Costs
1	66	$3,455	$442	$ 770	$2,160	$6,827
2	86	3,959	428	447	2,658	7,492
3	14	3,609	417	1,167	687	5,880
4	73	3,948	211	655	2,334	7,148
5	17	3,104	290	1,013	544	4,951
6	48	3,179	253	547	1,556	5,535
7	80	3,112	392	508	2,633	6,645
8	41	3,529	276	577	1,563	5,945
9	50	3,796	557	634	1,666	6,653
10	67	3,444	365	947	2,140	6,896
11	42	3,922	453	869	1,444	6,688
12	64	3,846	378	1,108	1,942	7,274
13	71	3,014	555	762	2,384	6,715
14	1	3,884	301	773	423	5,381
15	18	3,183	378	1,080	857	5,498
16	85	3,475	528	1,010	2,572	7,585
17	17	3,445	357	666	631	5,099
18	50	3,203	285	427	1,546	5,461
19	22	3,839	239	1,080	891	6,049
20	73	3,060	540	1,054	2,309	6,963
21	52	3,182	329	1,079	1,867	6,457
22	75	3,075	395	832	2,697	6,999
23	35	3,456	447	969	1,518	6,390
24	53	3,987	355	651	2,042	7,035
25	25	3,836	309	1,160	1,036	6,341
26	6	3,886	234	794	252	5,166
27	78	3,846	418	833	2,800	7,897
28	82	3,106	409	1,092	2,871	7,478
29	39	3,506	448	899	1,342	6,195
30	47	3,545	450	442	1,450	5,887
31	30	3,376	456	784	1,260	5,876
32	17	3,740	542	420	607	5,309
33	67	3,479	411	821	2,018	6,729
34	51	3,773	351	1,145	1,873	7,142
35	74	3,034	497	671	2,389	6,591
36	25	3,768	268	887	1,094	6,017
37	14	3,168	356	645	837	5,006
38	77	3,561	492	1,167	2,597	7,817
Average	48	$3,509	$390	$826	$1,671	$6,395

*Per 100,000 lines of computer code.

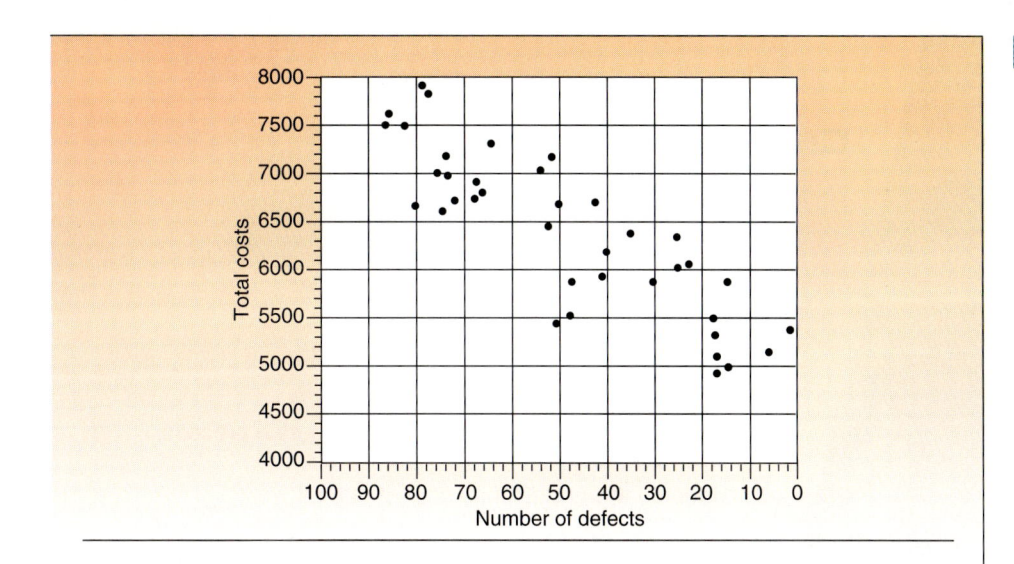

EXHIBIT 2
SDI Total Costs by Defects

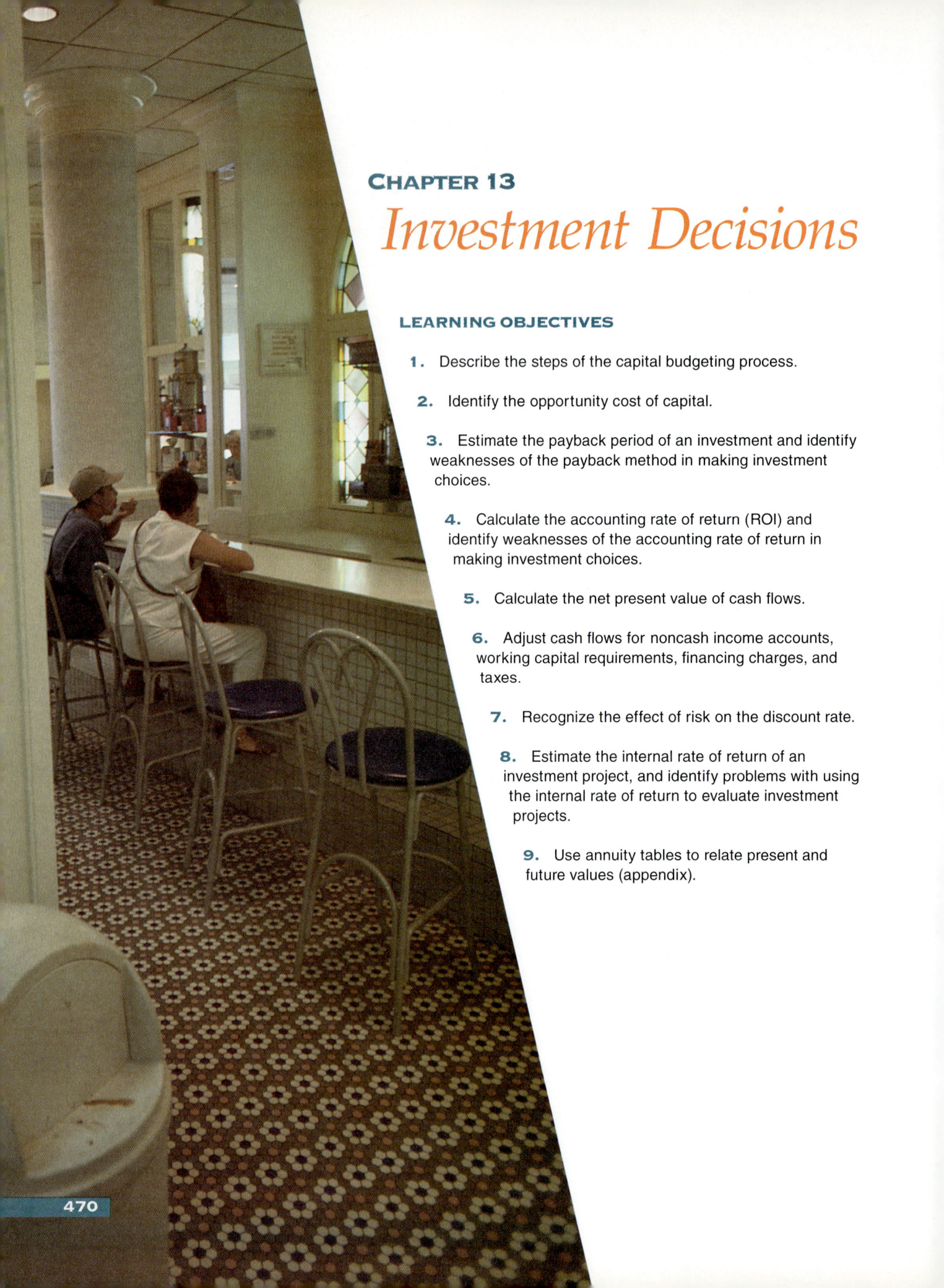

CHAPTER 13
Investment Decisions

LEARNING OBJECTIVES

1. Describe the steps of the capital budgeting process.

2. Identify the opportunity cost of capital.

3. Estimate the payback period of an investment and identify weaknesses of the payback method in making investment choices.

4. Calculate the accounting rate of return (ROI) and identify weaknesses of the accounting rate of return in making investment choices.

5. Calculate the net present value of cash flows.

6. Adjust cash flows for noncash income accounts, working capital requirements, financing charges, and taxes.

7. Recognize the effect of risk on the discount rate.

8. Estimate the internal rate of return of an investment project, and identify problems with using the internal rate of return to evaluate investment projects.

9. Use annuity tables to relate present and future values (appendix).

SLIM'S ICE CREAM PARLOR

Slim owns the only ice cream parlor in town. Slim eats a lot of his own ice cream and isn't so slim, but he recognizes that many people are concerned about their health and the fat content of ice cream. Therefore, Slim thinks a frozen yogurt machine might encourage more customers to come to his ice cream parlor. There is plenty of space to put the frozen yogurt machine and the additional business could be very profitable. He visits a supplier and finds that a new frozen yogurt machine costs $10,000. The machine would last for five years. Slim could pay cash for the machine but decides to borrow the amount from his bank at 8% interest.

To determine whether the frozen yogurt machine would be profitable, Slim made the following estimates of the impact of the machine on his reported income for each of the next five years:

Revenues from selling frozen yogurt	$5,000
Cost of ingredients	(1,500)
Additional power costs	(500)
Interest expense (.08)($10,000)	(800)
Straight-line depreciation on machine: $10,000/5 =	(2,000)
Profit per year	$ 200

Although these estimates indicate that the frozen yogurt machine will generate a profit, Slim is not sure that he has included everything in his calculations.

13.1 Long-Term Investment Decisions

Chapters 2 through 5 described different planning decisions and how management accounting can facilitate those planning decisions. Those decisions tended to have short-term implications. In other words, the cash flow effects of those decisions were resolved within a year of the decision. Long-term investment decisions tend to differ from short-term decisions in two ways: (1) a long-term investment decision usually involves a larger amount of cash outlay and has greater implications on the strategy of the organization and (2) a long-term investment decision has cash flow implications for many years.

The size and strategic implications of a long-term investment decision make those decisions much more critical to the organization. Therefore, the process of making a long-term investment decision is carefully controlled within organizations. The control aspects of the long-term investment decision are described in the next section.

The multiyear, cash-flow implications of a long-term investment decision cause additional complications in comparing the costs and benefits of the decision. Costs and benefits from different years are not directly comparable. The remaining part of this chapter and the appendix describe procedures for adjusting costs and benefits from different time periods to make them comparable.

The Capital Budgeting Process

Capital budgeting is a process of evaluating and choosing long-term investments. Because of the size of long-term investments, the organization should take special care in making these decisions. Typically, the capital budgeting process includes: (1) initiation or identification of the investment proposal, (2) ratification, (3) implementation, and (4) monitoring. These are the same steps in decision making described in Chapter 6.

The initiation process begins with the identification of possible investment opportunities. Different members of the organization can make proposals, but usually individuals with the most information are the initiators of investment proposals. Investment proposals include a description of the investment opportunity and the predicted effect on cash flows from the investment. Large investment proposals may also include the predicted effect on the balance sheet and income statement. Initiation is a planning process.

Once the proposal is developed, a ratification process begins. For control purposes, it is likely that different individuals in the organization are responsible for determining which investment proposals to accept. The parties responsible for ratifying a long-term investment proposal check to see if the cash-flow estimates are reasonable. Also, an analysis of the risk of the proposal is made. Because the long-term investment proposal may involve a substantial amount of cash, the economic viability of the organization may be at risk.

The parties responsible for ratification should also examine competitor reaction to the proposal. Initiators of long-term investment proposals often do not identify competitor reactions and assume that competitors will not change their behavior. In competitive markets, profitable projects are not easily found. Any investment project that appears profitable will soon have many competitors, which will drive down future cash inflows. The effect of competition should be recognized in estimating future cash flows. Firms must have some competitive edge, such as low cost manufacturing, excellent researchers, or quality customer service, to be able to consistently find investment projects that are profitable. When analyzing investment projects, it is important to understand the source of the expected profits.

Finally, ratification ensures that the investment is consistent with the goals of the organization. An investment proposal may appear to be profitable but could

Long-Term Investment Decisions

shift the emphasis of the organization away from its primary purpose. Ratification is a control process.

If the investment proposal is ratified, the next step is implementation. Cash and other resources are invested and operations related to the investment begin. Implementation is a planning process.

During and subsequent to the implementation stage, monitoring of the investment project occurs. The monitoring process determines whether the investment proposal is fulfilling expectations. If expectations are not being met, the investment project may be closed down before the planned termination. Once the investment project is completed, an audit of the project is performed to evaluate the performance of the managers and to determine appropriate adjustments to the capital budgeting process in the future. Monitoring is a control process.

These steps in the capital budgeting process are generally followed by all organizations with some minor variations. Cyto Technologies, a biotech company uses the process described in Figure 13.1 up to implementation.[1] Notice that there are several stages of ratification by the project approval team before the launch (implementation). The company would also have a monitoring process following the launch.

Accountants play many roles in the capital budgeting process. An accountant usually helps in putting together the investment proposal. At Cyto Technologies in Figure 13.1, the feasibility study in phase 2 includes a measure of the return on investment. In phase 3, product costs are estimated and final return on investment is estimated. The project approval team at Cyto Technologies includes the head of finance and accounting. Once ratified, an accountant identifies, measures, and communicates information to assist the implementation process. Accounting reports are also used in the monitoring process. Accountants should be active participants in all phases of the capital budgeting process.

Video stores seemed to be good small business investments initially, but gradually large stores like Blockbuster drove many mom-and-pop stores out of business.

Opportunity Cost of Capital

Chapter 2 defined the opportunity cost as the forgone opportunity of using a resource. The opportunity cost of using a resource depends on alternative uses of that resource. The opportunity cost is the basis for making planning decisions. If one is made better off by an action, in the sense that one is not forgoing a better alternative, then the proposed action is preferred.

The discussion in Chapter 2 on opportunity cost focused on decisions with short-term implications. The options to use labor or materials were assumed to occur during the same time period. There is no reason, however, to presume that all alternatives will occur in the same time period. One can defer accepting a current job offer and return to school for additional years before taking a job. The current stock of raw materials can be used in current production or else

FIGURE 13.1

Capital Budgeting Steps at Cyto Technology

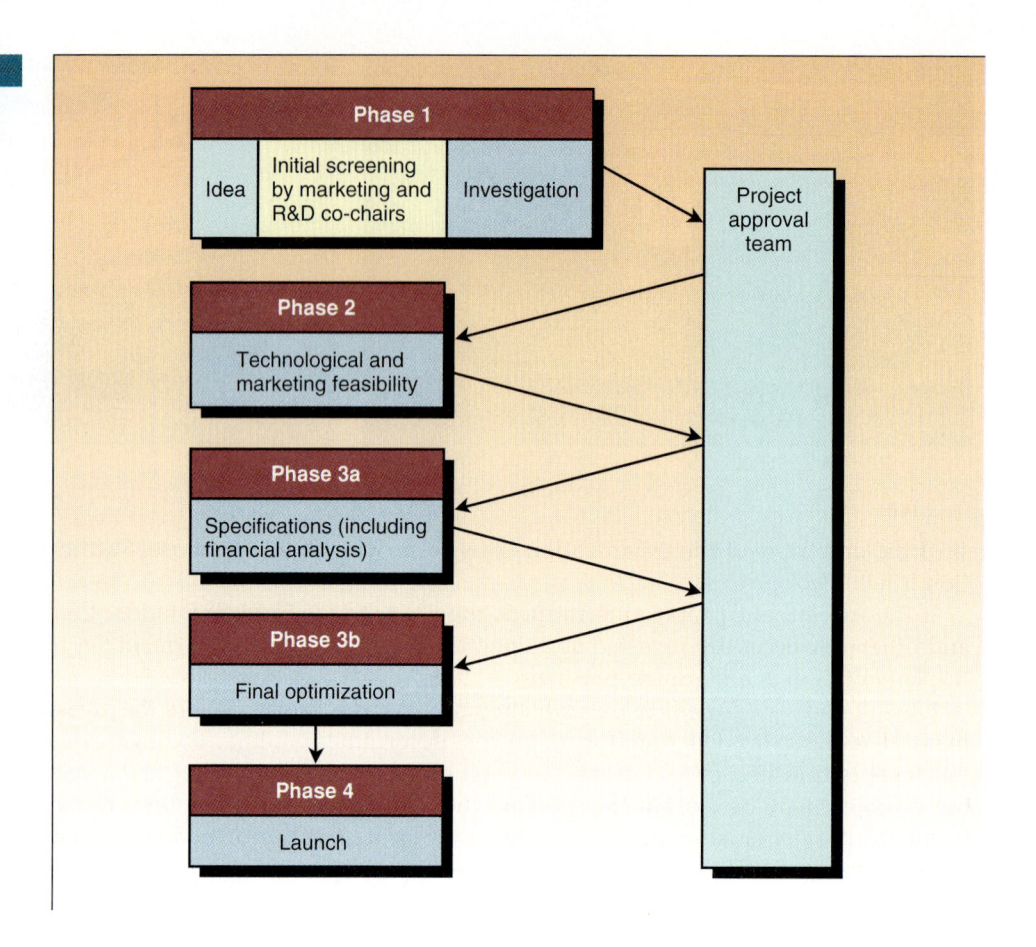

Phase 1: Idea | Initial screening by marketing and R&D co-chairs | Investigation

Phase 2: Technological and marketing feasibility

Phase 3a: Specifications (including financial analysis)

Phase 3b: Final optimization

Phase 4: Launch

Project approval team

---

stored and used next year. In general, all decisions have a time element. At any given point in time prior to accepting the pending decision, one always has the option of delaying or forgoing the decision and continuing to search for better alternatives. An alternative to all decisions is the "procrastination decision"— wait and hope something better emerges.

There are many decisions that explicitly involve a trade-off in cash inflows and cash outflows over time. For example, the decision to invest in research and development (R&D) involves postponing current cash payments to investors in order to fund R&D. Hopefully, the investment in R&D will lead to higher cash payments to investors in the future (when the R&D projects produce profitable new products). The decision to buy a government savings bond involves trading current consumption for future consumption. In fact, most decisions span several time periods and, therefore, involve cash flows over different time periods.

The decision to attend college and earn a degree involves comparing costs and benefits over time. Instead of working and earning a salary, one pays tuition in anticipation of a higher paying job in the future. One sacrifices current income and makes payments on books and tuition by investing in one's human capital in order to earn higher wages in the future. The sacrifices occur during the four years of college, while the benefits of higher wages accrue over the remainder of one's working career. The opportunity cost of going to college is what is forgone by not earning income now. The cash flows from the various alternatives occur in different time periods.

Calculating the opportunity cost of alternatives that involve cash flows occurring at different points of time is complicated because a dollar today is not equivalent to a dollar tomorrow. Time is money! A dollar received today can be invested and earn interest and is, therefore, worth more than a dollar tomorrow.

The **opportunity cost of capital** is a term used to describe the forgone opportunity of using cash. Like other resources, the opportunity cost of capital depends on whether the cash has another use and whether the cash is replaceable. Cash always has another use. If no other investments are available, the cash can be used to retire debt or pay dividends to the owners. Cash is also replaceable. Financial markets exist for issuing debt and stock. Therefore, the opportunity cost of capital is the replacement cost of cash or the cost of borrowing or issuing stock. The cost of borrowing money is the interest payment. The cost of issuing stock is the expected return to shareholders. The opportunity cost of capital is described in terms of a percentage return or an interest rate.

Not all organizations can borrow cash at the same interest rate. Those organizations that are more risky and less likely to repay the loan will have to pay a higher interest rate to borrow cash. The same is true with issuing stock. Shareholders of risky stock expect a higher return than shareholders of less risky stock. The relation between risk and the cost of capital is discussed later in the chapter. In the next few sections, the opportunity cost of capital is provided as an interest rate.

The purpose of recognizing the cost of capital is to make comparisons of cash flows over different time periods. The ability to compare cash flows over different time periods is extremely important in evaluating investment decisions. The analysis of investment alternatives involving cash flows received or paid over time is called capital budgeting.

The appendix in this chapter describes how to compare and aggregate cash flows that occur in different time periods. In general, cash now is worth more than cash in the future. The later the cash flows are received, the lower their present value. To compare cash flows in the future with cash flows in the present, the future cash flows must be discounted. The discount factor for a future cash flow is $1/(1 + r)^n$, where r is the opportunity cost of capital and n is the number of periods until the cash flow occurs. Note that the discount factor decreases with the opportunity cost of capital and the number of time periods. For example, if r equals 10% and n equals two years, the discount rate is $1/(1 + 0.10)^2$, or 0.826. One dollar received in two years is worth 82.6 cents today if the interest rate is 10%. If there is a higher opportunity cost of capital, say 12%, and more periods, say 4 years, the discount rate is $1/(1 + 0.12)^4$, or 0.636. One dollar received in four years at 12% is only worth 63.6 cents. The capital budgeting process should consider the opportunity cost of capital and discount future cash flows for comparison with present cash flows. The next section describes methods that treat future and present cash flows the same and do not discount future cash flows.

CONCEPT REVIEW

1. What are the steps in the capital budgeting process?
2. How does the opportunity cost of capital affect long-term investment decisions?

SLIM'S ICE CREAM PARLOR (CONTINUED)

Slim does not have a control problem in deciding to invest in the frozen yogurt machine. He is the sole employee and owner and will perform all the steps of the capital budgeting process. Slim recognizes, however, that he must include the opportunity cost of capital in his decision to invest in a frozen yogurt machine.

13.2 Investment Criteria Ignoring the Opportunity Cost of Capital

Some managers may find the discounting of future cash flows confusing or difficult. To make investment decisions, they may choose to use the payback method or the accounting rate of return on an investment (ROI) to make investment choices. These methods are described in this section.

Payback

A simple method of evaluating projects is the **payback** method. Payback is the number of years or months it takes for cash flows from an investment to equal the initial investment cost. Suppose a project's initial investment cost is $200,000 and subsequent yearly cash inflows are $50,000, $100,000, $100,000, and $200,000 after taxes. This project has a payback of two and one-half years. At the end of the second year, the project has returned $150,000 ($50,000 + $100,000). The third year cash flow is $100,000, or $50,000 per six months. Therefore, in two and one-half years, the cash inflows just equal the initial investment of $200,000. The great advantage of payback is its simplicity. It is easy to compute and to understand. One needs no assumptions about the appropriate opportunity cost of capital for the particular project. Simplicity, however, is also payback's handicap.

Payback ignores the opportunity cost of capital. Therefore, two projects are viewed as equally attractive if they have the same payback, even though all the payback may occur in the last year for one versus spread out evenly over time for the other. For example, suppose two projects each require $300,000 investments but one pays $100,000 for each of three years and the other pays nothing for two years and $300,000 in the third year. Each has a three-year payback, but the first is more valuable because the $100,000 payments in years one and two can be earning interest.

Payback also ignores all the cash flows beyond the payback period. Thus, payback ignores the "profitability" of the project. Two projects with the same investment and same cash flow per year up to the payback year have the same payback. But if one investment has no cash flows beyond the payback year and the other investment does, clearly the latter investment is better.

Finally, payback lacks a benchmark for deciding which projects to accept and which to reject. What payback cutoff should the firm use as a criterion for project selection? Is a three-year payback good or bad?

Some movies, such as Twister *and* Independence Day, *have fast payback periods of under a year, whereas other movies like* Cutthroat Island *may never pay back their investment.*

Some managers believe that it is very difficult to accurately forecast cash flows beyond three or four years. Thus, very little weight should be placed on these cash flows. Payback ignores these cash flows. One criticism of American managers is that they are too short-term oriented. They are not willing to take risks and to look at long-term payoffs. The exclusive use of payback to evaluate investment projects will tend to cause managers to focus on short-term cash flows and to ignore long-term rewards.

NUMERICAL EXAMPLE 13.1

A $400,000 investment in a motel has expected cash flows of $100,000 in each of the next 5 years. What is the payback of the investment? What does the payback method ignore?

■ **SOLUTION** The investment has a payback of 4 years, but the payback ignores the cash flows in the fifth year and the time value of money.

Accounting Rate of Return

Another method for project evaluation is the accounting rate of return, which is also called the **return on investment (ROI)**. The ROI of an investment project is the accounting income from the investment divided by the cost of the investment.

ROI = Income/Investment

The ROI formula looks quite simple, but there are some questions about how to measure the numerator and denominator. For example, the choice of different accounting methods will influence the income measure. Also, there is a question of whether to include interest and taxes in estimating income. In general, interest is not included in income, but there is less agreement on the treatment of taxes. Also, the investment could be measured in multiple ways. For example, the investment in the ROI formula is estimated using only fixed assets by some companies. Other companies include all assets as part of the investment. The investment may also be measured at the beginning or end of the income period or as an average over the income period.

The choice of how to measure income and investment for calculating the ROI should depend on how the ROI is being used. If the ROI is being used as a performance measure, the measures of income and investment should reflect controllability. If interest, taxes, current assets, or fixed assets are controllable, they should be included in the calculation of the ROI. If the ROI is being used for making a capital budgeting decision, then comparisons should be made with the opportunity cost of capital. Because interest is part of the opportunity cost of capital, it should be excluded from the income. The investment should include all assets because of the forgone opportunity of using the cash invested in the assets for other purposes.

How to estimate the ROI for an investment with income over many years is also unclear. An ROI could be measured for each year. For example, suppose a $10,000,000 investment is expected to yield income of $900,000 for each of the next five years. The straight-line depreciation method is used on the original investment, so the average investment declines each year. Table 13.1 shows the ROI for each year of this investment using the average investment each period.

The ROI increases from 10% the first year to 90% the last year. Because the investment is not described by a single ROI, the investment is difficult to compare with other investments.

478 Investment Decisions

TABLE 13.1

Average Net Income, Average Book Value of Investment, and Annual ROI

Year	Net Income	Average Book Value of Investment	ROI
1	$900,000	$9,000,000	10%
2	900,000	7,000,000	13%
3	900,000	5,000,000	18%
4	900,000	3,000,000	30%
5	900,000	1,000,000	90%

A multiperiod alternative of estimating the ROI of a project is to divide the average annual income over all the years of the average annual investment in the project:

$$\text{ROI} = \frac{\text{Average annual income from project}}{\text{Average annual investment in the project}}$$

$$= \frac{\$900,000}{\$5,000,000}$$

$$= 18\%$$

The ROI has the advantage of being easy to calculate once income and investment are defined. The ROI also relates to the firm's accounting statements, which are familiar to managers. The problem with using the ROI is that it can often lead to incorrect investment decisions.

The ROI results in incorrect decisions because it ignores the time value of money. In calculating the ROI, the average annual income from the project is computed. A dollar of income received today is treated the same as a dollar of income received in the future. The fact that these dollars are worth different amounts is ignored in computing accounting ROI.

The ROI also relies on accounting numbers rather than cash flows. For example, depreciation is often a major component of income, but depreciation has no cash flow implications other than its impact on income taxes. The following numerical example indicates how depreciation can influence the measurement of ROI.

NUMERICAL EXAMPLE 13.2

An investment of $300,000 causes cash inflows of $150,000 during each of the next three years. The investment is fully depreciated using the straight-line method over the three years. There are no other accrual effects, so the annual net income of the investment is $150,000 − $100,000, or $50,000. The average investment is used as the denominator to calculate the ROI. What are the ROIs for each year and what is the multiyear ROI? How would the sum-of-the-year-digits method affect the calculation of ROI?

■ **SOLUTION** Using straight line depreciation:

Year	Income	Average Investment	ROI
1	$50,000	$250,000	20%
2	50,000	150,000	33%
3	50,000	50,000	100%

The multiyear ROI is $50,000/$150,000, or 33%

The sum-of-the-year-digits method causes depreciation to be $150,000 in the first year, $100,000 in the second year, and $50,000 in the third year. Therefore, the ROI for each year is:

Year	Income	Average Investment	ROI
1	$ 0	$225,000	0%
2	50,000	100,000	50%
3	100,000	25,000	400%

The average annual income is $50,000, but the average investment over the three years is $100,000, so the multiyear ROI is $50,000/$100,000, or 50%. Note that accounting methods affect the ROI, making the ROI method less desirable.

CONCEPT REVIEW

1. What are the limitations of using the payback method to evaluate investments?
2. How can a multiyear ROI be calculated?
3. What are the limitations of using ROI to evaluate investments?

SLIM'S ICE CREAM PARLOR (CONTINUED)

Slim figures he should try all the methods of evaluating the frozen yogurt machine investment. To estimate the payback period, he must first estimate cash flows per year from his proposed investment. His original estimate of $200 of income per year includes $2,000 of depreciation expense, which does not involve any cash flows. Therefore, the cash flows per year of the $10,000 investment are estimated to be $2,200. The payback period is:

$$\$10,000/\$2,200 \text{ per year} = 4.55 \text{ years}$$

The ROI of the investment is calculated by taking the average investment over the five-year investment period and dividing by the annual income. The average investment is equal to $10,000/2, or $5,000. The estimated annual income of $200 includes an $800 interest expense that should be eliminated. The income before deducting the interest expense is $1,000. Therefore, the ROI for the frozen yogurt machine is:

$$\text{ROI} = \$1,000/\$5,000 = 20\%$$

Slim is not sure how to interpret either of these measures and recognizes that neither method includes the opportunity cost of capital. Therefore, he decides to continue reading.

13.3 The Net Present Value of Cash Flows

Capital budgeting decisions should consider the opportunity cost of capital. Future cash flows should be discounted when compared with present cash flows.

The discounting of future cash flows is accomplished through the following equation:

$$\text{Present value} = [1/(1 + r)^n] \times \text{Future cash flow}$$

where r is the opportunity cost of capital and n is the number of time periods that separate the present and the future cash flow. The opportunity cost of capital reflects the interest rate of borrowing money for the organization.

NUMERICAL EXAMPLE 13.3

Carbon Corporation, which has an opportunity cost of capital of 10%, is considering an investment project that should yield the following cash flows:

Year from Now	Cash Inflow
1	$44,000
2	50,000
3	20,000

What is the present value of these cash inflows?

■ **SOLUTION** The present value of the cash inflow is based on the equation: Present value = $[1/(1 + r)^n] \times$ Future cash flow

Cash Inflow	Discount Factor	Present Value
$44,000	$1/(1 + .1)^1 = .90909$	$40,000
50,000	$1/(1 + .1)^2 = .82645$	41,322
20,000	$1/(1 + .1)^3 = .75131$	15,026
Total present value of cash inflows		$96,348

The purpose of discounting future cash flows is to compare them with present cash flows. The **net present value** of an investment proposal compares all the cash inflows and outflows by discounting them to the present. An investment that has a positive net present value increases the value of the organization and should be made.

An investment generally involves a cash outflow in the present with subsequent future cash inflows. Because the initial investment outflow is already in present dollars, there is no need to discount the outflow. The present outflow can be compared with the discounted future cash inflows. In Numerical Example 13.3, the total present value of all the future cash inflows is $96,348. If the initial investment costs $100,000, the net present value is − $100,000 + $96,348, or −$3,652. The investment proposal has a negative net present value, and accepting the investment proposal will reduce the value of the organization. The costs (initial investment) are greater than the benefits (discounted future cash inflows).

If the initial investment for Numerical Example 13.3 is $80,000, then the net present value is − $80,000 + $96,348, or +$16,348. The investment proposal has a positive net present value and would increase the value of the organization. The benefits exceed the costs of the investment.

The general rule for making long-term investment decisions is to accept proposals that have a positive net present value and reject proposals that have a negative net present value. Other nonquantifiable factors should also be considered, such as the welfare of employees, the reaction of competitors, government actions, and the goals of the organization.

NUMERICAL EXAMPLE 13.4

A new drill press costs $20,000. The annual cost savings of having the new drill press are expected to be $8,000 over the next three years. At the end of the three years, the drill press is expected to be sold for $2,000. The borrowing rate for the company is 12%. What is the net present value of this investment?

■ **SOLUTION**

Year	Cash Flows	Discount Factor	Present Value
0	$-20,000	$1/(1 + .12)^0 = 1.00000$	$-20,000
1	8,000	$1/(1 + .12)^1 = 0.89286$	7,143
2	8,000	$1/(1 + .12)^2 = 0.79719$	6,378
3	$2,000 + $8,000	$1/(1 + .12)^3 = 0.71178$	7,118
Net present value			$ 639

The net present value of the investment in the drill press is positive. Therefore, the drill press should be purchased.

Estimating Cash Flows for Calculating Present Values

Future cash flows are discounted and compared with present cash flows to determine the net present value of an investment. If the net present value of the proposed investment is greater than zero, the investment should be undertaken. Although this concept appears straightforward, there are potential problems in estimating future cash flows. Considerable information must often be gathered to make reasonable estimates of future cash flows. Cash flows beyond five years are usually very difficult to predict accurately in a changing world. In addition to the uncertainty in estimating future cash flows, the factors described in this section also affect future cash flow estimates.

Discount Cash Flows, Not Accounting Earnings

Present value analysis is based on discounting cash flows, not accounting earnings. The reason for focusing on cash flows and not accounting earnings is because earnings contain accounting accruals and deferrals. The accounting process keeps certain cash flows out of earnings. The purchase cost of fixed assets is not treated as an expense until depreciated. That is, earnings do not contain amounts spent until the economic benefits of the investments are received. Likewise, sales are recorded when the legal liability arises, not when the cash is collected. Therefore, dollars *earned*, as computed by accounting earnings, do not reflect the dollars actually received. The reason we discount cash flows and not accounting earnings is because cash flows can be invested in the bank and thereby generate interest. Accounting earnings, however, cannot be used to open a bank account. You can't go to the store and buy soda and pretzels with accounting earnings, only cash.

Adjust Cash Flows to Reflect the Need for Additional Accounts Receivable and Inventory

Many businesses carry significant amounts of accounts receivable and inventories. Such inventories represent cash tied up that could be earning interest if invested in a bank. Therefore, cash invested in such inventories should be included in the investment in the business. Likewise, many businesses allow customers to make purchases on credit. In these cases, additional cash must be invested to finance these accounts receivable. On the other hand, to the extent

An investment in a new product such as Nabisco low-fat Pop-Tarts may affect sales of original Pop-Tarts.

that the firm acquires goods and services on credit, the accounts payable offset the cash needed to finance the current assets. The additional amounts invested in working capital (current assets − current liabilities) must also be included to derive the cash flows in the period.

Include Opportunity Costs but Not Sunk Costs

As in other planning decisions, opportunity costs should be used in capital budgeting. The opportunity cost of the investment may not be limited to the purchase price. A new investment project may also impose costs on other parts of the organization. For example, an investment in a new product may affect sales of other products. An investment in a new machine should consider the cost of disposing of the machine being replaced. If a new investment project uses existing resources, the benefit forgone of using those resources for some other project is part of the cost of the new investment. The opportunity cost concept is still valid with capital budgeting.

Sunk costs, on the other hand, should be ignored in capital budgeting. If a new investment project uses resources that have already been purchased and have no other uses, the purchase price of those resources should not be used to make an investment decision.

Exclude Financing Costs

The interest and principal payments on debt should not be included in the discounted future cash flows. The costs of financing the project are implicitly included in discounting the future cash flows. If the project has a positive net present value, then the cash flows from the project yield a return in excess of the firm's cost of capital, which more than compensates the firm for the financing costs. Dividend payments also should not be included in calculating cash outflows.

Taxes and Depreciation Tax Shields

Taxes are usually a very significant cash flow item in most discounted cash flow analyses. A corporate income tax rate of 34% implies that about a third of any project's profitability is taxed away. Therefore, the minimization of taxes becomes a very important element in capital budgets.

Most firms use different depreciation methods for external reports for shareholders and for the Internal Revenue Service (IRS). The IRS allows firms to elect straight-line depreciation for shareholder reports and accelerated depreciation for tax returns. There are other accounting methods that can cause the income reported to shareholders to differ from the firm's taxable income. For example, the expected cost of product warranties are included in financial reports to shareholders when the product is sold. However, the cost of the warranty work is included for tax purposes only when the actual warranty cost is incurred. When calculating a project's cash flows, it is important to use the tax accounting rules rather than the financial reporting rules for the shareholders to estimate income taxes. Taxes are a cash flow. The accounting rules used to compute taxes affect tax payments. The accounting methods used only for shareholder reports, however, do not affect tax cash flows.

The primary difference between cash flows and income for tax purposes is depreciation. **Depreciation** is the allocation of the historical cost of a fixed asset over time. The depreciation of the fixed assets is treated as an expense in calculating taxable income but is not a cash outflow. The cash outflow occurred when the fixed asset was purchased.

The amount of depreciation that can be recognized each year is determined by the tax code. Generally, organizations would like to recognize as much depreciation for tax purposes as possible to reduce income and, therefore, reduce their present tax liability. Depreciation is not a cash flow but affects cash flow through the calculation of taxable income. The reduction in cash payments due to depreciation is called the **depreciation tax shield**.

Some simple algebra illustrates the indirect cash flow effect of depreciation and the calculation of the tax shield.

Let:
- t = Tax rate
- R = Revenue
- E = All cash expenses (except depreciation)
- D = Depreciation (allowed for tax purposes)

Using this notation we can write down the following familiar formulas:

$$\text{Net income} = NI = (R - E - D)(1 - t)$$
$$\text{Taxes} = TAX = (R - E - D)t$$
$$\text{Cash flow} = CF = R - E - TAX$$
$$= R - E - (R - E - D)t$$
$$= (R - E)(1 - t) + Dt$$

Notice the last term in the cash flow equation, Dt, the depreciation tax shield. That is the annual depreciation charge, D, times the tax rate, t. The product of the two is *added* to the annual after-tax operating net cash flow, $(R - E)(1 - t)$, to arrive at the after-tax net cash flow. From the last formula, we can clearly see that the larger the depreciation expense, the higher is the firm's cash flow because the tax liability is lower. In this sense, depreciation is said to be a tax shield because it results in lower taxes and thus higher after-tax cash flow. The total amount of depreciation that can be deducted from taxes is limited to the original cost of the asset. Therefore, the sooner the depreciation is taken (assuming the firm has positive taxable income), the higher is the present value of the depreciation tax shield. Accelerated tax depreciation methods, which allow earlier recognition of depreciation, increase a project's net present value.

NUMERICAL EXAMPLE 13.5

An asset is purchased for $500,000. The asset has a five-year life and no salvage value. The tax rate is 34% and the interest rate is 5%. What is the present value of the tax shields under the straight-line and double-declining-balance depreciation methods?

TABLE 13.2

Comparing the Net Present Value of Depreciation Tax Shields of Straight-Line to Double-Declining-Balance Depreciation ($500,000 asset, no salvage, five-year life, 34% tax rate, 5% interest)

	Straight-Line Depreciation				Double-Declining-Balance Depreciation			
Year	Depreciation Expense	Tax Shield (Dt)	PV of Tax Shield	DDB Rate*	Book Value at Beg. of Yr.	Depreciation Expense	Tax Shield (Dt)	PV of Tax Shield
1	$100,000	$34,000	$ 32,381	0.4	$500,000	$200,000	$68,000	$ 64,762
2	100,000	34,000	30,839	0.4	300,000	120,000	40,800	37,007
3	100,000	34,000	29,370	0.4	180,000	72,000	24,480	21,147
4	100,000	34,000	27,972	0.4	108,000	43,200	14,688	12,084
5	100,000	34,000	26,640		64,800	64,800	22,032	17,263
	$500,000		$147,202			$500,000		$152,263

*DDB rate (double-declining-balance rate) is twice the straight-line rate, or 40% = $2 \times \frac{1}{5}$

■ **SOLUTION** Table 13.2 lays out the calculation of the present value of the tax shields under the straight-line and double-declining-balance depreciation methods. Double-declining-balance depreciation writes off the $500,000 original cost faster than straight-line depreciation. Therefore, its tax shield has a higher present value by $5,061. In other words, by using double-declining-balance depreciation instead of straight-line depreciation for tax purposes, the net present value of the project is increased by $5,061. This is about 1% of the asset's cost.

Adjusting the Discount Rate for Risk

In the previous sections, the opportunity cost of capital is provided as an interest rate. The opportunity cost of capital is the cost of replacing cash through borrowing or issuing stock. Because some organizations are less likely to repay loans, the opportunity cost of capital is higher for these organizations. Organizations that are more risky will have a higher cost of capital than organizations that are less risky. Investment projects that are more risky, thus making the organization

Success of ski resorts depends on the weather and the economy. The expected annual cash flow is an average of good and bad years.

riskier, should be treated as having a higher cost of capital. In other words, risky projects should be discounted at a higher interest rate than safe projects.

What we mean by risk, how it is measured, and how to choose risk-adjusted discount factors are the subjects of corporate finance. We will not concern ourselves with how to derive a risk-adjusted discount rate. For any given risky cash flow stream, we will assume that an equivalent risk-adjusted interest rate exists.

The risk of an investment occurs because there is uncertainty about future cash flows. The cash inflows of an investment depend on many factors that are not perfectly predictable. Future cash flows may depend on weather, the economy, the entry of competitors, or the fickle nature of customer demand. Because the cash flows are uncertain, one of many possible cash flows can result. Instead of discounting the highest or lowest cash flow that can occur, we discount the **expected** (or average) **cash flow.** For example, if the cash flows next year can be either $100 or $200 with equal probability, we would discount the expected cash flow of $150. The expected cash flows should be discounted using a risk-adjusted discount rate appropriate for the risk inherent in the project.

SLIM'S ICE CREAM PARLOR (CONCLUDED)

Slim now knows how to calculate the net present value of the investment in the yogurt machine, but he must reconsider his estimate of cash flows. Slim realizes that the machine is not the only investment he must make to provide frozen yogurt for his customers. He must also have some ingredients on hand to make the frozen yogurt. Slim estimates that the extra ingredients he will need to hold are relatively small and decides not to worry about that cost.

Slim also realizes that the opportunity cost of capital is implicitly included in the discounting process. The annual interest payments of $800 should not be included in the cash flow estimates to be discounted. The 8% interest rate does appear to be the correct risk-adjusted interest rate.

The space to be taken by the frozen yogurt machine had no alternative use, so no facility costs are applied to the investment project. Slim, however, needs to consider the effect the frozen yogurt will have on the sales of his other products. After careful consideration, he decides that the net effect on other sales of having frozen yogurt will be approximately zero. Some ice cream buyers will switch to frozen yogurt, but having frozen yogurt will bring in more customers, some who will buy ice cream.

Slim has forgotten to adjust his cash flow estimates for tax effects. The taxable income is $200 and the tax rate for Slim is 30%. Therefore, Slim must pay annual taxes of ($200)(.30), or $60. Slim's annual cash flow analysis after eliminating the depreciation and interest and adding the income taxes looks like the following:

Revenues from selling frozen yogurt	$ 5,000
Cost of ingredients	(1,500)
Additional power costs	(500)
Income taxes at 30%: (.30)($200)	(60)
Cash flows per year for five years	$ 2,940
Initial investment	$10,000

> Slim then estimates the present value of these cash flows over the next five years using a discount rate of 8%.
>
> | Year | Cash Flows | Discount Factor | Present Value |
> |------|-----------|-----------------|---------------|
> | 0 | $-10,000 | $1/(1 + 0.08)^0 = 1.00000$ | $-10,000 |
> | 1 | 2,940 | $1/(1 + 0.08)^1 = 0.92593$ | 2,722 |
> | 2 | 2,940 | $1/(1 + 0.08)^2 = 0.85734$ | 2,520 |
> | 3 | 2,940 | $1/(1 + 0.08)^3 = 0.79383$ | 2,334 |
> | 4 | 2,940 | $1/(1 + 0.08)^4 = 0.73503$ | 2,161 |
> | 5 | 2,940 | $1/(1 + 0.08)^5 = 0.68058$ | 2,001 |
> | Net present value | | | $ 1,738 |
>
> Based on the calculation of a positive net present value of $1,738, Slim is pleased to invest in the frozen yogurt machine.

CONCEPT REVIEW

1. Why should cash flows and not future earnings be discounted?
2. Why should accounts receivable and inventory levels be considered when making a capital budgeting decision?
3. Why should finance charges not be included when making a capital budgeting decision?
4. Why does depreciation act as a tax shield?
5. How does the risk of the investment project affect the discount rate used for capital budgeting.

13.4 Internal Rate of Return (IRR)

The **internal rate of return (IRR)** method for comparing different projects appears on the surface to be very similar to the net present value (NPV) method. The internal rate of return method finds the interest rate that equates the initial investment cost to the future discounted cash flows. In other words, the internal rate of return makes the net present value equal to zero. If the project's internal rate of return exceeds a certain cutoff rate (e.g., the project's cost of capital), the project should be undertaken.

The internal rate of return is quite easy to calculate if there is an initial cash outflow (the cost of the investment) followed by a cash inflow in one year. For example, suppose one can invest $1,000 today and receive $1,070 in a year. The internal rate of return (IRR) sets the investment cost equal to the discounted future cash flow:

$$\text{Investment cost} = (\text{Cash inflows in one year})/(1 + \text{IRR})$$

$$\$1,000 = \frac{\$1,070}{1 + \text{IRR}}$$

$$(1 + \text{IRR}) = \frac{\$1,070}{\$1,000}$$

$$\text{IRR} = 0.07 = 7\%.$$

In this very simple example, the internal rate of return on an investment of $1,000 today that generates a $1,070 payment in one year is 7%. If the cost of capital is 5%, then clearly this investment offers a return in excess of its opportunity cost. The net present value (NPV) of this investment is:

$$NPV = -\$1,000 + \frac{\$1,070}{1.05}$$

$$= -\$1,000 + \$1,019.05$$

$$= \$19.05$$

If the internal rate of return exceeds the opportunity cost of capital, the net present value of the investment is positive and the investment should be undertaken. If the internal rate of return is less than the opportunity cost of capital, the net present value of the investment is negative and the investment should be rejected.

The advantage of the internal rate of return method is that an investment project's return is stated as an interest rate. Some feel that saying a project's return is 14% is clearer than saying a project has a net present value of some monetary amount such as $628,623.

But the IRR and NPV methods do not always give consistent answers. The IRR and the NPV will potentially lead to different investment decisions if investments are mutually exclusive. Mutually exclusive investments are a group of investments of which only one can be chosen. For example, a manufacturing firm usually chooses only one of many possible methods to make a part. With mutually exclusive investments, a manager would like to rank the alternative investments. Consider the following two mutually exclusive investments:

1. Invest $1,000 today and receive $1,070 in one year.
2. Invest $5,000 today and receive $5,300 in one year.

We know from above that investment #1 has an IRR of 7% and a NPV of $19.05. The IRR of investment #2 is:

$$\$5,000 = \$5,300/(1 + IRR)$$

$$(1 + IRR) = \frac{\$5,300}{\$5,000}$$

$$IRR = 0.06 = 6\%.$$

Investment #2's NPV using a 5% cost of capital is:

$$NPV = -\$5,000 + \frac{\$5,300}{1.05}$$

$$= -\$5,000 + \$5,047.62$$

$$= \$47.62$$

Which investment is best? The IRR criteria says #1 is better because it has the higher IRR. But the net present value (NPV) criteria says #2 is better because it has the higher NPV. How should one decide? Which is more valuable, a rate of return or cash? Net present value indicates how much cash in today's dollars an investment is worth, or the *magnitude* of the investment's return. The IRR only indicates the *relative* return on the investment. A 20% return on $1,000 ($20) is preferable to a 200% return on $1 ($2). Therefore, the NPV provides the correct ranking.

The NPV and IRR methods may also rank investment projects differently because of a difference in the length of time or duration of cash flows. Consider the following two mutually exclusive investments:

1. Invest $1,000 today and receive $1,200 in one year.
2. Invest $1,000 today and receive $1,500 in three years.

The net present value of these two projects for different discount rates is presented in Figure 13.2. The internal rate of return of each of the two investments is the discount rate where each line crosses the x axis. For the first investment, the IRR is equal to 20%. For the second investment, the IRR is between 14% and

FIGURE 13.2
Comparing the NPV of Two Investments

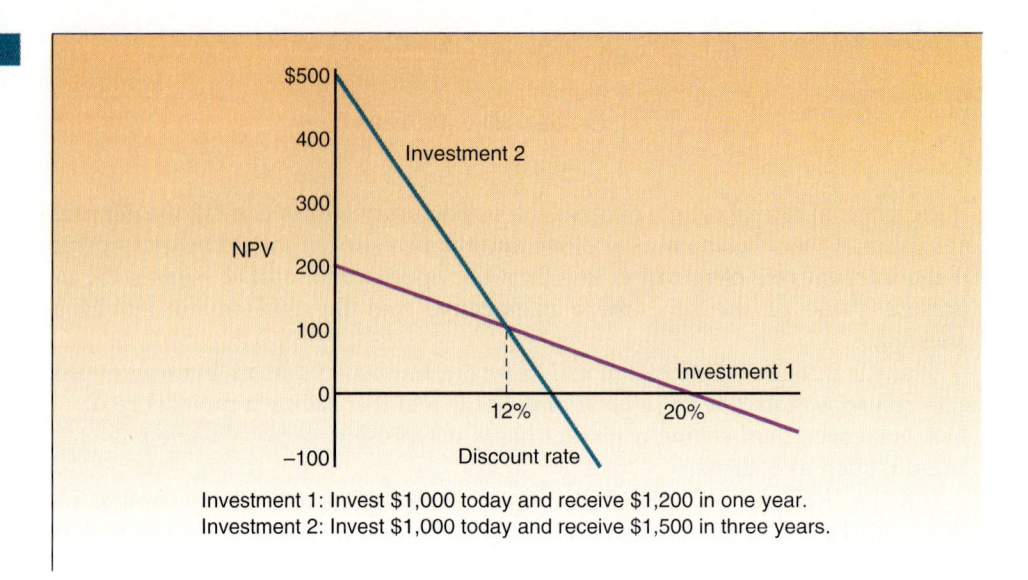

Investment 1: Invest $1,000 today and receive $1,200 in one year.
Investment 2: Invest $1,000 today and receive $1,500 in three years.

15%. Even though the IRR of the first investment is larger, the NPV of the second investment is higher if the discount rate is below 12%. Above 12% the NPV of the first investment is higher.

The net present values in Figure 13.2 decline as the discount rate rises because only the cash inflows are affected by the change in discount rate. The cash outflows that occur in the present are not affected by the discount rate. The cash inflows, however, occur in the future and their present values will decline with an increase in the discount rate. The net present value of investment 2 declines more rapidly because the present value of cash flows in the more distant future are more sensitive to changes in the discount rate.

Perhaps the most serious problem with the internal rate of return method is its implicit assumption regarding the *reinvestment rate.* The reinvestment rate is the interest rate used to compound cash flows received or paid over the life of the project. In the discounted cash flow method, each cash flow is discounted at the opportunity cost of capital. The implicit assumption is that intermediate cash flows are being reinvested at the opportunity cost of capital. If the opportunity cost of capital is expected to be higher or lower in future years, nonconstant discount rates can be used. The internal rate of return method assumes that all the intermediate cash flows are being automatically reinvested at the project's constant internal rate of return. Thus, the internal rate of return method implicitly assumes that all the intermediate cash flows can be invested in a stock of projects identical to the one being considered, and that the same internal rate of return can be achieved. If this is a one-time project, then there are no projects like it in the future that can be used in which to reinvest the project's cash flows. Therefore, the internal rate of return method overstates a project's rate of return if other investments with the same reinvestment rate do not exist. This is a serious problem with internal rate of return, making it very dangerous to use this method to evaluate alternative investments.

Another problem that may exist with the IRR is when an organization sets a **hurdle rate** higher than the cost of capital. A hurdle rate is a benchmark that is established by the organization as an investment criterion. In order to be acceptable, the planned IRR must be higher than the hurdle rate. For example, an organization may establish a hurdle rate of 20%, but the cost of capital is 10%. The organization will only accept investment proposals with a hurdle rate higher than 20%, but the organization is forgoing the opportunity to invest in projects with an IRR between 10% and 20%, which have positive NPVs.

The Poulan-Weedeater solar-powered lawnmower required several years to design and test. During this time a significant investment of cash was required to bring this product to market. How should Poulan decide which new projects to launch?

In summary, the internal rate of return provides the correct decision rule for investments if the cost of capital is used as the benchmark. If the internal rate of return is higher than the cost of capital, then the investment should be made. But the internal rate of return fails to duplicate the NPV ranking of mutually exclusive investment projects. Also, requiring investment projects to exceed a hurdle rate that is higher than the cost of capital forgoes the opportunity to invest in positive NPV projects. Therefore, the IRR should only be used with care.

Also, the internal rate of return is not always easy to calculate if there are unequal cash inflows over multiple years. Computers can be used to solve for the internal rate of return, but a trial and error method can also be used to approximate the internal rate of return. The trial and error method calculates the net present value for a particular discount rate. If the net present value is positive, a higher discount rate is tried. If the net present value is negative, a lower discount rate is tried. This process is continued until a discount rate is found that causes the net present value to be approximately zero.

WHAT'S HAPPENING

In a recent interview, the CEO of a large corporation stated that he only undertook projects with an IRR greater than 30%. Why has the corporation been downsizing in recent years?

NUMERICAL EXAMPLE 13.6

A company is considering an investment that requires an initial cash outlay of $100,000. The investment is expected to return $70,000 in the first year and $55,000 in the second year. What is the internal rate of return of the investment?

■ **SOLUTION** An initial estimate of 10% gives the following net present value (NPV):

$$-\$100,000 + [\$70,000/(1 + .1)] + [\$55,000/(1 + .1)^2] = \$9,090$$

Because the NPV is positive, a higher estimate for the internal rate of return is used, say 20%:

$$-\$100,000 + [\$70,000/(1 + .2)] + [\$55,000/(1 + .2)^2] = -\$3,473$$

Because the NPV is negative, a lower estimate for the internal rate of return is used, say 17%:

$$-\$100,000 + [\$70,000/(1 + .17)] + [\$55,000/(1 + .17)^2] = \$7$$

This NPV is very close to zero, so the internal rate of return is approximately 17%.

CONCEPT REVIEW

1. How is the internal rate of return determined?
2. What are some problems in using the internal rate of return to evaluate investments?

SLIM'S ICE CREAM PARLOR (CONTINUED)

Slim is thrilled with his new skills in using the time value of money, so he decides to calculate the internal rate of return of the frozen yogurt machine. He uses the trial and error method and begins with 8% to calculate the net present value.

Discount Rate	Net Present Value
8%	$1,738
10%	1,146
12%	599
14%	93
16%	−374

Slim finds that the internal rate of return is a little greater than 14%, which is above his opportunity cost of capital.

13.5 Capital Budgeting Methods Used in Practice

This section describes a survey of capital budgeting methods used in practice.[2] Five hundred large, publicly traded U.S. industrial firms were sampled in 1988 and 100 usable responses were obtained. Many of these same firms had responded to similar surveys in the past, allowing the researchers to study how the frequency of use of a method changed over time. Table 13.3 reports the results of these surveys. Two different types of capital projects were surveyed: expansion or new operations and replacement of existing assets. The following capital budgeting evaluation techniques were listed: discounting, accounting rate of return, payback, urgency, and other. Discounting includes both net present value and internal rate of return. Accounting rate of return and payback are the same as described earlier in the chapter. Urgency means the managers accept a project if the consequences of rejecting it have an immediate adverse effect on the firm. For example, if the Environmental Protection Agency cites the firm for a pollution violation and warns that fines will begin accruing unless the firm complies, then the decision to install pollution abatement equipment would be classified under urgency.

The first thing to note from Table 13.3 is the relatively high usage of discounting methods. In 1988, 87% of expansion projects and 60% of replacement projects were evaluated using discounting methods. Urgency is the method used in 23% of the replacement projects. The second fact to note from Table 13.3 is the rather dramatic increase in discounting methods from 1965 to 1988. The frequency of discounting methods has almost tripled over the 23-year period. Some or all of the following reasons may account for this trend: discounting methods are theoretically superior, they have been a mainstay in business school curriculums, and relatively cheap calculators and personal computers are available with programs

The Story of Managerial Accounting

Team Decisions Regarding Investing

One of the investment decisions the Irwin book team must make for the *Managerial Accounting* book is whether to have a preview before publication that includes some chapters to market the book. The preview is in color with a designed cover and is sent to most professors teaching management accounting. The chapters included in the preview are subject to minor revisions in the subsequent publication of the whole book. All these activities make the preview quite expensive. What information does each member of the *Managerial Accounting* book team bring to bear on this decision and how should this decision be made?

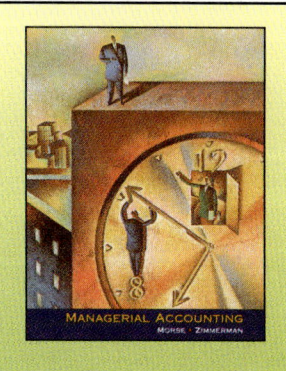

TABLE 13.3

Survey of Capital Budgeting Techniques Used in Practice

	1988	1980	1970	1965
Expansion/new operations				
Discounting	87%	71%	49%	31%
Accounting rate of return	4%	10%	25%	33%
Payback	4%	5%	16%	19%
Urgency	1%	1%	3%	6%
Other	4%	13%	7%	11%
Total	100%	100%	100%	100%
Replacement				
Discounting	60%	56%	35%	21%
Accounting rate of return	4%	7%	13%	15%
Payback	5%	4%	12%	12%
Urgency	23%	23%	32%	40%
Other	8%	10%	8%	12%
Total	100%	100%	100%	100%

Source: Klammer, Koch, and Wilner, "Capital Budgeting Pratices—A Survey of Corporate Use," *Journal of Management Accounting Research*, Fall 1991, Table 2, pp. 113–30.

that compute net present values and internal rates of return. Finally, when interest rates are high, as they were in the 1980s, discounting methods are more critical in comparing dollars from different time periods.

Net present value and internal rate of return are included under discounting in Table 13.3. If these are broken out separately, internal rate of return is more prevalent than net present value. As described above, the internal rate of return does not always rank projects in the same order as net present value. Given the survey findings, however, this disadvantage of the internal rate of return seems to be less important than its intuitive appeal.

13.6 Summary

1. **Describe the steps of the capital budgeting process.** The steps of the capital budgeting process include initiation, ratification, implementation, and monitoring.

2. **Identify the opportunity cost of capital.** The opportunity cost of capital is the forgone opportunity of using cash, which is generally the interest rate on borrowing money to replace the cash.

3. **Estimate the payback period of an investment and identify weaknesses of the payback method in making investment choices.** The payback period is the time required for the investment to generate cash flows equal to the initial investment. The payback method does not consider the time value of money or cash flows beyond the payback period.

4. **Calculate the accounting rate of return (ROI) and identify weaknesses of the accounting rate of return in making investment choices.** The accounting rate of return or ROI is the income from a project divided by the investment cost. The ROI is an accounting measure and does not consider the time value of money.

5. **Calculate the net present value of cash flows.** The net present value of cash flows is calculated by discounting all future cash flows to the present and comparing the present value of the cash inflows with the present value of the cash outflows.

6. **Adjust cash flows for noncash income accounts, working capital requirements, financing charges, and taxes.** Cash, not accounting income numbers, should be discounted to estimate the net present value of an investment. Income items such as depreciation do not reflect cash flows. New investments often require increased amounts of accounts receivable and inventory. Increases in accounts receivable and inventory caused by a new investment should be treated as part of the investment cost. Interest and principal payments on debt should not be included in the discounting of future cash flows because the discounting implicitly includes financing charges. And, taxes are an important part of cash flow estimates. Noncash expenses such as depreciation do affect cash flows indirectly through their effect on taxable income.

7. **Recognize the effect of risk on the discount rate.** The cash flows of higher risk investment projects should be discounted at a higher interest rate.

8. **Estimate the internal rate of return of an investment project, and identify problems with using the internal rate of return to evaluate investment projects.** The internal rate of return is the discount rate that sets the net present value of the cash flows equal to zero. The internal rate of return and net present value do not always rank investment projects the same. The difference in rankings could be due to the relative size of the investment and the duration of the cash flows. In addition, the internal rate of return method assumes that intermediate cash flows can be reinvested at the internal rate of return.

9. **Use annuity tables to relate present and future values (appendix).** The annuity tables allow for the calculation of the present value and future value of constant streams of cash over finite periods.

KEY TERMS

Capital budgeting A process of evaluating and choosing long-term investments.

Depreciation The allocation of the historical cost of a fixed asset over time.

Depreciation tax shield The reduction in taxes due to the reduction of taxable income through the use of depreciation.

Expected cash flow The sum of each cash flow that can occur weighted by its probability of occurrence.

Hurdle rate The benchmark rate of return that is established by the organization as an investment criterion.

Internal rate of return The discount rate that makes the net present value of an investment equal to zero.

Net present value The net present value of cash flows is calculated by discounting all future cash flows to the present and comparing the present value of the cash inflows with the present value of the cash outflows.

Opportunity cost of capital The return that could have been earned if the capital was invested in an equivalent risk instrument. Sometimes called *cost of capital.*

Payback The time required to generate cash inflows equal to the initial investment.

Return on investment (ROI) The income divided by the assets generating the income.

Appendix: Interest Rate Mathematics

This appendix develops the mathematical relations for converting cash flows received or paid at different times. By deriving the various formulas, the logic of the calculations is made clearer. In the following examples, the interest rate is given. Determining the appropriate interest rate to relate dollars from different time periods is discussed in the chapter.

Future Values

The *future value* of cash today is the initial amount plus interest that is earned during the interim period. If we assume an interest rate of 5% and an initial investment of $1,000, the future value of the $1,000 in one year is the initial investment of $1,000 plus interest of $50 (5% of $1,000), or $1,050. What is the future value of $1,000 in two years with an interest rate of 5%? At the end of the first year, one has $1,050 ($1,000 principal plus $50 of interest). This amount is then reinvested to yield $1,102.50 ($1,050 principal plus interest of $52.50). Of the $52.50 of interest in the second year, $50 is interest on the original $1,000 and

In some states, such as Colorado, you must specify at the time you buy a lottery ticket whether you want a lump-sum payment or payment over 20 years. How would you decide between receiving $50,000 a year for twenty years (a total of a million dollars) versus receiving $743,850 in a lump sum today?

$2.50 is interest on the first year interest ($50 × 5%). Or, at the end of the second year:

$1,000 + 2(0.05 × $1,000) + [0.05 × (0.05 × $1,000)] = $1,000 + $100 + $2.50 = $1,102.50

The fact that interest is earned on the interest in the second year is called *compounding*. The formulas we will derive are often called *compound interest formulas*. The future value of $1 at different interest rates for different periods of time is provided in Table 13A.5 at the end of the appendix.

We will now generalize the preceding illustration. Let PV represent the amount of money invested today at r% per year and let FV represent the amount that will be available at the end of the two years. The general formula relating present dollars to dollars in two years at r% per year is:

$$PV(1 + r)^2 = PV(1 + 2r + r^2) = FV$$

The $2r$ term represents interest for two years on the original investment of PV, and r^2 is the interest on the interest (compound interest). The general formula for leaving money in the bank for n years and allowing the interest to accumulate and earn interest is:

$$PV(1 + r)^n = FV \qquad \text{(Future value formula)}$$

All of the formulas of interest rate mathematics are just algebraic manipulations of this basic formula.

NUMERICAL EXAMPLE 13A.1

A mother, who recently gave birth to a daughter, has decided to put $1,000 in the bank for her daughter's college fund. The fund earns 6% a year for 18 years before being withdrawn from the bank, How much will the $1,000 be worth in 18 years?

■ **SOLUTION**
$$PV(1 + r)^n = FV$$
$$\$1,000(1 + 0.06)^{18} = \$2,854 = FV$$

The $1,000 will be worth $2,854 in 18 years.

Present Values

Suppose that instead of asking how much money a person will have at the end of n years, we ask how much money must be invested today at r% per year to have a defined future value at a specific future point in time? For example, how much money must someone invest today at a 5% interest rate to be able to buy a $25,000 boat in six years? The amount of money that must be invested today to equal a certain amount in the future at a given interest rate is called *present value* (PV). In present value calculations, the future value (FV) and interest rate (r) are known, but present value (PV) is unknown. Rearranging the future formula yields the present value formula:

$$PV = \frac{FV}{(1 + r)^n} \qquad \text{(Present value formula)}$$

To solve for the boat example,

$$PV = \frac{\$25,000}{(1 + 0.05)^6}$$

$$= \frac{\$25,000}{1.3401}$$

$$= \$18,655$$

Therefore, if a person invests $18,655 in the bank at 5% and allows the principal and interest to compound, at the end of six years that person will have $25,000. The present value of $1 received at different time periods in the future at different interest rates is provided in Table 13A.3 at the end of the appendix.

NUMERICAL EXAMPLE 13A.2

A recent college graduate would like to go back to school and get an MBA in 10 years. He estimates that a two-year MBA degree will cost $70,000, including living expenses, in 10 years. He can put money in a bank that will earn 5% annually for the next 10 years. How much money will he have to put in the bank today to have $70,000 in 10 years?

■ **SOLUTION**

$$PV = \frac{FV}{(1+r)^n}$$

$$= \$70{,}000/(1+0.05)^{10}$$

$$= \$42{,}974$$

The college graduate must deposit $42,974 in the bank today to have $70,000 in 10 years.

Present Value of a Cash Flow Stream

The future and present value formulas (which are the same formula) allow for the comparison of cash from different time periods. So far, we have been dealing with just a single cash flow invested today or received in the future. Now, suppose one has a series of cash flows occurring *at the end of each year* for the next n years. That is, FV_1 is the cash received at the end of the first year, FV_2 is the cash received at the end of the second year, and FV_n is the cash received at the end of the nth year. What is the present value of this cash flow stream? Apply the above present value formula to each cash flow and sum them together:

$$PV = \frac{FV_1}{(1+r)^1} + \frac{FV_2}{(1+r)^2} + \frac{FV_3}{(1+r)^3} + \ldots + \frac{FV_n}{(1+r)^n}$$

Suppose you are offered $500 at the end of the first year, $1,000 at the end of the second year, and $1,500 at the end of the third year. How much is this stream of cash flows worth today? Using the above formula:

$$PV = \frac{\$500}{(1+0.05)^1} + \frac{\$1000}{(1+0.05)^2} + \frac{\$1500}{(1+0.05)^3}$$

$$= \frac{\$500}{1.05} + \frac{\$1000}{1.1025} + \frac{\$1500}{1.157625}$$

$$= \$476 + \$907 + \$1{,}296$$

$$= \$2{,}679$$

Therefore, you would be indifferent between receiving the cash flow stream of $500, $1,000, and $1,500 in the next three years and $2,678.98 today if the interest rate is 5%.

Each of the cash flows, FV_t, is said to be *discounted* (or divided) by $(1+r)^n$ where n is the year in which the cash flow is received. Notice that $1 \div (1+r)^n$ is always less than one for all positive interest rates. Therefore, a dollar received in the future is worth less than a dollar today. We will see that discounting is central to the concept of comparing alternatives involving cash flows received at different points of time. By discounting the future cash flows from each alternative to present values (or dollars today), we can compare which alternative is best.

NUMERICAL EXAMPLE 13A.3

An insurance company is offering a new retirement policy. The insurance company is willing to pay $100,000 in 30 years, another $200,000 in 40 years, and a final payment of $300,000 in 50 years. What is the value of this retirement policy now to someone with an annual interest rate of 8%?

■ **SOLUTION** $PV = \$100,000/(1 + 0.08)^{30} + \$200,000/(1 + 0.08)^{40} + \$300,000/(1 + 0.08)^{50}$
$PV = \$9,938 + \$9,206 + \$6,396 = \$25,540$

The present value of the retirement policy is $25,540.

Perpetuities

A *perpetuity* is an infinite stream of equal payments received each year. Some government bonds issued by the British government promise to pay a fixed amount of cash each year forever. How much would investors be willing to pay for such bonds? All of the future payments, $FV_1, FV_2, \ldots, FV_n$ are the same and equal to FV. Substituting FV into the general formula yields:

$$PV = \frac{FV}{(1+r)^1} + \frac{FV}{(1+r)^2} + \frac{FV}{(1+r)^3} + \cdots$$

$$= \left(\frac{FV}{1+r}\right)\left(1 + \frac{1}{(1+r)^1} + \frac{1}{(1+r)^2} + \frac{1}{(1+r)^3} + \cdots\right)$$

From algebra, we know that the sum of an infinite series has the following expression:

$$\left(1 + \frac{1}{(1+r)^1} + \frac{1}{(1+r)^2} + \frac{1}{(1+r)^3} + \cdots\right) = \frac{1+r}{r}$$

Substituting this term into the above formula gives:

$$PV = \left(\frac{FV}{1+r}\right)\left(\frac{1+r}{r}\right)$$

$$PV = \frac{FV}{r} \qquad \text{(Perpetuity formula)}$$

This is the basic formula for a perpetuity, or an infinite cash flow stream, when the interest rate is $r\%$. If the British government bonds pay 100 pounds per year in perpetuity and the interest rate is 5%, then investors would be willing to pay:

$$PV = \frac{£100}{0.05}$$

$$= £2,000$$

NUMERICAL EXAMPLE 13A.4

Antonio's eccentric aunt had just died. He found he was included in the will. But instead of a lump sum payment, she left Antonio with an unusual contract through an insurance company. The insurance company must pay Antonio $1,000 per year beginning at the end of this year for an infinite number of years. When Antonio dies, his designated heir continues to receive these $1,000 payments. What is the present value of the contract if the interest rate is 8%?

■ **SOLUTION**

$$PV = \frac{FV}{r}$$

$$PV = \$1,000/.08 = \$12,500$$

The present value of the contract is equal to $12,500.

Annuities

An *annuity* is a stream of *equal* cash flows for a *fixed* number of years. Many financial instruments are annuities. For example, car loans and mortgage payments involve a fixed number of equal monthly payments. Corporate bonds pay a fixed amount twice a year over the term of the bond (usually 20 years). To derive the formula for an annuity, let FV again denote the annual cash flow received at the end of each of the next n years. The present value of an annuity of n cash flows of FV each:

$$PV = \frac{FV}{(1+r)^1} + \frac{FV}{(1+r)^2} + \frac{FV}{(1+r)^3} + \cdots \frac{FV}{(1+r)^n}$$

To derive the formula for this annuity stream, notice that mathematically an annuity is equivalent to the difference between the following two streams:

Year	0	1	2	3	...	n	$n+1$	$n+2$	...
Cash flow #1	0	FV	FV	FV	...	FV	FV	FV	
Cash flow #2	0	0	0	0	...	0	FV	FV	

That is, an annuity cash flow stream equals cash flow #1 minus cash flow #2. We know how to value cash flow #1 using the perpetuity formula:

$$\text{Present value of cash flow \#1} = \frac{FV}{r}$$

The present value of cash flow #2 is:

$$\text{Present value of cash flow \#2} = \left(\frac{1}{(1+r)^n}\right)\left(\frac{FV}{r}\right)$$

That is, the present value of cash flow #2 is the present value of a perpetuity discounted back from n years because the first perpetuity payment is not received for $n + 1$ years. The first term in the above formula discounts the value of the perpetuity to recognize that the first payment is not received immediately. Now take the difference between the two formulas:

$$\begin{aligned}\text{PV of an annuity} &= \text{PV of cash flow \#1} - \text{PV of cash flow \#2} \\ &= \frac{FV}{r} - \left(\frac{1}{(1+r)^n}\right)\left(\frac{FV}{r}\right)\end{aligned}$$

$$PV = FV\left(\frac{(1+r)^n - 1}{r(1+r)^n}\right) \qquad \text{(Present value of annuity formula)}$$

To illustrate the application of the formula, suppose a contract states that you are to receive $1,000 per year for 10 years. How large of a loan can you borrow today? The interest rate is 5%. What is the present value of the contract? Using our annuity formula we get:

$$PV = \$1{,}000 \left(\frac{(1.05)^{10} - 1}{0.05(1.05)^{10}} \right)$$

$$= \$1{,}000 \left(\frac{0.628895}{0.081445} \right)$$

$$= \$7{,}722$$

Another useful formula is the future value of an annuity. For example, if one invests $1,000 a year for 18 years, how much money will one have for a child's college education? We start with the present value of an annuity and then convert this amount to a future value by taking the present value formula for an annuity and multiplying it by $(1 + r)^n$. Or,

$$\text{Future value of annuity} = FV \left(\frac{(1 + r)^n - 1}{r(1 + r)^n} \right)(1 + r)^n$$

$$= FV \left(\frac{(1 + r)^n - 1}{r} \right) \quad \text{(Future value of annuity formula)}$$

To solve for how much money one will have for a child's education, using an interest rate of 5% we substitute into the above formula:

$$\text{Future value of annuity} = \$1{,}000 \left(\frac{(1.05)^{18} - 1}{0.05} \right)$$

$$= \$1{,}000 \, (28.132)$$

$$= \$28{,}132$$

Therefore, with interest left to accumulate in the bank, a person would have over $28,000 on an investment of $1,000 a year for 18 years at an interest rate of 5%. The future and present values of a $1 annuity for different interest rates and different periods of time are presented in Tables 13A.6 and 13A.4, respectively.

NUMERICAL EXAMPLE 13A.5

Karen Stark is considering the purchase of a home. She wants to borrow $100,000 from the bank. Instead of the normal monthly mortgage payments, the bank is willing to let Karen repay the loan in equal annual payments at 12% interest over the next 20 years. How much will Karen have to pay each year.

■ **SOLUTION**

$$PV = FV \left(\frac{(1 + r)^n - 1}{r(1 + r)^n} \right) \quad \text{or} \quad FV = PV \Big/ \left(\frac{(1 + r)^n - 1}{r(1 + r)^n} \right)$$

$$FV = \$100{,}000 \times \left(\frac{(1 + 0.12)^{20} - 1}{0.12(1 + 0.12)^{20}} \right)$$

$$FV = \$13{,}388$$

Karen will have to pay $13,388 at the end of each of the next 20 years.

Multiple Cash Flows per Year

So far we have considered only cash flows that occur once per year. How do we handle cash flows that occur more frequently, say monthly? We could add up the monthly flows and treat them as a single annual cash flow on the last day of the year. But this ignores the interest we could earn on the monthly receipts. To illustrate, consider the difference between the following two options: (1) receiving 12 monthly $1,000 payments or (2) receiving a single $12,000 payment at the end of the year. Before we can calculate which option is worth more, we first have to understand the relation between monthly and annual interest rates. If the annual interest rate is 5%, what is the interest rate per month? You might be tempted to say $0.05 \div 12 = 0.004166$, but this is wrong. A dollar invested at the monthly interest rate, r_m, must accumulate to the same amount at the end of the year as a dollar invested at the annual interest rate, r. Therefore, the following formula must hold:

$$(1 + r_m)^{12} = (1 + r)$$
$$(1 + r_m) = (1 + r)^{1/12}$$
$$r_m = (1 + r)^{1/12} - 1$$
$$= (1.05)^{1/12} - 1$$
$$= 0.004074$$

Now we can return to the original question and value the two options. The monthly interest rate just derived is 0.004074 and the annual interest rate is 0.05. Using the present value of the annuity formula to calculate the stream of 12 monthly $1,000 payments

$$FV\left(\frac{(1+r)^n - 1}{r(1+r)^n}\right) = \$1,000\left(\frac{(1.004074)^{12} - 1}{0.004074(1.004074)^{12}}\right)$$

$$= \$1,000\left(\frac{1.05 - 1}{0.004074(1.05)}\right)$$

$$= \$1,000(11.68817)$$

$$= \$11,688.17$$

The present value of the single $12,000 payment is:

$$\frac{FV}{(1+r)^n} = \frac{\$12000}{(1.05)^1} = \$11,428.57$$

Therefore, the 12 payments of $1,000 are worth $259.60 more today than a single $12,000 payment at an annual interest rate of 5%.

The preceding example illustrates that the earlier a payment is received, the more valuable the payment is. It also introduces the notion of the *compounding interval*. The compounding interval is the period of time in which interest is calculated and then compounded in the next period. The compounding interval could be a year, a month, or a day. The key point is that the annual interest rate cannot be used to discount cash flows received more frequently than yearly. Some banks quote interest rates in annual terms, say 5%, but then compound the interest monthly. In this case, the *effective* annual interest is:

$$\left(1 + \frac{r}{12}\right)^{12} - 1 = \left(1 + \frac{0.05}{12}\right)^{12} - 1$$

$$= (1.0041666667)^{12} - 1$$

$$= 0.05116$$

TABLE 13A.1
Example of Using Compound Interest Tables (Interest rate = 5%)

	Cash Flow In	Discount Factor	Source of Factor	Present Value
Years 1–20	$1,000	12.462	Table 13A.4	$12,462
Years 1–10	$1,000	7.722	Table 13A.4	7,722
Year 21	$3,000	0.359	Table 13A.3	1,077
Total present value				$21,261

Therefore, if the bank has a stated annual interest rate of 5% but compounds monthly, the *effective* interest rate is 5.116%. If the bank states that its interest rate is 5% but compounds interest *daily*, the *effective* annual rate is 5.127% [0.05127 = $(1 + 0.05/365)^{365} - 1$]. The preceding discussion illustrates that depositors wanting the highest *effective* interest rate will always choose the shortest compounding interval among banks offering the same stated annual interest rate.

NUMERICAL EXAMPLE 13A.6

Joe Swann has $5,000 to invest for two years. One bank offers a 5% annual rate compounded monthly and another bank offers 6% compounded annually. Which is the better investment?

■ **SOLUTION** A 5% annual rate is equivalent to a monthly rate of $(1 + 0.05)^{1/12} - 1$, or 0.0041558. The value of $5,000 over 24 months at 0.41558% is $5,000(1 + 0.0041558)^{24}$, or $5,523. The value of $5,000 over 2 years at an annual rate of 6% is $5,000(1 + 0.06)^2$, or $5,618. Investing the $5,000 at 6% annually has the higher future value.

It is not necessary to memorize the major formulas for converting cash flow streams into either present or future values. Tables at the end of the appendix contain the present and future values that correspond to the formulas. These tables greatly simplify the computation of present values. Also, most computer spreadsheet programs and hand-held calculators compute present values and future values. For example, suppose one wants to compute the present value of the following cash flows (at $r = 5\%$): $2,000 for the first 10 years, $1,000 for the next 10 years, and $3,000 at the end of year 21. Table 13A.1 lays out the calculations.

The first thing to note is that to simplify the calculations, the $2,000 stream for years 1–10 and the $1,000 stream for years 11–20 are equivalent to a $1,000 stream for the first 20 years and a $1,000 stream for the first 10 years. The discount factors for these two streams are taken from the annuity table later in this chapter (Table 13A.4). The single $3,000 payment in year 21 is discounted using the present value factor from the present value table (Table 13A.3). Adding the three discounted cash flows together yields a present value of $21,261.

NUMERICAL EXAMPLE 13A.7

Judy Radski is considering returning to school to get an MBA degree. Her current wages are $25,000. Tuition, books, and fees will cost $20,000 per year for two years. Upon completing the MBA, her starting salary will be $40,000. The MBA degree is expected to add $15,000 per year to her salary until retirement. However, she must give up two years of current salary while in graduate school plus pay tuition, books, and fees. At a current age

TABLE 13A.2
The Decision to Get an MBA Degree

		Net Cash Flow	Discount Factor	Present Value
Years 1–2	Forgone wages + cost of school	($45,000)	1.859	($ 83,655)
Years 1–30	Additional wages with MBA	$15,000	15.372	230,580
Years 1–2	Higher MBA wages not earned in first two years*	($15,000)	1.859	(27,885)
Net present value				$119,040

*The present value of $15,000 for two years is being deducted in this line because the line above includes the first two years.

of 31 and with an expected retirement age of 60, does it make sense to go back and get the MBA? The market rate of interest is 5%.

■ **SOLUTION** Table 13A.2 calculates the net present value of her MBA as the difference between the present value of the cash inflows and outflows.

In Table 13A.2 the additional wages of $15,000 are treated as an annuity beginning in year one and then a two-year annuity beginning in year one of $15,000 is subtracted. This is the simplest way of performing the calculation. The computations in Table 13A.2 assume that all cash flows occur at the end of the year. To keep the example simple, the additional wages from having the MBA degree are assumed to be constant at $15,000 per year over the career. Given these assumptions, the decision to get an MBA is worth $119,040 in today's dollars. That is, the present value of the additional wages from receiving the MBA is greater than the amount forgone (wages plus schooling costs) to acquire the degree.

SELF-STUDY PROBLEM

Avroland is an amusement park in California. They currently use a computer system to perform general accounting functions, including the tracking of ticket sales and payroll as well as employee and maintenance scheduling functions. The original system, when purchased two years ago, cost $300,000 and has been depreciated for tax purposes using straight-line depreciation with an expected useful life of four more years and a zero salvage value. However, due to recent expansion, the computer system is no longer large enough. Upgrading the system to increase the storage capacity and processing speed to accommodate the extra data processing demands would cost $65,000 and would become obsolete in four years. These system additions would also be depreciated using straight-line depreciation and would have a zero salvage value. The company's accountant estimates that the firm will increase operating spending by $28,000 a year after taxes for data processing, payroll (including Avroland personnel), and annual updates of software for the upgraded system. Alternatively, the firm could outsource payroll to a local payroll processing firm at the cost of $40,000 a year after taxes. This would free up enough capacity in the computer to prevent having to upgrade the machine. Assume a real cost of capital of 4% and a tax rate of 40%.

What should Avroland do?

Solution to Self-Study Problem

The relevant costs to Avroland for processing payroll internally are the cost of upgrading the computer plus the variable cost of processing the information minus the tax savings

TABLE 13A.3 Present Value of $1

Present value of $1 received at the end of n periods at an interest rate of i%

Periods	3%	4%	5%	6%	7%	8%	9%	10%	12%	14%	16%	18%	20%	25%	30%
1	0.971	0.962	0.952	0.943	0.935	0.926	0.917	0.909	0.893	0.877	0.862	0.847	0.833	0.800	0.769
2	0.943	0.925	0.907	0.890	0.873	0.857	0.842	0.826	0.797	0.769	0.743	0.718	0.694	0.640	0.592
3	0.915	0.889	0.864	0.840	0.816	0.794	0.772	0.751	0.712	0.675	0.641	0.609	0.579	0.512	0.455
4	0.888	0.855	0.823	0.792	0.763	0.735	0.708	0.683	0.636	0.592	0.552	0.516	0.482	0.410	0.350
5	0.863	0.822	0.784	0.747	0.713	0.681	0.650	0.621	0.567	0.519	0.476	0.437	0.402	0.328	0.269
6	0.837	0.790	0.746	0.705	0.666	0.630	0.596	0.564	0.507	0.456	0.410	0.370	0.335	0.262	0.207
7	0.813	0.760	0.711	0.665	0.623	0.583	0.547	0.513	0.452	0.400	0.354	0.314	0.279	0.210	0.159
8	0.789	0.731	0.677	0.627	0.582	0.540	0.502	0.467	0.404	0.351	0.305	0.266	0.233	0.168	0.123
9	0.766	0.703	0.645	0.592	0.544	0.500	0.460	0.424	0.361	0.308	0.263	0.225	0.194	0.134	0.094
10	0.744	0.676	0.614	0.558	0.508	0.463	0.422	0.386	0.322	0.270	0.227	0.191	0.162	0.107	0.073
11	0.722	0.650	0.585	0.527	0.475	0.429	0.388	0.350	0.287	0.237	0.195	0.162	0.135	0.086	0.056
12	0.701	0.625	0.557	0.497	0.444	0.397	0.356	0.319	0.257	0.208	0.168	0.137	0.112	0.069	0.043
13	0.681	0.601	0.530	0.469	0.415	0.368	0.326	0.290	0.229	0.182	0.145	0.116	0.093	0.055	0.033
14	0.661	0.577	0.505	0.442	0.388	0.340	0.299	0.263	0.205	0.160	0.125	0.099	0.078	0.044	0.025
15	0.642	0.555	0.481	0.417	0.362	0.315	0.275	0.239	0.183	0.140	0.108	0.084	0.065	0.035	0.020
16	0.623	0.534	0.458	0.394	0.339	0.292	0.252	0.218	0.163	0.123	0.093	0.071	0.054	0.028	0.015
17	0.605	0.513	0.436	0.371	0.317	0.270	0.231	0.198	0.146	0.108	0.080	0.060	0.045	0.023	0.012
18	0.587	0.494	0.416	0.350	0.296	0.250	0.212	0.180	0.130	0.095	0.069	0.051	0.038	0.018	0.009
19	0.570	0.475	0.396	0.331	0.277	0.232	0.194	0.164	0.116	0.083	0.060	0.043	0.031	0.014	0.007
20	0.554	0.456	0.377	0.312	0.258	0.215	0.178	0.149	0.104	0.073	0.051	0.037	0.026	0.012	0.005
21	0.538	0.439	0.359	0.294	0.242	0.199	0.164	0.135	0.093	0.064	0.044	0.031	0.022	0.009	0.004
22	0.522	0.422	0.342	0.278	0.226	0.184	0.150	0.123	0.083	0.056	0.038	0.026	0.018	0.007	0.003
23	0.507	0.406	0.326	0.262	0.211	0.170	0.138	0.112	0.074	0.049	0.033	0.022	0.015	0.006	0.002
24	0.492	0.390	0.310	0.247	0.197	0.158	0.126	0.102	0.066	0.043	0.028	0.019	0.013	0.005	0.002
25	0.478	0.375	0.295	0.233	0.184	0.146	0.116	0.092	0.059	0.038	0.024	0.016	0.010	0.004	0.001
26	0.464	0.361	0.281	0.220	0.172	0.135	0.106	0.084	0.053	0.033	0.021	0.014	0.009	0.003	0.001
27	0.450	0.347	0.268	0.207	0.161	0.125	0.098	0.076	0.047	0.029	0.018	0.011	0.007	0.002	0.001
28	0.437	0.333	0.255	0.196	0.150	0.116	0.090	0.069	0.042	0.026	0.016	0.010	0.006	0.002	0.001
29	0.424	0.321	0.243	0.185	0.141	0.107	0.082	0.063	0.037	0.022	0.014	0.008	0.005	0.002	0.000
30	0.412	0.308	0.231	0.174	0.131	0.099	0.075	0.057	0.033	0.020	0.012	0.007	0.004	0.001	0.000
35	0.355	0.253	0.181	0.130	0.094	0.068	0.049	0.036	0.019	0.010	0.006	0.003	0.002	0.000	0.000
40	0.307	0.208	0.142	0.097	0.067	0.046	0.032	0.022	0.011	0.005	0.003	0.001	0.001	0.000	0.000
60	0.170	0.095	0.054	0.030	0.017	0.010	0.006	0.003	0.001	0.000	0.000	0.000	0.000	0.000	0.000

TABLE 13A.4 Present Value of an Annuity

Present value of a stream of $1s received at the end of each of the next *n* periods at an interest rate of *i*%

Periods	3%	4%	5%	6%	7%	8%	9%	10%	12%	14%	16%	18%	20%	25%	30%
1	0.971	0.962	0.952	0.943	0.935	0.926	0.917	0.909	0.893	0.877	0.862	0.847	0.833	0.800	0.769
2	1.913	1.886	1.859	1.833	1.808	1.783	1.759	1.736	1.690	1.647	1.605	1.566	1.528	1.440	1.361
3	2.829	2.775	2.723	2.673	2.624	2.577	2.531	2.487	2.402	2.322	2.246	2.174	2.106	1.952	1.816
4	3.717	3.630	3.546	3.465	3.387	3.312	3.240	3.170	3.037	2.914	2.798	2.690	2.589	2.362	2.166
5	4.580	4.452	4.329	4.212	4.100	3.993	3.890	3.791	3.605	3.433	3.274	3.127	2.991	2.689	2.436
6	5.417	5.242	5.076	4.971	4.767	4.623	4.486	4.355	4.111	3.889	3.685	3.498	3.326	2.951	2.643
7	6.230	6.002	5.786	5.582	5.389	5.206	5.033	4.868	4.564	4.288	4.039	3.812	3.605	3.161	2.802
8	7.020	6.733	6.463	6.210	5.971	5.747	5.535	5.335	4.968	4.639	4.344	4.078	3.837	3.329	2.925
9	7.786	7.435	7.108	6.802	6.515	6.247	5.995	5.759	5.328	4.946	4.607	4.303	4.031	3.463	3.019
10	8.530	8.111	7.722	7.360	7.024	6.710	6.418	6.145	5.650	5.216	4.833	4.494	4.192	3.571	3.092
11	9.253	8.760	8.306	7.887	7.499	7.139	6.805	6.495	5.938	5.453	5.029	4.656	4.327	3.656	3.147
12	9.954	9.385	8.863	8.384	7.943	7.536	7.161	6.814	6.194	5.660	5.197	4.793	4.439	3.725	3.190
13	10.635	9.986	9.394	8.853	8.358	7.904	7.487	7.103	6.424	5.842	5.342	4.910	4.533	3.780	3.223
14	11.296	10.563	9.899	9.295	8.745	8.244	7.786	7.367	6.628	6.002	5.468	5.008	4.611	3.824	3.249
15	11.938	11.118	10.380	9.712	9.108	8.559	8.061	7.606	6.811	6.142	5.575	5.092	4.675	3.859	3.268
16	12.561	11.652	10.838	10.106	9.447	8.851	8.313	7.824	6.974	6.265	5.668	5.162	4.730	3.887	3.283
17	13.166	12.166	11.274	10.477	9.763	9.122	8.544	8.022	7.120	6.373	5.749	5.222	4.775	3.910	3.295
18	13.754	12.659	11.690	10.828	10.059	9.372	8.756	8.201	7.250	6.467	5.818	5.273	4.812	3.928	3.304
19	14.324	13.134	12.085	11.158	10.336	9.604	8.950	8.365	7.366	6.550	5.877	5.316	4.843	3.942	3.311
20	14.877	13.590	12.462	11.470	10.594	9.818	9.129	8.514	7.469	6.623	5.929	5.353	4.870	3.954	3.316
21	15.415	14.029	12.821	11.764	10.836	10.017	9.292	8.649	7.562	6.687	5.973	5.384	4.891	3.963	3.320
22	15.937	14.451	13.163	12.042	11.061	10.201	9.442	8.772	7.645	6.743	6.011	5.410	4.909	3.970	3.323
23	16.444	14.857	13.489	12.303	11.272	10.371	9.580	8.883	7.718	6.792	6.044	5.432	4.925	3.976	3.325
24	16.936	15.247	13.799	12.550	11.469	10.529	9.707	8.985	7.784	6.835	6.073	5.451	4.937	3.981	3.327
25	17.413	15.622	14.094	12.783	11.654	10.675	9.823	9.077	7.843	6.873	6.097	5.467	4.948	3.985	3.329
26	17.877	15.983	14.375	13.003	11.826	10.810	9.929	9.161	7.896	6.906	6.118	5.480	4.956	3.988	3.330
27	18.327	16.330	14.643	13.211	11.987	10.935	10.027	9.237	7.943	6.935	6.136	5.492	4.964	3.990	3.331
28	18.764	16.663	14.898	13.406	12.137	11.051	10.116	9.307	7.984	6.961	6.152	5.502	4.970	3.992	3.331
29	19.188	16.984	15.141	13.591	12.278	11.158	10.198	9.370	8.022	6.983	6.166	5.510	4.975	3.994	3.332
30	19.600	17.292	15.372	13.765	12.409	11.258	10.274	9.427	8.055	7.003	6.177	5.517	4.979	3.995	3.332
35	21.487	18.665	16.374	14.498	12.948	11.655	10.567	9.644	8.176	7.070	6.215	5.539	4.992	3.998	3.333
40	23.115	19.793	17.159	15.046	13.332	11.925	10.757	9.779	8.244	7.105	6.233	5.548	4.997	3.999	3.333
60	27.676	22.623	18.929	16.161	14.039	12.377	11.048	9.967	8.324	7.140	6.249	5.555	5.000	4.000	3.333
120	32.373	24.774	19.943	16.651	14.281	12.499	11.111	10.000	8.333	7.143	6.250	5.556	5.000	4.000	3.333
360	33.333	25.000	20.000	16.667	14.286	12.500	11.111	10.000	8.333	7.143	6.250	5.556	5.000	4.000	3.333

TABLE 13A.5 Future Value of $1

Future value of $1 invested today at i% interest and allowed to compound for n periods

Periods	3%	4%	5%	6%	7%	8%	9%	10%	12%	14%	16%	18%	20%	25%	30%
1	1.030	1.040	1.050	1.060	1.070	1.080	1.090	1.100	1.120	1.140	1.160	1.180	1.200	1.250	1.300
2	1.061	1.082	1.103	1.124	1.145	1.166	1.188	1.210	1.254	1.300	1.346	1.392	1.440	1.563	1.690
3	1.093	1.125	1.158	1.191	1.225	1.260	1.295	1.331	1.405	1.482	1.561	1.643	1.728	1.953	2.197
4	1.126	1.170	1.216	1.262	1.311	1.360	1.412	1.464	1.574	1.689	1.811	1.939	2.074	2.441	2.856
5	1.159	1.217	1.276	1.338	1.403	1.469	1.539	1.611	1.762	1.925	2.100	2.288	2.488	3.052	3.713
6	1.194	1.265	1.340	1.419	1.501	1.587	1.677	1.772	1.974	2.195	2.436	2.700	2.986	3.815	4.827
7	1.230	1.316	1.407	1.504	1.606	1.714	1.828	1.949	2.211	2.502	2.826	3.185	3.583	4.768	6.275
8	1.267	1.369	1.477	1.594	1.718	1.851	1.993	2.144	2.476	2.853	3.278	3.759	4.300	5.960	8.157
9	1.305	1.423	1.551	1.689	1.838	1.999	2.172	2.358	2.773	3.252	3.803	4.435	5.160	7.451	10.604
10	1.344	1.480	1.629	1.791	1.967	2.159	2.367	2.594	3.106	3.707	4.411	5.234	6.192	9.313	13.786
11	1.384	1.539	1.710	1.898	2.105	2.332	2.580	2.853	3.479	4.226	5.117	6.176	7.430	11.642	17.922
12	1.426	1.601	1.796	2.012	2.252	2.518	2.813	3.138	3.896	4.818	5.936	7.288	8.916	14.552	23.298
13	1.469	1.665	1.886	2.133	2.410	2.720	3.066	3.452	4.363	5.492	6.886	8.599	10.699	18.190	30.288
14	1.513	1.732	1.980	2.261	2.579	2.937	3.342	3.797	4.887	6.261	7.988	10.147	12.839	22.737	39.374
15	1.558	1.801	2.079	2.397	2.759	3.172	3.642	4.177	5.474	7.138	9.266	11.974	15.407	28.422	51.186
16	1.605	1.873	2.183	2.540	2.952	3.426	3.970	4.595	6.130	8.137	10.748	14.129	18.488	35.527	66.542
17	1.653	1.948	2.292	2.693	3.159	3.700	4.328	5.054	6.866	9.276	12.468	16.672	22.186	44.409	86.504
18	1.702	2.026	2.407	2.854	3.380	3.996	4.717	5.560	7.690	10.575	14.463	19.673	26.623	55.511	112.455
19	1.754	2.107	2.527	3.026	3.617	4.316	5.142	6.116	8.613	12.056	16.777	23.214	31.948	69.389	146.192
20	1.806	2.191	2.653	3.207	3.870	4.661	5.604	6.727	9.646	13.743	19.461	27.393	38.338	86.736	190.050
21	1.860	2.279	2.786	3.400	4.141	5.034	6.109	7.400	10.804	15.668	22.574	32.324	46.005	108.420	247.065
22	1.916	2.370	2.925	3.604	4.430	5.437	6.659	8.140	12.100	17.861	26.186	38.142	55.206	135.525	321.184
23	1.974	2.465	3.072	3.820	4.741	5.871	7.258	8.954	13.552	20.362	30.376	45.008	66.247	169.407	417.539
24	2.033	2.563	3.225	4.049	5.072	6.341	7.911	9.850	15.179	23.212	35.236	53.109	79.497	211.758	542.801
25	2.094	2.666	3.386	4.292	5.427	6.848	8.623	10.835	17.000	26.462	40.874	62.669	95.396	264.698	705.641
26	2.157	2.772	3.556	4.549	5.807	7.396	9.399	11.918	19.040	30.167	47.414	73.949	114.475	330.872	917.333
27	2.221	2.883	3.733	4.822	6.214	7.988	10.245	13.110	21.325	34.390	55.000	87.260	137.371	413.590	1,192.533
28	2.288	2.999	3.920	5.112	6.649	8.627	11.167	14.421	23.884	39.204	63.800	102.967	164.845	516.988	1,550.293
29	2.357	3.119	4.116	5.418	7.114	9.317	12.172	15.863	26.750	44.693	74.009	121.501	197.814	646.235	2,015.381
30	2.427	3.243	4.322	5.743	7.612	10.063	13.268	17.449	29.960	50.950	85.850	143.371	237.376	807.794	2,619.996
35	2.814	3.946	5.516	7.686	10.677	14.785	20.414	28.102	52.800	98.100	180.314	327.997	590.668	2,465.190	9,727.860
40	3.262	4.801	7.040	10.286	14.974	21.725	31.409	45.259	93.051	188.884	378.721	750.378	1,469.772	7,523.164	36,118.865

TABLE 13A.6 Future Value of an Annuity of $1

Future value of a stream of n $1s invested today at i% interest and allowed to compound for n periods

Periods	3%	4%	5%	6%	7%	8%	9%	10%	12%	14%	16%	18%	20%
1	1.000	1.000	1.000	1.000	1.000	1.000	1.000	1.000	1.000	1.000	1.000	1.000	1.000
2	2.030	2.040	2.050	2.060	2.070	2.080	2.090	2.100	2.120	2.140	2.160	2.180	2.200
3	3.091	3.122	3.153	3.184	3.215	3.246	3.278	3.310	3.374	3.440	3.506	3.572	3.640
4	4.184	4.246	4.310	4.375	4.440	4.506	4.573	4.641	4.779	4.921	5.066	5.215	5.368
5	5.309	5.416	5.526	5.637	5.751	5.867	5.985	6.105	6.353	6.610	6.877	7.154	7.442
6	6.468	6.633	6.802	6.975	7.153	7.336	7.523	7.716	8.115	8.536	8.977	9.442	9.930
7	7.662	7.898	8.142	8.394	8.654	8.923	9.200	9.487	10.089	10.730	11.414	12.142	12.916
8	8.892	9.214	9.549	9.897	10.260	10.637	11.028	11.436	12.300	13.233	14.240	15.327	16.499
9	10.159	10.583	11.027	11.491	11.978	12.488	13.021	13.579	14.776	16.085	17.519	19.086	20.799
10	11.464	12.006	12.578	13.181	13.816	14.487	15.193	15.937	17.549	19.337	21.321	23.521	25.959
11	12.808	13.486	14.207	14.972	15.784	16.645	17.560	18.531	20.655	23.045	25.733	28.755	32.150
12	14.192	15.026	15.917	16.870	17.888	18.977	20.141	21.384	24.133	27.271	30.850	34.931	39.581
13	15.618	16.627	17.713	18.882	20.141	21.495	22.953	24.523	28.029	32.089	36.786	42.219	48.497
14	17.086	18.292	19.599	21.015	22.550	24.215	26.019	27.975	32.393	37.581	43.672	50.818	59.196
15	18.599	20.024	21.579	23.276	25.129	27.152	29.361	31.772	37.280	43.842	51.660	60.965	72.035
16	20.157	21.825	23.657	25.673	27.888	30.324	33.003	35.950	42.753	50.980	60.925	72.939	87.442
17	21.762	23.698	25.840	28.213	30.840	33.750	36.974	40.545	48.884	59.118	71.673	87.068	105.931
18	23.414	25.645	28.132	30.906	33.999	37.450	41.301	45.599	55.750	68.394	84.141	103.740	128.117
19	25.117	27.671	30.539	33.760	37.379	41.446	46.018	51.159	63.440	78.969	98.603	123.414	154.740
20	26.870	29.778	33.066	36.786	40.995	45.762	51.160	57.275	72.052	91.025	115.380	146.628	186.688
21	28.676	31.969	35.719	39.993	44.865	50.423	56.765	64.002	81.699	104.768	134.841	174.021	225.026
22	30.537	34.248	38.505	43.392	49.006	55.457	62.873	71.403	92.503	120.436	157.415	206.345	271.031
23	32.453	36.618	41.430	46.996	53.436	60.893	69.532	79.543	104.603	138.297	183.601	244.487	326.237
24	34.426	39.083	44.502	50.816	58.177	66.765	76.790	88.497	118.155	158.659	213.978	289.494	392.484
25	36.459	41.646	47.727	54.865	63.249	73.106	84.701	98.347	133.334	181.871	249.214	342.603	471.981
26	38.553	44.312	51.113	59.156	68.676	79.954	93.324	109.182	150.334	208.333	290.088	405.272	567.377
27	40.710	47.084	54.669	63.706	74.484	87.351	102.723	121.100	169.374	238.499	337.502	479.221	681.853
28	42.931	49.968	58.403	68.528	80.698	95.339	112.968	134.210	190.699	272.889	392.503	566.481	819.223
29	45.219	52.966	62.323	73.640	87.347	103.966	124.135	148.631	214.583	312.094	456.303	669.447	984.068
30	47.575	56.085	66.439	79.058	94.461	113.283	136.308	164.494	241.333	356.787	530.312	790.948	1,181.882
35	60.462	73.652	90.320	111.435	138.237	172.317	215.711	271.024	431.663	693.573	1,120.713	1,816.652	2,948.341
40	75.401	95.026	120.800	154.762	199.635	259.057	337.882	442.593	767.091	1,342.025	2,360.757	4,163.213	7,343.858

from depreciating the upgraded machine. Outsourcing payroll costs $40,000 annually. Over the next four years, Avroland's cash flows would be as follows under the two possibilities:

Keep Payroll Inside

	Year 0	Year 1	Year 2	Year 3	Year 4	NPV
Cost of upgrade	$65,000					
Labor plus software		$28,000	$28,000	$28,000	$28,000	
Tax savings from depr*		($6,500)	($6,500)	($6,500)	($6,500)	
Total cash outflows	$65,000	$21,500	$21,500	$21,500	$21,500	
Discount rate	1.000	0.962	0.925	0.889	0.855	
Present value at 4%	$65,000	$20,683	$19,888	$19,113	$18,383	$143,067

Outsource Payroll

	Year 0	Year 1	Year 2	Year 3	Year 4	
Annual cost of service		$40,000	$40,000	$40,000	$40,000	
Discount rate	1.000	0.962	0.925	0.889	0.855	
Present value at 4%		$38,480	$37,000	$35,560	$34,200	$145,240

*$\dfrac{\$65{,}000}{4 \text{ years}} \times 40\% \text{ tax rate} = \$6{,}500$

Note that the depreciation of the original system will remain whether the system is upgraded or payroll is outsourced. Therefore, it is not relevant to the decision under consideration.

Since the net present value of the cash outflows is lower by keeping the payroll inside rather than outside the firm, the computer should be upgraded.

NUMERICAL PROBLEMS

NP 13–1: Decision with Discounting Cash Flows (LO 5; NE 3)
A law firm is considering firing one of the junior lawyers. The law firm presently has enough space for more lawyers but feels this junior lawyer is a net loss to the firm. To fire the lawyer, however, the firm would have to pay $100,000 now for severing the employee contract early. The lawyer currently brings in $200,000 per year in revenues with a salary of $80,000. The law firm, however, estimates that indirect costs related to the lawyer are $180,000 per year. The alternative is to wait two more years to fire the lawyer at the end of his contract and not make any severance pay. The discount rate is 10%.

What should the law firm do?

NP 13–2: Annuity (LO 5, 9) (Appendix)
Suppose the opportunity cost of capital is 10% and you have just won a $1 million lottery that entitles you to $100,000 at the end of each of the next 10 years.

a. What is the minimum lump-sum cash payment you would be willing to take now in lieu of the 10-year annuity?
b. What is the minimum lump sum you would be willing to accept at the end of the 10 years in lieu of the annuity?
c. Suppose three years have passed and you have just received the third payment and you have seven left when the lottery promoters approach you with an offer to "settle-up for cash." What is the minimum you would accept at the end of three years?
d. How would your answer to part a change if the first payment came immediately (at $t = 0$) and the remaining payments were at the beginning instead of at the end of each year?

NP 13–3: Retirement Decision and Annuities (LO 5, 9) (Appendix)

Mr. Jones intends to retire in 20 years at the age of 65. As yet he has not provided for retirement income and he wants to set up a periodic savings plan to do this.

If he makes equal annual payments into a savings account that pays 4% interest per year, how large must his payments be in order to assure that he will be able after retirement to draw $30,000 per year from this account until he is 80?

NP 13–4: Future Value of an Annuity (LO 5, 9)

A mother wants to put sufficient money in the bank to cover college expenses for her daughter in 15 years. She estimates that in 15 years $100,000 will be necessary to pay for college. The bank pays 8% compounded annually.

How much does she need to deposit each year to have sufficient money in 15 years?

NP 13–5: Compounding Interest (LO 5, 9)

Your grandfather put $1,000 in the bank for you 48 years ago. The bank paid 6% interest compounded annually during this time period.

How much is your grandfather's deposit worth today?

NP 13–6: Present Value of Interest and Principal (LO 5, 9)

You are thinking about borrowing $100,000 for 10 years at 12%. Annual interest payments are required at the end of each year, and the principal ($100,000) is to be repaid at the end of the 10 years.

What is the present value of the principal payment and what is the present value of the interest payments?

NP 13–7: Net Present Value and Internal Rate of Return (LO 5, 6, 8; NE 4, 6)

A company is considering buying a corporate jet for $5,000,000. The corporate jet will save employee time and eliminate the need to buy plane tickets. These benefits are worth approximately $800,000 per year. The cost of operating the plane is $100,000 per year. The plane will last for 10 years and be sold for $1,000,000 at the end of the 10th year. Assume an interest rate of 10% and no taxes.

a. What is the NPV of this project?
b. What is the internal rate of return of this project if the jet had zero value at the end of the 10th year?
c. Assume that the jet is depreciated $500,000 per year for the 10 years and is sold for $1,000,000 at the end of the 10th year. Also, assume that the tax rate on income is 40%. What is the NPV of the jet?

NP 13–8: Decision to Sell Division (LO 5, 9) (Appendix)

Several years ago your firm paid $25,000,000 for a small, high-technology company that manufactures laser-based tooth cleaning equipment, Clean Tooth. Unfortunately, due to extensive production line and sales resistance problems, the company is considering selling the division as part of a "modernization program." Based on current information, the following are the estimated accounting numbers if the company continues to operate the division:

Estimated sales revenues next 10 years	$500,000/year
Estimated cash expenses next 10 years	$450,000/year
Current offer for the division from another firm	$250,000

Assume:

a. Firm is in the 0% tax bracket (no income taxes).
b. There are no additional expenses associated with the sale.
c. After year 10, the division will have sales (and expenses) of 0.
d. Estimates are completely certain.

Should the firm sell the division for $250,000?

NP 13–9: Present Value of Payments (LO 5, 9) (Appendix)

Farmers in a valley are subject to occasional flooding when heavy rains cause the river to overflow. They have asked the federal government to build a dam upstream to prevent flooding. The construction cost of this project is to be repaid by the farm owners without interest over a period of 30 years. The costs are $300 an acre for a farm of 100 acres, a total of $30,000 to be repaid. No payments at all are to be made for the first five years. Then $1,000 is to be paid at the end of each year for 30 years to pay off the $30,000.

Is the farmer receiving a subsidy? Why? If the interest rate is 10%, what is the approximate present value of the subsidy (if any)? Show all calculations.

NP 13–10: Mortgage Payments and Refinancing (LO 5, 9) (Appendix)

You have just purchased a house and have obtained a 30-year, $200,000 mortgage with an interest rate of 10%.

- **a.** What is your annual mortgage payment, assuming you pay equal amounts each year?
- **b.** Assuming you bought the house on January 1, what is the principal balance after one year? After 10 years?

NP 13–11: Replacing or Modifying Equipment (LO 5, 6, 9) (Appendix)

The PQR Coal Company has several conventional and strip mining operations. Recently, new legislation has made strip mining, which produces coal of high sulfur content, unprofitable so those operations will be discontinued. Unfortunately, PQR purchased $1 million worth of earth-moving equipment for the strip mines two years ago, and this equipment is not particularly well suited to conventional mining.

Mr. Big, the president, suggests that since the equipment can be sold for $500,000 it should be scrapped. In his words, "I learned a long time ago that when you make mistakes, it's best to admit them and take your lumps. By ignoring sunk costs you aren't tempted to throw good money after bad. The original value of the equipment is gone."

A new employee, Mr. Embeay, has suggested that the equipment should be adapted to the conventional operations. He argues, "We are about to spend $800,000 on some new conventional equipment. However, for a smaller expenditure of $250,000 we can adapt the old equipment to perform the same task. Of course, it will cost about $20,000 per year more to operate over the assumed 10-year lives of each alternative. But at an interest rate of 10%, the inclusion of the present value of $20,000 per year for 10 years and the initial $250,000 is still less than $800,000 for new equipment. While it's true that we should ignore sunk costs, at least this way we can cut our losses somewhat."

Who's correct? Why?

NP 13–12: Student Loan Payments and Subsidies (LO 5, 9) (Appendix)

The National Direct Student Loan program (NDSL) allows college students to borrow funds from the federal government. The contract stipulates that the annual percentage rate of interest is 0% until 12 months after the student ceases his/her formal education (defined as at least half-time enrollment), at which time interest is 4% per year. The maximum repayment period is 10 years. For the purposes of the question below, assume that the student borrows $10,000 in the beginning of his/her first year of college and completes his/her education in four years. Loan repayments begin one year after graduation.

- **a.** Assuming that the student elects the maximum payment period, what are the uniform annual loan repayments? (Assume all repayments occur at the end of the year.)
- **b.** If the rate of interest on savings deposits is 6%, what is the minimum amount the student has to have in a bank account one year after graduation to make the loan payment calculated in part a?
- **c.** Are recipients of NDSL receiving a subsidy? If so, what is the present value of the subsidy when the loan is taken out?

NP 13–13: Value of a Home with an Assumable Mortgage (LO 5, 9) (Appendix)
A home identical to yours in your neighborhood sold last week for $150,000. Your home has a $120,000 assumable, 8% mortgage (compounded annually) with 30 years remaining. An assumable mortgage is one that the new buyer can assume at the old terms and continue to make payments at the original interest rate. The house that recently sold did not have an assumable mortgage; that is, the buyers had to finance the house at the current market rate of interest which is 15%.

What price should you ask for your home?

NP 13–14: Mortgage Department Decisions (LO 5, 9) (Appendix)
Suppose you are the manager of a mortgage department at a savings bank. Under the state usury law, the maximum interest rate allowed for mortgages is 10% compounded annually.

a. If you granted a $50,000 mortgage at the maximum rate for 30 years, what would be the equal annual payments?
b. If the bank's cost of capital is 12%, how much money does the bank lose by issuing the mortgage described in (a)?
c. The usury law does not prohibit banks from charging "points." One point means that the borrower pays 1% of the $50,000 loan back to the lending institution at the inception of the loan. That is, if one point is charged, the repayments are computed as in part a above, but the borrower receives only $49,500. How many points must the bank charge to earn 12% on the 10% loan?

NP 13–15: Decision to Make or Buy Electricity (LO 5, 9) (Appendix)
A firm that purchases electric power from the local utility is considering the alternative of generating its own electricity. The current cost of obtaining the firm's electricity from its local utility firm is $42,000 per year. The cost of a steam generator (installed) is $140,000 and the annual maintenance and fuel expenses are estimated at $22,000 per year. The generator is expected to last for 10 years, at which time it will be worthless. The cost of capital is 10% and the firm pays no taxes.

a. Should the firm install the electric generator? Why or why not?
b. The engineers have calculated that with an additional investment of $40,000, the excess steam from the generator can also be used to heat the firm's buildings. The current cost of heating the buildings with purchased steam is $21,000 per year. If the generator is to be used for heat as well as electricity, additional fuel and maintenance costs of $10,000 per year will be incurred. Should the firm invest in the generator and the heating system? Show all calculations.

NP 13–16: Internal Rate of Return (LO 5, 8; NE 4, 6)
Jasper, Inc., is considering two mutually exclusive investments (A and B). Alternative A has a current outlay of $300,000 and returns $360,000 next year. Alternative B has a current outlay of $165,000 and returns $200,000 next year.

a. Calculate the internal rate of return for each alternative.
b. Which alternative should Jasper take if the required rate of return for those projects in the capital market is 15%?
c. Why are the projects ranked differently in terms of internal rate of return and net present value?

NP 13–17: Decision to Sell or Keep an Asset (LO 5, 9) (Appendix)
Ab Landlord owns a dilapidated 30-year-old apartment building in Los Angeles. The net cash flow from renting the apartments last year was $200,000. He expects those net cash flows from renting the apartments to continue for the remaining useful life of the apartment building, which is 10 years. In 10 years the value of the property is expected to be $100,000. A developer wants to buy the apartment building from Landlord, demolish it, and construct luxury condominiums. He offers Landlord $1,500,000 for the apartments. Landlord's opportunity cost of capital is 16%. Assume there are no taxes.

Evaluate the developer's offer and make a recommendation to Ab.

NP 13–18: Decision to Replace a Machine (LO 5, 6, 9) (Appendix)   The Baltic Company is considering the purchase of a new machine tool to replace an older one. The machine being used for the operation has a tax book value of $80,000 with an annual depreciation expense of $8,000. The older machine tool is in good working order and will last, physically, for at least an additional 10 years. It can be sold today for $40,000 but will have no value if kept for another 10 years. The proposed new machine will perform the operation so much more efficiently that Baltic Company engineers estimate that labor, material, and other direct costs of the operation will be reduced $60,000 a year if it is installed. The proposed machine costs $240,000 delivered and installed, and its economic life is estimated to be 10 years with zero salvage value. The company expects to earn 14% on its investment after taxes (14% is the firm's cost of capital). The tax rate is 40%, and the firm uses straight-line depreciation.

Should Baltic buy the new machine?

NP 13–19: Investment in Pollution Control Devices (LO 5, 6, 9) (Appendix)   Overland Steel operates a coal burning steel mill in New York State. Changes in the state's air quality control laws will result in this mill incurring a $1,000 per day fine, which is paid at the end of the year, if it continues to operate. The mill currently operates every day of the year.

The mill was built 20 years ago at a cost of $15 million and has a remaining undepreciated book value of $3 million. The expected remaining useful life of the mill is 30 years.

The firm can sell the mill to a developer who wants to build a shopping center on the site. The buyer would pay $1 million for the site if the company demolishes and prepares the site for the developer. Demolition and site preparation costs are estimated at $650,000.

Alternatively the firm could install pollution control devices and other modernization devices at an initial outlay of $2.75 million. These improvements do not extend the useful life or salvage value of the plant, but they do reduce net operating costs by $25,000 per year in addition to eliminating the $1,000 per day fine. Currently, the net cash flows of sales less the cost of operating the plant are $450,000 per year before any fines.

Assume:

a. The opportunity cost of capital is 14%
b. There are no taxes.
c. The annual cash flow estimates given above are constant over the next 30 years.
d. At the end of the 30 years, the mill has an estimated salvage value of $2 million whether or not the pollution equipment is installed.

Evaluate the various courses of action available to management and make a recommendation as to which one is preferable. Support your conclusions with neatly labeled calculations where possible.

NP 13–20: Depreciation and Taxes (LO 5, 6; NE 5)   The Scottie Corporation has been offered a contract to produce 100 castings a year for five years at a price of $200 per casting. Producing the castings will require an investment in the plant of $35,000 and operating costs of $50 per casting produced. For tax purposes, depreciation will be on a straight-line basis over five years with a full year's depreciation being taken in both the beginning and ending years. The tax rate is 40% and the opportunity cost of capital is 10%.

Should Scottie accept the contract?

NP 13–21: Decision to Replace a Machine (LO 5, 6; NE 4, 5)   A punch press currently in use has a book value of $1,800 and is in need of design modification totaling $16,200, which would be recorded as a fixed asset and depreciated over its life. The press can be sold for $2,600 now, but it could be used for three more years if the necessary modifications are made, at the end of which time it would have no salvage value.

A new punch press can be purchased at an invoice price of $26,900 to replace the present equipment. Freight-in will amount to $800, and installation will cost $500. These expenses will be depreciated, along with the invoice price, over the life of the machine. Because of the nature of the product manufactured, the new machine also will have an expected life of three years and will have no salvage value at the end of that time.

Using the old machine, the operating profits before taxes and depreciation (revenues less costs) are $10,000 the first year and $8,000 in each of the next two years. Using the new machine, the operating profits before taxes and depreciation (revenues less costs) are $18,000 in the first year and $14,000 in each of the next two years.

Corporate income taxes are 40%, which is the same tax rate applicable to gains or losses on sales of equipment. Both the present and proposed equipment would be depreciated on a straight-line basis over three years. The opportunity cost of capital is 10%.

Should the company modify the old machine or purchase the new one?

NP 13–22: Capital Budgeting Decision (LO 5, 9) (Appendix)

The city of Toledo has received a proposal to build a new multipurpose outdoor sports stadium. The expected life of the stadium is 20 years and will be financed by a 20-year bond paying 8% interest annually. The stadium's primary tenant will be the city's Triple A baseball team, the Red Hots. The plan's backers anticipate that the site will also be used for rock concerts and college and high school sports. The city does not pay any taxes. The city's cost of capital is 8%. The costs and estimated revenues are presented below.

Cash Outflows:
Construction Costs	$12,000,000
General maintenance (including labor)	$250,000 per year

Cash Inflows:
Red Hots minimum lease payments	$650,000 per year
Concerts	$600,000 per year
College & high school sports	$ 50,000 per year

a. Should the city build the stadium? (Assume payments are made at the end of the year.)
b. The Red Hots have threatened to move out of Toledo if they do not get a new stadium. The city comptroller estimates that the move will cost the city $350,000 per year for 10 years in lost taxes, parking fees, and other fees. Should the city build the stadium now? State your reasoning.

NP 13–23: Payback Period (LO 3; NE 1)

The Kline Corporation is evaluating two investment projects: a tennis club and a squash club. The tennis club would require $10,000,000 to build. The management projects annual cash inflows from the tennis club to be $2,000,000. The squash club would be smaller and require $2,000,000 to build. The management projects annual cash inflows from the squash club to be $500,000.

a. What is the payback period for each of the investments?
b. Based on the payback period, which investment should be chosen?
c. What are the problems with making the investment decision based on the payback period?

NP 13–24: Accounting Rate of Return (ROI) (LO 4; NE 2)

The Kline Corporation in NP 13–23 is thinking about investing in either a tennis club or a squash club. The tennis club would cost $10,000,000 and generate annual cash flows of $2,000,000 per year. The initial cost of the tennis club would be depreciated over 10 years using straight-line depreciation. The squash club would cost $2,000,000 and generate annual cash flows of $500,000 per year. The initial cost of the squash club would be depreciated over 20 years using straight-line depreciation. Depreciation is the only adjustment to cash flow for the calculation of income for both investments. Each investment would have zero salvage value after being fully depreciated.

a. What is the ROI of each investment during the first year using beginning of the year investment as the denominator?
b. What is the multiyear ROI for each investment?
c. What are the problems with using ROI to evaluate investments?

NP 13–25: Adjusting Cash Flows for Accounts Receivable and Inventory (LO 7)   The Hammer Company is considering opening a new car dealership. The business would be completely funded by borrowing. At the end of the first two years, the new car dealership is expected to have account receivable balances of $50,000 and $75,000 and inventory balances of $300,000 and $400,000. Income for the first two years is expected to be $200,000 and $500,000.

How would the income numbers be adjusted for the accounts receivable and inventory balances if converting income into cash flows?

Discussion Problems

DP 13–1: Capital Budgeting and Opportunity Costs (LO 6)   Geico is considering expanding an existing plant on a piece of land it already owns. The land was purchased 15 years ago for $325,000 and its current market appraisal is $820,000. A capital budgeting analysis shows that the plant expansion has a net present value of $130,000. The expansion will cost $1.73 million and the discounted cash inflows are $1.86 million. The expansion cost of $1.73 million does not include any provision for the cost of the land. The manager preparing the analysis argues that the historical cost of the land is a sunk cost, and because the firm intends to keep the land whether or not the expansion project is accepted, the current appraisal value is irrelevant.

Should the land be included in the analysis? If so, how?

DP 13–2: Decision to Drop a Product (LO 6)   Declining Market, Inc., is considering the problem of when to stop production of a particular product in their product line. Sales of the product in question have been declining and all estimates are that it will continue to decline. Capital equipment used to manufacture the product is specialized, but can be readily sold as used equipment.

What is wrong, if anything, with a decision rule for this case which says:

> "Keep producing the product as long as its contribution to net earnings is positive."
> [Contribution to net earnings, where t is the tax rate, is $(1 - t)$ (sales − variable cost − depreciation on equipment used to manufacture product).]

DP 13–3: Postaudit of a Capital Budgeting Decision (LO 1)   The Sharp Razor Company invested in the production of a new type of razor blade three years ago. The production has been implemented and sales of the new razor blade have been going on for two years. The president of the company has asked the controller to perform a postaudit on the investment in the new type of razor blade. A postaudit is an examination of an investment after it has been made. The controller is complaining that the president just wants her to work overtime and there is no reason for this postaudit. She points out that the investment has already been made and is now a sunk cost.

How can a postaudit of a capital budgeting decision help an organization?

DP 13–4: Identifying the Opportunity Cost of Capital (LO 2)   Don Phelps recently started a dry-cleaning business. He would like to expand the business and have a coin-operated laundry also. The expansion of the building and the washing and drying machines will cost $100,000. The bank will lend the business $100,000 at 12% interest rate. Don could get a 10% interest rate loan if he uses his personal house as collateral. The lower interest rate reflects the increased security of the loan to the bank because the bank could take Don's home if he doesn't pay back the loan. Don currently can put money in the bank and receive 6% interest.

Provide arguments for using 12%, 10%, and 6% as the opportunity cost of capital for evaluating the investment.

DP 13–5: Payback Period and Risk (LO 3, 7)

The controller and the president are arguing about how to adjust for risk when evaluating investments. The president thinks the best way to evaluate risk is to measure the payback period of an investment. The shorter the payback period, the less the risk. The controller believes that the net present value should still be used to evaluate investments. To adjust for risk, the discount rate is simply increased.

Provide arguments for and against each of these alternative methods.

DP 13–6: Financing Charges and Net Present Value (LO 6)

The president of the company is not convinced that the interest expense should be excluded from the calculation of the net present value. He points out that, "Interest is a cash flow. You are supposed to discount cash flows. We borrowed money to completely finance this project. Why not discount interest expenditures?" The president is so convinced that he asks you, the controller, to calculate the net present value including the interest expense.

How can you adjust the net present value analysis to compensate for the inclusion of the interest expense?

CASE

C 13–1: Davenport Farms

Davenport Farms is a family-owned, fruit-growing operation. The farm currently includes 300 acres of orchards of apples, pears, and cherries and a warehouse for packing and storing fruit. Tom Davenport is the manager and owner of the farm, which has been in the family for several generations.

The operation of the farm requires a variety of heavy machinery including 10 tractors, 8 trucks of varying sizes, a sprayer for insecticides, and a bulldozer for removing tree stumps. The warehouse also has considerable equipment for grading, sorting, and packing the fruit. Part of the warehouse is dedicated to storage and is refrigerated in an atmosphere with low oxygen content to reduce spoilage.

Davenport Farms has 20 permanent employees to maintain the equipment, prune trees, apply insecticides, and irrigate the trees. During picking seasons, however, large numbers of migrant workers are hired for picking and working in the warehouse.

Davenport Farms has had several successful years and Tom is considering an expansion of the farm. Recently a 20-acre parcel adjacent to Davenport Farms has become available for sale for $100,000. The land is currently bare and would have to be developed for irrigation and planted with apple trees. Development of the land for irrigation would take several months and cost $20,000 in materials. Apple trees can be planted immediately after the land is developed. Tom assumes that his existing labor force can provide the labor for developing and planting the trees.

Tom has not decided whether he would plant dwarf apple trees or full-size apple trees. Dwarf apple trees produce fruit earlier (in the sixth year after planting) and require less space (100 per acre). The disadvantage is that dwarf apple trees do not last as long and will have to be replaced after 20 years. Full-size apple trees begin producing in the eleventh year after planting and are replaced after 40 years, but only 50 trees can be planted per acre. Annual cash expenses per acre are the same for each type of tree and each type of tree generates the same quantity of apples when producing. The cost of both types of seedling apple trees is $5 per tree. Tom plans to hold the land for 40 years and sell the land at the end of 40 years for $200,000. Tom has made the following estimates of costs and benefits of buying the land and planting either dwarf or full-size trees for the next 40 years:

	Planting Dwarf Trees	Planting Full-Size Trees
Land costs (now)	($100,000)	($100,000)
Development costs (now)	(20,000)	(20,000)
Planting costs:		
Dwarf: ($5/tree)(100/acre)		
(20 acres) = $10,000 now	(10,000)	
In 20 years	(10,000)	
Full size: ($5/tree)(50/acre)		
(20 acres) = $5,000 now		($5,000)
Stump removal and disposal:		
(in 20 years)	($100,000)	
Other cash expenses: ($20,000/year)		
(40 years) = $800,000	($800,000)	($800,000)
Cash revenues:		
Dwarf: ($70,000/year)		
(Years 6–20 and 26–40)	2,100,000	
Full size: ($70,000/year)		
(Years 11–40)		2,100,000
Sale of land	200,000	200,000
Total	$1,260,000	$1,375,000

Based on these estimates, the initial cash requirements to purchase and develop the land and plant dwarf trees is $130,000. If full-size trees are planted instead, the initial cost is $125,000. Tom has $40,000 of cash available to make this investment. The rest of the costs can be covered by a mortgage from the local bank. The local bank charges 10% interest for mortgages of this type. Tom will need to borrow $90,000 if he plants dwarf trees and $85,000 if he plants full-size trees. Tom figures his cost of capital is the interest rate that the bank charges.

Case Questions

a. Using net present value analysis, should Tom buy the land and, if so, which type of trees should he plant?
b. What other factors should be considered in making this land acquisition that are not captured in the present value analysis?

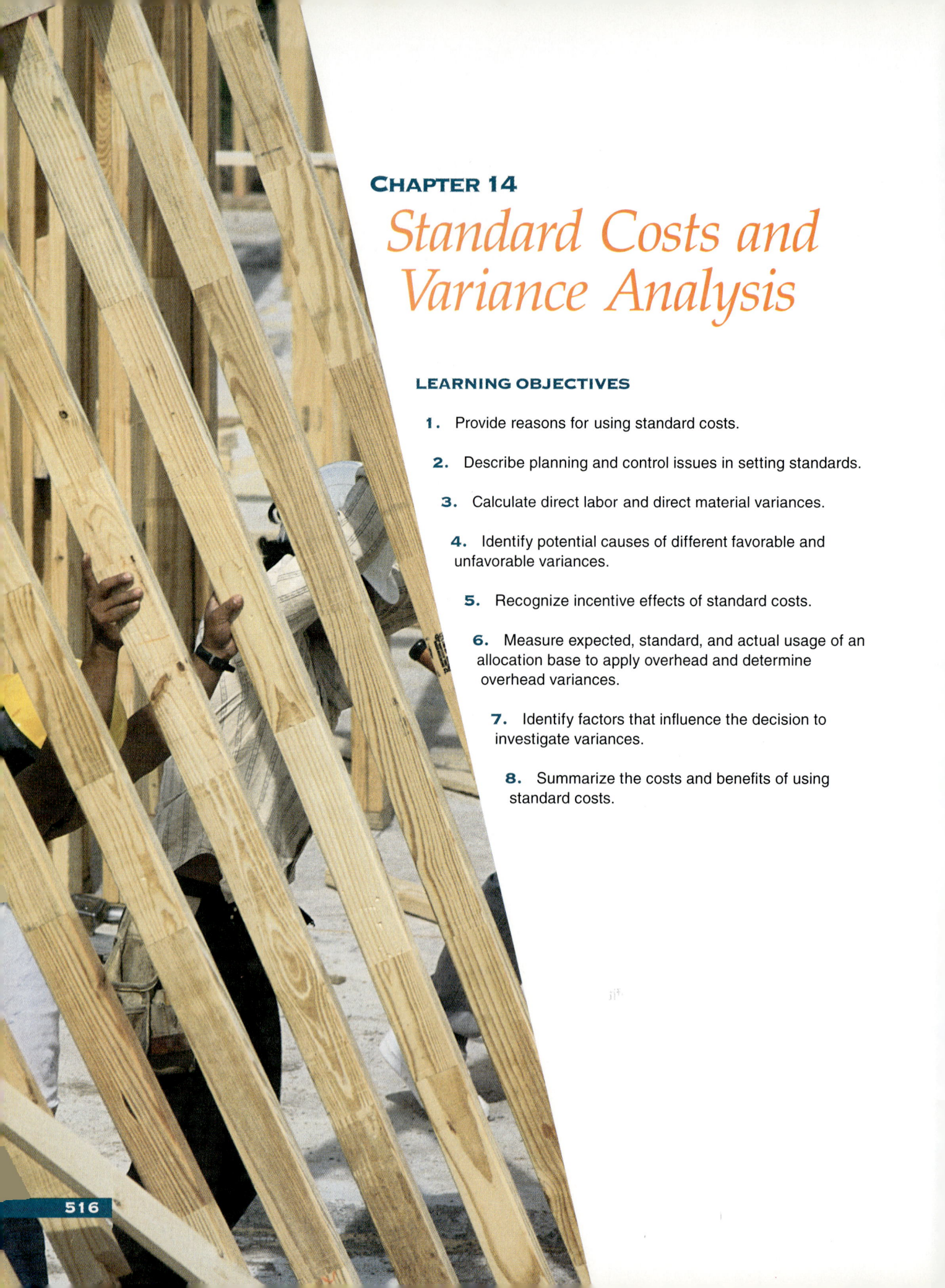

CHAPTER 14
Standard Costs and Variance Analysis

LEARNING OBJECTIVES

1. Provide reasons for using standard costs.

2. Describe planning and control issues in setting standards.

3. Calculate direct labor and direct material variances.

4. Identify potential causes of different favorable and unfavorable variances.

5. Recognize incentive effects of standard costs.

6. Measure expected, standard, and actual usage of an allocation base to apply overhead and determine overhead variances.

7. Identify factors that influence the decision to investigate variances.

8. Summarize the costs and benefits of using standard costs.

EDWARD ODELL, CONTRACTOR

Edward Odell started as a carpenter working on new homes. He soon tired of broken thumbnails and chilled bones and decided to become a contractor. He subcontracted with others to do most of the work on the new houses but maintained a crew to do the wood framing of the houses. Edward was successful while the local economy was doing well, but new housing starts are very sensitive to interest rates and the economy. There were times when he had to lay off his crew. Edward felt there must be something to do with the crew during downtime in the local economy, so he approached a Japanese company to export wall sections to Japan.

Traditional home construction in Japan had always conserved wood, which is a relatively scarce resource in Japan. But recently there has been increased demand for more substantial houses with walls built using 2' x 4's (1½ inches x 3½ inches) instead of smaller boards. Edward felt that he could successfully make and ship wall sections using 2' x 4's to Japan.

He received an initial order for 1,000 wall sections. The wall sections were 8 feet by 12 feet with sheetrock (dry wall) on one side. Edward bought some warehouse space and began construction. The first order was a real learning experience for Edward. The wall sections were relatively easy to make, but moving and shipping them led to many problems given their size and weight. Also, the Japanese company would only accept wall sections made of clear fir (no knots) even though the 2' x 4's would eventually be hidden behind the sheetrock and the exterior covering. Edward lost money on this first order, but the Japanese company was interested in more and larger orders. These orders were for a variety of different sizes of wall sections.

Edward felt he could do better the next time with a little more control of the manufacturing system. In particular, Edward felt he could save costs by reducing excess scrap and slack time for his workers. He had heard that standard costing systems might help him achieve those goals and make the new orders more profitable.

Edward reorganized his business by putting Jeff Pringle in charge of buying lumber, sheetrock, and other supplies. Barbara Kaplan was put in charge of the framing and Chet Slocum was assigned to manage the sheetrocking. Edward remained in charge of administration and marketing.

14.1 Standard Costs

Historical costs are useful for satisfying financial reporting: deriving unit product costs for valuing inventories (balance sheet) and cost of goods sold (income statement). Historical costs can also be a useful starting point for estimating opportunity costs. But historical costs do not provide any built-in controls or benchmarks as to what costs should be; they only state what the costs actually were. An over- or underabsorbed overhead number conveys some information about whether or not the plant has met expectations with respect to overhead. But there are no benchmarks as to whether direct labor or direct materials are too high or too low, except by comparing the actual numbers to the same numbers from prior periods.

Standard costs provide those benchmarks. They represent the expected future cost of a product, service, process, or subcomponent. Once standards are set, managers can gauge performance by comparing actual operating results against the standards. The difference between an actual and standard cost is called a **variance.** Variances provide useful information for senior management in determining whether the production system is operating efficiently. Variances are an important part of the control process. Variances are attention-getters. They alert senior managers that something is not going according to plan. Variances also provide information for performance evaluation. In addition to their role in control, standard costs are useful in making planning decisions such as product pricing decisions, make versus buy decisions, and plant resource allocation decisions.

This chapter describes the use of standard costs for planning and control. As seen in previous chapters, the conflict between planning and control also exists in standard cost systems. The focus of this chapter is on the costs and benefits of standard cost systems.

Reasons for Standard Costing

Historical costs can often prove misleading for planning purposes. They can be out of date if operating conditions, material prices, or wages have changed or are expected to change. Operating conditions in the past might not provide a valid basis for forecasting the future because new products are introduced or a new manufacturing process is implemented.

Standard costs are often used instead of historical costs in a wide variety of planning decision contexts: product pricing, contract bidding, outsourcing decisions, and assessing alternative production technologies. Standard costs are part of the budgeting system, which organizations use to coordinate their operating plans for the coming year. The estimated product cost at the beginning of the year is a standard cost. Standard costs convey information about product costs to the different parts of the organization. For example, marketing managers usually use standard costs for making selling decisions.

Standard costs also provide information for control. As part of the budgeting process, standard costs may be used as a form of contract among the managers of the organization. Manufacturing managers agree to supply a certain number of units of the product at a standard cost. Service department managers agree to supply their services at a standard cost. Managerial performance is evaluated based on the success of managers achieving these standard costs. Achieving standard costs can lead to bonuses and rewards.

Large variances between actual and standard costs indicate that a particular process differs significantly from what was expected when the standard was set. Variances are treated as signals indicating that processes may be out of control and corrective action is necessary. Not all variances necessarily indicate a problem. Variances may also indicate that the environment has changed and the standards are no longer appropriate. The variance itself will not tell the manager exactly what is wrong. Further investigation is usually necessary to determine the cause of the variance. **Management by exception** is a management strategy that focuses management effort on significant variances. When actual costs are close to the standard costs, managers assume that the process is operating as planned and no further investigation is necessary.

A survey in 1985 indicates that 85% of large publicly traded organizations use standard costs.[1] While standard cost systems are common in large organizations, some managers question the costs and benefits of these systems. Some firms are scaling back on their reliance on standard costs, changing how they estimate standard costs, or even abandoning their standard cost systems. The problems generally reflect the trade-off between using standard costs for planning decisions and control described in the next section.

Setting and Revising Standards

There is no commonly accepted method for deriving standard costs. Some experts argue that standard costs should be attainable, meaning the cost that is achievable if normal effort and environmental effects prevail. Others argue that standards should be those that will occur with extra effort. How difficult the standards should be to attain and how much weight to place on achieving the standards in performance evaluation are important issues in designing the firm's organizational structure. These issues involve trading off the costs and benefits of tight versus loose standards. In the aforementioned survey, 50% of the firms say they set standards to be the expected actual costs, yet difficult to attain; 42% say they set the standard based on average past performance; and 8% say they set the standard as the maximum theoretical efficiency level.[2]

If the standard cost is to reflect the opportunity cost of using a resource, setting and revising the standards requires communication with individuals with specific knowledge. The standard cost should contain all the specific knowledge pertaining to the resource. Standards that are the most accurate estimates of opportunity costs are the most useful in conveying information within the firm about alternative resource utilization.

But the accuracy of the standard as a measure of opportunity cost is often compromised for control reasons. Usually managers with the specific knowledge for updating the standard will be evaluated, at least in part, based on the difference between their actual performance and the standard. Managers are reluctant to reveal information that may later be used to penalize them.

Planning decisions require assembling the specialized knowledge that often only resides with the person or unit of the firm that later will be judged by the standard. For example, the purchasing department has the specialized knowledge to set the purchase price standard. But if the purchasing department also has the decision rights to set the purchase price standard, then the standard becomes less useful to evaluate the performance of the purchasing department manager. One solution is to separate the setting of the standard from ratifying and monitoring the standard.

Usually, the accounting or industrial engineering departments have the decision rights for setting or changing the standards. Individuals responsible for the standard cost variance have some ratification rights over the standards. Standards are then reviewed and revised each year as part of the annual budgeting cycle. In the study referred to above, 79% of the respondents said that three or more of the following groups participated in setting the standards: industrial engineering, purchasing, personnel, accounting, top management, and line managers with specific cost responsibility. Standard costs are reviewed for possible revision annually by 62% of the firms and quarterly by 15% of the respondents.[3]

A common approach for deriving standard costs is a bottom-up technique. Usually, the manager who will be held responsible for meeting the standard submits an initial estimate of the standard. These estimates are reviewed by industrial engineers, controllers, and higher level managers who ratify the standard. Sometimes industrial engineers submit the initial estimate of the standard. In all cases, setting and revising standards involve assembling specific knowledge from various individuals in the firm. The standard cost of each type of labor, material, and overhead is estimated, and the standard cost of the complete product is built up from the sum of these individual costs.

Target costing is a top-down approach. It starts with the long-run price, estimated by marketing, required to achieve a desired market share. From this price is subtracted the required return on investment (profits) to derive a total target product cost. This total target cost is then divided into subcomponent costs, including selling and distribution costs. These subcomponent costs become the targets or standards to be achieved if the firm is to meet its goals for market penetration, cost reduction, and return on capital. Target costs then become part of the performance evaluation system.[4]

Nissan first determines the target price to attract potential buyers to the new car model being designed. After deducting the desired profit margin from this target price, a target cost is derived. This total target cost is divided between design and engineering, manufacturing, sales and marketing. Within the manufacturing target cost, each part of the car such as the windshield and the engine block is assigned a target cost. "'This is where the battle begins.' The battle is an intense negotiating process between the company and its outside suppliers, and among departments that are responsible for different aspects of the product. The sum of the initial estimates may exceed the overall target cost by 20% or more. By the time the battle is over, compromises and tradeoffs by product designers, process engineers, and marketing specialists generally produce a projected cost that is within close range of the original target."[5]

This General Electric engineer is designing jet engines. GE uses target costing to drive costs down. GE decides what its customers like United Airlines will pay and then targets a lower cost to maintain its profits. By working with its suppliers and by eliminating unnecessary features, GE can lower its costs while preserving quality.

Once standards are set, they are used to judge performance by calculating the variance between the actual cost and the standard cost. In general, there are three sets of standard cost variances produced by most firms: direct labor variances, direct materials variances, and overhead variances. Because direct labor and materials are quite similar, their calculations and incentive effects are discussed together in the next two sections. Overhead variances are more complicated and are described generally in section 14.4. Specific overhead variance calculations are described in the appendix.

The variances described in this chapter are generic to a wide cross-section of applications. Each department, plant, and company will not use all the variances in this chapter. Some organizations will invent other variances. For example, sales variances may also be calculated. The variances used will be tailored to the organization's specific requirements. The purpose of the following discussion is to illustrate the types of variances possible and their advantages and disadvantages.

> **WHAT'S HAPPENING**
>
> Suppose Nissan plans to introduce a 2-passenger convertible with a target price to dealers of $22,000. Each car has a required profit of $1,500 and expected selling costs of $1,100. Calculate the target manufacturing cost.

CONCEPT REVIEW

1. Why do organizations use standard costing?
2. How are standards set?

EDWARD ODELL, CONTRACTOR (CONTINUED)

Edward Odell thinks that standard costing fits his business quite well. The business of making wall sections requires a series of repetitive actions by workers and the material requirements are fairly easy to measure. He hopes the standard costs will do two things for him: (1) determine product costs for the different sizes of wall sections so he can do a better job of pricing and (2) encourage managers and workers to use the materials and their time more efficiently.

To implement the standard costing system, Edward called in his managers and explained the problems. To encourage his managers to pay attention to the standards, he told them that he would give them bonuses if their departments did better than the standards. Jeff Pringle would be responsible for the material price variances and Barbara and Chet would be responsible for the direct labor variances and the material quantity variances. Then he asked them for input on establishing the standards. Jeff thought that lumber prices were going up in the future, so the standard price of the lumber should be higher than today's price. Barbara and Chet thought the standards should recognize some scrap and slack labor time.

Edward realized that his managers were not going to be completely forthcoming in establishing standards. Therefore, he decided to set the standards based on his knowledge of prices and the process of making wall sections. The following standards for direct labor and direct materials are used for making the 8 feet by 12 feet wall section:

Direct labor cost	$8/hour
Direct labor time per unit	3 hours
Material costs	
Lumber	$0.10/board foot
Sheetrock	$2/sheet
Material/unit	
Lumber	72 board feet
Sheetrock	3 sheets

The estimated direct cost per unit are:

Direct labor ($8/hour)(3 hours)	$24.00
Direct materials	
Lumber ($0.10/board foot)(72 board feet)	7.20
Sheetrock ($2/sheet)(3 sheets)	6.00
Total direct costs per unit	$37.20

14.2 Direct Labor and Direct Materials Variances

Variances are primarily used to identify problems within an organization in following a prescribed plan. Variances are calculated to help managers determine the cause and responsibility for the problem. By dividing variances into component variances, cause and responsibility become easier to identify. This section describes how standard cost variances for direct labor and materials are decomposed and calculated.

Direct labor and materials costs are composed of a price per unit and a quantity. In other words, the cost of direct labor is the wage rate per hour (price per unit) times the number of hours worked (quantity). The cost of direct materials used is the purchase price per unit of the materials times the quantity of units used. Any variance between the actual and standard costs is due to the actual price per unit and/or actual quantity used being different from the standard price or quantity. Recognizing the dual effect of price and quantity on costs allows the direct labor and materials variances to be decomposed into two parts: (1) variance due to the actual price per unit being different from the standard price per unit and (2) variance due to the actual quantity used being different from the standard quantity.

Direct Labor Variances

The **direct labor variance** is the difference between the actual direct labor costs and the standard direct labor costs for a period of time. The direct labor variance can be decomposed into a **wage rate variance** and a **labor efficiency variance.** The following equations define the wage rate and labor efficiency variances such that the sum of the two variances is equal to the direct labor variance.

Direct labor variance = Actual cost of labor − Standard cost of labor

$$= \left(\text{Actual wage rate} \times \text{Actual hours} \right) - \left(\text{Standard wage rate} \times \text{Standard hours} \right)$$

Wage rate variance = (Actual wage rate − Standard wage rate) × Actual hours

Labor efficiency variance = (Actual hours − Standard hours) × Standard wage rate

Direct labor variance = Wage rate variance + Labor efficiency variance

The wage rate variance focuses on the difference between the actual wage rate and the standard wage rate. The labor efficiency variance highlights the difference between the actual direct labor hours and the standard direct labor hours.

To demonstrate the calculation of direct variances, an example of the printing costs of the Smith Art Book is used. The standard costs to make a batch of 1,000 books are reported in Table 14.1.

The standard costs to make the 1,000 copies of the Smith Art Book are used as benchmarks for comparison with actual costs. Table 14.2 describes the actual costs.

The actual costs are $19,774, which is $126 less than the standard cost of $19,900. The $126 is called a **favorable variance.** A favorable variance occurs when the actual costs are less than the standard costs. An **unfavorable variance** occurs if actual costs are greater than standard costs.

The existence of a $126 favorable variance for the printing of the 1,000 copies of the Smith Art Book does not tell the manager much about the cause of the variance. To understand the total cost variance better, the cost variance can be broken into parts representing the prices and quantities of each of the inputs of

TABLE 14.1 Standard Cost Sheet

Smith Art Book: 1,000 copies

Direct Materials				Direct Labor			
Type	Qty.	Price	Amt.	Type	Hrs.	Wage	Amt.
Paper	800 lb.	$2	$1,600	Typesetters	80	$15	$1,200
Covers	1,000	$6	6,000	Printers	55	$40	2,200
Binding	500 lb.	$4	2,000	Binders	70	$20	1,400
Totals			$9,600				$4,800

Total direct materials	$ 9,600
Total direct labor	4,800
Total overhead ($100/printer hour)	5,500
Total cost	$19,900
Number of copies	÷1,000
Cost per book	$ 19.90

TABLE 14.2 Actual Cost Sheet

Smith Art Book: 1,000 copies

Direct Materials				Direct Labor			
Type	Qty.	Price	Amt.	Type	Hrs.	Wage	Amt.
Paper	810 lb.	$2.10	$1,701	Typesetters	85	$15.40	$1,309
Covers	1,005	$5.80	5,829	Printers	53	41.00	2,173
Binding	490 lb.	$4.20	2,058	Binders	72	$19.50	1,404
Totals			$9,588				$4,886

Total direct materials	$ 9,588
Total direct labor	4,886
Total overhead ($100/printer hour)	5,300
Total cost	$19,774
Number of copies	÷1,000
Cost per book	$ 19.77

TABLE 14.3

Relations among Direct Labor Variances

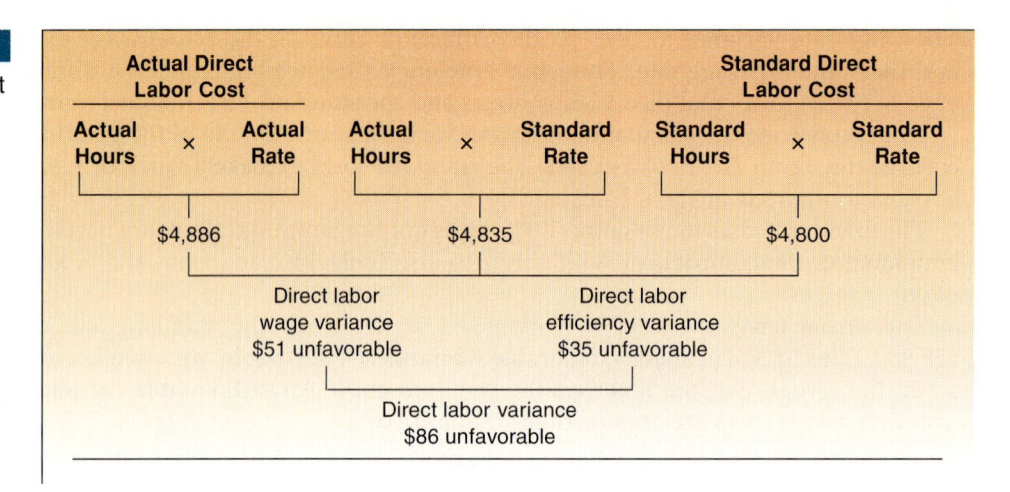

	Actual Direct Labor Cost				Standard Direct Labor Cost	
Actual Hours × Actual Rate		Actual Hours × Standard Rate		Standard Hours × Standard Rate		
$4,886		$4,835		$4,800		

Direct labor wage variance $51 unfavorable

Direct labor efficiency variance $35 unfavorable

Direct labor variance $86 unfavorable

---

the manufacturing process. For example, the direct labor variance for typesetters can be decomposed into a wage rate variance and a labor efficiency variance:

Wage rate variance = (Actual wage rate − Standard wage rate) × Actual hours

Typesetters	($15.40 − $15.00) × 85 =	$34 (unfavorable)
Printers	($41.00 − $40.00) × 53 =	53 (unfavorable)
Binders	($19.50 − $20.00) × 72 =	36 (favorable)
Total		$51 (unfavorable)

Labor efficiency variance = (Actual hours − Standard hours) × Standard wage rate

Typesetters	(85 − 80) × $15.00 =	$75 (unfavorable)
Printers	(53 − 55) × $40.00 =	80 (favorable)
Binders	(72 − 70) × $20.00 =	40 (unfavorable)
Total		$35 (unfavorable)

Notice that the sum of the wage variance and the efficiency variance ($51 + $35 = $86) is the difference between the total standard labor costs ($4,800) and the actual labor costs ($4,886). The relation among the direct labor variances is described in Table 14.3.

The variance analysis indicates that the unfavorable labor variances are primarily due to typesetter labor costs. The sum of the wage rate variance and the labor efficiency variance for printers is favorable and for binders only slightly unfavorable. The typesetter labor costs exceeded standard because (a) $0.40 more per hour was paid than expected and (b) 5 hours more typesetter hours were used than expected. If management believes that the standards are correct, then the typesetter labor variances indicate that the person responsible for assigning typesetters to the Smith Art Book assigned typesetters with a higher actual wage rate per hour than expected and that the person responsible for supervising the typesetters allowed more typesetting hours then expected. The costs of these two "errors" are $34 for paying too much per hour and $75 for using too many hours. Clearly, one's ability to draw these inferences depends on one's belief that the standards are indeed unbiased forecasts of what the typesetting wage rates should have been and how many hours of typesetting should have been used.

The foregoing analysis is illustrated graphically in Figure 14.1 In Figure 14.1, the rectangle $W_s \times H_s$ represents what the labor should have cost and the rectangle $W_a \times H_a$ represents what the labor actually cost. The total typesetting labor variance is the difference between what the typesetting actually cost and what it should have cost, $W_a H_a - W_s H_s$. This difference is the purple and orange shaded

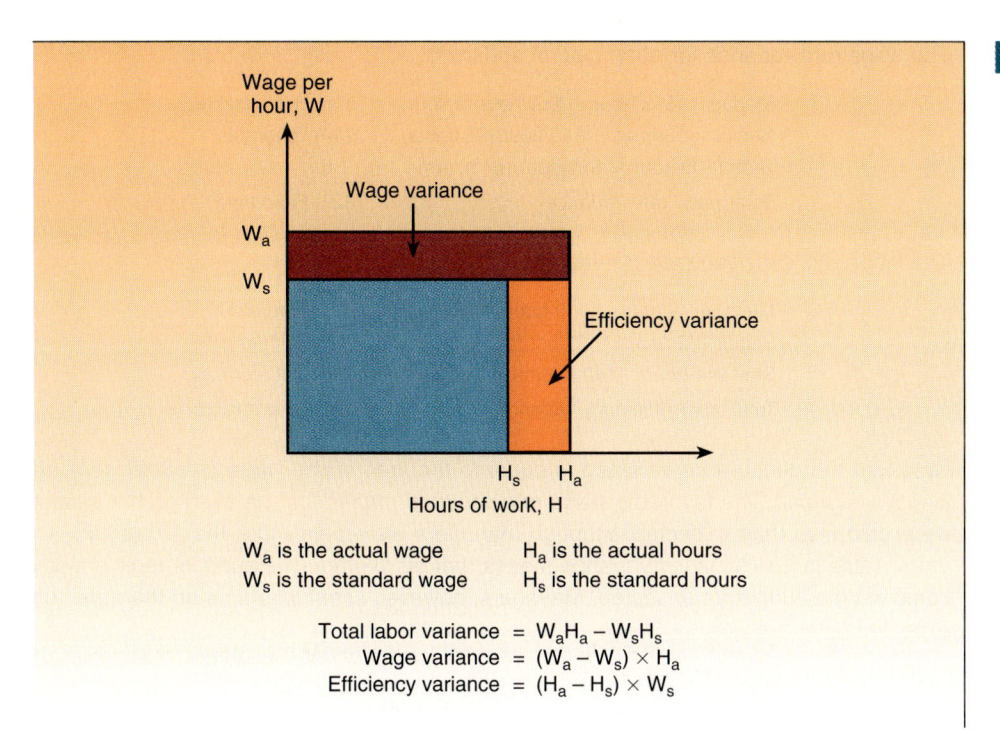

FIGURE 14.1
Direct Labor Variances

W_a is the actual wage
W_s is the standard wage
H_a is the actual hours
H_s is the standard hours

Total labor variance = $W_a H_a - W_s H_s$
Wage variance = $(W_a - W_s) \times H_a$
Efficiency variance = $(H_a - H_s) \times W_s$

areas in Figure 14.1. The two shaded areas are decomposed into a wage variance (the top purple rectangle) and an efficiency variance (the orange rectangle on the right).

NUMERICAL EXAMPLE 14.1

A CPA firm estimates that an audit will require the following work:

Type of Auditor	Expected Hours	Cost per Hour	Standard Costs
Manager	10	$50	$ 500
Senior	20	40	800
Staff	40	30	1,200
Totals	70		$2,500

The actual hours and costs were:

Type of Auditor	Actual Hours	Actual Cost per Hour	Actual Costs
Manager	9	$52	$ 468
Senior	22	38	836
Staff	44	30	1,320
Totals	75		$2,624

Calculate the direct labor, wage rate, and labor efficiency variances for each type of auditor and interpret the results.

■ **SOLUTION** The direct labor variance for each type of auditor is:

Type of Auditor	Actual Costs	Standard Costs	Direct Labor Variance
Manager	$ 468	$ 500	($32) Favorable
Senior	836	800	36 Unfavorable
Staff	1,320	1,200	120 Unfavorable
Totals	$2,624	$2,500	$124 Unfavorable

The wage rate variance for each type of auditor is:

Manager ($52/hour − $50/hour)(9 hours) = $18 Unfavorable
Senior ($38/hour − $40/hour)(22 hours) = (44) Favorable
Staff ($30/hour − $30/hour)(44 hours) = 0
Total wage rate variance ($26) Favorable

The labor efficiency variance for each type of auditor is:

Manager (9 hours − 10 hours)($50/hour) = ($50) Favorable
Senior (22 hours − 20 hours)($40/hour) = 80 Unfavorable
Staff (44 hours − 40 hours)($30/hour) = 120 Unfavorable
Total labor efficiency variance $150 Unfavorable

Note that the direct labor variance is equal to the sum of the wage rate and labor efficiency variances. The favorable wage rate variance means that on average the auditors were paid less than expected although managers were paid more than expected. The unfavorable labor efficiency variance means that on average the auditors took longer to complete the audit than expected. Managers, however, spent less time on the audit than expected.

Large variances, either favorable or unfavorable, can mean that the system is out of control. An accounting variance can indicate that either the operating unit deviated from an appropriate standard, or faulty assumptions were used to develop the standard. In the first case, supervisors of the direct labor did not operate at the levels assumed in the standards. Direct labor was used more or less efficiently than expected. In the second case, the standards were set at a level that could not be attained even if the supervisor used the direct labor as efficiently as possible. Just because a large unfavorable variance is reported does not mean that the person responsible is performing below expectations.

Large favorable variances are not necessarily good news because they could signal that quality is being reduced. For example, one way to generate favorable

These construction workers are pouring concrete footings for a new house. If they work slower than expected or run into unforeseen delays such as large rocks, there will be an unfavorable labor efficiency variance.

labor efficiency variances is to use too few labor hours and produce lower quality products. Likewise, favorable wage rate variances might mean that lower skilled, lower paid workers were used than expected; this too can mean that product quality is being compromised.

The personnel department is held responsible for the wage rate variance if that department has the decision rights for hiring workers with given job skills at a given standard wage rate. In other cases, the shop floor foreman is held responsible for wage rate variances if the foreman can schedule different workers with varying skills and wage rates to produce the product. If the foreman can change the mix of workers and thus the cost of the job by substituting more or less skilled workers at different wage rates, then the foreman is usually assigned the total direct labor variance and there is no reason to separately compute a wage variance and an efficiency variance except to provide information about what caused the labor variance.

The extent to which wage and efficiency variances are used to measure performance and the weight they receive in each manager's performance evaluation depends on the reliability of the underlying standards, the inherent variability of the wages and hours due to random fluctuations, and how much of the variance is potentially controllable by the manager. Some organizations place large weight on variances in performance evaluation, others place little or no weight on them.

Direct Materials Variances

Direct materials variances are similar to those computed for direct labor. As with direct labor, the total direct materials variance can be decomposed into a **price variance** and a **material quantity variance**. The calculations are identical to those for direct labor.

$$\text{Direct material variance} = \text{Actual cost of material} - \text{Standard cost of material}$$

$$= \left(\begin{array}{c}\text{Actual} \\ \text{price}\end{array} \times \begin{array}{c}\text{Actual} \\ \text{quantity}\end{array}\right) - \left(\begin{array}{c}\text{Standard} \\ \text{price}\end{array} \times \begin{array}{c}\text{Standard} \\ \text{quantity}\end{array}\right)$$

Price variance = (Actual price − Standard price) × Actual quantity

Quantity variance = (Actual quantity − Standard quantity) × Standard price

Direct material variance = Price variance + Quantity variance

Figure 14.2 illustrates how the total materials variance is decomposed into a material price variance and a material quantity variance, under the assumption that *all materials purchased are used immediately in production.* As in Figure 14.1, this difference is the purple and orange shaded areas in Figure 14.2.

The material price variance is typically one measure of the purchasing manager's performance. To be timely, the price variance should be calculated at the time the materials are purchased. The time of purchase may be different than the time the material is used. Other performance measures for the purchasing agent might include the percentage of on-time delivery of materials and material quality.

The quantity variance is one performance measure of the manager responsible for the efficient use of materials (usually the shop supervisor). Other performance measures for the shop supervisor include quality of output and timely manufacturing.

The calculation of material price variances can be demonstrated using the standard costs data for the Smith Art Book in Table 14.1 and the actual cost data in Table 14.2. The total direct material variance is $9,588 − $9,600, or $12 favorable. This variance can be decomposed into the material price variance and the

FIGURE 14.2
Direct Materials Variances (Materials used as purchased)

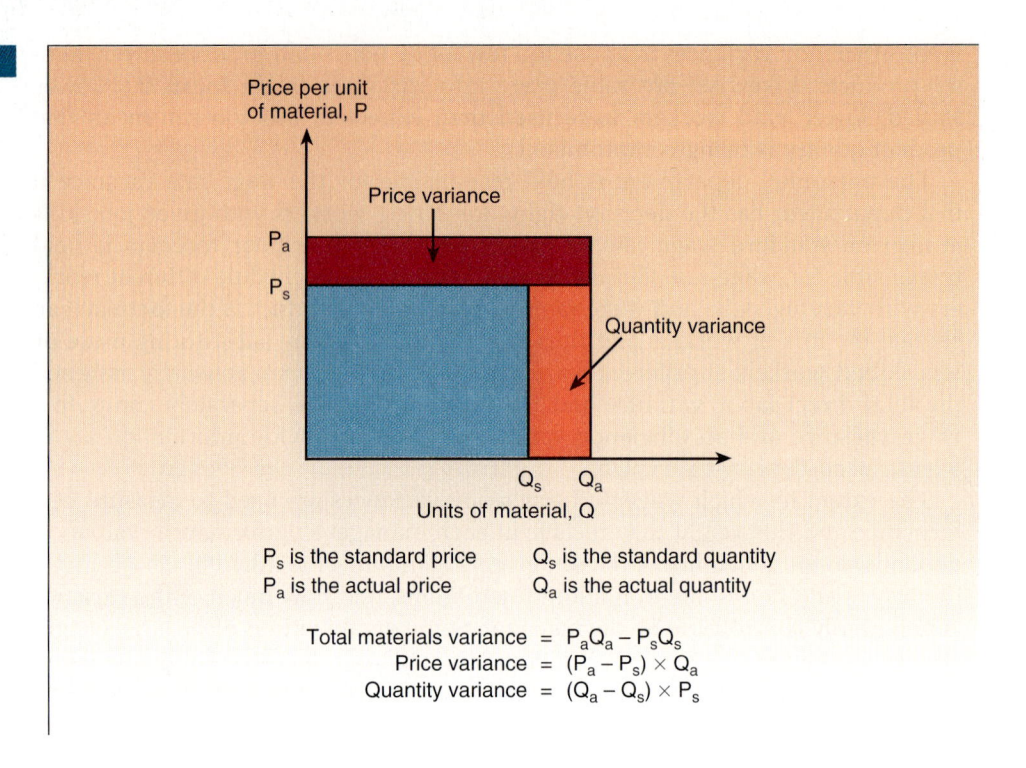

P_s is the standard price
P_a is the actual price
Q_s is the standard quantity
Q_a is the actual quantity

$$\text{Total materials variance} = P_a Q_a - P_s Q_s$$
$$\text{Price variance} = (P_a - P_s) \times Q_a$$
$$\text{Quantity variance} = (Q_a - Q_s) \times P_s$$

material quantity variance. The material price variances for each of the materials for the Smith Art Book are:

Material price variance = (Actual price − Standard price) × Actual quantity

Paper	($2.10/lb. − $2.00/lb.)(810 lbs.) =	$ 81 unfavorable
Covers	($5.80 − $6.00)(1,005) =	(201) favorable
Binding	($4.20 − $4.00)(490 lb.) =	98 unfavorable
Total material price variance		($ 22) favorable

The material quantity variance for each of the materials is:

Material quantity variance = (Actual quantity − Standard quantity) × Standard price

Paper	(810 lbs. − 800 lbs.)($2/lb.) =	$ 20 unfavorable
Covers	(1,005 − 1,000)($6.00) =	30 unfavorable
Binding	(490 lbs. − 500 lbs.)($4/lb.) =	(40) favorable
Total quantity variance		$ 10 unfavorable

Table 14.4 demonstrates the relation among the direct material variances.

In a standard cost system, materials are recorded in the raw material inventory accounts at standard cost. That is, inventory is stated at standard price, not actual price. The material price variance is recorded in a separate ledger account, which is usually written off to cost of goods sold at the end of the year instead of flowing through inventory and product costs. For example, suppose 100 pounds of copper are purchased for $12 per pound when the standard price is $10 per pound. The purchase is recorded in the raw material inventory account at $1,000 and the $200 difference is recorded in a separate materials price variance account. Future products using this copper are charged $10 not $12 per pound. By recording the $200 in a separate account and writing it off to cost of goods sold directly, the unit cost of the products using the copper are not affected by the $2 per pound price variation.

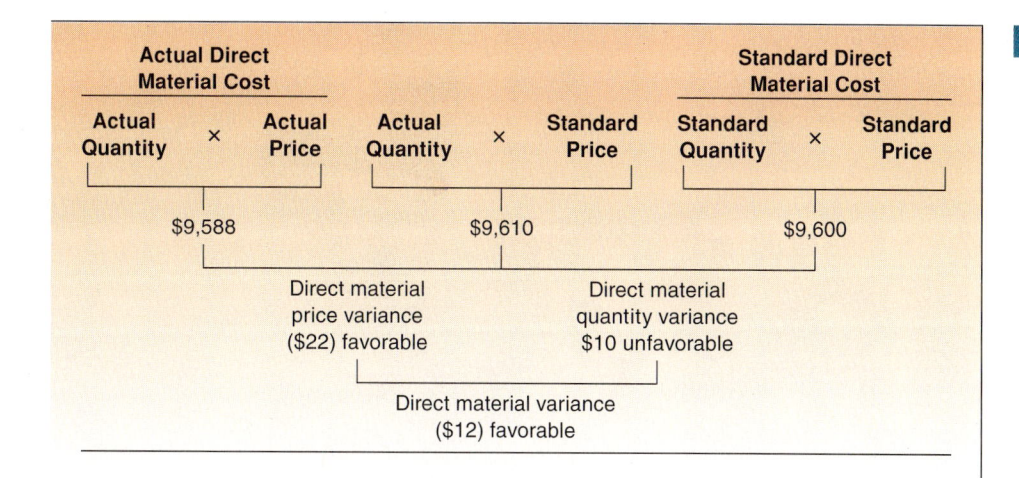

TABLE 14.4 Relation among Direct Material Variances

```
Actual Direct                                    Standard Direct
Material Cost                                    Material Cost

Actual     ×   Actual      Actual    ×  Standard    Standard   ×   Standard
Quantity       Price       Quantity     Price       Quantity       Price

    $9,588                    $9,610                   $9,600

              Direct material         Direct material
              price variance          quantity variance
              ($22) favorable         $10 unfavorable

                    Direct material variance
                         ($12) favorable
```

FIGURE 14.3 Direct Materials Variances (Materials purchased but not used yet)

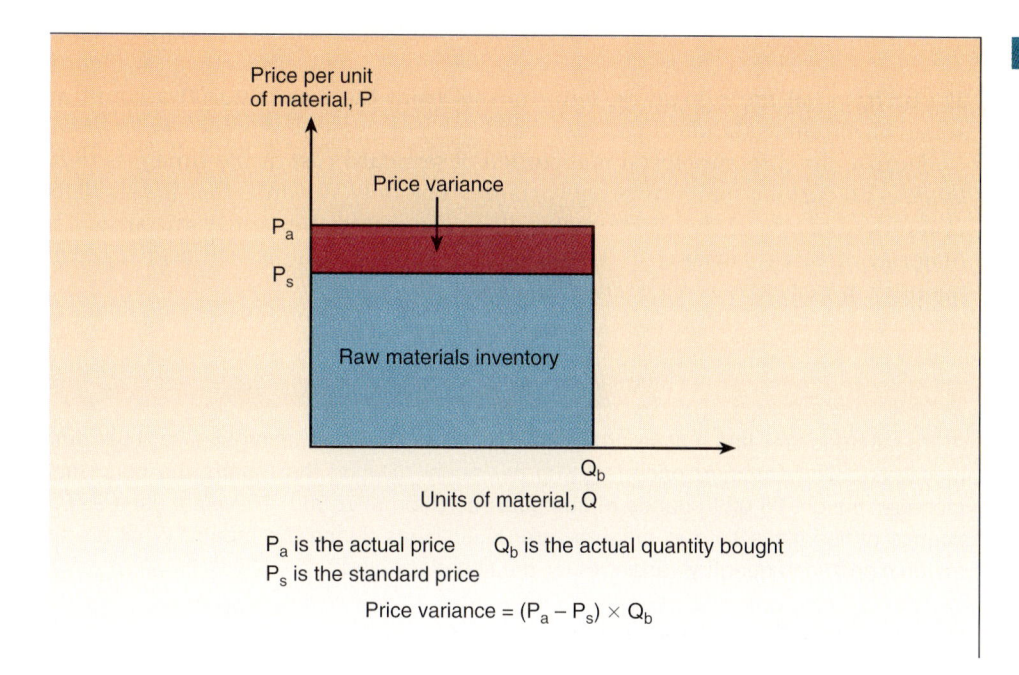

Price per unit of material, P

P_a — actual price
P_s — standard price

Price variance (shaded region above P_s)

Raw materials inventory (shaded region below P_s)

Q_b — Units of material, Q

P_a is the actual price Q_b is the actual quantity bought
P_s is the standard price

Price variance = $(P_a - P_s) \times Q_b$

The advantage of recording raw materials at standard cost is that downstream users in the plant only see standard costs. Likewise, labor is charged to products and jobs at standard cost. If standard costs are unbiased forecasts of future costs, then using standard costs gives downstream managers more accurate information regarding the opportunity cost of the raw material. Of course, this discussion assumes that standard prices are more accurate predictors of opportunity costs than actual prices. Using standard costs also reduces the risk borne by downstream "purchasers" of the product, such as the marketing department. Downstream users know at the beginning of the year what they will be charged for raw materials throughout the year. The use of standard costs thus removes uncontrollable factors from the performance measures of downstream users.

Figure 14.3 depicts the more usual case in which raw material is bought, placed in raw materials inventory, and then used at a later date. In Figure 14.3, the material price variance is removed as soon as the raw material is purchased. The raw materials inventory is then stated at the standard cost per unit. The price variance is reported as soon as the material is bought and not when the material is used at some later date. Once the material price variance is removed

This nursery customer is making a trade-off between quantity and price in selecting trees. A large tree costs more but covers more space than the cheaper small trees. How does this choice affect material, price, and quantity variances?

at purchase, all the remaining withdrawals from the raw material account are stated at the same standard cost per unit.

Because the direct material is recorded at standard cost at the time it is used, there is no further material price variance. The only variance that is calculated at the time of use of the direct materials is the material quantity variance. The material quantity variance is the difference between the actual and standard quantity of materials at the standard cost per unit.

NUMERICAL EXAMPLE 14.2

A tire manufacturer has a standard quantity of three pounds of fiberglass cord per automobile tire. The standard price is $1.00 per pound. During the month, the purchasing manager bought 98,000 pounds of fiberglass cord for $102,000. The plant used 95,000 pounds of fiberglass cord to manufacture 30,000 tires during the month. What are the material price and quantity variances for the fiberglass cord?

■ **SOLUTION** The material price variance is calculated at the time of purchase. The actual purchase price per pound is $102,000/98,000 = $1.04082/lb. Therefore, the material price variance is ($1.04082/lb. − $1.00/lb.)(98,000 lbs. = $4,000 unfavorable.

The material quantity variance is calculated when the material is used. In this case, 95,000 lb. were used. But (3 lb./tire)(30,000 tires), or 90,000 lb., should have been used according to the standard. The material quantity variance is (95,000 lbs. − 90,000 lbs.)($1/lb.), or $5,000 unfavorable.

The material price and quantity variances are often interrelated. For example, if substandard material is purchased at a price below the standard price, usually an unfavorable material quantity variance is generated because more material than standard is used. If a less expensive exterior house paint is purchased, more of it will probably be required to provide the same coverage as a higher quality, higher priced paint. A variance in one area is likely to be related to other variances. A favorable material price variance might cause an unfavorable material quantity variance, or a favorable labor efficiency variance from one type of labor might be the result of another unfavorable labor efficiency variance if another type of labor is substituted. A favorable materials price variance and resulting unfavorable materials quantity variance can cause unfavorable labor efficiency variances if extra material and labor are used due to the substandard materials.

Therefore, as a performance measurement system of the manufacturing process, the variances must be analyzed as an integrated whole.

CONCEPT REVIEW

1. What are the two components of direct labor and material costs?
2. What is the relation between standard and actual costs when the variance is favorable?
3. What type of manager is likely to be responsible for labor wage and efficiency variances?
4. What type of manager is likely to be responsible for material price and quantity variances?
5. Under what conditions would the material quantity variance be unfavorable?

ED ODELL, CONTRACTOR (CONTINUED)

The latest order to Ed Odell for 8 feet by 12 feet wall sections was for 3,000 units. Given the standards he set for constructing the wall sections, Ed Odell estimated that the total direct costs of making the 3,000 wall sections would be (3,000 units)($37.20/unit), or $111,600. Ed was pleased to find that the actual direct costs of completing the order were only $107,990. The total direct cost variance for the order was $111,600 − $107,990, or $3,610 favorable. He figured that the standard costing system was working. The following information used to calculate direct cost variances, however, made him wonder what was happening.

Purchases
    Lumber: 300,000 board feet at $0.09/board foot
    Sheetrock: 15,000 sheets of sheetrock at $1.90/sheet
Actual labor used: 10,000 hours at $7.00/hour
Standard labor: (3,000 units)(3 hours/unit)   9,000 hours
Actual direct material used:
    Lumber: 230,000 board feet
    Sheetrock: 9,100 sheets
Standard material:
    Lumber: (3,000 units)(72 board feet/unit)   216,000 board feet
    Sheetrock: (3,000 units)(3 sheets/unit)   9,000 sheets

The variances for direct costs for the order are:

Wage rate variance:	($7.00 − $8.00)(10,000 hours)	($10,000) Favorable
Labor efficiency variance:	(10,000 − 9,000)($8.00/hour)	8,000 Unfavorable
Material price variance for materials used for order:		
Lumber	($0.09 − $0.10)(230,000 board feet)	(2,300) Favorable
Sheetrock	($1.90 − $2.00)(9,100 sheets)	(910) Favorable
Material quantity variance:		
Lumber	(230,000 − 216,000)($0.10/board foot)	1,400 Unfavorable
Sheetrock	(9,100 − 9,000)($2/sheet)	200 Unfavorable
Total direct cost variance		($ 3,610) Favorable

Jeff Pringle, the purchasing manager was especially pleased. The material price variances for both the lumber and sheetrock were favorable, and Jeff

> estimated that the material price variance would be even higher if the material price variance was calculated based on the quantity purchased rather than the quantity used. Both Barbara Kaplan and Chet Slocum reported favorable wage rate variances to offset unfavorable labor efficiency and material quantity variances. They both claimed that the unfavorable quantity variances were due to poor quality materials.
>
> The variance analysis worried Ed Odell. The total cost of making the order was less than the total standard cost, but certain aspects of the analysis made him feel his problems weren't over. The managers' worrying about the quality of materials was especially bothersome given the Japanese customer's penchant for high quality. Also, Barbara and Chet had apparently hired lower waged workers to complete the order. Were these workers capable of producing work to meet the quality requirements of the customer? Also, why did Jeff purchase far more materials than were needed for the order? Eventually they would use the materials, but holding the inventory would be costly. Standard costing was proving to be more complex than expected.

14.3 Incentive Effects of Direct Labor and Materials Variances

Standard costs and variances, when used as part of the performance evaluation system, create incentives for managers to control costs; this is one of their intended purposes. Standards are part of the performance evaluation system, as described in Chapter 6. However, if the standard cost system is not designed properly and is not integrated consistently with the other parts of the performance evaluation and reward systems and the decision partitioning system, then dysfunctional behavior can result.

Standard cost variances when used as performance measures create subtle incentive effects. This section describes five: (1) the incentive to build inventories and/or to lower quality; (2) externalities; (3) discouraging cooperative effort; (4) mutual monitoring incentives; and (5) satisficing behavior.

Incentive to Build Inventories

Evaluating purchasing managers based on direct materials price variances creates incentives for these managers to build inventories. Price discounts are often granted for large volume purchases. Therefore, one way to generate favorable price variances is to purchase raw materials in lots larger than necessary for immediate production and hold these inventories until they are needed. However, it is costly to hold inventory because of warehousing, material handling, obsolescence, and financing costs.

One way to reduce the incentive to hold large inventories is to charge the purchasing department for the cost of holding inventories. For example, if the firm's opportunity cost of capital is 13% per year and warehousing and handling costs are 15% of the cost of the inventory per year, then charging the purchasing department 28% per year of the average dollar balance in raw materials inventory reduces the incentive to purchase in large lots. In other words, including inventory holding costs in the purchasing department's performance report reduces their incentives to buy large lots just to get price concessions.

Most firms do not charge purchasing managers for inventory holding costs because many holding costs are not part of the external reporting system. An alternative mechanism for controlling inventory-building behavior is to adopt rules such as just-in-time (JIT) purchasing rules described in Chapter 12. That is, the purchasing department can only order materials as they are needed for production.

Externalities

Externalities occur within an organization when the behavior of one individual affects other individuals within the organization. Purchasing managers can impose externalities on production by purchasing substandard materials. The lower quality materials often cause more labor hours and more skilled workers (paid higher wages) to process the substandard materials. The substandard materials impose downstream costs on the production managers because additional production resources are consumed for rework or machine downtime.

To offset the purchasing manager's incentive to acquire low-quality raw materials, purchases are inspected when received, engineering specifications are set for each product, and purchasing is not allowed to buy materials that deviate from these standards. Alternatively, part of the purchasing manager's performance evaluation can be tied to the amount of rework generated in production and/or the raw material quantity variance. The purchasing manager then has incentives to reduce rework and quantity variances by purchasing higher quality products. However, the purchasing manager can't control other reasons for rework and quantity variances, so including rework and quantity variances in the purchasing manager's evaluation may not be appealing to the purchasing manager.

Production managers also can impose externalities on purchasing by requesting that materials be purchased on short lead times and in small lot sizes to reduce the quantity of materials in storage. Also, by making frequent design changes, engineering can increase the actual price of the purchases. These are just a few examples of the types of externalities that purchasing and production can impose on each other.

A favorable dining experience at one outlet of a national chain can increase the likelihood of the customer frequenting other locations of that chain. If this family leaving McDonald's received good food and service at this outlet, they are more likely to frequent other McDonald outlets.

Discouraging Cooperative Effort

Evaluating individuals within an organization based on standard cost variances can discourage cooperative effort. In some firms every worker is evaluated based on a labor efficiency variance. In other words, the output of each individual is measured and compared with a standard to determine how the worker is rewarded. The workers in these factories are often reluctant to support others if their evaluation only reflects what they produce as an individual.

An alternative is to measure variances for a team or department within the organization. Team performance measures encourage cooperative effort but can lead to shirking on the part of some individuals. For example, a group student project for a class is given a single grade that is shared by all the participants in the group. Some individuals will take advantage of the group grading system by shirking their duties because they know other responsible students in the group will complete the group task.

To encourage cooperative effort and avoid shirking, many organizations calculate variances and measure performance at multiple levels. For example, an individual worker would be evaluated based on an individual labor efficiency variance and a departmental labor efficiency variance. Bonuses would be paid for both individual and group accomplishments.

Mutual Monitoring Incentives

The usual method of monitoring behavior within firms is for superiors to monitor subordinates. But another important form of monitoring occurs between managers who are not in a direct reporting relationship with each other. Monitoring can occur between managers at the same level in the same subunit or between managers in different subunits. Mutual monitoring occurs when managers or workers at the same level monitor each other.

If the purchasing department manager is held responsible for materials variance (including the quantity variance), then the purchasing manager has the incentive to monitor the production foreman's usage of materials. Likewise, the production foreman is monitoring the quality of the materials bought by the purchasing manager. By rewarding the purchasing manager on the basis of both the price and quantity variance, the purchasing manager will help devise ways in which the production manager can economize on materials, and the production manager will try to devise ways in which the purchasing manager can purchase materials to reduce the purchasing manager's costs. Therefore, in designing the performance evaluation and reward systems, one can create mutual monitoring incentives to encourage managers to acquire and utilize their specialized knowledge to improve the performance of another manager.

Satisficing Behavior

If standards are used as a benchmark for evaluating managers, the reward system is often tied to achieving the standard. If the manager works sufficiently hard to achieve the standard, a bonus is often paid to the manager. The problem with this type of reward system is that managers have incentives to achieve the standard, but go no further. This is called **satisficing behavior.** There is a further disincentive to perform beyond the standard. Next year's standards are usually based on past performance and would be harder to achieve if raised due to exceptional performance. The organization, of course, would like managers to continually improve and not stop when the standard is met.

Managers also need to react to competitors. If the manager is only focusing on the standard instead of the competition, the organization will not change to meet new demands. Rewarding managers for just achieving the standards tends

In the 1970s American motorcycle companies were complacent and just "met the standards" until Japanese brands such as Suzuki, Honda, and Kawasaki provided strong competition.

to make them think that the status quo is appropriate and does not promote innovation. Therefore, rewarding managers for meeting the standard is less appropriate in industries that are rapidly changing with new, innovative products. Also, the problem is not with using standards as performance measures but rather in how the compensation schemes reward performance. Compensation schemes should motivate managers to continuously improve beyond the standard with higher payments for greater improvement.

CONCEPT REVIEW

1. How do standard cost variances encourage the creation of excess inventory?
2. How does standard costing create externalities and discourage cooperative effort?
3. How can mutual monitoring be encouraged?
4. What is satisficing behavior and how is it related to standard costs?

EDWARD ODELL, CONTRACTOR (CONTINUED)

Ed Odell realized that his standard costing system did affect the behavior of his managers, but some behavior was perverse. Jeff Pringle was able to obtain favorable material price variances because he received discounts by purchasing more raw materials than required. To overcome this problem, Ed decided to charge Jeff for the average amount of raw materials in inventory.

The quality of the raw materials and the workmanship was another issue that Ed had to reconsider. Henceforth, incoming raw materials would have to pass an inspection. This would reduce the externalities imposed by Jeff on the other two managers. Also, Ed would retain the responsibility for hiring and training workers to try to improve the quality of workmanship.

Ed also decided to encourage cooperative behavior by tying part of the managers' bonuses to the profit of the whole company. Bonuses would be a percentage of total profit rather than a fixed amount if a certain level of profit were achieved. By making the bonuses a percentage of total profit, satisficing behavior on the part of managers would be less likely.

With these adjustments, Ed hoped that his standard costing system would lead to less perverse behavior. He still wanted to control direct costs but not at the risk of reduced quality, excess inventory costs, and management dissension.

14.4 *Overhead Standard Costs and Variances*

The previous discussion in this chapter described standards for direct labor and direct materials. Standards are also established for overhead costs. Overhead standard costs are used for both planning and control purposes. Standard overhead costs provide information about the cost of using overhead resources. Standard product costs used for pricing decisions include standard overhead costs. Standard overhead costs also provide benchmarks for evaluating managers who control overhead resources.

Overhead cost variances are more difficult to calculate and interpret than the direct material and labor variances because quantity and price are not inherent characteristics of overhead. Instead, quantity and price are defined in terms of the allocation base used to allocate overhead costs. The quantity of overhead is defined as the level of usage of the allocation base. The price of overhead is the application rate of the allocation base. The next section describes different measures of quantity for the allocation base. The following section describes variances in terms of budgeted, applied, and actual overhead. The calculations of specific overhead variances are left to the appendix.

Expected, Standard, and Actual Usage of the Allocation Base

Before describing overhead variances, it is useful to review some concepts and terminology involving the notion of volume. Most plants or departments within plants do not produce a single homogeneous product. Rather, a diverse set of outputs are manufactured. In this case, volume is not measured in terms of output but rather in terms of a common input such as direct labor dollars, machine time, or raw material dollars.

Once an input measure such as machine time is selected as the definition of volume in the plant or department, there are three different ways to quantify input volume: expected usage, standard usage, and actual usage of the input. The first volume measure, **expected usage,** is set at the beginning of the year based on the amount of production expected to occur during the year. Greater expected output volume implies greater expected input usage. If a car repair shop measures volume through the usage of direct labor hours, the expected direct labor hours are estimated at the beginning of the year based on an estimate of how many cars will be repaired during the year.

Expected usage of the allocation base is estimated for budgetary purposes. The overhead application rate is generally calculated by dividing the expected overhead costs by the expected usage of the allocation base.

Standard usage is the amount of the input used if each unit of product actually manufactured used precisely the standard units of input allowed. Given the output actually produced, standard usage measures how much input should

Auto service shops have standard usages or expected times to complete each type of job. A mechanic who works slower can't make the standard and causes an unfavorable variance. For example, the standard time to install this performance kit might be 45 minutes. If the mechanic takes an hour, an unfavorable labor efficiency variance is recorded.

have been used. For example, suppose direct labor hours are used as the allocation base. After each job is manufactured, the number of units actually produced times the standard number of direct labor hours per unit is the standard usage.

The third input volume concept is **actual usage.** This volume measure is the actual amount of an allocation base used (e.g., actual machine hours, actual direct labor hours, actual direct labor dollars).

The three input volume measures (expected, standard, and actual usage) differ in terms of when they are computed. Expected usage is estimated before the fiscal year begins and before production starts. Both standard and actual usages are computed after production is completed.

NUMERICAL EXAMPLE 14.3

The Pizza Company makes two types of frozen pizzas: pepperoni and cheese. The Pizza Company allocates overhead to these two products based on the number of direct labor hours. The direct labor hours per unit for making a pepperoni pizza is 5 minutes, or $1/12$ of an hour. The direct labor hours per unit for making a cheese pizza is 4 minutes, or $1/15$ of an hour. At the start of the year, the Pizza Company expected to make 12,000 pepperoni pizzas and 6,000 cheese pizzas. During the year, the Pizza Company actually made 9,000 pepperoni pizzas and 7,500 cheese pizzas. The time cards indicate that direct laborers worked for 1,300 hours. What are the total expected direct labor hours, standard direct labor hours, and actual direct labor hours?

■ **SOLUTION** Expected number of direct labor hours:

Pepperoni (12,000)(1/12)	1,000
Cheese (6,000)(1/15)	400
Total	1,400

Standard number of direct labor hours:

Pepperoni (9,000)(1/12)	750
Cheese (7,500)(1/15)	500
Total	1,250

Actual number of direct labor hours: 1,300

Budgeted, Applied, and Actual Overhead

In the previous section, three measures of usage of an allocation base are described. There are also three equivalent measures of overhead costs: budgeted, applied, and actual. **Budgeted overhead costs** (expected overhead costs) are the overhead costs expected at the beginning of the period. Budgeted overhead costs are estimated based on predictions about the level of operations of the organization during the coming period. Budgeted overhead costs are generally divided by the expected usage of the allocation base to calculate the application rate for the allocation base.

Applied overhead costs are the overhead costs that are applied to cost objects through the standard usage of the allocation base. In Chapter 10 the allocation of overhead occurs with the actual usage of the allocation base. With standard costing, however, the standard usage of the allocation base is used to allocate overhead costs. A standard costing system predetermines all the components (direct labor, direct materials, and overhead) of the product cost. If three direct labor hours (DLH) are the standard for making a particular product and direct labor hours are used as the allocation base, the overhead allocated to the product is three DLH times the application rate/DLH. Even though the product may have actually required four direct labor hours, the standard number of direct labor hours is used to apply the overhead.

The **actual overhead costs** are the actual costs of using overhead resources. These costs include cash outlays and depreciation of fixed assets.

Budgeted, applied, and actual overhead costs are usually different. Budgeted and applied overhead costs differ because the output (and, thus, the standard input usage) is different than expected. Only if the expected usage of the allocation base is equal to the standard usage of the allocation base, will the budgeted and applied overhead costs be equal.

The difference between applied (allocated) overhead costs and actual overhead costs is described in Chapter 10 as under- or overabsorbed overhead. In a standard costing system, the difference between the applied and actual overhead costs is called the **total overhead variance.** There are many factors that can cause the total overhead variance. Also, there are frequently multiple managers responsible for overhead resources. Therefore, partitioning the total overhead variance into components can allow for better identification of the cause and responsibility for the total overhead variance. One method of partitioning the total overhead variance is described in the appendix.

NUMERICAL EXAMPLE 14.4

A company makes two types of plastic pipe: 1-inch and 2-inch diameter. Overhead is allocated based on pounds of plastic in the pipe. The standards for the two types of pipe are:

Type	Standard Pounds/Unit	Expected Units	Expected Pounds of Plastic
1"	2	500,000	1,000,000
2"	3	600,000	1,800,000
Totals			2,800,000

The budgeted overhead for the period is $1,400,000. During the period, 450,000 units of 1-inch pipe are made using 1,050,000 pounds of plastic and 650,000 units of 2-inch pipe are made using 1,900,000 pounds of plastic. Actual overhead costs are $1,300,000. The application rate is $1,400,000/2,800,000 pounds, or $0.50/lb. What is the total overhead variance?

■ **SOLUTION** The total overhead variance is the difference between the actual overhead costs ($1,300,000) and the applied overhead costs. To calculate the applied overhead costs, the standard pounds of plastic must first be determined. The standard pounds times the application rate ($0.50/lb) is equal to the overhead applied.

Type	Standard Pounds/Unit	Actual Units	Standard Pounds of Plastic	Overhead Applied
1"	2	450,000	900,000	$ 450,000
2"	3	650,000	1,950,000	975,000
Totals			2,850,000	$1,425,000

The total overhead variance is $1,300,000 − $1,425,000, or $125,000 favorable.

Incentive Effects of Overhead Standards and Variances

Managers of overhead resources are responsible for providing quality services to the organization at the lowest possible cost. Standard costs for overhead are established, in part, to provide benchmarks for evaluating the managers of the overhead resources. If overhead standards are used for evaluation and rewarding managers, they will have an effect on the behavior of the managers.

The preferred effect of standard overhead costs is the reduction in overhead costs. The manager of the overhead resources can create favorable overhead variances by reducing overhead costs below the standard levels. Of course, maintaining the quality of the overhead service is still important to the organization, so there is a danger that the manager will inappropriately trade off cost savings and quality.

The other method of creating favorable overhead variances is to increase output. Increased output will increase the standard usage of the allocation base, which will increase the amount of overhead that is applied. If actual overhead costs don't increase proportionally with the allocation base, a favorable overhead variance will occur with increased output. For example, applied overhead costs will increase more rapidly than actual costs if some costs are fixed with respect to the allocation base.

One method of overcoming this overproduction incentive is to separate decision rights such that the overhead resource manager does not have control of output levels in the organization. If resource managers do not have control of output levels, they should only be evaluated by the portion of overhead variance caused by cost savings or overruns. Partitioning the overhead variances to identify responsibility for different portions of the overhead variance is discussed in the appendix.

CONCEPT REVIEW

1. How do expected, standard, and actual usages of the allocation base differ?
2. Why are standard overhead costs different from budgeted overhead costs?
3. What are some incentive effects of using overhead standards and variances for control?

EDWARD ODELL, CONTRACTOR (CONTINUED)

Once Ed Odell had designed a standard costing system to control the direct costs, he turned to overhead costs. Overhead costs were small when he was only a building contractor for new houses. He was able to work out of his house. The building of wall sections, however, forced him to rent a warehouse. In addition, he had more manager salaries and other indirect costs to pay. Overhead costs were rising more rapidly than his direct costs and he needed some mechanism to control the overhead.

During the budgetary process for the year, Ed estimated the total overhead costs for the company to be $400,000. He decided to use standard direct labor hours to allocate overhead to the various types of wall sections because direct labor hours were related to the number of managers, a major overhead expense. He estimated the company would use 100,000 standard direct labor hours based on expected production. The standard application rate, therefore, was $400,000/100,000 standard direct labor hours, or $4/standard direct labor hour.

Given that the 8 feet by 12 feet wall section had a standard of 3 direct labor hours per unit, the total standard hours for the order of 3,000 units was (3,000

> units)(3 direct labor hours/unit), or 9,000 hours. Other orders during the year caused an additional use of 86,000 standard direct labor hours, or a total of 95,000 standard direct labor hours. Therefore, during the year 95,000 standard direct labor hours × $4/direct labor hour, or $380,000 of overhead, were applied to products. The actual overhead for the year, however, was $405,000. Therefore, the overhead variance was $405,000 − $380,000, or $25,000 unfavorable.
>
> Ed Odell was unsure about what to do with this variance. It wasn't clear who was responsible for this variance. Many of the overhead decisions were actually his. He was also not sure whether the overhead costs were variable or fixed. The overhead variance required further investigation.

14.5 Variance Investigation

Calculating variances is only the first step in the process of making a decision using a standard costing system. Variances are calculated for planning and control purposes. In both cases, the variance by itself seldom provides sufficient information for making good decisions.

Variances are intended to identify problems in existing processes that require attention, but variances often occur when processes are operating correctly. Random fluctuations in the costs of material, labor, or overhead can cause a variance. A manager is seldom certain from the observation of a variance whether it is caused by a problem or a random fluctuation. Larger variances, however, are more likely to be associated with a problem than are smaller variances.

Small deviations between actual costs and standard costs are expected and unavoidable. But random variances will tend to offset each other over time. Positive random variances will approximately equal negative random variances, so aggregating random variances over time should lead to actual costs being close to standard costs. If variances do not offset each other over time, then the variances are likely caused by some other factor than randomness. Aggregating variances over time provides supervisors with more confidence about the origins of the variance.

Even if the manager knows a problem rather than random variation is causing a variance, the manager seldom can identify the nature of the problem by just looking at the variance. Looking at all of the variances provides more information. Certain combinations of variances are indicative of certain problems. For example, favorable material price variances and unfavorable material quantity and labor efficiency variances are consistent with the purchase of cheap, low quality materials. But even an analysis of all the variances does not reveal the complete story.

To understand the cause of variances, a manager must investigate the source of the variance. Investigations include questioning responsible parties and looking at noncost data such as percentage of defects and quality measures of raw materials.

The decision to investigate is a decision in itself. Investigations are often costly, involving labor and sometimes shutting down processes during the investigation. Therefore, not every nonzero variance should be investigated. The manager often uses a decision rule based on the size of the variance to decide when to investigate. Large variances are less

An engineer is making detailed measurements to determine why this electric motor does not meet specifications. Such in-depth examinations of a production process are often triggered by an unfavorable accounting variance.

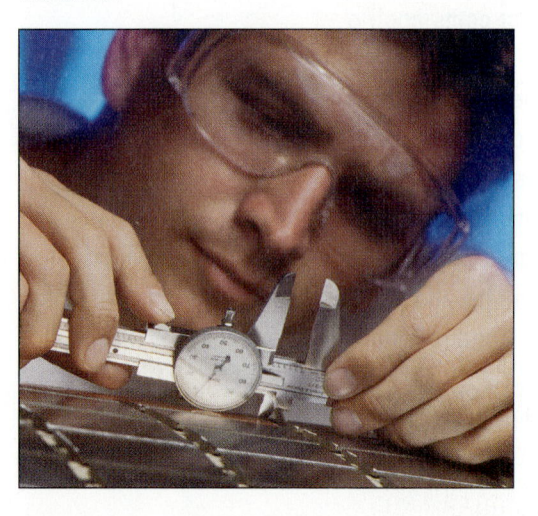

likely caused by random fluctuations and, therefore, are often deserving of further investigation. The problem is to decide how large the variance must be before investigation.

Factors that affect the decision rule to investigate variances include the size of the random fluctuations, the opportunity cost of investigation, the opportunity cost of not investigating, and the ease of correcting the problem if it exists. If random fluctuations tend to be very high, only very large variances would distinguish a variance caused by randomness from a variance caused by a problem. If the opportunity cost of investigation is high, the manager is much less likely to investigate smaller variances. If the opportunity cost of not investigating is also high, however, smaller variances are more likely to be investigated. For example, if the material quantity variance is caused by theft, a lack of investigation is likely to lead to further theft and a high opportunity cost to the organization. Therefore, small variances are likely to be investigated. Also, the ease of correcting the problem if it exists will also influence the decision to investigate. High correction costs mean that even if the problem is discovered, the organization may not fix the problem because the benefits are less than the costs. Therefore, there is less reason to investigate the problem. Instead, the organization may choose to change the standard. The new standard recognizes the existence of the problem, so the manager is not responsible for the variance that is too costly to fix.

CONCEPT REVIEW

1. Why are investigations of variances often appropriate?
2. What are some factors that influence the decision to investigate?

EDWARD ODELL, CONTRACTOR (CONCLUDED)

To investigate the $25,000 overhead variance, Ed Odell would have to use the assistant controller for 10 days. The assistant controller had some free time and was paid a fixed salary, so Ed figured the opportunity cost of using the assistant controller would be only about $400. The potential cost savings from correcting a problem with overhead could be much larger, but Ed is not sure that a problem exists. The variance could have been caused by not estimating the overhead costs or the number of standard direct labor hours correctly. Ed decides to go ahead with the investigation. The assistant controller finds that much of the variance is caused by misestimates but does find a way to save $1,000 per year by controlling the use of electricity more carefully. Therefore, Ed's decision to investigate saved $1,000 less the $400 investigation cost, or $600.

14.6 Costs and Benefits of Using Standard Costing Systems

Standard cost systems are costly to implement and operate. Not only must detailed standards be maintained for each labor and material input (standard prices and quantities), but these standards must be revised in a timely fashion. Rapid technological change and firms seeking continuous improvement (Total quality management programs are described in Chapter 12) cause standards to become obsolete quickly. In addition, it is expensive in terms of the opportunity cost of the manager's time to investigate cost variances.

NEC, a large diversified Japanese electronics firm, installed its standard cost system in the 1950s, when it was in a stable market supplying a small number of products, mainly telephones and switching equipment, to Nippon Telegraph & Telephone. But by the 1980s, NEC was supplying a vast number of different electronic products that are subject to rapid technological obsolescence in worldwide markets.[6]

It is very expensive to keep the standard costs up to date as products and the production technology changes. The life expectancy of any one cost standard is now much shorter. NEC still uses its standard cost system as a factory management tool but is not using standard costs on a product-by-product basis.

Standard cost systems also create incentive problems. Workers tend to focus on old standards rather than seeking continuous cost reductions. In addition, standard costing systems can cause overproduction and lower quality and discourage cooperative effort.

Standard cost variances are also not particularly timely. Cost variances are usually reported monthly or quarterly. This information may be too late to correct problems.

For many companies, however, the benefits of standard costs through improved control and planning decisions must exceed the costs of using standard costs. As mentioned earlier, a survey of large U.S. companies indicated that 85% use standard costs. A survey of 198 Japanese companies in four automated industries concludes that most Japanese firms are maintaining their standard costs.[7] The authors report that 70% of the firms in electronic and transportation equipment industries use standard costs, and 58% of the firms in chemical products and iron and steel manufacturing use standard costs.

While some companies might be abandoning their detailed standard cost systems, they are often maintaining some standard costs. These firms still see opportunities to use standard costs for planning and control purposes. A standard cost system must be designed carefully to maximize firm value. Carelessly designed standard cost systems that serve as performance evaluation schemes can lead to dysfunctional behavior.

The availability of extensive nonfinancial data generated by CAM allowed Milliken to simplify the existing variance reports and reduce the number of detailed cost standards estimated by industrial engineers, accountants, and production managers. However, Milliken still relies on standard costs for pricing decisions and performance evaluation. As described in Chapters 1, 6, and 12, the experience at Milliken illustrates how accounting systems are one part of the firm's planning and control systems. When technological change allows improvements in other parts of the planning and control systems, these changes are likely to affect the accounting system.

> **WHAT'S HAPPENING**
>
> One U.S. textile manufacturer, Milliken, substantially revised its standard cost system but did not eliminate it.[8] The firm installed computers and communications systems to improve manufacturing productivity by monitoring the production process. Computer-aided manufacturing (CAM) provided detailed data on output per machine, downtime, and the reason for the downtime. The CAM technology provided managers with daily detailed, nonfinancial information such as setup time. Besides changing its manufacturing systems (CAM) and accounting system (standard costs), what other changes do you think occurred at Milliken?

CONCEPT REVIEW

1. Why are standard costs difficult to implement in a rapidly changing business environment?
2. What evidence indicates that the benefits of using standard costs outweigh the problems of using standard costs for many organizations?

THE STORY OF MANAGERIAL ACCOUNTING

Team Decisions Regarding Standards

Richard D. Irwin has set standards to guide the *Managerial Accounting* book team. These standards are in the form of costs (development and production) and other quantitative measures (such as finish date, number of pages, and number of pictures). These standards were set after incorporating information from the different team members. Why did team members become more concerned about these standards as the project neared completion?

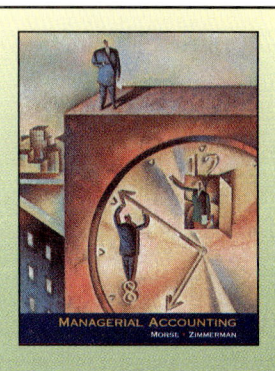

14.7 Summary

1. **Provide reasons for using standard costs.** Standard costs are used for planning purposes by communicating expected costs to members of the organization. Standard costs are also used for control by establishing benchmarks to evaluate processes and managers.

2. **Describe planning and control issues in setting standards.** For planning purposes, the person with the best knowledge of a process should establish standards. Conflict exists, however, if that individual is also evaluated based on those standards.

3. **Calculate direct labor and direct material variances.** Direct labor and material variances are divided into variances related to differences between actual and standard prices and variances related to differences between actual and standard quantities.

4. **Identify potential causes of different favorable and unfavorable variances.** All variances are potentially due to incorrect standards. Favorable price variances (standard prices greater than actual prices) could also be caused by purchasing large amounts of materials to get discounts or purchasing lower quality items. Unfavorable price variances (actual prices more than standard prices) could be caused by paying for rush orders or paying for higher quality materials or labor. Favorable quantity variances (actual quantity used less than the standard quantity) could be caused by efficient use of labor or materials or using higher quality labor or materials. Unfavorable quantity variances (actual quantity used greater than the standard quantity) could be caused by the inefficient use or theft of direct resources or use of lower quality labor or materials.

5. **Recognize incentive effects of standard costs.** Standard costs have the potential to cause overproduction and lower quality, externalities imposed on other parts of the organization, uncooperative effort, mutual monitoring, and satisficing behavior.

6. **Measure expected, standard, and actual usage of an allocation base to apply overhead and determine overhead variances.** Budgeted numbers at the beginning of the period are used to calculate the expected usage of the allocation base and the application rate. Standard usage is the standard input per unit times actual units produced and is used to apply overhead. Actual usage is measured throughout the period based on the observed usage of the allocation base. The total overhead variance is the difference between the actual overhead and the overhead applied.

7. **Identify factors that influence the decision to investigate variances.** The decision to investigate a variance is based on the size of the random variation, the opportunity cost of investigation, the opportunity cost of not investigating, and the ease of correcting the problem if it exists.

8. **Summarize the costs and benefits of using standard costs.** Standard costs can improve planning and control, but standard costing systems are costly to implement and adjust if the product mix is changing rapidly. Standard costs also potentially cause adverse incentive effects such as overproduction and satisficing behavior depending on how the performance reward systems use the standard costs.

KEY TERMS

Actual overhead costs Indirect costs actually incurred by the organization.

Actual usages The number of times an allocation base is actually used.

Applied overhead costs The dollar amount of overhead allocated to different products or other cost objects.

Budgeted overhead costs The expected indirect costs used to establish application rates.

Direct labor variance The difference between actual and standard labor costs.

Direct materials variance The difference between actual and standard material costs.

Expected usage The number of times an allocation base is expected to be used.

Favorable variance Occurs when actual costs are less than standard costs.

Fixed overhead budget variance The difference between budgeted and actual fixed overhead (appendix).

Fixed overhead variance The difference between applied and actual fixed overhead (appendix).

Fixed overhead volume variance The difference between applied and budgeted fixed overhead (appendix).

Labor efficiency variance The difference between actual and standard direct labor hours times the standard wage rate.

Management by exception A management style of focusing on unusual cost variances.

Material price variance The difference between the actual price and standard price of raw materials times the actual quantity used or purchased.

Material quantity variance The difference between the actual and standard quantity of materials used times the standard price.

Satisficing behavior Employees seeking satisfactory levels of performance measures without trying to excel.

Standard costs Benchmarks based on expected future costs.

Standard usage The number of times a cost driver is expected to be used given the actual number of units of output.

Target costing Choosing a cost goal given a competitive sales price and an expected profit margin.

Total overhead variance The difference between total actual and applied overhead.

Unfavorable variance Occurs when actual costs are greater than standard costs.

Variable overhead efficiency variance The difference between actual and standard usage of the allocation base times the standard application rate for variable overhead (appendix).

Variable overhead spending variance The difference between actual and standard application rates for variable overhead times the actual usage of the allocation base (appendix).

Variable overhead variance The difference between the actual and applied variable overhead (appendix).

Variance The difference between actual and standard costs.

Wage rate variance The difference between the actual wage rate and the standard wage rate times the actual hours.

Appendix: Overhead Variances

The total overhead variance is the difference between the applied overhead and the actual overhead. There are many reasons for a nonzero overhead variance. Standards and application rates could be wrong. The production could be greater or less than expected. Overhead departments may not be operating efficiently. Further information about the cause of the total overhead variance can be created by partitioning the total overhead variance into components.

A common procedure is to partition the total overhead variance into variances related to variable and fixed overhead. The **variable overhead variance** is defined as the actual variable overhead less the applied variable overhead or:

$$\text{Actual Variable Overhead} - \text{Applied Variable Overhead}$$
$$U_a VR_a - U_s VR_s$$

where

U_a = Actual usage of the allocation base
VR_a = Actual variable overhead application rate
(Actual variable overhead cost/actual usage of the allocation base)
U_s = Standard usage of the allocation base
VR_s = Standard variable overhead application rate

The equation for the variable overhead variance is similar to the equations for the direct costs. The usage of the allocation base is a quantity measure and the application rate is a price for using the allocation base. Therefore, the variable overhead variance can also be divided into a price and quantity variance.

The **variable overhead spending variance** is a price variance caused by the actual application rate being different than the standard application rate:

$$\text{Variable overhead spending variance} = U_a(VR_a - VR_s)$$

For managers responsible for the efficient provision of variable overhead resources, the standard application rate is a benchmark for evaluating performance. An unfavorable variable overhead spending variance indicates the actual variable costs are higher per unit of the allocation base than expected. An unfavorable variance doesn't mean the manager of the overhead resources is doing a poor job. Overhead resources may have become more expensive than expected or the quality of the overhead services provided are very high. An unusual variance, however, can be used as a signal to investigate.

The **variable overhead efficiency variance** is a quantity variance related to the usage of the allocation base:

$$\text{Variable overhead efficiency variance} = VR_s(U_a - U_s)$$

The standard usage of the allocation base determines the amount of variable overhead that is applied. If actual usage of the allocation base is greater than the standard usage, variable overhead is underabsorbed and the variable overhead efficiency variance is unfavorable. The responsibility for the variable overhead efficiency variance should generally rest with the users of the allocation base. For example, the variable overhead costs of the personnel department are often allocated to production departments based on standard direct labor hours. The manager of the production department is generally responsible for the difference between the actual and standard direct labor hours. The manager of the personnel department, however, could be responsible if the quality of the hiring led to direct labor not being able to achieve standards. Once again a further investigation is necessary to determine if a problem exists and who is responsible.

The **fixed overhead variance** is the actual fixed overhead less the applied fixed overhead. Fixed overhead, unlike variable overhead, should not change with the allocation base. The fixed overhead variance can be divided into two more variances: the **fixed overhead budget variance** and the **fixed overhead volume variance.** Managers responsible for fixed overhead resources are generally evaluated based on the difference between actual fixed overhead expenditures and budgeted fixed overhead, which is the fixed overhead budget variance. An unfavorable fixed overhead budget variance indicates that more resources are expended on fixed overhead than expected.

If the fixed overhead variance is divided to obtain a fixed overhead budget variance, the following equations indicate that the remaining fixed overhead variance is the budgeted fixed overhead less the applied fixed overhead or the fixed overhead volume variance:

$$\text{Fixed overhead variance} = \text{Actual fixed overhead} - \text{Applied fixed overhead}$$

$$= (\text{Actual fixed overhead} - \text{Budgeted fixed overhead}) + (\text{Budgeted fixed overhead} - \text{Applied fixed overhead})$$

$$= \text{Fixed overhead budget variance} + \text{Fixed overhead volume variance}$$

The fixed overhead volume variance can also be written as:

$$\text{Budgeted fixed overhead} - \text{Applied fixed overhead} = U_e FR_s - U_s FR_s = FR_s(U_e - U_s)$$

where

U_e = Expected (or budgeted) usage of the allocation base
FR_s = Standard fixed overhead application rate
U_s = Standard usage of the allocation base

The difference between the expected usage and the standard usage of the allocation base is due to the volume of output being different than expected. If the number of units produced is less than expected, the standard usage of the allocation base is less than expected. Therefore, less fixed overhead costs are applied than expected, and the volume variance is unfavorable. Given that the volume variance depends on the output of the organization, the manager responsible for fixed overhead resources should not be responsible for the volume variance. The manager in control of output should be responsible for the volume variance. The manager will have an incentive to overproduce because increased output will make the volume variance more favorable as more fixed costs get applied.

NUMERICAL EXAMPLE 14A.1

A company that services office machines applies variable and fixed overhead to jobs based on standard labor hours. The company has the following budget numbers related to the allocation base:

Type of Service	Expected Service Units	Standard Labor per Service Unit	Total Expected Labor Hours
Copiers	5,000	1 hour/unit	5,000 hours
Fax machines	1,000	2 hours/unit	2,000 hours
Total			7,000 hours

The standard numbers related to the allocation base given actual output are:

Type of Service	Actual Service Units	Standard Labor per Service Unit	Total Standard Labor Hours
Copiers	4,500	1 hour/unit	4,500 hours
Fax machines	1,100	2 hours/unit	2,200 hours
Total			6,700 hours

The actual number of labor hours used to service the copiers and fax machines was 6,800 hours. Budgeted and actual variable and fixed overhead costs were:

Overhead	Budgeted Costs	Actual Costs
Variable	$20,000	$22,000
Fixed	15,000	14,000

Calculate the application rates for variable and fixed overhead, the amount of variable and fixed overhead applied, the variable overhead spending and efficiency variances, and the fixed overhead budget and volume variances.

■ **SOLUTION** The application rates are calculated by dividing the budgeted (or expected) overhead by the expected usage of labor hours:

Variable overhead application rate = $20,000/7,000 hrs. = $2.857/hr.
Fixed overhead application rate = $15,000/7,000 hrs. = $2.143/hr.

The applied fixed and variable overhead is calculated by multiplying the application rates times the standard hours:

Variable overhead applied = (6,700 hrs.)($2.857/hr.) = $19,142
Fixed overhead applied = (6,700 hrs.)($2.143/hr.) = $14,358

The variable overhead variance is the difference between the actual variable overhead ($22,000) and the applied variable overhead ($19,142), or $2,858 unfavorable. The variable overhead variance can be further divided into the variable overhead spending variance and the variable overhead efficiency variance. The actual application rate for variable overhead is the actual variable overhead costs ($22,000) divided by the actual labor hours (6,800), or $3.235/hr.

Variable overhead spending variance = $U_a(VR_a - VR_s)$
= 6,800 hrs.($3.235/hr. − $2,857/hr.)
= $2,570 unfavorable

Variable overhead efficiency variance = $VR_s(U_a - U_s)$
= $2.857/hr.(6,800 hrs. − 6,700 hrs.)
= $286 unfavorable

The sum of these two variances is equal to $2,856 unfavorable, which differs from the variable overhead variance $2,858 because of rounding error.

The fixed overhead variance is the difference between the actual fixed overhead ($14,000) and the applied fixed overhead ($14,358), or $358 favorable. The fixed overhead variance can be divided into the fixed overhead budget variance and the fixed overhead volume variance.

Fixed overhead budget variance = Actual − Budgeted fixed overhead
= $14,000 − $15,000
= $1,000 favorable

Fixed overhead volume variance = Budgeted − Applied fixed overhead
= $15,000 − 14,358
= $642 unfavorable

The sum of the fixed overhead budget and volume variances is equal to the total fixed overhead variance.

SELF-STUDY PROBLEM

The Tippa Canoe Company makes fiberglass canoes. The fiberglass resin is initially molded to the shape of a canoe, then sanded and painted. Metal or wooden seats and frames are added for stability. The Tippa Canoe Company was started several years ago in the owner's garage. The owner, Jeff George, did a lot of the initial manual labor with the help of a few friends. The company has since expanded into a large warehouse and new employees have been hired. Because of the expansion, Jeff is no longer directly involved with production and is concerned about his ability to plan for and control the company. He is considering the implementation of a standard cost system.

a. Describe the procedures Jeff should use in setting standards for direct labor and direct materials.
b. Describe how Jeff could use standards for planning purposes.
c. Describe how Jeff could use standards for motivating employees and problems in using standards as performance measures.
d. Why are some of Jeff's friends who worked with him from the beginning not very excited about a change to a standard cost system?

Solution

a. Direct material standards should be established for the fiberglass resin and the wood and metal for the seats and the frame. For planning purposes, the standards for quantity and price should reflect expectations, but Jeff is no longer familiar with production and must ask some employees about expected quantities and prices. The purchasing manager has information on prices and the manufacturing manager has information on quantities. The direct labor standards are based on expectations from the personnel manager and the manufacturing manager.
b. If accurate estimates of prices and quantities are provided, Jeff can use the information to plan for cash flows. Also, the standards can be used to plan for appropriate inventory levels given planned manufacturing efforts.
c. The standards can be used as benchmarks to evaluate the performance of employees. A problem with using standards as performance measures is the difficulty of obtaining accurate standards from the individuals being evaluated. Standards can also provide incentives to increase inventories, discourage cooperative behavior, and lead to satisficing behavior.
d. Some of Jeff's friend who are still working in the expanded organization will probably be unhappy with the standard costing system because they will no longer be judged directly by their friend Jeff but through standards that appear impersonal and lacking in trust. Jeff's friends, however, must recognize that Jeff can no longer directly observe what is happening in the company. Standard costing systems are not established because of a lack of trust; standard costing systems are used to convey information among the different members of the organization.

NUMERICAL PROBLEMS

NP 14–1: Direct Material Variances (LO 3; NE 2)

Todco planned to produce 3,000 units of its single product, Teragram, during November. The standard specifications for one unit of Teragram include six pounds of material at $0.30 per pound. Actual production in November was 3,100 units of Teragram. The accountant computed a favorable materials purchase price variance of $380 and an unfavorable materials quantity variance of $120.

Based on these data, calculate how many pounds of material were used in the production of Teragram during November.

(CMA adapted)

NP 14–2: Direct Material Variances (LO 3, 4; NE 2)   Medical Instruments produces a variety of electronic medical devices. Medical Instruments uses a standard cost system and computes price variances at the time of purchase. One product, a thermometer, measures patient temperatures orally. It requires a silver lead with a standard length of five inches per thermometer. To make the leads, hollow silver tubing is purchased at $4 per inch, cut into the required length, and then assembled into the thermometer.

There was no silver tubing in inventory when a batch of 200 themometers was scheduled for production. Twelve hundred inches of silver tubing were purchased for $4,680 by the purchasing department for this 200-unit batch of thermometers, and 1,100 inches were used in production.

Compute the materials price and quantity variances for silver tubing and comment on the meaning of each.

NP 14–3: Direct Variances (LO 3; NE 1, 2)   Arrow Industries employs a standard cost system in which direct materials inventory is carried at standard cost. Arrow has established the following standards for the direct costs of one unit of product.

	Standard Quantity	Standard Price	Standard Cost
Direct materials	8 pounds	$1.80 per pound	$14.40
Direct labor	0.25 hour	$8.00 per hour	2.00
			$16.40

During May, Arrow purchased 160,000 pounds of direct material at a total cost of $304,000. The total factory wages for May were $42,000, 90% of which were for direct labor. Arrow manufactured 19,000 units of product during May, using 142,500 pounds of direct material and 5,000 direct labor hours.

a. Calculate the direct materials price variance for May.
b. Calculate the direct materials quantity variance for May.
c. Calculate the direct labor wage rate variance for May.
d. Calculate the direct labor efficiency variance for May.

(CMA adapted)

NP 14–4: Raw Material Variances (LO 3; NE 2)   Thirty-six thousand pounds of plastic pellets were purchased for $8,640. These pellets are used in injection molding machines to produce plastic parts. The pellets have a standard cost of $0.25 per pound. Thirty thousand pounds of these pellets were used in two jobs. The first job called for 14,000 pounds of pellets but actually used 15,000 pounds. The second job also used 15,000 pounds but it called for 15,500 pounds. The company uses a standard cost system, calculates price variances at purchase, and had no beginning inventory of this plastic pellet.

At the conclusion of the two jobs and before any more of the plastic pellets are used (and before proration or write-off of variances), prepare a table that indicates the financial disposition of the historical cost of the pellets (i.e., account for the $8,640).

NP 14–5: Direct Labor Variances (LO 3; NE 1)   Hospital Software sells and installs computer software used by hospitals for patient admissions and billing. Each client engagement involves Hospital Services taking their proprietary software and modifying it for the specific demands of the client. Prior to each installation, Hospital Software estimates the number of hours of programming time each job will require and the cost of the programmers. Programmers record the amount of time they spend on each engagement, and at the end of each installation, variance reports are prepared.

For the Denver General Hospital account, Hospital Software estimates the following labor standards:

	Standard Hours	Standard Rate/hr.
Junior programmer	85	$23
Senior programmer	33	$31

After the job was completed, the following costs were reported:

Junior programmer (98 hours)	$2,352
Senior programmer (36 hours)	$1,044

Calculate the labor efficiency and labor wage rate variances for the junior and senior programmers on the Denver General Hospital account.

NP 14–6: Standard Costs (LO 1, 2, 3)
Ogwood Company is a small manufacturer of wooden household items. The Corporate Controller plans to implement a standard cost system for Ogwood. The controller has information from several co-workers that will assist him in developing standards for Ogwood's products.

One of Ogwood's products is a wooden cutting board. Each cutting board requires 1.25 board feet of lumber and 12 minutes of direct labor time to prepare and cut the lumber. The cutting boards are inspected after they are cut. Because the cutting boards are made of a natural material that has imperfections, one board is normally rejected after cutting for each five that are accepted. Four rubber foot pads are attached to each good cutting board. A total of 15 minutes of direct labor time is required to attach all four foot pads and finish each cutting board. The lumber for the cutting boards costs $3 per board foot, and each foot pad costs $0.05. Direct labor is paid at the rate of $8 per hour.

a. Develop the standard cost for the direct cost components of the cutting board. The standard cost should identify the (1) standard quantity, (2) standard rate, and (3) standard cost per unit for each direct cost component of the cutting board.
b. What are the advantages of standard cost systems?
c. Explain the role of each of the following persons in developing standards:
   (1) Purchasing manager
   (2) Industrial engineer
   (3) Cost accountant

(CMA adapted)

NP 14–7: Direct Materials Variance (LO 3, 4; NE 1, 2)
Howard Binding manufactures two types of notebooks, large and small. The large and small notebooks are made of the same cloth cover (direct material) but of different quantities. The standard cost sheet for each is:

	Large	Small
Cloth covering	3 feet @ $0.30/ft	2 feet @ $0.30/ft
Ring holder	1 @ $0.12 each	1 @ $0.12 each
Direct labor	0.15 hour @ $6.00/hr	0.10 hour @ $6.00/hr

At the beginning of the month, the purchasing department bought 35,000 feet of cloth for $10,850. There were no beginning inventories. During the month, 5,000 large and 8,000 small notebooks were produced. The production records for the month indicate the following actual production quantities:

	Large	Small
Cloth covering	16,000 feet	15,500 feet
Ring holders	5,000 @ $0.12 each	8,000 @ $0.12 each
Direct labor	800 hours @ $5.80/hr	780 hours @ $6.10/hr

a. Calculate the cloth covering price variance (1) at purchase and (2) when the materials are actually used.

b. Discuss why the two price variances calculated in part a above differ and which is superior (and why).

NP 14–8: Budgeted, Standard, and Actual Machine Hours (LO 6; NE 3)

The Toronto Engine Plant of Eastern Corporation manufactures engine blocks for automobiles. Three types of engine blocks are produced: four-, six-, and eight-cylinder blocks. An engine block is the basic component of an automobile engine and contains the cylinders into which the pistons are fitted. After assembling the block with the head, pan, pistons, spark plugs, rods, camshaft, and valves, the motor is ready to be fitted with the fuel and exhaust systems and installed in the automobile. The engine block is cast from a single block of steel. The cylinders are bored by high-precision computer-controlled machine tools, and then other machine tools tap and thread the block to attach the other engine components. The cylinder boring department is the key process after the engine block is cast.

Overhead is tracked to departments. The allocation base in the cylinder boring department is machine hours, or the number of hours each block spends in the computer-controlled machine tool having its cylinders bored. Each of the three motor blocks requires the following standard machine hours per block:

4-cylinder blocks	0.50 machine hours per block
6-cylinder blocks	0.70 machine hours per block
8-cylinder blocks	0.90 machine hours per block

Each block requires some setup time to mount and correctly position the block in the computer-controlled machine tool. Hence, an eight-cylinder block does not require twice the machining time of a four-cylinder block. Also, a cylinder in a four-cylinder block is larger and requires more boring time than does a cylinder in a six- or eight-cylinder block.

At the beginning of the year, management forecasts the number of blocks to be manufactured based on the projected unit sales of car models requiring four-, six-, and eight-cylinder engines. The plant plans to produce 95,000 engine blocks using 67,500 machine hours. The expected production by block type and the standard machine hours per block are given in the following table.

Calculation of Expected Usage of Machine Hours—Toronto Engine Plant's Cylinder Boring Department

Product	Expected Production	Standard Machine Hours per Block
4-cylinder blocks	25,000 blocks	0.50
6-cylinder blocks	40,000 blocks	0.70
8-cylinder blocks	30,000 blocks	0.90
	95,000 blocks	

Expected machine hours

During the year, production plans change as customer preferences become known. An unexpected increase in gasoline taxes causes consumers to shift toward smaller, more fuel-efficient automobiles with smaller engines. Fewer eight-cylinder engines are made and more four- and six-cylinder engines are manufactured. The following table presents the actual operating results for the year.

Calculation of Actual and Standard Machine Hours—Toronto Engine Plant's Cylinder Boring Department

Product	Actual Blocks Produced	Actual Machine Hours
4-cylinder	27,000	14,200
6-cylinder	41,000	29,000
8-cylinder	28,000	25,000
	96,000	68,200

What are the budgeted, standard, and actual machine hours?

NP 14–9: Expected, Standard, and Actual Volume and Volume Variance (LO 9; NE 3) (Appendix)   Printers, Inc., manufactures and sells a midvolume color printer (MC) and a high-volume color printer (HC). MCs require 100 direct labor hours to manufacture each printer and HCs require 150 direct labor hours. At the beginning of the year, 700 MCs are scheduled for production and 500 HCs are scheduled. At the end of the year, 720 MCs and 510 HCs were produced. Fourteen hundred hours too many were used in producing MCs and 3,000 hours fewer than standard were used to manufacture HCs. The flexible overhead budget is $2.9 million of fixed costs and $10 per direct labor hour.

Calculate

a. Expected volume.
b. Standard volume.
c. Actual volume.
d. Overhead rate.
e. Fixed overhead volume variance and discuss its meaning.

NP 14–10: Direct Variances (LO 3, 4; NE 1, 2)   ColdKing Company is a small producer of fruit-flavored frozen desserts. For many years, ColdKing's products have had strong regional sales on the basis of brand recognition. However, other companies have begun marketing similar products in the area, and price competition has become increasingly important. John Wakefield, the company's controller, is planning to implement a standard cost system for ColdKing and has gathered considerable information from his co-workers on production and materials requirements for ColdKing's products. Wakefield believes that the use of standard costing will allow ColdKing to improve cost control and make better pricing decisions.

ColdKing's most popular product is raspberry sherbet. The sherbet is produced in 10-gallon batches, and each batch requires six quarts of good raspberries. The fresh raspberries are sorted by hand before entering the production process. Because of imperfections in the raspberries and normal spoilage, one quart of berries is discarded for every four quarts of acceptable berries. Three minutes is the standard direct labor time for sorting that is required to obtain one quart of acceptable raspberries. The acceptable raspberries are then blended with the other ingredients; blending requires 12 minutes of direct labor time per batch. After blending, the sherbet is packaged in quart containers. Wakefield has gathered the following pricing information:

- ColdKing purchases raspberries at a cost of $0.80 per quart. All other ingredients cost a total of $4.50 per 10-gallon batch.
- Direct labor is paid at the rate of $9 per hour.

- The total cost of material and labor required to package the sherbet is $0.38 per quart.

a. Develop the standard cost for the direct cost components of a 10-gallon batch of raspberry sherbet. The standard cost should identify the
  (1) Standard quantity
  (2) Standard rate
  (3) Standard cost per batch
  for each direct cost component of a batch of raspberry sherbet.
b. As part of the implementation of a standard cost system at ColdKing, John Wakefield plans to train those responsible for maintaining the standards in the use of variance analysis. Wakefield is particularly concerned with the causes of unfavorable variances.
  (1) Discuss the possible causes of unfavorable materials price variances and identify the individual(s) who should be held responsible for these variances.
  (2) Discuss the possible causes of unfavorable labor efficiency variances and identify the individual(s) who should be held responsible for these variances.

(CMA adapted)

NP 14–11: Overhead Variances (LO 9) (Appendix)

Turow Trailers assembles horse trailers. Two models are manufactured, G7 and V8. While labor intensive, the production process is not very complicated. The single plant produces all the trailers. Forty-eight work teams of two or three workers assemble entire trailers. Sixteen foremen supervise the work teams. Material handlers deliver all the parts needed for each trailer to the work team. Personnel, accounting, inspection, purchasing, and tools are the other major overhead departments. Some operating statistics for 1994 and 1995 are provided below:

	1994	1995
Expected denominator volume (direct labor hours)	1 million	1 million
Flexible budget:		
Fixed overhead	$2.1 million	$2.2 million
Variable overhead per direct labor hour	$7	$8
Units produced:		
G7	11,000	8,000
V8	12,000	6,000
Standard direct labor hours per unit of:		
G7	40	40
V8	50	50
Actual variable overhead incurred	$7.0 million	$6.1 million
Actual fixed overhead incurred	$2.0 million	$2.0 million
Actual direct labor hours	1 million	0.7 million

a. Calculate all the overhead variances for both 1994 and 1995.
b. Discuss who in the plant should be held responsible for each of the overhead variances.

NP 14–12: Variance Calculations (LO 3, 4, 9; NE 1, 2) (Appendix)

Betterton Corporation manufactures automobile headlight lenses and uses a standard cost system. At the beginning of the year, the following standards were established per 100 lenses (a single batch).

	Input	Amount
Direct material	100 lbs. @ $2.00/lb.	$200
Direct labor	5 hours @ $18/hr.	90
Factory overhead:		
Fixed overhead	$4 per direct labor hour	20
Variable overhead	$6 per direct labor hour	30
Total cost per batch of 100 headlight lenses		$340

Expected volume per month is 5,000 direct labor hours for January and 105,000 headlight lenses were produced. There were no beginning inventories. The following costs were incurred in January:

Fixed factory overhead		$ 39,000
Variable factory overhead		$ 20,000
Direct labor	5,400 hours	$ 99,900
Direct material used	102,000 lbs.	
Direct material purchased	110,000 lbs.	$209,000

a. Calculate the following variances:
   (1) Variable overhead spending variance
   (2) Fixed overhead volume variance
   (3) Fixed overhead budget variance
   (4) Variable overhead efficiency variance
   (5) Direct materials price variance at purchase
   (6) Direct labor efficiency variance
   (7) Direct materials quantity variance
b. Discuss how the direct materials price variance computed at purchase differs from the direct materials price variance computed at use and the advantages and disadvantages of each.

NP 14–13: Fixed Overhead Volume Variance (LO 9) (Appendix)

Shady Tree produces two products, M1s and M2s. There are no beginning inventories or ending work-in-process inventories of either M1s or M2s. A single plantwide overhead rate is used to allocate overhead to products using standard direct labor hours. This overhead rate is set at the beginning of the year based on the following flexible budget: fixed factory overhead is forecast to be $3 million and variable overhead is projected to be $20 per direct labor hour. Management expects plant volume to be 200,000 standard direct labor hours. The following are the standard direct labor hours for each product:

SHADY TREE MANUFACTURING
Direct Labor Standards per Product

	M1	M2
Standard direct labor hours per unit	3	5

The variable overhead variances and fixed overhead budget variance for the year were zero. The following table summarizes operations for the year:

SHADY TREE MANUFACTURING
Summary of Operations for the Year

	M1	M2
Units produced	30,000	12,000
Units sold	20,000	10,000

a. Calculate the plantwide overhead rate computed at the beginning of the year.
b. Calculate the fixed overhead volume variance for the year.
c. What is the dollar impact on accounting earnings if the fixed overhead volume variance is written off to cost of goods sold?
d. What is the dollar impact on accounting earnings of prorating the fixed overhead volume variance to inventories and cost of goods sold compared to writing it off to cost of sales?
e. Suppose at the beginning of the year, management at Shady Tree Manufacturing wants to increase accounting earnings in a particular year without changing

production or sales levels. Describe how they might do this (assuming their external auditors would allow such action). Use the facts presented above to illustrate your answer.

NP 14–14: Variances and Absorption and Variable Costing (LO 3, 9)

The Mopart Division produces a single product. Its standard cost system incorporates flexible budgets and assigns indirect costs on the basis of standard direct labor hours. At the expected volume of 4,000 direct labor hours, the standard cost per unit is as follows:

Selling price	$38.00
Direct materials, 3 lb. @ $5	$15.00
Direct labor, 0.4 hr. @ $20	8.00
Variable indirect costs, 0.4 hr @ $6	2.40
Fixed indirect costs, 0.4 hr @ $4	1.60
Total	$27.00

For the month of March, the following actual data were reported:

Units produced	9,000.00
Number of direct labor hours	3,800.00
Actual wage rate	$ 20.50
Direct materials used (pounds)	28,000.00
Average price of materials used	$ 5.50
Average selling price	$ 38.75
Number of units sold	8,800.00
Variable indirect costs	$21,500.00
Fixed indirect costs	$15,800.00
Variable selling & administrative costs	$34,500.00
Fixed selling & administrative costs	$28,000.00

There was no beginning inventory.

a. Analyze the results of operations for the month of March. Support your analysis with both reason and data. Exposition and easy-to-follow tables count.
b. Present two income statements in good format using absorption costing and variable costing net income.
c. Reconcile any difference in net income between the two statements.
d. What is the opportunity cost of the unused normal capacity?

NP 14–15: Variance Calculations (LO 3, 4, 9; NE 1, 2) (Appendix)

Anpax, Inc., manufactures two products, L7 and Q2. Overhead is allocated to products based on machine hours. Management uses a flexible budget to forecast overhead. For the current year, fixed factory overhead is projected to be $2.75 million and variable factory overhead is budgeted at $20 per machine hour. At the beginning of the year, management developed the following standards for each product and made the following production forecasts for the year:

ANPAX, INC.
Current Year Standards and Production Forecasts

	Products	
	L7	Q2
Budgeted number of units produced	25,000	35,000
Production standards:		
Direct labor per unit	10 hours @ $15/hour	12 hours @ $15/hour
Direct materials per unit	85 lb. @ $1/lb	95 lb @ $1/lb
Machine hours per unit	4 hours	5 hours

There were no beginning or ending inventories. Actual production for the year was 20,000 units of L7 and 40,000 units of Q2. Other data summarizing actual operations for the year are given below:

Direct labor	700,000 hours	$9.8 million
Direct materials	5.0 million lbs.	$5.5 million
Machine hours	270,000 hours	
Fixed overhead	$3.4 million	
Variable overhead	$5 million	

a. Calculate the fixed overhead rate for the current year.
b. Calculate materials and labor variances. Report only quantity (efficiency) variances and price variances.
c. Calculate the overhead variances.
d. Your boss (a nonaccountant) asks you to explain in nontechnical terms the meaning of each overhead variance.

Discussion Problems

DP 14–1: Criticism of Standard Cost Variances (LO 1, 2)   Critically evaluate the following quotation:

> More research is needed to explain the tenacity with which businesses cling to accounting performance information. More empirical research into the consequences of managing information is also in order, but there already is much evidence that businesses impair their competitiveness and profitability today by managing with the information found in standard cost variances, flexible budgets, product costs, return on investment, and more. Less well understood is why 'world-class' manufacturing companies persist in using accounting-based financial performance measures.

[Source: H. T. Johnson, "Performance Measurement for Competitive Excellence," *Measure for Manufacturing Excellence*, ed. R. Kaplan (Boston: Harvard Business School Press, 1990), p. 84.]

DP 14–2: Labor Efficiency Ratio (LO 2, 5)   A number of companies use the following ratio to measure operating efficiency:

$$\frac{\text{Earned direct labor dollars}}{\text{Actual direct labor dollars}}$$

Earned direct labor dollars are the number of units produced times the standard direct labor dollars per hour. For example, the machine department produced four jobs today:

Job #	Number of Units Produced	Standard Labor Dollars per Unit	Earned Direct Labor Dollars
101	100	$3	$ 300
102	200	2	400
103	150	1	150
104	100	2	200
Total earned direct labor dollars			$1,050

Actual direct labor dollars for today are $1,350.

$$\frac{\text{Earned direct labor dollars}}{\text{Actual direct labor dollars}} = \frac{1,050}{1,350} = 0.777$$

The higher the ratio, the more output per actual direct labor dollar. Operating managers are rewarded for high values of this ratio. Discuss the advantages and disadvantages of using this ratio to measure and reward performance of factory management.

DP 14–3: Setting Standard Costs (LO 2)   Associated Media Graphics (AMG) is a rapidly expanding company involved in the mass reproduction of instructional materials. AMG is organized into a number of production departments responsible for a particular stage of the production process, such as copyediting, typesetting, printing, and binding. An engineering department provides technical assistance to the various production units. Ralph Davis, owner and manager of AMG, has made a concentrated effort to provide a quality product at a competitive price with delivery on the promised due date. Expanding sales have been attributed to this philosophy. Davis is finding it increasingly difficult to supervise personally the operations of AMG and is beginning to institute an organizational structure that would facilitate management control.

One change recently made was the designation of operating departments as cost centers, with control over departmental operations transferred from Davis to each departmental manager. However, quality control still reports directly to Davis, as do the finance and accounting functions. A materials manager was hired to purchase all raw materials and to oversee the inventory handling (receiving, storage, etc.) and record-keeping functions. The materials manager is also responsible for maintaining an adequate inventory based upon planned production levels.

The loss of personal control over the operations of AMG caused Davis to look for a method of efficiently evaluating performance. Dave Cress, a new cost accountant, proposed the use of a standard cost system. Variances for material, labor, and manufacturing overhead could then be calculated and reported directly to Davis.

a. Assume that Associated Media Graphics (AMG) is going to implement a standard cost system and establish standards for materials, labor, and manufacturing overhead. Identify and discuss for each of these cost components:
    (1) Who should be involved in setting the standards.
    (2) The factors that should be considered in establishing the standards.
b. Describe the basis for assignment of responsibility under a standard cost system.

(CMA adapted)

DP 14–4: Standard Overhead Rates (LO 9)   Spectra, Inc., produces personal computer color monitors. The firm makes 19-inch monitors with the following cost structure:

Direct materials	$220
Direct labor	$150

Because of the rapidly changing market for computer monitors, standard costs, overhead rates, and prices are revised quarterly. While the direct labor component of standard cost has been relatively constant over time, direct material costs, especially the cost of the circuit boards, fluctuate widely. Therefore, for pricing purposes, management reviews costs each quarter and forecasts next quarter's costs using the current quarter's cost structure. They also use this method for revising overhead costs each quarter. Overhead is applied to products using direct labor cost. Fixed overhead is incurred fairly uniformly over the year. The overhead rate next quarter is the ratio of actual overhead costs incurred this quarter divided by this quarter's direct labor cost. Data for the last six quarters are:

	1995				1996		
	Q1	Q2	Q3	Q4	Q1	Q2	Q3
Actual unit sales	200	200	190	180	190	250	
Total direct labor	$ 30,000	$ 30,000	$28,500	$27,000	$28,500	$ 37,500	
Actual overhead	$101,000	$102,000	$98,000	$95,000	$97,000	$118,000	
Overhead rate	$3.35	$3.37	$3.40	$3.43	$3.52	$3.40	$3.15

The president of the company, responding to the auditor's suggestion that they set their projected costs on an annual basis, replied: "Annual budgeting is fine for more static companies like automobiles. But the computer industry, especially peripherals, changes day by day. We have to be ahead of our competitors in terms of changing our product price in response to cost changes. If we waited eight months to react to cost changes, we'd be out of business."

Do you agree with the president or the auditor? Critically evaluate Spectra's costing system. What changes would you suggest, and how would you justify them to the president?

DP 14–5: Overhead Variances (LO 2, 9)

Western Sugar processes sugar beets into granulated sugar that is sold to food companies. They use a standard cost system to aid in the control of costs and for performance evaluation. To compute the standards for next year, the actual expense incurred by expense category is divided by the bushels of sugar beets processed to arrive at a standard cost per bushel. These per bushel standards are then increased by the expected amount of inflation forecast for that expense category. This year, Western Sugar processed 63 million bushels of beets. The calculation of next year's standard costs are:

WESTERN SUGAR
Standard Costs for Next Year
(thousands of dollars)

	This Year's Cost	Cost per Bushel	Inflation Adjustment	Standard Cost per Bushel
Direct labor	$ 33,000	$0.524	4%	0.544
Sugar beets	58,000	0.921	3.5%	0.953
Variable overhead	24,000	0.381	5%	0.400
Fixed overhead	43,000	0.683	2%	0.696
Total	$158,000	$2.509		$2.593

Next year, actual production is 68 million bushels. At the end of next year, the following report is prepared:

WESTERN SUGAR
Actual Result Compared to Standard Next Year
(thousands of dollars)

	Actual Cost	Standard Cost per Bushel	Standard Cost	Variance
Direct labor	$ 38,100	$0.544	$ 36,992	1,108U
Sugar beets	64,829	.953	64,804	25U
Variable overhead	28,211	.400	27,200	1,011U
Fixed overhead	45,227	.696	47,328	2,101F
Total	$176,367	$2.593	$176,324	$43U

Senior management was not surprised at the small variances for labor and sugar beets. The processing plant has very good operating controls and there had been no surprises in the sugar beet market or in the labor market. Their initial forecasts proved to be good. They were delighted to see the favorable total overhead variance ($1,090F = $1,011U + $2,101F). Although variable overhead was over budget, fixed overhead which was below budget more than offset the over-budget variable overhead. There was no major change in the plant's production technology to explain this shift (such as increased automation), and therefore senior management was prepared to attribute the favorable total overhead variance to better internal control by the plant manager.

a. What do you think is the reason for the overhead variances?
b. Is it appropriate to base next year's standards on last year's costs?

CASES

C 14–1: Volume Measures

The gear cutting department of Universal Transmissions cuts the teeth into gears. These gears are then finished in other departments and assembled into farm and construction equipment transmissions (tractors, combines, bulldozers). The department contains three identical cutting machines that were purchased two years ago. Each machine is expected to be used 2,400 hours a year. The production budget for the year is:

Gear Cutting Department
Budgeted Production
For 1/1/96–12/31/96

Gear Type	Budgeted Production (No. of gears)	Standard Minutes/Gear	Budgeted Minutes
A7474	965	36	34,740
B7682	290	21	6,090
C4983	993	24	23,832
D7575	514	44	22,616
F8390	733	39	28,587
H6363	547	54	29,538
H8983	989	32	31,648
J3839	354	33	11,682
K9828	546	52	28,392
L2738	922	48	44,256
L7378	494	26	12,844
L9383	313	11	3,443
M7483	199	52	10,348
M8992	950	50	47,500
Q2839	423	52	21,996
R093	588	37	21,756
S2829	719	45	32,355
S2882	488	25	12,200
T8390	373	57	21,261
U1920	185	34	6,290
Y7382	647	37	23,939
Total			475,313

The operating budget for the Gear Cutting Department for 1996 is:

Gear Cutting Department
Operating Budget
For 1/1/96–12/31/96

	Fixed Costs	Variable Costs/ Machine Hour
Cutting oil		$ 3.21
Depreciation	$ 632,000	
Engineering	232,890	
Maintenance	69,840	4.56
Operators	25,400	36.34
Plant overhead	124,400	1.20
Utilities	26,800	2.21
Total	$1,111,330	$47.52

Costs in the Gear Cutting Department are assigned to gears based on standard gear-cutting machine minutes. At the beginning of the year, the cost per minute on the gear-cutting machines is set by dividing budgeted costs in the department (budgeted fixed costs plus budgeted variable costs per machine minute times projected minutes for the year) by projected minutes for the year. The following table summarizes actual operations by gear type:

Gear Cutting Department
Summary of Operations
For 1/1/96–12/31/96

Gear	Actual Production	Standard Minutes/Gear	Standard Minutes of Volume	Actual Minutes of Volume	% Variance Actual from Standard
A7474	1,041	36	37,476	41,528	11%
B7682	304	21	6,384	6,160	−4%
C4983	937	24	22,488	24,671	10%
D7575	543	44	23,892	26,359	10%
F8390	724	39	28,236	29,546	5%
H6363	544	54	29,376	26,970	−8%
H8983	958	32	30,656	29,631	−3%
J3839	331	33	10,923	10,142	−7%
K9828	596	52	30,992	28,823	−7%
L2738	1,007	48	48,336	49,494	2%
L7378	536	26	13,936	14,484	4%
L9383	335	11	3,685	3,936	7%
M7483	208	52	10,816	10,657	−1%
M8992	1,020	50	51,000	55,543	9%
Q2839	462	52	24,024	23,125	−4%
R093	603	37	22,311	22,761	2%
S2829	675	45	30,375	28,110	−7%
S2882	447	25	11,175	12,371	11%
T8390	351	57	20,007	19,989	0%
U1920	191	34	6,494	6,332	−2%
Y7382	585	37	21,645	20,167	−7%
Total			484,227	490,799	

Case Questions

a. Identify all the various measures of volume (e.g., actual volume) that can be used in the Gear Cutting Department for 1996. For each volume measure identified, provide the 1996 empirical magnitude.

b. Calculate the cost per minute in the Gear Cutting Department for 1996.

c. An outside company offers to provide gear cutting for gear #A7474 for $63 per gear. This includes pick-up and delivery and they guarantee the same quality and timeliness of delivery as the Gear Cutting Department. Analyze the outside offer and make a recommendation as to whether or not the offer should be accepted. Be sure to identify any assumptions underlying your recommendation.

C 14–2: Direct Material Variance Analysis

Maidwell Company manufactures washers and dryers on a single assembly line in its main factory. The market has deteriorated over the last five years and competition has made cost control very important. Management has been concerned about the materials cost of both washers and dryers. There have been no model changes in the past two years and economic conditions have allowed the company to negotiate price reductions for many key parts.

Maidwell uses a standard cost system in accounting for materials. Purchases are charged to inventory at a standard price, and purchase discounts are considered an administrative cost reduction. Production is charged at the standard price of the materials used. Thus, the price variance is isolated at time of purchase as the difference between gross contract price and standard price multiplied by the quantity purchased. When a substitute part is used in production rather than the regular part, a price variance equal to the difference in the standard prices of the materials is recognized at the time of substitution in the production process. The quantity variance is the actual quantity used compared to the standard quantity allowed with the difference multiplied by the standard price.

The materials variances for several of the parts Maidwell uses are unfavorable. Part No. 4121 is one of the items that has an unfavorable variance. Maidwell knows that some of these parts are defective and will fail. The failure is discovered during production. The normal defective rate is 5% of normal input. The original contract price of this part was $0.285 per unit; thus, Maidwell set the standard unit price at $0.285. The unit contract purchase price of Part No. 4121 was increased $0.04 to $0.325 from the original $0.285 due to a parts specification change. Maidwell chose not to change the standard, but treated the increase in price as a price variance. In addition, the contract terms were changed from payment due in 30 days to a 4% discount if paid in 10 days or full payment due in 30 days. These new contractual terms were the consequence of negotiations resulting from changes in the economy.

Data regarding the usage of Part No. 4121 during December is as follows:

Purchases of Part No. 4121	150,000 units
Unit price paid for purchases of Part No. 4121	$0.325
Requisitions of Part No. 4121 from stores for use in products	134,000 units
Substitution of Part No. 5125 for Part No. 4121 to use obsolete stock (standard unit price of Part No. 5125 is $0.35)	24,000 units
Units of Part No. 4121 and its substitute (Part No. 5125) identified as being defective	9,665 units
Standard allowed usage (including normal defective units) of Part No. 4121 and its substitute based upon output for the month	153,300 units

Maidwell's material variances related to Part No. 4121 for December were reported as follows:

Price variance	$7,560.00 Unfavorable
Quantity variance	1,339.50 Unfavorable
Total materials variances for Part No. 4121	$8,899.50 Unfavorable

Bob Speck, the purchasing director, claims the unfavorable price variance is misleading. Speck says that his department has worked hard to obtain price concessions and purchase discounts from suppliers. In addition, Speck has indicated that engineering changes have been made in several parts increasing their price even though the part identification has not changed. These price increases are not his department's responsibility. Speck declares that price variances no longer measure the Purchasing Department's performance.

Jim Buddle, the manufacturing manager, thinks the responsibility for the quantity variance should be shared. Buddle states that manufacturing cannot control quality associated with less expensive parts, substitutions of material to use up otherwise obsolete stock, or engineering changes that increase the quantity of materials used.

The accounting manager, Mike Kohl, has suggested that the computation of variances be changed to identify variations from standard with the causes and functional areas responsible for the variances. The following system of materials variances and the method of computation for each was recommended by Kohl.

Variance	Method of Calculation
Economics variance	Quantity purchased times the changes made after setting standards. Standards were the result of negotiations based on changes in the general economy.
Engineering change variance	Quantity purchased times change in price due to part specifications changes.
Purchase price variance	Quantity purchased times change in contract price due to changes other than parts specifications or the general economy.
Substitutions variance	Quantity substituted times the difference in standard price between parts substituted.
Excess usage variance	Standard price times the difference between the standard quantity allowed for production minus actual parts used (reduced for abnormal scrap).
Abnormal failure rate variance	Abnormal scrap times standard price.

Case Questions

a. Discuss the appropriateness of Maidwell Company's current method of variance analysis for materials and indicate whether the claims of Bob Speck and Jim Buddle are valid.

b. Compute the materials variances for Part No. 4121 for December using the system recommended by Mike Kohl.

c. Indicate who would be responsible for each of the variances in Mike Kohl's system of variance analysis for materials.

(CMA adapted)

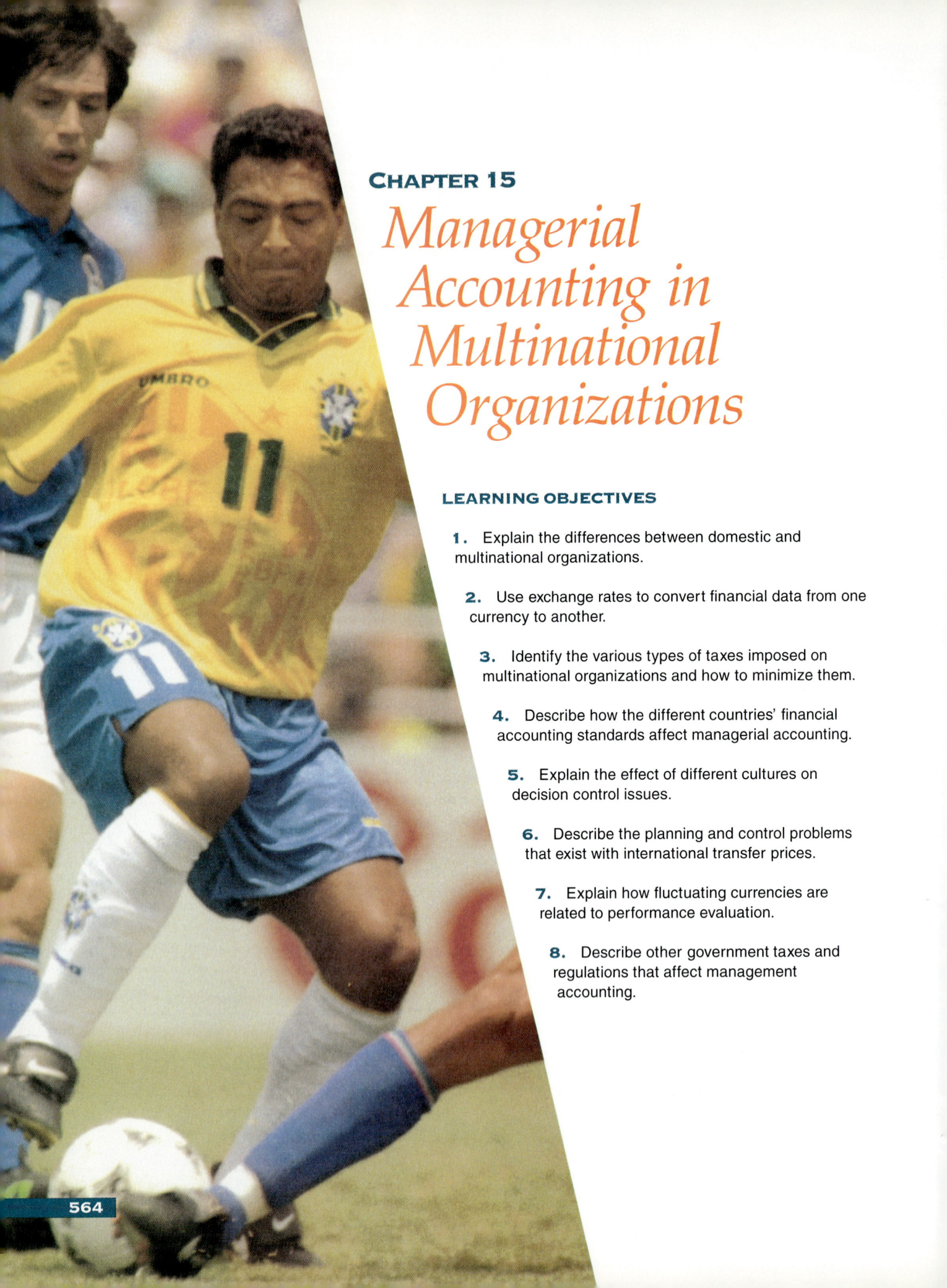

CHAPTER 15
Managerial Accounting in Multinational Organizations

LEARNING OBJECTIVES

1. Explain the differences between domestic and multinational organizations.

2. Use exchange rates to convert financial data from one currency to another.

3. Identify the various types of taxes imposed on multinational organizations and how to minimize them.

4. Describe how the different countries' financial accounting standards affect managerial accounting.

5. Explain the effect of different cultures on decision control issues.

6. Describe the planning and control problems that exist with international transfer prices.

7. Explain how fluctuating currencies are related to performance evaluation.

8. Describe other government taxes and regulations that affect management accounting.

SOCCER STARS

Ramon Perez and John Williams were college roommates and All-American soccer players in college in southern California. Ramon is from Mexico City and John from Los Angeles. After graduation they played professional soccer and made their respective national teams. They remained close friends and decided to become partners in a soccer-related business. In 1994 they formed a company called Soccer Stars that had two retail stores, one in Mexico City and the other in Los Angeles. To capitalize on the growing interest in soccer and the contacts they made playing soccer, Ramon and John pay soccer stars to sign various collectibles such as photographs, soccer balls, trading cards, hats, and so forth. Then Soccer Stars sells the autographed items in their retail stores in Mexico City and Los Angeles.

Soccer Stars is incorporated in Mexico with a U.S. wholly owned subsidiary, the Los Angeles store. Ramon operates the Mexico City store and John the Los Angeles store. Both Ramon and John secure autographs from soccer players when their teams are in town. For example, when the Italian team was playing in Los Angeles, John paid three top stars $50 for each signature. Each one signed 40 soccer balls. John paid $6,000 [$50 × 3 × 40] for these autographs. The 40 balls cost an additional $320. Thus, the total cost for the autographed items was $6,320. Twenty-five of the autographed balls were shipped to the Mexico City store and the remainder are for sale in the Los Angeles store.

Ramon and John each draw a salary from Soccer Stars and split the remaining profit equally. Ramon draws his salary in Mexican pesos and John's salary is in U.S. dollars. When John and Ramon set the respective wages, one peso was worth $0.18; or, 5.5555 pesos were worth one dollar.

$$1 \text{ peso} = \$0.18$$

$$\frac{1}{\$0.18} = 5.5555 \text{ pesos per dollar}$$

$$5.5555 \text{ pesos} = \$1.00$$

(The symbol for the Mexican peso is Ps. Thus, 10 pesos is denoted as Ps10.) This year Ramon's salary is Ps160,000 and John's is $28,800 U.S. (Ps160,000 × $0.18). Thus, John and Ramon were each drawing equivalent value salaries when the peso was worth $0.18.

Last year, Ramon's salary was Ps160,000. But since the peso was worth $0.20 last year, John's salary was $32,000 (Ps160,000 × $0.20). John and Ramon are discussing various ways of dealing with the fluctuations in the peso-dollar exchange rate and the effects these fluctuations are having on their business.

15.1 International Trade and Multinational Organizations

Trade is now expanding worldwide. More and more of the goods and services we buy are from outside our borders and more of our goods and services are purchased by foreign buyers. Look at the clothes you are wearing. Most of them are produced overseas. Shoes are made in Singapore, T-shirts in Guatemala, jeans in South Korea, and baseball caps in Costa Rica. Even though the clothes are manufactured outside the United States, they are sold by U.S. companies such as Nike and Starter. Pizza Huts, McDonalds, and Burger Kings have stores stretching from Beijing to Cape Town. Microsoft software products are universally used. There are few cities in the world where you cannot buy a roll of Kodak film or receive CNN and MTV broadcasts.

There are a variety of ways firms become involved in international trade. The simplest form of international trade is through an import or export transaction. For example, an American wine store wants to purchase German wine to sell in the U.S. There are several methods of obtaining the German wine. The wine store can purchase wine directly from the German winery, purchase the wine from an American importer, or purchase the German winery and send some of the German wine to the American wine store. Each method of purchasing German wine has its own advantages and disadvantages in terms of contracting and transaction costs.

The cost of importing these German wines into the U.S. depends on whether they are imported through a wine agent or purchased directly from the German winery.

Purchasing directly from the German winery requires the American wine store to negotiate contracts with the owners of the German winery. The American wine store will also have to arrange shipping and prepare the appropriate paperwork for importing the wine into the United States. Import tariffs must be paid to the U.S. government. The American wine store may also have to pay in German marks. These procedures would be too costly if the American wine store only wanted to buy a few cases of wine.

Purchasing through an American wine importer reduces the contracting and transaction costs. The wine importer negotiates contracts with the German winery, arranges all the necessary import paperwork, and pays all the import tariffs. The American wine store pays the American wine importer in U.S. dollars. The main disadvantage of using a wine importer is the higher price that must be paid for the wine.

Another method of buying German wine is for the American wine shop to buy the German winery and ship some of the wine to the U.S. Purchasing the German winery alleviates the need to negotiate over wine prices, but other contracting and transaction costs exist. The American wine store must manage the German winery by hiring German nationals to manage the winery or send American managers over to Germany. The American owners must learn German customs, political constraints, and possibly learn to speak German to effectively oversee its German employees. In addition, the German winery is operating with German marks. Internal performance measures and contracts with vendors may be in German marks even though the American wine store wants to maximize profit in U.S. dollars.

Purchasing the German winery does have many advantages. The American wine store is assured a long-term supply of wine and has more control over quality. Owning the German winery allows for greater control over costs.

If the benefits outweigh the costs and the American wine shop buys the German winery, the wine shop becomes a multinational organization. A **multinational firm** is an organization that has operating units, such as manufacturing plants, retail outlets, or distribution warehouses, in more than one country. A company importing or exporting goods is not a multinational firm because it only has an operating unit in one country. Multinational firms exist because they find it is less costly to contract across international borders within the same organization than through markets. For example, Ford profits by selling cars in Canada that are manufactured and assembled in Canada instead of manufacturing all the cars in the United States and exporting some of them to Canada. By having manufacturing plants in both the United States and Canada (as well as other countries), Ford is a multinational firm.

This chapter describes how managerial accounting changes when the firm becomes multinational. The managerial accounting system must adapt to differences in currencies, taxing authorities, accounting standards for external reporting, and cultures. These differences create additional complexities for making planning decisions and control. In this chapter we examine these differences and how they affect transfer pricing and performance evaluation.

SOCCER STARS (CONTINUED)

Soccer Stars is a multinational firm because it has operating units in two separate countries (Mexico and the United States). Being a multinational firm, Soccer Stars must transact in both Mexican pesos and U.S. dollars, pay taxes in two different countries, deal with different financial accounting requirements, and respond to different cultural factors.

568 *Managerial Accounting in Multinational Organizations*

CONCEPT REVIEW

1. Describe various ways firms can engage in international trade.
2. What is a multinational organization and how does it differ from a domestic organization that imports or exports products?

15.2 Different Currencies

Each country has its own monetary system with its own currency. For example, the United States has the dollar, Mexico the peso, Britain the pound, and Brazil the cruzeiro. Even though Canada and Australia call their currency the "dollar," a Canadian dollar is different from an Australian dollar and both differ from a U.S. dollar.

Each country has it own currency because each country's government prints and controls its own money supply. The U.S. government prints dollars that are used to settle transactions in the United States. A U.S. merchant does not have to accept 20 Australian dollars for a shirt costing U.S. $20 because an Australian dollar is not legal tender for transactions in the United States. If the merchant accepted Australian dollars for the sale, she would have to convert the Australian dollars into U.S. dollars in order to purchase other goods in the United States. And 20 Australian dollars do not convert to U.S. $20.

Exchange Rates

The price at which one currency can be converted to another currency is called an **exchange rate.** They are the rates large international banks are willing to exchange one currency for another. Banks charge a fee for this service. Table 15.1 lists the exchange rates between U.S. dollars and other major currencies as reported in *The Wall Street Journal* on June 13, 1996.

There are two columns in this table for each currency. The first column of numbers is the value of one unit of the foreign currency in U.S. dollars. For example, the Australian dollar is worth 79 cents in U.S. dollars. The second column is how many foreign currency units is equal to one U.S. dollar. From this table

In the Bank of Tokyo's foreign exchange trading room, clients call the bank's traders to buy or sell foreign currencies. Traders locate someone else willing to trade the same currency and arrange for the exchange. All of this occurs in seconds via computers.

TABLE 15.1

Foreign Exchange Rates for One U.S. Dollar (as of 6/13/96)

	U.S. Dollar Equivalent	Currency per U.S. $
Australia (dollar)	0.79	1.26
Britain (pound)	1.53	0.65
Canada (dollar)	0.73	1.37
China (renminbi)	0.12	8.34
France (franc)	0.19	5.12
Germany (mark)	0.65	1.53
Hong Kong (dollar)	0.13	7.74
India (rupee)	0.03	34.94
Israel (shekel)	0.31	3.27
Italy (lira)	0.0006	1547
Japan (yen)	0.009	109
Mexico (peso)	0.13	7.59
Netherlands (guilder)	0.58	1.72
Poland (zloty)	0.37	2.72
South Korea (won)	0.001	794
Switzerland (franc)	0.79	1.26

(the second column of numbers), we see that one U.S. dollar converts to about 1.26 Australian dollars, about 5.12 French francs, about 1,547 Italian lira, about 109 Japanese yen, or about 794 South Korea wons. Notice, we use the term "about" because these exchange rates fluctuate constantly in world markets depending on the demand and supply for currencies. If you travel to Italy and use a credit card to make purchases, Visa/MasterCard automatically converts your charges in lira to U.S. dollars using the exchange rate on the day of the charge. Thus, foreign charges made on several different days will be converted at slightly different exchange rates.

Organizations use published exchange rates to estimate the cost of a product or service made in another country. For example, suppose a Swiss organization wants to buy an American car that costs US$20,000. Using the exchange rates in Table 15.1, the car should cost the Swiss organization (1.26 Swiss francs per US$)(US$20,000), or 25,200 Swiss francs. If the Swiss organization waits another month before buying the American car, the exchange rate most likely will change. Exchange rates usually are subject to the supply and demand for the currencies. If more people want Swiss francs than U.S. dollars, the U.S. dollar will lose value relative to the Swiss franc. The exchange rate will change so that U.S.$1 will be worth less Swiss francs, say, 1.16 Swiss francs per U.S.$. Then the American car will cost the Swiss organization (1.16 Swiss francs per US$)(US$20,000), or 23,200 Swiss francs. To convert from one currency to another, use the exchange rate where the numerator is the currency you are converting to and the denominator is the currency you are converting from.

NUMERICAL EXAMPLE 15.1

A shirt made in the U.S. costs U.S.$20. What is the cost of the shirt in South Korean won and Italian lira using the exchange rates in Table 15.1?

■ **SOLUTION** The cost of the shirt in South Korean won is (794 won per U.S.$)(U.S.$20), or 15,880 won. The cost of the shirt in Italian lira is (1,547 lira per U.S.$)(U.S.$20), or 30,940 lira.

If an organization desires to exchange other currencies into U.S. dollars, the first column of numbers is used. One German mark is worth 0.65 U.S. dollars. Notice that each column of numbers is roughly the inverse of the other column. Except for small transaction costs, dollars can be converted to another currency or that currency can be converted to dollars by taking the inverse (dividing into one) of the exchange rates in Table 15.1. For example, the exchange rate of 1.53 German marks per U.S.$ is equivalent to 1.53 German marks per U.S.$, or U.S.$0.65 per German mark.

NUMERICAL EXAMPLE 15.2

A U.S. organization wants to buy cloth from India that costs 800,000 Indian rupees. What is the cost in U.S. dollars using the exchange rates in Table 15.1?

■ **SOLUTION** The exchange rate of Indian rupees into U.S. dollars is U.S.$0.03 per Indian rupee. The cost of the cloth is (U.S.$0.03 per Indian rupee)(800,000 Indian rupees), or approximately U.S.$24,000.

An important cornerstone of this book is the concept of opportunity cost. Foreign currency exchange rates are good examples of opportunity costs. Suppose you are in Hong Kong when one U.S. dollar can be converted to 7.7 Hong Kong dollars. You are standing outside a restaurant and deciding whether to enter and eat a meal for 77 Hong Kong dollars. What are you forgoing by eating? You forgo 77 Hong Kong dollars. But you acquired these Hong Kong dollars by converting $10 U.S. dollars into Hong Kong currency. The opportunity cost of the meal is the U.S.$10 you gave up to acquire the Hong Kong currency.

Managerial Importance of Exchange Rates

Exchange rates are extremely important for a country's economy. If exchange rates change to make a country's currency more valuable, the currency is said to appreciate. The appreciation of a country's currency makes its goods more expensive for foreign customers and imports of foreign goods cheaper for domestic consumers. Domestic consumers are made better off when their country's currency appreciates, but domestic producers of exports are harmed because the cost of their products in foreign markets is higher.

WHAT'S HAPPENING

Interest rates on 10-year government bonds in Italy are 13% and in the United States interest rates on comparable government bonds are 7%. Why would anyone invest in U.S. government bonds at 7% if they can invest at 13% in Italy? (Note: assume there is no difference in default risk between U.S. and Italian government bonds.)

Fluctuating foreign exchange rates have many important implications for managers of multinational firms. Many multinational firms have manufacturing facilities located in different countries. In this way, if a particular foreign currency appreciates in value, thereby increasing the export cost of the manufactured goods, the multinational can shift production to countries whose currencies have not appreciated. Likewise, if labor rates fall in one country relative to another country, the multinational can shift production to the country with the relative decline in labor rates, assuming other costs, quality, and exchange rates remain unchanged. Thus, managers of multinational firms seeking to produce the best products at the lowest possible costs constantly monitor exchange rate movements.

Multinational organizations face a number of issues arising from having operations spanning different currencies. Not only is cash management more difficult because multiple currencies are involved, but performance evaluation and transfer pricing are more complicated. For example, does the firm maintain a single-currency accounting system to evaluate all its foreign subsidiaries, and if so, which currency is used? Is all performance evaluation reported in a single currency or is each operating unit's performance reported in its domestic currency? These and other management accounting questions are addressed in later sections of this chapter.

Soccer Stars (continued)

> Soccer Stars ended the year with a profit in each store after paying both Ramon and John their salaries. At that time, the exchange rate was 6 pesos to the dollar. The Mexico City store reported profits of Ps102,000 and the Los Angeles store had profits of $13,000. The Los Angeles store's profits of $13,000 is equivalent to Ps78,000 ($13,000 × 6 pesos per dollar). Thus, Soccer Stars' total profits are Ps180,000 which are split evenly between the two partners, each receiving Ps90,000. But John doesn't want pesos, he wants dollars. John's Ps90,000 profits is equivalent to $15,000. But his store only made $13,000 in profits. So, Ramon must send John another $2,000. Therefore, Ramon must convert Ps12,000 into $2,000 by going to his local bank and selling Ps12,000 to receive a $2,000 check he can send to John. After this transaction, Ramon has Ps90,000 remaining from his profits (Ps102,000 − Ps12,000) and John has $15,000, which is equivalent to Ps90,000.

CONCEPT REVIEW

1. Why can't Canadian dollars be used to make purchases in the United States?
2. What is an exchange rate?
3. What does it mean when one currency appreciates against another currency?

15.3 Multiple Taxing Authorities

Companies engaged in international trade face a variety of taxes levied by multiple taxing authorities. Each country in which the multinational operates has the opportunity to impose taxes on the multinational. Minimizing the various taxes is an important consideration in making management decisions. Three of the most important taxes facing multinational organizations are corporate income taxes, value-added taxes, and tariffs. The corporate income tax is discussed in this section and value-added taxes and tariffs are described in the appendix.

Each country in which the multinational corporation operates taxes the income of the corporation. Each country's corporate income tax laws are different. In general, however, multinationals are taxed on the income generated in each country in which they operate. For example, Ford car plants in Canada are taxed on the income their plants generate in Canada even though Ford headquarters are in the United States.

NUMERICAL EXAMPLE 15.3

Ajax, an international corporation, operates in two countries, France and Spain, and has profits in both—$100,000 in France and $200,000 in Spain. Both countries' profits have been converted to U.S. dollars to simplify the example. Suppose France has a corporate income tax rate of 25% and Spain 35%. If each country only taxes that portion of Ajax's income earned in its jurisdiction, what is Ajax's total tax payment?

■ **SOLUTION** Ajax's total tax payment is $95,000 calculated as follows:

	France	Spain	Total
Income earned in country	$100,000	$200,000	$300,000
Corporate tax rate	25%	35%	
Taxes paid	$ 25,000	$ 70,000	$ 95,000

If each country only taxes the income earned in its country, income is only taxed once. In deciding what portion of the organization's profit is associated with each country in Numerical Example 15.3, Ajax has an incentive to shift income from Spain, where it is taxed at 35%, to France, where income is taxed at only 25%. One way to do this is via corporate cost allocation. The next example illustrates how cost allocations can lower worldwide taxes.

NUMERICAL EXAMPLE 15.4

In calculating the income earned in both the French and Spanish companies in Numerical Example 15.3, corporate headquarters costs of $80,000 were allocated to the two subsidiaries. Corporate headquarters costs consist of Ajax's chief executive officer and all of her expenses. She oversees and coordinates the operations in both countries. Based on the tax laws in France and Spain, these headquarters staff costs can be allocated to the subsidiaries and deducted from income before calculating income taxes. The tax laws allow either number of employees in each country or total sales in each country to be used to allocate headquarters costs. The following table provides data on these two allocation bases.

	France	Spain	Total
Number of employees	30	30	60
Percent employees	50%	50%	100%
Allocated headquarters costs	$ 40,000	$ 40,000	$ 80,000
Revenues	$900,000	$2,700,000	$3,600,000
Percent revenue	25%	75%	100%
Allocated headquarters costs	$ 20,000	$ 60,000	$ 80,000

In calculating the income earned in each country in Numerical Example 15.3, Ajax used number of employees. What is the effect on taxes if revenues are used to allocate corporate headquarters expense instead of number of employees?

■ **SOLUTION** The following table illustrates the effects of changing allocation bases on taxes.

	France	Spain	Total
Allocated costs (employees)	$40,000	$40,000	$80,000
Allocated costs (revenues)	$20,000	$60,000	$80,000
Increase (decrease) in taxable income	$20,000	($20,000)	0
Corporate tax rate	25%	35%	
Increase (decrease) in taxes	$ 5,000	($ 7,000)	($ 2,000)

If instead of using number of employees as the allocation base, Ajax uses revenues, the French company's expenses fall by $20,000 and its taxable income rises by $20,000. At a 25% tax rate, the French company pays $5,000 more in taxes. However, the Spanish company's allocated costs rise by $20,000 and hence its taxable income falls by $20,000. The Spanish company's tax bill falls by $7,000 ($20,000 × 35%). The net result is Ajax saves $2,000 in taxes. Every dollar cost shifted from France to Spain causes $0.10 to be saved in taxes (35% − 25%). Since $20,000 was shifted by changing the cost allocations between France and Spain, the company saved $2,000 in taxes.

SOCCER STARS (CONTINUED)

Soccer Stars incurred legal costs of $1,400 getting import-export licenses from both the Mexican and American authorities. The corporate income tax rate is 35% in Mexico and 40% in the United States. In deciding how to allocate the legal costs between the Mexico City store and the Los Angeles store, Ramon and John decide that based on the total revenues of the two stores, $1,000 will be charged to the Los Angeles store and $400 to the Mexico City store. Since both stores have taxable income, they want to allocate most of the legal costs to the store that has the highest tax rate, the Los Angeles store (40%) versus Mexico City store (35%), assuming the tax authorities in the United States and Mexico allow this allocation.

15.4 Accounting Standards for External Reporting

The accounting rules for external reporting followed by companies in the United States are not the same rules followed by companies in other countries. Companies all around the world prepare balance sheets and income statements. However, these financial statements are usually not comparable. The language in the statements is the local language, not necessarily English. The currency is the local currency. The terminology can be different; certain accounts can mean different things. The amount of information disclosed about certain transactions such as leases and pensions is likely different from U.S. statements. In some countries, financial reporting is done primarily for tax purposes. And finally, the accounting rules used to calculate the amounts are often different.

For example, research and development expenditures can be treated as an asset in Japan but must be expensed in the United States. Also, German accounting practices are more conservative than those in the United States because German corporations recognize future losses and expenses sooner than required by U.S. accounting rules. UK companies make occasional revaluations of buildings and land to market value; U.S. rules preclude such revaluations except after certain mergers. While there are international bodies seeking to standardize accounting rules across countries, these efforts have had very little impact. Most countries do not wish to cede control of their accounting rules to an international body.[1]

A subsidiary of a multinational corporation operating in a foreign country might have to prepare financial statements following the accounting rules of that country. These rules can differ from those of the parent corporation, thereby requiring a conversion to different accounting rules before forwarding financial statements to the parent.

WHAT'S HAPPENING

Do you think it is ethical for a multinational company to choose cost allocations to minimize its tax liability, even if such allocations are within the legal tax guidelines of the host countries? How does a multinational corporation determine what is its fair share of taxes and how much in taxes must be paid to remain a responsible corporate citizen?

These business people meeting in an airport use their cellular phone and notebook computers to stay in touch with their offices and customers all over the world. These are just two of the technological innovations contributing to the global expansion of business.

Foreign subsidiaries operating in countries with different financial accounting standards must decide which country's accounting standards to use to measure the subsidiary's performance. Suppose a Japanese pharmaceutical company has a subsidiary in the United States. The subsidiary has a research and development department that spent $450 million last year developing and testing new drugs. According to U.S. accounting rules, this $450 million is treated as period expense and reduces last year's income by $450 million. But according to Japanese accounting rules, this $450 million is recorded as an asset and amortized over its useful life. If the U.S. subsidiary's amortization of prior year's R&D expenditures is $375 million, the managers of the Japanese U.S. subsidiary would want to base their performance evaluation on Japanese accounting rules for R&D. Japanese accounting rules would increase their reported income this year by $76 million over income reported by U.S. accounting rules. If the Japanese parent adopts U.S. accounting standards for evaluating its U.S. subsidiary, it reduces the incentive of their U.S. managers to invest in R&D, unless some other component of their U.S. managers' compensation scheme or performance measure is adjusted. Moreover, if the local accounting standards are used to measure subsidiary performance, comparability across subsidiaries in different foreign countries becomes more difficult. For this reason, most multinationals adopt a single country's accounting standards, usually where the parent is headquartered, to measure the performance of all their foreign subsidiaries.

Besides tax and financial accounting differences, countries have different laws regulating business. The appendix describes a few of the more important laws that affect managerial accounting: domestic content requirements, hard currency restrictions, and antidumping regulations.

SOCCER STARS (CONTINUED)

Soccer Stars owns depreciable assets such as computers, cash registers, shelving and display cases, and telephones in both Mexico and the United States. To minimize bookkeeping costs, Ramon and John decide to

> use the same depreciation methods for taxes and internal reporting. Soccer Stars depreciates its Mexican assets by straight-line depreciation and its U.S. assets by accelerated depreciation. However, using different depreciation methods for similar assets distorts the relative profitability of the two stores. The Mexico City store would appear to be more profitable than the Los Angeles store in the early years because the Mexico City store is being charged relatively less depreciation.

15.5 Cultural Differences

Beliefs, values, and goals often differ across countries and subcultures within the same country. People behave differently and react to situations differently depending on the norms of the culture in which they have been raised. A nation's culture is a product of its religious beliefs, history, and economic circumstances. Language is also an important dimension of its culture. A number of studies have found cultural differences across nations. Dutch passengers are more likely than Belgians to greet strangers when entering a train. Japanese and Israeli cultures emphasize group (or collective) versus individual orientation, whereas the United States and Australia emphasize individualism. French workers are less likely than Canadian workers to break a company rule, even if it is in the company's best interest.[2] Even within the same country there can be cultural differences. The Italian subcultures of Rome and Florence differ as do those of New York City and Indianapolis in the United States.

A January 5, 1996, *Wall Street Journal* article describes how U.S. firms such as Goldman, Sachs & Co. and J.P. Morgan & Co. now dominate worldwide financial transactions. Seven of the top ten firms underwriting global stock offerings and advising clients on global mergers are U.S. companies.

Cultural advantages are one reason advanced for the U.S. dominance. "American frontier spirit, appetite for risk, can-do attitudes and rags-to-riches dreams explain U.S. success in global finance." Also contributing to the U.S. success is the fact that U.S. capital markets are far less regulated than other countries. This has allowed U.S. firms to innovate new financial transactions, (such as mortgage-backed securities, at home before exporting these ideas abroad.

Cultural differences can affect managerial accounting systems in several ways. The Japanese collective orientation fosters their approach to teams, participative decision making, and quality circles. Quality circles are routine meetings of production workers to develop improved manufacturing processes. Accounting systems requiring team input will be more difficult to implement in cultures that stress the individual. Many U.S. control systems are built around monitoring individual contributions and not collective contribution. An important, but unanswered, question is the extent to which successful accounting systems developed in one culture can be exported to a different national culture.[3] For example, team performance measures are common in Japan to encourage

WHAT'S HAPPENING

Large multinational companies often have a separate legal company established in each country where they operate. This wholly owned subsidiary is responsible for all accounting functions within the country such as billing customers, collecting payments, making disbursements, and issuing financial reports. With improved computers and telecommunications such as high-speed phone lines, many multinationals are establishing regional accounting centers that handle all the accounting transactions within the region. At one firm, its European accounting center handles the billing, disbursements, and even telephone inquiries for 14 European subsidiaries. Customers calling a local phone number have their calls routed to Ireland where operators answer their questions regarding billing in the local language of the caller. The customer is unaware the operator is in a different country. How does this European accounting center in Iceland relate to Figure 12.1?

At this Hitachi shipyard in Japan, morning exercises on the dock help build team loyalty.

cooperation. Will they work in the U.S. or will American workers insist on individual performance measures?

In many countries, paying bribes to government officials is part of their culture. Such "grease payments" for relaxing laws or for expediting transactions are required to conduct business in some countries. In the United States, the Foreign Corrupt Practices Act (FCPA) makes it illegal for U.S. companies to bribe foreign officials to abuse their power to benefit the firm. However, the FCPA allows small "grease payments" if they expedite trade. In order to comply with the FCPA, U.S. companies must maintain strong internal controls, including record-keeping systems that document that illegal payments were not paid to foreign officials.

SOCCER STARS (CONTINUED)

Studies have shown that Mexican workers have a lower tolerance to ambiguity than American workers. Mexican workers respond more favorably to detailed operating rules than American workers because company rules are one way to reduce ambiguity workers face. Ramon and John, aware of these cultural differences, decide to write a more detailed and complete set of operating policies for the Mexico City store employees than for the Los Angeles store.

CONCEPT REVIEW

1. Why do multinational organizations face multiple taxing authorities?
2. Give some examples of international accounting standard differences.
3. Describe some cultural differences between two countries.

15.6 International Transfer Pricing Issues

Chapter 7 describes the importance of transfer pricing within organizations. A transfer price is the amount one internal operating unit charges another for transferring a good or service between units. For example, if a manufacturing

This photo shop in Venezuela sells Kodak products purchased from the Kodak South American subsidiary, which imported them from the U.S. For each product imported, a transfer price is set between Kodak and its South American subsidiary. Why must Kodak set a transfer price on each product imported into Venezeula?

division produces a product and transfers it inside the firm to a sales division that sells it to an external customer, the transfer price is an expense to the sales division and a revenue to the manufacturing division.

Transfer prices are used to measure the performance of internal units of the organization that are exchanging intermediate goods and services. Transfer prices help provide incentives to coordinate decentralized operating units. Some of the common methods for calculating transfer prices include external market prices, full costs, variable costs, and negotiated prices.

With a purely domestic firm, choosing the "best" transfer price involves looking at how transfer pricing affects the selling and buying divisions' incentives. If too high a price is set, the buyer purchases too few units and if too low a price is set, the seller produces too few units. Transfer pricing, which is already a complicated choice problem, becomes even more complicated for a multinational. Besides worrying about internal incentives, domestic and foreign taxes and political considerations are affected. This section outlines some of the more important international aspects of transfer pricing.

What's Happening

In some cultures, auditing is a useful method of helping resolve conflicts between owners and managers. After controlling for a variety of economic variables, one study finds that former British colonies have a higher proportion of auditors in the population and Moslem countries a smaller proportion of auditors than an average country.[4]

Tax Minimization

If a multinational company transfers products between two countries with different corporate income tax rates, the multinational will try to set a transfer price to minimize its joint tax liability. One way to do this is to recognize more of the profits in the country with the lowest tax rate. If the country of the supplying division has the lowest tax rate, a higher transfer price transfers profit to the supplying division and lowers after-tax profit. If the country of the purchasing division has the lowest tax rate, a lower transfer price transfers profit to the purchasing division and lowers after-tax profit.

NUMERICAL EXAMPLE 15.5

Suppose Pepsi ships 5,000 units of syrup from the United States to a foreign country subsidiary where carbonated water is added and the mixture is canned and sold.

Suppose the U.S. income tax rate is 40% and the foreign country's tax rate is 20%. The variable cost to manufacture and ship the syrup is $14 per unit. It costs the foreign subsidiary an additional $10 per unit to add the water, can, and sell the drink for $80 per unit. All costs are variable. The following table summarizes the tax rates, final sales price, operating costs, and units transferred. To simplify the example, the foreign country's sales have been converted to U.S. dollars.

	U.S.	Foreign Subsidiary
Tax rate	40%	20%
Units transferred & sold	5,000	5,000
Variable cost per unit	$14	$10
Variable cost	$70,000	$50,000
Selling price per unit		$80
Revenue from final sales		$400,000

If Pepsi can select a transfer price of $16 per unit or $18 per unit, which one should Pepsi select?

■ **SOLUTION** The following table calculates the total tax liability of Pepsi if the syrup is transferred at $16 per unit.

	U.S.	Foreign Subsidiary	Total
Revenue from transferring syrup @ $16	$80,000		
Revenue from final sales		$400,000	
Cost of syrup transferred		80,000	
Variable cost	70,000	50,000	
Income before taxes	$10,000	$270,000	
Taxes	$ 4,000	$ 54,000	$58,000

From the preceding table, Pepsi's total tax liability is $58,000 if the transfer price is set at $16 per unit. If the transfer price is set at $18 per unit, the following table shows that the total tax liability rises to $60,000.

	U.S.	Foreign Subsidiary	Total
Revenue from transferring syrup @ $18	$90,000		
Revenue from final sales		$400,000	
Cost of syrup transferred		90,000	
Variable cost	70,000	50,000	
Income before taxes	$20,000	$260,000	
Taxes	$ 8,000	$ 52,000	$60,000

Pepsi's taxes are higher with the $18 transfer price because profits are shifted out of the low tax foreign subsidiary to the high tax U.S. parent. By selecting $16 instead of $18 as the transfer price, Pepsi saves $2,000 of taxes.

Because transfer pricing is often an effective way for multinational organizations to shift taxes to lower income tax jurisdictions, government officials monitor closely firms' transfer pricing methods. Tax authorities in both the importing and exporting countries scrutinize the transfer pricing schemes used. Moreover, there are numerous tax treaties between countries that specify the general transfer pricing methods that can be used by companies conducting business in the two countries covered by the treaty. Thus, while firms have some discretion in setting transfer prices, they are constrained by existing tax laws and treaties.

SOCCER STARS (CONTINUED)

John Williams paid $6,320 for 120 autographs on 40 soccer balls. One unautographed soccer ball costs $8. With three autographs at $50 each, the autographed ball has a total cost of $158. This ball has a retail price in the United States of $320. When this ball is exported to the Mexico City store, it is sold for Ps2000. The U.S. store is subject to a combined federal and state income tax rate of 40%. Mexico imposes a 35% income tax on Mexican companies. John and Ramon must set a transfer price on the autographed ball imported into Mexico. They want to minimize the total taxes paid on the transfer and sale of the soccer ball in Mexico. After consulting their accountant, they determine that the best transfer price on the ball is the cost to John of the ball and autographs ($158). Another alternative is to use as the transfer price the U.S. retail price of the ball ($320). The following table illustrates the total taxes paid using the cost of the ball and its retail price as alternative transfer prices (six pesos can be exchanged for one dollar).

	Alternative Transfer Prices	
	Cost	Retail
Transfer price in U.S. dollars	$158.00	$320.00
Amount in pesos (exchange rate 6:1)	Ps 948.00	Ps1920.00
Cost	$158.00	$158.00
U.S. profit on export	$ 0.00	$162.00
U.S. income tax on export (40%)	$ 0.00	$ 64.80
U.S. tax in pesos (exchange rate 6:1)	Ps 0.00	Ps 388.80
Selling price in Mexico	Ps2000.00	Ps2000.00
Transfer price	Ps 948.00	Ps1920.00
Mexico profits before taxes	Ps1052.00	Ps 80.00
Mexico tax on profits (35%)	Ps 368.20	Ps 28.00
Total U.S. and Mexico taxes	Ps 368.20	Ps 416.80

As can be seen from the above table, Soccer Stars saves about Ps49 (about $8) per soccer ball in taxes by using the cost of the soccer ball ($158) instead of its retail price ($320) as the transfer price.

Political Considerations

Taxes and tariffs are important considerations in setting transfer prices of goods shipped among multinational subsidiaries. Political considerations can also influence the transfer pricing decision. If the local government is threatening to expropriate the assets of high-profit, foreign-owned companies, these companies may want to choose high transfer prices for their imports and low transfer prices for their exports. These actions reduce the apparent profitability of their foreign operations. This might reduce the attractiveness to the government of seizing the foreign-controlled company. Also, transfer prices which lower reported profits might forestall entry by local competitors.

Trade-Offs with Planning Decisions and Control

As discussed earlier, domestic organizations try to set transfer prices for performance evaluation purposes in such a way as to get the buying and selling divisions to exchange the number of units that maximize the organization's overall profits. But in multinational firms, income taxes and political considerations force managers to choose a transfer price that trades off planning for taxes and political purposes with control. One solution is to choose a transfer price that partially satisfies planning and control functions within the multinational but is optimal for neither purpose. If multinationals choose transfer prices solely to minimize taxes, they must devise alternative measures of performance to motivate managers of foreign subsidiaries. Instead of relying on accounting profits affected by transfer prices to measure and reward the performance of its subsidiary managers, organizations might want to use revenues, production costs, and market share as performance measures.

If income taxes and political considerations have a significant effect on choice of transfer pricing methods, several consequences arise. Some firms become more centralized because they cannot rely on transfer prices to create appropriate decentralized incentives. Other firms may use one transfer price, such as market value, for internal evaluation and a different transfer price, such as full cost, for tax reporting. However, using different transfer prices for internal evaluation and taxation increases bookkeeping costs and creates confusion among the managers as to which transfer price is "right."

SOCCER STARS (CONTINUED)

To minimize total taxes, John and Ramon have been using the U.S. cost of the autographed balls as the transfer price for balls purchased in the United States and transferred to Mexico. Since the U.S. tax rate (40%) is higher than the Mexican tax rate (35%), the U.S. cost as the transfer price causes all the profits to be realized in Mexico and taxed at the lower rate. However, this historical cost transfer price does not reflect the opportunity cost of the balls when imported to Mexico. The U.S. retail price is the amount forgone when the ball is transferred. Ramon and John realize that the historical cost of the balls is not the best measure to use for decentralized decisions. However, taxes are also an important consideration. Since Soccer Stars is small and Ramon and John talk each day about what merchandise is selling in each store, they decide to continue to use the historical cost of U.S. merchandise as the transfer price. The opportunity cost of the merchandise will continue to be exchanged verbally. While this system will work for now, they also understand that once Soccer Stars adds more retail outlets in additional countries, they will have to reexamine the transfer pricing decision.

CONCEPT REVIEW

1. For a product transferred between two subsidiaries of a multinational firm operating in two foreign countries, how would you set the transfer price to minimize the combined income tax liability?
2. How do international taxation and political considerations affect multinational organizations' decision planning and control systems?

15.7 Performance Evaluation

Chapter 6 described the importance of performance evaluation as one leg of the three-legged stool that determines the organization's structure. Assigning decision rights and rewarding performance are the other two legs of the stool. Multinational organizations like all organizations must design organizational structures that provide incentives for their employees to work towards the goals of the organization. Unlike purely domestic firms, multinational firms face an additional issue, the currency to be used to evaluate performance. As described in this section, the choice of currency affects the risk managers face thereby influencing their incentives to manage this risk.

Honda Motors is a Japanese company that owns Honda America, a U.S. subsidiary. Honda America manufactures and sells many of the cars sold in the United States. Honda Motors must decide what currency (dollars or yen) should be used to evaluate the managers of Honda America. To focus on the central issue, consider the case of a single Honda car manufactured entirely with U.S. parts and sold in America. The car cost $15,000 to manufacture and sell and Honda America sells the car for $20,000 to a dealer. Assume that one dollar is equivalent to 100 yen, so Honda America has a profit of $5,000, or 500,000 yen ($5,000 × 100 yen per dollar), per car.

If exchange rates remain constant, managers are indifferent to the choice of currency to use as the performance measure. But suppose the exchange rate goes to 80 yen to a dollar. Assume Honda America is still making a profit of $5,000 per car. If the yen is used to evaluate Honda America *and* the current exchange rate of 80 yen to a dollar is used to translate Honda America's profits of $5,000, then only 400,000 yen ($5,000 × 80 yen per dollar) are earned. The depreciation of the dollar relative to the yen has caused Honda Motors' profits to fall from 500,000 to 400,000 yen per car.

The question becomes, who bears the risk of exchange rate fluctuations? If Honda America's performance is judged based on yen at current exchange rates, the local mangers bear the risk of exchange rate fluctuations. If Honda America's performance is based on the local currency, the U.S. dollar, the risk of exchange fluctuations is borne by the parent corporation, Honda Motors.

This English craftsman is cutting leather for Jaguar automobile seats. Ford, a U.S. company, owns Jaguar, a U.K. company. Jaguars are made in the U.K. and exported to countries around the world. Should the French managers responsible for importing and selling Jaguars in France be evaluated in U.S. dollars, U.K. pounds, or French francs?

The Story of Managerial Accounting

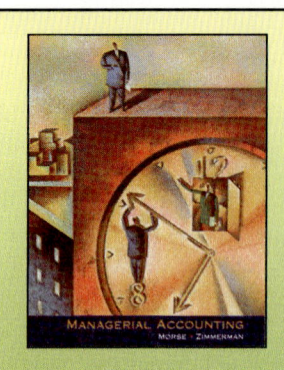

Team Decisions Regarding International Activities

Jeff, the team leader, and Heather, the marketing manager, began investigating opportunities for international sales of *Managerial Accounting* at an early stage in the planning process. International sales of textbooks is an important contributor to profit. Several professors in Australian universities have expressed interest in adopting *Managerial Accounting* for their classes. What additional factors should Peggy, the accountant, consider in estimating the profit of sales in Australia?

One argument for basing performance evaluation on the local currency is that the local manager cannot prevent fluctuations in exchange rates. Exchange rates are set in worldwide markets. Hence, local managers should not be held accountable for exchange rate risk. If their performance is based on exchange rate fluctuations and they are risk averse, they will try to reduce this risk. One way to reduce this risk is by buying or selling currencies to offset their exchange risk. However, such currency transactions generate transactions costs. For example, Honda America can hedge its risk if evaluated in yen in the following way. As soon as it sells a car, Honda America goes to a bank and converts the $5,000 of profit into 500,000 yen. Then if the dollar depreciates against the yen, Honda America has locked in the profits in yen. However, it is costly to exchange small amounts of currencies. Honda, because of its size, can get a better rate on translating dollars into yen than Honda America.

Most multinational companies tend to evaluate their local managers using the local currency, not the parent's currency. Thus, most multinationals do not force the local managers to bear the exchange rate risk. But some multinationals evaluate their subsidiaries after translating each subsidiary's performance into the parent's currency. By forcing the subsidiary to bear the exchange rate risk, they want the local manager to manage the risk through the buying and selling of currencies to offset their exchange risk.

Honda Motors, the parent company, can probably bear this risk at lower cost than Honda America. Honda Motors has worldwide operations and hence holds a diversified portfolio of assets in many different currencies. This diversified global portfolio helps dampen the effect of exchange rate movements in any one currency. Secondly, the shareholders of Honda Motors can also reduce the dollar-yen exchange risk by holding a diversified portfolio of stocks. If the yen appreciates against the dollar, some of Honda investors' other securities will rise, offsetting the decline in Honda America's profits.

The parent company can usually reduce the risk more efficiently (at less cost) than the managers of a foreign subsidiary. Therefore, it is usually not a good idea to evaluate the managers of a foreign subsidiary in terms of the parent's currency. If managers are evaluated in a foreign currency, they will attempt to reduce the exchange risk through numerous costly currency transactions.

Two vice presidents from Bank of America describe the important role of budgeting foreign exchange rates. In their article, they describe how firms with foreign subsidiaries must estimate the future exchange rate in order to convert the foreign subsidiary's financial plans back to the parent's currency. This "budget rate" is a key planning assumption and has multiple uses within the firm. It is used to convert foreign earnings into U.S. dollars and to evaluate subsidiary performance. The budget rate can affect product pricing, which country manufactures the product, and where the materials are sourced. It also affects how the risk of exchange rate fluctuations is borne between the foreign subsidiary and the parent corporation.[5]

Soccer Stars (concluded)

Soccer Stars pays both Ramon and John the same peso salary, Ps160,000. John's salary is then converted to U.S. dollars at the prevailing exchange rate when John is paid. In addition, any remaining profits are split evenly. John's salary in U.S. dollars has been declining because the dollar value of the peso has been falling. John must have U.S. dollars to live in the United States. Thus, any change in the dollar-peso exchange rate affects the number of dollars John has to purchase U.S. goods and services. Exchange rate fluctuations affect Ramon's standard of living indirectly because foreign imported goods now require more pesos to purchase.

To shift some of the exchange rate risk borne by John, Ramon and John decide to fix John's salary in U.S. dollars at $30,000 per year (about Ps167,000 when the peso is worth $0.18). If the exchange rate fluctuates, John is still paid $30,000. However, Soccer Stars will pay more or less than Ps167,000. Suppose the peso falls to $0.15. Soccer Stars will have to convert 200,000 pesos to pay John's $30,000 salary. This is Ps33,000 pesos more than had the exchange rate remained at $0.18 per peso. Because John and Ramon are joint owners of Soccer Stars, they share the Ps33,000 higher cost. Ramon now bears about half the exchange rate risk and John the other half.

CONCEPT REVIEW

1. How does the choice of local versus parent's currency affect the exchange rate risk borne by the local manager?
2. Give some reasons why most multinational firms use the local currency to evaluate their local operations.

15.8 Summary

1. Explain the difference between domestic and multinational organizations. Multinational organizations have operations in several foreign countries. Each country has its own currency which means the multinational is exchanging one currency for another when goods or services are exchanged across countries. Having operations in different countries exposes the multinational to multiple taxing authorities. Multinationals must operate in countries with different customs and cultures that affect the behavioral expectations of the workers and customers.

2. **Use exchange rates to convert financial data from one currency to another.** To convert prices stated in the local currency to a foreign currency, take the amount stated in the local currency and multiply it by the exchange rate expressed as the number of foreign currency units per local currency unit.

3. **Identify the various types of taxes imposed on multinational organizations and how to minimize them.** When a multinational manufactures a product in England and sells it in France, both the British and French governments require the multinational to file income tax returns. In some cases, more than one government can tax the same income. This causes double taxation. To reduce the total taxes paid to all governments, multinationals locate operations and choose accounting and transfer pricing methods that shift income into those tax jurisdictions with the lowest tax rates. However, tax authorities and tax agreements among countries constrain multinationals' choice of accounting and transfer pricing methods.

4. **Describe how the different countries' financial accounting standards affect managerial accounting.** The financial accounting rules followed by companies in the United States are not the same rules followed by companies in other countries. For example, research and development can be capitalized in Japan, but not in the United States. The foreign subsidiary's financial reports must be converted before they can be consolidated with the parent's records. The performance evaluation of the foreign subsidiary depends on whether the foreign or the domestic accounting standard is used.

5. **Explain the effect of different cultures on decision control issues.** People differ in their beliefs, values, language, and goals because of their different religions, history, and economic circumstances. These cultural differences vary across countries. For example, Japanese culture fosters more collective actions. In the United States, there are more individualistic processes. These cultural factors seem to affect the decision control systems used by organizations operating in the particular culture. Japanese decision control systems tend to be based more on team output and team decision making (e.g., quality circles) than in the United States.

6. **Describe the planning and control problems that exist with international transfer prices.** In domestic organizations, transfer pricing involves looking at how transfer pricing affects the selling and buying divisions' incentives. Transfer prices should be equal to the opportunity cost of transferring one more unit to appropriately motivate decentralized decision making. But international transfer prices also determine the taxes to be paid in different countries. The choice of international transfer prices must trade off these planning and control issues.

7. **Explain how fluctuating currencies are related to performance evaluation.** Most multinationals evaluate their foreign subsidiaries in terms of the local currency, not the parent's currency. This reduces the risk of foreign exchange movements borne by the local managers. With lower risk, there is less reason for the local manager to engage in costly buying and selling of foreign currencies.

8. **Describe other government taxes and regulations that affect management accounting.** Value-added taxes (VAT) are levied on labor and overhead costs of the manufacturer and require detailed cost records to be maintained. Tariffs are paid on the value of the products imported into the country, which in turn depend on the transfer price. Domestic content requirements cause the

management accounting system to track the original source (country of origin) of the parts and materials in the final product. Finally, hard currency restrictions and antidumping laws require detailed cost records.

KEY TERMS

Antidumping regulations Government regulations that prohibit foreign companies from selling goods in the domestic country at prices below average cost. (Appendix)

Domestic content requirements These rules specify the percentage of the final product that must be produced domestically in order for the imported good to qualify for lower tariffs. (Appendix)

Exchange rate The price at which one currency can be exchanged for another currency.

Multinational firm A firm with operating units in more than one country.

Tariffs Taxes imposed by governments on goods imported into a country as a percentage of the value of the import. (Appendix)

Value-added tax (VAT) This is a tax on the difference between what the manufacturer sells the product for and the cost of the materials used to produce the product. (Appendix)

Appendix: Other Government Taxes and Regulations

Tax systems are but one way countries differ. In addition, countries differ in their laws regulating the conduct of business within their borders. There are many business regulations that differ across countries. Some of these regulations such as corporate income taxes and financial accounting standards were described in the chapter. This appendix describes a few others that affect multinational organizations' management accounting systems: value-added taxes (VAT), tariffs, domestic content requirements, hard currency restrictions, and antidumping regulations.

Value-Added Taxes (VAT)

Some countries do not rely on corporate income taxes to raise revenue but rather use a value-added tax; other countries use both. The **value-added tax (VAT)** is based on the value added (labor and overhead) by each stage in the production process. Each intermediate producer of the product pays the VAT and passes the tax on to the purchaser. For example, suppose a company assembles computer circuit boards and sells them to computer companies that assemble the final PC. The circuit board assembler buys chips and a board for $20, assembles them, and sells them for $50. Suppose the VAT is 15%. The board assembler's value added is $30 ($50 − $20), and the value-added tax is $4.50 (15% × $30) on the board. This company's VAT causes the firms' accounting systems to carefully track material purchases from labor and overhead acquisitions in order to provide accurate records for VAT calculations.

The United States does not have a VAT, but in Europe it is widely used. The VAT varies from country to country. In Denmark and Sweden it is 25% and in Holland it is 22%. Across Europe, it averages about 17%. The value-added tax is similar to a sales tax in that it is a tax on the product and not a tax on profits. In the United States, sales tax is added to retail purchases in many parts of the country.

Tariffs

Tariffs are taxes levied on goods by the importing country. Tariffs are a tax on the value of the imported good and thus increase the price to the consumer of the importing country. For example, the United States has relatively low tariffs on imported automobiles but a 25% tariff on small trucks. Besides being a source of revenue for the government, tariffs protect the locally produced products from foreign competition. Tariffs protect local producers at the expense of consumers in the same country who pay higher prices for imported products. When tariffs in all countries are reduced, prices fall and both imports and exports expand. The lowering of tariffs, however, will harm organizations that can't compete in an international market.

Besides affecting income taxes, transfer pricing also affects tariffs. If a multinational transfers products between two operating units, the importing unit pays a tariff on the imported good. The tariff is based on the transfer price established on the product. For example, suppose a multinational transfers a product with a transfer price of $100 to a subsidiary in a country with a 25% tariff. The importing subsidiary pays $25 and the total cost of the product is $125. If the transfer price is lowered to $80, the tariff is reduced to $20. Thus, to reduce tariffs, multinationals will try to keep transfer prices low. But low transfer prices drive up the income taxes paid by the importing subsidiary. Therefore, not only must tariffs be considered, but so too must the income tax rates of the two countries.

Import tariffs affect the firm's strategy and organizational structure. If tariffs are high, the multinational may decide to create a wholly owned subsidiary to manufacture the product locally rather than import it and pay the higher tariffs. Thus, tariffs, like other taxes, affect the organization's decisions regarding where to manufacture the product.

Domestic Content Requirements

Many countries try to protect their local industry by imposing **domestic content requirements** which specify the percentage of the final product that must be produced domestically. For example, the North American Free Trade Agreement (NAFTA) provides for lower tariffs on products manufactured or grown regionally within the United States, Canada, and Mexico. To implement these rules, a product's origin must be determined, which in some cases is not so obvious. Consider the nationality of a Honda where the parts come from both Japan and the United States, are assembled in Mexico, and finished in Canada. The rules-of-origin for this car require careful accounting of the product's costs by source of origin. While there are numerous exceptions, NAFTA generally provides that a product will receive preferential tariffs if its regional content (from Canada, United States, or Mexico) is not less than 50% of its cost.

In some cases, foreign companies importing products are required to purchase a certain fraction of the product domestically to receive preferential tax or tariff treatment. Some companies set up domestic operations in foreign countries that assemble final products from parts imported from abroad to gain the preferential treatment. The important point is that domestic content requirements cause firms to redesign their product costing accounting systems to track the cost by country of origin of each product.

Hard Currency Restrictions

Some developing countries have a shortage of foreign exchange—currencies of other countries, especially U.S. dollars. Foreign exchange allows these countries to purchase imported goods such as oil and medical supplies. To conserve its foreign exchange balances, these countries often restrict dividends foreign subsidiaries operating in their country can remit back to their multinational parent.

Transfer pricing policies are affected when companies operate in countries with hard currency restrictions. If a country restricts foreign companies from withdrawing profits from their country, setting a high transfer price allows the multinational to withdraw its "profits" in the form of a "cost."

Antidumping Regulations

International treaties and local laws prevent foreign companies from selling products in their markets at prices below the company's average cost. These restrictions are known as **antidumping regulations.** A common belief is that some foreign companies with excess capacity dump their products into foreign markets at low prices. This forces the local firms out of business so the foreign firm can charge prices above average cost in the long run. Antidumping regulations are an attempt to promote fair competition but may actually reduce competition from foreign firms. However, the fact remains that some governments, including the United States, have antidumping laws. Firms doing business in foreign countries must be prepared to produce cost accounting records that demonstrate that they are not dumping products in the foreign country at prices below average cost.

NUMERICAL PROBLEMS

NP 15–1: Income Taxes and Transfer Prices (LO 3, 6; NE 5)   Refer to the box on page 579. Suppose the Mexican corporate income tax rate is 55% instead of 35%. How would the analysis of Soccer Stars transfer price change? In particular, what transfer price should Soccer Stars set on the soccer ball exported from the United States?

NP 15–2: Foreign Exchange Rates (LO 2; NE 1, 2)   Using the exchange rates in Table 15.1 (page 569), answer the following questions:

a. How many French francs will one U.S. dollar buy?
b. How many U.S. dollars will one French franc buy?
c. How many German marks will one French franc buy? (Hint, convert francs to dollars and then dollars to marks.)

NP 15–3: Foreign Exchange Conversions (LO 2; NE 2)   In Hong Kong, a BigMac Meal costs HK$16, a McDonalds milkshake is HK$6.5, and two medium Pizza Hut pizzas are HK$99. How much are these items in U.S. dollars? (The exchange rate is 7.73 Hong Kong dollars per U.S. dollar.)

NP 15–4: Taxing Worldwide Income and Foreign Tax Credits (LO 3; NE 3)   Like the United States, Mexico taxes Mexican multinational firms based on their worldwide income and gives a tax credit for foreign taxes paid. A foreign tax credit is a reduction in a firm's domestic tax liability for taxes paid to foreign governments. Otel is a Mexican petro-chemical company with a Costa Rican subsidiary. Otel's worldwide profits before taxes are Ps18,500,000. Their Costa Rican profits are Ps8,000,000. The tax rates in Mexico and Costa Rica are 35% and 45%, respectively. Calculate Otel's total tax liability and the average tax rate paid by Otel.

NP 15–5: International Transfer Pricing and Tariffs and Taxes (LO 3, 6, 8; NE 5) (Appendix)   Phipps manufactures circuit boards in Division Low in a country with a 30% income tax rate and transfers them to Division High in a country with a 40% income tax. An import duty of 15% of the transfer price is paid on all imported products. The import duty is not deductible in computing taxable income. Each circuit board's full cost is $1,000, variable cost $700, and selling price by Division High $1,200. The tax authorities in both countries allow firms to use either variable cost or full cost as the transfer price.

Analyze the effect of full cost and variable cost transfer pricing methods on Phipps' cash flows.

NP 15–6: Performance Measures and Exchange Rates (LO 2, 7)

Hochstedt is a German firm with a wholly owned U.S. subsidiary. The parent firm manufactures and exports products from Germany to its U.S. subsidiary for sale in the United States. Hochstedt also has wholly owned subsidiaries in 14 other countries. The firm has a 35% cost of capital requirement on its foreign subsidiaries. Hochstedt invested $5.8 million in the U.S. operation three years ago. The investment consisted of land, building, equipment, and working capital. Today, the book value of the investment is $6 million. The balance sheet for the U.S. subsidiary is:

HOCHSTEDT U.S. SUBSIDIARY
Balance Sheet
Current Year
(millions)

Current assets		$0.5		
Building and equipment			Equity of parent	$6.0
Cost	3.0			
Accumulated depreciation	0.6	2.4		
Land		3.1		
Total assets		$6.0	Total equity	$6.0
Current investment in U.S. subsidiary stated in marks at the historical exchange rate when the investment was made (1.40DM per $ × $6)				DM8.4

When it started the U.S. operation, Hochstedt invested 8.12 million ($5.8 × 1.4) German marks when the exchange rate was 1 U.S. dollar = 1.40 marks ($1 = DM1.4). The exchange rate over the current year has been constant at $1 = DM1.57.

For the current calendar year, a summary of the operations of the U.S. subsidiary is:

HOCHSTEDT
U.S. Subsidiary
Current-Year Operations

U.S. sales	$14 million
U.S. expenses (including depreciation)	$ 8 million
Imports from parent sold in the year	DM6.2 million

The U.S. subsidiary imported from the parent DM6.2 million of product that it sold for $14 million and incurred expenses in the U.S. of $8 million. Ignore taxes.

a. Senior management of Hochstedt is interested in comparing the profitability of its various foreign wholly owned subsidiaries. Prepare a performance report for the U.S. subsidiary for the current year.
b. List and discuss some of the issues that management must address in designing a measure of performance for its foreign subsidiaries.

NP 15–7: Current Exchange Rates (LO 2)

As an exercise, look up in today's paper, the current foreign exchange rates for those currencies listed in Table 15.1. Which exchange rates are most different from those in Table 15.1. What do you think has caused these changes?

NP 15–8: International Taxation (LO 3; NE 3, 5)

A multinational firm, MNE, operates in two countries, X and Y, with tax rates of 40% and 10% respectively. Production costs are exactly the same in each country. The following table summarizes the operating data for the two subsidiaries of MNE. (All data have been converted to dollars to simplify the example.)

	Subsidiary in Country X	Subsidiary in Country Y
Tax rate	40%	10%
Units sold	100	200
Unit cost	$10	$10
Selling price per unit	$20	$20

a. If each operating unit of MNE produces and sells only in its local country and each is treated as being a separate company and pays taxes only in the country of its operations, what is MNE's total tax bill?

b. Suppose that MNE's subsidiary in country Y manufactures all the output sold in both countries. It ships the output to the MNE subsidiary in country X that sells the product. The transfer price is set at $20. There are no costs of shipping the units from Y to X. If each country only taxes profits occurring within its jurisdiction, again calculate MNE's total tax liability.

c. Now suppose that the MNE's subsidiary in country X manufactures all the output sold in both countries. It ships the output to the MNE subsidiary in country Y that sells the product. Again, there are no costs of shipping the units from X to Y. If each country only taxes profits occurring within its jurisdiction, what transfer price must be set to minimize MNE's total tax liability?

NP 15–9: Exchange Rates and Performance Evaluation (LO 2, 7)

Hillsborough Bikes makes a single, very high quality mountain bike that has a unique, patented frame. Hillsborough sells 2,800 units in the United States for $738 each and exports 1,250 units to Japan for 76,500 yen each.

The Hillsborough bike is made from components purchased in the United States, Japan, and Germany. The current cost of each bike is detailed in the following table.

HILLSBOROUGH BIKES
Unit Cost Data

	Source	Cost	Dollar Cost
Frame and handlebar	U.S.	187 dollars	$187.00
Pedals and cranks	German	22 marks	14.67
Gears	Japanese	8975 yen	89.75
Derailers	Japanese	6300 yen	63.00
Seat	German	28 marks	18.67
Brakes	Japanese	4650 yen	46.50
Rims	Japanee	13570 yen	135.70
Tires	U.S.	48.75 dollars	48.75
Assembly labor	U.S.	67.85 dollars	67.85
Overhead	U.S.	33.49 dollars	33.49
Packaging	U.S.	13.38 dollars	13.38
Total cost			$718.76

The dollar costs in this table are based on the dollar-yen exchange rate of 100 and the dollar-mark exchange rate of 1.5.

The dollar depreciates against both the yen and mark. The new exchange rates are 91 yen per dollar and 1.4 marks per dollar. They are currently capacity constrained because they can only produce 4,050 frames per year. They also have fixed contracts to sell 2,800 bikes in the United States. They expect to continue to sell 1,250 bikes in Japan at 76,500 yen each.

a. Prepare an income statement showing how much profit Hillsborough was making under the old exchange rates of 100 yen and 1.5 marks per dollar.
b. Prepare an income statement showing how much profit Hillsborough will make under the new exchange rates of 91 yen and 1.4 marks per dollar.
c. Write a short memo to management explaining how the new exchange rates will affect their profit and reconcile any change in profit.
d. Include in your memo any suggested management changes Hillsborough should investigate to further exploit the new exchange rates.

NP 15–10: Accounting Standards and Performance Evaluation (LO 4, 7)

MicroChip designs and manufactures integrated circuits for medical instruments. It has a wholly owned subsidiary in Japan that also does research and development and manufacturing and sales. The statement below summarizes the Japanese and U.S. operations:

	(all amounts in millions)	
	Subsidiary in Japan (yen)	U.S. Operations (dollars)
Revenue	980	33
Expenses (net of R&D)	630	25
R&D	310	5
Operating profit	40	3

In the United States, R&D expenses are not capitalized but rather are expensed when incurred. In Japan, R&D is capitalized and amortized. MicroChip's Japanese subsidiary operating profit of 40 million yen follows Japanese accounting standards for R&D. The subsidiary's R&D expense is calculated as follows:

Beginning balance of R&D	2,500
New R&D added during the year	600
Total R&D	3,100
Amortization rate per year	10%
R&D expense	310

a. Prepare a statement that evaluates MicroChip's Japanese and U.S. operating performance in U.S. dollars using U.S. accounting standards. Note: the exchange rate is 110 yen to the dollar.
b. Discuss the implications of the difference in accounting for R&D in the U.S. and Japan.

DISCUSSION PROBLEMS

DP 15–1: Opportunity Cost and Foreign Exchange (LO 2)

A friend of yours says, "A Canadian relative of mine died and left me $10,000 Canadian. But I don't want to convert this to U.S. dollars because I'll lose 30%." (Assume the U.S.-Canadian exchange rate is 0.70.) How do you respond?

DP 15–2: Exchange Rates and Performance Evaluation (LO 7)

Monsanto is a worldwide chemical company. In the 1980s Monsanto noticed that sales were declining in certain foreign markets. The local managers in these markets were asked to increase their advertising and marketing expenditures to try to stem the decline. When the senior managers in the United States looked at accounting reports of advertising and marketing expenditures in these markets, these expenditures were declining. Monsanto had the accounting practice of converting all foreign currencies into U.S. dollars before reporting the foreign results to U.S. senior managers. The dollar had been strengthening against the local currencies in those foreign markets whose Mansanto managers were asked to increase their advertising and marketing expenditures. When asked why they had not increased these expenditures, the foreign managers were confused and said they had increased the expenditures. Explain the apparent inconsistency between the foreign managers and the accounting reports used by the senior U.S. managers.

DP 15–3: Budgeting for International Start-Ups (LO 2, 7)

Veriplex manufactures process control equipment. This 100 year-old German company has recently acquired a former East German firm that has a design for a new proprietary process control system. A key component of the new system to be manufactured by Veriplex is called the VTrap, a new line of precision air-flow gauges.

Veriplex uses tight financial budgets linked to annual bonuses to control its manufacturing departments. Each manufacturing department is a cost center. The VTrap gauge is being manufactured in Veriplex's Gauge Department which also manufactures an existing line of gauges. The Gauge Department is responsible for introducing VTrap which has been in development in the Gauge Department since the beginning of the year. The Gauge Department's budget for the current year consists of two parts: DM 6.60 million for manufacturing the existing line of gauges and DM 0.92 million to develop and manufacture VTrap.

The new gauge will be manufactured using much of the same equipment and personnel as the existing gauges. VTrap is an integral part of the proprietary process control system Veriplex hopes will give it a sustainable competitive advantage. Top management is heavily committed to this strategy. Senior engineering staff are always in the Gauge Department working with the manufacturing personnel to modify and refine both the gauges' design and the production processes to produce them. (Note: Engineering Department costs are not assigned to the Gauge Department.)

By the end of the fiscal year, the Gauge Department spent DM 1.30 million on the VTrap program and DM 6.39 million on existing gauge production. Both the new and existing gauge lines achieved their target production quotas and quality goals for the year.

a. Prepare a financial statement for the Gauge Department that details its financial performance for the fiscal year just completed.
b. Upon further investigation of the financial results, you discover that DM 0.15 million of the VTrap budget was for special tooling being supplied by an Italian firm. The contract for the tooling specified that payment would be for 165 million lira. When the contract was signed, one mark was worth 1,100 lira. When the tooling bill was paid, one mark bought 1,200 lira. Revise the financial performance report in (a) above in light of these new facts. Discuss the differences in the two reports and what they mean.
c. You discover similar patterns in other departments between new and existing products and their budgets and actual costs. What are some possible reasons why the pattern in the Gauge Department is not an isolated occurrence but rather has occurred with other new product introductions and is likely to occur with future new product introductions.

DP 15–4: International versus Domestic Difference (LO 1, 3, 5)

A U.S. manager was heard to say, "I don't understand all the fuss about studying international business. Los Angeles has multiple languages and cultures and inflation is like changing exchange rates, both raise comparability problems. We have operations in all 50 states and thus have to deal with multiple taxing authorities. Since we have been successful in the U.S., I have no doubt we will be successful internationally."

How would you respond to this manager?

Endnotes

Chapter 1
1. *The Wall Street Journal*, February 2, B 2:5.
2. *The Wall Street Journal*, March 7, B 11:1.
3. K. Walker and T. Zinsli, "Coors Shenandoah: Brewing a Better Start-Up Operation," *Journal of Cost Management* 7, no. 2 (Summer 1993), pp. 5–12.
4. S. Garner, *Evolution of Cost Accounting to 1925* (Montgomery, Ala.: University of Alabama Press, 1954) and A. Chandler, *The Visible Hand* (Cambridge, Mass.: Harvard University Press, 1977).
5. S. Harrison, "Not Just Bean Counters Anymore," *Management Accounting*, March 1993, pp. 29–32.
6. S. Harrison, "The Most Natural Thing to Do", *Management Accounting*, March 1995, pp. 22–26.
7. *The Wall Street Journal*, April 20, 1995, A 1:5.

Chapter 4
1. M. Crane and J. Meyer, "Focusing on True Costs in a Service Organization," *Management Accounting*, February 1993, pp 41–45.
2. T. Hobdy, J. Thomson, and P. Sharmon, "Activity-Based Management at AT&T," *Management Accounting*, April 1994, pp 35–39.
3. *The Wall Street Journal*, February 27, 1995, B 8B:5.

Chapter 5
1. R. Drtina, "The Outsourcing Decision", *Management Accounting*, March 1994, pp 56–62.
2. *The Wall Street Journal*, November 29, 1995, B 8:2.

Chapter 6
1. A. Maslow, *Motivation and Personality* (New York: Harper & Row, 1954).
2. R. Kaplan and D. Norton, "The Balanced Scorecard—Measures that Drive Performance," *Harvard Business Review,* January-February 1992.
3. *The Wall Street Journal*, February 22, 1994.
4. *The Wall Street Journal*, April 12, 1996, A4.

Chapter 7
1. A. Chandler, *The Visible Hand* (Cambridge, MA: Harvard University Press, 1977), pp. 445–449.
2. S. Tulle, "The Real Key to Creating Wealth," *Fortune*, September 20, 1993, pp. 38–50.
3. In 1989, Kodak reorganized Ultra Technologies and merged it back into Consumer Products. In 1990, Kodak sold the battery business to a group of private investors.
4. *The Wall Street Journal*, October 20, 1995, B 4:3.

Chapter 8
1. R. Drtina, S. Hoeger, and J. Schaub, "Continuous Budgeting at the Hon Company," *Management Accounting*, January 1996, pp 20–24.
2. M. Shields and S. Young, "Antecedents and Consequences of Participative Budgeting: Evidence on the Effects of Asymmetrical Information," *Journal of Management Accounting Research*, 1993, pp. 265–80.
3. A. Christie, M. Joye, and R. Watts, "Organization of the Firm: Some Survey Results," unpublished working paper, University of Rochester (1993).
4. W. Cress and J. Pettijohn, "A Survey of Budget-Related Planning and Control Policies and Procedures, Journal of Accounting Education 3 (Fall 1985), pp. 65–66.

Chapter 9
1. C. Thompson, *How to Find Factory Costs* (Chicago: A. W. Shaw Company, 1916), p. 105. Quoted by S. Garner, *Evolution of Cost Accounting to 1925* (Montgomery, Alabama: University of Alabama Press, 1954), pp. 170–71.
2. When the units in inventory are sold, the indirect costs allocated to these units are charged to income. Thus, managers cannot continually increase earnings by allocating excessive indirect costs to units in inventory without building inventories.

3. P. Carroll, "The Failures of Central Planning—at IBM," *The Wall Street Journal*, January 28, 1993, p. A14.

Chapter 10

1. A. Chandler, *The Visible Hand* (Cambridge, Mass.: Harvard University Press, 1977), pp. 267–68.
2. R. Howell, J. Brown, S. Soucy, and A. Seed, *Management Accounting in the New Manufacturing Environment* (Montvale, N.J.: National Association of Accountants, 1987).
3. R. Banker, G. Potter, and R. Schroeder, "An Empirical Analysis of Manufacturing Overhead Cost Drivers," *Journal of Accounting & Economics* 19 (February 1995), pp. 115–37.
4. U. Karmarkar, P. Lederer, and J. Zimmerman, "Choosing Manufacturing Production Control and Cost Accounting Systems," *Measuring Manufacturing Performance*, R. Kaplan, ed. (Boston: Harvard Business School, 1989).
5. I. Kim and J. Song, "U.S., Korea, and Japan: Accounting Practices in Three Countries," *Management Accounting*, August 1990, p. 26–30.

Chapter 11

1. D. Swenson, "The Benefits of Activity-Based Cost Management to the Manufacturing Industry," *Journal of Management Accounting Research*, Fall 1995, pp. 167–80.
2. T. Hiromoto, "Another Hidden Edge—Japanese Management Accounting," *Harvard Business Review*, July–August 1988, pp. 4–7.
3. *The Wall Street Journal*, November 8, 1995, B 4:3.

Chapter 12

1. The following papers discuss and present evidence regarding the interdependencies among organizational structure, capital structure, and accounting choice outlined in this section and summarized in Figure 12.1: A. Christie, M. Joye, and R. Watts, "Organization of the Firm: Theory and Evidence," unpublished working paper, University of Rochester (1990); C. Smith and R. Watts, "The Investment Opportunity Set and Corporate Financing, Dividend, and Compensation Policies," *Journal of Financial Economics* 32 (1992); and J. Gaver and K. Gaver, "Additional Evidence on the Association between the Investment Opportunity Set and Corporate Financing, Dividend, and Compensation Policy," *Journal of Accounting and Economics* 16 (1993), pp. 125–60.
2. *The Wall Street Journal*, September 20, 1993, pp. A3–4.
3. Chris Ittner and Robert Kaplan, "Texas Instruments: Cost of Quality (A)," Harvard Business School Case 9-189-029.
4. J. Mathews and P. Katel, "The Cost of Quality," 9/7/92, pp. 48–49.
5. *The Wall Street Journal*, December 12, 1995, A 21:3.
6. W. Turk, "Management Accounting Revitalized: The Harley-Davidson Experience," in B. Brinker, ed. *Emerging Practices in Cost Management* (Boston: Warren, Gorham & Lamont, 1990), pp. 155–66.
7. R. Calvasina, E. Calvasina, and G. Calvasina, "Beware of Accounting Myths," *Management Accounting* (December 1989), pp. 41–45.
8. R. Kaplan, "John Deere Component Works (A)," Harvard Business School Case 9-187-107.

Chapter 13

1. S. Kalagnanam and S. Schmidt, "Analyzing Capital Investments in New Products," *Management Accounting*, January 1996, pp. 31–36.
2. T Klammer, B Koch, and N Wilner, "Capital Budgeting Practices—A Survey of Corporate Use," *Journal of Management Accounting Research* (Fall 1991), pp. 113–130.

Chapter 14

1. W. Cress and J. Pettijohn, "A Survey of Budget-Related Planning and Control Policies and Procedures," *Journal of Accounting Education* 3 (Fall 1985), p. 66.
2. W. Cress and J. Pettijohn, p. 66. A related study finds, "a large majority of profit center budget targets are set so they can and will be achieved." [K Merchant, *Rewarding Results: Motivating Profit Center Managers* (Boston: Harvard Business School Press, 1989), p. 30].
3. W. Cress and I. Pettijohn, p. 74.
4. See Y. Kato, "Target Costing Support Systems: Lessons from Leading Japanese Companies," *Management Accounting Research* 4 (March 1993) pp. 33–47; T. Hiromoto, "Another Hidden Edge—Japanese Management Accounting," *Harvard Business Review* (July–August 1988), pp. 22–26; and M. Sakurai, "Target Costing and How to Use It," *Journal of Cost Management for Manufacturing Industry* (Summer 1989) pp. 39–50.
5. F. Worthy, "Japan's Smart Secret Weapon," *Fortune*, August 12, 1991, pp. 72–75.
6. T. Hiromoto, "Another Hidden Edge—Japanese Management Accounting," *Harvard Business Review* (July–August 1988).
7. P. Scarbough, A. Nanni, Jr., and M. Sakurai,

"Japanese Management Accounting Practices and the Effects of Assembly and Process Automation," *Management Accounting Research* 2 (March 1991), pp. 27–46.
8. J. Edwards, C. Heagy, and H. Rakes, "How Milliken Stays on Top," *Journal of Accountancy,* April 1989, pp. 63–74.

CHAPTER 15

1. Ray Ball, "Making Accounting International: Why, How, and How Far Will It Go?" *Journal of Applied Corporate Finance* 8 (Fall 1995), pp. 19–29.
2. Geert Hofstede, *Culture's Consequences: International Differences in Work-Related Values* (London: Sage Publications Ltd, 1980). Also see J. Birnberg and C. Snodgrass, "Culture and Control: A Field Study," *Accounting, Organizations and Society* 13 (1988), pp. 447–464.
3. Chee Chow, Michael Shields, and Yoke Kai Chan, "The Effects of Management Controls and National Culture on Manufacturing Performance: An Experimental Investigation," *Accounting, Organizations and Society* 16 (1991), pp. 209–26.
4. Dale Morse, "Explaining the International Supply of Auditors," *International Journal of Accounting* 28 (1993), pp. 347–355.
5. A. Miyamato and S. Godfrey, "Foreign Exchange Budget Rates: How They Can Affect the Firm" *Journal of Applied Corporate Finance* 8 (Fall 1995), pp. 115–20.

Thoughts on "What's Happening" Questions

Chapter 1

Page 7 McDonald's is able to provide faster service if they have inventory on hand when the customer orders. The disadvantage is that hamburgers may go to waste if not ordered within a reasonable time. Burger King can accommodate special orders more easily, but takes longer to service customer orders. Recently both companies have developed quicker ways of cooking hamburgers so that both fast service and special orders can be accommodated.

Page 14 Financial and tax issues take more precedence in smaller organizations because they are required by banks, external shareholders and taxing authorities. Smaller organizations may also not have as many control problems because the owner can easily observe all the employees. Managerial accounting efforts are often delayed until they are required by the organization to maintain control. Managers of small organizations often don't recognize the benefits of or have the time for managerial accounting.

Page 18 The engineers did not trust the organization's accounting system to give them accurate information for their own needs.

Page 22 Undergraduate accounting programs tend to emphasize public accounting because of the visibility of large CPA firms and the CPA examination. Also, financial accounting, auditing, and tax have prescribed and detailed rules that must be learned. Management accountants must understand financial accounting, auditing and tax as well as management accounting procedures.

Chapter 2

Page 38 The sales of General Motors cars did not stop with the strike. As long as the customers can find the car of their choice on the lot, there are no lost sales. An accurate figure on lost sales should consider only those customers who chose to go to another company to buy a car because of either no inventory or in support of the strikers.

Page 38 Financial statements are not just for planning purposes. They are also used to measure the performance of the managers of the firm. Historical costs might be better representations of how the managers performed.

Page 45 There is a large fixed cost in making an airplane. Factories must be constructed, parts purchased, planes designed, and marketing channels and customers identified before a plane can be sold.

Chapter 3

Page 69 Management accountants must identify ways that they can generate additional revenues by supporting value-added activities or reduce costs by identifying and reducing non-value-added activities.

Chapter 4

Page 103 Microsoft felt that the cost of additional testing of Windows 95 would reduce the costs of servicing customers who encounter problems with the product.

Page 106 By taking multiple "snapshots" of the organization, Fireman's Fund can estimate the amount of labor time spent on different products using the proportion of snapshots that a worker is working on a particular product. That proportion times the total labor time of the worker is the estimate of direct labor by that individual on that product.

Chapter 5

Page 142 Selling below average cost may be a reasonable decision for an organization when operating below capacity. In general, prices should be above the variable cost, which is less than the average cost when below capacity.

Page 152 One answer is that airlines had been applying unavoidable costs to the losing flights. These unavoidable costs did not disappear when the flights were dropped. The other possibility is that customer use of flights is linked. A customer whose flight from New York to Chicago is dropped will not take the airline's flight from Chicago to Los Angeles.

Chapter 6

Page 172 Central planners of a central economic planning system require information about all facets of the economy in order to plan efficiently. Controlling such an organization is very difficult.

Page 179 A coach is not in complete control of the win/loss record. Factors such as injuries and playing a "hot" team are not under the coach's control. The coach, however, is responsible for recruiting and preparing the basketball players for games and should be evaluated based on those performance measures.

Chapter 7

Page 199 The economy should only affect the presidential elections to the extent that the president is responsible for the economy. Some people would argue that the president has little control over an economy that is very decentralized like in the United States.

Page 203 In general, bonuses based on profit is a reasonable approach, but for Sears it had an unexpected consequence. In automotive repairs the employees can increase short-run profit by identifying problems that don't exist or faking repairs. Customers can not easily recognize if they are being tricked.

Page 209 Very few investment projects can promise a 30% return. Therefore, little money was reinvested and assets were sold when they could not return 30%.

Page 210 We know from Chapter 6 that all organizations have systems that partition decision rights, measure performance, and reward performance. These three systems are like a three-legged stool. If a firm adopts EVA, this is a change in their performance measurement system. It is likely that the other two legs of the stool are being changed as well: the partitioning of decision rights and the rewarding of performance.

Page 219 It is not the best use of resources to have highly paid scientists performing secretarial tasks. One thing Bellcore did was to reduce the transfer price. They did this by subtracting some fixed costs such as office rent, property taxes, and insurance from the transfer price for secretarial services.

Chapter 8

Page 241 Detailed budgets for environmental projects are developed as a control device to monitor the managers responsible for the project and to document to the government agencies the organization's compliance with the government's regulations.

Page 242 The Japanese yen has appreciated against the dollar. This causes their profit margins in yen to be squeezed. They can raise the dollar price of their cars, but this reduces the demand for their cars. Alternatively, they can reduce their costs. Japanese auto makers did both.

Page 244 Requiring several levels to approve the budget is a way to both monitor lower level managers and to communicate planning information to senior managers who can then better coordinate the various operations of the organization.

Page 248 By using budgeted exchange rates, Bank of America removes the risk of exchange rate fluctuations from its managers. Since managers cannot control exchange rate fluctuations, imposing this risk on them makes them worse off.

Page 251 Political appointees usually have no prior experience in the governmental units. Therefore, zero-based budgeting is a good way for the appointees to gain more information about the organization.

Page 261 Chevron's daily cash balances can be in the hundreds of millions of dollars. By estimating the cash flows accurately, the company can place most of the cash in over-night interest-bearing accounts. The over-night interest on $100,000,000 can be over $10,000.

Chapter 9

Page 291 By reimbursing costs, there was no incentive for hospitals to reduce costs. Hospital costs rose sharply.

Page 297 After changing its cost allocation system, IBM re-evaluated the strategy of its PC business and changed its marketing and pricing strategy to be more competitive.

Page 308 Total profits actually fell after closing what appeared to be unprofitable rail lines. Closing these lines eliminated the revenues they generated, but not all the costs assigned to these lines were saved when they were closed. The labor contracts required workers be reassigned to other lines.

Chapter 10

Page 346 The cost of products in retail and wholesale organizations is primarily the purchase price. Overhead and labor can not be easily traced to the different products, so it is easier to treat those costs as period costs.

Page 351 Most of the cost of electronics plants are direct material (66%) indicating that these plants purchase a lot of subcomponents and raw materials. Overhead is high (25% of product cost) and three times larger than direct labor (8%) indicating that these plants employ a significant amount of automation.

Chapter 11

Page 401 Accounting's claim to adding value is improving planning decisions and helping in control.

Chapter 12

Page 452 ISO 9000 certification does not actually check product quality. It certifies that the firm has a written process for documenting its quality. If a firm says that half of our products are defective and has written policies, procedures, and methods to document that half of their products are defective, then this firm can be ISO 9000 certified.

Page 457 In the past, direct labor was a larger component of total product cost than it is today. Therefore, controlling labor costs through the use of detailed direct labor standards and variances while time consuming and costly paid off in lower product costs. But at only 10% of total product costs, a large direct labor savings today results in only a small change in product costs.

Chapter 13

Page 489 A 30% internal rate of return is very difficult to achieve. Therefore, the company would make very few new investments.

Chapter 14

Page 521 The target manufacturing cost is $22,000 − $1,500 − $1,100, or $19,400.

Page 542 Milliken is likely to have changed its business strategy, how it partitions decision rights, and its compensation plans.

Chapter 15

Page 570 Italian government bonds will pay a higher interest rate because the market expects the lira to depreciate against the dollar. Although the annual interest paid in lira by the Italian bonds remains constant in the future, these lira are converted into fewer dollars in the future as the lira:dollar exchange rate falls.

Page 573 Ethical questions have few right or wrong answers, partly because there is no general agreement as to what constitutes ethical behavior. In terms of deciding whether a particular cost allocation or a company's share of taxes is ethical, managers must consider at least the following two points. First, if the firm pays more in taxes, can it survive in a competitive marketplace? If competitors are paying lower taxes and therefore setting lower prices, other firms must follow or else they will be forced out of business. Second, the news media has an incentive to publish stories about firms seeking to shirk their fair share of taxes. These stories are more popular if it appears there is an intent to deceive by the use of some extreme cost allocation procedure. Therefore, in choosing cost allocation procedures that affect taxes, managers must consider the likely adverse public relations such allocations will generate if they are reported by the press.

Page 575 Figure 12.1 illustrates how technological innovation causes organizational change. Consolidating all their separate European accounting offices into a single center located in Ireland is an organizational change. The technological changes allowing this consolidation are advances in computers and telecommunications, in particular, low-cost, reliable high-speed phone lines.

Page 577 Some cultures have alternatives to auditors to resolve conflicts between owners and managers such as religious or political leaders. Some countries also have fewer absentee owners or use banks infrequently, so the auditing of external financial statements is less necessary.

Answers to Concept Reviews

Chapter 1

Pages 7–8
1. Management accounting must adapt to changes in the organization, which is changing because of technological changes and global competition.
2. Technological innovations allow an organization to communicate information better and operate more efficiently.
3. Global competition forces organizations to continually innovate to keep ahead of their customers.
4. TQM is a philosophy of continually lowering costs and improving the provision of services and products to customers.
5. The value chain identifies the critical processes necessary to serve the customer.

Page 10
1. Organizations form to achieve goals that cannot be attained individually.
2. The three basic processes are the assignment of decision rights, the measurement of performance, and the rewarding of individuals.

Page 12
1. The role of the manager is to make planning decisions and control other decisions within the organization.
2. Not all individuals within an organization will work toward the common goals of the organization without control.

Page 15
1. Management accounting provides information for improved planning decisions.
2. Management accounting helps align the interests of the members of the organization with the goals of the organization by measuring performance.
3. External users of the accounting system include external shareholders, banks, and governmental bodies.

Page 18
1. The communication of information within the organization is affected when the same information is used to evaluate members of the organization.
2. Historical costs may differ from the market value of an asset.
3. Maximizing profit based on historical cost is not always consistent with maximizing shareholder wealth.

Page 19
1. Multiple accounting systems allow for different systems to focus on planning, control, and external reporting.
2. Multiple accounting systems are expensive to operate and may be confusing to the members of the organization.

Page 20
1. The growth of large corporations and the separation of managers and owners made management accounting more important.
2. The nature of each organization leads to different demands on the accounting system.

Page 24
1. The controller is responsible for the organization's accounting system while the internal auditors monitor the organization to determine if prescribed operational procedures are being followed.
2. A code of ethics provides direction for management accountants when making a subjective decision that affects multiple stakeholders.

Chapter 2

Page 39
1. Only differential costs and benefits are relevant to a decision because all the other costs and benefits are the same for each alternative.
2. Future costs and benefits are not known for certain and often involve factors that are not easily quantified in dollar terms.
3. The alternative use of resources should be considered in determining the opportunity cost.
4. Sunk costs are the effect of past decisions that can't be changed.

Pages 42–43
1. The cost of starting operations and making the first few units includes the purchase and setting-up of machinery and training of labor.

2. When the capacity of resources is reached, the cost of additional use of those resources becomes very high.
3. The marginal cost identifies the cost of making one more unit and should be used for making a decision of whether to make additional units.
4. The average cost does not provide the cost of making additional units and shouldn't be used in deciding whether to increase output.

Page 46
1. The fixed cost does not change with the rate of output.
2. Variable costs approximate the marginal cost at a normal rate of operations.
3. Historical costs are objective and easy to measure and may be useful for control purposes.

Page 48
1. The cost of information is the cost of acquiring and analyzing the information.
2. The benefit of information comes from improved planning decisions.

Chapter 3

Page 75
1. Cost objects are chosen based on what decision is being made.
2. Product mix and pricing decisions use product and service costs.
3. The cost of activities can be used to determine if the activity should be outsourced or if there is an alternative activity that is cheaper and more effective.
4. The value chain identifies the critical activities necessary to satisfy the customer. Activities that are not on the value chain are potential sources of cost savings.
5. The cost of a subunit can be used to evaluate the manager responsible for the subunit.
6. Treating customers as cost objects allows for the identification of profitable customers and customers who may be causing losses.
7. Supplier costs are affected by the cost of the part, the quality of the part, timely delivery, and negotiation costs.
8. Shareholders use financial reports to evaluate top-level managers and make investment decisions with respect to the organization.

Page 78
1. Direct costs are the easiest to trace to a cost object.
2. Indirect costs are common to multiple cost objects.
3. A cost driver identifies the cause of the indirect cost.

Page 84
1. The account classification method separates accounts into variable and fixed. The summation of the costs of all of the fixed accounts is the fixed cost and the summation of the costs of all of the variable accounts divided by the expected output is the variable cost per unit of output.
2. The visually-fitted line represents the relation between past costs and outputs. The intercept on the cost axis represents the fixed cost and the slope represents the variable cost per unit.

Chapter 4

Page 105
1. Most costs are committed during the design and engineering stage.
2. The various stages in a product's life cycle are: initial planning and proposal (including marketing surveys), designing and engineering the product or service (including comparisons with leading competitors' products and services), manufacturing the product or providing the service, and finally distributing the product or service and providing customer service activities.

Page 108
1. Direct product costs are commonly classified as direct material and direct labor.
2. Direct material costs are estimated by looking at materials required and supplier prices. Direct labor costs are estimated by estimating the time required to make the product and the labor rates.

Page 111
1. Indirect product costs are costs that are not directly associated with a single cost object.
2. Unit-level costs vary with the number of units. Batch-level costs vary with the number of batches. Product-level costs vary with the number of products. Facility-level costs are fixed except when additional facilities are added.

Page 117
1. Estimated indirect costs are divided by the estimated usage of the cost driver to determine an application rate. The application rate then becomes the cost of using the cost driver.
2. The problem with applying indirect costs using a single cost driver is that not all indirect costs necessarily vary with usage of that cost driver. Therefore, the estimated product costs will not necessarily be a good estimate of the opportunity cost.

Page 122
1. The first step of ABC is identifying activities and cost drivers for each activity. The estimated costs of each activity is divided by the estimated usage of its respective cost driver to determine an application rate for each cost driver. Costs are then applied based on the usage of the cost drivers by the different products.
2. ABC recognizes different levels of indirect costs and generally provides a more accurate estimate of the cost of a product. ABC, however, is more costly to estimate.

Chapter 5

Page 142
1. Producing the quantity at which marginal cost equals marginal benefit maximizes value.
2. Cost-based pricing is used in regulated industries and when the supplier does not want to bear the risk of making a product with an uncertain cost.
3. The lower boundary in making a pricing decision is approximated by the variable cost.

Page 149
1. The basic equation for CVP analysis is: Profit = (Price per unit) (Number of units) − (Variable cost per unit) (Number of units) − Fixed costs
2. The purpose of break-even analysis is to estimate the output quantity necessary to have a zero profit to see if the project is potentially profitable.
3. The major assumptions of CVP analysis include a separation of costs into fixed and variable and constant prices and variable cost per unit over the relevant range of output.
4. To use CVP analysis with multiple products, constant proportions or a "basket" of the multiple goods must be assumed.

Page 155
1. Incremental costs should be considered in adding a product.
2. Avoidable costs identify those costs that would be eliminated if the product is dropped.
3. If the purchase price of the product is less than the cost of making the product, the product should be purchased.
4. A product should be processed further if incremental revenues are greater than incremental costs.
5. Organizations prefer to sell products with higher contribution margins per unit.

Chapter 6

Page 173
1. The two internal roles of management accounting are improving planning decisions and assisting in control.
2. Larger organizations have greater control problems because there are more individuals to motivate to act in the best interest of the organization.

Page 176
1. Top-level managers delegate some of their decision rights to subordinates who delegate some of their decision rights to their subordinates.
2. People with the best knowledge have the capabilities to make the best planning decisions.
3. By transferring knowledge to managers who will act in the best interests of the organization, the linking of knowledge and decision rights and control are both achieved.

Page 182
1. The costs include time and effort. The benefits include monetary rewards, status, and relationships with people with similar interests.
2. Monitoring costs are incurred to assist in the control of the organization.
3. Performance measures are used to evaluate individuals and subunits of an organization.
4. A good performance measure is consistent with the goals of the organization and reveals the actions of the individual being evaluated.
5. Good performance measures should lead to extra rewards.

Page 184
1. The three systems are the assignment of decision rights, the measurement of performance, and the rewarding of individuals.
2. Accounting plays a major role in measuring performance.

Page 188
1. The four steps of the decision process are initiation (planning), ratification (control), implementation (planning), and monitoring (control).
2. Separation of planning and control activities allows for mutual monitoring.

Chapter 7

Page 200
1. The controllability principle rewards and penalizes each member of an organization for only those activities that they can control.
2. The advantage of a relative performance measure is that comparisons can be made across individuals facing a similar environment. The disadvantage is that there are always winners and losers no matter how all the managers did, which may lead to competition among managers rather than cooperation.

Page 203
1. A cost center either has a fixed set of inputs from which to maximize outputs or a fixed output to be achieved by minimizing the cost of inputs.
2. Minimizing cost may have adverse effects on quality, so quality measures should be used in conjunction with cost measures.
3. Profit centers normally have control over both inputs and sale of outputs.

Page 212
1. The profit of investment centers does not normally include interest on long-term debt, so performance measures should capture the cost of capital.
2. ROI allows for the comparison of performances across managers of different amounts of assets and is in the form of an easily understood percentage. The problems include measurement errors due to the use of

historical costs, manipulation, incentives to underinvest, and not including the value of cash flows.
3. Residual income has all of the problems of ROI except underinvestment. Residual income has the advantage of explicitly recognizing the cost of capital.
4. Many responsibility centers have characteristics of more than one type of responsibility center. For example, managers of some responsibility centers have the decision rights to make minor expansions of their responsibility center, but don't have decision rights for large expansions.

Page 222
1. Transfer pricing allows decentralized managers to make transfer decisions among themselves. The transfer price should equal the opportunity cost of providing the product or service to ensure that the appropriate decision is made that benefits the whole organization.
2. Transfer prices provide managers with information on the cost of internal services so they can plan accordingly. Transfer prices can also be used to reduce taxes when operating in more than one taxing authority.

CHAPTER 8
Page 245
1. Budgeting facilitates the transfer of information within the organization to improve planning decisions. Budgeting also forces managers to plan in a periodic manner.
2. The budget is used to distribute decision rights by specifying how much can be spent on different items. Budgeting also establishes benchmarks for evaluating performance.
3. The gathering of information for planning purposes is influenced by how the information is to be used for evaluating performance.

Page 252
1. Short-run budgets are both planning and control tools. Long-run budgets reduce managers' focus on short-term performance and are primarily used for planning purposes.
2. A line item budget restricts the decision rights of a manager by forcing the manager to make purchases in prespecified amounts.
3. The cost of budget lapsing is the need to continually budget for multi-period projects and not allowing managers to make trade-offs across different time periods. The benefit of budget lapsing is greater control on short-term spending.
4. Managers who can control the size of operations should be evaluated based on static budgets, while managers who do not control the size of operations should be evaluated based on flexible budgets.
5. Zero-base budgeting is useful when there is a new manager and there is a greater need of information flow.

Page 263
1. The first step of the budget process is normally the estimation of sales.
2. Production requirements are equal to sales plus expected ending inventory less beginning inventory.
3. A financial budget identifies the cash flows to and from investors and creditors of the organization.
4. Pro forma financial statements are the expected financial statements at the end of the budgeting period.

CHAPTER 9
Page 289
1. Cost allocation is the assignment of costs of internal services such as maintenance or data processing to the users of those services such as production units.
2. Common resources are used by multiple cost objects. Therefore, common resources are difficult to trace to cost objects.

Page 294
1. Allocating costs of all manufacturing overhead to products is traditionally done for external financial and tax reporting.
2. Organizations prefer to allocate as much overhead as possible to products that are being produced under cost reimbursement contracts.

Page 296
1. Cost allocations should approximate the opportunity cost of using the overhead resource for planning purposes.
2. Cost allocations are used to communicate information to and penalize the party causing the externality (assuming it is negative).

Page 299
1. Cost allocations may coincide with the distribution of resources and limit the amount of resources that the manager controls.
2. Cost allocations affect the performance measures of managers and discourage managers from using the allocation base used to allocate the costs.
3. Mutual monitoring is monitoring that is performed by peers within the organization. Cost allocations are like prices that occur within the organization and reveal the efficiencies of other units within the organization.

Page 308
1. Cost objects are chosen depending on the type of decision being made.
2. A cost pool is an aggregation of costs related to a specific activity.
3. The allocation base is used to distribute costs of a cost pool among the different cost objects.

4. The application rate is the estimated size of the cost pool divided by the estimated usage of the allocation base.
5. As the cost objects use the allocation base, costs are allocated to the cost objects based on the application rate.
6. A cost driver reflects the cause of the costs in the cost pool while the allocation base may be chosen for control reasons. Both are used to apply costs of common resources to multiple cost objects.

Page 310
1. The purpose of segment reporting is to measure the performance of different subunits and groups of products of the organization.
2. Transactions with other subunits of the organization affect the segment reports of the interacting subunits. For segment reports these transactions should be treated as if they are with external parties.

CHAPTER 10

Page 341
1. The two types of production processes are job order production and continuous flow production.
2. Job order costing is used for job order production and process costing is used for continuous flow.

Page 344
1. The job-order cost sheet records direct materials, direct labor, and overhead.
2. The overhead costs are added based on the use of an allocation base.

Page 348
1. Once production begins a work-in-process account begins receiving costs.
2. At the end of production the costs are transferred to the finished inventory account.
3. At the time of sale the costs are transferred to cost of goods sold.

Page 358
1. Actual overhead costs or usage of the allocation base may be different than estimated.
2. Over- and under-absorbed overhead reflect how actual operations differed from expected operations and may be used to adjust future estimates. These future estimates are used in making product mix and pricing decisions. Over- and under-absorbed overhead may also reflect control problems.
3. Over- and under-absorbed overhead can be treated as (1) cost of goods sold, (2) prorated among work-in-process, finished goods, and cost of goods sold, or (3) eliminated by recalculating the application rate using actual numbers and reallocating the overhead.
4. Multiple allocation bases yield more accurate product costs if products use overhead resources in different ways.

Page 362
1. The primary purpose of process costing is to identify the average cost of the product.
2. Equivalent unit calculation is used when there are partially completed units at the beginning and end of the accounting period.

Page 367
1. The schedule for cost of goods manufactured generates the costs transferred to finished goods. The cost of goods sold is calculated by adding the costs transferred to finished goods to the beginning inventory of finished goods less the ending inventory of finished goods.
2. FIFO assumes that cost of the early units of inventory should be transferred to cost of good sold first. LIFO assumes that the cost of the latest units of inventory should be transferred to costs of goods sold first. The weighted-average cost method combines the costs of the beginning and recently added inventory.

CHAPTER 11

Page 391–392
1. Overproduction leads to more fixed costs being retained in inventory and a higher short-term profit.
2. The cost of extra inventory could be charged to the person responsible for the inventory decision or JIT could be used.
3. By definition, the marginal use of a resource that is a fixed cost is zero. Any time a manager is charged through a cost allocation for using a fixed cost resource, the manager will tend to use less of the resource.
4. The death spiral is caused by dropping products but not avoiding costs that are then allocated to the remaining products.

Page 394
1. The application rate is equal to the estimated overhead costs divided by the usage of the allocation base when operations are at capacity.
2. The proportion of fixed costs allocated is equal to the proportion of capacity used.
3. The advantage is identifying the cost of unused capacity and not burdening existing products or departments with costs due to capacity decisions. Using practical capacity still does not alleviate the overproduction problem.

Page 397
1. Fixed costs are treated as period expenses.
2. Variable costing removes the incentive to overproduce and identifies the contribution margin.
3. Variable costing may lead to problems in identifying fixed and variable costs. Variable costing still requires the choice of an allocation base.

Page 405
1. ABC is a full absorption costing system and fixed costs can be transferred to inventory and out of the income statement with overproduction.
2. ABC requires the identification of multiple overhead activities and greater recordkeeping on usage of cost drivers.
3. The value chain is composed of the activities that add value to the customer. Non-value-added activities are sources for cost reduction.
4. ABC may not be appropriate for organizations with only a small proportion of overhead or uniform products. ABC may also lead to control problems because of changes in performance measures.

Page 409
1. Joint products come from a common resource in predetermined proportions. Joint costs are the cost of the common resource and the cost of splitting the resource into the joint products.
2. Joint costs are common to all joint products and can not be separately identified with one joint product.
3. A joint product should be processed further if the incremental revenues are greater than the incremental costs.

Chapter 12

Page 442
1. Major forces affecting organizations recently include technological innovations and global competition.
2. Investment opportunities are determined by the asset structure, customer base, and nature of knowledge creation.
3. The organizational structure interacts with the investment opportunities. The investment opportunities affect the organizational structure, but the organizational structure can be changed through different incentives to affect the investment opportunities.
4. Planning decisions allow for more efficient methods of creating and selling products, which adds value to the organization.
5. The role of management accounting is to assist in control and planning decisions. The management accounting system must change as the organization changes.

Page 458
1. Productivity is generally measured by dividing outputs by inputs.
2. Productivity measures identify efficient uses of resources and are used to motivate managers. Aggregating different inputs and outputs, however, require prices and changing prices can influence productivity measures. Productivity measures may also promote overproduction and don't explicitly recognize quality.
3. The philosophy of TQM is to continually lower costs and provide better products and improved service for customers.
4. The four categories of quality costs are: prevention, appraisal, internal failure and external failure.
5. The advantages of JIT include reduced inventory and storage costs and a quicker response to customer demand through faster throughput times.

Chapter 13

Page 475
1. The steps in the capital budgeting process are initiation or identification of investment opportunities, ratification, implementation, and monitoring.
2. The opportunity cost of capital represents the forgone opportunity of the cash invested in the project generating a return on another investment. The opportunity cost of capital is used to discount future cash flows.

Page 479
1. The payback period does not use the time value of money and does not recognize cash flows beyond the payback period.
2. A multi-year ROI is calculated by dividing the annual average income by the average investment during the life of the investment.
3. ROI does not recognize the time value of money and is influenced by accounting methods.

Page 486
1. Cash flows should be discounted because they can be invested and generate a return.
2. Most capital budgeting decisions have an effect on the level of other asset accounts. More cash invested in accounts receivable and inventory generates an opportunity cost of capital.
3. Finance charges are implicitly recognized by the discount rate.
4. Depreciation lowers income which reduces cash that must be paid in taxes. Therefore, depreciation affects cash through income taxes.
5. Higher risk projects should be discounted by higher interest rates.

Page 490
1. The internal rate of return is the discount rate on cash flows that sets the net present value to zero.
2. The internal rate of return may cause incorrect decisions when mutually exclusive investment choices must be made. Also the internal rate of return may be difficult to calculate.

Chapter 14

Page 521
1. Organizations use standard costing to communicate expected costs for planning purposes. The primary

reason, however, is to control processes and individuals by using standard costs as benchmarks.
2. There is no generally accepted method for setting standards. Some organizations set standards very tightly and others set standards that are easily attainable. Information from those with knowledge about the processes should be obtained to establish standards.

Page 531
1. The two components are quantity and unit prices.
2. A favorable variance means that standard costs are greater than actual costs.
3. The personnel manager is likely to be responsible for the labor wage variance and the operations manager should be responsible for the efficiency variance.
4. The material price variance is the responsibility of the purchasing manager and the quantity variance is the responsibility of the operations manager.
5. The material quantity variance is unfavorable when more material is used than the standard. It can be caused by carelessness in using the material or poor quality material.

Page 535
1. Purchasing managers can reduce the material price variance by purchasing large amounts to get discounts.
2. If a manager is only responsible for one variance, that manager will act in a way to influence that variance to the detriment of the rest of the organization. An example is a purchasing manager purchasing low quality material to obtain a favorable price variance, but the quantity variance will likely be unfavorable when employees try to work with the poor quality material.
3. By making managers responsible for multiple variances that they have some effect, they will monitor other managers that influence those variances.
4. Satisficing behavior occurs when employees only work hard enough to satisfy standards.

Page 539
1. The expected usage is based on estimates at the beginning of the period. The standard usage is based on the standard per unit times the actual units. The actual usage is what occurs.
2. Standard overhead costs differ from budgeted overhead costs because the expected usage of the allocation base is different than the actual usage.
3. Overhead standards are intended to motivate managers to use overhead resources efficiently. Favorable fixed overhead variances, however, can be obtained through overproduction.

Page 541
1. Variances represent deviations from plans and should be understood by managers.

2. The decision to investigate depends on the size of random fluctuations, the opportunity cost of investigation, the opportunity cost of not investigating, and the ease of correcting the problem if it exists.

Page 542
1. Standard costs are frequently based on past experiences and take time to institute. A rapidly changing business environment means that there is not a long history to refer and not enough time to institute a standard costing system.
2. Standard costs are still being used by a large number of companies.

CHAPTER 15

Page 568
1. Firms become involved in international trade through simple import or export transactions or by establishing direct operations in a foreign country.
2. A multinational firm is an organization that has operating units, such as manufacturing plants, retail outlets, or distribution warehouses, in more than one country. A company importing or exporting goods is not a multinational firm because it only has an operating unit in one country.

Page 571
1. A U.S. merchant does not have to accept Canadian dollars because Canadian dollars are not legal tender for transactions in the United States.
2. An exchange rate is the price at which one currency can be converted to another currency.
3. If a currency appreciates against another currency, the appreciated currency can buy more of the depreciated currency. The appreciation of a country's currency makes its goods more expensive for foreign customers and imports of foreign goods cheaper for domestic consumers.

Page 576
1. Companies engaged in international trade face multiple taxing authorities because each country in which the multinational operates has the legal rights to impose taxes on the organizations operating within its jurisdiction.
2. Research and development expenditures can be treated as an asset in Japan but must be expensed in the United States. German accounting is more conservative than U.S. accounting because German corporations recognize future losses and expenses sooner than required by U.S. accounting rules. UK companies make occasional revaluations of buildings and land to market value, whereas U.S. rules preclude most revaluations.
3. Japanese and Israeli cultures emphasize group (or collective) versus individual orientation, whereas in the United States and Australia, individualism is more dominant.

Page 580

1. Set the transfer price to recognize more of the profits in the country with the lowest tax rate. If the country of the supplying division has the lowest tax rate, a higher transfer price transfers profit to the supplying division and lowers after-tax profit. If the country of the purchasing division has the lowest tax rate, a lower transfer price transfers profit to the purchasing division and lowers after-tax profit.
2. If the local government is threatening to expropriate the assets of high-profit, foreign-owned companies, these companies may want to choose high transfer prices for their imports and low transfer prices for their exports. If multinationals choose transfer prices solely to minimize taxes or for political considerations, they must devise alternative measures of performance to motivate managers of foreign subsidiaries.

Page 583

1. If managers are evaluated in a foreign currency of their parent instead of their own local currency, they bear the risk of exchange rate fluctuations.
2. Using the local currency to evaluate the manager of the local operations reduces the risks of exchange rate fluctuations borne by the local manager. The local manager cannot prevent fluctuations in exchange rates. Hence, they should not be held accountable for currency revaluations. If their performance is based on exchange rate fluctuations and they are risk averse, they will try to reduce this risk. One way to reduce this risk is by buying or selling currencies to offset their exchange risk. However, such currency transactions generate transactions costs. The shareholders or the corporation can bear this risk at lower cost than the local manager.

Photo Credits

Chapter 1

Page 2 John Thoeming
5 Michael Rosenfeld/Tony Stone Images
7 John Thoeming
8 John Thoeming
8 John Thoeming
15 Courtesy of Boeing Corporation
20 Copyright General Motors Corporation; used with permission
22 Courtesy of Bell South Corporation

Chapter 2

Page 30 John Thoeming
33 John Thoeming
34 John Thoeming
35 John Thoeming
36 Kinko's is a registered trademark of Kinko's Graphics Corp. and is used with permission
40 Courtesy of United Airlines
47 John Thoeming

Chapter 3

Page 60 Eric Millette
63 Courtesy of Mrs. Fields' Cookies
65 Courtesy of Brothers Gourmet Coffee, Inc.
69 Tony Stone Images
71 The Image Bank
73 William Crow/Sonoco
75 Tony Stone Images
80 Left: John Thoeming
80 Right: Tony Stone Images

Chapter 4

Page 100 Brett Froomer/The Image Bank
102 Susan Van Etten/Stock Boston
105 Courtesy of the Boeing Corporation
106 Tony Stone Images
110 Gary Gladstone/The Image Bank
112 Shumsky/The Image Works
119 Courtesy of Deere & Company

Chapter 5

Page 134 Courtesy of the Hillendale Bed & Breakfast
137 John Thoeming
139 John Thoeming
141 John Thoeming
145 John Thoeming
150 Peter Pearson/Tony Stone Images
152 Courtesy of Sun Microsystems
157 Mitch Kezar/Tony Stone Images

Chapter 6

Page 170 John Thoeming
174 Chuck Keeler/Tony Stone Images
178 John Thoeming
180 John Thoeming
181 Courtesy of Chrysler Corporation

Chapter 7

Page 196 Tony Stone Images
199 AP Photo
201 John Thoeming
204 Ben Glass/Motion Picture & Television Archive
206 AP Photo/Steven Senne
211 Tony Stone Images
213 Courtesy of Weyerhaeuser Company

Chapter 8

Page 238 Tony Stone Images
240 Tony Stone Images
243 Courtesy of Hon Company
247 Bob Daemmrich/The Image Works
249 AP Photo
254 Tony Stone Images
259 Greenlar/The Image Works
260 John Thoeming

Photo Credits

Chapter 9

Page 286	Bob Daemmrich/The Image Works
288	Jeff Greenberg/Peter Arnold, Inc.
293	John Edwards/Tony Stone Images
296	Hiroyuki Matsumoto/Tony Stone Images
301	Charles Thatcher/Tony Stone Images
304	David R. Frazier/Tony Stone Images
309	John Thoeming

Chapter 10

Page 338	Keith Wood/Tony Stone Images
342	Barbara Filet/Tony Stone Images
346	Bruce Forster/Tony Stone Images
347	Paul Chesley/Tony Stone Images
351	Andrew Sacks/Tony Stone Images
355	Bob Daemmrich/The Image Works
359	Rich LaSalle/Tony Stone Images

Chapter 11

Page 384	Gabriel M. Covian/The Image Bank
386	John Thoeming
388	John Thoeming
393	F. Pedrick/The Image Works
399	Okoniewski
400	Courtesy of United Parcel Service
404	Michael Salas/The Image Bank
407	Graeme Norways/Tony Stone Images

Chapter 12

Page 435	Bob Daemmrich/The Image Works
437	Joe Sohm/The Image Works
438	Glenn Turner
443	Juan Silva/The Image Bank
447	Courtesy of Motorola Corporation
449	BMW Manufacturing/William H. Struhs
456	David Frazier/Tony Stone Images
457	John Thoeming

Chapter 13

Page 470	John Thoeming
473	John Thoeming
473	John Thoeming
476	CS/Motion Picture & Television Archives
482	John Thoeming
484	Mark Junak/Tony Stone Images
489	AP Photo
493	John Thoeming

Chapter 14

Page 516	Zigy Kaluzny/Tony Stone Images
520	Michael Rosenfeld/Tony Stone Images
526	A. T. Willett/The Image Bank
530	John Thoeming
533	John Thoeming
534	Howard Boylan/Tony Stone Images
536	Tim Bieber/The Image Bank
540	Kaluzny & Thatcher/Tony Stone Images

Chapter 15

Page 564	AP Photo/Thomas Kienzle
566	John Thoeming
568	Mike Blank/Tony Stone Images
574	Dan Bosler/Tony Stone Images
576	Martin Rogers/Tony Stone Images
577	Rob Crandall/The Image Works
581	Andy Sacks/Tony Stone Images

INDEX

A

ABC/Capital Cities, 35
Absorption costing, 338–383, **363**
   alternatives to, 391–406
      activity-based costing; *see*
         Activity-based costing (ABC)
      practical capacity, overhead
         allocation based on, 392–395
      variable costing; *see* **Variable costs/costing**
   criticisms of, 384–392
      allocation base, underuse of, 389–390, 394
      overproduction incentives, 386–389, 394–395
      product costs, misleading, 390–391
   death spiral and, 390–391, **411**
   job order systems; *see* **Job order systems**
   process cost systems; *see* **Process cost systems**
Accelerated depreciation, 483–484
Accounting/Accountants; *see also* Accounting systems
   and capital budgeting, 473
   in decentralized organizations; *see* Decentralized organizations
   financial, 13, **25**
   management; *see* **Management accounting**
   responsibility, 200, **224**
   tax, 13, 14–15, **25**
      cost allocation and, 291
      LIFO and, 366
Accounting systems
   compared, 13
   and JIT processes, 456–457
   multiple, 18–19, 294
   multiple-purpose, trade-offs
      external reporting *vs.* control, 17
      planning decisions *vs.* control, 16, 220, 388, 405
      planning decisions *vs.* external reporting, 16–17, 75
   organizational change and, 183–184
   purposes served by, 13
   role of, 12–15, 441–442
      control, 14

      external users, 14–15
      performance measures, 179–180
      planning decisions, 13–14, 456
Accounts, classification of, 79–82
Activities; *see also* **Value chain**
   cost drivers; *see* **Cost drivers**
   cost of, planning decisions related to, 67–70
   non-value-added; *see* **Non-value-added activities**
   outsourcing of; *see* **Outsourcing**
   value-added; *see* **Value-added activities**
Activity-based costing (ABC), 117–122, **123,** 398–399; *see also* **Activity-based management (ABM)**
   acceptance of, 403–406
   advantages, 119–120
   book team and, 409
   and incentive to overproduce, 403
   opposition to, 184
   problems with, 120–122
      book team and, 122
   single cost drivers *vs.*, 120–121
Activity-based management (ABM), 120, **123, 411;** *see also* **Activity-based costing (ABC)**
   control implications of, 401–403
   cost drivers, choosing, 402
   and organizational complexity, 399–401
   planning decisions through, 399–401
   process management and, 400, **411**
   value chain and, 401
Actual overhead costs, 538, **544**
Actual usage, 537, **544**
Allegheny Ludlum Steel Co., 397
Allocation bases, 299, **311**
   actual usage of, 537, **544**
   choosing, for cost allocation, 301–303
   cost drivers; *see* **Cost drivers**
   departmental, 357
   expected usage of, 536–537, **544**
   input volume measures, 536–537
   for joint costs, 411–412
   multiple, for overhead costs, 354–356
   standard usage of, 536–537, **544**
   underuse of, absorption cost systems and, 389–390, 394
   and variable costing, 397

American Express, 67
American Institute of Certified Public Accountants (AICPA), 290
Annuities, 497–498
   future value table, 505
Antidumping regulations, 585, 587
Application rates
   calculation of, for cost allocation, 303–306
   overhead, 349–351
      departmental, for two-stage cost allocation, 357–359
      with multiple allocation bases, 354–356
      practical capacity of allocation base and, 392–395
      recalculating, 353–354
Applied overhead costs, 537–538, **544**
Appraisal costs, 450, **460**
Asset structure, 438–439, **460**
AT&T, 63, 120, 211, 219
Automatic teller machines (ATMs), 7
Average costs, 42, **49**
   absorption cost systems and, 386–388
   and incentive to overproduce, 403
Avoidable product costs, 152, **160**
   and planning decision simplification, 85

B

Balanced scorecard, 179–180, **189**
Balance sheets, budgeted, 262–263
Ball, Ray, 595
Banker, R., 594
Bank of America, 249, 582–583
Bank of Tokyo, 568
Batch-level costs, 109, **123**
Bausch & Lomb, 180
Behavior
   ethical; *see* **Ethics**
   modifying, 297–298
   satisficing, 534–535, **544**
   self-interested, 177
Bellcore, 219
BellSouth, 22, 23
Bell Telephone, 441
Benchmarking, 103, **123**

Benefits, 32, **49**; see also **Cost/benefit analysis**
   differential, 33, **49**
   externalities, 296, **311**
   identification/measurement of, 34–35
Bingham, R., 318n
Birnberg, Jacob, 595
Blockbuster Video, 473
BMW, 449
Boeing Corp., 14, 15, 105, 152
Bonus plans, organizational change and, 182–184
Bottlenecks, 157–158, **160**
Bottom-up budgeting, 244
Brand-name capital, 438
Break-even analysis, 144–146, **160**
Briggs & Stratton, 211
British Rail, 308
Brothers Gourmet Coffee Bar, 65
Brown, J., 594
Budgeted overhead costs, 537, **544**
Budget lapsing, 247–249, **266**
Budgets/Budgeting, 238–285
   benefits of, 240
   book team and, 263
   bottom-up, 244
   capital; see **Capital budgeting**
   CEO in charge of, 244
   committees for, 244
   for control, 241–243
      and planning trade-offs, 243–245
   defined, 240, **266**
   for employee motivation, 241
   flexible, 249–250, **266**
   incremental, 251–252, **266**
   kaizen costing, 242
   lapsing of, 247–249, **266**
   line-item, 245–246
   long-run, 245–246
   master; see **Master budget**
   monthly cash flow, 266–268
   participative, 244, **266**
   as performance measure, 241–242
   for planning decisions, 240–241
      and control trade-offs, 243–245
   for problem resolution, 245–252
   short-run, 245–246
   static, 249–250, **266**
   strategic planning and, 245–246
   top-down, 244
   variances, 241–242, **266**
   zero-base (ZBB), 251–252, **266**
Burger King, 7, 8, 447, 566
By-products, 409, **411**
   joint cost allocation for, 412

C

Calvasina, E., 594
Calvasina, G., 594
Calvasina, R., 594
Capacity, 49
   opportunity costs of exceeding, 41
   practical, 392–395, **411**
Capital
   brand-name, 438
   opportunity cost of; see **Opportunity cost of capital**
Capital budgeting, 470–514, **492**; see also **Investment opportunities**
   accountants' role in, 473
   book team and, 491
   case study, 513–514
   implementation stage, 473
   initiation process, 472
   internal rate of return; see **Internal rate of return (IRR)**
   long-term investment decisions, 472
   master budget illustration, 258
   methods used in practice, 489–491
   net present value of cash flows; see **Net present value (NPV)**
   process of, 472–473
   project evaluation
      opportunity cost of capital, 473–475
      payback method, 476–477, **493**
      return on investment (ROI); see **Return on investment (ROI)**
   ratification process, 472–473
Carlson, D., 68n
Carnegie, Andrew, 19, 343
Carroll, P., 594
Carter, Jimmy, 252
Case studies
   capital budgeting, 513–514
   cost allocation, 334–337
   cost estimation, 97–98
   direct material variance analysis, 560–562
   ethical behavior, 29
   indirect product costs, 131–132
   master budget, 283–285
   motivation, employee, 193–194
   opportunity costs, 58–59
   overhead costs
      and dropping product with joint costs, 427–429
      in new factory, 426–427
      over- and underabsorbed overhead cost flows, 380–383
      variable, choosing cost drivers to reflect, 429–430
   product planning decisions, 169
   quality costs, 467–469
   volume measures, 559–560
Cash flows
   annuities, 497–498
   budgeting
      spreadsheet analysis, 266–268
      statements for, 260–262
   expected, 485, **493**
   net present value of; see **Net present value (NPV)**
   perpetuities, 496–497
   present value of, 495–498
      multiple per year, 499–501
CBS, 35
Certified management accountants (CMAs), 23
Chan, Yoke Kai, 595
Chandler, A., 593, 594
Change, organizational
   book team and, 23
   framework for, 182–184, 436–442
   investment opportunities; see **Investment opportunities**
   and management accounting, 19–21, 441–442, 458–459
   organizational structure, 440
   planning decisions, 440
   and global competition, 6–8, 20–21, 436–437
   innovations
      just-in-time (JIT) processes; see **Just-in-time (JIT) processes**
      productivity measurement, 443–446
      total quality management; see **Total quality management (TQM)**
   for quality, 448
   technological change, 20–21, 436–437
      computers, 5
      information systems, 4–5
      materials requirement planning (MRP), 455, **460**
Chevron, 261
Chow, Chee, 595
Christie, A., 593, 594
Chrysler, 181–182, 215
CNN, 566
Coca-Cola, 211
Common costs, 106, **123**
Compensation contracts, 440
   book team and, 186
   performance measures and, 181–182
Competition
   cost-based pricing and, 140
   global; see Global competition
Compound interest, 494
   and multiple cash flows per year, 499–501
Computer-assisted design (CAD), 5, **25**
Computer-assisted manufacturing (CAM), 5, **25**, 542
Computer-integrated manufacturing (CIM), 5, **25**
Computers
   and organizational change, 5
   spreadsheet analysis, monthly cash flow budgets, 266–268
Constraints
   bottlenecks, 157–158, **160**
   capacity, 41
   product mix decisions with, 155–159
   theory of, 156–159, **160**
Contracts
   cost-based pricing and, 139–140
   employee, rewarding performance through, 181–182
Contribution margin per unit, 143, **160**
   product mix decisions with constraints and, 155–156
Control, 11–12, **25**, 172–173
   activity-based management (ABM) implications, 401–403
   budgeting for, 241–243, 247
   case study, 193–194
   cost allocation for, 296–299
   decision rights; see **Decision rights**
   and external reporting trade-offs, 17

Control **(continued)**
    hierarchies, 186
    historical costs and, 17, 45
    incentive to overproduce, mitigating, 388–389, 395
    internal system for, 186–187, **189**
    kickbacks, 187
    and line-item budgets, 247
    management accounting for, 14, 172
    monitoring, 12, **25**, 185, **189**
    and multiple allocation bases, 356
    and organizational goals; *see* Goals, organizational
    over- and underabsorbed overhead, 351
    performance measures; *see* **Performance measures**
    and planning decisions
        separation from decision control, 184–187
        trade-offs between, 16, 220, 243–245, 388, 580
    process costing for, 361–362
    system examples, 186–187
    theory of constraints and, 158
    transfer pricing and, 214, 220–221
Controllability principle, 198–200, **223**
    and cost allocation, 289
    and transfer pricing, 214
Controllable costs, 198–200, **223**
Controllers, 21–22, **25**
Coors, 5
Corning, Inc., 259
Cost Accounting Standards Board (CASB), 293
Cost allocation, 286–337
    absorption costing; *see* **Absorption costing**
    basic steps of, 299–308
        1. defining cost objects, 299–300
        2. accumulating indirect costs in cost pools, 300–301
        3. choosing allocation base, 301–303
        4. estimating application rate, 303–306
        5. allocating costs to cost objects, 307–308
    book team and, 310
    case study, 334–337
    and controllability principle, 289
    defined, 288, **311**
    ethical considerations, 288–289
    with fixed costs, 350–351
    of joint costs; *see* **Joint costs**
    multiple methods for, 294
    multistage, 300–301, **311**
    reasons for, 289–299
        control purposes, 296–299
            behavior modification, 297–298
            decision rights allocation, 297
            mutual monitoring, 298, **311**
            performance measures, 297–298
        external requirements, 290–294
            cost reimbursement contracts, 291–293

            shareholders, reports to, 290–291
            taxable income, reporting of, 291
        planning purposes, 294–296
            communication of cost data, 295–296
            externalities and, 296
            opportunity cost estimation, 294–295
            tracing costs, 75–78, 85
                with cost drivers, 76–78, 111–117
                      disadvantages, 115–117
                      process steps, 111–115
        segment reporting and, 308–310
    of service department costs, 312–316
        direct method, **311**, 312–313
        reciprocal method, **311**, 315–316
        step-down method, **311**, 313–315
    two-stage, 357–359
Cost-based pricing, 138–140
Cost/benefit analysis, 49
    of customers, 71–72
    for decision planning, 32–39
    differential costs/benefits, 33
    for information gathering, 46–48
    of joint processes, 407–408
    opportunity costs; *see* **Opportunity costs**
    product mix decisions and, 64
    of subunits, 70–71
    and sunk costs, 38
Cost centers, 200–202, **223**
    identification of, 212
Cost drivers, 76–78, **87**
    choice of, ABM and, 402
    tracing indirect product costs with, 111–117
    and ABC, compared, 120–121
Cost estimation, 60–98
    case study, 97–98
    cost drivers; *see* **Cost drivers**
    cost objects; *see* **Cost objects**
    direct labor, 107, **123**
    direct product costs, 106–108
    of fixed and variable costs, 78–84
        by account classification, 79–82
        by regression analysis, 87–89
        by visually fitted historical costs, 82–84
    for planning decisions, 62–75
        activity costs, 67–70
        customer costs, 71–72
        period costs, 74–75
        product costs, 62–67
        subunit costs, 70–71
        suppliers, 72–74
    by tracing costs, 75–78, 85, 111–117
Costner, Kevin, 204
Cost objects, 62, **87**, 288, **311**
    defining, for cost allocation, 299–300
    of planning decisions, 85
    subunits as, 71
    suppliers as, 73
    time periods as, 74–75
    tracing costs to, 75–78, 85

Cost of goods manufactured, 364–367
Cost of goods sold, 74–75, **87**
    adjusting, for over- or underabsorbed overhead, 352
    and alternative cost flow inventory methods, 364–367
    estimating, 260
Cost pools, 300–301, **311**
    choosing allocation base for, 301–303
    fixed costs in, 305–306
    multiple overhead, 354–356
Cost reimbursement contracts, 291–293
Cost(s), 49
    allocating; *see* **Cost allocation**
    appraisal, 450, **460**
    average, per unit, 42
    avoidable, 85, 152, **160**
    batch-level, 109, **123**
    common, 106, **123**
    controllable, 198–200, **223**
    customer, 71–72
    CVP and; *see* **Cost-volume-profit (CVP) analysis**
    differential, 33, **49**, 85
    direct; *see* **Direct costs**
    external failure, 450, **460**
    externalities, 296, **311**
    facility-level, 110, 120, **123**
    financing, 482
    fixed, 43–45, **49**
    historical; *see* **Historical costs**
    identification/measurement problems, 35
    incremental, 85, 136–137, **160**
    indirect; *see* **Indirect costs**
    internal failure, 450, **460**
    joint; *see* **Joint costs**
    marginal; *see* **Marginal costs**
    monitoring, 177–178
    opportunity; *see* **Opportunity costs**
    overhead; *see* **Overhead costs**
    prevention, 450, **460**
    product-level, 109, **123**
    purchasing, 73
    quality, 450–451, 467–469
    sunk, 38–39, **49**
    unit-level, 109, **123**
    variable; *see* **Variable costs/costing**
Cost-volume-profit (CVP) analysis, 142–149, **160**
    break-even analysis, 144–146, **160**
    constant sales prices and, 148
    graph of, 147–148
    multiple products and, 149
    opportunity cost approximation and, 148
    optimal quantity/price determination and, 148
    problems with, 148–149
    profit equation, 142–143
    specified profit, achieving, 146–147
    after-tax, 160
    time value of money and, 148–149
Crane, M., 593
Cress, W., 593, 594
CSX, 211

Index

Cultural differences, multinational firms and, 575–576
Customer base, 439, 460
Customers
  costs of, 71–72
  quality defined by, 448
  satisfaction of
    JIT processes and, 455–456
    quality and, 447, 449
Cutthroat Island, 476
Cyto Technologies, 473, 474

D

Daihatsu, 242
Dan Post Boot, 355
Death spiral, 390–391, 411
Decentralized organizations
  controllability principle, 198–200, **223**
  responsibility accounting, 200, **224**
  responsibility centers; *see*
    Responsibility centers
  transfer pricing; *see* **Transfer pricing**
Decision rights, 9, 25
  assignment of, 173–174, 440
  cost allocations and, 197
    of cost center managers, 200–202
  of investment center managers, 204–205
  knowledge and, 174–176
  line-item budgets and, 247
  organizational change and, 182–184
  and planning decision process, 184–188
  of profit center managers, 202–203
  responsibility centers and, 200–201
Defects
  measuring quality by, 448–449
  opportunity cost of, 450
  zero defects concept, 447–448
Delta Air Lines, 409
Demand, cost-based pricing and, 139
Department of Defense, 291
Depreciation, 492
  accelerated, 483–484, **492**
  double-declining-balance, 484
  economic, 304
  and NPV analysis, 482–484
  straight-line, 483–484
Depreciation tax shield, 483–484, 492
Diamler-Benz, 5
Differential benefit, 33, 49
Differential costs, 33, 49
  and planning decision simplification, 85
DiGabriele, A., 326n
Direct costs, 87, 106–108
  tracing to cost objects, 75–78, 85
Direct labor, 106–107, **123**
  cost of, job order systems and, 345–346
Direct labor variances, 522–527, 544
  composition of, 522–523
Direct materials, 106–107, **123**
Direct materials variances, 527–531, 544
  case study, 560–562

Direct method, of cost allocation, **311,** 312–313
Direct product costs; *see* **Direct costs**
Discount rates, 475
  risk-adjusted, 484–486
Disney, 35
Domestic content requirements, 585, 586
Double-declining-balance depreciation, 484
Drtina, R., 593
Dumping, 142, 160
  regulations against, 587
Du Pont, 19, 207–209, 304, 309
Du Pont, Pierre, 207–209

E

Eastman Kodak, 211, 235–236, 245–246, 566, 577, 593
Economic depreciation, 304
Economic value added (EVA); *see* **Residual income**
Edgar Thompson Steel Works, 343
Edwards, J., 595
E.I. Du Pont de Nemours Powder Co.; *see* Du Pont
Eisenstadt, M., 318n
Empowerment, worker, 10, **25**
Engel, J., 430n
Equivalent units, 360, **363**
Ethics, **25**
  case study, 29
  cost allocation and, 288–289
  IMA code of, 23–24
  and management accounting, 22–24
  of outsourcing, 69–70
Exchange rates, 568–570, **585;** *see also* Foreign currency
  managerial importance of, 570–571
  and performance evaluation, 581–583
Expected cash flow, 485, 493
Expected usage, 536–537, 544
External failure costs, 450, 460
Externalities, 296, 311, 533
External reporting, 13, 14–15; *see also* Financial statements
  and control trade-offs, 17
  cost allocation and, 290–291, 294
  historical costs and, 16–17
  by multinational firms, 573–575
  over- and underabsorbed overhead, 351–352
  and planning decision trade-offs, 16–17, 75
  of profits, CVP analysis *vs.*, 143
  segment reporting in, 309
  of taxable income, 291

F

Facility-level costs, 110, 120, **123**
Factories, changes caused by JIT, 454–455
Favorable variance, 241–242, **266,** 523, **544**
Financial accounting, 13, **25**
  external users of, 14–15
  period costs and, 74–75

Financial Accounting Standards Board (FASB), 14, 16, 290
Financial budget, master budget illustration, 258–259
The Financial Executive, 189–190
Financial statements; *see also* External reporting
  budgeted (pro forma), 259–263, **266**
  balance sheet, 262–263
  cash flow statement, 260–262
  income statement, 260
Financing costs, future cash flow estimation and, 482
Fireman's Fund, 106
First-in, first-out (FIFO) method, 260, 361, **363,** 365–367
Fixed costs, 49
  cost allocation with, 350–351
  in cost pools, 305–306
  estimation of
    by account classification, 79–82
    by regression analysis, 87–89
    by visually fitted historical costs, 82–84
  and opportunity cost approximation, 43–45
  and rate of output, 85
Fixed overhead budget variance, 544, 546
Fixed overhead variance, 544, 546
Fixed overhead volume variance, 544, 546
Flexible budgets, 249–250, **266**
Florida Power & Light, 451–452
Ford Motor Co., 40, 63, 215, 567, 571, 581
Foreign Corrupt Practices Act (FCPA), 576
Foreign currency, 568–571
  exchange rates; *see* **Exchange rates**
  hard currency restrictions, 587
Foreign exchange markets, 585; *see also* **Exchange rates**
Future value
  of annuities, 498, 505
  of cash, 493–494, 504

G

Gardner, M., 302n
Garner, S., 593
Gaver, J., 594
Gaver, K., 594
General Electric, 520
Generally accepted accounting principles (GAAP), 13, 14, 290
  indirect product costs and, 109
  joint cost allocation, 407, 411
General Motors, 9, 19, 20, 38, 69–70, 213, 215
Global competition
  and organizational change, 6–8, 20–21, 436–437
  quality and, 447
Goals, organizational
  allocation bases and, 302
  individual goals *vs.*, decision rights and, 174–175

Goals **(continued)**
    motivating individuals toward, 176–182
        activity-based management and, 402
        budgeting and, 241
        case study, 193–194
        compensation contracts, 181–182, 440
        monitoring costs and, 177–178, **189**
        performance measurement; *see* **Performance measures**
    self-interested behavior, 177
The Goal, 156
Godfrey, S., 595
Goldman, Sachs & Co., 575
Goldratt, Eliyahu, 156
Goodwill, customer, cost-based pricing and, 140
Government regulations
    antidumping regulations, **585**, 587
    cost-based pricing and, 139–140
    domestic content requirements, **585**, 586
    hard currency restrictions, 587

H

Hard currency restrictions, 587
Harley-Davidson, 457
Harrington, L., 227
Harrison, S., 593
Harvard Business Review, 179
Heagy, C., 595
Hewlett-Packard, 457
Hierarchies
    for control, 186
    of responsibility centers, 204–205
Hiromoto, T., 594
Historical costs, **25**
    opportunity costs *vs.*, 45–46
    performance measures and, 179
    planning decisions and, 16–17
    popularity of, 45
    standard costs *vs.*, 518
    visually fitted, for cost estimation, 82–84
Hitachi, 405, 576
Hobdy, T., 593
Hoeger, S., 593
Hofstede, Geert, 595
Hon Co., 242–243
Honda Motors, 534, 581–582
Howell, R., 594
Hurdle rate, 488, **493**

I

IBM, 172, 235–236, 297, 449
Implementation, 185, **189**
Income, taxable, reporting of, 291, 366
Income statements, budgeted, 260
Incremental budgets, 251–252, **266**
Incremental costs, 136–137, **160**
    and planning simplification, 85
Incremental revenues, 136–137
Independence Day, 476

Indirect costs, 87
    activity-based costing; *see* **Activity-based costing (ABC)**
    allocating; *see* **Cost allocation**
    batch-level, 109, **123**
    case study, 131–132
    cost pools of, 300–301
    facility-level, 110, 120, **123**
    nature of, 108–111
    overhead; *see* **Overhead costs**
    product-level, 109, **123**
    unit-level, 109, **123**
Indirect product costs; *see* **Indirect costs**
Individual goals, 176–177
    and self-interested behavior, 177
    vs. organizational goals, decision rights and, 174–175
Information
    benefit and cost of, 46–48
    materials requirement planning (MRP), 455, **460**
    planning decisions and, 13–14
    technology and, 4–5
Initiation, 185, **189**
Institute of Management Accountants (IMA)
    CMA certification, 24
    code of ethics, 23–24
Intel, 447–448
Interest rates
    as opportunity cost of capital, 475
Internal auditors, 22, **25**
Internal control system, 186–187, **189**; *see also* **Control**
Internal failure costs, 450, **460**
Internal rate of return (IRR), 486–490, **493**
    hurdle rate, 488, **493**
    NPV method *vs.*, 487–488
    problems with, 488–489
    reinvestment rate and, 488
Internal Revenue Service (IRS), 13, 14, 16, 247
    depreciation and, 482–483
International Organization of Standards (ISO), 452
International trade, 566–568; *see also* **Multinational firms**
Inventories
    costing methods, 364–367
        first-in, first-out (FIFO), 260, 361, **363**, 365–367
        JIT processes and, 457–458
        last-in, first-out (LIFO), 260, 361, **363**, 365–366
        specific identification valuation method, 365–366
        weighted-average cost method, **363**, 365–367
    future cash flow estimation and, 481–482
    incentives for building, 532–533
    reducing, 389
Investment centers, 204–212, **223**
    decision rights and, 204
    identification of, 212
    opportunity cost of capital and, 205

    performance measures for
        multiple, 211–212
        residual income, 209–211, **224**
        return on investment (ROI); *see* **Return on investment (ROI)**
Investment opportunities, 437–440, **460**; *see also* **Capital budgeting**
    asset structure and, 438–439
    customer base and, 439
    external forces and, 436–437
    knowledge creation and, 439
    NAFTA and, 437
ISO 9000 certification, 452
Ittner, Chris, 594

J

Jaguar, 581
Job-order cost sheets, 341–342, 345–346
Job order systems, 341–359, **363**
    accounts, cost flows through, 345–348
    important features of, 343
    job-order cost sheets, 341–342, 345–346
    labor costs, 345–346
    material costs, 346
    overhead costs; *see* **Overhead costs**
    schematic of, 345
John Deere, 119, 459
Joint costs; *see also* **Joint products**
    allocation of, 407–409, 411–414
        by-products and, 412
        GAAP recommendations, 407, 411
        net realizable value method, 412–413, 414
        physical measure method, 412, 413
        relative sales value method, 412, 413
    defined, 407, **411**
Joint products, 406–410, **411**
    by-products, 409, **411**
    costs of; *see* **Joint costs**
Joyce, M.J., 333n
Joye, M., 593, 594
J.P. Morgan & Co., 575
Juran, Joseph, 447
Just-in-time (JIT) processes, 7, **25**, 453–458
    accounting system changes for, 456–457
    factory changes caused by, 454–455
    for inventory reduction, 389
    materials requirement planning (MRP) and, 455, **460**
    popularity factors, 455–456
    problems with, 457–458
    and supplier relationships, 455
    throughput time, 453–454, **460**
    traditional systems *vs.*, 453–454
    wasted (non-value-added) time, 454

K

Kaizen costing, 242
Kalagnanam, S., 594
Kaplan, Robert S., 26, 179, 593, 594
Karmarkar, U., 594

Katel, P., 594
Kato, Y., 594
Kawasaki, 534
Kickbacks, 187
Kim, I., 594
Kinko's, 37
Klammer, T., 491, 594
Kmart, 187
Knowledge
  creation of, investment opportunities and, 439
  and decision rights, 174–176
  standard cost setting and, 519
  transference of, 175–176
Koch, B., 491, 594

L

Labor, direct; *see* **Direct labor**
Labor efficiency variance, 522–527, **544**
La Leche League, 32
Lammers, L., 302n
Last-in, first-out (LIFO) method, 260, 361, **363**, 365–366
Lead-loss pricing, 140, **160**
Lederer, P., 594
Lewis, R., 227
Line-item budgets, 246–247
Lonczak, D., 318n
Long-run budgets, 245–246
Ludlow Co., 73

M

McDonald's, 7, 8, 63, 446–447, 533, 566
McDonnell Douglas, 451–452
Make-or-buy decisions; *see* **Outsourcing**
Management accounting, 25
  accountants, types of, 21–22
  adaptation of, 458–459
    book team and, 459
  for control, 14, 172
  ethics and, 22–24
  evolution of, 19–21
  innovations and, 442–458
    just-in-time (JIT) processes; *see* **Just-in-time (JIT) processes**
    productivity measurement, 443–446
    total quality management; *see* **Total quality management (TQM)**
  and organizational change, 4–8, 20–21, 441–442, 458–459
  for planning decisions, 13–14
  problems, signs of, 459
  quality costs and, 451
  role of, 441–442
Management by exception, 519, **544**
Managers
  decision rights of, 200–205
  motivating, with ABM, 402
  role of, 10–12
Marginal costs, 41–42, **49**, 137
  and rate of output, 85
Marketing, and control/planning budget trade-offs, 243–244
Marshall Field's, 19

Maslow, A., 176, 593
Master budget, 252, **266**
  case study, 283–285
  construction of
    budgeted (pro forma) financial statements, 259–263, **266**
    balance sheet, 262–263
    cash flow statement, 260–262
    income statement, 260
  capital investment budget, 258
  financial budget, 258–259
  firm description, 253
  process overview, 253–255
  production budget, 256–257
  sales budget, 255–256
  selling and administration budget, 257–258
Material price variance, 527–531, **544**
Material quantity variance, 527–531, **544**
Materials, direct; *see* **Direct materials**
Materials requirement planning (MRP), 455, **460**
Mathews, J., 594
Merchant, K., 594
Merkel, H., 333n
Meyer, J., 593
Microsoft, 33, 64, 103, 566
Milliken, 542
Miyamato, A., 595
Monitoring, 12, **25**, 185, **189**
  mutual, 298, **311**, 534
Monitoring costs, 177–178, **189**
Monthly cash flow budgets, 266–268
Morse, Dale, 595
Motivation; *see* Goals, organizational
Motorola, 447, 455
Mrs. Field's, 63
MTV, 566
Multinational firms, 564–591, **585**
  antidumping regulations, **585**, 587
  cultural differences and, 575–576
  domestic content requirements, **585**, 586
  external reporting, accounting standards for, 573–575
  Foreign Corrupt Practices Act (FCPA), 576
  and foreign currencies; *see* Foreign currency
  international trade and, 566–568
  multiple taxing authorities, 571–573
  performance evaluation in, 581–583
    book team and, 582
  tariffs, **585**, 586
  taxes and; *see* Taxes
  transfer pricing issues, 576–580
    planning decisions/control trade-offs, 580
    political considerations, 579
    tax minimization, 577–579
Multiple accounting systems, 18–19, 294
Multistage cost allocation, 300–301, **311**
Mutual monitoring, 298, **311**, 534

N

Nabisco, 482

Nanni, A., Jr., 595
NEC, 542
Net present value (NPV), 475, 479–486, **493**; *see also* Present value
  future cash flows, estimating, 481–484
    accounting earnings and, 481
    accounts receivable and, 481–482
    depreciation tax shield, 483–484, **492**
    inventory and, 481–482
    tax considerations, 482–483
  IRR method *vs.*, 487–488
  risk-adjusted discount rates, 484–486
Net realizable value method, of joint cost allocation, **411**, 412–413, 414
Niederpreum, G., 430n
Nike, 69, 438, 566
Nippon Telegraph & Telephone, 542
Nissan, 520, 521
Non-value-added activities, 6–7, **25**, 69, **411**
  activity-based management and, 401
Non-value-added time, 454
North American Free Trade Agreement (NAFTA), 6, 437, 586
Norton, D., 179, 593

O

Opportunity cost of capital, 205, **223**, 473–475, **493**
  ignoring, 476–479
  net present value of cash flows; *see* **Net present value (NPV)**
  risk and, 210, 484–486
Opportunity costs, 35–38, **49**
  approximations of, 43–46
    CVP analysis and, 148
    fixed and variable costs, 43–45
    historical costs, 45–46
  for transfer pricing
    control problems, 220
    with external competitive market, 216–218
    without external competitive market, 218–220
  of capital; *see* **Opportunity cost of capital**
  case study, 58–59
  cost allocation and, 294–295
  and CVP analysis, 143
  of defective products, 450
  of exceeding capacity, 41
  foreign exchange rates as, 570
  framework of, for planning decisions, 85
  future cash flow estimation and, 482
  of holding inventory, 387
  identification/measurement of, 36–38
  of information, 47
  of initiating operations, 40
  of joint products, 407–408
  of normal operations, 40–41
  and planning decisions, 38, 85
  product costs and, in absorption cost systems, 390–391

Opportunity costs **(continued)**
  and rate of output, 40–43
    graphical analysis, 41
Organizations
  accounting systems, role of, 12–15, 441–442
  activity-based management; *see* **Activity-based management (ABM)**
  asset structure of, 438–439, **460**
  change and; *see* **Change, organizational**
  complexity of, 399–401
  control; *see* **Control**
  customer base of, 439, **460**
  decentralized; *see* **Decentralized organizations**
  decision rights, 9, **25**
  efficiency of, 6–7
  financial reports of, 14–15
  investment opportunities of; *see* **Investment opportunities**
  just-in-time (JIT) processes; *see* **Just-in-time (JIT) processes**
  knowledge creation, 439
  managers, role of, 10–12
  multinational; *see* **Multinational firms**
  nature of, 8–10
  service, value chains of, 68
  stakeholders of, 9, **25**
  structure of, 9–10, 440
    change and, 182–184, 436
    investment opportunities and, 437–440
    management accounting and, 441–442
    TQM and, 452
  subunits of, 70–71
  total quality management; *see* **Total quality management (TQM)**
  value chain and; *see* **Value chain**
  worker empowerment, 10, **25**
Outsourcing, 69–70, **87,** 152–153
Overabsorbed overhead, 349–352, **363**
  case study, 380–383
Overhead costs, 106, **123**
  activity-based costing (ABC) and, 398
  actual, 537–538, **544**
  applied, 537–538, **544**
  budgeted, 537, **544**
  case studies, 426–430
  in job order systems, 346
    allocating by departments, 357–359
    allocating to jobs, 348–359; *see also* **Cost allocation**
    multiple allocation bases, 354–356
    over- and underabsorbed, 349–352, **363**
      accounting for, 352–354
      application rate, recalculating, 353
      case study, 380–383
      cost of goods sold, adjusting, 352
      proration, 352, **363**
    practical capacity, allocation based on, 392–395

Overhead variances, 536, 538–539, 545–548
  total, 538, **544**
Overproduction, incentives for, 386–389, 394
  activity-based costing (ABC) and, 403
  mitigating, 388–389, 395, 539
  overhead variances and, 538–539

P

Participative budgeting, 244, **266**
Payback, 476–477, **493**
Pepsi, 438
Perez, M., 326n
Performance measures, 25, 178–180, **189**
  accounting numbers as, 179
  balanced scorecard, 179–180, **189**
  budgeted, 241–242
  compensation contracts and, 181–182
  controllability principle, 198–200, **223**
  cost allocations and, 297–298
  for cost centers, 201–202
  dysfunctional management behavior and, 459
  foreign exchange rates and, 581–583
  for investment centers
    multiple measures, 211–212
    residual income, 209–211, **224**
    return on investment (ROI), 206–209, **224**
  for JIT organizations, 456
  in multinational firms, 581–583
    book team and, 582
  multiple, 211–212
  organizational change and, 182–184, 440
  and organizational goals, 9
  overproduction and, 388–389, 394
  productivity measures as, 445
  for profit centers, 203
  quality-based criteria for, 451
  relative, 198–199, **224**
  responsibility centers and, 200–212
  target costing and, 520
  transfer pricing as, 214
    book team and, 221
  variances as, 527
    incentive effects, 532–535
Period costs, 74–75, **87**
Perpetuities, 496–497
Pettijohn, J., 593, 594
Philip Morris, 139
Physical measure method, of joint cost allocation, **411,** 412, 413
Pizza Hut, 566
Planning decisions, 32–59
  through activity-based management, 399–401
  activity-based costing and, 120–121
  activity cost-related, 67–70
    outsourcing; *see* **Outsourcing**
  book team and, 86
  budgeting for, 240–241
  and control, 184–188
    trade-offs between, 16, 243–245, 388, 405, 580

  using cost/benefit analysis; *see* **Cost/benefit analysis**
  cost objects of, 85
  costs associated with, 85
  customer cost-related, 71–72
  decentralized, transfer pricing and, 215, 220–221
  estimating costs for; *see* **Cost estimation**
  and external reporting trade-offs, 16–17, 75
  historical costs and, 16–17, 45
  improving, 295–296
  and joint costs, 407–408
  management accounting and, 13–14, 459
  of managers, 10–11
  opportunity costs and; *see* **Opportunity costs**
  organizational value and, 440
  period cost-related, 74–75
  process of
    and decision control process separation, 184–188
    steps in, 185
    team-based, 23
  product; *see* **Product planning decisions**
  product cost-related
    pricing; *see* **Pricing decisions**
    product mix; *see* **Product mix decisions**
    target costing, 66–67, **87**
  quality costs and, 451
  rate of output, 40–43
  simplification of, 85
  subunit cost-related, 70–71
  sunk costs and, 38
  supplier-related, 72–74
  value chain and, 67–68
Potter, G., 594
Poulan-Weedeater, 489
Practical capacity, 411
  overhead allocation based on, 392–395
Predatory pricing, 140, 160
Present value
  of annuities, 497–498, 503
  of cash, 494–495, 502
  of cash flow streams, 495–498
    multiple, per year, 499–501
  net; *see* **Net present value (NPV)**
  of perpetuities, 496–497
  tables, 502–503
Prevention costs, 450, **460**
Pricing decisions, 64–66, **87,** 136–142
  book team and, 158
  cost-based, 138–142
  CVP analysis and, 148
  dumping, 142, **160**
  and joint costs, allocated, 407
  lead-loss pricing, 140, **160**
  lower boundary, cost as, 140–142
  over- and underabsorbed overhead and, 351
  poor management accounting system and, 459
  predatory pricing, 140, **160**

Pricing decisions (continued)
productivity measurement and, 444–445
transfer pricing; *see* **Transfer pricing**
for value maximization, 136–138
Process cost systems, 359–362, **363**
for control, 361–362
equivalent units, 360, **363**
and work-in-process, 360–361
Processes; *see* Activities
Process management, 400, **411**
Product costs, 62, **87**
activity-based costing; *see* **Activity-based costing (ABC)**
activity costs and, 70
avoidable, 85, 152, **160**
direct; *see* **Direct costs**
indirect; *see* **Indirect costs**
misleading
absorption cost systems and, 390–391
variable costing and, 396
planning decisions related to pricing; *see* **Pricing decisions**
product mix; *see* **Product mix decisions**
target costing, 66–67, **87**
product life cycle and, 102–105
Production budget, master budget illustration, 256–257
Productivity measurement, 443–446
Product-level costs, 109, **123**
Product life cycle, 123
and product costs, 102–105
benchmarking, 103, **123**
Product mix decisions, 62–64, **87,** 149–155
adding product/service, 150–151
with constraints, 155–159
dropping product/service, 151–152
death spiral, 390–391, **411**
and joint costs, allocated, 407
make-or-buy, 152–153
outsourcing, 69–70, **87,** 152–153
over- and underabsorbed overhead and, 351
poor management accounting system and, 459
promotion, 154–155
sell or process further, 153–154
joint products, 408–409
Product planning decisions, 134–169
break-even analysis, 144–146, **160**
case study, 169
CVP analysis; *see* **Cost-volume-profit (CVP) analysis**
pricing; *see* **Pricing decisions**
Products
defective; *see* Defects
design of, for quality, 448
joint; *see* **Joint products**
multiple, CVP analysis and, 149
Profit
estimation of; *see* **Cost-volume-profit (CVP) anaaysis**
as performance measure, 203
productivity and, 445
specified, achieving, 146–147

after-tax, 160
Profit centers, 202–203, **224**
identification of, 212
Pro forma (budgeted) financial statements, 259–263, **266**
Proration, 352, **363**
Purchasing costs, suppliers and, 73

Q

Quaker Oats, 211, 309
Quality; *see also* **Total quality management (TQM)**
costs of, 450–451
case study, 467–469
different meanings of, 446–448
and global competition, 447
ISO 9000 certification, 452
measuring, 448–449
performance measurement and, 451
traditional approach to, 447
zero defects concept, 447–448

R

Rakes, H., 595
Rate of output
costs associated with, 85
CVP analysis and, 148
opportunity costs and, 40–43
relevant range of, 43–44, **49**
Ratification, of decisions, 185, **189**
investment proposals, 472–473
Raw materials, 106–107
Reciprocal method, of cost allocation, **311,** 315–316
Regression analysis, 87–89
Reinvestment rate, 488
Relative performance measurement, 198–199, **224**
Relative sales value method, of joint cost allocation, **411,** 412, 413
Relevant range, of output, 43–44, **49**
Research and development, opportunity cost of capital and, 474
Residual income, 209–211, **224**
Responsibility accounting, 200, **224**
Responsibility centers
cost allocations to, 297
cost centers, 200–202, **223**
hierarchy of, 204–205
identification of, 212
investment centers; *see* **Investment centers**
profit centers, 202–203, **224**
transfer pricing and; *see* **Transfer pricing**
Return on investment (ROI), 224, 493
capital project evaluation, 477–479
decomposition of, 208
as performance measure, 206–209
Revenue, incremental, 136–137
Reward systems
compensation contracts, 181–182, 440
organizational change and, 182–184
Richard D. Irwin, Inc., 23, 47, 69, 86, 310, 409, 543

Risk
discount rates adjusted for, 484–486
opportunity cost of capital and, 210, 484–486
Rivera, N., 326n
Rolls Royce, 446
Ryetown Steel, Inc., 429–433

S

Sakurai, M., 594, 595
Sales budget, master budget illustration, 255–256
Satisficing behavior, 534–535, **544**
Sayers, B., 318n
Scarbough, P., 595
Schaub, J., 593
Schmidt, S., 594
Schroeder, R., 594
Sears, 19, 203, 301
Securities and Exchange Commission (SEC), 13, 16, 290
Seed, A., 594
Segment reporting, 308–310, **311**
Selling and administration budget, master budget illustration, 257–258
Sell or process further decisions, 153–154
joint products, 408–409
Service cost, 62, **87;** *see also* **Product costs**
Service departments, allocating costs of, 312–316
Service organizations, value chains of, 68
Shareholders, financial reports to, 290–291, 294
Sharmon, P., 593
Shields, Michael, 593, 595
Short-run budgets, 245–246
Siviy, P., 227
Smith, C., 594
Smithkline-Beecham, 5
Snapple Beverage Corp., 309
Snodgrass, C., 595
Song, J., 594
Sonoco Products Co., 73
Soucy, S., 594
Specific identification inventory valuation method, 363, 365–366
Spector, S., 227
Spreadsheet analysis, monthly cash flow budgets, 266–268
Stakeholders, 9, **25**
Standard costs/costing, 516–522
book team and, 543
costs and benefits, 541–542
defined, 518, **544**
overhead, 535–539
reasons for using, 518–519
setting and revising, 519–521
target costing and, 520
variances; *see* **Variances**
Standard usage, 536–537, **544**
Starbucks, 65
Starter, 566
Static budgets, 249–250, **266**
Stein, J., 430n
Step-down method, of cost allocation, **311,** 313–315

Stewart, G. Bennett, III, 278
Straight-line depreciation, 483–484
Strategic planning, 245–246, **266**
    book team and, 47
Subunits, organizational, 70–71
Sunk costs, 49
    and cost/benefit analysis, 38–39
    future cash flow estimation and, 482
Sun Microsystems, 152, 153
Suppliers
    JIT processes and, 455
    planning decisions related to, 72–74
Suzuki, 534
Swenson, D., 594

T

Target costing, 66–67, **87**, 520, **544**
Tariffs, 585, 586
Tax accounting, 13, 14–15, **25**
    cost allocation and, 291
Taxes
    minimizing, 577–579
    and multinational firms, 571–573
        tariffs, **585,** 586
        transfer pricing issues, 577–579
        value-added taxes (VAT), **585,** 585–586
    and net present value analysis, 482–484
    reporting of income, 291, 366
Technology, and organizational change, 4–5, 20–21, 436–437
Tektronix, 18, 298
Texas Instruments, 450
Theory of constraints, 156–159, **160**
Thompson, C., 593
Thomson, J., 593
Throughput time, 453–454, **460**
Time value of money, 148–149
Time Warner Entertainment, 441
Tolomeo, C., 326n
Top-down budgeting, 244
Total overhead variance, 538, **544**
Total quality management (TQM), 6, **25,** 446–453; see also Quality
    costs of quality
        categories, 450–451
        identification and measurement, 448–452
    elements of, 448
    multidisciplinary task forces, 452
    restructuring of organization for, 452
Toyota, 7, 66–67, 242, 446
Tracing costs
    direct, 75, 85
    indirect, 75–78, 85
        with cost drivers, 76–78, 111–117
Transfer pricing, 212–222, **224**
    for control, 214
    for decentralized planning decisions, 215, 220–221
    fixed costs and, 219
    full-cost, 219
    international, 576–580
        domestic vs., 220–221
        planning decisions/control

        trade-offs, 580
        political considerations, 579
        tax minimization, 577–579
    methods compared, 220–221
    negotiated, 220
    opportunity cost estimation and control problems, 220
        with external competitive market, 216–218
        without external competitive market, 218–220
    as performance measure, 214
        book team and, 221
    reasons for, 213–214
    segment reporting and, 308–310
    variable costs and, 219
Tulle, S., 593
Turk, W., 594
Twister, 476
Twombly, J., 326n

U

Ultra Technologies, 211, 593
Underabsorbed overhead, 349–352, **363**
    case study, 380–383
Unfavorable variance, 241–242, **266,** 523, **544**
United Airlines, 40
Unit-level costs, 109, **123**
UPS, 400
U.S. Steel, 19, 343, 440
Usiatynski, S., 333n
US West, 441
USX, 440

V

Value
    maximizing, pricing and, 136–138
    organizational, planning decisions and, 440
Value-added activities, 67–69, **411**
    activity-based management and, 401
Value-added tax (VAT), 585, 585–586
Value chain, 6–7, **25, 87**
    and activity-based management, 401
    of different organizations, 401
    planning decisions and, 67–68
Variable costs/costing, 43–45, **49,** 395–398, **411**
    allocation base selection and, 397
    estimation of
        by account classification, 79–82
        by regression analysis, 87–89
        by visually fitted historical costs, 82–84
    overproduction incentives and, 395
    per unit, **49**
        and opportunity cost approximation, 43–45
    product costs and, 396–397
    and rate of output, 85
    transfer pricing and, 219
Variable overhead efficiency variance, 544, 545
Variable overhead spending variance,

    544, 545
Variable overhead variance, 544, 545
Variances, 241–242; see also **Standard costs/costing**
    defined, **266,** 518, **544**
    direct labor, 522–527, **544**
    direct materials, 527–531, **544**
    favorable, 241–242, **266,** 523, **544**
    investigating, 540–541
    labor efficiency, 522–527, **544**
    management by exception and, 519, **544**
    material price, 527–531, **544**
    material quantity, 527–531, **544**
    overhead; see **Overhead variances**
    and performance measurement, 527
        incentive effects, 532–535, 538–539
            cooperative effort, discouraging, 533–534
            externalities, 533
            inventory building, 532–533
            mutual monitoring, 534
            overproduction, 539
            satisficing behavior, 534–535, **544**
    unfavorable, 241–242, **266,** 523, **544**
    wage rate, 522–527, **544**
Visa/MasterCard, 569
Volume measures, 536–537
    case study, 559–560

W

Wage rate variance, 522–527, **544**
Walker, K., 593
Wallace Co., 452
The Wall Street Journal, 47, 568, 575, 593, 594
Wasted time, 454
Watts, R., 593, 594
Weighted-average cost method, for inventory valuation, **363,** 365–367
Westinghouse, 35
Weyerhaeuser Corp., 213
Whirlpool, 211
Wilner, N., 491, 594
"Woodstock 94," 248
Worker empowerment, 10, **25**
Work-in-process, process costing and, 360–361
Worthy, F., 594

X

Xerox, 301, 447

Y

Young, S., 68n, 593

Z

Zero-base budgets (ZBB), 251–252, **266**
Zero defects concept, 447–448
Zimmerman, Jerold L., 594
Zinsli, T., 593
Zytec, 405